Learning:

Processes

Learning:

Processes

Melvin H. Marx, Editor

University of Missouri, Columbia

The Macmillan Company

Collier-Macmillan Limited, *London*

First Printing

Library of Congress catalog card number: 69-12744

THE MACMILLAN COMPANY
COLLIER-MACMILLAN CANADA, LTD.,
TORONTO, ONTARIO

Printed in the United States of America

Foreword

The three volumes in this set were planned to provide comprehensive, up-to-date coverage of the wide range of behavioral functions generally referred to as learning. Obviously such an enterprise can be only partially achieved within the various limitations necessarily imposed upon the editor and writers. But it is my hope that we have achieved a reasonably satisfactory treatment of a wide sector of the very broad spectrum of learning problems. The books were planned on the premise that it is no longer possible for one psychologist to be fully expert in all the areas of so broad and diversified a field as learning. Expert coverage of the major facets of the field has therefore been attempted by having a large number of separate authors each contribute a section on his own special subject. Variations in the time of receipt of the final manuscripts within each volume account for some differences in the nature and scope of literature coverage by the various authors.

Here I will briefly indicate some of the general considerations that were used in planning the volumes and then describe the specific intent of each of the volumes. More detailed descriptions of the particular volumes are provided in the introductions to them. The introductory sections are also designed to orient the reader in each subject

matter by brief surveys of relevant background materials.

The general intent of each of the several sections in a volume is to present the highlights of the special subject matter. Each section has therefore been written by a psychologist who is himself an active researcher in the field.

The books are aimed at the advanced undergraduate. The question that was suggested to each author as the criterion for coverage and level of difficulty was, "What should a college senior graduating with a major in psychology know about this subject?" Each section was intended to be an independent, self-sufficient unit, including introductory or orienting material, a review of the major propositions and principles in the area, discussion of key questions and salient contributions, and finally some consideration of the future, with special regard to critical research needs.

The three volumes may be differentiated, briefly, as to their content and objectives. *Learning: Processes* is intended to emphasize the *description* of behavioral changes commonly called learning, and closely related fundamental behavioral phenomena (transfer, retention, stimulus generalization). *Learning: Interactions* is intended to emphasize the interrelationships between

v

behavior changes produced by behavior itself ("learning") and certain intimately connected functions (motivation, perception, concept formation, and personality) as well as how such behavior changes operate across phyla and how they are neurophysiologically mediated. *Learning: Theories* is intended to emphasize the interpretation of the fundamental learning processes, ordered in terms of the type of theoretical method used, or of key constructs.

A word about the technical organization of the sections. In order to make the books maximally useful each section has been given a high degree of self-sufficiency. The glossary, suggested further readings, and references for each section are placed at the end of that section. There is a minimal degree of overlap in these materials. A comprehensive index, with extensive cross-referencing, should help to tie the sections together.

The symbols S (for subject) and E (for experimenter) have been used throughout the books because of the great frequency with which these terms occur.

I am grateful to a number of persons for their aid in the preparation of these volumes. The specific acknowledgments to publishers and authors for their kind permission to reprint materials are given in each volume. My colleagues have been generous with their time and helpful with their critical suggestions. Most of all, I wish to express my deepest gratitude to my wife, Kathleen, for her indefatigable assistance in the effort required to keep the contributors writing and in the endless technical details involved in the preparation of each volume for the publisher. I hope that the appearance of the volumes will be partial repayment to her for her patience and perseverance throughout the many long hours she has spent on this project.

M. H. M.

Columbia, Missouri

Preface

The overall objective of this volume is to provide a description of the behavioral processes which are commonly referred to under the general term *learning*.

The introductory section contains material of general interest (Chapter 1) and a brief discussion of the free-operant procedure (Chapter 2). The latter is included as a special topic because of the failure of contributors to produce a section on this topic and the feeling that at least the essence of free-operant research should be in the book.

The first half of the book is concerned mainly with the more basic learning processes. The section on instrumental learning presents a broad scheme under which the great variety of instrumental processes can be classified. The next section concerns classical conditioning, which is superficially at least the simplest form of learning process. The problem of stimulus generalization is then treated, in detail, because of its relationship to the previous topics.

The second half of the book concerns somewhat more complex processes. The section on verbal learning deals in a simple and straightforward manner with this uniquely human form of behavior. The section on transfer and retention is placed next. The discussion of these fundamental processes logically follows the treatment of verbal learning mainly because the great bulk of research on transfer and retention has utilized verbal learning material. The book is completed by the section on motor behavior.

M. H. M.

Contents

I

Learning Processes

Melvin H. Marx

University of Missouri, Columbia

1

Introduction

Historical Overview

This brief overview is presented to introduce some conceptual order into the welter of widely different behaviors that are subsumed under the rubric *learning*. Research techniques and procedures now in use have generally developed over the past few decades, and many reflect the kinds of problems that were then under active investigation. Furthermore, the objectives of learning researches have changed over the decades and an appreciation of these changes will help in the understanding of today's research objectives.

The intensive and systematic scientific investigation of learning has been primarily an activity of the twentieth century. From the vantage point of today's position in history, one may discern two major historical phases leading to the contemporary situation. These will be very roughly sketched, with the understanding that only the most salient developments are treated and that many important issues are therefore ignored. Moreover, they have relevance primarily for the United States, where there has been the most intensive investigation of instrumental learning (as contrasted with

classical conditioning, most intensively studied in the U.S.S.R.).

Descriptive period. The fundamental need in the early researches was for reasonably well-controlled data. There was therefore an emphasis mainly upon empirical, as opposed to rational or even theoretical, procedures. Good examples are provided by Thorndike (1898), who performed the first systematic investigation of animal instrumental learning, and Bryan and Harter (1897), who studied the acquisition of skill in telegraphy. Although some interpretation of data was attempted, the data themselves were largely collected without much concern for prior interpretations. In other words, theories did not dictate research plans. Rather, the major objective was the collection of a large amount of data representing the manner in which various tasks are learned.

Theoretical period. Subsequent to World War I, there was a phase of research on learning marked by a very great concern for theoretical issues. As a matter of fact, theory was the exclusive concern of a surprisingly large number of researchers. Most of the theoretical discussion, and the research that was directly stimulated by it, centered around the opposed theoretical positions of Hull (1943) and Tolman (1932). Many attempts at "crucial" experiments were made, and it was not until the late 1950's that interest in this kind of research began to show a marked decline. One reason for this decline was the growing disenchantment with Hullian theory, which had been most influential, and the realization that the originally clear-cut theoretical differences did not survive the accumulation of empirical evidence. In other words, as the theories were modified they tended more and more to converge toward a common ground capable of encompassing the major facts of an empirical sort. In this process experimentation aimed at theoretical differentiations did of course play a key role. Nevertheless, there was growing recognition of the need for data that were not so closely associated with specific theoretical issues.

Contemporary period. During the present decade, theoretically stimulated research cannot be said to have passed entirely from the picture, but it certainly enjoys a much more secondary position. Two new, or at least newly emphasized, kinds of research are more prominent.

The first of these, the emphasis upon data collection *per se* in the absence of explicit theoretical interests, is in a sense a reversion to the first period described. To some extent this contemporary emphasis does probably represent the recognition of the need for detailed descriptions of behavior changes. More importantly, however, the contemporary atheoretical tendency reflects both a strong reversion from the overemphasis on theory of the previous period, and the growing influence of Skinner (1938, 1961) and the operant conditioning movement. (Operant conditioning is described in Chapter 2 of this section.) There is widespread and explicit acceptance of the proposition that data are valuable independent of the theory that spawned them.

The second of the relatively new movements in the contemporary picture reflects a different reaction to the earlier theoretical efforts. This is the emphasis upon smaller theoretical problems, and the attempt to build "miniature systems" rather than to test grand theoretical structures. From another point of view, however, this present emphasis may be considered as a development from the systematic functionalism of the earlier day, with its focus on *problems* rather than theories.

Whatever its origin, the contemporary focus on problems and limited theory is much to be encouraged, for it would seem to be putting learning research more in line with the conventional procedures of science which have proved so successful in other fields of endeavor. Statement of this bias should not be considered as an attempt to deprecate or to eliminate any of the other kinds of research emphases—certainly we have room for all approaches that give any kind of promise—but rather as an expression of faith in the emphasis on problems and functions as being generally most likely to be scientifically fruitful.

Basic Definitions of Learning

Lay definitions. Lay definitions of learning focus on the acquisition of either knowledge (mainly verbal learning) or skill (mainly motor learning). Although these kinds of learning are indeed important (see Sections V and VII), they by no means include all the behavior processes that are included in the term *learning* as psychologists use it. Moreover, they have one additional serious shortcoming. Learning is not necessarily improvement, as often seems to be assumed by the layman.

General technical definition. All-encompassing technical definitions of so complex a term as *learning* are difficult if not impossible. At least two major kinds of usages of the term may be distinguished. In the first usage, most relevant for the present volume, *learning* refers to ongoing behaviors, and to changes in behavior. In the second usage, it refers to some kind of internal events which are presumed to underlie the behavior processes. This latter usage is most relevant for the interpretive treatments in *Learning: Theories.*

Accepting for present purposes the directly behavioral kind of definition, we can most usefully and generally define learning as *a relatively enduring change in behavior which is a function of prior behavior* (*usually called practice*). [For an extended treatment of the problem of the definition of learning, consult Kimble, (1961, Chapter 1).] Although this general definition may not satisfy everyone, and needs to be qualified, it nonetheless does indicate the basic meaning normally associated with the concept. It is especially appropriate in connection with the term *processes*, as used in the present volume. A process is defined as "any phenomenon which shows a continuous change in time." This volume is therefore concerned with the various types of behavioral changes, or processes, which can be identified as resulting at least to some extent from previous behavior of the individual and as therefore being classifiable as learning.

Qualifications and distinctions. Certain qualifications need to be made before the definition of the term *learning* can be considered reasonably complete. Learning must be distinguished from other processes which produce behavioral changes but not as a function of prior behavior in any directly relevant manner. Learning is also commonly distinguished from certain superficially very similar behavioral changes where different underlying mechanisms are assumed to operate.

With regard to the first kind of distinction, there are several causes of behavior changes which need to be excluded from the definition stated earlier. Among these are maturation (or growth), fatigue, drug and dietary effects, disease effects, and adaptation.

Maturation produces behavior changes by means of changes in bodily structure, on a genetic basis and without regard for previous experience. We are all familiar with the marked changes in behavior that typically occur at certain critical periods in development (for example, adolescence). Although these changes are certainly subject to some influence from previous experience, and therefore may be said to have been influenced to some extent by learning, nevertheless they are basically a function of a different kind of causative factor (for example, hormone secretion) which is largely independent of previous experience.

The same statement can be made for each of the other exclusions, with the possible exception of adaptation, and for similar reasons. Fatigue operates to reduce behavior output by means of lactic acid accumulated in the musculature and not adequately removed by the circulatory system. Drugs and dietary factors operate more or less directly on the sensory, neural, or effector mechanisms. Disease processes may also affect any of the organ systems and so influence behavior.

The distinction between these various kinds of processes and learning is an important one both practically and theoretically. It is important in practice because the actions which need to be taken to correct behavior changes differ markedly. For example, a child whose poor school learning is thought to be due to insufficient preparation will be given a certain kind of treatment (say, additional practice sessions). However, if his performance is actually due to organic factors (say, hearing loss from disease) this kind of treatment will be of small value. Many similar, commonplace examples should be evident to the reader. Theoretically this kind of distinction is important because we are concerned with correct identification of the conditions underlying behavior and behavior change.

Confusions which occur as a result of insufficient knowledge or analysis are of course detrimental to this objective.

One further distinction should be introduced at this point. This is the distinction between learning and performance. Although learning cannot be measured in the absence of behavior, or performance, nevertheless it is also true that lack of performance does not necessarily indicate lack of learning. Before learning can be demonstrated behaviorally, some degree of motivation must be present. Thus an S which has learned some particular response (say, recital of a poem) will not perform appropriately unless adequately motivated. The complex relationships between learning and motivation, as reflected in varying performance, are touched upon at various points in the present text and are directly treated in one section of *Learning: Interactions.*

Distinguishing learning from adaptation is also difficult. Indeed, some would hold that no such distinction should be made and that adaptation is properly to be considered as learning. Which of these positions will ultimately be accepted will depend upon a great deal more information about the underlying mechanisms than is now available. Meanwhile, a brief description of adaptation should indicate the basis for its separate status.

Adaptation may be of two types, sensory or motor. Sensory adaptation refers to the progressive loss in sensory effectiveness suffered by stimuli over time. Olfactory adaptation in which originally noxious stimuli (for example, packing-house odors) quickly cease to be smelled offers a familiar illustration. Motor adaptation, commonly called *habituation*, refers to a decrement in response to a particular stimulus that occurs merely from the presentation of the stimulus. A familiar example of this phenomenon is the gradual reduction in the startle reaction (and presumably the underlying fear or emotional response) typically exhibited by animals persistently exposed to loud, sudden noises or other forms of strong stimulation.

The behavior shown in habituation is related to that shown in sensory adaptation in that in both cases there is reduced response. However, in the case of the latter process the response is often but not necessarily a verbal one—indicating the extent to which the persistence of an originally effective stimulus has resulted in sensory decrement—whereas in habituation an overt and nonverbal response is involved and the sensory experience of the S is not directly assessed by the E. The mechanism underlying sensory adaptation consists of changes in the sensory system, either in the sense organ itself or in the sensory parts of the brain. The mechanism of habituation presumably involves associative functions of the brain.

There are certain behavioral processes (for example, pseudoconditioning, sensitization) that are similar to learning but that are commonly held to be fundamentally different. The difference depends upon a somewhat finer technical definition than the one previously given. This more refined definition holds that the behavior changes identified as learning are not simply a function of past experience or prior behavior, but are also a reflection of a specific connection between a stimulus situation (usually labeled S) and the specified responses (usually labeled R). Learning then is identified as a change, usually but not always an increment, in the S-R relationship—that is, a change in the manner in which responses are now made to stimuli. A large number of illustrations of this more specific kind of learning definition will be found in the chapters that follow.

The Learning Task

The diversity of behavior processes that can be subsumed under the rubric *learning* is almost as great as the diversity of behavior itself. However, each learning experiment can be considered to be a "task" for the *S*. Consequently, a tremendous variety of tasks have been investigated, in *S*s ranging from one-celled organisms to groups of human beings, by researchers in the field of learning. The sections that follow provide some idea of this great diversity. Section II presents a detailed breakdown of the variety of learning tasks that involve instrumental learning, and Section III describes the variety of tasks used in classical conditioning studies. (The distinction between classical and instrumental conditioning and learning is made in these sections, and especially in Section II.) Human verbal and motor learning is described in Sections V and VII, respectively. Here certain of the more important general considerations concerning learning tasks will be discussed.

Simplification of task. One of the more prominent trends in instrumental learning research over the past half century has been the very marked tendency toward investigation of increasingly simplified tasks. The first tasks used in instrumental learning research were relatively complex. For example, Thorndike placed a cat in a so-called puzzle box, illustrated in Figure 1-1, in which many different kinds of responses could be made but only one response was instrumental in opening the box and allowing *S* to obtain a reward placed outside. Even more complex was the original maze, devised by Small around 1900, for the study of learning in the rat. The early models contained a large number of choice points and blind alleys, requiring *S* to learn a complex of right and left turns.

The evolution of the maze provides an interesting illustration of the trend toward simplification. This evolution is shown schematically in Figure 1-2. After several decades of using the complex forms, such as the multiple-T maze, investigators began to turn to what is generally called the T-maze —a *single* stem or alley and one choice point. Use of the single-choice-point test on

successive trials provides information on the manner in which a single discrimination is learned, and so permits the investigator to obtain less contaminated data than he can obtain from those tests in which multiple discriminations have to be made. The popularity of the T-maze and the gradual decline of interest in the multiple-T maze attest to the degree of the conviction among investigators that it is preferable to study the presumed unit of learning before attacking the more complex problem of how such units are combined in learning.

The next step was the removal of the T, or choice point of the apparatus. The straightaway, or runway, became a preferred instrument for many types of investigation. It measures simply the starting latency and running speed of *S* without requiring any explicit choice among incompatible responses. In other words, *S* merely starts and runs with varying speed. Furthermore, whereas the earliest runways tended to be extremely long (Hull even placed one in a corridor because of space limitations in rooms), the later runways have tended to be relatively short.

This shift from the T-maze, which provides mainly a measure of response choice, to the runway, which provides measures of response latency and response duration, reflects an important shift also in the kind of research problem investigated. Choice measures clearly represent learning, in the sense of newly acquired S-R relationships, as well as motivation. Latency and speed measures are more commonly coming to be interpreted as primarily motivational in character (see Spence, 1956, 1960; Logan and Wagner, 1965; Marx, 1966), in the sense that they reflect the activation of the associative (S-R) relationships.

The culmination of the reduction of length of runway may be considered to be the box, which is no runway at all. But this further step in the direction of spatial reduction cannot really be considered to be a part of the evolution of the "maze." That

(a)

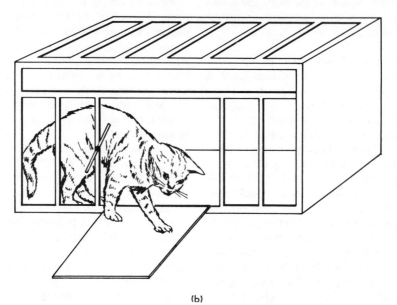

(b)

Figure 1-1.   Two views of the cat in the puzzle box. Panel (a) shows *S* performing the necessary instrumental act that opens the door; panel (b) shows the escape response. This response enables *S* to obtain the incentive (not shown), which was generally placed outside the box in the early research.

change must be attributed to a reduction in the complexity of the original Thorndikian puzzle box, rather than a truncating of the runway. Research by Skinner in the 1930's and the 1940's was responsible for popularizing this new instrument. As described in

Chapter 2, the Skinner box is a markedly simplified chamber, sound- and light-proofed, containing usually only a single object for manipulation (a "manipulandum"). The great advantage of this simplification is the high degree of experi-

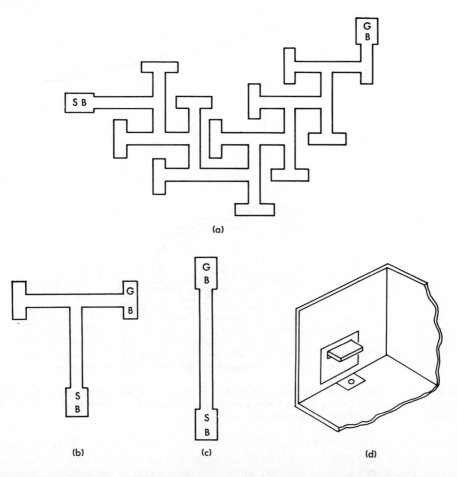

Figure 1-2. Evolution of the maze and view of the rat operant conditioning box. SB = startbox; GB = goalbox. Panel (a) shows the hypothetical floor plan of a multiple-T maze with ten choice points; note that at any choice point each path looks the same to S. Panel (b) shows the floor plan of a T maze. Panel (c) shows the floor plan of a runway. Panel (d) is an enlarged, cutaway view of a typical operant (Skinner) box for the rat, which may be considered to be a kind of goalbox not requiring locomotion; the operation of the manipulandum (bar) provides an incentive available through the magazine opening, shown below.

mental control of extraneous stimulation. Automation of the operation of the box also helps to generate data which typically show a high degree of regularity.

It is tempting to extend the trend just described by pointing to the introduction of an implanted electrode into S's brain. Figure 1-3 shows a rat S pressing a bar with intracranial stimulation (ICS) as the reinforcer. Each response produces a small electric pulse to the brain. Ss thus reinforced have been observed to work until literally exhausted, making thousands of instrumental responses. Such strictly internal stimulation obviously eliminates the need for any external environmental manipulations whatsoever, beyond the requirement that S makes some minimal response to activate the electrode. Although this procedure can hardly be considered to

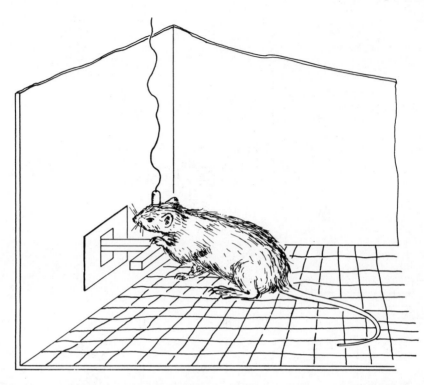

Figure 1-3. Schematic cutaway view of a rat in an ICS (intracranial self-stimulation) experiment. Depression of the bar provides a tiny electrical charge to a brain center by means of the attached electrode.

represent a further deliberate reduction of complexity of overt response required of *S*, it nonetheless does seem to offer the ultimate in such reduction.

The trend toward simplification of response has been true of instrumental, rather than classical, conditioning. The specific, "part" responses measured in classical conditioning, typically to discrete stimuli, have been until recently relatively simple.

"Rote" learning, characteristic of human verbal learning investigations, has seen a very similar reduction in complexity. The earlier investigations were prone to utilize long, complex tasks such as poems, or in the time of Ebbinghaus, lists of "nonsense" syllables. Ebbinghaus' invention of the nonsense syllable was of course a major step forward, because it greatly reduced the variably meaningful associations brought in

by real words. An even more important step in the direction of simplification, and increased power of analysis, came with the explicit separation of stimulus and response terms, as by means of the *paired-associate* paradigm. Again, the great popularity of this technique which permits a variety of manipulation of stimulus and response conditions, attests to the strong motivation of researchers to achieve a maximum degree of analysis (see Sections V and VI) and to investigate elementary as well as more complex phenomena.

Dimensionalization of tasks. There is obviously a great variety of tasks used in learning experiments—and a still greater variety of tasks which show learning in everyday life. Learning tasks can be ordered along a large number of dimensions. As the more detailed discussion in Section VI shows, a dimensional analysis of learning tasks is an important prerequisite to the development of effective analyses of learning, and especially to the relating of learning measures to other variables. Some of the ways in which such a dimensional analysis can be made will be suggested.

Learning tasks vary along the dimension of sensory-motor versus verbal components (for example, a finger maze at the sensory-motor end of the continuum and a poem or set of nonsense syllables at the verbal end); rote versus ideational components (for example, a list of nonsense syllables and a riddle, for the two continuum ends, respectively); a single principle for solution versus multiple principles; and so on. Note that these dimensions are far from orthogonal; rather, there are complex interactions between the various dimensions.

Although dimensionalization of learning tasks has long been recognized as a necessary procedure for certain types of laboratory tasks (for example, motor skills), it has not been equally recognized as important for the many kinds of nonlaboratory learning situations and for the learning processes that occur in everyday life. If such more complex situations are to be effectively analyzed, the learning processes found there must also be dimensionalized (whether or not that particular term is used to represent the analysis).

Task instructions. With human Ss, the task instructions are typically made explicit, so that the S knows what is expected of him. With animal Ss, the task instructions are implicit in the situation. That is, E "tells" S what is expected of him by manipulations of the environment. To take a simple example, depriving a rat of food and then allowing him to discover food pellets at the end of a runway is a way of letting him know what is expected.

Such implicit instructions in animal learning research are obviously used as a means of motivating S and insuring that his performance will be of the sort that E

wishes to measure. One should not assume, however, that in the case of human Ss all of the motivation is carried in the formal instructions. The recent demonstrations of bias in experimental situations (see Rosenthal, 1966) provide clear evidence of the potency of situational variables in human and animal research. Moreover, it is a serious mistake to assume that human Ss will naturally be motivated to learn, formally or informally, merely because there is a learning task presented (see Marx and Tombaugh, 1967, Chapter 7). More attention is needed than is often given to the effective motivating conditions in human learning research.

Phases of Learning Experiments

Just as the scientific definition of learning differs from the lay definition, so the laboratory investigation of learning differs from the everyday learning situation. In addition to the all-important matter of control of variables, characteristic of laboratory research generally, the typical learning experiment consists of a number of more or less well-defined phases. Although these vary from one experiment to another, there is sufficient commonality to permit the following general comments.

Pretraining phase. The pretraining phase is the phase during which various preliminary steps are taken, in advance of the training proper. In human research, for example, the S will be given his instructions, and may be given special preliminary treatment necessary before data can be collected (for example, placement of electrodes in physiological learning experimentation). The purpose of this treatment may be in part to produce emotional adaptation to the situation, much as in the case of animal research.

With animal Ss, the pretraining phase is more likely to be more extended. Ss may be put on food or water deprivation, for motivational purposes, and perhaps allowed to explore the apparatus. Magazine training, in which *S* is permitted to eat from the mechanism which delivers the food reinforcements, is a common and important form of pretraining.

Training phase. This is the primary phase of the learning experiment, during which the learning that is the fundamental objective of the research is acquired. *Acquisition* is the technical term that is often used to describe this learning, whether it is of nonsense syllables by a human *S* or the running response by a rat *S*.

The kinds of measures used vary with the type of learning task. Where a more complex task is employed, such as learning a poem or a list of nonsense syllables by the human *S* or learning how to reach an incentive in a multiple-unit maze or a puzzle box by the animal *S*, acquisition may be measured simply in terms of errors made or time required. Number of correct responses per trial may also be measured.

These relatively gross measures tend to be replaced, in more analytic research, by measures of choice (when selective or discrimination learning is involved) or by various intensive measures of response strength. The latter are by far the most popular in contemporary animal research and are also frequently used in human research. The main intensive measures are *response rate* (number of responses per unit time), *frequency of occurrence* (per trial unit) of the referent (learned) response, *latency* of response (the time between the stimulus and the response), and response *amplitude* (the force or energy with which the response is made). More details on this kind of measure are discussed in Section II, within the framework of instrumental conditioning.

Test phase. In some studies, where acquisition *per se* is the only objective of the research, there may be no further experimentation beyond the training phase proper. More often, however, there is some

sort of test phase introduced after training in order to assess the effects of whatever variables were manipulated.

In conditioning studies, the test phase is frequently an *extinction* period, during which all experimental conditions are the same as they were in training except that the reinforcement is not presented. In practice, for example, this means that the animal *S* is not given the food pellet at the end of the runway, or after pressing the bar, as he had been during training; or that the human *S* who has learned the eye blink response to a puff of air is now tested without that (reinforcing) stimulus. It is apparent that extinction tests can be administered only after reinforced training. More detailed accounts of the various reinforcing operations are provided in the later sections of this book, and discussions of the theoretical accounts of reinforcement are provided in *Learning: Theories*.

Other ways of testing involve the application of *retention* and *transfer* sessions, fully described in Section VI. Because of the important conceptual relationships between the learning process itself and these types of test some discussion here also is indicated.

Learning, retention, and transfer. In a narrow sense, *learning* refers to the acquisition of behavior (that is, to the development of new S-R connections, as discussed earlier). The relationship of the acquisition process to various kinds of subsequent measures, also treated in Section V and Section VI, merits some introductory comments.

In a rough manner, the terms *learning*, *retention*, and *transfer* are relatively simple to separate. *Learning* refers to behavior changes that can be identified as functions of behavior itself ("practice"); *retention* refers to the persistence of learning over some time interval (and is the obverse of "forgetting"); and *transfer* refers to the influence that prior learning has upon some new learning.

Viewed in terms of the processes themselves, however, the situation is somewhat more complicated than might be suggested by these descriptions. For example, it is apparent upon reflection that without retention there could be no learning; that is to say, unless the effects of one trial or response persist until the next trial or response, over a period of time, they cannot have the effect upon subsequent behavior that we have identified as learning. Thus, learning and retention can be seen as merely two sides of the same coin—or two representations of one underlying process, whatever its nature.

To carry this analysis one step further, the distinction between retention and transfer can also be largely eliminated; or, to put it a different way, what is referred to as retention (upon which, we have just concluded, learning necessarily depends) is really transfer. This conclusion follows if we distinguish in the usual manner between retention and transfer tests on the basis of whether or not there has been a change in testing conditions. If there has been no change, we speak of retention, because retention is assumed to be a test of behavior change under the same conditions as learning. On the other hand, if there has been a deliberate change in testing conditions, such as the introduction of an entirely new task, then we speak of transfer. But if we recognize that in spite of our best intentions there is always *some* change in testing conditions—if nothing else a change from aging and other internal functions, within organisms—then we must agree that all behavior tests are really, from this point of view, tests of transfer rather than of learning or retention.

These arguments raise serious questions about the *ultimate* advisability of making any clearcut distinctions among these operationally separable processes. Nevertheless, in terms of experimental manipulations and the corresponding conceptualizations, learning, retention, and transfer are clearly and usefully distinguishable. For example, the distinction between learning and retention—and especially between

spaced learning trials and retention trials—is entirely arbitrary. Whether a given investigator is measuring learning (that is, acquisition) or retention depends primarily upon his own intention, and how he defines his experimental operations. It is clearly possible for exactly the same experimental operations to be labeled "learning" in one case and "retention" in another (that is, the relearning type of retention test). This situation, although potentially confusing from a superficial semantic point of view, merely reflects the fact that, as emphasized earlier, there is no natural way of separating the influence of retention from learning. Moreover, the distinction between retention and transfer also needs to be made in terms of E's intentions and manipulations. If there is a deliberate effort made to change conditions, as there necessarily is in transfer experimentation, then the term *transfer* is justified; if, on the other hand, there is no such intention, and conditions are minimally varied, the term *retention* is justified. But again the relativity of these terms, and the fundamental processes they identify, must be kept in mind if realistic appraisals of research and conceptualizations are to be made.

General Issues

Here a small number of issues that cut across various learning tasks and problems are briefly discussed.

Is there a single learning process? One of the more striking observations that has been made concerning learning is that there is such a tremendous variety in behaviors that are learned, or contain significant learned components. As a matter of fact, there is scarcely a human behavior that is not either learnable or markedly influenced by learning.

A basic question is whether there is a single kind of learning process. From the standpoint of elegance—conceptual and theoretical—the concept of *the* learning process, as opposed to multiple learning processes, is indeed attractive. This motivation to subsume under a single concept, or set of concepts, all of the diverse behavioral data collectively called learning has been a potent force underlying much theoretical argumentation.

Attractive as the prospect of a single process is, from the standpoint of scientific parsimony, we are hardly justified in accepting it in the absence of a great deal more compelling evidence than is presently available. As a matter of fact, the opposite strategy seems to be strongly indicated: on operational grounds alone it is necessary to accept the manifest multiple processes as separate *until* they can be shown to be functions of the same underlying mechanisms (which, presumably, will ultimately be neurophysiological or neurochemical. Moreover, such combinations as seem justified on the basis of the data should be done cautiously and without undue extrapolation beyond the data.

The present text will provide occasional examples of integrating principles which do permit some such subsumption. But the focus of this volume is empirical. Generally we are concerned with the various learning processes as they are observed and manipulated, and the question of their fundamental similarity is left to other treatments (for example, the companion volume on *Learning: Theories*, where this kind of problem is more directly treated).

Convergence of methodologies: focus on mechanisms. As was apparent in the brief historical overview, there have been two markedly contrasting methodologies used in learning research. On the one hand, the early investigators tended to make a direct, frontal attack upon learning phenomena, using such gross measures as errors and time to complete the task. On the other hand, the more recent trend has been toward much more analytic attacks on simpler problems, utilizing restricted stimulus and response samples and measures specific to single responses.

There are many recent signs of a marked trend toward the convergence of these contrasting methodologies. Illustrations of this are to be found especially in the recent changes noted, in Chapter 2, in the free-operant movement. The most important factor in this convergence of methodologies is the renewed attention paid to specific problems, and in particular to the mechanisms underlying behavior. This convergence upon mechanisms is seen as a most fruitful means of accelerating progress, and in achieving a useful rapprochement between theory-oriented and data-oriented approaches. One especially nice consequence of this tendency is that investigators are becoming increasingly freer to choose the apparatus and procedure that best fits their particular problem rather than remain tied to those which happen to have been developed and used in the laboratories and/or conceptual frameworks within which they were trained and are working.

Generalizability of principles. One of the most vexing problems confronting psychology is the question of how far from the obtained data generalizations may be reliably made, and to what extent even well-established principles based upon work on a given kind of S can be safely generalized to other kinds of Ss. The discussion of this problem here complements the treatment of another facet of the problem, focusing on the interaction of variables, in Chapter 3.

In its most obvious and common form, this question relates to the use of animal Ss and the problem of generalizing to humans. Here a tremendous amount of distortion and misunderstanding has been generated. Learning research has concentrated heavily on a relatively small number of species, mainly using the rat, and, more recently, the pigeon. Learning researchers have been attacked from two sides. On the one hand, those who emphasize human problems have not hesitated to point out the questionability of generalizing from animal data to human behavior. On the other hand, those who are concerned with comparative problems (for example, Beach, 1950) have taken the profession to task for not investigating a wider range of animal forms so that a true comparative psychology can be developed.

In considering the merits of these various arguments let us proceed by reviewing briefly the major reasons for the investigation of infrahuman forms. These may be listed under three major points.

First, animals are used as *S*s in order simply to increase our knowledge of the animals themselves. This objective is often an important one, with some applicability in psychology (see, for example, Skinner, 1960; Verhave, 1966c; and Cumming, 1966 for applications of operant research made possible by detailed knowledge of the pigeon's capabilities). Nevertheless, it is probably the least important reason for the study of animals in psychology.

Second, animals are studied for comparative purposes—that is, to learn more about the full range of their capacities and functions, and to analyze the initiation and development of particular organ systems and processes (for example, the nervous system, discrimination learning, and so on). From this point of view, it cannot be denied that there has indeed been, at least until recently, a marked reluctance on the part of learning researchers to study a wide variety of animal forms. But is it legitimate to criticize any researcher for investigating what he finds interesting? As will be explained later, most of the investigators who utilize animals in their research do so not because of any special comparative interests—nor in many cases, because of any special interest in the applicability of their findings to humans. Thus the burden of improvement of this situation would seem to fall upon those who profess themselves to be directly concerned about

comparative psychology, rather than upon those who are not so directly concerned. Fortunately, promising starts are being made along these lines, stimulated most importantly, perhaps, by the rapprochement of experimentalists within psychology and the group of animal-behavior researchers called ethologists within zoology (see Schoenfeld and Baron, 1965).

The special comparative objective involving humans is of primary interest to many persons, within as well as outside psychology, and especially to students of psychology. These persons, with their strong interest in practical affairs, often have great difficulty in seeing the usefulness of research on lower animals, especially at a time when psychology is being called upon to help resolve so many pressing human needs. Several rejoinders can be made to this questioning attitude. For one thing, the same answer can be given as was mentioned earlier with regard to the comparative criticism—namely, let those who are so interested in human applications do that work, but let others, who are not so concerned, go their own way. (See Hilgard, 1964; Marx and Tombaugh, 1967, Chapter 8; and Hilgard and Bower, 1966, Chapter 16 for discussions of the problem of interesting and training educators in learning research that will be more directly relevant to everyday teaching procedures.) Furthermore, it can be pointed out that generalizations are never completely safe and that generalizing from infrahuman to human is on the same continuum as all generalizations. One cannot safely assume that merely because human *S*s are used the results are *ipso facto* widely applicable to human problems. As a matter of fact, as psychology students should know, it is not even safe to generalize from time to time for the same individual. Obviously, the degree of safety varies widely in these situations, but it is always safest to be extremely cautious about generalizing. Finally, and most important, the animal researcher will point to his primary goals, as described immediately following, and will hope that some glimmer of understanding will shine through.

The third use of animals in behavioral research is as tools for the study of the various behavioral functions in which psychologists are interested. From this point of view, which is assuredly a dominant one in experimental psychology and should at least be recognized by nonexperimental psychologists, the particular type of Ss used is of strictly secondary concern. The major objective is the development of the kind of lawful relationships among variables which is the ultimate goal of all science. And it is sometimes very difficult for this kind of so-called pure researcher to see why he cannot be allowed to proceed on his own way, working with humans or animals or whatever (for example, computers, as in certain research on problem solving). Rats and pigeons are popular, partly for reasons of historical accident— they were selected for research, proved satisfactory, and now have a huge accumulation of important knowledge—and partly for reasons of convenience (ease of obtaining, maintenance, and so on) as well as special applicability (for example, the rat is unusually well suited to maze learning, the pigeon to discrimination of hues, and so on).

These factors are less dramatic than the giant salivary cell of the fruitfly, *Drosophila melanogaster*, which makes this organism so attractive to the geneticist—so much so that the entire modern science of genetics can be said to have been developed largely on the basis of knowledge gained from investigation of this single organism; they are also less dramatic than the extraordinarily large optical cell of the *Limulus* crab, which attracts visual research to this particular animal form. But the considerations which make the rat and the pigeon, or any other species, attractive to the researcher should be evaluated in the light of the objectives of those researchers—and not the objectives of the critic. Viewed in this light, the concentration of learning researchers upon the rat and the pigeon becomes more understandable.

All this is not to deny the need for extensive investigations of an increasingly wider range of animal forms, for the purpose of improving the generalizability of our knowledge of behavioral functions like learning as well as for purely comparative purposes. Ultimately, psychology will need to have both the *intensive* investigation of particular behavioral functions, most conveniently performed upon a small number of animal forms, and the *extensive* investigation of a wider variety of animal forms. And there have been within recent years some encouraging signs (for example, Bitterman, 1960, 1965) that progress along the latter front is accelerating.

2

The Free Operant

Stemming from the work of B. F. Skinner (1938, 1961), the operant-conditioning movement, whose task is sometimes described as the "functional analysis of behavior," has become an increasingly visible and viable force within psychology. This development has been reflected in the formation and growth of a special journal, *The Journal of the Experimental Analysis of Behavior*, in 1958, and more recently by the formation of a new division of the American Psychological Association, the Division for the Experimental Analysis of Behavior (see Skinner, 1966b).

This chapter provides a brief description of the more important aspects of the operant-conditioning movement considered in relationship to the older and more orthodox methodologies in learning research.

Free-Operant Instrumental Training

An *operant* is a response which is *emitted* by S, without any particular forcing stimulus, rather than elicited, as by a reinforcing (unconditioned) stimulus. The latter process defines a respondent, the type of response involved in classical conditioning.

The free operant should be contrasted with the usual discrete-trial procedure. The pivotal distinction is whether or not the S is able to respond repeatedly within a training session. In free-operant training S is free to respond at any time without the restrictions normally imposed by the discrete-trial procedure.

As an illustration of such restrictions, consider the runway. Once S has traversed the runway and entered the goalbox he is not immediately free to run again. In the ordinary runway, he must be removed from the goalbox and returned to the startbox (usually after being placed during the intertrial interval in a separate waiting chamber).

In the free-operant experimental situation developed by Skinner (1938) a maximal amount of freedom for a response is obtained. The sound-proofed, ventilated chamber is purposely stripped down to the barest essentials. Performance of the referent response (the one to be measured) is thereby encouraged by reducing the opportunity for other overt responses. For

Figure 2-1. Cutaway view of pigeon at key in operant-conditioning box. Feeding magazine, offering grain for reinforcement, is shown open at bottom.

example, for the rat S, ordinarily all that is available within the chamber for manipulation is a bar, or lever, the pressing of which defines the referent response. Such a device is commonly called a manipulandum, sometimes an operandum. For the pigeon S, a disk (called a key) is lighted from behind, and the pecking of it defines the referent response. Similar simple responses are required of other animals. Such a device is depicted in Figure 2-1, for the pigeon. (Figures 1-3 and 2-3 show rats in boxes with bars as manipulanda.)

If the referent response is not made within a reasonable time, in initial training, responding can be facilitated by such techniques as smearing small amounts of food on the bar, for the rat, or placing a small spot in the transilluminated key, for the pigeon. These operations are very simple illustrations of the free-operant training procedure called shaping, a description of which follows.

A wider variety of manipulanda can of course be used with human Ss, but even here a simple bar or button is sufficient. Operant procedures are commonly applied to many categories of human behavior, and especially to the behavior of children and psychiatric patients. Reinforcement, as with candy pellets for children or cigarettes or coins for adults, is effective even when it follows the response in the absence of any verbal instructions.

The response rate measure. An important consequence of the freedom permitted in responding is that the most appropriate response measure becomes the rate at which the referent response is made. The rate measure is the only one that has been emphasized by Skinner, and by many of his more orthodox followers. Rate of response has been customarily measured by a special recording device, called a *cumulative recorder*. This consists of a continuously rotating drum across which a marking pen is pulled slowly. Each response steps the pen slightly (see Figure 2-2, p. 21). The rate at which the response is performed is therefore indicated by the slope of the line —a perfectly horizontal line indicating no responses at all (as in complete extinction). Although the cumulative recorder is still the prime measuring device in certain laboratories (see Skinner, 1966a, 1966b; Dinsmoor, 1966; Verhave, 1966b), in other operant laboratories it is now being used mainly as a monitoring device and as a means of producing records of responses for visual inspection.

The great emphasis in free-operant research on the response-rate measure raises questions about the comparative advantages of this measure. Although much has been made by free-operant proponents of the similarities between this measure and measures in other sciences (for example, Honig, 1966a), it is difficult to agree with the more extreme positions advanced (for example, Skinner's 1966b contention that response rate operates in "real time" and is therefore more meaningful than "trial-to-trial" measures). The major features of rate as a measure of response are that it provides a stable and yet sensitive measure of continuous behavior. Its stability is a function of the relatively great amounts of time that are used in training the S, and its sensitivity to the effects of even very subtle variables (for example, slight amounts of drugs, which may produce discernible behavioral changes, in response rate, before gross physiological changes occur) is a matter of empirical demonstration.

From one point of view the absence of such events as the opening and closing of doors in the apparatus may be regarded as at least in part responsible for the allegedly greater regularity of free-operant behavior, once it is well established. From another point of view, however, the organism's own behavior, allowed to occur without restrictions imposed by E, may be regarded as containing certain intrinsic confounding.

For example, responses associated with the consuming of food can interfere with making a subsequent instrumental response, as Platt and Spence (1967) have shown. The discrete-trial procedure has the advantage of controlling this kind of behavior by restricting it to a specified time span. Measures such as response latency and amplitude can then be taken from a common starting point (provided, say, by the opening of the start door in the runway). Acquisition curves based on such better-controlled measures may be regarded as superior in this respect to those provided by free-operant rate measures. Furthermore, it can be argued that if the same amount of time is made available to S in the discrete-trial situation, a corresponding regularity of behavior can be obtained (with S adapting to the external events such as door operations in much the same way perhaps as he adjusts his rate of response in the free-operant situation). We may conclude that for certain purposes response rate is an unexcelled measure, whereas for other purposes it is not as useful as alternative measures.

Schedules of reinforcement. As used by Skinner and the operant-conditioning group, the term *reinforcement* is essentially descriptive. That is to say, it is not intended to imply any hypothetical behavioral mechanism but refers merely to the fact that when a response is followed by certain kinds of stimulus consequences—the reinforcement operation—it is strengthened. Such strengthening, which is the key process in free-operant research, is identified with increased rate of responding or increased control of the behavior. (See Hilgard and Bower, 1966, Chapter 14, for a recent discussion of the theoretical issues concerning the reinforcement mechanism, and also *Learning: Theories*.)

A fundamental variable commonly manipulated in free-operant research is the scheduling of reinforcement (Ferster and Skinner, 1957). Reinforcers can be given following every response, producing continuous reinforcement (CRF), or intermittently after responses (IRF). The latter operation produces what is sometimes called, outside the free-operant framework, partial reinforcement (PRF) or aperiodic reinforcement (APR).

There are four basic intermittent reinforcement schedules. Two of these are *ratio* schedules, in which reinforcement frequency is determined by the number of responses made. A fixed-ratio (FR) schedule provides reinforcement after some *set* number of responses, and a variable-ratio (VR) schedule after *varying* numbers of responses. The counterpart *interval* schedules are the fixed-interval (FI), which provides reinforcement for the first response following a *set* interval of time from the last reinforcement, and the variable-interval (VI), which provides reinforcement for the first response following *varying* intervals of time from the last reinforcement. Variable schedules are identified by numbers representing the means of the values used (for example, VR 5 refers to a schedule with a mean ratio requirement of five responses, and VI 1 min. refers to a schedule with a mean interval of one minute between successive reinforcements).

Some of the more commonly observed behavioral results of the basic schedules may be noted. Ratio schedules customarily produce an especially high rate of responding, and this is particularly true of the VR schedule (see slot-machine behavior in humans for a clear illustration from everyday life). Fixed-interval schedules usually produce a gradual acceleration in responding toward the end of the interval. The cumulative record shows a concave inclination which is called a *scallop*. Finally, all of the intermittent schedules result in markedly increased resistance to extinction, compared to CRF.

Figure 2-2 shows representative cumulative records for each of these four basic schedules of reinforcement.

A very great variety of complex schedules of reinforcement is possible when the basic schedules are combined. For example, a *mixed* schedule is one in which the schedule changes within a test period (for example, FR 5, VI 2 min.) in the absence of any associated external cues; if the latter are present, a *multiple* schedule results.

Other complications of the early free-operant procedure have been developed to produce an intriguing richness of experimental manipulation. For example, the *time-out* (or blackout) operation takes S out of the experimental situation. Time out can be response correlated, and then may serve as a punishment, or as a means of avoiding the initial situation. (Thus, the pigeon which has been on an especially difficult ratio schedule is provided with a separate key which when pecked turns out the light on the main key and removes the possibility of reinforcement.) The best recent single sources of detailed accounts of the current free-operant procedures and results are the collection of essays edited by Honig (1966b) and the selected readings edited by Verhave (1966a).

Shaping. Perhaps the most important of the procedural variations introduced by the free-operant researchers is that called *shaping*. Shaping refers to the judicious use of selective reinforcement to develop new responses and combinations of responses. The basic process in shaping is "successive approximation." This phrase merely means that in reinforcing S the E waits until behavior similar to that which is to be developed occurs. In other words, if one wishes to reinforce the raising of the right wing in a pigeon, he does not normally wait until the wing is fully and clearly raised but rather until it is raised just a small amount —and then immediately reinforces (in this case, operates the grain magazine). This process continues by additional relatively small steps as the desired behavior is more and more closely approximated. Eventually, given sufficient care and patience on the part of E, the desired behavior is obtained.

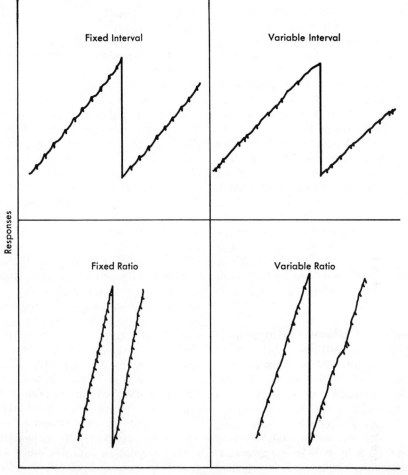

Figure 2-2. Representative cumulative records of the four fundamental schedules of reinforcement. The paper moves from right to left as the record is made. Each response steps the response (stepping) pen toward the top of the page. The slash marks occurring in each record represent reinforcements, and the vertical line represents the resetting of the response pen. Note the scallops in FI recording, the linear appearance of the VI curve representing uniform response rate, and the high rate generated by FR, especially, and by VR.

Obviously, an instrumental response cannot be reinforced until it occurs. Because eliciting stimuli are not used in free-operant research the initial rate, called the *operant level*, must sometimes be increased by such "artificial" means as shaping. Some of the more interesting applications of shaping are evident in the techniques of animal training, generally used with more or less effectiveness but without explicit rationale by animal trainers. (See Breland and Breland, 1966, for a systematic treatment of this topic.)

Impressive behavioral repertoires can be

developed by successive shaping procedures
—for example, "ping-pong" playing by
pigeons, dropping balls through hoops by
rats, and the like. Perhaps the most
fascinating incident involves Skinner's
wartime project on training pigeons as
"bombardiers" (see Skinner, 1960). Although the project was rendered unnecessary by the use of atomic weapons to
end the war with Japan, this work did seem
to offer some practical promise. The
pigeon S was trained to peck at a lighted
display in such a manner as to keep a
projectile on target. More mundane uses of
pigeons in industry, as assembly-line
inspectors of pharmaceutical and electronic
materials, are recounted by Verhave
(1966c) and by Cumming (1966). These
tasks utilize the extraordinarily fine visual
discrimination of which the pigeon is
capable.

"Superstitious" behavior. What Skinner
(1948) called "superstitious" behavior in
the pigeon affords another illustration of
the potency of reinforcement. In this
case the "selection" of a response to
be strengthened is entirely adventitious.
Whereas shaping refers to the case in which
E selects a response and succeeds in getting
S to perform it by successive approximation, superstitious behavior is investigated
in situations in which reinforcement is
programmed independently of the S's
behavior. For example, food is offered every
thirty seconds irrespective of what S
happens to be doing. Nevertheless, S often
adopts a relatively stereotyped behavior
pattern during the thirty seconds between
food presentations. The presumption is that
the reinforcement operation "selects"
some particular response (for example,
raising of the left leg by the pigeon) which
happens to occur close to the time of food
reinforcement. A single food reinforcement
increases the rate of this particular response
sufficiently to make it probable that it will
again occur shortly, and so be likely to be
reinforced again.

The Problem of Acquisition

One of the interesting aspects of free-
operant research utilizing the response-rate
measure is that so little direct experimentation has been performed on the problem of
learning, or response acquisition, itself.
With the exception of such work as Skinner's
(1948) demonstration of "superstitious"
behavior, some of the research on discrimination training, and certain research
on avoidance training, especially that using
the Sidman schedule (Sidman, 1953),
acquisition of the response has not been
much emphasized as a problem in its own
right. Rather, the focus is on an analysis of
control of behavior by various variables.

Although operant conditioning is generally considered to involve learning, as the
term *conditioning* very plainly indicates, a
question as to the aptness of such a
classification may nonetheless be raised.
Performance of an already well-learned
response is most commonly what is
manipulated in such research, and most of
the effects observed are functions of what
are often interpreted as motivational factors.

A limitation of the free-operant procedure with regard to the generation of
regular acquisition data was noted in the
preceding discussion of the interference
with the instrumental response by responses made to the reinforcer, particularly
the food reinforcer (see Platt and Spence,
1967). Apart from this limitation there has
seemed to be a lack of concern among most
operant conditioners for acquisition data.
A major reason for this lack of interest in
acquisition, as compared with performance,
is the general feeling that before meaningful experimental variations can be introduced there must be a highly stable,
learned response, as indicated by the
regularity of its rate of emission. In a recent
paper on free-operant methodology, for
example, Dinsmoor (1966, p. 423) emphasizes this point: "*If the experimenter fails
to establish an appropriate base-line perform-*

ance for each of his subjects, his entire experiment may be vitiated and all his efforts wasted."

With such a requirement it is hardly surprising that more has not been done on the problem of response acquisition. This is especially unfortunate in that an experimental analysis of the shaping process, so much emphasized in informal discussion and demonstration by the free-operant researcher, would seem to offer an unusually fertile field for systematic, analytic research. Transitions among schedules of reinforcement offer one related problem where systematic research with free-operant techniques has been performed and could well be increased.

The argument for a relative position on this issue, viewing any change in performance as acquisition, has been ably made by Sidman (1960). He asks, for example, "Is acquisition of behavior from a zero baseline, if indeed a zero baseline is available, any less a special condition than its acquisition from a more active state?" (1960, p. 117). Whether or not a theoretical zero baseline exists, however, the fact remains that organisms do acquire *new* stimulus-response relationships, and such acquisition is the focus of much research in the field of learning.

Another facet of the free-operant position on acquisition, at least as investigated by other techniques, may be seen in Skinner's comments on learning curves. He holds that the shape of learning curves using time or error measures "tells us little or nothing about the processes of conditioning and extinction. . . . It merely describes the rather crude overall effects of adventitious contingencies . . ." (Skinner, 1966a, p. 17). Although there may well be a good basis for questioning some such data, this statement overlooks the fact that there are other ways of introducing order into experimental research than the free-operant procedure. Moreover, it is the task of scientific research to uncover the determinants of the gross and complex learning

process, such as is represented by the kinds of curves criticized by Skinner. In this process, useful information concerning acquisition and extinction can result from the systematic manipulation of experimental variables in the discrete-trial as well as the free-operant procedure. As indicated previously, each methodology has both strengths and weaknesses.

The Emphasis on the Individual *S*

The operant conditioning group has consistently maintained that if sufficient experimental control is exercised over behavior there is no need for large groups of *S*s. Large groups and statistical analyses of data are normally used, according to this argument, to cover up deficiencies in experimental control (see Sidman, 1960). Experimental reports in the operant *Journal of the Experimental Analysis of Behavior* customarily involve very small numbers of *S*s, who are typically trained and tested over relatively long periods of time.

An important purpose of this approach is the desire to predict the behavior of individual *S*s, rather than groups of *S*s. Sidman (1952) has been particularly insistent on this point and has demonstrated that the mathematical functions obtained from groups of *S*s cannot be used to predict the behavior of individuals. However, the replication of experimental results by additional individual *S*s is an acceptable procedure.

Few experimental psychologists would disagree with the position that it is preferable to exercise stringent experimental controls, directly eliminating variability in data attributable to extraneous conditions, but this objective is more readily aspired to than achieved. Experimental problems vary widely in their susceptibility to controls. Furthermore, complex interactions exist among the experimental variables under investigation and certain other variables, interindividual differences as well as treatment conditions (see Chapter 3). Although these interactions must be recognized, and need to be investigated, they cannot be predicted in advance of the data. Dependence upon one or two Ss per treatment condition may therefore seriously mislead an E, save perhaps for some of the simpler problems.

Beyond these considerations, it is often difficult, and sometimes impossible, to use a single S for more than one experimental treatment, as is customarily done in free-operant research. This is obviously true when experimentally naive Ss are indicated. In this respect operant researchers have been criticized for neglecting the possible contaminating role of complex past experiences, often incompletely reported, of their Ss (for example, Grant, 1958).

In spite of these cavils, the operant-conditioning stress on the individual S has had a most salutary effect on the methodology and point of view of the more traditional researchers. Although group research has not been discarded, Es now not only attempt to use smaller numbers of Ss wherever possible, but also, and more important, pay much more attention to the individual learning data that are obtained in large group experiments. Moreover, interpretations of group data are much more carefully made, with concern for the possible pitfalls of using averaged data when individual behavior is really involved.

Stimulus Control of Behavior: Discrimination Learning

As Skinner has pointed out, stimuli may be said to "control behavior" in three major ways. First, they *elicit* certain responses, as in the classical-conditioning procedure; second, they *reinforce* responses, as in instrumental learning; and third, they *cue* behavior, as in discrimination learning. This latter term is generally used to refer to any kind of learning procedure in which particular stimuli, or cues, come to exercise differential or selective control over responses.

Stimulus control plays a key role in free-operant research. According to Skinner's early (1938) formulation, a positive discriminative stimulus (S^D) is one which "sets the occasion for" a response to be reinforced. That is, through learning S begins to respond in the presence of the S^D because of selective reinforcement; and, contrariwise, *not* to respond in the presence of a negative stimulus (conventionally labeled S^Δ) because of extinction. Development of this kind of stimulus control is much emphasized in the "functional analysis of behavior" by operant researchers.

Discrimination learning may, more generally, be categorized on the basis of the temporal relationship of the cue presentation into (1) *successive* and (2) *simultaneous* procedures. In the successive design, the cues to be discriminated are presented on separate occasions. In the simultaneous procedure, these cues are presented together and a choice required.

Successive-discrimination procedures may be further categorized on the basis of whether a simple yes/no (or go/no go) response is required—that is, S either responds to the positive cue or fails to respond to the negative cue—or differential responses of a positive sort are required for reinforcement—for example, a left turn in a T-maze for a dark cue and a right turn for a bright cue.

Perhaps the most exciting recent development within the area of discrimination learning has been the demonstration by Terrace (1963a, 1963b, 1966b) of "errorless discrimination." In the Terrace procedure a pigeon is initially trained to respond to the positive cue. The negative cue is presented weakly (that is, the response key is very dimly lit) at first, so as not to encourage a response. A progressively more strongly lit negative cue can then be used, with S never responding to it. An S so trained may discriminate perfectly (that is, make very few or no responses at all to the negative cue) in contrast to the S trained in the usual manner with full simultaneous or successive presentation of both cues. This technique has been and promises to continue to be a most fruitful means of experimentation (see Terrace, 1966b; Hilgard and Bower, 1966; Chapter 15 and Section IV of this volume). The errorless discrimination research not only raises questions about the orthodox view of discrimination learning as dependent upon extinction of the negative response tendency, but also has important implications for efficiency of discrimination training.

For the most part psychologists investigating discrimination learning have not been interested in purely perceptual matters, and have therefore used what they thought to be clearly discriminable cues (in order to investigate the role of various factors in the rate of acquisition of the discrimination). Recently, however, there has developed a renewed interest in the perceptual and attentional factors involved in such learning. These researches and their rationales are reviewed in the recent learning-theory text by Hilgard and Bower (1966, Chapter 15; see also Mackintosh, 1965), and in the section on cognitive learning theory in *Learning: Theories*. Further discussion of the techniques of discriminative instrumental conditioning is to be found in Sections II and IV of this volume.

Controlled-Operant (Discrete-Trial) Instrumental Training

Psychologists have developed a wide variety of controlled-operant, or discrete-trial, learning devices. Certain of the older and more orthodox of these are described in Chapter 1 and in Section II. It is important to recall that the restriction on opportunity to respond is the key distinction between the two types of instrumental

procedures. Thus, the primary characteristic of the free operant is the use of the free-response-rate measure. Other characteristics may be regarded as secondary and as a function of the use of a relatively simplified test compartment with restricted locomotion. The controlled operant in the Skinner-type experimental chamber seems to offer a nice compromise. As developed for the rat S, it utilizes a retractable bar. The presentation and retraction of this bar define a trial. Retraction of the bar can be effected either by S, by pressing, or by E, by experimental program after a predetermined period of time if pressing does not occur.

One recent multiple-bar setup (Marx *et al.*, 1965) can be used to measure choice behavior, in the manner demonstrated in Figure 2-3. In this application the back bar is presented to initiate a trial. When it is pressed once (or several times, if a higher response ratio is required), it retracts and the other two bars, on the right and left sides, appear. When one of these is pressed, both retract and the appropriate feeding magazine operates to present a reinforcement. After an interval of time the back bar is again presented, to initiate the next trial. If on any trial an insufficient number of barpresses occur, the bar is programmed to retract automatically (after an arbitrary time limit) thus ending the trial (much as a rat is removed from a runway after some arbitrary time limit). This apparatus permits not only a great variety of testing conditions (for example, short delay of reinforcements on one side versus long delay on the other, high reward versus low reward, and so on), but also simulation of other training and testing procedures (for example nonchoice performance such as is involved in the runway, by using only the back bar and one side bar with associated magazine).

The use of this kind of controlled-operant procedure combines the advantages of the discrete-trial methodology and the conditioning box. The latter advantages are the following:

Figure 2-3. A multiple-bar operant box designed for discrete-trial experimentation. The rat S has pressed the center bar (behind S) to bring out the two side bars in a choice situation. The feeding mechanism is in the floor directly below each bar.

1. High degree of environmental control, thus assuring less interference from extraneous stimulation. (This feature can of course be provided in a runway or a maze, but with more difficulty.)

2. Good adaptation of S to the test environment (very difficult to obtain in an apparatus where extensive locomotion occurs, even with environmental controls).

3. Reduced handling by E, and consequent reduction of emotionality in S, especially between trials. (This feature is especially difficult to accomplish outside of the box.)

4. Automated programming and recording (possible to some extent but less readily accomplished in the runway or maze).

5. More exact control of the reinforcement operation, as by precisely timed presentation and withdrawal of the feeding magazine (possible in the goalbox of a runway but more difficult to achieve normally because of the variation in S's rate of approach to the magazine).

With regard to the problem of response measures, what are the advantages of the controlled-operant procedure? As suggested earlier, they are mainly that a different kind of control can be achieved of S's behavior when measures other than response rate are used, or when response rate is measured over relatively short periods of time (discrete trials). In the typical free operant, for example, interresponse time (IRT) can be obtained, and is being increasingly used; but this measure, although valuable, is not the same kind of latency measure as is customarily used in discrete-trial research. A more uniform measure of response strength can be obtained when each latency measure is based upon the same formal starting point (introduction of bar, or presentation of stimulus cue) and when interfering responses are minimized. Similarly, measures of probability of response (either in a choice or a nonchoice situation), response amplitude, duration of response, and errors are more readily taken in the discrete-trial situation. Although Skinner (1966b) has minimized the role of these measures, they are nonetheless considered to be of value by many investigators and are widely used in a variety of learning problems.

Typically, discrete-trial experiments utilize a small number of daily trials for each *S* and require a relatively small amount of time per *S* (in contrast to free-operant procedures where usually a large amount of time is given each *S*, but a small number of *S*s is used). In order to avoid sequential effects trials are sometimes spaced as widely as one day apart, although more often trials are spaced at intervals of up to one minute. Massed trials (minimal spacing of fifteen or less seconds) are sometimes used for tests, because massing seems to be more sensitive to the effects of some variables (for example, Cogan and Marx, 1965). One of the advantages of the controlled-operant multiple-bar set-up described previously is that all of the *S*s in an experiment can be run each day (using eight boxes simultaneously). This not only makes possible the completion of the experiment in less time than when separate squads are run, successively, but also reduces variability in *S*s (all can be drawn from same population) and experimental conditions (effects of extraneous laboratory variables that change over time are minimized). These advantages of the Skinner-box procedure are all independent of the discrete-trial variable and can be found in free-operant research.

In the typical discrete-trial instrumental training all of the experimental *S*s are given a set number of training trials, after which test trials are administered. Sometimes, however, *S*s are trained to a criterion of mastery, at which point the test is introduced. An obvious advantage of the former procedure is that it permits an easy control of number of reinforcements and trials and that it is relatively simple and straightforward to use. Its major dis-

advantage is that it will almost invariably allow overtraining of some *S*s as well as undertraining of others, because it does not take account of individual differences in learning rate. The use of a criterion of mastery, with each *S* being treated individually, overcomes this particular objection. However, this is more cumbersome to apply and has the further disadvantage that numbers of trials and of reinforcements differ from *S* to *S*.

Trends Toward Integration

A number of interesting trends may be discerned with regard to the increasing integration of the Skinnerian group with the mainstream of American experimental psychology. Three of these will be noted.

First, there has been a very large amount of adaptation of free-operant techniques, and their incorporation into other types of instrumental-learning situations (for example, the use of "free behavior" by Logan, 1964; the development of automated controlled-operant conditioning boxes by Marx *et al.*, 1965).

Second, there has been a marked increase within the movement of research with human *S*s, from normal as well as psychiatric populations. Although the surge of interest in the teaching machine as a special device seems to have diminished, interest in programmed learning has not. But the most significant recent development has been the rapid expansion of behavioral modification, or behavior therapy, as it is more often called within the field of clinical psychology (Ullman and Krasner, 1965). This movement has had a strong impact upon many clinicians whose backgrounds have been far removed from operant conditioning. Behavior therapy, which essentially involves a direct behavioral attack upon deviant symptoms without much in the way of explicit concern for inner variables, does involve more than operant procedures, but these are a fundamental part of the movement as it is presently constituted.

Third, within the operant-conditioning group, there has developed gradually a broadening of interests (see Honig, 1966b) as well as a growing concern with matters of interpretation, in marked contrast with the earlier, strictly atheoretical Skinnerian position. The extent to which this trend has grown was indicated by a session on "The Theory of Reinforcement Schedules" at the 1966 national convention of the American Psychological Association—

chaired by none other than B. F. Skinner himself.

As a result of these recent developments, the operant-conditioning movement appears to be well started on the process of integration with the older, more orthodox methodologies within psychology. As it succeeds in influencing psychologists from other conceptual and procedural frameworks, and in shaping their behaviors, it will necessarily lose much of its original identity—just as have most of the historically important movements as they have contributed to the growth of the science.

Glossary

acquisition. The process by which a new response is learned through practice.

adaptation. The decrement in a sensation or response resulting from its repeated elicitation by a stimulus.

behavior therapy. Application of operant-conditioning procedures to the modification of everyday human problems; reinforcement is used selectively to modify behavior in a clinical setting.

conditioning. A kind of learning in which an originally ineffective stimulus comes to elicit (classical conditioning) or set the stage for (operant conditioning) a particular response.

conditioning, classical. Associative learning in which the reinforcement is given contiguously with the response but independently of its occurrence.

conditioning, instrumental. Associative learning in which reinforcement is contingent upon the making of a response.

conditioning, operant. Instrumental conditioning in which S "emits" the learned response in the absence of any particular eliciting stimulus.

contiguity theory. The proposition that association of stimulus and response is sufficient to produce learning.

controlled operant. An emitted response which S is permitted to make only at certain times (in a discrete-trial procedure).

crucial experiment. An experiment intended to make possible a critical decision between alternative theoretical accounts.

discrete trial. The use of intertrial intervals, providing separate trials, in a learning experiment.

discrimination. The process of differentiating among stimuli.

discriminative stimulus. A cue which has been associated with either reinforcement (positive discriminative stimulus, or S^D) or nonreinforcement (negative discriminative stimulus, or S^Δ) and which has therefore acquired control over S's behavior.

E. Abbreviation for experimenter.

effector. An organ of response (muscle or gland).

empirical. Relating to sensory experience.

extinction. The procedure whereby S is allowed to make the previously learned response but in the absence of the previous reinforcement; the reduction in learned performance resulting from such a procedure.

free operant. A response whose emission leaves S in a position to make further such responses immediately (for example, pressing a bar in a box, as contrasted with running down a runway).

functionalism. A psychological system which stresses the function and utility of behavior.

habituation. Adaptation of a motor response.

learning. Relatively enduring change in behavior which is a function of prior behavior ("practice").

manipulanda. Objects in an experimental situation by means of which *S* can effect changes in the environment.

maturation. The development (growth) of structure and function in an organism as a direct result of its biological inheritance.

modality. A form of sensory experience (for example, vision, audition).

motivation. The conditions within an organism that activate it in some particular behavior.

nonsense syllable. A relatively meaningless verbal stimulus, usually consisting of a consonant-vowel-consonant (CVC) combination, which was invented by Ebbinghaus as a means of studying the acquisition of verbal associations.

operant level. Rate of response prior to any reinforcement.

paradigm. A fundamental design for a specific type of experiment.

performance. The behavior of *S*; a function of appropriate motivation as well as learning.

pseudoconditioning. The strengthening of the relationship between a response and a previously neutral stimulus by means of repeated elicitation of the response by another stimulus in the absence of pairing of the two stimuli.

retention. The maintenance of learning over a period of time following acquisition.

S. Abbreviation for subject.

sensitization. Strengthening of a response normally made to the conditioned stimulus, after training in which conditioned and unconditioned stimuli are not paired.

shaping. An operant experimental procedure in which selective reinforcement is used to train *S*, by means of successive approximations, in some new behavior.

superstitious behavior. Operant responding in which there is only an accidental connection between the response and the appearance of a reinforcer.

transfer. The influence that prior training has upon subsequent learning.

variable. A category of objects or events; a factor or condition conceptualized for purposes of scientific investigation.

References

Beach, F. A. The snark was a Boojum. *Amer. Psychol.*, 1950, **5**, 115–124.

Bitterman, M. E. Toward a comparative psychology of learning. *Amer. Psychol.*, 1960, 15, 704–712.

Bitterman, M. E. Phyletic differences in learning. *Amer. Psychol.*, 1965, **20**, 396–410.

Breland, K. & Breland, Marian. *Animal behavior.* New York: Macmillan, 1966.

Bryan, W. L., & Harter, N. Studies in the physiology and psychology of the telegraphic language. *Psychol. Rev.*, 1897, **4**, 27–53.

Cogan, D. C., & Marx, M. H. The effect of intermittent presentation of goalbox cues on resistance to extinction under spaced and massed conditions. *Psychol. Rec.*, 1965, **15**, 169–173.

Cumming, W. W. A bird's eye glimpse of men and machines. In R. Ulrich, T. Stachnik, & J. Mabry (Eds.), *Control of human behavior.* Glenview, Ill.: Scott, Foresman, 1966.

Dinsmoor, J. A. Operant conditioning. In Sidowski, J. B. (Ed.), *Experimental methods and instrumentation in psychology.* New York: McGraw-Hill, 1966, 421–450.

Ferster, C. B., & Skinner, B. F. *Schedules of reinforcement.* New York: Appleton-Century-Crofts, 1957.

Grant, D. A. Review of *Schedules of reinforcement* by C. B. Ferster & B. F. Skinner. *Contemporary Psychology*, 1958, **III**, 328–329.

Hilgard, E. R. A perspective on the relationship between learning theory and educational practices. Ch. 17 in E. R. Hilgard (Ed.), *Theories of learning and instruction.* Yearb. Natl. Soc. Stud. Educ., 1964, **63**, Part I, 402–418.

Hilgard, E. R., & Bower, G. H. *Theories of learning*. 3rd ed. New York: Appleton-Century-Crofts, 1966.

Honig, W. K. Introductory remarks. In W. K. Honig (Ed.), *Operant behavior: Areas of research and application*. New York: Appleton-Century-Crofts, 1966a.

Honig, W. K. (Ed.), *Operant behavior: Areas of research and application*. New York: Appleton-Century-Crofts, 1966b.

Hull, C. L. *Principles of behavior*. New York: Appleton-Century-Crofts, 1943.

Kimble, G. A. *Hilgard and Marquis' Conditioning and Learning*. 2nd ed. New York: Appleton-Century-Crofts, 1961.

Logan, F. A. The free behavior situation. In D. Levine (Ed.), *Nebraska symposium on motivation*. Lincoln: Univer. of Nebraska Press, 1964.

Logan, F. A., & Wagner, A. R. *Reward and punishment*. Boston: Allyn & Bacon, 1965.

Mackintosh, N. J. Overtraining, reversal, and extinction in rats and chicks. *J. comp. physiol. Psychol.*, 1965, **59**, 31–36.

Marx, M. H. The activation of habits. *Psychol. Rep.*, 1966, **19**, 527–550.

Marx, M. H., & Tombaugh, T. N. *Motivation: Psychological principles and educational implications*. San Francisco: Chandler, 1967.

Marx, M. H., Tombaugh, T. N., Hatch, R. S., & Tombaugh, Jo W. Controlled operant conditioning boxes with discrete-trial programming for multiple experimental use. *Percept. mot. Skills*, 1965, **21**, 247–254.

Platt, J. R., & Spence, K. W. Intertrial interval and response-competition in discrete-trials lever-pressing. *Amer. J. Psychol.*, 1967, **80**, 110–114.

Rosenthal, R. *Experimenter effects in behavior research*. New York: Appleton-Century-Crofts, 1966.

Schoenfeld, W. N., & Baron, S. H. Ethology and experimental psychology. *Science*, 1965, **147**, 634–635.

Sidman, M. A note on functional relations obtained from group data. *Psychol. Bull.*, 1952, **49**, 263–269.

Sidman, M. Avoidance conditioning with brief shock and no exteroceptive warning signal. *Science*, 1953, **118**, 157–158.

Sidman, M. *Tactics of scientific research*. New York: Basic Books, 1960.

Skinner, B. F. *The behavior of organisms*. New York: Appleton-Century-Crofts, 1938.

Skinner, B. F. Superstitions in the pigeon. *J. exp. Psychol.*, 1948, **38**, 168–172.

Skinner, B. F. Pigeons in a pelican. *Amer. Psychol.*, 1960, **15**, 28–37.

Skinner, B. F. *Cumulative record*. Rev. ed. New York: Appleton-Century-Crofts, 1961.

Skinner, B. F. Operant behavior. In W. K. Honig (Ed.), *Operant behavior*. New York: Appleton-Century-Crofts, 1966a.

Skinner, B. F. What is the experimental analysis of behavior? *J. exp. anal. Behav.*, 1966b, **9**, 213–218.

Spence, K. W. *Behavior theory and conditioning*. New Haven: Yale Univer. Press, 1956.

Spence, K. W. *Behavior theory and learning*. Englewood Cliffs, N. J.: Prentice-Hall, 1960.

Terrace, H. S. Discrimination learning with and without "errors." *J. exp. Anal. Behav.*, 1963a, **6**, 1–27.

Terrace, H. S. Errorless transfer of discrimination across two continua. *J. exp. Anal. Behav.*, 1963b, **6**, 223–232.

Terrace, H. S. Behavioral contrast and the peak shift: Effects of extended discrimination training. *J. exp. Anal. Behav.*, 1966a, **9**, 613–617.

Terrace, H. S. Stimulus control. In W. K. Honig (Ed.), *Operant behavior: Areas of research and application*. New York: Appleton-Century-Crofts, 1966b.

Thorndike, E. L. Animal intelligence: An experimental study of the associative processes in animals. *Psychol. Monogr.*, 1898, **2**, No. 8.

Tolman, E. C. *Purposive behavior in animals and men*. New York: Appleton-Century-Crofts, 1932.

Ullman, L. P., & Krasner, L. *Case studies in behavior modification*. Holt, Rinehart, & Winston, 1965.

Verhave, T. (Ed.), *The Experimental analysis of behavior*. New York: Appleton-Century-Crofts. 1966a.

Verhave, T. An introduction to the experimental analysis of behavior. In T. Verhave (Ed.), *The Experimental analysis of behavior*. New York: Appleton-Century-Crofts, 1966b.

Verhave, T. The pigeon as a quality-control inspector. *Amer. Psychol.*, 1966c, **21**, 109–115.

Suggested Readings

Catania, A. C. (Ed.), *Contemporary Research in Operant Behavior*. Glenview, Ill.: Scott, Foresman, 1968. An emphasis on animal experiments marks this recent volume.

Deese, J., & Hulse, S. H. *The psychology of learning*. New York: McGraw-Hill, 1967. A recent revision of one of the better texts.

Honig, W. K. (Ed.), *Operant behavior: Areas of research and application*. New York: Appleton-Century-Crofts, 1966. Up-to-date contributions by many of the leading operant conditioners.

Melton, A. W. (Ed.), *Categories of human learning*. New York: Academic Press, 1964. A contributed volume reflecting the recent expansion of research on human learning.

Millenson, J. R. *Principles of behavioral analysis*. New York: Macmillan, 1967. This high-level introductory text has a very strong (operant) learning orientation.

Kimble, G. A. (Ed.), *Foundations of conditioning and learning*. New York: Appleton-Century-Crofts, 1967. A valuable historical treatment of the fundamental works in the field.

Kimble, G. A. *Hilgard and Marquis' Conditioning and Learning*. 2nd. ed. New York: Appleton-Century-Crofts, 1961. A popular text, concentrating on empirical data from animal research.

Reynolds, G. S. *A Primer of Operant Conditioning*. Glenview, Ill.: Scott, Foresman, 1968. An introduction to procedures and principles in operant conditioning.

Sidman, M. *Tactics of Scientific research*. New York: Basic Books, 1960. A stimulating treatment by a leading operant tactician.

Skinner, B. F. *Cumulative record*. Rev. ed. New York: Appleton-Century-Crofts, 1961. The best of Skinner, accumulated over about three decades.

Ulrich, R. E., Stachnik, T. J., & Mabrey, J. H. (Eds.), *Control of Human Behavior*. Glenview, Ill.: Scott, Foresman, 1968. Descriptions of varied attempts at management of human behavior by application of operant conditioning.

Verhave, T. (Ed.), *The Experimental Analysis of Behavior*. New York: Appleton-Century-Crofts, 1966. Another in the recent collections of readings in operant conditioning.

II

Instrumental Conditioning

M. R. D'Amato

Rutgers University

Instrumental Conditioning: Introduction*

Classical Conditioning Versus Instrumental Learning

Distinguishing classical conditioning from other forms of learning is not an overly difficult task. To be sure the line of demarcation is not always sharp (for example, Kimble, 1964, p. 38), but the blurry spots are relatively few. One familiar and often reliable landmark is whether application of the reinforcing stimulus depends on S's behavior. When reinforcement comes S's way regardless of his behavior one can be fairly sure of being within the boundaries of classical conditioning. If, on the other hand, S must do something to earn the reinforcing stimulus —in which case we say that reinforcement is "response contingent"—the chances are good that one has passed beyond the limits of classical conditioning into the broad

* Some of the material in this section is drawn from an undergraduate text in experimental psychology which is being prepared under contract with the McGraw-Hill Book Company.

Much of the research referred to in this section was supported by National Science Foundation grants GB-1515, GB-2784 and GB-4011.

expanse of *instrumental learning*. The latter term is meant to refer collectively to *all types of learning other than classical conditioning*.

There are, of course, other useful signs that aid orientation. Classical conditioning most usually involves effectors of the autonomic nervous system, though the conditioned eyeblink response is one clear exception. Also in classical conditioning, the response to be conditioned is under E's control by means of the unconditioned stimulus (UCS). Stated differently, on the response side the raw materials of classical conditioning are *elicited*, rather than *emitted*, responses (Skinner, 1938, pp. 19ff), the response to be conditioned (or something close to it) being directly elicitable by the UCS.

Categorizing behavior that lies beyond the realm of classical conditioning is, however, quite another matter. Anyone attempting to break off instrumental conditioning from other forms of learning involving response-contingent reinforcement must be content with a ragged edge. As a recent volume devoted entirely to the subject makes clear, we are still at a loss to define unambiguously the functional differences that might exist among the different categories of instrumental learning (Melton, 1964). Not that meaningful functional differences do not exist; we simply have not yet discovered enough of them. Conceivably, sharp distinctions among categories of instrumental learning could also be drawn from a sufficiently general and detailed theory of behavior. But considering present accomplishments in this area, aid and comfort seems less likely to be forthcoming from this source than from empirically determined patterns of functional differences.

Nevertheless, in the interest of establishing a taxonomy of learning one can always fall back on operational specification of categories. That is, if two learning paradigms involve significantly different operations the learning processes they tap are assumed to differ in some significant way and so the paradigms are placed in, or made to define, different categories of learning. The three criteria used to set off classical conditioning from other forms of learning were operational criteria. I agree with Kimble (1964), however, that if categories so defined are to be of any deep significance sooner or later functional differences must be adduced as well. What constitutes significant operational differences is often notoriously difficult to tell. And conversely, important operational difficulties may exist where determined scrutiny seems to indicate none.

By "functional" differences one refers to important differences in the way the same (or analogous) independent variables affect behavior. To cite one example, partial reinforcement schedules (schedules in which reinforcement is withheld on a percentage of the trials) severely retard acquisition of certain classically conditioned responses (Fitzgerald, 1963; Kimble, 1961, p. 103). Yet these same schedules only temporarily depress acquisition of an instrumentally conditioned response and may even lead to higher levels of performance. As another illustration, the amount of reward employed as reinforcement is an exceedingly important variable determining speed of running in a straight alley as well as rate of bar pressing. This same variable, however, has surprisingly little effect on the rate at which a visual discrimination is acquired, raising the suspicion that somewhat different learning processes are involved in the former and latter situations.

However, it must be stressed that disparity in the effects of a single independent variable does not necessarily imply differences in underlying processes; such isolated instances could easily be the result of trivial differences in procedures, apparatus, and so on. Much more convincing for the delineation of separate categories of learning is the formation by a number of independent variables of different *patterns* of effects. Operational differences in learning paradigms that do not enjoy accompanying behavioral (functional) differences might be of value as classificatory aids, but they are likely to be of little help in the task of analyzing fundamental learning processes and may even impede this undertaking by implying differences in underlying processes where none exist.

In the paragraphs that follow we shall introduce an operational criterion which will be of value in separating instrumental conditioning from other forms of instrumental learning. And, in the next chapter, we shall be able to demonstrate that this operational criterion also accommodates certain important functional differences between instrumental conditioning (so defined) and other classes of instrumental learning.

Like velocities in physics, behavior has *direction* and *magnitude*. If a pigeon pecks one of two keys facing it we may ask *which* key it pecked (response direction) and *how fast* or with *what force* it pecked (response magnitude). Despite the obviousness of this distinction and its relevance for a variety of experimental results, psychologists have been unaccountably tardy in giving it due recognition. Perhaps one factor deferring such recognition is the implicit—frequently, explicit—assumption that laws of learning are independent of the response systems upon which they are formulated.

Response Magnitude. Of course for a response to have magnitude it must have direction as well; it must be identified. When, however, only a single response class is recorded and reinforced by E, response direction is fixed and only response magnitude is subject to variation and measurement. In the straight alley there is only one response class—that of traversing the alley from start to goal box—which is recorded and reinforced by E. Variation can occur in response magnitude only, for example, in how fast S runs to the goal box. As a second illustration, a monkey given a single lever to press for food reinforcement may engage in all sorts of behavior, but because only his lever-pressing responses are recorded and reinforced, response direction is held constant. It is response magnitude, perhaps response rate or latency, that provides the data of experimental interest.

Magnitude measures may be divided into two classes, those that are *reinforcement-correlated* and those that are *reinforcement-uncorrelated*. In the first class there is a direct relationship between response magnitude and receipt of reinforcement. In the runway, for example, running speed and receipt of reinforcement are perfectly correlated in that the faster S runs, the faster it receives access to the reward in the goal box. For many reinforcement schedules the major dependent variable in the Skinner-box setting, response rate, also is reinforcement-correlated: the higher the rate the sooner reward is received.

In contrast, most often response *force* is reinforcement-uncorrelated (or only slightly correlated), inasmuch as a certain minimum force applied to the manipulandum activates the feeder mechanism and forces of greater magnitude have no effect whatever on receipt of reinforcement. The same is normally true for response duration,

a minimum duration of activation of the manipulandum being required and longer durations having no effect on the delivery of reinforcement. It is quite feasible to convert response force and duration into reinforcement-correlated measures, arranging things experimentally so that the greater the force exerted or the longer the duration of response, the faster reward is made available to S. Contingencies of this nature are rarely, if ever, used. However, Notterman and Mintz (1965), in their recent extensive analysis of response force in the bar-press situation, investigated a somewhat different kind of correlation between force and reinforcement, namely, one in which *amount* of reward is correlated with response force. DRL schedules (Ferster and Skinner, 1957) are examples where the usual correlation between response rate and reinforcement, or between response speed and reinforcement (Logan, 1961), is reversed by requiring that S withhold his response for a certain minimum length of time.

From among the many different measures of response magnitude that exist—response rate, latency, force, amplitude, displacement, duration, and so on—several are often simultaneously available for measurement. It is uncommon, however, that more than one measure of response magnitude is seriously studied within the same experiment, so that our knowledge of how different indicators of response magnitude covary with variations in important independent variables is still very rudimentary (see Herrick and Bromberger, 1965; Kobrick, 1956). Quite likely the clustering of measures of response magnitude will hinge on the nature and extent of the correlation with reinforcement enjoyed by each of the separate indicators. This is an important problem area, one which, because of recent technological advances in response measurement and data processing, ought soon to escape its past neglect.

Response Direction. When identification of S's response is the important dependent variable, one is dealing with response direction. In principle, S chooses between two or more well-defined alternatives, and the basic datum consists of the classification of S's response within the permissible alternatives.

Though also available for measurement, indicators of response magnitude are usually completely ignored when E's first interest is in response direction. In verbal learning experiments, for example, where almost always the important datum is the identity of the verbal response given by S, how fast or how loud S responds (measures of response magnitude) is rarely bothered with. Among the few exceptions are certain word-association tests, for which the identification of the verbal response given and its latency are both of importance.

Utilization of both direction and magnitude measures occurs somewhat more frequently in animal studies, where, for example, response speed may be recorded in a T-maze as well as S's choice. Not uncommonly in such situations, response direction and response magnitude react differently to the experimentally manipulated variables.

Instrumental Conditioning Defined

At the outset let us face the fact that no definition of instrumental conditioning—or of any other category of learning for that matter—is going to be completely satisfactory. Apart from the problem of capturing closely the thing to be defined, if a definition is to enjoy useful precision it will have to suffer a certain amount of arbitrariness. These difficulties acknowledged, we take as our definition of instrumental conditioning any learning (1) *based on response-contingent reinforcement* and (2) *not involving choice among experimentally defined alternatives*. The requirement that reinforcement be response contingent quali-

fies the learning as instrumental, and the specification that the behavior be nonchoice means that only a single response class exists and that the dependent variable must be framed in terms of response magnitude. If the task presented S involves choice among a set of alternatives, we are not dealing with instrumental conditioning. Later we will suggest other categories for simple choice behavior.

Before applying our definition of instrumental conditioning we should refine it somewhat by making a distinction on the stimulus side. The straight alley, an apparatus in which a rat is given the task of running down a length of runway to obtain reward in the goal box, is a well-used instrumental conditioning situation. Imagine that a light above the alley were turned on during those trials on which food was to be found in the goal box and extinguished on trials when the goal box was unbaited. Soon this (discriminative) cue would come to regulate the rat's running behavior in that S would run to the goal box quickly when the light was illuminated, showing little interest in traversing the alley when the light was extinguished. The presence of the discriminative stimulus has a profound influence on S's behavior, though the behavior remains nonchoice, that is, does not involve a choice among alternatives. We shall choose to consider this situation also one of instrumental conditioning, but, to distinguish it from those in which exteroceptive discriminative stimuli are not employed, we will refer to it as an instance of *discriminative* instrumental conditioning. Consequently, we recognize two major subclasses of instrumental conditioning, *nondiscriminative* and *discriminative*. In both the behavior is nonchoice and reinforcement is response contingent, but in the latter a discriminative cue is associated with the availability of reinforcement.

It may be objected that, contrary to our dichotomy, there is no such thing as "nonchoice" behavior, every response being a choice among alternatives, no matter how ill defined the latter might be. A rat not running down the straight alley is doing something else, sitting, sniffing, and so on. A child not delivering marbles into the experimental receptacle is engaged in other behavior, looking around him, examining the marbles, and so on. It is only that in some cases we are interested enough in at least some of the alternatives to note and record them, whereas in others we are not. There is a sense in which this argument is correct, indeed, is logically correct. If S is not performing the instrumental response he must be engaged in alternative behavior, which may be considered to have been "chosen" over the instrumental response.

But not all sets of alternatives are equivalent. A rat not running a straight alley because, say, the discriminative cue is absent on that trial, is engaging in a class of alternatives (sitting, grooming, sniffing, and so on) that bears little similarity to the instrumental response required in the situation, running. At a commonsense level, the alternatives to the instrumental response "chosen" by the rat are not for the purpose of arriving at the reinforcement. It is quite different in the case of a monkey—to mix phylogenetic levels—who must choose between lifting stimulus object A or B for the raisin that is under one of them. Here the alternatives (choosing either A or B), potentially at least, are both routes to reinforcement, and on each trial the animal chooses one or the other of the two alternatives available to him.

It is perhaps unnecessary to labor the point further, though it should be added that classical conditioning also is restricted to nonchoice behavior. A single response, that elicited by the UCS, comprises the behavior of interest; accordingly, the dependent variables must be framed in terms of response magnitude, as indeed they are. Typical dependent variables are amount of salivation, magnitude of the GSR, and other such "intensive" measures. Even occurrence or nonoccurrence of the conditioned response may be considered a magnitude measure, because fundamentally it is based on response latency. It may be apparent that if the present analysis is accepted it becomes possible to define the entire class of conditioning simply as *acquisition involving nonchoice behavior*.

Varieties of Instrumental Conditioning Procedures

A number of different experimental procedures have conventionally been included under the rubric of instrumental conditioning (see, for example, Grant, 1964, pp. 8–13; Kimble, 1961, pp. 65–71; see also Bitterman, 1962). It is the purpose of the present section to describe the more important of these within the context of the definition of instrumental conditioning offered previously. The section also provides a bird's-eye view of some of the topics to be covered in the succeeding two chapters.

An exceedingly important variable in instrumental conditioning is the nature of the reinforcing stimulus, whether it is "positive" or "negative." Positive reinforcers (S^{R+}) are defined at bottom as stimuli which S will work to attain. Conversely, negative reinforcers (S^{R-}) are stimuli which S will work to be rid of; they are often referred to as *aversive* or *noxious* stimuli. In some cases a stimulus can act as both a positive and a negative reinforcer, depending on circumstances. For example, a weak electric shock which ordinarily would serve as a negative reinforcer can be converted to a positive reinforcer by appropriate pairing with a potent S^{R+}, say food.

Because of the extremely important role played by the "sign" of the reinforcing stimulus, it is reasonable to subclassify further instrumental conditioning in terms of the nature of the reinforcement employed. By forming all possible pair combinations of the two operational criteria—employment of positive or negative reinforcement, and presence or absence of a discriminative stimulus—we arrive at four major types of instrumental conditioning. A brief discussion of each follows.

Instrumental Conditioning with Positive Reinforcement

Nondiscriminative Instrumental Conditioning. This is the procedure that is often called reward training. With animal Ss the reward is usually food or water; with humans (often children) it may be money, a trinket, or a piece of candy. The positive reinforcer may either be "primary"—that is, presumably unlearned (food, water, and so on); or it may be "secondary" or "conditioned"—its rewarding properties being traceable to past learning (money, tokens, goal boxes in which food was previously obtained, and so on). There seems to be no compelling reason to distinguish, as is sometimes done, among conditioning procedures in terms of whether the reinforcement employed is primary or conditioned, because the effects on behavior of both are closely comparable.

The straight alley has been a favorite setting for research in this type of instrumental conditioning, rivaled only by the Skinner box and related apparatuses. Most of the research employing Skinner boxes has involved "free responding" rather than discrete trials. The first technique leaves S free to make the instrumental response at his own pace, whereas the second regulates each opportunity to respond (a trial). With children and adults as experimental subjects, instrumental conditioning often occurs within the context of such simple tasks as placing marbles in an aperture, playing a slot machine, and so forth.

Discriminative Instrumental Conditioning. In this variety of instrumental conditioning a cue signals the availability of reinforcement, and eventually S comes to execute the instrumental response vigorously in the presence of the cue but weakly, if at all, in its absence. Referred to the straight alley situation, the stimulus associated with reward and hence called the positive stimulus $(S+)$, might be a white alley, in which case the stimulus associated with nonreinforcement, the "negative" stimulus $(S-)$, is likely to be a black alley. The S is run on the two alleys in a quasirandom order, usually 50 per cent of the trials being conducted on each alley, and soon S's behavior reveals that it discriminates reward as available only in the white alley. Goodness of discrimination is generally determined by comparing response speed in $S+$ with speed in $S-$.

This type of instrumental conditioning is often referred to as "successive" discrimination conditioning, because S responds to $S+$ and $S-$ in succession. Successive discrimination is to be contrasted with "simultaneous" discrimination, where $S+$ and $S-$ are presented simultaneously, as, for example, in a two-choice situation. Because choice between alternatives is always involved, simultaneous discrimination does not qualify as instrumental conditioning.

In the Skinner box situation successive discrimination conditioning is arranged in a precisely analogous manner; however, here the positive stimulus is usually referred to as the "discriminative" stimulus (S^D), and the counterpart of $S-$ is S^Δ (S-delta). Response rate is usually the dependent variable of interest so that ordinarily goodness of discrimination is assessed by comparing rate of responding in S^D with rate in S^Δ.

A serious complication for our definition of instrumental conditioning arises here and it should be acknowledged. The richness of discriminatory behavior which can be developed by appropriate schedules of reinforcement even when the instrumental behavior is nonchoice is well known.

Simply because choice among alternatives is not involved, must all of this behavior be classified as instrumental conditioning? It is possible, though perhaps not likely, that there are functional similarities running through all discrimination learning based on nonchoice behavior, however complex, which argue convincingly for their inclusion within the category of instrumental conditioning. A second possibility is that in order to maintain reasonable homogeneity and cogency for this category some restrictions will have to be placed on the stimulus side, perhaps that only a single S^D and a single S^Δ be involved. However, any such cleavage should split off categories which are separated by meaningful functional differences.

A similar problem, though perhaps with fewer ramifications, arises in the case of nondiscriminative conditioning where, though manipulated discriminative stimuli are lacking, the scheduling of reinforcement can take on many and varied forms, some quite complex, as in "mixed" schedules (Ferster and Skinner, 1957). It remains to be seen whether there are important functional similarities running through the behavior generated by all such schedules—basically because of the fact that only a single response class is involved—or whether the behavior is too richly varied to be profitably encompassed within the category of instrumental conditioning.

Instrumental Conditioning with Negative Reinforcement

Nondiscriminative Instrumental Conditioning. When reinforcement is positive the contingencies between response and reinforcement are limited in that, almost always, S works under some schedule or another to obtain reinforcement. With negative reinforcement, on the other hand, more possibilities appear, and there are three in particular which have received a good bit of attention: punishment, escape, and avoidance conditioning.

If a particular response acts to produce a negative reinforcer the paradigm is one of *punishment*. More precisely, in punishment the *application* of the aversive stimulus is contingent upon the execution of a member of a specific response class. For example, a pigeon accustomed to pecking a key to obtain food might later be greeted with an electric shock each time that it makes the instrumental response. To cite a more familiar example, children are ordinarily scolded, if not worse, for uttering obscenities in the presence of their parents. Note that the aim of punishment is not the acquisition of an instrumental response but rather the weakening or elimination of a response already in S's repertoire in some strength.

In *escape* conditioning the negative reinforcer is applied independently of S's behavior; execution of a specific response then terminates S^{R-}. The grid floor of an experimental chamber housing a rat might suddenly be electrified and S must press the bar in order to terminate the noxious stimulus. As a second example, a perceptive child may terminate abruptly his mother's ire by a look of unusually deep remorse, or by another acquired stratagem.

Finally, in *avoidance* conditioning performance of the instrumental response at the appropriate time allows S to prevent or postpone for a time the appearance of the negative reinforcer. A disgruntled motorist pays an exorbitant $15 parking fine only to prevent the unpleasant consequences of failing to do so. In laboratory situations, S might press a lever, withdraw a limb, or remove himself to a different location in order to avoid an impending aversive event.

All three conditioning procedures—punishment, escape, and avoidance—are possible in nondiscriminative situations, a point that is obvious in the case of punishment and escape. In nondiscriminative avoidance conditioning, S^{R-} is applied periodically unless S makes the required instrumental response, which postpones the negative reinforcer for a period of time. Named after the individual who first reported its use, it frequently is referred to as the *Sidman procedure*.

All three procedures employ nonchoice behavior; consequently, the dependent variables must be expressed in terms of response magnitude, usually response latency or response rate. Choice among alternatives can be introduced into these conditioning procedures, in which case they would fall beyond the scope of instrumental conditioning.

Discriminative Instrumental Conditioning. In *discriminated punishment* a cue signals when execution of the instrumental response is likely to produce S^{R-}. If the pigeon whose key pecks led to shock as well as to food were afforded a cue which indicated when responding was likely to lead to S^{R-}, S would soon put this information to good advantage and respond only in the absence of the stimulus. And to continue a "real-life" example cited previously, although punishment of swearing behavior is likely to occur if parents are at hand, the same utterances under different stimulus conditions—say, in the presence of peers—are in no such danger.

Discriminated escape conditioning is a completely feasible instrumental conditioning procedure, but it seems to have found little use in the laboratory. In this variant a cue would signal when escape from the negative reinforcer was possible; performance of the instrumental response in the absence of the cue would have no effect on S^{R-}

In *discriminated avoidance conditioning* a cue signals the impending S^{R-}, and performance of the instrumental response soon enough after the appearance of the cue enables S to avoid the aversive stimulus. An apparatus widely used in studies of discriminated avoidance learning is the "shuttle box," so called because S remains

in one compartment of this apparatus until the discriminative stimulus appears, which, if shock is to be avoided, S takes as the signal to move into the other compartment. After a time the stimulus appears again, and S can again avoid S^{R-} by removing himself within the allotted time to the first compartment. By "shuttling" back and forth between the two compartments in response to the discriminative stimulus, S is able to stay out of harm's way.

The major dependent variable in studies of discriminated avoidance conditioning is the percentage of trials on which S makes an avoidance response, that is, responds soon enough after the appearance of the discriminative cue to avoid S^{R-}. Actually this measure is one of response magnitude, because it is based directly on response latency. If the latency of a response, measured from the onset of the discriminative cue, is shorter than the interval separating onset of S^{R-} from onset of the cue (the so-called CS–UCS interval), the response counts as an avoidance response; if it is longer, S falls victim to the aversive stimulus and the response, an escape response, merely terminates S^{R-}

Extinction Processes in Instrumental Conditioning

Our discussion of instrumental conditioning has been restricted thus far to acquisition processes. However, extinction of an instrumental response is of even greater interest to many investigators, and in the subsequent two chapters we will have a good deal to say about this topic.

The operation of extinction as applied to positively reinforced instrumental responses is well defined and unique. It consists simply of the withholding of S^{R+}, which results, of course, in the weakening of the instrumental response. When referred to conditioning with negative reinforcement, this uniqueness is lost, and extinction after escape, punishment, and avoidance conditioning can in each case refer to at least two different operations. Extinction of an escape response, for example, may be conducted either by the complete removal of S^{R-} from the experimental situation, or, quite the opposite, by applying the negative reinforcer throughout a trial sequence, it no longer being terminated by the instrumental response. The first procedure is much more common than the second. More than a single option also exists for extinction after punishment and avoidance conditioning. In Chapter 5 we shall deal with these various extinction operations in some detail, as well as the question of their interrelationship.

Other Forms of Instrumental Learning

It will be of value in later discussions to distinguish forms of instrumental learning which appear to be closest to instrumental conditioning. The nearest kin seems to be simple choice situations based on spatially distinct alternatives, as provided for example by a T-maze, or by a pair of manipulanda (bars, levers, and so on). Here again an option arises with respect to the presence or absence of exteroceptive discriminative stimuli (also called *discriminanda*). If these are lacking the correct and incorrect responses are defined in terms of spatial (or response) characteristics; for example, the left arm of a T-maze might be the correct one. Acquisition of choice behavior based on alternatives which are differentiated by means of spatial (or response) characteristics only is often called *selective learning* or *spatial discrimination*. Because of the lack of discriminanda, we shall refer to this category as *nondiscriminative choice learning*. Where the alternatives available to S are defined by discriminative cues, we shall use the term *discriminative choice learning*. Of course in the latter, S must attend to the discriminanda if he is to solve the problem.

As the number of alternatives in choice learning increases, the more complex the learning processes tapped tend to become. "Oddity" learning (learning to choose the singular member of a group of stimuli) requires at least three discriminanda; "matching from sample" (choosing from among a group of stimuli the one that matches the specimen provided by E) often employs more. It is sometimes useful to distinguish between choice situations involving only two alternatives and those incorporating a larger number. When we wish to emphasize that we are referring to the former type, we shall use the terms *simple* choice behavior, *simple* discrimination learning, and so on.

Role of Instrumental Conditioning in Behavior Analysis

In view of the apparent simplicity of the instrumental conditioning situation it is not unreasonable to wonder about the relevance of this area for other, more complex (and perhaps more interesting), behavioral situations. To those who have devoted much time and effort to research in instrumental conditioning the justification has been an abiding faith in the existence of fundamental "laws" of learning having general, if not universal, application. These laws of learning, or laws of behavior, as they are often referred to, are the analogue in psychology to fundamental laws in physics and chemistry. And just as the latter have been strikingly successful in permitting the control and prediction of complex physical and chemical events, many psychologists believe that basic laws of behavior, once "discovered," will contribute significantly to the understanding and control of more complex behavioral events.

However, looking for basic laws of behavior is one thing; finding them is quite another. Unlike the physicist and chemist, the psychologist must deal with a subject matter over which he often has distressingly little control and about whose background and history—of trivial interest to the physicist and chemist but of critical importance to the psychologist—he is likely to be woefully uninformed. Both considerations nudge the psychologist in search of basic laws of learning to the animal level where, though admittedly one white rat is by no means identical to all others, such problems are vastly simplified and where there are few restrictions concerning the kinds and ranges of variables that can be investigated.

Also seen standing in the way of the discovery of fundamental laws of learning are needless complexities in the learning tasks presented S. Even so patently simple a situation as the T-maze produces many complications for an investigator bent on close analysis. The multiple T-maze, now largely abandoned, was hopelessly complex. On the other hand, classical and instrumental conditioning, with their nonchoice and limited discriminative features, seemed to offer learning situations reduced to essentials. Perhaps because of the greater degree of technical competence in instrumentation and surgery required by many classical conditioning procedures—Pavlov was a physiologist by training—or perhaps because of attitudes derived from American functionalism, of the two classes of conditioning techniques instrumental conditioning came to be preferred in this country as the research tool from which to fashion the basic laws of learning. An enormous amount of research directed toward this end was, and still is, conducted within settings provided by straight alleys, shuttle boxes, Skinner boxes, and like apparatuses.

Interaction of Variables in Psychological Research

Granting, however, that the use of animal Ss and simplified behavioral situations strips away many layers of complexity, does E therefore necessarily find himself closer to the roots of behavior? This difficult and troublesome question cannot be discussed adequately here, but certain aspects of the problem bear mentioning.

First to be faced is the unpleasant, but pervasive, fact that in psychology the data bearing on empirical relationships are seldom unequivocal; though consensuses do appear, experimental evidence is rarely unanimous. The basis for discordant experimental results is not necessarily inadequate research design or execution, though of course such deficiencies are at times sufficient cause. Much more often the culprit is nothing more than the inherent complexity of behavioral processes, even in so "impoverished" a situation as instrumental conditioning.

Perhaps we should be a little more explicit as to what is meant by "complexity." Not only is the number of variables determining a behavioral event relatively large, as compared to, say, physical or chemical events; in addition, the variables often interact in such a way as to restrict severely generalization of results from one set of conditions to another.

As an illustration, the question "Does resistance to extinction of a nondiscriminative instrumental response increase with increasing amounts of training?" seems a reasonable enough inquiry to put to empirical test. An investigator pursuing this problem on a straight alley is likely to find, if he uses a rather large food reward, that resistance to extinction is actually *reduced* by relatively large amounts of training. If, on the other hand, a small reward is employed an affirmative answer is the more probable outcome. Apparently, then, whether resistance to extinction is found to increase with increasing amounts of training *depends on the particular values that E happens to choose for a number of other variables in the situation*, amount of reward, and perhaps type of instrumental response, among them. The original question is not as reasonable as it first appeared and must be qualified to take cognizance of those variables which, in their interaction with amount of training, determine how the latter variable will affect resistance to extinction.

Framed in more general terms, questions of the sort "How does variable X affect behavior Y?" will often produce "conflicting" results if the effect of X on Y depends importantly on another variable, say Z. It is convenient to refer to X's dependence on Z as "interaction," that is, variables X and Z "interact" in determining behavior Y. If variables X and Z do not interact, then the effects on Y of manipulations of variable X will be essentially independent of the value maintained with variable Z. (Something less general than *statistical* interaction is intended here, because the kind of interactions that cause particular trouble are those in which the *direction* of the effect of variable X on behavior Y depends on the value of variable Z operating: for some values of Z increasing X enhances Y, whereas for others, X might exert no effect on Y or even be detrimental.)

Returning to the point that prompted the present discussion, a good deal of the apparently discordant results in psychological research can be traced to unsuspected interactions between two or more variables. Though their discovery—with present research methods more often a matter of accident than of design—and verification are often extremely illuminating, such interactions complicate vastly the task of piecing together fundamental empirical relationships. At the present stage of theoretical development there simply is no way of knowing in advance whether a once or twice obtained empirical relationship will hold when changes are made in such variables as experimental task and procedures, motive-incentive conditions, age, sex, and strain of Ss, to say nothing of their phylogenetic level (see D'Amato and Schiff, 1965).

If it turns out that there is a reasonable limit to the number and extent of such interactions, then it should be possible ultimately to elaborate basic laws of learning, as well as theories constructed from them, that will enjoy sufficient generality to allow their profitable use in the analysis of behavior significantly more complex than that from which they were derived. If, on the other hand, the number of interacting variables that importantly qualify most empirical relationships is so large that it is impractical to encompass them sufficiently to attain the required degree of generality, then probably there will be much less to be gained from the search for "basic" laws of learning. Though research in simplified behavioral situations might still yield broad principles having general relevance for more complex behavioral situations (such as the deleterious effects on acquisition of delayed reinforcement), the fashioning of *specific* relationships which transfer directly to complex behavior, as specific physical laws formulated under simplified conditions carry over exactly to complex physical events, would seem to be precluded. The guilding principle in this event would be to stay as close as possible to the behavior of interest.

It is still too early to tell which eventuality is likely to prevail, or, probably more accurately, what blend of the two possible approaches will prove most fruitful. Psychology is a very young science with its major technical refinements and substantive discoveries still ahead of it. Considering the enormous power and economy that basic laws of behavior would confer, continued sanguinity toward the first approach seems in order.

Summary

A number of distinctions and definitions were introduced in the present chapter as the domain of instrumental conditioning was staked out. First, instrumental *learning* was taken to include all acquisition in which reinforcement is *response contingent*. Instrumental *conditioning* was then defined to be that portion of instrumental learning in which the behavior under study is *nonchoice*, that is, does not involve choice between experimentally defined alternatives. Because only a single response class exists in instrumental conditioning, response *direction* is inapplicable and the dependent variables must be framed in terms of response *magnitude*. Four general types of instrumental conditioning were described, based on the nature of the reinforcement employed (positive or negative) and on the presence or absence of discriminative cues. With negative reinforcement three paradigms have received a good deal of attention: punishment, escape, and avoidance conditioning. All three are possible in the nondiscriminative and the discriminative forms.

Close to instrumental conditioning is *simple nondiscriminative choice learning*, which was defined as acquisition in a two-choice situation with no manipulated discriminative cues. When discriminative cues, or *discriminanda*, are provided to define the correct and incorrect alternatives, we progress to *simple discriminative choice learning*. Deletion of the qualifier *simple* means that more than two alternatives may be involved.

The important concept of *interaction* between variables was introduced in connection with the frequent difficulty of replicating experimental results. If the effect of an independent variable on some dependent variable turns out to depend importantly on the status of a second independent variable, we say that the two independent variables *interact* in their effects on the dependent variable. The bearing that interaction of variables has on the possibility of formulating basic laws of learning having direct application to complex behavioral events was pointed out.

Instrumental Conditioning with Positive Reinforcement

The present chapter is devoted to an examination of some of the variables that importantly affect acquisition and extinction in positively reinforced instrumental conditioning. Of the large number of variables that have been investigated, we will focus on only a few, magnitude of reward, drive (motivational) level, delay of reinforcement, schedule of reinforcement, and level of acquisition training. There are some interesting interrelationships among these five variables which, in part, account for their selection; moreover, all have been the target of a good bit of research effort. In the course of the chapter we shall also become acquainted with some of the theoretical formulations that have been advanced to accommodate the known influence of these and other variables of importance.

Effects of Several Variables on Nondiscriminative Instrumental Conditioning

We turn our attention first to nondiscriminative conditioning and begin by considering the acquisition process.

Nondiscriminative Acquisition

Rate of Acquisition Versus Asymptote. Two processes can be distinguished in the acquisition of a conditioned response, *rate* of acquisition and *asymptote*. Asymptote refers to a relatively stable "terminal" level of performance, whereas *rate* reflects the rapidity with which the asymptote is reached. Figure 4-1 illustrates how acquisition curves can differ in rate, asymptote, or both.

It is difficult, if not impossible, to be sure that acquisition of a response has reached asymptote in the technical sense of that word, that further training would not improve performance. Consequently, the term *asymptote* must be taken with a grain of salt, interpreted to mean a point in acquisition where rate of acquisition has been reduced to a negligibly low value.

Where the data warrant we will indicate whether a given relevant variable influences rate of acquisition, asymptote, or possibly both.

Magnitude of Reward. The size of the reward, or incentive, used has an important and somewhat complex effect on

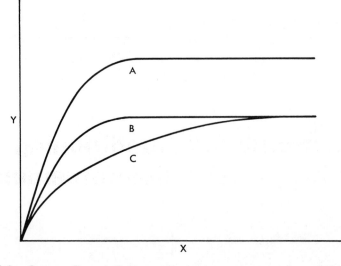

Figure. 4-1. Curves B and C have the same asymptote but different rates of approach. Curves A and B have different asymptotes but the same rate. Curves A and C differ in both rate and asymptote.

instrumental conditioning, both in acquisition and in extinction. Though many questions still remain, we now understand the action of this variable in instrumental conditioning much more fully than we did a few years ago.

Before proceeding, a word about the methods by which magnitude of reward is manipulated. With hungry Ss the commonest procedure is to vary the weight or the volume of solid and liquid nutrients. If E wishes to hold volume constant, perhaps to control for the amount of consummatory activity, concentration of a liquid nutrient, such as sucrose solution, is manipulated. In recent years a unique and extremely potent reward has become available through the use of direct electrical stimulation of certain centers of the brain. Animals with electrodes implanted in these areas will perform an instrumental response diligently and almost endlessly in order to receive electrical brain stimulation (Valenstein and Beer, 1964). By manipulating the intensity of the electrical stimulation, as well as other parameters of the stimulating current, precise control may be ob-

tained over the magnitude of this unusual reward.

SIMPLE EFFECTS OF REWARD MAGNITUDE. Turning now to the effects of reward magnitude on instrumental conditioning, the first generalization of importance is that, within wide ranges of amount of reward and training level, asymptotic performance is positively related to reward magnitude: *the greater the magnitude of reward, the higher the acquisition asymptote.*

Representative data are presented in Figure 4-2. Hungry rats ran down a straight alley to obtain access to 2.5, 5.0, or 10 per cent concentration of sucrose solution. It is clear from the figure that despite extensive training (ninety-nine trials at one trial per day), the three groups of Ss remained separated in their running speeds throughout acquisition. With suitable experimental controls, this is a result that is obtained repeatedly (Kintsch, 1962; Kraeling, 1961; Spence, 1956, p. 131).

In the studies just cited each S was exposed to only a single reward magnitude, so that experience with different reward magnitudes was eliminated as a factor in these experiments. We have used the term *simple effects* to emphasize this condition. The generalization that in instrumental conditioning magnitude of reward and asymptotic performance are positively related applies most exactly to the simple effects of reward magnitude.

CONTRAST EFFECTS OF REWARD MAGNITUDE. When *S* is made to experience more than one value of the independent variable —in the present instance, more than one magnitude of reward—the term *contrast effects* shall be used to refer to the observed influence of the independent variable.

1. *Initial shifts*. A number of studies have investigated what happens in instrumental conditioning when reward magnitude is shifted abruptly to higher and lower values. Their results provide us with a second generalization, namely, that *initial shifts in magnitude of reward will be matched by rapid shifts in performance to conform to*

the new reward magnitude. The rapidity of the adjustment in performance depends on a number of factors, among them the type of reward employed. Apparently, sucrose solutions of varying concentrations but of fixed quantity result in more sluggish shifts than either electrical brain stimulation or different quantities of dry food (Homzie and Ross, 1962). Nevertheless, sooner or later instrumental performance adjusts itself to the prevailing reward magnitude.

2. *Repeated shifts*. A question of some importance for the range of applicability of the first generalization cited is: What happens when *S* is exposed repeatedly to a number of different reward magnitudes? Does performance of the instrumental response continue to adjust itself appropriately to the changing reward magnitudes? The answer is that it usually does.

The data of Figure 4-3, obtained from a rat with electrodes implanted in the median

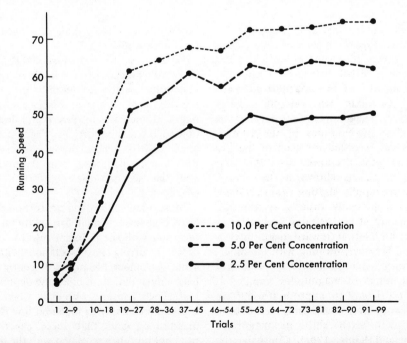

Figure 4-2. Running speed as a function of magnitude of reward (concentration of sucrose solution). Note that the three curves arrive at different asymptotes. (Reprinted with permission from Kraeling, D. Analysis of amount of reward as a variable in learning. *J. comp. physiol. Psychol.*, 1961, **54**, 560–565.)

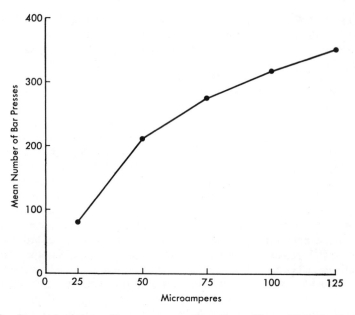

Figure 4-3. Bar-pressing performance as a function of intensity of electrical brain stimulation. (Data courtesy of S. S. Steiner, Schering Corporation, Bloomfield, N.J.)

forebrain bundle, illustrates this point (also see Schrier, 1965). On each of four days S pressed a lever for electrical brain stimulation, which varied between 25 and 125 microamperes (μa), in steps of 25 μa. Each of the five values was randomly determined daily. The number of responses made in the last five minutes of the 10-min. periods was recorded for each of the five intensities and averaged over the four training days. As shown in the figure, despite the rapidly shifting reward values, there is a perfectly orderly relationship between rate of bar pressing and intensity of brain stimulation (reward magnitude).

When, however, training with the different reward magnitudes is very prolonged and the range of magnitudes sampled is rather restricted, an appropriate shift in performance may occur only for a brief period with each shift in magnitude (Keesey and Kling, 1961). Consequently, the relationship between reward magnitude and asymptotic instrumental performance stated earlier is perhaps more valid for the

simple effects of magnitude of reward than for contrast effects.

3. *"Elation" and "depression" effects.* At times adjustments to new levels of reward magnitude, particularly initial adjustments, tend to overshoot their mark, rising too high with increases in reward and descending too low with reductions. The first effect, apparently less general than the second, has been picturesquely called the elation effect and the second, the depression effect (Zeaman, 1949).

Most often elation and depression effects have been investigated for an initial shift only and with the different reward magnitudes occurring in association with the same instrumental response. Recently it has been shown that elationlike and depression-like effects can be obtained when S is exposed repeatedly to high and low reward magnitudes, and that these experiences need not both be associated with the instrumental response undergoing conditioning. To illustrate, Pieper and Marx (1963) allowed three groups of rats to consume fixed amounts of sucrose solutions varying in concentration, 4 per cent sucrose by weight in one group of Ss, 11.3 per cent for the second, and 32 per cent for the third. After experiencing the "prefeeding" reward assigned them, Ss stayed in the Skinner box, where they had to press a bar to receive further reward. The important point is that in the bar pressing, magnitude of reward was identical for all three groups, the 11.3 per cent concentration. This two-stage procedure—prefeeding with a small amount of the 4, 11.3, or the 32 per cent solution followed by bar pressing for the

11.3 per cent solution—was repeated daily for twenty-eight days. What the investigators wished to determine was whether prefeeding with different sucrose concentrations would have an effect on the conditioning of the bar-press response, which, as we have noted, always led to the same reward.

The results of the experiment are shown in Figure 4-4. It is clear that the three groups eventually came to bar-press at considerably different rates, the ordering of the groups suggesting the operation of elationlike and depressionlike effects. One

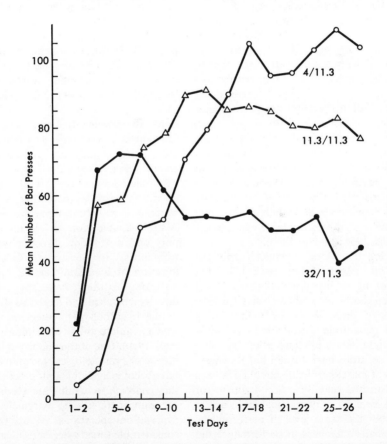

Figure 4-4. Bar-pressing performance as a function of sucrose solution concentration experienced during prefeeding. The figure on the left refers to the prefeeding sucrose concentration; the figure on the right, the concentration which was the reward for bar pressing. (Reprinted with permission from Pieper, W. A., and Marx, M. H. Effects of within-session incentive contrast on instrumental acquisition and performance. *J. exp. Psychol.*, 1963, **65**, 568–571.)

must conclude from these and related data that, even for the rat, the reinforcing value of a particular reward depends not only on its absolute properties but also on the relation it bears to previously experienced rewards (see Black, 1968).

Conceivably the basis of elation and depression effects is motivational, increases in reward giving rise to motivational increments and decreases to motivational decrements. Later in this chapter we shall present a different interpretation of the depression effect.

4. " *Varied* " *magnitude of reward.* Let us suppose that shifts in reward magnitude are made rapidly and unpredictably; for example, 50 per cent of a day's trials are conducted with a relatively large reward and 50 per cent with a smaller reward, the sequence of trials being determined by chance. Will the asymptotic performance of *S*s be representative of the large reward, the small reward, or will it be appropriate for an intermediate reward magnitude? The answer appears to be that it will most nearly resemble the performance level characteristic of the average of the two reward magnitudes, as though *S* "averages out" the reward magnitudes (Logan, Beier, and Ellis, 1955; Logan, 1960).

IMPLICATIONS. One conclusion from the work on magnitude of reward is that behavior in an instrumental conditioning situation can be controlled closely for long periods of time simply by manipulating reward magnitude. Although this conclusion might seem obvious after the fact, things need not have turned out that way. The *S*s of our experiments could have been so constituted that they would run to, or press a lever for, any reasonable reward at just about the same level of performance, or, if small differences in performance did occur early in acquisition, these would rapidly disappear with continued training. That such behavior does not ordinarily occur has implications for the kind of theory that is likely to prove successful in

accounting for behavior in the instrumental conditioning situation.

A second, more theoretical, implication of the preceding results drawn by some is that the magnitude of reward variable has its major influence on ongoing behavior and affects more permanent "habit structures" little, if at all. The rapid shifts in instrumental performance to conform to the prevailing reward magnitude has been interpreted to mean that this variable determines the extent to which a habit is exercised or performed rather than influencing the strength of the habit itself. In more technical terminology, amount of reward is thought to affect *performance* rather than *learning* (see, for example, Kimble, 1961, pp. 4–5). If reward magnitude influenced the learning process itself, presumably its effects on behavior would be more lasting than they have proved to be.

Drive (Motivational) Level. The motivational level of *S* is another variable that has an important influence on instrumental conditioning. Normally drive level is manipulated by some sort of deprivation operation, such as depriving *S* of food, water, a sexual or social partner, and so on. Also available for drive manipulation purposes are more direct physiological techniques, for example, subcutaneous injection of hypertonic saline solution to instigate the thirst drive, or even more directly, chemical and electrical stimulation of the hypothalamic centers of the brain which regulate thirst and hunger (Grossman, 1960). One of the important potentialities of the physiological techniques, which have become available only recently, is that they enable *E* to manipulate *S*'s drive level, say hunger or thirst, extremely rapidly; deprivation operations require, of course, considerable time to become effective.

SIMPLE EFFECTS OF DRIVE LEVEL. There is a remarkable similarity between the simple effects of drive level on instrumental conditioning and those of magnitude of reward. Hold magnitude of reward constant and

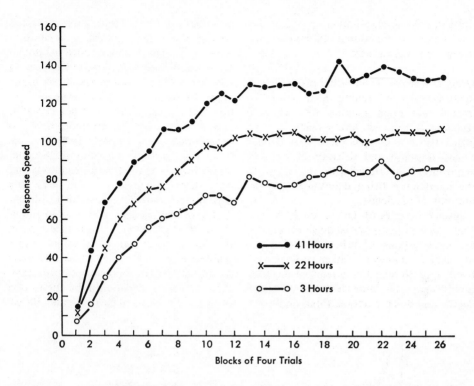

Figure 4-5. Instrumental performance as a function of hours of food deprivation, magnitude of reward held constant. (Data from Davenport, J. W. Choice behavior as a function of drive strength and rate of learning. Unpublished Ph.D. dissertation, State Univer. Iowa, 1956.)

manipulate drive level, say by varying the number of hours of food deprivation, and in all probability a set of acquisition curves will result that is indistinguishable from that obtained when magnitude of reward is varied. The curves in Figure 4-5, obtained from hungry rats in an elevated platform apparatus, show the same prolonged separation as those in Figure 4-2. Drive level, then, also exerts a strong influence on asymptotic instrumental performance and, as with reward magnitude, within wide limits *the more intense the drive the higher the performance asymptote.*

CONTRAST EFFECTS OF DRIVE LEVEL. Rapid shifts in drive level are more difficult to realize by conventional means than corresponding shifts in reward magnitude;

consequently, we have much less information on how well performance in instrumental conditioning tracks shifts in motivation. As demonstrated in Figure 4-6, however, the evidence available suggests that instrumental performance is as sensitive to changes in drive level as it is to alterations in reward magnitude. The current availability of physiological methods of manipulating motivation makes it likely that a great deal more information on the contrast effects of drive level will become available in the near future.

Note in Figure 4-6 that there is little over- or undershoot in the groups experiencing a shift in motivational level (Groups 2-22 and 22-2). An effect parallel to the elation and depression found with reward magnitude apparently does not occur with shifts in drive level, pointing up one of the few important functional differences between these two variables.

Delay of Reward. The normal procedure in instrumental conditioning is to reward *S* immediately upon making the required response. If, however, a time delay is interposed between completion of the conditioned response and delivery of reward, acquisition is interfered with, the extent of the interference being determined by the duration of the delay.

SIMPLE EFFECTS OF DELAY OF REWARD. Figure 4-7 presents the acquisition curves for three groups of rats running to an identical food reward which was delayed for 0, 3, or 30 sec. after *S* reached the goal box. There are three features of these curves that deserve notice. First, and most

important, a clear separation develops among the three groups, a separation showing no sign of convergence. Although the 0-sec. delay group does not appear to have arrived at asymptote, the curves of the figure are demonstrative of the generalization that *asymptotic performance in instrumental conditioning is inversely related to the duration of reward delay*, the longer the delay, the lower the asymptote. Second, unlike the effects of reward magnitude and drive level (Figures 4-2 and 4-5), the performance differences to which different delays of reward give rise emerge rather slowly. It is as though performance early in training is governed by variables other than reward delay, which takes hold only somewhat later in the acquisition process. Finally, there is evidence in the curves of a drop-off in performance in the 30-sec.

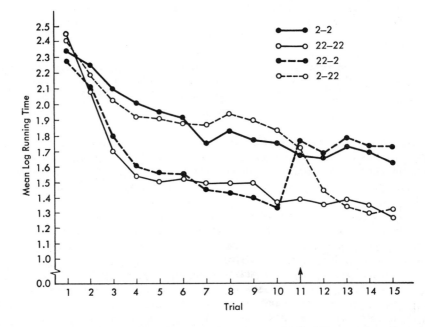

Figure 4-6. These data were obtained in a ten-unit T-maze, rather than in an instrumental conditioning apparatus. However, they do illustrate that instrumental performance (running time) reacts rather quickly to shifts in drive level. At the point indicated by the arrow, Group 2-22 was shifted from 2 hours hunger to 22 hours; the reverse shift occurred for Group 22-2. (Reprinted with permission from Hillman, B., Hunter, W. S., and Kimble, G. A. The effect of drive level on the maze performance of the white rat. *J. comp. physiol. Psychol.*, 1953, **46**, 87–89.)

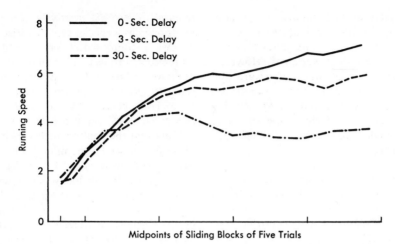

Figure 4-7. Running performance as a function of delay of reward. (Reprinted with permission from Logan, F. A. *Incentive.* New Haven: Yale Univer. Press, 1960.)

delay group: for the first time we encounter *nonmonotonicity* in a curve relating performance level to amount of practice.

One possible interpretation of the preceding results is that in initial acquisition performance is controlled primarily by the prevailing motive-incentive conditions, and because these are constant across groups, the behavior in the three groups is comparable. As learning progresses and *S* begins to discriminate the reward delay, a measure of aversiveness becomes associated with the latter (perhaps through a mechanism such as frustration—discussed subsequently), which either limits asymptotic behavior to a value below that possible with zero delay, or, if the delay is relatively long, actually causes a decline in the level of performance already achieved.

CONTRAST EFFECTS. Suppose *S*s trained with a long delay of reward are suddenly shifted to a short delay. How does instrumental performance adjust itself to the new delay? Unfortunately, the evidence is far from consistent.

1. *Initial shifts.* One result seems firm: *S*s shifted to a shorter delay adjust their performance to conform to the more favorable delay (Harker, 1956). Moreover,

under certain circumstances such *S*s will exceed the performance levels of *S*s run consistently with the shorter delay, producing behavior resembling an elation effect (Sgro and Weinstock, 1963). Shifts from a short (1-sec.) to a long (10-sec.) delay, however, sometimes fail to result in a performance decrement (Harker, 1956).

2. *Varied delay of reward.* When delay of reward is shifted abruptly and unpredictably between two values, unlike the results obtained with reward magnitude for the corresponding operation, the usual result is that *S*'s performance arrives asymptotically at the level typical for the *shorter* delay. As may be seen in Figure 4-8, a group of *S*s trained on a straight alley with a 1-sec. delay on 50 per cent of its trials and a 9-sec. delay on the other 50 per cent ultimately performed at the same level as achieved by a group run on all trials with the shorter of the two delays. A third group that experienced a delay of 5 sec. on all trials turned out to be the slowest of the three groups. (Note again the nonmonotonicity in the last group.)

Summary. To summarize briefly the effects of reward magnitude, drive level, and reward delay on the acquisition of a non-discriminative instrumental response, we have seen that response magnitude is quite sensitive to all three variables. However, compared with magnitude of reward and drive level, delay of reward shows certain clear differences of detail, suggesting that the mechanisms underlying the effects of these variables are themselves different, at least in part.

Other Variables. Nondiscriminative instrumental conditioning is, of course, affected by a number of other variables, such as schedules of reinforcement, intertrial interval, response effort, and so on. At least some of these variables are potentially reducible to the three already discussed. For example, a random partial reinforcement schedule could be considered as a limiting case of varied magnitude of reward where, on some trials, reward magnitude is reduced to zero. Alternatively, it might be interpreted as a special case of varied delay of reward, composed of zero reward delay on reinforced trials and "infinite" delay on nonrewarded trials. Inasmuch as randomly rewarded Ss often perform asymptotically at a level comparable to continuously reinforced Ss (Ss rewarded on all trials), it appears that the analogy with varied delay of reward might be the more fitting of the two. It will be recalled that varied delay (between two equally likely values) tends to produce asymptotic performance that is appropriate for the shorter of the two delays, whereas varied magnitude of reward usually leads to asymptotic performance that falls below the level attained by the more favorable of the two magnitudes.

For a discussion of other variables that influence instrumental conditioning, sources such as Kimble (1961) and Logan (1960) may be consulted.

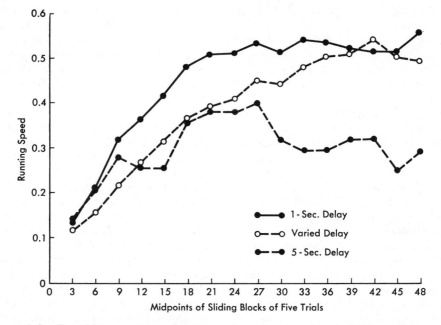

Figure 4-8. Running speed as a function of constant and varied delay of reward. The varied delay group experienced a 1-sec. delay on 50 per cent of its trials and a 9-sec. delay on the other 50 per cent. (Reprinted with permission from Logan, F. A., Beier, E. M., and Ellis, R. A. Effect of varied reinforcement on speed of locomotion. *J. exp. Psychol.*, 1955, **49**, 260–266.)

Nondiscriminative Extinction

Perhaps more attention has been paid to extinction in instrumental conditioning than to acquisition. The factors governing the persistence of a response in the absence of reinforcement is a topic having a good deal of theoretical and practical significance. In a sense, however, the operation of extinction—by definition the removal of the reinforcing stimulus—is simply a special case of reward contrast effects in which reward magnitude is shifted from some positive value to zero. And in all probability the data relating to extinction will be found to dovetail with the results obtained when shifts are between two nonzero reward magnitudes. To cite a specific illustration of this point, it is often found that performance during the early trials of extinction is poorer than on later trials. Recalling our discussion of contrast effects of reward magnitude, this result may be attributed to an initial depression effect from which Ss recover on later extinction trials.

The Concept of Frustration. Before proceeding to the data of extinction it is convenient to introduce here an explanatory mechanism which has proved quite fruitful in the interpretation of many aspects of conditioning and extinction in instrumental conditioning—the concept of frustration. To get to this notion, however, we must first become acquainted with a related idea, the fractional anticipatory goal response.

THE FRACTIONAL ANTICIPATORY GOAL RESPONSE. Suppose that S runs off repeatedly a stimulus-response (S-R) sequence which terminates in reward (S^{R+}), which we symbolize as

$$S_1\text{-}R_1, S_2\text{-}R_2, \ldots, S_n\text{-}R_n \to S^{R+} \to R_G.$$

The S-R sequence may be a chain of stimuli and responses comprising the running response (in a straight alley), the bar-pressing response, or any other instrumental sequence. The terminal response in the sequence, R_G, is the goal response that is appropriate to the reward employed, eating, drinking, and so on. Part of the goal response will depend closely on S^{R+}, in the sense that its likelihood of occurring in the absence of the reward object is very slight. For example, the peristaltic movements of the gullet which form a component of the goal response to a food reward are not likely to occur unless food is present and ingested.

On the other hand, a portion of R_G is not so directly tied down to the reward. Salivation regularly accompanies eating but clearly it can occur in the absence of ingesting food, as happens when one anticipates a preferred food. This part or "fraction" of the total goal response, the "detachable" component of R_G, may be symbolized as r_G.

Because r_G is detachable from R_G, it is available for conditioning to various stimuli in the experimental situation. For example, it is to be expected that with repeated trials r_G would become (classically) conditioned to the cues immediately preceding reward. In terms of our symbolized S-R sequence, S_n would come to elicit not only R_n, a link in the instrumental response chain, but also r_G. Moreover, either through further conditioning or through the mechanism of stimulus generalization, stimuli very early in the S-R chain would also come to evoke r_G. Thus

$$S_1\text{-}R_1, S_2\text{-}R_2, \ldots, S_n\text{-}R_n$$
$$\quad r_G \qquad r_G \qquad\qquad r_G$$

Because the r_G response comes to be elicited very early in the S-R sequence, and therefore "anticipates" S^{R+}, it is called the *fractional anticipatory goal response*. Inasmuch as any response made by S may be assumed to have stimulus consequences—proprioceptive feedback and the like—the fractional anticipatory goal response always appears with an associated stimulus component s_G, that is, $r_G\text{-}s_G$. There are certain special properties assigned to s_G, but these need not concern us now. The important point is that the r_G-s_G mechanism is an objective way of capturing the notion that after a number of rewarded trials S comes to anticipate, or to expect, a reward as a consequence of performing the instrumental response. Psychologists have not been unanimous as to the ontological footing of the r_G-s_G mechanism. Some believe it to be simply a theoretical tool on the level of an intervening variable and others assign it an existential status. Recently, attempts have been made to measure actual anticipatory responses (for example, anticipatory licking) and relate these to instrumental behavior (Deaux and Patten, 1964).

THE FRUSTRATION MECHANISM. It is at this point that the notion of frustration enters. If, after conditioning r_G to the components of the S-R sequence, reward is omitted, it is assumed that a primary frustration response, R_F, occurs. In ordinary terms, frustration is assumed to be an unconditioned response which occurs when an anticipated reward fails to materialize.

One of the important properties assigned R_F is that it is assumed to give rise to a drive state, which, like other "irrelevant" drives (drives not appropriate to the reward object being employed), summates with the relevant motivation to produce in S a heightened drive state.

This assumed property of frustration has been supported by evidence of the following sort. Rats are trained on a runway which has two goal boxes, GB_1 and GB_2, the latter being some distance beyond GB_1. On an initial series of trials S finds reward in both goal boxes. Then comes a series of test trials on some of which S still finds reward in GB_1 (and GB_2), but on others reward is given only in GB_2. The critical datum is the speed with which S runs to GB_2 after having failed to find food in GB_1. Is this speed greater than when food is presented in GB_1, as should be the case if the frustration presumably experienced in GB_1 owing to the omission of food there resulted in a

drive increment? (We must recall here that response magnitude is sensitive to differences in drive level.) Most relevant experiments agree in showing a "frustration effect," that is, faster running to GB_2 after S has experienced nonreward in GB_1 (Amsel and Roussel, 1952).

A second property assigned to frustration is a mechanism providing for the *anticipation* of frustration—the fractional anticipatory frustration response. Just as R_G was assumed to have a conditionable component r_G, the primary frustration response R_F is assumed to possess a detachable portion, r_F, which is available for classical conditioning to stimuli that occur early in the S-R chain. Thus, after one or more frustrating experiences r_F may become conditioned to, and elicited by, stimuli occurring relatively early in the response chain, which is to say S would anticipate being frustrated. And in further analogy with the fractional anticipatory goal response, r_F has its distinctive stimulus consequences s_F, so that the complete anticipatory frustration mechanism is r_F-s_F.

It is a reasonable assumption—and there are supporting data as well—that frustration stimuli are aversive, in the sense that normally S will avoid frustrating situations if at all possible. Granting this assumption, it follows that S will ordinarily act in such a way as to avoid stimuli that produce fractional anticipatory frustration responses, that is, stimuli which elicit the expectation of frustration.

Because they act in opposite ways, it is important to distinguish between the two effects of frustration just discussed. On the one hand, the *experience* of frustration leads to a motivational increment that serves to *augment* the magnitude of immediately following responses. On the other hand, the *anticipation* of frustration, because of its assumed aversiveness, will often *reduce* response magnitude in instrumental conditioning, inasmuch as S will tend to avoid or postpone making responses which intensify anticipatory frustration (r_F-s_F). In attempting to predict the role of frustration in any specific situation one must, therefore, assess which of these two processes will be predominant.

The concept of frustration, as defined here, is useful in explaining in an informal way many of the facts of instrumental conditioning and extinction. For example, we have seen that when S is shifted to a smaller reward one often obtains a depression effect, a drop in performance below that maintained by Ss that have always experienced the smaller reward. Applying the frustration hypothesis to this result one would assume that on encountering the smaller reward a "mild" frustration response occurs. Although we defined the frustration hypothesis in terms of a transition to zero reward, it is a reasonable generalization that frustration will also occur, but to a lesser extent, if a significant reduction in reward is imposed, not necessarily to a zero value (Bower, 1962). Through stimulus generalization, or perhaps rapid conditioning, the anticipatory frustration response is evoked in some measure by the stimuli occurring early in the appropriate S-R chain. Because the nearer S progresses to the goal box, the stronger r_F-s_F becomes, and because *anticipatory* frustration is assumed to be aversive, it seems a fair inference that Ss shifted to smaller rewards will, at least temporarily, run slower than Ss whose speed is regulated by reward magnitude uncomplicated by anticipatory frustration responses.

Other deductions are possible in this situation. We know that frustration cannot develop until an appropriate anticipatory goal response has been conditioned to the S-R chain. Accordingly, a depression effect should not occur if the reward shift takes place very early in training. Later in the chapter we shall cite further applications of the frustration hypothesis, but now let us turn our attention to some of the variables that affect importantly the extinction process in nondiscriminative conditioning.

Drive Level. Variables having to do with the nature of the reinforcement employed (for example, amount, delay, and schedule of reinforcement) can, by definition, be manipulated only during acquisition, because in extinction reward is unavailable. On the other hand, variables that are independent of the reinforcement operation (for example, drive level, intertrial interval, and response effort) may be studied for their effects on extinction separately for manipulations taking place during acquisition and during extinction. In the case of motivational level the consensus is that drive manipulations restricted to the acquisition period have little effect on later resistance to extinction when proper controls are employed (see Kimble, 1961, pp. 411–16). This much could have been guessed from our discussion of acquisition where we noted that, though nondiscriminative instrumental behavior was sensitive to differences in contemporary drive level, it tended to adjust itself rapidly to motivational shifts. Extinction just provides the added complication of a concurrent shift of reward to zero magnitude.

We might also expect from the acquisition data that differences in drive level operating during the extinction process itself would prove effective in influencing resistance to extinction, and indeed this is actually the case (Horenstein, 1951). Consequently, the influence wrought by drive level on extinction may be considered simply as an extension of its effects on acquisition.

Amount of Acquisition Training. It is an almost universal assumption that the greater the amount of training, the stronger the habit. Instrumental conditioning is no exception and so it has been generally assumed that the strength of a conditioned response is a monotonic function of the amount of training afforded the conditioned behavior. In many quarters resistance to extinction has been taken to be a fair measure of the strength of a conditioned response, generating the implication that as the amount of training given an instrumental response increases, so ought resistance to extinction. For many years learning theorists rested in the comfort of the knowledge that this putative relationship was actually the case. Recently, however, unmistakable evidence has been obtained showing that in certain experimental situations resistance to extinction is *reduced* by higher levels of acquisition training (for example, Birch, 1965; North and Stimmel, 1960; Ison, 1962). Because it is known that in these situations, at very low levels of training, resistance to extinction increases with increasing practice, the implication is that the two variables are nonmonotonically related. That is, at relatively low acquisition levels both increase together, but at higher levels resistance to extinction decreases with further increases in amount of training.

One complicating aspect of this relationship is that, almost without exception, level of acquisition training and resistance to extinction have been found to be *monotonically* related in the Skinner box setting. To cite one example, D'Amato, Schiff, and Jagoda (1962) carried training to a maximum of 1,600 reinforced bar-press responses distributed over thirty-two days and found an essentially monotonic function between acquisition level and resistance to extinction (solid line, Figure 4-10, p. 69). The basis of this striking disparity is not altogether clear, though there is some evidence that it might have to do with the magnitudes of the rewards employed, a variable to which we now turn.

Magnitude of Reward. The effect of reward magnitude on resistance to extinction presents a confused picture until one realizes that it is impossible to consider this variable in isolation of all others. The question, "How does reward magnitude affect resistance to extinction?" is simply too open-ended, too unspecific to be adequately answered. In the terminology of

Chapter 3, amount of reward interacts importantly with level of training, nature of the dependent variable employed, and possibly other variables as well, in determining resistance to extinction.

Earlier work suggested that resistance to extinction of the running response was increased by large magnitudes of reward, but then the very opposite result was obtained in quite similar experimental situations (Armus, 1959; Hulse, 1958). To confuse matters further, Hill and Spear (1962), attempting to resolve the discrepancy, thought that reward magnitude might interact with the intertrial interval in determining resistance to extinction. They found, however, that their larger reward *increased* resistance to extinction for both of the intertrial intervals employed by them.

The results of the studies just cited, as well as those of certain others, can be explained if we assume that in the straight alley amount of training interacts with reward magnitude in determining resistance to extinction. The nature of the hypothesized interaction is shown in Figure 4-9 for two reward values. With a small reward resistance to extinction is assumed to be monotonically related to acquisition level. With larger magnitudes of reward, on the other hand, the function turns nonmonotonic.

If there is any validity to this hypothesis it would explain why Skinner-box studies uniformly produce monotonic functions relating resistance to extinction to reward magnitude, because without exception the reward employed in such studies is relatively small. It would also explain why Armus (1959) and Hulse (1958) found large reward to lead to less resistance to extinction than small reward, whereas Hill and Spear (1962) encountered just the opposite: the first investigators used relatively large numbers of acquisition trials (*B* in Figure 4-9), but Hill and Spear used relatively few (*A*). Note from the graph that for some intermediate value of training, there should

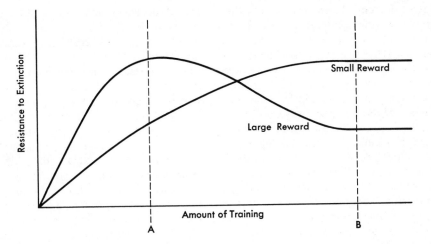

Figure 4-9. Assumed interaction between reward magnitude and amount of training in determining resistance to extinction. Note that with a relatively small amount of training (A) large reward will lead to more resistance to extinction than a small reward; when training is very substantial, however, this relationship is reversed (B).

be no difference between large and small reward. As yet, the relations postulated in Figure 4-9 have not been verified completely, but partially confirming evidence is now available (Birch and Valle, 1967; Ison and Cook, 1964; but see Hill and Wallace, 1967).

An important lesson which comes out of this discussion is that one must be exceedingly careful about extrapolating experimental results beyond the range of values sampled. One must be continually aware that in any experiment a large number of possibly relevant variables are held constant, usually at arbitrary values. Whether, and to what extent, the obtained results will generalize beyond these unavoidable boundaries is a question that should always receive close attention.

Even if the sort of interaction portrayed in Figure 4-9 were to receive confirmation, the role of reward magnitude in the extinction of an instrumentally conditioned response would by no means be thereby completely settled, for it is obviously possible that other interacting variables might be discovered. For example, the effect of reward magnitude and amount of

training on resistance to extinction might be a function of the specific behavioral measure employed, the set of functions shown in Figure 4-9 applying to, say, running time, and perhaps a somewhat different set of functions to response latency.

There is no reason to be discouraged by the complexity confronting us even at the comparatively "simple" level of instrumental conditioning. First, being aware that such interactions as illustrated in Figure 4-9 exist should disabuse us of an oversimplified approach toward behavioral analysis and temper appropriately our empirical generalizations. Perhaps more important, as these interactions become clear they place us on guard as to the sort of interactions we should look for in other situations. It seems plain, for example, that before E thinks too generally about an interesting finding obtained in an instrumental conditioning setting he ought to wonder whether his result is bound to the particular training level (or reward magnitude) employed in his study.

A more consoling consideration is the hope that eventually, as the level of our analysis deepens, the empirical interactions themselves will become deducible from a limited set of theoretical principles or concepts. It has been suggested, for example, that where nonmonotonicity between acquisition level and resistance to extinction occurs, this result can be understood in terms of the interplay between the r_G-s_G and the r_F-s_F mechanisms (Clifford, 1964). It will be recalled that the development of frustration depended on the prior establishment of r_G-s_G. Other things equal, it is reasonable to suppose that the fractional anticipatory goal response will be stronger after high levels of training than after low levels. As a consequence, one might suppose that after intensive acquisition training Ss will encounter more disruptive frustration upon confronting extinction trials than comparable Ss allowed lesser amounts of acquisition training.

One difficulty with this formulation is, of course, that it does not accommodate the known importance of reward magnitude. However, it is not inconsistent to suppose further that the strength of r_G-s_G is positively related to magnitude of reward, so that nonmonotonicity will, other things equal, be in evidence at lower levels of training, when reward magnitude is high. Conceivably, with very small rewards—as used in the Skinner-box studies—an enormous amount of training is necessary to effect substantial differences in the fractional anticipatory goal response and hence in the extent of the frustration experienced in extinction.

The point of this discussion is not to present a favorable prospectus for the frustration hypothesis, but rather to illustrate that even a relatively simple interrelationship between two assumed underlying processes can engineer a plausible explanation of a complicated structure of behavioral data (see Theios and Brelsford, 1964).

Delay of Reward. In attempting to assess the role of delay of reward on subsequent resistance to extinction two methodo-

logical problems arise which, though of considerable importance, can only be mentioned here. Recall that delay of reward had a powerful influence on asymptotic performance in acquisition. Because Ss experiencing different reward delays during acquisition are likely, as a consequence, to enter extinction at different performance levels, it is not unambiguous as to what one should take as his measure of "resistance to extinction." Absolute level of responding will not do generally, but corrections for disparities in initial response levels are not always easy to justify. Though the problem has not been completely solved, some practical guidelines have been established (Anderson, 1963). For present purposes it is sufficient that we be aware of the problem and be on guard that proffered differences in rate of extinction reflect more than simply differences in response strength at terminal acquisition. Obviously this caveat applies as well to variables other than delay of reward.

The second methodological problem concerns the manner in which reward delay is manipulated. Actually, there is a whole cluster of methodological problems involved here, but we will cite only one, goal-box confinement time during acquisition and during extinction. Where delay of reward has been manipulated by subjecting Ss to different waiting periods in the goal box prior to the receipt of reinforcement, the duration of goal-box confinement to be employed during extinction must be given careful consideration. If, for example, delays of 15 and 30 sec. had been used in acquisition, an extinction goal-box confinement time of 30 sec. might operate against differences being obtained in extinction (see Tombaugh, 1966).

VARIED DELAY OF REWARD. Although the methodological problems just cited complicate interpretation of the available data, the results arising from *varied* delay of reward seem rather consistent: resistance to extinction is increased when delay of reward is introduced on a portion of the training trials (Schoonard and Lawrence, 1962). To be effective the delay must be substantial, in rats in the order of 20 to 30 sec. (Logan, 1960, p. 191). Apparently, the effect holds whether the confinement time during extinction is very brief or maintained for a period of time corresponding to the delay interval.

CONSTANT DELAY OF REWARD. The results obtained with constant delay of reward, that is, with all acquisition trials of a given condition conducted under the same reward delay, are less conclusive (Fehrer, 1956; Logan, 1960; Marx, McCoy, and Tombaugh, 1965). Here the problem of goal-box confinement time during extinction appears to be more critical, though, unfortunately, the designs of most relevant experiments do not permit direct analysis of the contribution of this variable.

Capaldi and Bowen (1964) manipulated reward delay and goal-box confinement time independently (15 and 30 sec.) and found that the 30-sec. delay resulted in greater resistance to extinction than the shorter delay. However, this outcome was limited to the case where goal-box confinement was 15 sec.; with a 30-sec. confinement period differences in delay of reward experienced during acquisition had no discernible effect on resistance to extinction.

In conclusion, despite the lack of unanimity in the available data the clear consensus is that where delay of reward does have an effect, it acts to *increase* resistance to extinction.

In a way this is an unexpected result inasmuch as delay of reward interferes, often markedly, with the establishment and maintenance of an instrumental response. However, this is not the first time that we have found resistance to extinction to be at variance with response measures based on acquisition performance. A comparatively large reward raises instrumental asymptotic performance, but in some cases it results in reduced resistance to extinction. It appears that resistance to extinction and response

vigor measured during acquisition cannot both be direct measures of "response strength" (which may be defined as the inferred strength of an instrumental response resulting from its acquisition history). In their extension of the theory of cognitive dissonance to the data of instrumental conditioning, Lawrence and Festinger (1962) lean heavily for support on this apparent disparity.

Schedules of Reinforcement. One of the most potent variables affecting resistance to extinction is the schedule or pattern of reinforcement experienced during acquisition. Reinforcement can be administered according to a number of different schedules, but the one of primary interest here is a "random partial reinforcement schedule," or, in operant terminology, a "variable ratio" schedule. In such schedules reinforcement is presented on a percentage of trials, often 50 per cent, the reinforced and nonreinforced trials being programmed in a random or a quasirandom sequence. The major point of interest is that resistance to extinction is increased, often remarkably so, with partial reinforcement schedules, a phenomenon often referred to as the partial reinforcement effect (PRE).

The PRE has received a great deal of attention from researchers and theorists for the same reason that the nonmonotonicity sometimes found between acquisition level and resistance to extinction has attracted interest, because of the paradox that in both instances an assumed measure of response strength, resistance to extinction, fails to be in direct correspondence with variables—amount of training in the one case and percentage of reinforcement in the other—naturally thought to be means of manipulating the strength of an instrumentally conditioned response. The theoretical effort expended in trying to bend this result into harmony with conventional learning theory has been of comparatively large proportions (see Lewis, 1960).

In one form or another, hypotheses arising from the Hullian orientation have ascribed the PRE to differential stimulus generalization effects, the argument being that a partial reinforcement schedule better prepares S for the stimulus conditions which are to be confronted during extinction.

The frustration hypothesis is one such interpretation and has been applied to the PRE in some detail (Amsel, 1962). The gist of the argument is that, owing to the non-reinforced trials of a partial reinforcement schedule, S experiences frustration during acquisition and in some measure becomes accustomed to making the instrumental response in the presence of cues characteristic of frustration (s_F). Partially reinforced Ss are therefore less disrupted during extinction by anticipatory frustration responses than are continuously reinforced Ss, who in extinction encounter frustration for the first time. This oversimplified presentation does not do justice to Amsel's careful treatment of the topic, and the reader is referred to his paper for a more complete discussion.

Theoretical accommodation aside, the PRE is one of the most robust results in instrumental conditioning. Unlike so many other phenomena in instrumental conditioning in which often a number of variables interact in many and sometimes inexplicable ways, the PRE is obtainable under an extremely wide range of conditions and organisms. There is some question whether it occurs in fish, but at the mammalian level it has something of the status of a behavioral law.

Other Variables. There are, of course, a number of other variables that affect significantly the extinction process, for example, the effortfulness of the instrumental response, the intertrial interval, and so on. But it is safe to say that the most important variables determining the rate of extinction of a nondiscriminative instrumental response are those relating to the conditions of reinforcement.

Summary. The facts of extinction, even in the relatively simplified situation of instrumental conditioning, are, as we have seen, rather complex. The frustration hypothesis, including the fractional anticipatory frustration response, is probably one of the most useful explanatory mechanisms available. It is applicable to the partial reinforcement effect, to the interaction between magnitude of reward and level of training in determining resistance to extinction, and, possibly, to the influence of delay of reward. Still, there are difficulties which face this approach on the empirical and theoretical side (Hill, 1968; Lawrence and Festinger, 1962, Chapter 5).

Although theorists have had available to them for some time mechanisms for handling S's anticipations concerning reward conditions—mechanisms such as the fractional anticipatory goal response—the locus of extinction has been generally assumed to reside ultimately in the S-R relation, that is, between the instrumental response and the "eliciting" stimulus. Theorists have generally set themselves the task of explaining why R is no longer conditioned to, or elicited by, S. Possibly this emphasis has been misplaced. If S's response is governed by his anticipation of the reward contingencies (such anticipations need not be on the "conscious" level), then the strength of the instrumental response will depend on the nature and strength of these anticipations, and perhaps our attention should be aimed more directly toward how environmental events alter them, rather than toward the S-R "bond." Thus, for example, a partial reinforcement schedule leads to greater resistance to extinction, perhaps not because r_F becomes part of the stimulus eliciting the instrumental response, but rather because this schedule strengthens directly the anticipatory goal response itself. The theory of cognitive dissonance, as applied by Lawrence and Festinger (1962), illustrates one approach in which the focus of attention in instrumental conditioning is shifted away from the S-R bond to what might be termed the S-S^R relation. Their theory is primarily concerned with how certain classical variables alter this relationship, for example, how they increase the "attractiveness" of the goal object for S.

Effects of Several Variables on Discriminative Instrumental Conditioning

Our treatment of discriminative instrumental conditioning will be comparatively brief, for the reasons that first, many less data are available in this area, and second, many of the obtained results are deducible from the principles established in nondiscriminative conditioning.

Acquisition

Magnitude of Reward. The effects of reward magnitude on discriminative instrumental conditioning are just what we would expect from the data obtained in the simpler, nondiscriminative, case. We know, for example, that asymptotic running speed in a straight alley is directly related to reward magnitude. Consequently, if one group of Ss is trained on a discriminative instrumental task (a "successive" discrimination) with relatively small reward and a second with a larger reward, any measure of discrimination that is based on response speed should show better discrimination learning in the second group.

The reasoning is simple. Both groups receive zero reward in S− (say, a white alley), and so, apart from contrast effects, running speed in the presence of this stimulus should be comparable in the high and low reward groups. However, the former group receives a larger reward in S+ (a black alley, say) than the latter group and should therefore run faster in this alley. Results confirming this expectation have been obtained in the straight alley (Bower and Trapold, 1959), and corresponding data based on response rate have been reported in the Skinner-box setting (Stebbins, 1959).

Observe that contrast effects, to the extent that they operate in discriminative instrumental conditioning, serve to increase further the differences in running speeds to S+ and S− in the high and low reward groups and thus accentuate the influence of reward magnitude on discriminative instrumental conditioning (see Bower, 1961).

The conclusion, then, is that because response intensity is sensitive to reward magnitude, discriminative instrumental conditioning will be facilitated by increasing magnitudes of reward.

Drive Level. The role of drive level in discriminative instrumental conditioning is not so easily deduced from its effects in the nondiscriminative case. We have seen that asymptotic performance is positively related to drive level in nondiscriminative conditioning. However, Ss trained on a discriminative conditioning task under relatively high drive will be operating under the higher motivation both when responding to S+ and to S−. As a consequence, the facilitation exerted by the higher drive level will apply in both instances and it becomes a matter of whether performance is enhanced more when responding to S+ or to S−.

Another way of framing this problem is in terms of interaction between reward magnitude and drive level in determining response strength. In our discussion of the role of drive level in nondiscriminative conditioning we pointed out its facilitating effects in the context of a single reward magnitude. If the facilitating effects of this variable were, in some sense, about the same for all magnitudes of reward, including zero reward, then motivational level could not affect discriminative conditioning, because S's performance would be augmented (under high drive) as much in S− as in S+.

There is, however, a further complication that is best presented by an example. A frequently used measure of the goodness of an operant discrimination is the "discrimination ratio," namely the ratio of the rate of responding in S^Δ to the rate in S^D, that is, S^Δ/S^D. Where discriminative behavior is completely absent, the discrimination ratio will be close to one, while in the case of perfect discrimination the ratio goes to zero. Now suppose that the effect of drive level on response rate were independent of reward magnitude in the sense that for all magnitudes of reward the effect of drive was to multiply response rate by a certain factor. Thus, for example, in a specific situation, if low drive (perhaps four hours of food deprivation) led to a rate of, say, 100 responses per minute, high drive (twenty-four hours of deprivation) would multiply this rate by, let us say, a factor of 1.2. Granting that high drive has this effect for all reward magnitudes, including zero reward, it is clear that discrimination performance, as defined by the discrimination ratio, would not be affected by drive manipulations. To illustrate, in terms of the figures just cited, if S has a discrimination ratio of 0.6 under low drive, his ratio upon being shifted to high drive would remain 0.6, because response rate in S^Δ as well as rate in S^D would be multiplied by the assumed factor of 1.2.

It must be noted, however, that if a measure of discrimination were employed which was based on the *difference* between response rates in S^Δ and S^D, then, according to the above assumed action of drive, this variable would indeed affect the measured discrimination. Consequently, whether or not drive is found to influence discriminative conditioning will depend, in part at least, on one's measure of discrimination performance.

In the operant situation, where the discrimination ratio is usually employed, the evidence bearing on the role of drive in discriminative conditioning is sparse and somewhat inconsistent. Dinsmoor (1952)

found that response rate in S^D was augmented by increasing drive levels about as much, proportionately, as rate in S^Δ. His results imply, therefore, that drive level has little effect on discriminative conditioning. On the other hand, Gray (1965), in a more recent study, obtained results suggesting that discriminative performance is impaired by higher drive levels.

In the straight alley and related apparatuses discrimination performance must be based on time scores rather than on response rate; for example, running times, starting latencies, and the like. The practice here has been to measure goodness of discrimination in terms of *differences* between, say, running time in $S+$ and in $S-$. Ratios of such measures are rarely, if ever, used, though they are much more comparable to the discrimination ratio.

We stated previously that the problem of the role of drive in successive discrimination can be referred to the nondiscriminative case by considering the question of whether drive level and reward magnitude interact in determining response strength. If in nondiscriminative conditioning the facilitating effect of increasing drive level were the same—in terms of time score *differences* —for all values of reward magnitude including zero reward, then we could not reasonably expect motivational level to affect discriminative conditioning in any important way. There have been a number of experiments addressed to this problem, but unfortunately, sometimes these two variables have been found to interact in determining running speed and related measures (Kintsch, 1962) and sometimes not (Reynolds and Pavlik, 1960). The basis of the interaction, when found, is that in terms of performance differences the facilitory effect of drive is greater the larger the reward. If such a result could be generally anticipated, then we would expect performance in discriminative conditioning, when measured in terms of differences in responding to $S+$ and to $S-$, to be facilitated by increasing drive levels. There is some evidence that, under certain special conditions at least, this is the case (Spence, Goodrich, and Ross, 1959).

In spite of the sparsity of the relevant data some conclusions and guesses can be made about the role of drive in instrumental discriminative conditioning. First, because manipulations of drive level encompass both the positive and the negative stimulus, response augmentation occurs with respect to both discriminanda at the higher drive levels, and this tends to reduce the effect of the drive variable no matter how goodness of discrimination conditioning is measured. Second, measures of discrimination based on differences are much more likely to produce a positive relationship between discriminative conditioning and motivational level than measures based on ratios. Indeed, it is possible for the former to show a positive relationship between the two variables while the latter points toward the very opposite conclusion (see Gray, 1965, Table 1). Third, because drive level and reward magnitude have been often found to interact in determining response strength in nondiscriminative conditioning, it is to be expected that this variable will frequently turn out to be positively related to discrimination conditioning where, as on the straight alley, measures of discrimination goodness are based on response differences. Finally, there are probably a number of other variables that modulate the relationship between drive and discriminative conditioning, but our knowledge of these is still rudimentary.

Other Variables. Of the many other variables that affect discriminative instrumental conditioning we will touch on only a few.

DELAY OF REWARD. The role of reward delay in discriminative conditioning apparently has not been investigated, possibly because the outcome, qualitatively at least, is obvious. From what we know about

this variable in the nondiscriminative case, discriminative conditioning is bound to be impeded if a delayed, rather than an immediate, reward were associated with S+. Similarly, if a delayed rather than zero reward were to be associated with S−, discriminative conditioning would doubtlessly be interfered with.

INTENSITY OF THE POSITIVE STIMULUS. Intensity of the CS has been shown to be a relevant variable in classical conditioning. The question thus arises as to whether a comparable effect holds for instrumental conditioning. Recently it has been shown that in an operant discrimination the intensity of S^D (white noise) is positively related to discriminative performance (Gray, 1965), so that apparently this variable does have a similar effect in classical and instrumental conditioning.

RELATIVE EXPOSURE TO THE POSITIVE AND NEGATIVE STIMULUS. The nature of discriminative instrumental conditioning is such that S+ (or S^D) and S− (S^Δ) are presented to S in serial order, the relative amount of exposure to each stimulus being essentially an arbitrary decision. A natural, and for some purposes convenient, arrangement is to program equal numbers of S+ and S− trials, or, in the operant case, equal times in S^D and S^Δ. It is reasonable to inquire, nevertheless, whether a more efficient distribution of training experience can be arranged, whether experience with one of the stimuli is more critical than experience with the other.

It has been shown in both the straight alley (Notterman, 1951) and the Skinner box (Sherman, Hegge, and Pierrel, 1964) that discriminative performance is enhanced by increasing amounts of exposure to the negative stimulus, the amount of training with the positive stimulus held constant. In the second study cited data were also presented which suggested that a given amount of training on S^Δ had a relatively constant effect on the discrimination ratio over a considerable range of training in S^D. In other words, it appears that performance in successive discrimination situations is governed more importantly by conditioning which takes place in the presence of the negative stimulus than by the reactions associated with the positive cue.

One does not have to look far for an explanation of this result. Granting that the instrumental response itself is easily conditioned in most instrumental situations (running down an alley, pressing a bar, and so on), not much training is required to establish the response at a fairly high strength. On the other hand, the other requirement of a successive discrimination, namely, to withhold the instrumental response in the presence of the negative stimulus, will depend on a good bit of training because S "has nothing to lose" in responding also to the negative cue. In more technical terms, the contingency between the instrumental response and reward results in, first, the establishment and strengthening of the instrumental response, which naturally generalizes from the positive stimulus to the negative cue. The complementary process in discriminative conditioning, extinction of the instrumental response in the presence of the negative stimulus, comes later and depends, of course, on experience with nonreinforced responding to $S-$ (S^Δ). And the more of such experience, the faster this process is established (see D'Amato and Jagoda, 1960).

Generalizing this line of reasoning, it is apparent that variables which encourage extinction in nondiscriminative conditioning will, when operating in association with the negative cue, facilitate discriminative conditioning; similarly, variables which augment performance in nondiscriminative conditioning, when they occur in conjunction with the positive stimulus, will also enhance discriminative conditioning. An interesting conjecture is that, generally speaking, the first class of variables is more powerful than the second.

Extinction

Discriminative training presents more options in extinction than was the case for nondiscriminative conditioning. During extinction of a discriminative response, S's experience with the discriminanda may be restricted to the former $S+$, to the former $S-$, or both stimuli may be encountered, in the same or in different arrangements as prevailed during acquisition. Nevertheless relatively few relevant data are available within this setting, and of those that do exist many were collected for reasons other than an interest in the extinction process itself (Black, 1965; Sperling, 1962). Our discussion of this topic will therefore be brief.

Extinction After Discriminative Training. A question of some interest is whether discriminative conditioning leads to greater resistance to extinction of an instrumental response than a comparable amount of nondiscriminative training. As pointed out by Jenkins (1961), early in discriminative training the reinforcement schedule *with respect to* S'*s response* is effectively one of partial reinforcement, because some responses (those executed in $S+$) are reinforced and others (those occurring in $S-$), are not. Accordingly, reasoning from the partial reinforcement effect found in nondiscriminative conditioning one might suspect that discriminative conditioning would result in augmented resistance to extinction. Jenkins (1961), working with discrete trials in a Skinner-box setting, got just such a result. Pigeons trained on a successive discrimination problem responded more to the the former $S+$ in later extinction than Ss whose training had been nondiscriminative. A similar result was obtained by D'Amato, Schiff, and Jagoda (1962), in a Skinner-box study employing free responding rather than discrete trials.

On the other hand, augmented resistance to extinction was not observed after

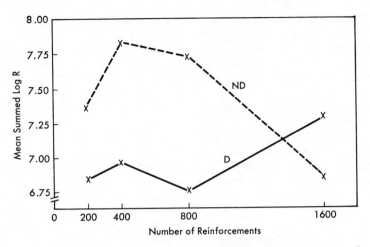

Figure 4-10. Bar-pressing performance in extinction (expressed as a logarithmic measure) as a function of number of reinforcements and type of instrumental conditioning, discriminative (D) vs. nondiscriminative (ND). (Reprinted with permission from D'Amato, M. R., Schiff, D., and Jagoda, H. Resistance to extinction after varying amounts of discriminative or nondiscriminative instrumental training. *J. exp. Psychol.*, 1962, **64**, 526–532.)

discrimination conditioning in a straight alley (Birch, Allison, and House, 1963). A possible explanation of this discrepancy is that the discrimination facing S in the last study was learned too soon for the non-reinforced responding on S− trials to generalize to S+ trials. Although successive discrimination training in a straight alley is such that ordinarily S executes the instrumental response on every trial, if S differentiates between the discriminanda at an early point in training, the reinforcement events of S+ and S− trials cannot be expected to coalesce into a quasipartial reinforcement schedule. The indicated conclusion is that discriminative conditioning is likely to result in augmented resistance to extinction when the discrimination task is not too easily acquired.

Amount of Acquisition Training. We have seen that within the confines of the Skinner-box setting resistance to extinction of a nondiscriminative response is monotonically related to acquisition level. Apart from the possible role that reward magnitude

might play in accounting for the observed monotonicity, it appears that even with the usual small rewards employed in such situations the relation can be altered radically by discriminative training. D'Amato, Schiff, and Jagoda (1962) compared the effects of discriminative and nondiscriminative training on the resistance to extinction of a bar-pressing response. As mentioned earlier, with nondiscriminative training they found resistance to extinction and acquisition level to be monotonically related up to 1,600 reinforced responses. With discriminative training, however, the function obtained between the two variables was clearly nonmonotonic (dotted line, Figure 4-10).

One possible explanation of this result is that at lower acquisition levels resistance to extinction of a discriminative response is inflated by the fortuitous partial reinforcement experience associated with discrimination training. However, with prolonged training Ss form a stable discrimination and as a consequence experience what is effectively a continuous reinforcement schedule. Conceivably this experience, if extensive, counteracts the effects of the earlier quasipartial reinforcement schedule. This otherwise promising explanation flies in the face of the consistent finding that, in nondiscriminative situations, even a substantial amount of continuous reinforcement does not reduce resistance to extinction significantly (Sutherland, Mackintosh, and Wolfe, 1965). Consequently, the result may depend on some aspect of the discriminatory behavior itself rather than on a concomitant fortuitous partial reinforcement experience.

Summary. There is a close continuity between the facts of nondiscriminative and discriminative instrumental conditioning. At bottom this confluence is due to the circumstance that both situations focus upon the same behavioral manifestation, response magnitude, and the variables which affect response magnitude in the one situation, influence it in much the same way in the other. In a real sense discriminative instrumental conditioning is simply a generalization of nondiscriminative conditioning. Apart from contrast effects—whose influence can, as we have seen, be worked out in the nondiscriminative case—the relationships established in nondiscriminative conditioning may be expected to hold as well for the discriminative case.

Furthermore, what we have defined as discriminative conditioning is itself a special case of the more general paradigm in which S is presented serially with two discriminatively different situations having different "payoffs." The more favorable situation, that associated with the larger reward, we label $S+$ and the less favorable, $S-$. The still wider generalization to more than two differentiable situations with varying payoffs is apparent.

There is one immediate pitfall to this increasing generalization. Is zero reward located on the continuum of reward values, being only a "reward" of particularly small magnitude, or does it have

unique properties? We have encountered some evidence favoring the former view; namely, a frustration effect also occurs upon reduction of a reward to a nonzero value (Bower, 1962). But in the ability of even very small rewards to sustain conditioned behavior apparently indefinitely, we seem to come upon imposing counterevidence. Animals will work for very long periods for the smallest rewards, which are insufficient to maintain them physically. Yet, as we know, instrumental behavior soon collapses when reward is reduced to zero. Here is a point at which the assumed continuity between zero and nonzero reward values needs to be investigated further.

Although we cannot in these chapters consider instrumental learning in any detail, it will be useful to pause for a moment to inquire into the role played by the familiar variables, reward magnitude and drive level, in simple instrumental learning. In doing so we will encounter complications which illustrate the difficulties standing in the way of generalizing the results of instrumental conditioning to instrumental learning. At the same time we should be able to see that the facts of instrumental conditioning are by no means inapplicable to simple instrumental learning.

Magnitude of Reward. A substantial number of experiments have had the aim of determining the role of reward magnitude in simple discriminative instrumental learning (see Chapter 3). The results appear confusing, but some degree of order can be brought out of them.

Several experiments employing rats as Ss failed to produce differences in the learning of a simple visual discrimination task when manipulating amount of reward (McKelvey, 1956; Reynolds, 1949). It appeared from these studies that if the reward was of sufficient size to motivate S to learn the discrimination problem, S tended to learn independently of reward magnitude. On the other hand, studies appeared in the literature showing that with monkeys as *S*s reward magnitude did indeed influence acquisition of a discrimination task, larger rewards facilitating learning (Schrier and Harlow, 1956).

Apart from the fact that these two sets of studies are obviously correlated with differences in the phylogenetic level of the *S*s employed, there was a difference in design which could have accounted for the conflicting results. In the rat studies separate groups of *S*s were used under the high reward and low reward conditions, constituting what may be called between-groups or separate-groups designs. A different design was employed in the studies in which monkeys served as experimental *S*s. Each monkey was tested under each of the reward values investigated, so that a given monkey might learn problem A under low reward and problem B under high reward. This sort of experimental design may be referred to as a within-group or a single-group design. There is no longer any doubt that these two designs can lead to quite divergent results when the same independent variables are investigated (D'Amato, 1955; D'Amato, Lachman, and Kivy, 1958; Grice and Hunter, 1964). Indeed, our knowledge of contrast effects should alert us to this possibility.

In any event, it appears to be the case that magnitude of reward is very much more likely to influence simple discrimination learning when a single-group, rather than a separate-groups, design is employed. Schrier (1958) investigated this possibility with monkeys and found that with the former design amount of reward was directly related to discrimination performance; with a separate-groups design, on the other hand, amount of reward did not show a uniform relationship with discrimination performance, and in general there was less of an overall influence. Precisely the same kind of interaction between the effect of reward magnitude on discriminaion learning and the type of research design employed was reported by Lawson (1957).

The mechanism responsible for these differences observed with between- and within-group designs is not at all clear, though it is apparent that contrast effects might be at work. In Schrier's (1958) study, for example, the greatest divergence between his two design groups occurred at the lowest amount of reward employed, the group experiencing the single-group design being substantially inferior to the corresponding separate-groups *S*s. This suggests the operation of a depression effect, and if such were the case it would help to account for the greater sensitivity shown toward the reward magnitude variable by single-group designs (with or without accompanying elation effects).

Whatever the interpretation, however, it is clear that within the separate-groups design—which was the design employed in the instrumental conditioning studies that revealed asymptotic performance to be directly related to reward magnitude—instrumental conditioning is much more sensitive to variations in reward magnitude than is simple discriminative instrumental learning, and the same holds true for discriminative instrumental conditioning. This fact naturally poses a serious problem for theorists who hope to derive, as a matter of principle, instrumental learning from instrumental conditioning. Furthermore, running time differences, that is, differences in response magnitude, have been reported in discrimination studies in which reward variations had no effect on choice behavior (McKelvey, 1956).

Drive Level. We have seen that drive level also importantly influenced nondiscriminative instrumental conditioning. Its effect on discriminative conditioning was not unambiguous, however, perhaps in part because of the different measures of goodness of discrimination that have been employed. Nevertheless, despite occasional exceptions (Eisman, Aismow, and Maltzman, 1956), the majority of studies which have manipulated drive level within a simple discriminative learning situation have found this variable to be ineffectual in influencing discriminative performance, irrespective of the type of design employed (Hillman, Hunter, and Kimble, 1953; Meyer, 1951; Miles, 1959). As with reward magnitude, the failure of drive level to influence choice behavior has occurred in situations where response magnitude has proved sensitive to motivational differences (Hillman, *et al.*, 1953; Lachman, 1961).

True, a mechanism exists within the Hull-Spence theory by means of which one could account for the failure of drive level to influence discrimination learning, at least under certain specified conditions (Spence, Goodrich, and Ross, 1959). It appears, however, that these conditions are not characteristic of the many studies which have failed to show drive level to be an effective variable in simple discrimination learning, so we have here a second instance which provides difficulties for the transition from instrumental conditioning to instrumental learning.

Nondiscriminative Instrumental Learning. There is a further complication. As it turns out, simple nondiscriminative choice behavior (that is, acquisition of simple spatial discriminations) *is* affected by reward magnitude, and reliably so (Pubols, 1961; Wike and Farrow, 1962). Apparently nondiscriminative instrumental learning forms somewhat of a bridge between instrumental conditioning and discriminative instrumental learning. The fact that stimulus comparison does not play an important role in nondiscriminative learning (*S* can commit himself to a choice long before reaching the choice point), whereas such a process is critically involved in discriminative instrumental learning, might be the key to understanding why nondiscriminative instrumental learning shares some of the properties of instrumental conditioning.

The Hull-Spence Theory of Instrumental Conditioning

Our treatment of instrumental conditioning has largely sidestepped discussion of formal theories in instrumental conditioning. The best known and most widely applied of these is the Hull-Spence theory, which, after Hull's death in 1952, was carried forward singlehandedly by Spence. The prominent role played by this theory in the area of instrumental conditioning requires that we give it some consideration, though a detailed treatment cannot be offered here. We will describe the Hull-Spence theory by showing how it can handle a number of the facts of instrumental conditioning with which we are already familiar.

To begin with, the theory is based on a family of theoretical constructs, often referred to as *intervening variables*, by means of which manipulated independent variables are ultimately related to observed behavior. These intervening variables are meant to embody, in a relatively precise way, those processes or factors which importantly determine performance in instrumental conditioning. The fact that motivational level—or in a specific case, hunger deprivation—is an important factor in instrumental conditioning is taken account of by incorporating into the theory the coordinate intervening variable D (*drive*). The more elementary fact that performance in instrumental conditioning improves with training—that learning occurs—is accommodated by the intervening variable H, or *habit strength*.

Having postulated a number of theoretical constructs, each one subsuming a large class of empirical operations presumably homogeneous in their effects on the conditioning process, the critical task then is to interrelate these constructs in a way that leads to successful prediction of instrumental behavior. As an illustration, let us trace out how these constructs are combined to obtain the known result that asymptotic performance in instrumental conditioning is directly related to motivational level.

First, looking at the intervening variable habit strength a little closer we find that it is tied down to the conditions of training by the following equation:

$$H = A(1 - 10^{-iN})$$

In this defining equation N stands for the number of training trials and hence provides the bridge between H and the empirical world. The symbol A, a constant characteristic of the individual learner, determines the limiting value of H, that is, its asymptote. And i, again a function of the individual, is the rate parameter, specifying the rapidity with which acquisition asymptote is reached (Spence, 1956, pp. 93–95). We see, therefore, that the "negative growth" function so often observed in instrumental conditioning curves is built directly into the construct H.

To continue the theoretical development, habit strength and drive are assumed to combine multiplicatively to determine one of the terminal intervening variables in the construct chain, *excitatory potential* (E). Thus, $E = H \times D$. Such dependent variables as response speed, latency, and amplitude are tied directly to E and its derivatives.

The fact that variations in drive affect asymptotic performance in instrumental conditioning now follows directly. The higher the motivational level (the longer the period of deprivation), the greater the value of D, and because manipulation of D is essentially equivalent in its effect to manipulation of A, the greater the motivation the higher the performance asymptote.

Also entailed in this theoretical formulation is the implication that *rate* of acquisition will not be influenced by drive manipulations. Although we had little to say about this aspect of acquisition curves in our earlier discussion—mainly because the available evidence is not as unequivocal as

in the case of asymptotic performance (Davenport, 1965)—drive level and reward magnitude appear to have little, if any, effect on acquisition rate (see Figures 4-2 and 4-5). So this feature of the Hull-Spence theory also seems congruent with the tenor of the available data.

Simple effects of reward magnitude, which, it will be recalled, closely resembled the corresponding drive level effects, are handled in a similar fashion. Manipulations of reward magnitude are reflected in a construct called *incentive motivation*, K. For example, the larger the amount of reward employed the higher the value of K. This new construct is joined with the others in the postulated relation $E = H(D + K)$. Consequently, variations in magnitude of reward are reflected by variations in K and these in turn, just as was the case for D, imply differences in acquisition asymptote but not in rate (see Black, 1965).

In the case of contrast effects of reward magnitude additional concepts, such as anticipatory frustration, are necessary to accommodate elation- and depression-like manifestations. The fractional anticipatory goal response r_G-s_G, it might be noted here, is thought by Spence to be the mechanism underlying incentive motivation. That is, the purpose of K is to mirror the strength of r_G-s_G, and variables which affect K do so because they play a role in determining the strength of the anticipatory goal response.

It will be recalled that, compared to magnitude of reward and drive level, delay of reward showed some clear differences in its role in instrumental conditioning. For one thing performance differences emerged more slowly with different delays; and for another, with longer delays performance not uncommonly fell off with increasing training. Clearly, delay of reward will have to enter the theory in a different way from drive level and reward magnitude if these differences are to be accommodated. Such is the case. Delay of reward is thought to be one of the independent variables determining an inhibitory factor I, which, in substracting from excitatory potential, produces what is termed *effective* excitatory potential ($\bar{E}$). Thus,

$$\bar{E} = E - I = H(D + K) - I$$

This inhibitory factor is also presumed to be a function of the number of delay of reward trials encountered. Although the exact way in which these two classes of independent variables determine I has not been specified, it is entirely possible to relate them monotonically to I and still have deducible the two effects of reward delay under consideration.

The Hull-Spence theory extends immediately to discriminative instrumental conditioning in the assumption that the theory applies separately to $S+$ and to $S-$. Of course, contrast effects and generalization between $S+$ and $S-$ act to complicate the derivation of the "positive" and "negative" excitatory potentials, but these difficulties are relatively minor.

Perhaps enough has now been said to give the reader some feeling of the general approach of the Hull-Spence theory of instrumental conditioning (see Spence, 1956, for further information). The theory, as we have already pointed out, has by no means had its horizons limited to conditioning. Explicit methods have been proposed by means of which the response magnitude measures of discriminative conditioning can be transformed to derive, hopefully, the choice measures characteristic of simple instrumental learning (Spence, 1958; Spence, Goodrich, and Ross, 1959). As yet, however, these attempts toward the solution of what must be acknowledged to be an extremely difficult and complex task, have met with only limited success.

Summary

Our sampling of research areas in positively reinforced instrumental conditioning, although by no means extensive, has been sufficient to show that a considerable amount of effort has been expended in this enterprise. The rewards, in terms of empirical and theoretical knowledge, perhaps have not been startling, but they have been steady. Recognition that such diverse operations as comprise the manipulation of drive level and amount of reward affect instrumental performance in very similar ways, and the embodiment of this correspondence into a formal theoretical statement, is no small accomplishment. The casting of so anthropomorphic a concept as frustration into an objective, scientific mold, defining its essential characteristics in such a way as not to rob it of its everyday significance, drawing inferences from its sharpened definition which may be investigated (and often validated) at various levels from rat to man, all within the short period of some fifteen years, must be regarded as a respectable accomplishment regardless of one's theoretical persuasion.

In some cases enlightenment consists chiefly in pointing to opportunities that remain to be developed. We have seen how close, conceptually and empirically, nondiscriminative and discriminative instrumental conditioning stand to each other, and we even know something about the kinds of complications one may expect when comparing the two. It would seem possible, therefore, to develop a quantitative theory based on nondiscriminative conditioning which will predict in detail the facts of discriminative instrumental behavior. This quite feasible enterprise remains to be exploited.

On the other hand, the facts of instrumental conditioning have clearly shown that certain of our preconceptions concerning the regularities and "lawfulness" of behavior which may be expected even in so simple a situation as instrumental conditioning have been naive. The empirical relationships that can boast substantial freedom from limitations imposed by situational and related parameters are very few. Multivariable interactions can be expected to be the rule, not the exception, and this fact complicates greatly our search for, and the means by which we shall express, regularities in instrumental behavior. But if disillusionment must precede wisdom, we are at least past the first phase. The knowledge that such interactions are to be expected will probably alter our future research strategies in such a way as to provide for their appraisal at the very outset of our research efforts. And as pointed out earlier, as our theoretical analysis becomes more acute the characteristics of such interactions should more often be forecasted by theoretical considerations.

5

Instrumental Conditioning with Negative Reinforcement

Unlike our approach in the last chapter, we will here present at the outset a theoretical account of some of the mechanisms assumed to be implicated in instrumental conditioning with negative reinforcement. This formulation will provide a valuable frame of reference within which to view the empirical facts and principles that follow.

Motive-Incentive Conditions Under Negative Reinforcement

When positive reward is employed as the reinforcing agent it is usually a simple matter to designate exactly the motive-incentive conditions operating in the conditioning of a bit of behavior. Motivation most often derives from some sort of deprivation procedure, and the incentive, of course, is simply the positive reinforcer employed—food, water, and so on. However, in conditioning with negative reinforcement the reinforcing agent is often not at all easy to specify. What is the reinforcing event on a trial in which S successfully avoids S^{R-}? This question in particular has spurred the development of a number of

theoretical approaches by means of which the motive-incentive mechanisms underlying conditioning with negative reinforcement might be conceptualized. The one to be described here has proven quite fruitful over the years, during which time it has gained rather widespread acceptance, explicit and implicit. Originally proposed to accommodate avoidance conditioning, its range of application will be seen to be much wider.

The Fractional Anticipatory Pain Response —Fear. In escape conditioning, where S's task is to remove himself from S^{R-}, the source of his motivation is evident. It arises from S^{R-} itself, which is applied until the escape response is made, terminating the aversive stimulation. But in punishment and avoidance conditioning the presence of S^{R-} cannot always be appealed to as providing the motivational or reinforcing basis of S's behavior. A well-punished response may fail to occur for a considerable time even though punishment has been long discontinued; and as already noted, by definition S spares himself S^{R-} when he performs an avoidance response. To provide for a motivating and reinforcing mechanism which operates in the absence of S^{R-}, the present formulation enlists an anticipatory mechanism that captures in a relatively objective way the intuitive notion of fear or anxiety.

Aversive stimuli, such as electric shock or intense visual, auditory, and thermal stimulation, arouse in S a state of pain or discomfort which S will ordinarily attempt to alleviate, just as he attempts to alleviate hunger or thirst. Let us refer to the response complex elicited by S^{R-} as R_P, "P" standing for pain or discomfort. Part of R_P is detachable from S^{R-} in the sense that it can occur in the absence of its normal eliciting stimulus, much as we assumed that a portion of the goal and frustration response complexes r_G and r_F, were detachable from their primary eliciting stimuli. As usual, we refer to this component as r_P and, as before, we assume that r_P is conditionable to stimuli which precede or signal the onset of S^{R-}. In further correspondence with the anticipatory goal and frustration responses, we refer to r_P as the *fractional anticipatory pain* (or discomfort) response.

The parallel between the fractional anticipatory pain response and the everyday notions of fear and anxiety may be apparent. Like r_P, these terms are usually employed to refer to the anticipation of a painful event or, more generally, an event capable of producing distress or discomfort. In what follows we shall use the terms *anticipatory pain response, fear* and *anxiety* interchangeably.

Because r_P is a portion of R_P it is a reasonable assumption that S will attempt to avoid stimuli which elicit r_P, just as S attempts to avoid S^{R-} itself. More exactly, stimuli that evoke in S the anticipatory pain mechanism r_P-s_P will be responded to as aversive stimuli, avoided by S where possible or terminated or reduced when avoidance is not allowed. Such stimuli may therefore be termed *conditioned* or *secondary aversive stimuli*. By way of contrast, stimuli that elicit the anticipatory *goal* response will be sought out or approached by S; they are therefore called *conditioned* or *secondary reinforcing stimuli*.

To recapitulate, a primary aversive stimulus S^{R-} elicits in S a primary pain or discomfort response, R_P, which has a detachable and conditionable component, r_P. This response, along with its proprioceptive stimulus concomitant s_P, comprises the fractional anticipatory pain response, or more simply, fear or anxiety. Cues which signal the onset of primary aversive stimuli become conditioned aversive stimuli because they become conditioned to, and elicit, r_P-s_P. Fear, as we all know, is not a very pleasant experience. Further on in the chapter we shall employ the r_P-s_P mechanism to interpret a number of facts arising from conditioning with negative reinforcement.

The fractional anticipatory pain response has been identified with certain response components of the autonomic nervous system, for example, the heart rate, respiratory, and circulation changes initiated by release of adrenalin. The associative mechanism through which r_P becomes conditioned has been assumed therefore to be classical conditioning. This is another point of correspondence between r_P and the fractional anticipatory goal and frustration responses. It will be recalled that both of the latter responses were also assumed to become associated through classical conditioning procedures. Though it was not mentioned in our earlier discussion, presumably this implies that the autonomic nervous system also plays an important role in the origin of r_G and r_F. The extremely close correspondence between r_P and r_F suggests that there should be some points of close similarity in the roles played by anticipatory pain and frustration responses in instrumental conditioning. Later we shall point out a striking illustration bearing on this expectation.

It should be pointed out that the preceding formulation differs in terminology, though probably not in substance, from most accounts of the role played by fear or anxiety in conditioning with negative reinforcement. The terminology employed here serves to highlight the common conceptual status of. r_G, r_F, and fear (r_P). Some authors have maintained that the unconditioned reaction to a strong S^{R-} includes not only pain but fear as well, and that the conditioned anticipatory fraction of this total reaction be termed *anxiety* to distinguish it from the unconditioned fear component (Solomon and Wynne, 1954, p. 354). Because there are at present no operations by which fear and anxiety may be distinguished, and because, as will be pointed out later, negative reinforcers need not evoke a pain reaction, the formulation of fear as an anticipatory pain or discomfort response is preferred by the writer.

Positive and Negative Reinforcement Compared

In a sense, the terms *positive* and *negative* reinforcement project misleading connotations. If by *reinforcement* we mean a stimulus situation which tends to strengthen behavior sequences upon which it is contingent, then clearly all reinforcement is positive. All reinforcement must be comprised of stimulus situations attractive to S. There is, in fact, a very tight logical correspondence between the origin and function of the motive-incentive events which occur during positively reinforced instrumental conditioning and those that transpire during conditioning with negative reinforcement. With positive reinforcement a drive state is induced by some sort of deprivation procedure, whether this be deprivation of food, of a social partner, or of adequately varied sensory stimulation. The incentive, it follows, is the restoration of the commodity denied S—food, a companion, and so on. With negative reinforcement, on the other hand, motivation is instilled by the application of a stimulus that causes S some degree of pain

or discomfort. And in this case removal, or reduction in the intensity, of the unpleasant stimulation constitutes the basis of reinforcement.

But because hunger, thirst, and other such "appetitive" drives implicated in positive reinforcement may be considered to cause in S discomfort or distress, and because the corresponding reward objects serve to reduce in some measure these unpleasant sensations, it is apparent that the structure of motive-incentive conditions in positive reinforcement is similar, if not identical, to that of negative reinforcement. What then, if any, are the essential differences between the motive-incentive conditions operating in these two types of conditioning situations?

Of the several obvious divergences that come to mind, the one having the most significant consequences has to do with differential rates of drive induction. In virtually all applications of negative reinforcement the drive inducing stimuli are so managed that drive onset is very abrupt, practically instantaneous. Aversive intensities of electric shock, light, noise, cold, and so on, are applied to S at the outset, causing him immediate pain or discomfort. It should be noted, however, that this is not an inherent feature of negative reinforcement. Any terminally aversive stimulus, including electric shock, can be administered in gradually increasing intensities, reaching aversive levels only after a substantial period of time.

In contrast with the normally abrupt action of aversive stimuli, deprivation procedures require considerable time in order to achieve effective motivational levels. But here too a reversal of normal events is possible in the use of physiological methods of manipulating appetitive drives, which, as we pointed out in the last chapter, offer the promise of enabling E to induce such motivational states very quickly. Thus, although in practice there exists an extreme contrast in the rates of drive induction attained under positive and negative reinforcement, in principle this divergence is subject to manipulation, even to the point of being reversed from its normal order.

One significant consequence which flows from the different rates of drive induction is that certain conditioning procedures, notably punishment and avoidance conditioning, are not feasible with the motive-incentive conditions of positive reinforcement. The reason is that, although appetitive drives may be considered to cause discomfort or distress to *S*, their rates of induction are so slow by ordinary deprivation procedures that it is difficult to associate a specific stimulus with the onset of these drive states or to arrange for sharply discriminable contingencies between them and a specific bit of behavior. To take avoidance as an illustration, if a strong thirst drive could be instigated (and removed) immediately in *S*, and if a cue were made to signal the onset of this artifically produced thirst, then doubtless *S* would learn to "avoid" the thirst by making an appropriate instrumental response when the signaling cue appeared. And referred to punishment, a response that produced the artifically induced thirst would doubtlessly be suppressed, just as if it had produced more conventional primary aversive stimuli. Consequently, the implausibility of having deprivation states serve as primary aversive stimuli stems directly from their gradual onset.

There are many other obvious differences between positive and negative reinforcement but, on analysis, none of them seem to be useful means of differentiating the two. One might maintain, for example, that with negative reinforcement the source of motivation is confounded with the source of reward. Shock is applied to institute drive and then removed to produce reward; thus a very large reward is not possible in a mildly shock-motivated *S*. This argument is not very convincing, however, because it is plain that the upper limit of the reward possible in positive

reinforcement is also dictated by the extent of the drive operating in *S*. It is not possible, for example, to reward a two-hour food-deprived *S* to the same maximal extent as a twenty-four-hour deprived individual.

Neither is it useful to differentiate positive and negative reinforcement on the basis that in the first case a commodity is removed to produce motivation and restored to provide reward, while just the opposite order prevails for negative reinforcement. A rat swimming through cold water to get to a warmer goal box is clearly involved in conditioning with negative reinforcement. Yet it is reasonable to maintain that the animal's motivation arises from his being deprived of heat, which is restored in the warmer goal box.

Finally, it probably also is largely irrelevant that primary aversive stimuli are often painful. True, strong intensities of visual, auditory, and thermal stimuli, as well as electric shock, are capable of producing pain in *S*, although the usual ranges of hunger, thirst, and other deprivation states achieved by normal deprivation procedures do not trespass upon the pain threshold. Nevertheless, conditioning with negative reinforcement is often conducted with primary aversive stimuli that do not provoke pain, and although the presence of pain undoubtedly accentuates certain aspects of negative reinforcement, its effects appear to be more quantitative than qualitative.

In conclusion, it appears that the single essential feature distinguishing negative from positive reinforcement is that the onset of drive is instantaneous in the one case and quite prolonged in the other. From this one crucial difference many divergences then appear.

Because of their different motivational structures, the patterns of reward employed with positive and negative reinforcement are quite different. In positively reinforced conditioning *E* usually reinforces *S* on each trial with a reward magnitude that reduces his drive state by a relatively small quantity (usually because E wishes to "conserve" S's motivation from trial to trial). With negative reinforcement, on the other hand, reinforcement on each trial is often "complete," the aversive stimulus being removed (or avoided) entirely. When comparing conditioning under positive and negative reinforcement this difference in the manner in which incentives are administered must be kept in mind.

Though the notion that positive and negative reinforcement are essentially equivalent processes presently can claim little direct supporting evidence, it should prove a useful working hypothesis. The central assumption, that all significant differences between positive and negative reinforcement arise from the vastly different rates of induction (and reduction) of appetitive and aversive drives, is easily subject to test on the side of S^{R-}. There is nothing to prevent E from paralleling appetitive drives, in both their onset and reduction characteristics, with appropriately chosen primary aversive stimuli. The reverse attack, mimicking the growth and reduction rates of primary aversive drives with appetitive drives, is more difficult technically. But it too should be possible by taking advantage of modern physiological techniques, through which thirst, and perhaps hunger, can be induced directly via electrical and chemical stimulation of the central nervous system.

Escape Conditioning

Reflecting the fact that research in the area of negative reinforcement has centered around the paradigms of escape, punishment, and avoidance conditioning, the organization of this chapter will depart in some measure from that adopted in the last chapter. The major sections of the present chapter will revolve around these three paradigms, rather than around a few,

centrally important, empirical variables. Nevertheless, where possible, parallels will be drawn to the conclusions and principles stated in the preceding chapter.

In a recent compilation of references pertinent to instrumental escape conditioning, fewer than twenty references bear publication dates of 1950 or earlier (Woods, 1965). The number of items in this bibliography increases about six-fold over the next fifteen years, with the period 1960–1965 producing approximately as many published items as all previous years. Thus, after a long period of neglect, research in escape conditioning is increasing in popularity. Despite the recent upsurge, however, our knowledge in this area is extremely spotty; seldom will we find the kind of firm generalizations that were possible with positively reinforced conditioning.

Acquisition in Escape Conditioning

Magnitude of Reward. Escape conditioning, better than punishment or avoidance training, lends itself to an analysis of the kinds of variables investigated in the case of conditioning with positive reinforcement. To investigate with negative reinforcement the role of reward (incentive) magnitude on response strength, one might, for example, run Ss in a straight alley under a fixed shock level, say 400 volts (applied through an appropriate current-limiting resistor). In analogy with conditioning with S^{R+}, S would be rewarded by a reduction in shock intensity when he arrived in the goal box. Reducing the goal-box shock level to different values provides an operation which bears a close correspondence to manipulations of positive incentives, such as amount of food reward.

Just such an experiment has been performed a number of times, with the usual outcome that asymptotic running speed is positively related to amount of shock reduction (Bower, Fowler, and Trapold,

1959; Campbell and Kraeling, 1953). A similar result has been found with thermal aversive stimuli (Woods, Davidson, and Peters, 1964). Consequently, at least with respect to its simple effects, incentive magnitude appears to play similar roles in negatively and positively reinforced instrumental conditioning.

There are many less data available relating to contrast effects arising from incentive shifts in negative reinforcement. From those that do exist it appears that the phenomena of elation and depression do not occur with negative reinforcement. Bower, Fowler, and Trapold (1959) shifted Ss from large reward (200 volts reduction) to small (50 volts reduction) and vice versa, and found that although Ss adjusted their running speeds rather quickly to the new reward magnitudes there was no evidence of the over- or undershooting that define elation and depression effects.

The currently indicated conclusion seems to be that although negative reinforcement parallels positive reinforcement in the simple effects of reward magnitude, and perhaps also with respect to rapid adjustments to shifts in magnitude (but see Howe, 1961), contrast effects may not occur with S^{R-}. It will be recalled, however, that contrast effects, particularly the elation effect, also failed to occur under certain circumstances with positive reward. Conceivably, the same variables that preclude their occurrence with S^{R+} operate more generally in the case of S^{R-}.

Another possibility is that with negative reinforcement contrast effects are masked by the fact that normally on each trial S experiences two rewards in sequence rather than a single reinforcement, as is the case in positive reinforcement. In the Bower, Fowler, and Trapold study, for example, after receiving its large or small incentive in the goal box, S was removed from the latter and placed in the start box; during this interval S^{R-} was, of course, reduced to zero. Consequently, S experienced on each trial either the reward sequence large-small or small-large. Repeated experience with these contrasting reward magnitudes could have caused Ss to adapt to shifts in incentive magnitude. If so, when the "small" reward Ss were shifted to a large goal-box reward they would show no elation effect because they had already experienced in the experimental situation many transitions from small to large rewards. This interpretation would be supported by results showing that contrast effects obtained with positive reinforcement become attenuated with repeated shifts in reward magnitude; data bearing directly on this issue are few, however. Perhaps Pieper and Marx (see Figure 4-4) would have observed a reduction in contrast effects had they carried training further. And the reverse argument holds for those Ss that were shifted from a large to a small goal-box reward.

It is, of course, quite possible to arrange for more comparable incentive conditions when testing for effects of reward magnitude shifts in positive and negative reinforcement. With positive reinforcement, a second reward might be given to S upon its removal from the goal box, a reward of a size that would sum the goal-box and post-trial incentives to a constant and relatively large magnitude. Conversely, with negative reinforcement the second reward might be eliminated by maintaining S at the goal-box shock intensity throughout the intertrial interval, until the moment the next trial begins. Whether contrast effects would be obtained under such modifications or whether a greater consistency in contrast effects would emerge under positive and negative reinforcement remains to be seen.

Drive Level. With negative reinforcement, drive level is usually manipulated by varying the intensity of the primary aversive stimulus. To investigate the role of drive level on instrumental conditioning incentive magnitude must, of course, be held constant, a precondition achieved by reducing S^{R-} a constant amount. Drive level and constant reward magnitude thus defined, the resulting data are not what we would expect from our knowledge of how variations in appetitive drives affect instrumental conditioning.

Campbell and Kraeling (1953) ran different groups of rats on a straight alley with shock levels varying between 200 and 400 volts. Each group received a constant 100-volt shock reduction as reward upon entry into the goal box. They found that running speed in their escape situation was inversely related to shock (drive) level. One possible explanation of this result is that strong shock might have caused S to engage in responses which reduced somewhat the aversive stimulus while competing with the instrumental sequence, responses such as jumping, pressing down on its paws to increase the contact area (thereby reducing current density), and so on. Supporting this view is the fact that Ss in the 400-volt group did not increase their average running speed over the fifteen training trials given them; rather, they showed a slight declining trend.

A more consonant result was obtained by Woods, Davidson, and Peters (1964), who used cold water as the source of drive in their Ss. Although asymptotic speed of swimming to a reward of warmer water was not affected by temperature variations between 15 and 25 degrees C., it increased when the alley water temperature was reduced to 12 degrees C. In these comparisons incentive magnitude, defined in terms of the difference in temperature between the "alley" and "goal box" water, was held constant.

It appears, therefore, that if the opportunity for S to reduce the severity of S^{R-} by engaging in responses which simultaneously compete with the instrumental response is eliminated, drive level may turn out to play a similar role in positive and negative reinforcement. Obviously, however, the relevant data are quite scanty.

Delay of Reward. Figure 5-1 depicts the running speed curves of six groups of rats running down a straight alley charged with 250 volts; upon reaching the goal box S^{R-} was terminated after various delays ranging from 0 to 16 sec. It is apparent from the curves that asymptotic speed is inversely related to reward delay, and in this respect the data are in harmony with the corresponding results from conditioning with positive reinforcement. Note, however, that nonmonotonicity does not occur to any substantial degree in any of the curves. It will be recalled that nonmonotonicity was commonly encountered with delays of positive reward (Figures 4-7 and 4-8). Possibly, nonmonotonicity would have been obtained if training had been continued beyond twenty-eight trials.

As a second possibility, perhaps the critical factor operating again relates to motive-incentive differences. In the Fowler and Trapold study every trial ended with complete reward, which is to say S^{R-} was ultimately reduced to zero after S reached the goal box. This procedure contrasts with the corresponding operation employed in studies cited earlier, in which a small food reward was given on each trial, reducing the hunger drive by an insignificant degree. In view of this sharp disparity in reinforcement procedures, the question arises as to whether nonmonotonicity would disappear in positively reinforced conditioning if a very large food reward were used. Or conversely, would it appear in escape conditioning if reward were reduced to a relatively small value?

Delay of reward, it might also be noted here, plays an important, if somewhat complex role in punishment. As we shall later see, depending on circumstances, an immediate punishment can be either more or *less* effective than a delayed punishment.

Summary. Although in their general effects the three variables discussed display important similarities in positively and negatively reinforced conditioning, it is clear that the correspondence is far from perfect. There is no evidence of contrast effects with shifts in

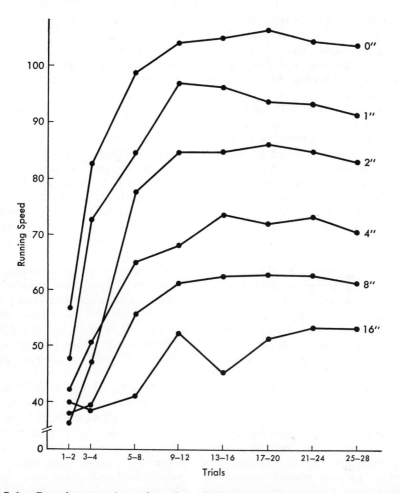

Figure 5-1. Running speed as a function of the delay (in sec.) of shock termination. (Reprinted with permission from Fowler, H., and Trapold, M. A. Escape performance as a function of delay of reinforcement. *J. exp. Psychol.*, 1962, **63**, 464–467.)

the magnitude of S^{R-}, nonmonotonicity with substantial delays of negative reinforcement has not yet been reported, and, finally, drive level effects are not as marked nor as reliably obtained as with positive reinforcement. Perhaps all these points of divergence would disappear if the motive-incentive conditions operating in negative reinforcement were made to parallel more closely those characteristic of the analogous positive reinforcement paradigms. To achieve this goal a close analysis is required of the motive-incentive patterns operating

in the two conditioning situations which are to be placed in correspondence. As yet, however, only the barest beginning has been made in this direction.

Extinction in Escape Conditioning

Extinction is a concept which has its genesis and major application in the area of positive reinforcement. The motive-incentive conditions implied by the operation of extinction in the latter context are that (1) the magnitude of S^{R+} be reduced to zero and (2) the motivational state (as produced by the deprivational procedure) be unchanged. The last requirement is implicit, but nevertheless essential. Parallel conditions are obtained in escape conditioning by having the instrumental response no longer terminate S^{R-}. Primary reinforcement is thereby eliminated while maintaining primary drive. As noted in the first chapter of this section, however, employment of this extinction procedure is rare. More commonly S^{R-} is eliminated entirely during "extinction" trials, a procedure which abolishes primary drive as well as primary reward. Where one is seeking parallels in the effects of various independent variables upon the extinction of positively and negatively reinforced conditioning, these two quite different extinction procedures must be distinguished. Elimination of primary reward, but not primary drive, would seem to provide the extinction paradigm more closely analogous to extinction with positive reinforcement. We shall consider briefly both extinction operations.

Extinction as Removal of Primary Reward. One of the most interesting relationships arising from our earlier discussion of extinction with positive reinforcement was the interaction of amount of reward and level of acquisition training in determining resistance to extinction. Does an equivalent interaction hold for negative reinforcement? The answer is that we simply do not know; the relevant literature is extremely meager. Campbell (1959) trained partially restrained rats in a Skinner-box-type apparatus to poke their heads through a hole and depress a lever to turn off shock delivered to their tails. Number of reinforced trials was varied between 0 and 500. During a subsequent 15-min. extinction period, throughout which S^{R-} was applied continuously, a *monotonic* relation was obtained between the number of instrumental responses made (resistance to

extinction) and amount of prior escape training.

Several comments are in order here. First, inasmuch as during training reinforcement was complete—each escape response terminated S^{R-}—the suggestion is that incentive magnitude was of comparatively large proportions. A possibly mitigating factor, however, is that the shock employed apparently was rather mild. Second, because trials in a Skinner-box setting seem to be less efficacious in obtaining the kinds of effects presently under consideration, it is possible that 500 training trials is an insufficient number to demonstrate nonmonotonicity in escape conditioning.

In a study recently completed in our laboratory, James Fazzaro varied escape training in a Skinner-box setting between 200 and 1,600 trials, distributed 100 trials per day. He used as S^{R-} a pulsating or "discontinuous" shock (0.2 sec. on time, 2.0 sec. off time) of approximately 0.8 milliamperes (ma). Discontinuous shock, which has been found to facilitate avoidance learning markedly (D'Amato, Keller, and DiCara, 1964), was used in the present context as a means of providing a strongly aversive, not overly disorganizing, S^{R-}. Extinction entailed five daily 10-min. periods during which the escape response, bar pressing, no longer terminated S^{R-}. In Figure 5-2 the results, in terms of the total number of responses made during the five extinction sessions, are presented for the four groups of the experiment. It is clear that there is no evidence of nonmonotonicity in the data.

In the light of Fazzaro's results it is unlikely that the monotonicity obtained by Campbell (1959) was due either to inadequate magnitude of reward (see Stavely, 1966) or to an insufficiently high degree of training. His data also suggest a reinterpretation of the general failure to find nonmonotonicity in Skinner-box settings when reinforcement is positive. Contrary to a previous conjecture, these failures may not

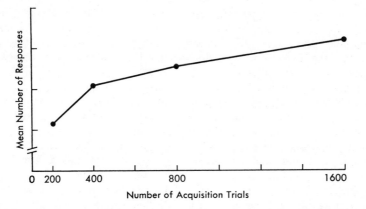

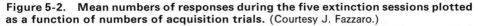

Number of Acquisition Trials

Figure 5-2.   Mean numbers of responses during the five extinction sessions plotted as a function of numbers of acquisition trials. (Courtesy J. Fazzaro.)

be the result of the fortuitous fact that studies utilizing Skinner boxes tend to employ small food rewards; rather, they may point to a fundamental difference between Skinner-box apparatuses and runway devices. Possibly, the relevant variable operating is the amount of effort required in the two situations to execute the instrumental response, or, perhaps, competing responses are more likely to occur in one situation than in the other. (Distracting stimuli are much more prevalent in runway apparatuses, which, in general, maintain poorer environmental control than is the case for Skinner-box situations.) Whatever the cause, it is clear that the interactive relationship between level of training and amount of reward in determining resistance to extinction needs to be tested under a much wider range of conditions before it can be safely generalized from the runway to other instrumental conditioning situations or, farther afield, to negatively reinforced conditioning.

Extinction as Removal of S^{R-}. If, after S has been trained to escape S^{R-} the negative reinforcer is removed from the experimental situation, eliminating the basis of primary motivation as well as primary reward, will S respond at all during such "extinction" trials? The answer is yes, and

for an explanation of why the instrumental response continues to occur in the absence of primary drive and primary reward we must recall the fractional anticipatory pain mechanism, $r_P\text{-}s_P$.

The explanation begins with the assumption that during escape training $r_P\text{-}s_P$, or fear, becomes conditioned to the cues of the apparatus in the presence of which S was shocked or endured other negative reinforcers, for example, the stimuli occurring in the start box or the alley of a runway apparatus. Carrying this illustration further, during a subsequent extinction trial, even though S^{R-} is no longer present, fear presumably occurs in some measure in both the start box and the alley, providing the motivational thrust for the escape response.

Moreover, when S arrives in the goal box its fear is reduced in part or in whole because of the goal box's status, acquired during training, as a cue associated with shock termination. Because fear reduction, like reduction of S^{R-}, is rewarding, the instrumental response should be strengthened during such an "extinction" trial. Thus, we come to grips with quite a different problem, namely, why should S ever stop responding during this sort of extinction procedure? The answer is that eventually the fear itself extinguishes. Remember that fear, $r_P\text{-}s_P$, is classically conditioned to apparatus cues, the un-conditioned stimulus being shock, or more generally, S^{R-}. Since S^{R-} never occurs during the extinction procedure being considered, we have at hand a necessary and sufficient condition for extinction of a classically conditioned response, namely, removal of the unconditioned stimulus. With the eventual extinction of r_P-s_P the motivating and reinforcing basis of S's responding collapses, and the instrumental response soon follows suit.

This interpretation has a direct bearing on an interesting bit of behavior which some have termed *masochism*, others giving it the more neutral appellation *vicious cycle* or *self-punitive* behavior. The experimental situation is as follows. Rats are first trained on a simple escape response in a runway. During these trials S is placed in the start box and after a few seconds shock is applied to the floor of the alley *and of the start box*. After the establishment of the escape response there then ensues a series of extinction trials carried out under one of two different conditions. One group of Ss is extinguished by the removal of S^{R-} procedure; these Ss never again encounter shock in the runway. The second group of Ss no longer is shocked in the start box but shock is applied in a section of or through-out the alley portion of the runway, for example, in the first 8 in. of the alley (Martin and Melvin, 1964). Now the remarkable fact is that, contrary to common sense, the Ss that experience shock in the alley take *longer* to extinguish than those that do not. That is, they do not do the sensible thing of staying put in the start box, in which they never are shocked during extinction; rather they venture out of the start box, are shocked, then continue on their way to the goal box. We seem faced here with the paradox that punishment serves to strengthen, rather than to weaken, an instrumental response.

Although there are several possible interpretations of this interesting result (Brown, Martin, and Morrow, 1964; see

Melvin, 1964), the one appearing to enjoy most support is expressed in terms of the anticipatory pain mechanism (fear). To state this explanation in a few words, it is assumed that the group of Ss for which shock no longer occurs in the runway extinguishes in accordance with the preceding description for the removal of S^{R-} procedure. The superior resistance to extinction of the second, experimental, group of Ss is then ascribed to the fact that the shock which they encounter during their extinction trials serves to maintain the fear response (r_P-s_P) at a relatively high level.

Let us be a bit more specific. When a rat of the experimental group is placed in the start box on an extinction trial, it experiences the anticipatory pain mechanism, the s_P portion of which during training was associated with running to the goal box (where both S^{R-} and fear were terminated or reduced). Even though, during extinction, the start box is no longer electrified, fear alone is sufficient to initiate the escape response. When S emerges from the start box and is shocked in the alley, he continues his run to the goal box, terminating again both S^{R-} and fear. In short, the shock (or an alternate S^{R-}, see Melvin and Martin, 1966) experienced by S on these "extinction" trials greatly attenuates extinction of the fear response, which, as we have seen, must be eliminated if the instrumental response is to be extinguished.

If S is shocked during every trial on which it emerges from the start box, thus maintaining the fear response, why should extinction ever occur? The answer to this reasonable question is that the fear elicited by the start box, which motivates initiation of the escape response, itself gradually extinguishes, inasmuch as shock never occurs there. As the fear begins to extinguish S takes longer and longer to leave the start box and, consequently, the fear generated there is reduced more and more. It has been shown, in fact, that if the electrified portion of the alley is far removed from the start box, rather than being adjacent to it, the facilitative effect of shock on resistance to extinction is very much attenuated (Martin and Melvin, 1964).

We see, then, that the anticipatory pain mechanism provides us with a reasonable and consistent explanation of the foregoing, "self-punitive" behavior.

Summary. We have by no means discussed all the points of possible parallel between escape conditioning and conditioning with positive reinforcement that have come under investigation. For example, the partial reinforcement effect has been obtained with escape conditioning (Bower, 1960). Also, a number of studies have concerned themselves with the question of how well certain behavioral properties characteristic of fixed ratio schedules under positive reinforcement are retained when reinforcement is negative (Winograd, 1965). Inasmuch as most of the properties of standard operant reinforcement schedules have been worked out under positive reinforcement, the more general issue arises as to the extent to which these properties are independent of the sign of the reinforcer. As already emphasized, however, in making such comparisons E must be on guard that the motive-incentive conditions under negative reinforcement correspond as closely as possible to those normally prevailing when reinforcement is positive.

Punishment

In the first chapter of this section we defined punishment as response-contingent aversive stimulation. At times, however, the term is also applied to the application of aversive stimulation without any requirement of response contingency. As an illustration, S might be busy pressing a bar to obtain food when, either unheralded or perhaps preceded by an appropriate signal, shock is applied to the grid floor, quite

independently of what S is doing at the moment. Where a stimulus signaling the onset of shock is employed, S comes in short order to cease his instrumental activity upon its onset, adopting a posture of freezing and crouching in anticipation of S^{R-}; apparently, the cue has become a conditioned stimulus for fear. The response suppression elicited by this stimulus has been called the *conditioned emotional response* (CER). There has been a good bit of research effort devoted to the CER, which has proved a very useful behavioral tool in a number of research areas. We shall not discuss here the CER (more generally, response-noncontingent aversive stimulation) but will restrict ourselves to the response-contingent case, which, for us, shall define punishment.

Punishment has a very long history, as long as man himself, who undoubtedly always has used punishment in an effort to influence the behavior of others. Law and order, whether local or national, rely heavily for their maintenance on a calculated system of punishments. Nevertheless differences of opinion with respect to the efficaciousness of punishment have probably always existed. The spare-the-rod-and-spoil-the-child school has always had its opposition, though probably never as strong as during the last half century. In spite of the very important role played by punishment in the affairs of men, only recently has it come under steady research efforts in the laboratory.

Most accounts of punishment start with Thorndike, who was one of the first to give a systematic account of the role of punishment in learning. Thorndike has been called a "connectionist," one who views the learning process as the establishment of "connections" or "bonds" between stimuli and responses. Within this orientation Thorndike (1913) originally maintained that positive reinforcement strengthened stimulus-response connections, whereas punishment, or negative reinforcement, weakened such connections.

This symmetry in the effects of positive and negative reinforcement upon learned associations was pleasing but not destined to stand up to relevant empirical data. Later Thorndike (1932) modified his view about the role of punishment, holding that it weakened S-R connections little, if at all. With this change in view Thorndike became one of the first of modern psychologists to disparage the usefulness of punishment in behavior control, though it was left for Skinner to develop and stress the point. In any event, for a time the major research question posed in the investigation of punishment was whether it was an effective agent in the elimination of a conditioned response, a topic having obvious practical consequences. Experiments by Estes (1944) and Skinner (1938, p. 154) fortified the view that punishment was an ineffective device for the elimination of unwanted behavior and that extinction was by far the better alternative. During the last several years our understanding of the effects of punishment has increased considerably, both with respect to empirical and theoretical matters. Let us turn now to this development.

Acquisition Processes in Punishment

Punishment as Passive Avoidance Learning. The paradigm of punishment presupposes the existence of a goal-directed response in some strength. In the laboratory this response is usually a conditioned instrumental response established by positive reinforcement—pressing a bar, running down a runway, and so on. If this conditioned response is conceived of as an S-R association, and if punishment is conceded to have no effect on the bond or association itself, how then shall we conceptualize the well-established empirical result that punishment suppresses the behavior upon which it is contingent? How shall we

interpret the known fact that, penalized with a sufficiently noxious stimulus, S will no longer lead to R if R in turn leads to S^{R-}?

A number of theoretical approaches have been advanced to handle this problem (see Church, 1963). We will describe here only one of these, the avoidance hypothesis which has been proposed by Mowrer (1960). This hypothesis makes use of the fractional anticipatory pain mechanism, or fear, in establishing both the motivation and incentive for the response suppression that normally follows punishment.

Suppose, then, that S has learned in a given situation to make an instrumental response which secures for him some sort of positive reinforcement, and suppose that conditions are altered so that the response now also produces an aversive stimulus, S^{R-}. After a few such experiences S will either show hesitancy in making the instrumental response or desist from it altogether. On an intuitive level the explanation is clear: S simply is afraid to make the response because he "knows" that it will lead to the aversive event. The achievement of the present hypothesis is that it incorporates this commonsense explanation within a systematic objective theoretical approach. Or as Mowrer has put it in a closely related context:

Our "rediscovery" of phenomena which, it seems, are as old as mammalian life itself may not seem like much of an accomplishment; and certainly there is every reason to be appropriately modest about it. But in one respect, there is real progress here: these phenomena are now being identified in a *systematic conceptual framework* and their definition is in terms of *clear-cut, empirical operations* [Mowrer, 1960, p. 166].

According to the avoidance hypothesis, as a result of punishment, fear, in the form of the r_P-s_P mechanism, becomes conditioned to the proprioceptive stimuli characteristic of the instrumental, punished, act. Thus, when S begins to perform the instrumental response the resulting proprioceptive stimulation elicits r_P-s_P, or fear. Cessation of the instrumental response, on the other hand, results in a cessation of fear because the proprioceptive stimuli to which fear has become conditioned are themselves terminated. Because fear reduction is reinforcing, the act of terminating or diminishing in intensity the instrumental, punished, response is thereby reinforced. As fear becomes conditioned to proprioceptive stimuli occurring earlier and earlier in the instrumental response sequence, cessation of the latter will tend to occur at an earlier and earlier point. Eventually, if the conditioned fear is sufficiently antedating, only the merest fragment of the response sequence will occur before fear intervenes and motivates termination of the instrumental response.

Because in deferring from initiating or completing the instrumental response S is acting to avoid S^{R-}, Mowrer has suggested that punishment may be viewed as a form of avoidance conditioning. However, the avoidance response is not an active, explicit response specified by E, but rather the more "passive" reaction of *not* responding. He has suggested, therefore, that punishment be called *passive* avoidance learning and that the behavior characteristic of the usual avoidance paradigm be termed *active* avoidance conditioning (Mowrer, 1960).

The preceding interpretation squares with a number of the facts of punishment conditioning. For example, if application of S^{R-} were delayed too long at the completion of the response to be punished, its effectiveness in suppressing behavior should (under certain conditions) be reduced, because conditioning of fear to the proprioceptive stimuli characteristic of the instrumental act would thereby be impaired. This deduction has been upheld in laboratory experiments on animals (delay of punishment gradient), and it embodies a useful principle of child rearing discovered independently by many parents.

On the debit side, it is difficult to see how this account of punishment can handle the response suppression which occurs with CER training. In the latter, it will be recalled, S^{R-} is applied independently of S's behavior. Consequently, because termination of the instrumental response does not in any way affect the appearance of S^{R-}, cessation of the instrumental response sequence cannot be reinforced by fear reduction. It would seem that intense fear has the ability to suppress behavior generally, even when S^{R-} is not correlated with a specific bit of behavior. Response suppression, or partial immobility, apparently is a quite general response to intense fear, present at many phylogenetic levels, including man. Perhaps the CER data can be reconciled with the avoidance hypothesis of punishment by assuming that strong fear, whether generated from response-contingent aversive stimulation or not, has the initial effect of suppressing behavior generally. When, however, S^{R-} is response correlated the fear eventually differentiates out, so to speak, and becomes associated primarily, if not solely, with the proprioceptive consequences of the response which leads to punishment.

Factors Affecting Intensity of Response Suppression. Because response suppression is the major behavioral result of punishment, let us sample a few of the important variables determining the amount of suppression likely to be obtained. The first variable to be discussed, perhaps the most obviously relevant one, is intensity of S^{R-}

INTENSITY OF S^{R-} There are three generalizations relating to the effect of intensity of the aversive stimulus which are rather well established. First, with mildly aversive stimulation, response suppression is likely to be slight; further, as punishment conditioning continues the instrumental response recovers, often completely (Azrin, 1960a; Rachlin, 1966). Second, with aversive stimulation of moderate intensity suppression is greater, and although partial recovery of the response may occur, response strength is not likely to return to its prepunishment state (Appel and Peterson, 1965). There is a moral here, namely, if mild punishment is to remain effective it must be used sparingly. The child who reacts with near indifference to his parents' repeated scoldings or slaps is an illustration of mild punishment made ineffective through overuse.

Finally, with severe punishment response suppression may be complete and permanent. As an illustration, Appel (1961) punished the bar-pressing response in two squirrel monkeys who had been trained to respond for a food reward during eight-hour training sessions. After a single session in which Ss were shocked for making the instrumental response, their response rates fell almost to zero and stayed there for the following fifty experimental sessions, *even though shock was eliminated during the last thirty sessions.* The monkeys were very highly motivated for food, having been reduced to 60 per cent of their normal body weight. Yet they preferred to endure eight straight hours in the experimental chamber without food rather than perform the instrumental response, which might result in shock. Complete and lasting response suppression has also been obtained with pigeons (Azrin, 1960a) and rats (Storms, 1962).

These results from animal investigations have some direct implications for the proper use of punishment in the control of human behavior. First, punishment has the effect of suppressing the punished response and advantage can be taken of this respite to redirect behavior into more acceptable channels. Mild punishment has the advantage that it does not precipitate intense fear, which is likely to impede attempts toward rechanneling behavior. Second, as we have already noted, in order to remain effective, mild and moderate punishment must be used sparingly. Finally, where one is dealing with incorrigible behavior, seemingly immune to the usual behavioral-

control methods, the results obtained with strong punishment are suggestive.

It seems possible that strong punishment, employed in conjunction with other techniques, might turn out to be an efficient and effective means of suppressing and eventually eliminating incorrigible and chronic behavioral problems which, at present, are unresponsive to more conservative behavioral-control techniques. The goal of a therapeutic program based on negative reinforcement would be to have the fear generated by S^{R-} work back through the instrumental chain to its earliest portions and eventually to the very act of thinking about the prohibited activities.

There are, of course, a number of important problems facing any attempt to use strong aversive stimuli in the control and treatment of behavioral problems. First of all, the ability of the patient to discriminate the conditions under which punishment is administered could defeat the whole procedure. The alcoholic or drug addict might very well come to fear alcohol or drugs in a therapeutic situation, where he knows he will be punished for partaking of them, but be bothered little if at all by fear of such activity when outside the clinic. This problem, really one of inadequate generalization of the fear elicited in the clinic, has its no less important counterpart in the necessity to obtain a degree of differentiation of the experimentally induced fear. We wish the fear or anxiety elicited by S^{R-} to remain associated with the proprioceptive and other stimuli characteristic of the undesirable behavior, whether the patient is in or out of the clinic. On the other hand, we must require that the fear be extinguished to other, irrelevant, components of the patient's behavior. Appel's monkeys, for example, were generally fearful as the result of their experience with intense punishment. They cowered in one corner of the experimental cages, doing nothing, and showed signs of fear even outside the experimental situation.

Recently, a series of studies was reported in which electric shock was employed as a means of modifying the behavior of autistic children (Lovaas, Schaeffer, and Simmons, 1965). Painful electric shock was used as punishment in an attempt to suppress such "pathological" behaviors as self-stimulation and temper tantrums, and as negative reinforcement in an escape-avoidance situation designed to establish social responsiveness. These investigators met with some success, though they encountered the sort of problems discussed previously. [For a critique of their work see Breger (1965).]

Electric shock, as well as other aversive stimuli, has been used with some success in the treatment of sexual deviations. A recent review of this topic has been provided by Feldman (1966).

In order to place the use of strong punishment, and other aversive techniques, in the control of human behavior on a more substantial footing, investigations on the animal level are required in which the variables which control both generalization and differentiation of the fear generated by S^{R-} are isolated and interrelated.

STRENGTH OF THE PUNISHED RESPONSE. Other things constant it is a reasonable assumption that the degree of response suppression arising from punishment will be a function of the strength of the punished response. This expectation turns out to be justified, but the kind of relationship which apparently holds is not at all what intuition would suggest. At least two studies have reported that rats given a relatively large amount of reward training prior to the introduction of S^{R-} are, compared to Ss given smaller amounts of training, *less* resistant to the effects of punishment; the former Ss show, in other words, *more* response suppression (Karsh, 1962; Miller, 1960). In Miller's experiment, for example, rats were trained on a runway to obtain food, and after either twenty-one or thirty-eight days of such training shock was introduced in the goal box (in addition to food) on each trial. The effect of the shock

was to reduce the running speed in the second group of animals to a much greater degree than in the first.

The interpretation of this result is not clear, but if it turns out to hold generally the outlook for the use of punishment in the control of long-standing habits is more promising than common sense would lead us to suspect.

DELAY OF PUNISHMENT. As already mentioned, the effects of delay of punishment are somewhat complex. Generalizing from the data which we discussed in connection with delay of reward in positive reinforcement and in escape conditioning, we might suppose that the effectiveness of S^{R-} in a punishment situation would be reduced as the period of time intervening between execution of the instrumental response and application of S^{R-} increases. If, however, we consider closely the fractional anticipatory pain mechanism, another possibility comes into view. Given that a period of time, say 30 sec., intervenes between completion of the instrumental response and the appearance of S^{R-}, it is likely that after sufficient training the anticipatory pain response, fear, will become conditioned to stimuli characteristic of the 30-sec. preshock interval. When this occurs S would come to anticipate shock during the 30-sec. delay interval and be fearful. Granting that this is the case, the aversiveness of S^{R-} might actually be enhanced when it is delayed, because in addition to the shock itself, S must contend with the fear which arises from its anticipation.

As a matter of fact, when given a choice between immediate and delayed punishment, both rats (Knapp, Kause, and Perkins, 1959; but see Perkins, Levis, and Seymann, 1963) and humans (Badia, McBane, Suter, and Lewis, 1966; D'Amato and Gumenik, 1960) prefer the immediate punishment (shock). Because all the experiments just cited involved choice between experimentally defined alternatives, there is a question about their relevance for punishment in instrumental conditioning. Will immediate S^{R-} suppress behavior more effectively than delayed negative reinforcement in a punishment paradigm restricted to instrumental conditioning?

Our knowledge of the workings of the r_P-s_P mechanism should alert us to the possibility that amount of punishment training will be an important factor in determining the relative effectiveness of immediate and delayed punishment. If the extent of such training is rather slight, conditioning of r_P-s_P to the cues of the delay interval may not occur to a degree sufficient to elicit intense fear during the preshock interval. Under such circumstances immediate punishment should prove more effective than delayed punishment in suppressing behavior, simply because the contingency between the instrumental response and S^{R-} will be recognized more quickly. The general implication is that any factor which delimits S's experience with the conditions of punishment will tend also to reveal immediate punishment as more effective than delayed punishment.

It is interesting that experiments supporting the concept of a simple delay-of-punishment gradient have employed rather few punishment trials, too few to allow for the conditioning of fear to the preshock interval (Banks and Vogel-Sprott, 1965; Baron, 1965; Kamin, 1959). The writer knows of no study in which delay of punishment has been investigated with levels of training high enough to guarantee fear conditioning to the preshock interval, if indeed such a process occurs when punishment is delayed in instrumental conditioning. The anticipated result of such a study would be that, initially, a delay-of-punishment gradient would appear, with response suppression being greater for the shorter delays of S^{R-}. With continued training, however, the shape of the gradient should become altered with the point of maximum suppression shifting from zero to nonzero delays of punishment. Quite likely, intensity of S^{R-} would also

prove to be a relevant variable in this situation, though its effects are hard to anticipate.

OTHER VARIABLES. There are, of course, a number of other variables that influence the extent of response suppression obtained in punishment conditioning, for example, the point in the instrumental response sequence at which punishment is applied, the proportion of responses punished, and so on. Generally speaking, however, these variables are not likely to be as potent as those already discussed, and in some cases their effects may be reducible to some combination of the three variables, strength of S^{R-}, delay of S^{R-}, and strength of the punished response. Church's (1963) review may be consulted for a discussion of some of these variables, as well as for a general survey of the area of punishment. Attention should also be called to Solomon's (1964) recent and interesting overview of punishment, and to Azrin and Holz's (1966) excellent discussion of the topic from the operant point of view.

Extinction Processes in Punishment

Unlike the other negative reinforcement paradigms, punishment does not establish an instrumental response of its own; its effect, as we have seen, is to suppress to a greater or lesser degree an instrumental response established and maintained by positive reinforcement. It is the strength of this response which is manipulated during studies of extinction. One interesting question, for example, is whether a positively reinforced instrumental response established in the presence of punishment is more or less resistant to extinction (when both S^{R+} and S^{R-} are eliminated) than a response acquired without negative reinforcement. Another question of practical as well as theoretical significance is whether *extinction* of a positively reinforced response can be facilitated by the use of punishment during the extinction period.

One may also look at the other side of the coin, extinction of the *effects* of punishment. In this case S^{R+} is maintained and S^{R-} is eliminated, interest being focused on the *recovery* of the instrumental response. In terms of our previous analysis, we may say that extinction of r_P-s_P is at issue here. We touched on this question in the last section, where we saw that with severe punishment recovery of the instrumental response may not occur for long periods; extinction of r_P-s_P apparently is extremely slow when S^{R-} has been intense. The present section will deal only with the question of how punishment affects resistance to extinction.

Effect of Punishment Applied During Extinction. If during extinction the instrumental response, in addition to no longer leading to S^{R+}, is punished, will extinction be facilitated? Clearly, punishment ought to suppress the instrumental response during extinction just as it does during acquisition. But that is not the issue. The question is whether the applied punishment will leave a "residue" of suppression so that, when terminated, a permanent weakening of the instrumental response is left behind. The answer appears to be that, unless S^{R-} is relatively strong (Boe, 1966; Estes, 1944), punishment applied temporarily during extinction will have little effect on the course of extinction (Skinner, 1938, p. 154).

The explanation of this result follows rather directly from the r_P-s_P mechanism. When punishment is applied during extinction the instrumental response suffers weakening from two sources, elimination of S^{R+} and introduction of response-contingent S^{R-}. When S^{R-} is mild the contribution from the latter source is relatively small. In fact, the response suppression observed upon introduction of mild punishment might not be due entirely to the aversive character of S^{R-}; a part of such suppression might be attributable to the sudden introduction of a "novel" stimulus.

Controls for the evaluation of the "suppression" arising from this source are rare. In any event, during the period that punishment is applied r_P-s_P (fear) becomes conditioned in some measure to the proprioceptive consequences of the instrumental response, and whether or not resistance to extinction will suffer upon the removal of S^{R-} depends on the strength of this conditioning. With mild punishment, fear conditioning is presumably quite weak and extinguishes rapidly after withdrawal of S^{R-}; hence, overall resistance to extinction is affected little, if at all. With strong or intense punishment, on the other hand, r_P-s_P is more firmly established and upon removal of punishment extinguishes so slowly that an effect is seen on the customary measures of resistance to extinction.

Effect of Punishment Applied During Acquisition on Subsequent Resistance to Extinction. We have just seen that if moderate or intense punishment is introduced during extinction, even temporarily, resistance to extinction is likely to be impaired. Suppose, however, that an instrumental response is *acquired* under the burden of punishment, which is removed during subsequent extinction. Will resistance to extinction be augmented by the punishment which accompanied acquisition of the instrumental response? Does response acquisition in the face of punishment lead to a kind of response "fixation"?

There have been a number of studies which have shown just that: Ss who acquired an instrumental response while being punished were later more resistant to extinction than controls who never experienced punishment. As an illustration, Brown and Wagner (1964), in a study to which we shall return later, ran one group of rats on a runway with food reward and a second group with food plus shock, 50 per cent of the acquisition trials being punished. During a subsequent extinction series (S^{R-} now eliminated) the formerly punished group turned out to be more resistant to extinction than the nonpunished Ss. A similar result was obtained by Karsh (1964) within the Skinner-box setting.

Granted that punishment applied during acquisition of an instrumental response augments subsequent resistance to extinction, how shall this result be interpreted? Does punishment applied during acquisition somehow strengthen the response over and above the strengthening contributed by S^{R+}, or is the augmented resistance to extinction due not so much to the application of punishment as to its removal? To enlarge on the latter possibility, if termination of punishment were generally accompanied by something of an elation effect, then the observed enhanced resistance to extinction might simply be due to the fact that punishment is terminated during extinction, rather than to a direct effect of punishment on the acquisition of the instrumental response. Unfortunately, controls for the evaluation of enhanced responding upon termination of punishment during extinction are not usually included in relevant studies. It is true that in our discussion of incentive shifts in escape conditioning we made the point that elationlike effects were not observed in such conditioning. But it does not necessarily follow that an elationlike effect does not occur in punishment. As a matter of fact, Azrin (1960b) has reported that pigeons pecking a key to obtain food showed an increase in their response rate when the punishment which attended each key peck was terminated (see Rachlin, 1966). On the other hand, in Karsh's (1964) study, although the required control group was absent, there was some evidence that an elation effect, if operating, was not likely to have been very important.

Let us assume for the moment that the enhanced resistance to extinction associated with the application of punishment during the acquisition of an instrumental response is not an artifact caused by the removal of punishment during extinction, but rather is indicative of a genuine effect of punishment on response acquisition. Although there are a number of mechanisms by means of which punishment could exert such an influence on subsequent resistance to extinction (Lawrence and Festinger, 1962), one plausible and interesting possibility is that punishment applied during acquisition augments subsequent resistance to extinction simply because there is a degree of commonality between punishment and extinction. As we shall now see, there are several studies which support this view.

Similarities Between Punishment and Extinction. In our discussion of the anticipatory pain mechanism, r_P-s_P, we noted that it and the anticipatory frustration response, r_F-s_F, had in common a number of formal properties. Both their mode of establishment and their aversive properties were seen to be rather similar. Shifting to the intuitive level, although one can certainly distinguish between the anticipation of frustration and the anticipation of pain, the emotional responses attending both types of experiences have some degree of commonality. Perhaps it is more than terminological convenience that a slap to the backside and the dispatching to bed without supper are both called punishment. Withdrawal of privileges, a frequent form of "punishment," probably would not be effective unless accompanied by feelings of frustration.

The assumption, then, is that punishment and extinction have overlapping behavioral effects because anticipatory frustration (r_F-s_F) and fear (r_P-s_P), the mechanisms assumed to mediate the manifestations of these operations, are themselves partially overlapping. The laboratory evidence supporting functional similarities between fear and anticipatory frustration takes several different forms. One approach has been to show that certain drugs have a similar effect on behavior mediated by anticipatory frustration and behavior mediated by fear. For example, alcohol and sodium amytal, although depressants, are known to facilitate behavior that has become suppressed through punishment (Barry and Miller, 1962). Presumably these drugs are effective because they inhibit or reduce the fear which underlies suppression of the instrumental response.

If fear and anticipatory frustration bear fundamental similarities to each other, drugs that reduce fear ought to reduce anticipatory frustration as well. Barry, Wagner, and Miller (1962) put this hypothesis to test by determining whether alcohol and sodium amytal increased resistance to extinction of an instrumental response established under positive reinforcement. In accordance with the assumptions underlying the anticipatory frustration mechanism, Ss extinguished after a continuous reinforcement schedule ought to experience considerable frustration upon encountering nonreward, and in short order the fractional anticipatory response should become conditioned to (in the case of a runway) the cues of the start box and alley. Because anticipatory frustration (s_F) is aversive and because the nearer to the goal box S proceeds, the stronger the stimulus component becomes, the effect of anticipatory frustration will be to interfere with the instrumental response. Put differently, S will try to "avoid" anticipatory frustration by avoiding the cues which elicit it. If, therefore, alcohol and sodium amytal administered during extinction actually reduce anticipatory frustration, the treated Ss ought to run faster (be more resistant to extinction) than controls that receive a placebo injection. As shown in Figure 5-3, exactly this was found. Animals extinguished under either alcohol or sodium amytal extinguished much more slowly than controls (see also Wagner, 1963).

If, indeed, there is a significant similarity between the anticipatory frustration and pain responses can we substitute, in some measure, one for the other? In more operational terms, can punishment and nonreinforcement be used, at least in part, interchangeably? Brown and Wagner

(1964), addressing themselves to this question, sought to determine whether punishment applied during the acquisition of an instrumental response would act like nonreinforcement in increasing subsequent resistance to extinction (a point we have already discussed) and conversely, whether nonreinforcement experienced during acquisition would later render Ss more resistant to the suppressive effects of punishment.

In their experiment three groups of rats were trained on a runway under one of three conditions. One group (Group C) received a food reward on each trial and never experienced punishment during acquisition training. A second group (Group N) was a partially reinforced group that encountered food on only 50 per cent of its trials: it also never experienced punishment during acquisition training. The last group (Group P) was continuously reinforced with respect to S^{R+}, but on 50 per cent of its trials (precisely those trials on which Group N was nonrewarded) this group encountered both food *and* shock in the goal box. After acquisition was completed each of the three groups was divided into two equated subgroups and each subgroup exposed to one of two testing conditions. One of the testing conditions was plain extinction, all three subgroups receiving neither S^{R+} nor S^{R-} during the extinction trials. Under the second testing condition all three subgroups received both S^{R+} and S^{R-} (punishment) on every test trial.

If anticipatory frustration and fear are partially equivalent mechanisms and if, as assumed, frustration plays a central role in extinction, the group that was punished during acquisition (Group P) ought to extinguish more slowly than the continuously reinforced Ss (Group C). Of course, Group N ought to be more resistant to extinction than Group C; this is merely the partial reinforcement effect. If r_F-s_F and r_P-s_P are completely equivalent processes, there should be no difference between Group P and Group N.

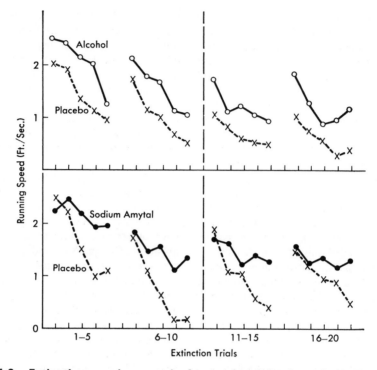

Figure 5-3. Extinction running speed of rats after injection of alcohol, sodium amytal, or placebo. After Trial 10 the alcohol and placebo groups were divided in two, half of each group receiving alcohol during Trials 11–20 and half, placebo; the same manipulation occurred for the sodium amytal and placebo groups shown in the lower graph. Observe that extinction performance adjusted itself rapidly to the current drug condition, both alcohol and sodium amytal resulting in faster running. (Reprinted with permission from Barry, H., III, Wagner, A. R., and Miller, N. E. Effects of drugs on approach-avoidance conflict tested repeatedly by means of a "telescope alley." *J. comp. physiol. Psychol.*, 1962, **55**, 201–210.)

As for the second test, conducted with S^{R+} and S^{R-} applied on every trial, one would naturally expect the best performance in the group that had been punished during acquisition (Group P). If, however, enduring nonreinforcement during acquisition produced effects similar to those arising from punishment, then the formerly nonreinforced group (Group N) ought to be less suppressed than Group C by the punishment encountered during testing.

As may be seen in Figure 5-4, these predicted results were obtained. In the extinction test, Group P was superior to Group C. Note, however, that Group P is closer in its performance to Group C than to Group N. In the right half of the figure we see that in the test involving punishment the ordering of the groups is P, N, and, last, C with Group N approximately midway between the other two groups.

These results, consistent and attractive as they are, would be somewhat more forceful if certain controls had been employed. We have already alluded to one type of control group that would be desirable in the test conducted under extinction. Because for Group P both S^{R+} *and* S^{R-} are eliminated during extinction, contribution of an elation effect (with respect to S^{R-}) should be ruled out, or at least assessed, as a contributing factor to

Group P's superiority over Group C. A related control group would have been desirable for the test conducted under punishment, namely, a group shifted from 50 per cent to 100 per cent reinforcement on S^{R+} without the accompaniment of punishment. It seems possible that a shift from 50 to 100 per cent reward, as occurred in Group N, would by itself be sufficient to augment performance over a group of Ss always experiencing a continuous reinforcement schedule (Group C). The possibility to be ruled out is an elation effect based on an enrichment of the prevailing positive reinforcement schedule.

There are a number of studies which are germane to this question but their results are conflicting. Shifting Ss from 50 per cent partial reinforcement to 100 per cent reinforcement has been reported to lead to an enhancement in performance (Harris, Smith, and Weinstock, 1962); more often, however, such an effect has not been observed (Badia, 1965; Jenkins, 1962). One difficulty is that, after even a moderate amount of training, partially reinforced Ss come to respond with considerable vigor, sometimes exceeding the performance of continuously reinforced Ss. Under the circumstances a "ceiling" effect may

operate to attenuate the facilitative effect of shifting from a poor to a richer reinforcement schedule.

Despite the qualifications just mentioned, the pattern of results obtained in the investigations cited points decidedly to a significant and meaningful partial equivalence between the r_F-s_F and r_P-s_P mechanisms, or more operationally, between extinction and punishment. This suggests the interesting possibility of viewing extinction not as a process *sui generis*, but rather as a special case of punishment. The weakening of the instrumental response which attends normal extinction procedures may be considered a form of response suppression in which the "punishment" consists of nonreinforcement, or perhaps more exactly, of the frustration which attends nonreinforcement. Such an interpretation can draw for support on at least a few parallels between punishment and extinction (in addition to those already cited). Recall that Miller (1960) found that a higher level of acquisition training prior to the introduction of punishment led to more response suppression than a lesser amount of training. Now recall that in the previous chapter we pointed out that in the runway, at least, resistance to extinction

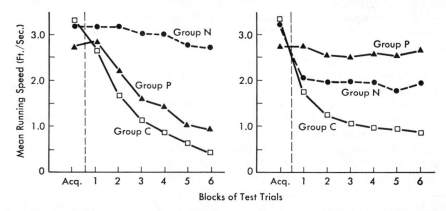

Figure 5-4. **Mean running speeds on the last day of acquisition and subsequent daily blocks of six test trials under conditions of extinction or punishment (see text).** (Reprinted with permission from Brown, R. T., and Wagner, A. R. Resistance to punishment and extinction following training with shock or nonreinforcement. *J. exp. Psychol.*, 1964, **68**, 503–507.)

seems to be nonmonotonically related to acquisition level. The analogy between these two results from disparate areas is clear and appealing.

A somewhat different interpretation of the partial reinforcement effect also arises from this reorientation. As we have already pointed out, Miller (1960) was able to induce in his Ss a marked resistance to the suppressive effects of punishment by first exposing them to a series of gradually increasing shocks. If we think of a partial reinforcement schedule as a means of exposing S gradually to the punishing experience of frustration, we lay hold of a second interesting parallel between extinction and punishment.

There is also a conceptual advantage to be gained by thinking of extinction as a means of inducing response suppression. Theorists would no longer be obliged to "explain" extinction in terms of some sort of a reorganization between stimulus and response. The association may be permitted to remain intact, weakening of the instrumental response being attributed to response suppression arising from the conditioning of anticipatory frustration to the proprioceptive consequences of the instrumental act (see Leitenberg, 1965). Of course, eventually one would have to deal with extinction of the anticipatory mechanisms themselves. One could not go on forever relying on suppressive mechanisms to account for the decline of once dominant instrumental behavior. However, the anticipatory mechanisms (that is, r_G-s_G) are assumed to be conditioned by means of classical conditioning procedures, and it may very well be that here "true" conditioning occurs. Associations or bonds are perhaps here established and destroyed by the reinforcement contingencies appropriate to classical conditioning (see Mowrer, 1960). Be that as it may, there are a number of interesting and intriguing implications in the view that extinction, or rather the weakening of an instrumental response which occurs as a result of the extinction operation, is a form of response suppression.

Avoidance Conditioning

We turn now to the final topic of this chapter, avoidance conditioning. If escape and punishment conditioning have been relatively neglected research areas during the recent past, avoidance learning has had more than its fair share of attention. A bibliography of the number of researches conducted in the last twenty years employing avoidance conditioning paradigms would doubtlessly run to many hundreds, and the rate of output shows no sign of declining. After a one-sided emphasis on discriminated avoidance conditioning, nondiscriminated avoidance conditioning came into its own through the invention of the "Sidman" technique (for a review of free-operant avoidance see Sidman, 1966). Both types of paradigms have been used extensively in purely behavioral analyses of avoidance learning, as tools in psychophysiological and psychopharmacological research, and in other enterprises. Despite the mountains of data compiled, however, our conception of the processes underlying avoidance conditioning has not changed very much during the last couple of decades. The most widely accepted analysis of avoidance learning goes by the name of "two-factor" or "two-process" theory, a formulation which is largely responsible for the conceptualization of fear as an anticipatory classically conditioned response.

Avoidance conditioning was first investigated in the context of classical conditioning procedures, and the terminology applied to the avoidance paradigm in instrumental conditioning bears the stamp of this origin. Despite the fact that the instrumental response usually cannot be considered to be an unconditioned response to the experimentally manipulated aversive stimulus, the latter is nevertheless always referred to as an *unconditioned stimulus* (UCS) rather than a negative reinforcer, S^{R-}. Similarly, the cue signaling the aversive stimulus is not referred to as a discriminative stimulus, as it very well might be, but as the *conditioned stimulus* (CS). Although for adherents of two-factor theory there is a certain justice to the classical conditioning nomenclature, a compromise in terminology might serve their theory more accurately. If the discriminative cue continues to be referred to as the CS but the aversive stimulus has its designation changed to S^{R-}, we perhaps would thereby capture the notion that classical conditioning and instrumental conditioning are both involved in avoidance learning, as well as indicating that the avoidance response is not necessarily an unconditioned response to the aversive stimulus. We shall, however, leave the initiation of this terminological reform to others.

Two-Factor Theory of Avoidance Conditioning

Before proceeding to this interpretation, let us review the essentials of a discriminative avoidance conditioning paradigm. A signal of some sort, the conditioned stimulus, precedes the aversive stimulus (usually shock) by a period of time, very often in the neighborhood of 5 sec. The aversive stimulus is termed the *unconditioned stimulus* (UCS), and the interval separating onset of the CS from onset of the unconditioned stimulus is referred to as the CS–UCS interval. The instrumental response, which may be bar pressing, wheel turning, running, or jumping from one compartment to another, or any of a variety of other responses, is called an avoidance response (or a *conditioned response*, CR) if it occurs prior to the termination of the CS–UCS interval, that is, prior to the onset of the UCS. Under usual procedures such a

response terminates the CS and results in the omitting of the UCS on that trial. When the instrumental response postdates the onset of the UCS it is termed an escape response and by ordinary procedures serves to terminate both the CS and the UCS.

According to two-factor theory, classical conditioning and instrumental conditioning are both involved in the establishment of an avoidance response. Classical conditioning serves the function of associating the anticipatory pain response, fear, to the CS, a process which is accomplished very rapidly and because it is based on classical conditioning, requires only the pairing of the CS and UCS in a favorable temporal order. Instrumental conditioning, for its part, is assigned the task of associating the instrumental response to the CS in sufficient strength for it to occur early enough to antedate the UCS. What constitutes the reinforcement for this association has caused a good bit of controversy. Escape trials present no problem because on such trials the instrumental response serves to terminate the UCS; consequently, the association between the CS and the instrumental response may be considered to be reinforced by the latter event. On avoidance trials, however, the UCS cannot be appealed to as providing a source of reinforcement, and so either one must assume that the instrumental response is weakened on such trials or that the reinforcing event lies elsewhere. Some have assumed that avoidance of the UCS is by itself sufficient to constitute a reinforcing event. However, this position has proved unpalatable to many because it appears to require that *S* have an expectation (not in the objective sense of an anticipatory response) about the occurrence of shock. In other words, failure to be shocked can be reinforcing only if *S* expects such treatment. Two-factor theory appeared to discover a way of circumventing such expectations by appealing to fear reduction, brought about by CS termination, as the reinforcing event on avoidance trials.

There is a distinction that needs to be made here between CS termination and the reduction or termination of fear which is assumed by two-factor theorists to follow upon the former. It is completely possible to hold, as indeed many have maintained, that CS termination (or termination of proprioceptive cues associated with the UCS) is the sole reinforcement for avoidance responses, without any mention of fear arousal or fear reduction (Schoenfeld, 1950). According to this point of view, any stimulus that comes to signal a primary negative reinforcer (S^{R-}) becomes a secondary negative reinforcer. And just as a response which escapes S^{R-} is reinforced by termination of the primary negative reinforcer, a response which allows S to escape a secondary negative reinforcer is likewise reinforced by termination of the latter. In other words, proponents of this view are simply accepting the empirical fact that secondary negative reinforcers can strengthen responses which terminate them, without theorizing as to the basis of this source of reinforcement. In the context of two-factor theory, however, CS termination is reinforcing only if it leads in turn to fear reduction or termination. For further details on this distinction, as well as an interesting account of the origin of two-factor theory, see Solomon and Brush (1956).

The rationale is simple enough. Fear is presumed to be elicited by the CS; an avoidance response terminates the CS and by eliminating the stimulus which elicited fear results in a reduction, if not total deletion, of the fear itself. Fear reduction, coming *after* the instrumental response, serves to reinforce the latter in the normal manner of instrumental conditioning.

The central point, then, is that two-factor theory does not accept avoidance of the UCS *per se* as constituting a reinforcing event; rather, it is *escape* of the anxiety instigated by the CS which serves as the reinforcement for the instrumental response on avoidance trials. This is a fascinating conjecture, a feature of two-factor theory which has made it attractive to many. But as we shall see shortly, despite the empirical support that seems to accrue to this position, there is a real question whether the basis of reinforcement on avoidance trials resides solely in the termination of the CS.

A Brief Appraisal of Two-Factor Theory

Before turning to a consideration of some of the relevant data, there is a logical point to be made. If one takes two-factor theory completely seriously, there really is no such thing as avoidance learning. A response that serves to avoid an aversive event does so quite accidentally, according to two-factor theory (and related theories which stress termination of secondary aversive stimuli). The motivation for such a response is *escape* from the fear that is generated by the CS, and reinforcement is the associated fear reduction. In more intuitive terms, an avoidance response is not made for the "purpose" of avoiding the UCS, nor does the latter event have anything to do with the strengthening of an avoidance response. Logically, then, either two-factor theory is correct and there is no such thing as "true" avoidance learning or, alternatively, termination of the CS (with attending fear reduction) cannot be the sole basis of reinforcement in avoidance conditioning.

Empirical support for two-factor theory, most of it indirect, converges from a number of different directions. Avoidance learning is frequently more difficult to obtain with trace conditioning than with delayed conditioning procedures (Mowrer and Lamoreaux, 1951). The reason is that, presumably, with trace conditioning the opportunity for the instrumental response to terminate the CS is either much reduced or eliminated altogether. Avoidance conditioning is also put at a disadvantage when the CS is programed to be of fixed duration rather than being response terminated (Mowrer and Lamoreaux, 1942). Similarly, extinction of an avoidance response has been shown to progress much more slowly when the CR is closely associated with CS termination than when CS termination precedes the instrumental response (Kamin, 1954). A different line of evidence shows that acquisition of an avoidance response is sometimes interfered with by drugs and surgical techniques thought to attenuate anxiety reactions. (Wynne and Solomon, 1955).

But the sum and substance of these studies, and the many others like them which are interpreted as supporting two-factor theory, is that avoidance conditioning is facilitated, sometimes markedly, by response termination of the CS and by the maintenance of "normal" anxiety or fear reactions (which presumably mediate the reinforcing effect of CS termination). In no case, however, has CS termination been shown to be *necessary* for avoidance learning. And never has avoidance conditioning suffered total abolition by interference with anxiety reactions. These are facts which must be kept in mind when judging the adequacy of two-factor theory and related interpretations of avoidance conditioning.

Principles of Anxiety Conservation and Partial Irreversibility. In a detailed elaboration of two-factor theory, Solomon and Wynne (1954) proposed two modifications which they felt were necessary to accommodate certain avoidance conditioning data that appeared to them not tractable to two-factor theory as it then stood. The breadth of their analysis and their ingenious extensions of the theory provide another kind of support for the two process interpretation. They noted that in previous experimental work (Brush, Brush, and Solomon, 1955) they observed that when a shock UCS assumed "traumatic" intensities, Ss often failed to extinguish an

avoidance response despite prolonged extinction testing. In these studies dogs were trained in a shuttle box to avoid intense shock, a task which they usually mastered in only a few trials. Even though the CS–UCS interval was as long as 10 sec., in short order the latencies of the CRs shrank down to 1.5 sec. or so. Moreover, the mean latencies often continued to decrease during subsequent extinction trials, which might number 200 or more.

A second observation that seemed at variance with unmodified two-factor theory was that "overt signs of anxiety rapidly disappeared while the dogs were becoming more and more stereotyped in their jumping and their latencies to the CS were shortening" (Solomon and Wynne, 1954, p. 359). They further observed that if "anxiety was being reduced by jumping, the anxiety reduction certainly was not evident at that stage."

Another detail of their data which seemed to require explanation outside of two-factor theory was that if a "dog happened to have an abnormally long latency on a particular trial, he typically acted 'upset' immediately *after* the instrumental response had occurred, and jumped very quickly on the next few trials" (p. 359).

In the light of these apparent strains on two-factor theory Solomon and Wynne attempted to provide theoretical relief in the form of a "principle of anxiety conservation." According to this principle fear was not an inevitable response to the CS. If S responded fast enough at the onset of the CS, fear might not have a chance to develop to any significant proportions; in common parlance, S responds before he has a chance to become afraid. Coupling this assumption with the assumption that extinction of a classically conditioned response occurs only if the CR is performed on the trial on which the UCS is omitted, they concluded that weakening of the fear reaction will not take place on extinction trials which stimulate very short response latencies. On such trials, consequently, anxiety is "conserved."

This principle is useful in explaining the fact that little or no overt sign of fear was observed when Ss were jumping rapidly to the CS, and also accommodates the third observation mentioned previously, that Ss did manifest anxiety reactions after jumps having long latencies. Furthermore, because fear presumably occurs on such trials and its reduction serves to reinforce the preceding instrumental response, the shorter latencies observed on subsequent trials is also accommodated.

Although the principle of anxiety conservation provides a mechanism for stretching out the extinction phase of avoidance conditioning, it cannot, of course, incorporate the failure of extinction to occur at some point in testing, if indeed traumatic avoidance conditioning is "inextinguishable." True, the fear reaction would not be weakened on trials which elicit fast CRs, but without fear there is no basis for continued reinforcement of the instrumental response, and so on such trials the CR should undergo weakening. Response latencies will increase to the point that eventually anxiety has time to occur, and at this point some weakening of the fear reaction will take place as well as some strengthening of the instrumental response. Eventually, however, all the anxiety must drain away.

In recognition of this fact and convinced that the avoidance response in their Ss was essentially inextinguishable by ordinary extinction procedures, Solomon and Wynne proposed a second principle, the "principle of partial irreversibility of anxiety" as a way out of the dilemma. The notion is that an anxiety reaction conditioned by a traumatic UCS simply does not ever extinguish completely. Some residue always remains to serve as reinforcement for the instrumental response.

The necessity for the principle of partial irreversibility of anxiety seems doubtful, even for UCSs of traumatic intensity. In the first place, avoidance learning motivated by traumatic UCSs does not always lead to

"inextinguishability" or even to an excessive degree of resistance to extinction. Kamin (1954), for example, in a study previously cited found that after trace conditioning with a 20-sec. CS–UCS interval, extinction was accomplished within a reasonable number of trials. And even considering those conditions under which some Ss fail to extinguish, others treated in an identical fashion extinguish within the number of test trials set by the E.

Furthermore, "inextinguishability" has been found with shock intensities as low as 0.7 milliamperes (ma), a fraction of the approximately 10 ma that was used in the studies that suggested to Solomon and Wynne the principle of partial irreversibility (Brush, 1957). As Brush points out, this result discredits the plausibility of the partial irreversibility principle, which was based in part on the assumption that extremely intense UCSs produce qualitatively different effects—perhaps at the neurological level—than more moderate intensities. Brush's suggestion is probably correct that the extreme resistance to extinction found in his study and others like it is due to the fact that the experimental situation during extinction permitted response termination of the CS for all instrumental responses, *whether or not they constituted avoidance (anticipatory) response.* In Brush's study, for example, although the CS–UCS interval during acquisition was only 10 sec., during extinction the CS (lowering the barrier door and extinguishing the light in the compartment occupied by S) remained in force until S responded or until 2 min. elapsed (which defined a failure to respond). In other words, even when S failed to emit a CR (jumping within 10 sec.) his response was reinforced by CS termination. This procedure is to be contrasted to one in which, during extinction, the CS acts for only the duration of what was the CS–UCS interval during acquisition, which in the present example would have been 10 sec. Had the door been lowered and the light illuminated when S failed to jump within 10 sec. doubtless many more, and perhaps all, Ss would have extinguished within the 200 trials allowed them. In my own laboratory, where we have had a good bit of experience with discriminated bar-press avoidance learning, we have found, in sharp contrast to the results just described, extraordinarily rapid extinction of even well-established and long-standing avoidance behavior. We have worked with (discontinuous) shock levels up to 30 ma and have never failed to observe orderly extinction in our Ss (see D'Amato, Fazzaro, and Etkin, 1967).

The magnified resistance to extinction which response termination of the CS can bring about is further evidence of the potent reinforcing ability of this variable. But if CS termination can reinforce the instrumental response it can perform the same function for other responses, responses which may compete with the instrumental behavior. When CS termination is correlated with behavior other than the instrumental response, such behavior will be strengthened and very likely compete subsequently with the instrumental response. This seems to account for the fact that avoidance behavior extinguishes very rapidly with our extinction procedure, and in all probability this is why the 20-sec. CS interval group of Kamin's (1954) trace conditioning study extinguished so fast. Having again granted the potency of CS termination as a reinforcing agent we should, however, stress once more that this fact does not by itself imply that CS termination is *necessary* for avoidance conditioning.

The principle of anxiety conservation, although somewhat more appealing than partial irreversibility, also has its difficulties. The supposition that weakening of a classically conditioned response occurs only on trials on which the CR is evoked is probably incorrect. Many years ago Pavlov (1927) described a phenomenon of extinction "below zero." Pavlov was referring to the fact that the recovery of an extinguished salivary conditioned response could be inhibited by administering extinction trials beyond the point where S failed to give any response at all to the CS. This would appear to be a clear counterexample to the principle of anxiety conservation. Another difficulty is that if it is assumed the fear reaction does not occur on trials on which anxiety is "conserved," or that it occurs to a very insignificant extent, one then has the problem of accounting for the motivational basis of such avoidance responses. Unmodified two-factor theory has the attractive property that with a single concept, conditioned fear, it provides both the motivation and the reinforcement for avoidance behavior.

Termination of the CS and Avoidance of the UCS as Factors in Avoidance Conditioning. In the standard discriminative avoidance conditioning paradigm, termination of the CS and avoidance of the UCS are confounded as possible sources of reinforcement. That is, when S's response antedates the UCS it usually serves both to terminate the CS and to avoid the UCS. Strengthening of the avoidance response could therefore be due to either of these factors or to some combination of the two. If two-factor theory is correct, reinforcement should be due solely to response termination of the CS.

Kamin (1956) made the first attempt to untangle these two potential sources of reinforcement in a study that manipulated independently CS termination and UCS avoidance. In his study four groups of rats were trained in a shuttle box on a simple avoidance task. On escape trials (trials on which the instrumental response postdated the UCS) all groups were treated identically: the escape response resulted in the termination of both the CS and the UCS. On avoidance trials (trials on which S made a CR) the treatment afforded the four groups was quite different. For one group, the Terminate-CS group, the CR benefited S only by terminating the CS; the UCS was delivered at its appointed time (five seconds after the onset of the CS) and S had to leave the compartment he occupied in order to terminate the shock. Kamin reasoned that if two-factor theory were completely correct, the Terminate-CS animals ought to be as reinforced on "avoidance" trials as Ss for whom a CR both terminated the CS and avoided the UCS. The latter Ss, called the "Normals," comprised the second group of the experiment.

For a third group of Ss (the "Avoid-UCS" group) avoidance responses did not terminate the CS, which continued acting for the full five seconds of the CS–UCS interval; however, such responses did serve to avoid the UCS. If avoidance of the UCS *per se* is a factor in avoidance learning then this group ought to show some learning of the avoidance task despite the fact that CRs do not lead immediately to termination of the CS. A fourth group (the "Classical" group) was allowed neither the benefit of CS termination nor UCS avoidance on trials on which a CR was made. In this group, even when the instrumental response antedated the UCS, the CS was maintained; at the end of the CS–UCS interval shock was delivered and S had to escape the latter by running into the un-occupied compartment.

The results of this experiment are shown in Figure 5-5 for the 100 trials of training. As one would expect, the Normal group shows by far the best avoidance performance, and the Classical group, the worst. The Terminate-CS and Avoid-UCS groups are intermediate, and though the latter group does somewhat better than the former during the last forty training trials, the difference between the two groups is far from achieving statistical significance.

Taken at face value, the results of this experiment imply that both factors, CS termination and UCS avoidance, contribute to the avoidance performance observed in the Normal group. Kamin points out,

however, that it is quite possible to rationalize away the failure of CS termination to appear as the sole reinforcing agent. Perhaps, he conjectures, the Terminate-CS group did not achieve the level of performance attained by the Normals because CRs in this group suffered a sort of delayed punishment. If, for example, S performed a CR 4 sec. after the onset of the CS, the UCS, delivered 1 sec. later, would serve as a punishment for the instrumental response. Clearly this factor should depress responding in the Terminate-CS group.

A contrasting facilitory effect, may, according to Kamin, be expected to operate in the Avoid-UCS group. Although the CS does not in this group terminate with the execution of a CR, some benefit should derive from the fact that often the CS terminated within a second or two after completion of an avoidance response. If, as an illustration, S completed a CR within three seconds after the onset of the CS, termination of the CS would have followed two seconds later. Though admittedly the reinforcing effect of such a delayed CS termination might not be as great as an immediately terminating CS, some strengthening of the CR might nevertheless be forthcoming from this source (see Kamin, 1957).

There is another aspect of this study that bears mentioning. It will be recalled that in all groups the CS and UCS both terminated upon execution of an escape response. If CS termination on escape trials is an important factor in determining the *emergence* of avoidance responding (see Kamin *et al.*, 1959), it is not difficult to see that all four groups would have profited equally from this factor (disregarding different numbers of escape trials); as a consequence, any effects arising from manipulations performed on avoidance trials would tend to be masked. In any event, it is perfectly clear that no unambiguous conclusions concerning the respective roles of CS termination and UCS avoidance are possible on the basis of this study. We may

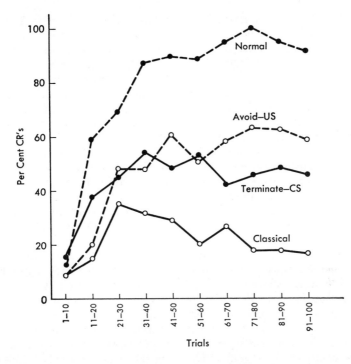

Figure 5-5. Per cent conditioned responses over the 100 avoidance acquisition trials. The four groups differ with respect to the treatment received on CR trials, that is, trials on which the instrumental response was performed prior to the onset of the UCS (see text). (Reprinted with permission from Kamin, L. J. The effects of termination of the CS and avoidance of the US on avoidance learning. *J. comp. physiol. Psychol.*, 1956, **49**, 420–424.)

conclude, as we already know from other sources, that CS termination is a powerful reinforcing event in avoidance conditioning. But whether UCS avoidance plays a role, indeed perhaps even a *necessary* role, remains an open issue.

Some Arguments Against Two-Factor Theory. There are a number of pieces of evidence, again all indirect, that can be brought to bear against the two-factor interpretation of avoidance conditioning. They take the form of disconfirming both the necessity and the sufficiency of CS termination in avoidance acquisition, and denying the central role assigned by two-factor theory to fear conditioning. The first line of attack, implying as it does that UCS avoidance is an important reinforcing

event in avoidance learning, is equally effective against two-factor theory and related approaches that reduce avoidance learning to escape from secondary aversive stimuli. The second strikes more particularly at two-factor theory.

AVOIDANCE CONDITIONING WITHOUT RESPONSE-PRODUCED CS TERMINATION. One fact seems clear. Avoidance conditioning is possible with procedures that preclude the possibility of CS termination by the avoidance response. Perhaps the clearest example of this is the Sidman procedure (Sidman, 1953), a variety of nondiscriminative avoidance conditioning in which an experimentally produced CS is not employed. Often the UCS is an inescapable brief pulse of shock, so that the instrumental response does not even serve to escape the UCS. Nevertheless, it is beyond question that very respectable levels of avoidance performance can be obtained with this procedure in rats, monkeys, and other organisms.

It really is quite difficult to see how two-factor theory, or any interpretation that places the burden of avoidance learning on escape from secondary aversive cues, can accommodate Sidman avoidance conditioning in any satisfactory way. It is characteristic of this procedure that shocks are delivered at regular intervals, say every 10 sec., unless S makes the instrumental response, which postpones the next shock a fixed interval of time, say 20 sec. Possibly one could assert that the time interval separating shocks serves as the CS, and as the interval from the last shock wears on, S becomes more and more anxious. Finally he makes the instrumental response, which somehow reduces his anxiety (because it terminates the CS?). Such an interpretation seems rather contrived, to say the least. Carried to its logical conclusion, it would seem impossible ever to deny the existence of a CS, for one could always be postulated within the organism. And having hypothesized the existence of a CS, hypothesizing its termination is a natural complement. Much the same argument applies to those interpretations which look to proprioceptive cues as the source of secondary aversive stimuli.

Trace conditioning with CSs of such short duration that response termination of the CS is impossible presents a similar difficulty. A nice illustration of this point is a recent study by Taub, Bacon, and Berman (1965) in which monkeys learned a trace avoidance response (arm flexion) although disadvantaged by deafferentation of their responding limb (which was kept out of sight of S). These animals could neither see nor, presumably, feel the arm that was performing the instrumental response, and there was no possibility whatever of response-produced CS termination. Though not up to unoperated controls, all of the operated Ss reached an 80 per cent criterion

of avoidance conditioning. The experiment has relevance for more than the two-factor theory of avoidance learning, but it does show that avoidance learning can occur in the absence of response termination of an exteroceptive CS as well as in the face of total impoverishment of sensation from the response sequence constituting the instrumental response.

FAILURE TO OBTAIN AVOIDANCE CONDITIONING WITH RESPONSE-PRODUCED CS TERMINATION. If the Sidman procedure and trace conditioning show that response-produced CS termination is not a necessary requirement of avoidance conditioning, numerous failures to acquire an avoidance response despite long training with CS termination procedures suggest that neither is it sufficient. In one study, for example, rats were trained on a total of better than 7,000 trials distributed over a four-month period under procedures which appeared to be quite favorable for avoidance conditioning (D'Amato and Schiff, 1964). Yet half of the rats tested failed to average more than 16 per cent avoidances in any one session, even though they escaped quickly and each instrumental response terminated the CS. As Turner and Solomon (1962) have pointed out, failures to learn are not uncommon in avoidance conditioning (and may occur even among human Ss); characteristically, however, such failures are ignored by E. Turner and Solomon attempted to accommodate theoretically this unexpected aspect of avoidance conditioning within a framework consistent with two-factor theory. However, the nature of their theory is such that it does not seem an appropriate explanation for the learning failures which occur in the discriminated bar-press avoidance situation (see D'Amato, Keller, and Biederman, 1965).

One difficulty facing proponents of UCS avoidance as the effective reinforcing agent in avoidance conditioning is in accounting for the *emergence* of avoidance responses. An "avoidance" response (better called an *anticipatory* response) must first occur before UCS avoidance can serve as a reinforcing event. As we have seen CS termination is very influential in producing anticipatory responses, but we have also seen that factors can operate to prevent response-produced CS termination from serving this role.

Conversely, factors other than CS termination can be taken advantage of to encourage early emergence of anticipatory responses. D'Amato, Keller, and DiCara (1964) showed, for example, that avoidance conditioning could be improved dramatically by employing as the UCS a discontinuous rather than a conventional continuous shock. At least in the bar-press situation, this modification of the UCS is extremely powerful in stimulating emergence of anticipatory responding.

To summarize this argument, complete failures to acquire what appears to be a simple avoidance response in situations allowing for response-produced CS termination clearly show that the latter factor is not sufficient for the development of avoidance conditioning. In order for UCS avoidance to serve as a reinforcing agent the instrumental response must somehow be made to antedate the UCS. If conditions are such that CS termination is not sufficient to serve this purpose other means must be exploited, and one such alternative method is discontinuous shock. The suggestion, then, is that response-produced CS termination often turns up as an important factor in avoidance conditioning simply because it encourages emergence of anticipatory responding, which, once it occurs, is reinforced by the UCS avoidance for which it is responsible. In a very real sense *S must first avoid before he can learn to avoid.*

INVERSE RELATIONSHIP BETWEEN SHOCK INTENSITY AND AVOIDANCE CONDITIONING. Another, circumstantial, bit of evidence not congruent with two-factor theory is the repeated finding that rate of avoidance conditioning is *inversely* related to shock intensity. Manipulating shock intensity

between the extremes of very mild and quite strong shock, Moyer and Korn (1964), Bolles and Warren (1965), Levine (1966), and D'Amato and Fazzaro (1966) all found avoidance conditioning to develop most rapidly at the *lowest* shock intensity employed. This result is somewhat embarrassing to two-factor theory, which must concede that fear conditioning is more intense at the higher shock levels. And though the theory might not be obliged to predict that avoidance conditioning and shock level be positively related for all intensities—obviously with very strong shock disorganization might become a disrupting factor—it nevertheless ought to predict that short of this point stronger shock should facilitate avoidance acquisition.

Adherents of UCS avoidance are in a better position with respect to this finding. Their interpretation would be that whether or not higher shock intensities act to facilitate avoidance acquisition depends on the relationship that exists between shock level and emergence of anticipatory responses. If strong shock carries with it behavioral effects that suppress anticipatory responding, avoidance behavior simply will never get started. Apparently, moderate to strong shock does just that, at least in the rat. The mechanism operating appears to be the conditioning of response suppression (crouching and freezing behavior) to the CS, a suppression that inhibits a wide range of behavior, the instrumental response included (D'Amato and Fazzaro, 1966). As a result of this conditioning, when a CS associated with relatively strong shock appears *S* responds by freezing and crouching, often remaining in this posture until the onset of the UCS. Emergence of anticipatory responses thus precluded, avoidance behavior never really gets started. As strong a factor as response-produced CS termination is in encouraging anticipatory responses, it can be completely neutralized in the rat by strong or even moderate shock levels.

DISAPPEARANCE OF FEAR SYMPTOMS WITH WELL-ESTABLISHED AVOIDANCE BEHAVIOR. Another set of observations incongruent with two-factor theory has to do with avoidance maintenance (in distinction to avoidance acquisition). To be consistent two-factor theory must require that the maintenance of even long-established avoidance behavior be based on fear arousal and reduction, though the intensity of the fear reaction may become attenuated to some unspecified irreducible minimum. Turning first to ordinary experience, it does not seem to be the case that the vast repertoires of avoidance behaviors maintained in our daily lives require for their evocation the elicitation of fear and for their reinforcement, fear reduction. We stop at a red traffic signal not because that stimulus evokes in us fear which is reduced by bringing the automobile to a halt, but rather because we wish to avoid the unpleasant consequences which failing to stop might cause us. It is entirely conceivable that when first learning to drive something of an anxiety reaction was indeed elicited by a red traffic signal, but all traces of such a reaction appear to be completely extinguished in most experienced drivers. Similarly, largely based on an anxiety motive instilled by his parent, a child may initially learn to stop before crossing a thoroughfare and look about for approaching automobiles. But what adult approaching an avenue first experiences fear, stops, looks about, crosses the street, and then experiences fear reduction?

The same point can be made in a more objective way by observing animals who have mastered an avoidance conditioning task. After a reasonable amount of experience in the experimental situation such animals show no outward indication of fear when the CS appears, and may even make the instrumental response with a degree of deliberation that one is tempted to interpret as nonchalance. The disappearance of fear symptoms in animals well practiced at an avoidance task is an observation that

has been made many times (Woodworth and Schlosberg, 1954, p. 675). Obviously, without an independent criterion of anxiety —a limitation that two-factor theorists are often reminded of—there is no sure way of determining whether or not fear does extinguish entirely in the course of protracted training. The evidence, slim as it is, is that if anxiety is occurring it is too mild to be reflected in overt symptoms or, in the case of humans, in experience.

The most direct evidence bearing on this point is contributed by a study by Kamin, Brimer, and Black (1963), in which the intensity of fear generated in a shuttle-box avoidance task was monitored by the conditioned suppression observed in a CER situation. They found that as the avoidance acquisition criterion was made more stringent the conditioned suppression observed in CER tests first increased and then *decreased*. Furthermore, Ss tested after meeting an extinction criterion of failing to avoid on five successive trials showed considerable conditioned suppression, suggesting that extinction of avoidance behavior *precedes* extinction of the fear response. These investigators conclude that their data "reveal a considerable lack of parallelism between fear and instrumental behavior, and thus encourage speculation that variables other than fear of the CS are largely responsible for the maintenance of avoidance behavior" (p. 501).

Further inferential evidence on this score may be derived from the fact that highly practiced Ss may avoid on 99 per cent or more of their trials. We know that instrumentally conditioned responses can be maintained at fair levels with reinforcement ratios as little as one in 100. But usually Ss must be shaped for a time in order for this behavior to be sustained on such an impoverished reinforcement schedule. So far as we know, classically conditioned (appetitive) responses differ from their instrumental counterparts in that they do not react well to low reinforcement ratios.

Pavlov (1927), for example, observed that it was very difficult to obtain salivary conditioning if the unconditioned stimulus were not applied on every second or third trial. Granting that this last observation does not necessarily hold for fear conditioning and granting further that the anxiety complex may include skeletal as well as autonomic components, it seems unlikely that anxiety could play a very significant role in the maintenance of highly successful avoidance behavior acquired rapidly and motivated by a mild to moderate UCS.

Summary

Perhaps "crucial" evidence is not available but nevertheless the arguments and evidence reviewed in the last section warrant further evaluation of the view that the necessary and sufficient condition for acquisition and maintenance of avoidance behavior is UCS avoidance (see Bolles, Stokes, and Younger, 1966). This point of view will be unpalatable to those who hold to an "escape" interpretation of avoidance learning. One primary motivation for maintaining the latter theoretical position is to circumvent the necessity of considering the absence of an event as a reinforcing stimulus, which appears to require that S first possess an expectation about the event in question. But an objective accounting of avoidance conditioning need no longer be obliged to avoid concepts based on S's "expectations." We have observed in the last chapter the widespread use made of the anticipatory goal and frustration responses by the most respected of behaviorists. Indeed, fear itself is an anticipatory response and therefore in the nature of an expectation.

There seems to be no reason why reinforcing properties of UCS avoidance could not also be interpreted in terms of events which follow upon anticipatory responses (for example, r_P-s_P). The primary frustration response R_F, it will be recalled, was postulated to be an unconditioned response which occurred when the anticipatory goal response did not lead to its accustomed reward object. Following a parallel line of development, one might hold that when S expects a negative reinforcement (that is, r_P-s_P is elicited by stimuli in the situation) and it does not materialize, an unconditioned response of "relief" occurs, a response which, in contrast to frustration, possesses positive reinforcing properties and serves to reinforce the avoidance response (see Mowrer, 1960).

In conditioning situations employing positive reinforcement the absence of S^{R+} (after its consistent appearance) is usually easily discriminated by S, who simply no longer finds food in its accustomed place. In avoidance conditioning, however, the deletion of S^{R-} may under certain circumstances be much more difficult to discriminate. For example, in trace conditioning, discrimination of the absence of S^{R-} would hinge on S's ability to discriminate the duration of the CS–UCS interval, because in trace conditioning neither the onset nor the termination of the UCS is correlated with an exteroceptive cue. Possibly this is one reason why CS termination is such an important factor in avoidance conditioning: it provides a stimulus situation which aids S to discriminate the omission of the UCS.

The object of the preceding paragraphs is not to present a theory of avoidance conditioning based on UCS avoidance, but rather to indicate one possible approach by means of which UCS avoidance can be admitted as an essential ingredient of avoidance conditioning by recourse to concepts no less objective than those already in wide use among certain "hard-nosed" behaviorists.

Throughout this chapter parallels between conditioning with negative and positive reinforcement have come up repeatedly. At the very outset we tried to show that the motive-incentive conditions of both types of conditioning procedures are, at least conceptually, quite similar. The most crucial difference, it will be recalled, was that with negative reinforcement drive induction (as well as reduction) occurs much more rapidly than is the case for positive reinforcement. A number of important consequences could be traced to this one incongruence.

As for the behavioral data themselves, we witnessed a number of parallels between nondiscriminative conditioning with positive reinforcement and its negative reinforcement counterpart, escape conditioning. Where divergences were observed, many of these could have arisen from procedural differences or from asymmetrical drive induction rates.

On the theoretical side, the anticipatory goal response r_G-s_G emerged as an ubiquitous explanatory tool in the accounting of the facts of instrumental conditioning with positive reinforcement. An analogous role was played by fear, or more generally, the anticipatory pain or discomfort response r_P-s_P. Pushing this correspondence even further, just as the disconfirmation of r_G-s_G was assumed to result in an unconditioned frustration state, R_F, the possibility was pointed out of using to conceptual advantage the notion that disconfirmation of r_P-s_P leads to an unconditioned "relief" response (R_R). But whereas R_F is essentially a negatively reinforcing condition, R_R is presumed to be positively reinforcing. Obviously the next step is to place in correspondence r_F-s_F and an anticipatory relief response r_R-s_R, the former being

somewhat aversive in nature, the latter positive.

The point of multiplying anticipatory mechanisms is that instrumental conditioning appears to require some means of accounting for the fact that such behavior is influenced importantly by S's expectations concerning future events. There is nothing mysterious or loose-thinking about this; it is no more than recognition of the simple fact that knowledge of past relationships to some extent governs present behavior. It would be a simple matter to construct a robot rat that would learn to perform a specific response in order to obtain "reinforcement" and be so regulated that when reinforcement was eliminated it relinquished its "learned" response. But the "frustration" which befalls a real rat when he first encounters nonreward would be alien to its robot counterpart. Possibly the robot could be modified to produce the kinds of behavior that have been attributed to frustration. But in doing so doubtlessly a mechanism would have to be built into the robot which served to compare present reinforcement conditions with related past experience. Fractional anticipatory responses are just such a mechanism.

If the empirical data arising from instrumental conditioning have done nothing else they have shown clearly that an account of instrumental behavior *in stimulus-response terms* must include mechanisms which allow for behavior based on anticipation of future events. The major problem posed by this task is its accomplishment in an objective and nontrivial way.

Glossary

avoidance conditioning. A form of conditioning in which performance of the instrumental response at the appropriate time (during the CS–UCS interval) serves to prevent or postpone for a time the appearance of S^{R-}

CS (conditioned stimulus). In classical conditioning, the stimulus which, having been paired with the UCS, ultimately comes to evoke the conditioned response; in instrumental conditioning, the stimulus complex to which the instrumental response is presumed to be associated.

discriminative instrumental conditioning. An instrumental conditioning situation in which the availability of reinforcement is correlated with a distinctive stimulus complex.

DRL (differential reinforcement of low rates) schedule. A reinforcement schedule in which essentially S must withhold the instrumental response for some period of time in order to obtain reinforcement.

escape conditioning. A form of conditioning in which S^{R-} is applied by E independently of S's behavior, and performance of a specific response terminates the negative reinforcer.

instrumental conditioning. Any learning based on response-contingent reinforcement that does not involve choice among experimentally defined alternatives.

nondiscriminative instrumental conditioning. Instrumental conditioning in which the presence or absence of reinforcement is not correlated with distinctive stimuli.

punishment conditioning. A form of conditioning in which application of S^{R-} is contingent upon the execution of a specific response.

r_F (fractional anticipatory frustration response). A detachable portion of the primary frustration response, R_F, which can become conditioned to stimuli that occur early in the stimulus-response "chain."

R_F (primary frustration response). An unconditioned response which is assumed to occur when r_G does not lead to its accustomed reward.

r_G (fractional anticipatory goal response). A "detachable" component of the total goal response which, through (classical) conditioning, becomes associated to stimuli that occur early in the stimulus-response "chain." An objective way of capturing the notion that after a number of rewarded trials S comes to anticipate, or to expect, a reward as a consequence of performing the instrumental response.

r_P (fractional anticipatory pain—or discomfort—response). A detachable portion of the primary pain (or discomfort) response, which can become conditioned to stimuli occurring early in the stimulus-response "chain." An objective mechanism to handle the everyday notion of fear, which may be thought of as an expectancy of pain or discomfort.

S^D and $S+$. A "discriminative" and "positive" stimulus, respectively, associated with the availability of reinforcement in an operant (free responding) situation as compared to, in the second case, a discrete trials arrangement.

S^Δ and $S-$. Stimuli associated with unavailability of reinforcement in the operant (free responding) and discrete trials situations, respectively.

S^{R-}. A "negative" reinforcer; essentially a stimulus object or situation which S will perform work to be rid of.

S^{R+}. A "positive" reinforcer; in effect, a stimulus object or situation which S will in some sense work to attain.

UCS. In classical conditioning, the stimulus which elicits the response that is to become conditioned; in instrumental conditioning (most often in avoidance conditioning), the stimulus, usually shock, employed to motivate the instrumental response.

References

Amsel, A. Frustrative nonreward in partial reinforcement and discrimination learning: some recent history and a theoretical extension. *Psychol. Rev.*, 1962, **69**, 306–328.

Amsel, A., & Roussel, J. Motivational properties of frustration: I. Effect on a running response of the addition of frustration to the motivational complex. *J. exp. Psychol.*, 1952, **43**, 363–368.

Anderson, N. H. Comparison of different populations: resistance to extinction and transfer. *Psychol. Rev.*, 1963, **70**, 162–179.

Appel, J. B. Punishment in the squirrel monkey *Saimiri sciurea*. *Science*, 1961, **133**, 36.

Appel, J. B., & Peterson, N. J. Punishment: effects of shock intensity on response suppression. *Psychol. Rep.*, 1965, **16**, 721–730.

Armus, H. L. Effect of magnitude of reinforcement on acquisition and extinction of a running response. *J. exp. Psychol.*, 1959, **58**, 61–63.

Azrin, N. H. Effects of punishment intensity during variable-interval reinforcement. *J. exp. Anal. Behav.*, 1960(a), **3**, 123–142.

Azrin, N. H. Sequential effects of punishment. *Science*, 1960(b), **131**, 605–606.

Azrin, N. H., & Holz, W. C. Punishment. In W. K. Honig (Ed.), *Operant behavior: Areas of research and application.* New York: Appleton-Century-Crofts, 1966. Pp. 380–447.

Badia, P. Effects of drive, reinforcement schedule, and change of schedule on performance. *J. exp. Psychol.*, 1965, **69**, 292–297.

Badia, P., McBane, B., Suter, S., & Lewis, P. Preference behavior in an immediate versus variably delayed shock situation with and without a warning signal. *J. exp. Psychol.*, 1966, **72**, 847–852.

Banks, R. K., & Vogel-Sprott, N. Effect of delayed punishment on an immediately rewarded response in humans. *J. exp. Psychol.*, 1965, **70**, 357–359.

Baron, A. Delayed punishment of a runway response. *J. comp. physiol. Psychol.*, 1965, **60**, 131–134.

Barry, H., III, & Miller, N. E. Effects of drugs on approach-avoidance conflict tested repeatedly by means of a "telescope alley." *J. comp. physiol. Psychol.*, 1962, **55**, 201–210.

Barry, H., III, Wagner, A. R., & Miller, N. E. Effects of alcohol and amobarbital on performance inhibited by experimental extinction. *J. comp. physiol. Psychol.*, 1962, **55**, 464–468.

Birch, D. Extended training extinction effect under massed and spaced extinction trials. *J. exp. Psychol.*, 1965, **70**, 315–322.

Birch, D., Allison, J. K., & House, R. F. Extinction performance following discrimination training. *J. exp. Psychol.*, 1963, **65**, 148–155.

Birch, D., & Valle, F. P. Resistance to extinction in the runway following a shift from small to large reward. *J. comp. physiol. Psychol.*, 1967, **63**, 50–53.

Bitterman, M. E. Techniques for the study of learning in animals: analysis and classification. *Psychol. Bull.*, 1962, **59**, 81–93.

Black, R. W. Differential conditioning, extinction, and secondary reinforcement. *J. exp. Psychol.*, 1965, **69**, 67–74.

Black, R. W. On the combination of drive and incentive motivation. *Psychol. Rev.*, 1965, **72**, 310–317.

Black, R. W. Shifts in magnitude of reward and contrast effects in instrumental and selective learning: A reinterpretation. *Psychol. Rev.*, 1968, **75**, 114–126.

Boe, E. E. Effect of punishment duration and intensity on the extinction of an instrumental response. *J. exp. Psychol.*, 1966, **72**, 125–131.

Bolles, R. C., Stokes, L. W., & Younger, M. S. Does CS termination reinforce avoidance behavior? *J. comp. physiol. Psychol.*, 1966, **62**, 210–207.

Bolles, R. C., & Warren, J. A., Jr. The acquisition of bar press avoidance as a function of shock intensity. *Psychon. Sci.*, 1965, **3**, 297–298.

Bower, G. H. Partial and correlated reward in escape learning. *J. exp. Psychol.*, 1960, **59**, 126–130.

Bower, G. H. A contrast effect in differential conditioning. *J. exp. Psychol.*, 1961, **62**, 196–199.

Bower, G. H. The influence of graded reductions in reward and prior frustrating events upon the magnitude of the frustration effect. *J. comp. physiol. Psychol.*, 1962, **55**, 582–587.

Bower, G. H., Fowler, H., & Trapold, M. A. Escape learning as a function of amount of shock reduction. *J. exp. Psychol.*, 1959, **58**, 482–484.

Bower, G. H., & Trapold, M. A. Reward magnitude and learning in a single-presentation discrimination. *J. comp. physiol. Psychol*, 1959, **52**, 727–729.

Breger, L. Comments on "Building social behavior in autistic children by use of electric shock." *J. exp. res. Person.*, 1965, **1**, 110–113.

Brown, J. S., Martin, R. C., & Morrow, M. W. Self-punitive behavior in the rat:

facilitative effects of punishment on resistance to extinction. *J. comp. physiol. Psychol.*, 1964, **57**, 127–133.

Brown, R. T., & Wagner, A. R. Resistance to punishment and extinction following training with shock or nonreinforcement. *J. exp. Psychol.*, 1964, **68**, 503–507.

Brush, F. R. The effects of shock intensity on the acquisition and extinction of an avoidance response in dogs. *J. comp. physiol. Psychol.*, 1957, **50**, 547–552.

Brush, F. R., Brush, E. S., & Solomon, R. L. Traumatic avoidance learning: the effects of CS-US interval with a delayed-conditioning procedure. *J. comp. physiol. Psychol.*, 1955, **48**, 285–293.

Campbell, B. A., & Kraeling, D. Response strength as a function of drive level and amount of drive reduction. *J. exp. Psychol.*, 1953, **45**, 97–101.

Campbell, S. L. Resistance to extinction as a function of number of shock-termination reinforcements. *J. Comp. physiol. Psychol.*, 1959, **52**, 754–758.

Capaldi, E. J., & Bowen, J. N. Delay of reward and goal box confinement time in extinction. *Psychon. Sci.*, 1964, **1**, 141–142.

Church, R. M. The varied effects of punishment on behavior. *Psychol. Rev.*, 1963, **70**, 369–402.

Clifford, T. Extinction following continuous reward and latent extinction. *J. exp. Psychol.*, 1964, **68**, 456–465.

D'Amato, M. R. Secondary reinforcement and magnitude of primary reinforcement. *J. comp. physiol. Psychol.*, 1955, **48**, 378–380.

D'Amato, M. R., & Fazzaro, J. Discriminated lever-press avoidance learning as a function of type and intensity of shock. *J. Comp. physiol. Psychol.*, 1966, **61**, 313–315.

D'Amato, M. R., Fazzaro, J., & Etkin, M. Discriminated bar-press avoidance maintenance and extinction in rats as a function of shock intensity. *J. comp. physiol. Psychol.*, 1967, **63**, 351–354.

D'Amato, M. R., & Gumenik, W. E. Some effects of immediate versus randomly delayed shock on an instrumental response and cognitive processes. *J. abnorm. soc. Psychol.*, 1960, **60**, 64–67.

D'Amato, M. R., & Jagoda, H. Effects of extinction trials on discrimination reversal. *J. exp. Psychol.*, 1960, **59**, 254–260.

D'Amato, M. R., Keller, D., & Biederman, G. Discriminated avoidance learning as a function of parameters of discontinuous shock. *J. exp. Psychol.*, 1965, **70**, 543–549.

D'Amato, M. R., Keller, D., & DiCara, L. Facilitation of discriminated avoidance learning by discontinuous shock. *J. comp. physiol. Psychol.*, 1964, **58**, 344–349.

D'Amato, M. R., Lachman, R., & Kivy, P. Secondary reinforcement as affected by reward schedule and the testing situation. *J. comp physiol Psychol*, 1958, **51**, 737–741

D'Amato, M. R., & Schiff, D. Long-term discriminated avoidance performance in the rat. *J. comp. physiol. Psychol.*, 1964, **57**, 123–126.

D'Amato, M. R., & Schiff, D. Overlearning and brightness-discrimination reversal. *J. exp. Psychol,*, 1965, **69**, 375–381.

D'Amato, M. R., Schiff, D., & Jagoda, H. Resistance to extinction after varying amounts of discriminative or non-discriminative instrumental training. *J. exp. Psychol.*, 1962, **64**, 526–532.

Davenport, J. W. Choice behavior as a function of drive strength and rate of learning. Unpublished Ph.D. dissertation, State Univer. Iowa, 1956.

Davenport, J. W. Distribution of M and i parameters for rats trained under varying hunger-drive levels. *J. genet. Psychol.*, 1965, **106**, 113–121.

Deaux, E. B., & Patten, R. L. Measurement of the anticipatory goal response in instrumental runway conditioning. *Psychon. Sci.*, 1964, **1**, 357–358.

Dinsmoor, J. A. The effect of hunger on discriminated responding. *J. abnorm. soc. Psychol.*, 1952, **47**, 67–72.

Eisman, E., Asimow, A., & Maltzman, I. Habit strength as a function of drive in a brightness discrimination problem. *J. exp. Psychol.*, 1956, **52**, 58–64.

Estes, W. K. An experimental study of punishment. *Psychol. Monogr.*, 1944, **57**, (3, Whole No. 263).

Fehrer, E. Effects of amount of reinforcement and of pre- and postreinforcement delays on learning and extinction. *J. exp. Psychol.*, 1956, **52**, 167–176.

Feldman, M. P. Aversion therapy for sexual deviations: a critical review. *Psychol. Bull.*, 1966, **65**, 65–79.

Ferster, C. B., & Skinner, B. F. *Schedules of reinforcement.* New York: Appleton-Century-Crofts, 1957.

Fitzgerald, R. D. Effects of partial reinforcement with acid on the classically conditioned salivary response in dogs. *J. comp. physiol. Psychol.*, 1963, **56**, 1056–1060.

Fowler, H., & Trapold, M. A. Escape performance as a function of delay of reinforcement. *J. exp. Psychol.*, 1962, **63**, 464–467.

Grant, D. A. Classical and operant conditioning. In A. W. Melton (Ed.), *Categories of human learning.* New York: Academic Press, 1964, Pp. 1–31.

Gray, J. A. Relation between stimulus intensity and operant response rate as a function of discrimination training and drive. *J. exp. Psychol.*, 1965, **69**, 9–24.

Grice, G. R., & Hunter, J. J. Stimulus intensity effects depend upon the type of experimental design. *Psychol. Rev.*, 1964, **71**, 247–256.

Grossman, S. P. Eating or drinking elicited by direct adrenergic or cholinergic stimulation of the hypothalamus. *Science*, 1960, **132**, 301–302.

Harker, G. S. Delay of reward and performance of an instrumental response. *J. exp. Psychol.*, 1956, **51**, 303–310.

Harris, S. J., Smith, M. G., & Weinstock, S. Effects of nonreinforcement on subsequent reinforced running behavior. *J. exp. Psychol.*, 1962, **64**, 388–392.

Herrick, R. M., & Bromberger, R. A. Lever displacement under a variable ratio schedule and subsequent extinction. *J. comp. physiol. Psychol.*, 1965, **59**, 392–398.

Hill, W. F. An attempted clarification of frustration theory. *Psychol. Rev.*, 1968, **75**, 173–176.

Hill, W. F., & Spear, N. E. Resistance to extinction as a joint function of reward magnitude and the spacing of extinction trials. *J. exp. Psychol.*, 1962, **64**, 636–639.

Hill, W. F., & Wallace, W. P. Reward magnitude and number of training trials as joint factors in extinction. *Psychon. Sci.*, 1967, **7**, 267–268.

Hillman, B., Hunter, W. S., & Kimble, G. A. The effect of drive level on the maze performance of the white rat. *J. comp. physiol. Psychol.*, 1953, **46**, 87–89.

Homzie, M. J., & Ross, L. E. Runway performance following a reduction in the concentration of a liquid reward. *J. comp. physiol. Psychol.*, 1962, **55**, 1029–1033.

Horenstein, B. R. Performance of conditioned responses as a function of strength of hunger drive. *J. comp. physiol. Psychol.*, 1951, **44**, 210–224.

Howe, E. S. The effect of an increased versus a decreased reduction in shock used as incentive. *Amer. J. Psychol.*, 1961, **74**, 462–466.

Hulse, S. H., Jr. Amount and percentage of reinforcement and duration of goal confinement in conditioning and extinction. *J. exp. Psychol.*, 1958, **56**, 48–57.

Ison, J. R. Experimental extinction as a function of number of reinforcements. *J. exp. Psychol.*, 1962, **64**, 314–317.

Ison, J. R., & Cook, P. E. Extinction performance as a function of incentive magnitude and number of acquisition trials. *Psychon. Sci.*, 1964, **1**, 245–246.

Jenkins, H. M. The effect of discrimination training on extinction. *J. exp. Psychol.*, 1961, **61**, 111–121.

Jenkins, H. M. Resistance to extinction when partial reinforcement is followed by regular reinforcement. *J. exp. Psychol.*, 1962, **64**, 441–450.

Kamin, L. J. Traumatic avoidance learning: the effects of CS-US interval with a trace-conditioning procedure. *J. comp. physiol. Psychol.*, 1954, **47**, 65–72.

Kamin, L. J. The effects of termination of the CS and avoidance of the US on avoidance learning. *J. comp. physiol. Psychol.*, 1956, **49**, 420–424.

Kamin, L. J. The gradient of delay of secondary reward in avoidance learning. *J. comp. physiol. Psychol.*, 1957, **50**, 445–449.

Kamin, L. J. The delay-of-punishment gradient. *J. comp. physiol. Psychol.*, 1959, **52**, 434–437.

Kamin, L. J., Brimer, C. J., & Black, A. H. Conditioned suppression as a monitor of fear of the CS in the course of avoidance training. *J. comp. physiol. Psychol.*, 1963, **56**, 497–501.

Kamin, L., Campbell, D., Judd, R., Ryan, T., & Walker, J. Two determinants of the emergence of anticipatory avoidance. *J. comp. physiol. Psychol.*, 1959, **52**, 202–205.

Karsh, E. B. Effects of number of rewarded trials and intensity of punishment on running speed. *J. comp. physiol. Psychol.*, 1962, **55**, 44–51.

Karsh, E. B. Punishment: effect on learning and resistance to extinction of discrete operant behavior. *Psychon. Sci.*, 1964, **1**, 139–140.

Keesey, R. E., & Kling, J. W. Amount of reinforcement and free-operant responding. *J. exp. Anal. Behav.*, 1961, **4**, 125–132.

Kimble, G. A. *Hilgard and Marquis' conditioning and learning.* New York: Appleton-Century-Crofts, 1961.

Kimble, G. A. Categories of learning and the problem of definition: comments on Professor Grant's paper. In A. W. Melton (Ed.), *Categories of human learning.* New York: Academic Press, 1964, Pp. 32–45.

Kintsch, W. Runway performance as a function of drive strength and magnitude of reinforcement. *J. comp. physiol. Psychol.*, 1962, **55**, 882–887.

Knapp, R. K., Kause, R. H., & Perkins, C. C. Immediate versus delayed shock in T-maze performance. *J. exp. Psychol.*, 1959, **58**, 357–362.

Kobrick, J. L. The relationships among three measures of response strength as a function of the numbers of reinforcements. *J. comp. physiol. Psychol.*, 1956, **49**, 582–585.

Kraeling, D. Analysis of amount of reward as a variable in learning. *J. comp. physiol. Psychol.*, 1961, **54**, 560–565.

Lachman, R. The influence of thirst and schedules of reinforcement-nonreinforcement ratios upon brightness discrimination. *J. exp. Psychol.*, 1961, **62**, 80–87.

Lawrence, D. H., & Festinger, L. *Deterrents and reinforcement.* Stanford, Calif.: Stanford Univer. Press, 1962.

Lawson, R. Brightness discrimination performance and secondary reward strength as a function of primary reward amount. *J. comp. physiol. Psychol.*, 1957, **50**, 35–39.

Leitenberg, H. Is time-out from positive reinforcement an aversive event? *Psychol. Bull.*, 1965, **64**, 428–441.

Levine, S. UCS intensity and avoidance learning. *J. exp. Psychol.*, 1966, **71**, 163–164

Lewis, D. J. Partial reinforcement: a selective review of the literature since 1950. *Psychol. Bull.*, 1960, **57**, 1–28.

Logan, F. A. *Incentive.* New Haven: Yale Univer. Press, 1960.

Logan, F. A. Discrete-trials DRL. *J. exp. Anal. Behav.*, 1961, **4**, 277–279.

Logan, F. A., Beier, E. M., & Ellis, R. A. Effect of varied reinforcement on speed of locomotion. *J. exp. Psychol.*, 1955, **49**, 260–266.

Lovaas, O. I., Schaeffer, B., & Simmons, J. Q. Building social behavior in autistic children by use of electric shock. *J. exp. res. Person.*, 1965, **1**, 99–109.

Martin, R. C., & Melvin, K. B. Vicious circle behavior as a function of delay of punishment. *Psychon. Sci.*, 1964, **1**, 415–416.

Marx, M. H., McCoy, D. F., Jr., & Tombaugh, J. W. Resistance to extinction as a function of constant delay of reinforcement. *Psychon. Sci.*, 1965, **2**, 333–334.

McKelvey, R. K. The relationship between training methods and reward variables in brightness discrimination learning. *J. comp. physiol. Psychol.*, 1956, **49**, 485–491.

Melton, A. W. (Ed.) *Categories of human learning.* New York: Academic Press, 1964.

Melvin, K. B. Escape learning and "vicious-circle" behavior as a function of percentage of reinforcement. *J. comp. physiol. Psychol.*, 1964, **58**, 248–251.

Melvin, K. B., & Martin, R. C. Facilitative effects of two modes of punishment on resistance to extinction. *J. comp. physiol. Psychol.*, 1966, **62**, 491–494.

Meyer, D. R. Food deprivation and discrimination reversal learning by monkeys. *J. exp. Psychol.*, 1951, **41**, 10–16.

Miles, R. C. Discrimination in the squirrel monkey as a function of deprivation and problem difficulty. *J. exp. Psychol.*, 1959, **57**, 15–19.

Miller, N. E. Learning resistance to pain and fear: effects of overlearning, exposure, and rewarded exposure in context. *J. exp. Psychol.*, 1960, **60**, 137–145.

Mowrer, O. H. *Learning theory and behavior.* New York: Wiley, 1960.

Mowrer, O. H., & Lamoreaux, R. R. Avoidance conditioning and signal duration—a study of secondary motivation and reward. *Psychol. Monogr.*, 1942, **54**, (5, Whole No. 247).

Mowrer, O. H., & Lamoreaux, R. R. Conditioning and conditionality (discrimination). *Psychol. Rev.*, 1951, **58**, 196–212.

Moyer, K. E., & Korn, J. H. Effect of UCS intensity on the acquisition and extinction of an avoidance response. *J. exp. Psychol.*, 1964, **67**, 352–359.

North, A. J., & Stimmel, D. T. Extinction of an instrumental response following a large number of reinforcements. *Psychol. Rep.*, 1960, **6**, 227–234.

Notterman, J. M. A study of some relations among aperiodic reinforcement, discrimination training, and secondary reinforcement. *J. exp. Psychol.*, 1951, **41**, 161–169.

Notterman, J. M., & Mintz, D. E. *Dynamics of response.* New York: Wiley, 1965.

Pavlov, I. P. *Conditioned reflexes.* (Translated by G. V. Anrep) Oxford: Oxford University Press, 1927. (Dover Edition 1960).

Perkins, C. C., Levis, D. J., & Seymann, R. Preference for signal-shock vs. shock-signal. *Psychol. Rep.*, 1963, **13**, 735–738.

Pieper, W. A., & Marx, M. H. Effects of within-session incentive contrast on instrumental acquisition and performance. *J. exp. Psychol.*, 1963, **65**, 568–571.

Pubols, B. H., Jr. The acquisition and reversal of a position habit as a function of incentive magnitude. *J. comp. physiol. Psychol.*, 1961, **54**, 94–97.

Rachlin, H. Recovery of responses during mild punishment. *J. exp. Anal. Behav.*, 1966, **9**, 251–263.

Reynolds, B. The relationship between strength of a habit and the degree of drive present during acquisition. *J. exp. Psychol.*, 1949, **39**, 296–305.

Reynolds, W. F., & Pavlik, W. B. Running speed as a function of deprivation period

and reward magnitude. *J. comp. physiol. Psychol.*, 1960, **53**, 615–618.

Schoenfeld, W. N. An experimental approach to anxiety, escape and avoidance behavior. In Hoch, P. H., & Zubin, J. (Eds.) *Anxiety.* New York: Grune and Stratton, 1950.

Schoonard, J., & Lawrence, D. H. Resistance to extinction as a function of the number of delay of reward trials. *Psychol. Rep.*, 1962, **11**, 275–278.

Schrier, A. M. Comparison of two methods of investigating the effect of amount of reward on performance. *J. comp. physiol. Psychol.*, 1958, **51**, 725–731.

Schrier, A. M. Response rates of monkeys (*Macaca mulatta*) under varying conditions of sucrose reinforcement. *J. comp. physiol. Psychol.*, 1965, **59**, 378–384.

Schrier, A. M., & Harlow, H. F. Effect of amount of incentive on discrimination learning by monkeys. *J. comp. physiol. Psychol.*, 1956, **49**, 117–122.

Sgro, J. A., & Weinstock, S. Effects of delay on subsequent running under immediate reinforcement. *J. exp. Psychol.*, 1963, **66**, 260–263.

Sherman, J. G., Hegge, F. W., & Pierrel, R. Discrimination formation as related to the amount of S^Δ training. *Psychon. Sci.*, 1964, **1**, 43–44.

Sidman, M. Avoidance conditioning with brief shock and no exteroceptive warning signal. *Science*, 1953, **118**, 157–158.

Sidman, M. Avoidance behavior. In W. K. Honig (Ed.), *Operant behavior: Areas of research and application.* New York: Appleton-Century-Crofts, 1966. Pp. 448–498.

Skinner, B. F. *The Behavior of organisms.* New York: Appleton-Century-Crofts, 1938.

Solomon, R. L. Punishment. *Amer. Psychologist*, 1964, **19**, 239–253.

Solomon, R. L., & Brush, E. S. Experimentally derived conceptions of anxiety and aversion. In M. R. Jones (Ed.), *Nebraska symposium on motivation:1956.* Lincoln: Univer. Nebraska Press, 1956. Pp. 212–305.

Solomon, R. L., & Wynne, L. C. Traumatic avoidance learning: the principles of anxiety conservation and partial irreversibility. *Psychol. Rev.*, 1954, **61**, 353–385.

Spence, K. W. *Behavior theory and conditioning*. New Haven: Yale Univer. Press, 1956.

Spence, K. W. Behavior theory and selective learning. In M. R. Jones (Ed.), *Nebraska symposium on motivation: 1958*. Lincoln: Univer. Nebraska Press, 1958.

Spence, K. W., Goodrich, K. P., & Ross, L. E. Performance in differential conditioning and discrimination learning as a function of hunger and relative response frequency. *J. exp. Psychol.*, 1959, **58**, 8–16.

Sperling, S. E. Extinction effects following nondifferential reinforcement of an irrelevant stimulus. *J. exp. Psychol.*, 1962, **63**, 50–56.

Stavely, H. E., Jr. Effects of escape duration and shock intensity on the acquisition and extinction of an escape response. *J. exp. Psychol.*, 1966, **72**, 698–703.

Stebbins, W. C. Relation of amount of primary reinforcement to discrimination and to secondary reinforcement strength. *J. comp. physiol. Psychol.*, 1959, **52**, 721–726.

Storms, L. H., Boroczi, C., & Broen, W. E. Punishment inhibits an instrumental response in hooded rats. *Science*, 1962, **135**, 1133–1134.

Sutherland, N. S., Mackintosh, N. J., & Wolfe, J. B. Extinction as a function of the order of partial and consistent reinforcement. *J. exp. Psychol.*, 1965, **69**, 56–59.

Taub, E., Bacon, R. C., & Berman, A. J. Acquisition of a trace-conditioned avoidance response after deafferentation of the responding limb. *J. comp. physiol. Psychol.*, 1965, **59**, 275–279.

Theios, J., & Brelsford, J. Overlearning-extinction effect as an incentive phenomenon. *J. exp. Psychol.*, 1964, **67**, 463–467.

Thorndike, E. L. *Educational psychology*. Vol. II. *The psychology of learning*. New York: Teachers College, Columbia University, 1913.

Thorndike, E. L. Reward and punishment in animal learning. *Comp. Psychol. Monogr.*, 1932 (8, Whole No. 39).

Tombaugh, T. N. Resistance to extinction as a function of the interaction between training and extinction delays. *Psychol. Rep.*, 1966, **19**, 791–798.

Turner, L. H., & Solomon, R. L. Human traumatic avoidance learning: theory and experiments on the operant-respondent distinction and failures to learn. *Psychol. Monogr.*, 1962, **76** (40, Whole No. 559).

Valenstein, E. S., & Beer, B. Continuous opportunity for reinforcing brain stimulation. *J. exp. Anal. Behav.*, 1964, **7**, 183–184.

Wagner, A. R. Sodium amytal and partially reinforced runway performance. *J. exp. Psychol.*, 1963, **65**, 474–477.

Wike, E. L., & Farrow, B. J. The effects of magnitude of water reward on selective learning and habit reversal. *J. comp. physiol. Psychol.*, 1962, **55**, 1024–1028.

Winograd, E. Escape behavior under different fixed ratios and shock intensities. *J. exp. Anal. Behav.*, 1965, **8**, 117–124.

Woods, P. J. A bibliography of references relevant to instrumental escape conditioning. Distributed privately, 1965.

Woods, P. J., Davidson, E. H., & Peters, R. J. Instrumental escape conditioning in a water tank: effects of variations in drive stimulus intensity and reinforcement magnitude. *J. comp. physiol. Psychol.*, 1964, **57**, 466–470.

Woodworth, R. S., & Schlosberg, H. *Experimental psychology*. New York: Holt, Rinehart, and Winston, 1954.

Wynne, L. C., & Solomon, R. L. Traumatic avoidance learning: acquisition and extinction in dogs deprived of normal peripheral autonomic functioning. *Genet. Psychol. Monogr.*, 1955, **52**, 241–284.

Zeaman, D. Response latency as a function of the amount of reinforcement. *J. exp. Psychol.*, 1949, **39**, 466–483.

Suggested Readings

The research literature in instrumental conditioning, like that in other active areas of psychological investigation, is rocketing to orbital proportions. Rather than presenting a list of suggested readings which emphasizes empirical developments, therefore, the following selections were chosen on the basis that they represent a range of general approaches to the study and conceptualization of instrumental conditioning.

Campbell, B. A., & Church, R. M. (Eds.), *Punishment and aversive behavior*. New York: Appleton-Century-Crofts, 1969.

Hull, C. L. *Principles of behavior*. New York: Appleton-Century-Crofts, 1943.

Lawrence, D. H., & Festinger, L. *Deterrents and reinforcements*. Stanford, Calif.: Stanford Univer. Press, 1962.

Logan, F. A. *Incentive*. New Haven: Yale Univer. Press, 1960.

Mowrer, O. H. *Learning theory and behavior*. New York: Wiley, 1960.

Spence, K. W. *Behavior theory and conditioning*. New Haven: Yale Univer. Press, 1956.

III

Classical Conditioning

I. Gormezano

University of Iowa

John W. Moore

University of Massachusetts

6

History and Method

As early as 1897, Pavlov, the Russian physiologist, noted in the course of his investigations of digestive processes that stimuli which regularly preceded the appearance of food to a dog (for example, the sight of the food pan, the smell of food, the sound of footsteps of the approaching *E*) came to elicit "psychic" salivary and gastric secretions (Pavlov, 1902). Although other investigators of digestive processes had observed these "psychic" secretions (Babkins, 1949, p. 301), systematic investigation of the phenomenon waited upon Pavlov's particular genius to appreciate its significance. To Pavlov the occurrence of "psychic" secretions revealed adaptive behavior of the animal to its external and internal environment and, more importantly, it appeared to him to provide an objective and powerful method for investigating the functions of the cerebral cortex. Although Pavlov was awarded the Nobel prize in 1904 for his investigations of glandular and neural factors in digestion, he expended his entire remaining efforts, from 1902 until his death in 1936, on an empirical elaboration of these "psychic" secretions and on a theory of cortical function.

By the time Pavlov's work first became known in the United States (Pavlov, 1906; Yerkes and Morgulis, 1909) he had already collected and organized a large body of data. Though his experimental findings were limited to the salivary responses in dogs, Pavlov was the first to employ procedures and concepts such as conditioning itself, conditioned and unconditioned stimuli, reinforcement, irradiation (stimulus generalization), extinction, spontaneous recovery, and differentiation or discrimination. His concepts were later employed by others in analyzing a wide range of behavior extending from individual behavior to social action. In spite of the broad uses made of his work, Pavlov's impact upon psychologists of learning was not so much his "discovery" of conditioned responses but his elucidation of the many conditions affecting the formation and retention of these learned responses and the formulation of an objective terminology for their description. Pavlov's terms are in fact still regarded by most investigators of learning as being among the most basic descriptive units of behavior, applicable even in learning paradigms other than classical conditioning.

Concept of the Reflex and Conditioned Reflex

In spite of the anticipations of conditioning in the writings of the Greek philosophers, its tradition is directly traceable to the philosophical writing of Descartes. In 1660, Descartes developed his concept of a reflex to describe stereotyped, innate muscular responses following sensory stimulation, which he assumed was "reflected" back out from the brain (that is, from the pineal gland). Further study by physiologists revealed that reflexes present in already decapitated animals could be abolished by destruction of the remaining spinal cord, leading to the conclusion that the "seat of reflection" was in the spinal cord. Whytt, in 1751, expanded the concept of the reflex to include not only muscular responses, but also such autonomic responses as salivation and pupillary responses to light. Bell, in 1811, and Magendie, in 1822, providing further development, elaborated the anatomical concept of the reflex-arc. Subsequent physiologists of the eighteenth and nineteenth centuries studied the various phenomena of reflex action in decapitated or decerebrated animals under the assumption that consciousness was abolished by destruction of the brain and that the observed absence of spontaneous activity precluded "voluntary" movement. The remaining responses of the organism to sensory stimulation were then attributed to the automatic mechanisms of the reflex-arc. (See Fearing, 1930, for a detailed treatment of the history of research on the reflex.)

Although investigators of the eighteenth and nineteenth centuries restricted their study of reflexes to spinal preparations, this was not construed as meaning that only the spinal cord had reflexes, but simply that physiology had not yet acquired the means for reliably studying reflexes of the cerebral hemispheres. Sechenov, the father of modern Russian physiology, was impatient with this restriction of method and asserted there were reflexes of the brain as well as of the spinal cord. While working in Barnard's laboratory he produced inhibition of reflexes in the frog by the application of salt solutions and crystals to various parts of the brain stem and cut surfaces of the brain. From these observations Sechenov (1863) set forth his hypothesis of reflex action of the brain which set the basis for the principal philosophical and scientific assumptions of the Russian physiological tradition. This hypothesis looked upon the function of the brain as a reflex process involving sensory input, activity within the central nervous system, and efferent outflow. H. Jackson, the British neurologist, arrived at a similar theoretical position independent of Sechenov, but it was from Sechenov that Pavlov received his inspiration (Babkin, 1949, p. 283).

Sechenov was correct, of course, in asserting that reflexes could occur when the brain was intact or following cranial nerve stimulation. However, his assertions blurred the distinction that had been made between stereotyped, innate responses following sensory stimulation that were dependent on or independent of the state of consciousness. To the classical physiologist, spinal preparations provided the defining condition for the absence of the state of consciousness. On the other hand, Sechenov asserted that any "involuntary" response (in the sense of being automatized) is a reflex whether or not it depends upon the state of consciousness. Sechenov did differentiate, however, between the spinal reflexes of classical physiology and his proposed "reflexes" of the brain. These latter reflexes he called "acquired reflexes" because they were a function of the previous learning history of the animal. But, in the hands of Sechenov, this new concept had no experimental operations to distinguish its historical antecedents from those of spinal reflexes. It was Pavlov, accepting Sechenov's definition of an "acquired reflex," who provided the experimental operations for defining and investigating them. Pavlov (1927) later substituted the term *unconditioned reflex* for *reflex* and *conditional reflex* for *acquired reflex*, thus maintaining the classical physiologist's distinction of a reflex while providing the new defining conditions for an "acquired reflex."

Historically, social philosophers, as well as some psychologists, have erroneously considered Pavlov's conditioned reflex, like the spinal reflex preparation of the classical physiologist, to be an involuntary, automatic, and unconscious response. This misconception has apparently arisen from a failure to recognize the operational distinction between reflexes and conditioned reflexes. As yet, there is little satisfactory evidence to indicate that conditioned reflexes can be obtained in spinal preparations (Kellogg, 1947). Furthermore, even when the organism's brain is intact, conditioned reflexes have not met the contemporary physiologist's criteria for definition as a reflex. To determine whether in an intact organism a response classifies as a reflex, the physiologist first measures the latency, duration, and other topographical characteristics of the response to the adequate stimulus in a decapitated, anaesthetized, or spinally transected animal. If he obtains essentially the same response in the unanaesthetized, intact animal, he infers that the response can be properly classified as a reflex. Although unconditioned reflexes in the classical conditioning experiment may meet this criterion, conditioned reflexes have not. Thus, starting with the early interests of American psychologists in comparing the conditioned reflex with the unconditioned reflex (Schlosberg, 1928), it was, and is now more generally, recognized that the conditioned reflex differs in many respects from the unconditioned reflex.

Classical Conditioning and Learning

The early history of the influences of Pavlov's research and those of his more psychologically oriented Russian contemporary, Bekhterev, on American psychology has been elegantly portrayed by Kimble (1961). Briefly, Watson (1916), sensing its importance as an objective method for the study of behavior, advocated the use of classical conditioning to replace the method of introspection. Watson, in later writings (1925), employed the concept of conditioning as a central theoretical construct in which complex learning was considered to be a chaining of conditioned reflexes. Watson asserted that the unconditioned reflex was the basic unit of innate behavior and the conditioned reflex the basic unit of learned behavior. Smith and Guthrie (1921) recognized the unfortunate connotation of the term *conditioned reflex* as automatic, unconscious, and involuntary and advocated the now generally employed term (among American psychologists) *conditioned response*.

Following Watson's writings, the employment of classical conditioning as a concept denoting a specific theoretical process gained great systematic importance in learning and behavior theory. Guthrie (1930, 1935) was probably the most effective advocate of the position that classical conditioning is the ideal vehicle for a contiguity interpretation of learning. Hull (1929, 1937, 1943), like Watson, consistently employed classical conditioning as a theoretical process, and from the detailed knowledge of conditioned responses gained from his own research, developed a system of definitions, postulates, and theorems, from which he generalized to instrumental conditioning and selective learning. Spence (1956), Razran (1957), and Mowrer (1960) have been the contemporary broad interpreters of classical conditioning, whereas Estes (1950, 1959) has stimulated some limited theoretical applications of statistical learning theory to classical conditioning (Theios and Brelsford, 1966). It will be interesting to see whether the latter kind of approach is productively developed.

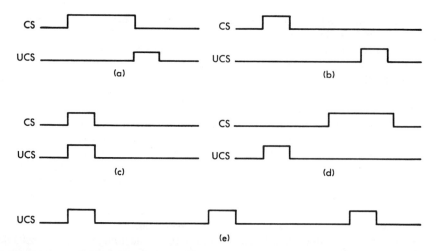

Figure 6-1. Various temporal arrangements of the CS and UCS in the classical-conditioning paradigm. The upward and downward deflections indicate the onset and offset of stimuli, respectively.

Classical Conditioning Paradigms

Although Pavlov restricted his investigations to the salivary response in dogs, the classical conditioning paradigm has been extended to studies involving organisms as low in the phylogenetic scale as planarians (flatworms) and to organisms as high as man. The responses employed have included motor responses ranging from gross approach or withdrawal movements to the relatively precise eyelid response, and the recording of such bioelectric signals as emanate from the heart (EKG), brain (EEG), and skin (GSR). Despite the variety of organisms and response systems employed, the amount of research involving classical conditioning has lagged considerably behind other methods for investigating learning processes.

The essential feature of classical conditioning is a set of experimental operations involving an unconditioned stimulus (UCS) which reliably produces a measurable unconditioned response (UCR) and a conditioned stimulus (CS) that has been shown by test not to produce the UCR. The CS and UCS are then presented repeatedly

to the organism in a specified order and temporal spacing, and a response similar to the UCR develops to the CS that is called the conditioned response (CR). Although various temporal arrangements of the CS and UCS characterize the classical conditioning paradigm, what distinguishes it from instrumental conditioning is that presentation or omission of the UCS is independent of CR occurrence. By contrast in the instrumental conditioning paradigm a contingent relationship exists such that occurrence of the response results in the presentation or omission of the reinforcing event.

The variety of forms of the classical conditioning experiment that arise from the order and temporal spacing of the CS and UCS are presented in Figure 6-1. When the CS is initiated before the onset of the UCS and remains on at least until UCS onset, the procedure is described as *delay* conditioning (Figure 6-1a). If the CS is terminated before UCS onset, the procedure is described as *trace* conditioning (Figure 6-1b). When the CS and UCS are coextensive in time, *simultaneous* conditioning results (Figure 6-1c). If in repeated pairings the UCS precedes the CS, the procedure is described as *backward* conditioning (Figure 6-1d); and when just the UCS is presented alone at a constant time interval, the interval between presentations serves as the CS for *temporal* conditioning (Figure 6-1e).

Classical conditioning has been subclassified on the basis of the type of UCS employed. Classical conditioning is called *classical reward conditioning* if the UCS employed is a positive reinforcer and *classical defense conditioning* with a negative reinforcer (Spence, 1956). Technically, the notation positive and negative reinforcer requires independent assessment of the UCS in an instrumental conditioning situation. It should be apparent, however, that the relative efficacy of positive reinforcers in classical reward conditioning is more likely to be related to the antecedent motivational state of the organism than negative reinforcers, which are considered to provide their own motivation.

Anticipatory instructed conditioning and *sensory preconditioning* are additional subdivisions of classical conditioning (Grant, 1964). The reference experiment for anticipatory instructed conditioning involves the formation of CRs based upon the instructed voluntary squeezing of a rubber bulb in response to a sound stimulus (Ivanov-Smolensky, 1933). The sound stimulus is preceded regularly by some neutral CS, and gives in effect a reaction-time experiment with a constant foreperiod signaled by CS onset. The occurrence of bulb-squeezing responses to the CS prior to or in the absence of the sound stimulus constitutes the CR. Although it is commonly assumed that the UCS must be some stimulus that produces the response reflexively without previous learning (as may be true in most cases of classical reward and defense conditioning), the only requirement within the framework of a classical conditioning experiment is that some manipulable stimulus reliably produce the desired response.

The basic paradigm for *sensory preconditioning* initially involves presenting two neutral stimuli, CS_1 and CS_2 (for example, a buzzer and a light) together for a large number of trials. CS_1 is then repeatedly paired with a UCS until a CR is established to CS_1; CS_2 is presented and if the CR occurs, sensory preconditioning has been demonstrated. If sensory preconditioning is revealed the inference is made that some learned connection between CS_1 and CS_2 was established in the preconditioning (first) phase of the experiment which facilitated the transfer of the CR from CS_1 to CS_2.

The *conditioned emotional response* (CER) experiment may also be subsumed under classical conditioning. Like the sensory preconditioning experiment, it involves an assessment of the effects of classical conditioning training by the employment of a transfer paradigm. The CER consists of the suppression of on-going operant behavior in the presence of a warning signal (CS) which has preceded shock (UCS). In the reference experiment (Hunt and Brady, 1951) rats received daily bar-pressing sessions in a Skinner box for water reinforcement. When a stable rate of bar pressing was attained on a partial reinforcement schedule, paired CS–UCS presentations of a sound and shock were superimposed in the Skinner box (or in a separate box with an electrified grid). An assessment was then made of the extent of suppression of the on-going bar-pressing response in the presence of the CS. In this paradigm the assumption is made that the interference with the on-going bar-pressing response is the result of incompatibility between the CR (the conditioned emotional response) established to the CS by CS–UCS pairings and the on-going operant behavior (Estes and Skinner, 1941). Although an assessment of CS–UCS pairings on the conditioned emotional response is made only indirectly, the CER technique has been employed to assess the effects of a variety of classical conditioning parameters with surprising quantitative sensitivity (Kamin, 1965).

Methodological Considerations

CR and UCR Measurement

The response to the UCS in most classical conditioning paradigms is rarely a single discrete response; usually is it a constellation of UCRs, and the investigator must decide which of these responses he wishes to observe. The decision is governed in part by the reliability of occurrence of the UCR, the degree of instrumentation involved, the organism, and whether some response systems evoked by the UCS (and paired with the CS) are more sensitive to change than others. For these as well as theoretical reasons, some investigators concentrate upon one response system, whereas others may take concurrent measurement of several. Generally, the investigator will select, define, and measure responses which are maximally sensitive to parametric manipulation. Whether one or several response systems are under observation, the investigator must also make every effort to ensure that response systems concurrently activated by UCS occurrences are not obscuring the influence of the independent variables on the relevant response systems, for example, the influence of respiration on heart rate.

Given that the appropriate parameters for conditioning have been selected, repeated pairings of the CS and UCS will produce a change in some measurable aspect of the CR from some initial base level to some terminal level, and this change constitutes an index of conditioning. The acquisition of CRs has been assessed according to their frequency, latency, amplitude, and magnitude. Generally, investigators have settled upon the response measure found to have the most sensitive and ordered relationship to the number of CS and UCS pairings. In salivary and GSR conditioning, for example, the amplitude or magnitude measure is most widely employed. In *magnitude measurement* the

"extent" of the responses is summed and divided by the total number of conditioning trials. Thus, this measure involves averaging responses of zero "extent." In *amplitude measurement*, however, the extent of the responses are averaged only for obtained responses. Because it is desirable to make frequency and "extent" measures as independent as possible, the amplitude measure should be employed. Amplitude and latency are descriptive measures of the CR, whereas frequency refers to the number of CRs relative to the number of trials. Another descriptive measure of the CR is *recruitment*, which is generally defined as the time elapsing between initiation of the response and the time at which the response reaches maximum amplitude. For most response systems the recruitment measure would have a high positive correlation with the amplitude measure.

CS-UCS Interval

Although the interstimulus interval between the onset of the CS and the onset of the UCS affects the rate of conditioning, the exact relationship is not known for each type of conditioning paradigm. Current empirical data suggest that for classical defense conditioning the optimal interval (that is, the interval producing the fastest rate of conditioning) is perhaps as short as 0.25 to 0.50 sec., whereas, for other classical conditioning paradigms (for example, classical reward conditioning) the information is not yet firmly available. Nevertheless, by employing an interstimulus interval at least as long as the usual latency of the CR, one can observe the course of conditioning on every trial by examining the occurrence of CRs in the interval between CS-onset and the presentation of the UCS (that is, anticipatory CRs). If, however, one wishes to employ the optimal interval for conditioning then certain difficulties arise. The CR latencies of autonomic responses (for example, salivary and GSR) commonly average 2 to 5 sec. and those of skeletal responses (for example, eyelid and leg flexion) average 0.2 to 0.5 sec. Consequently, when autonomic response systems are employed, anticipatory CRs generally cannot be observed with CS–UCS intervals less than 2 to 3 sec. Under such circumstances investigators frequently measure CRs on interspersed test trials in which the UCS is omitted, or in an extended series of extinction trials. The utilization of test trials can, however, markedly alter the course of conditioning, and the measurement of CRs on extinction trials does not permit an assessment of the growth of conditioning. Whether one should employ the short but optimal interstimulus interval or longer than optimal interval will generally depend, then, upon the strategic interests of the investigator.

CR Specification

It is commonly assumed that the CS is a neutral stimulus which acquires its response producing capabilities through its pairing with the UCS. However, for many organisms the CS elicits a constellation of reflex responses (for example, GSR, eyeblink, cardiac, and vascular reactions) which have been referred to as orienting reflexes, and have been studied in their own right (Sokolov, 1963). If one of the response systems reflexively elicited by the CS is the one whose course of conditioning is under observation, then the reflex response to the CS is referred to as an alpha response. Generally, a careful detailing of the latency, duration, and amplitude of the alpha response, as well as a determination of its course of habituation, can provide a basis for eliminating it from consideration as a CR. This can be accomplished by employing a control group given CS-alone presentations. Alpha responses are usually of a shorter latency than CRs: hence, if a

sufficiently long CS–UCS interval is employed, both responses can be observed in the interval and scored accordingly. However, the latency of CRs will vary not only as a function of the CS–UCS interval, but also with other conditioning parameters (for example, number of conditioning trials and intensity of the UCS). Therefore, problems arise when the parameters employed may lead to the occurrence of CRs in the latency range of the alpha response. Under such conditions a common procedure is to precede conditioning trials with repeated presentations of the CS until the alpha response is markedly reduced or no longer occurs. The difficulty with such a procedure is that a single CS–UCS pairing may often be sufficient to reinstate the alpha response.

The reinstatement or augmentation of the alpha response through the experimental operation of CS–UCS pairings is referred to as *sensitization*. To aid in distinguishing reinstated alpha responses from CRs a classical discrimination procedure is employed in which one stimulus (the positive CS) is paired with the UCS and another (the negative CS) is not. If the responses to the positive and negative stimuli are similar prior to acquisition training, then conditioning is presumed to be demonstrated by a difference in the amplitude or frequency of responding to the positive stimulus. Another approach to the problem of sensitization of alpha responses is to employ a control group receiving the same number of presentations of the CS and UCS as the experimental group, but with the CS and UCS presented alone in a random fashion. Differences in responding to the CS, between the experimental and the control group, are then used to assess conditioning. It should be noted, however, that both of these procedures involve the assumption that sensitization effects are not uniquely determined by the CS–UCS interval. Furthermore, these procedures do not eliminate the occurrence of augmented or reinstated alpha responses, but simply permit an assessment of their contribution to responses scored as CRs.

Once the alpha response has been eliminated from consideration, the possible contribution of other sources of nonassociative responses to CR measurement must be assessed. If the UCS is presented one or more times prior to the presentation of the CS (particularly if the UCS is noxious), the procedure may frequently result in the occurrence of responses to the CS that are quite indistinguishable from CRs. Such a procedure is called *pseudoconditioning* and the resulting responses are traditionally treated as separate from those acquired by classical conditioning because of their occurrence in the absence of previous CS–UCS pairings. The mechanism producing pseudoconditioned responses is not known at present; however, it is clearly a result of UCS presentations and might therefore be expected to contribute to the responses scored as CRs.

The presentation of the UCS can have another possible nonassociative effect in that it may operate to elevate the spontaneous rate of emission of the response system under investigation. To assess the spontaneous rate of occurrence of the response, a control group may be employed in which neither the CS nor UCS is presented and the interval of observation employed would be comparable to the CS–UCS interval of the experimental group. To assess the effects of UCS presentations, another control group is given the same number of UCS presentations (at the same intertrial interval) as the experimental group and a determination made of the number of responses occurring in the interval of observation before UCS-onset. A comparison of response frequency between the group given no stimulation and that given only UCS presentations permits an assessment of the effects of the UCS on spontaneous emissions of the response. Another approach to the problem of spontaneous responses involves correcting for their contribution to response frequency in a CS–UCS conditioning group. This has been done by adjusting conditioning-trial CR frequencies on the basis of response rate in a comparable pretrial interval (see Fitzgerald, 1963; Lipkin and Moore, 1966).

A single control-group procedure has been employed to control for both pseudoconditioned and spontaneous responses. The procedure involves presenting CS-alone and UCS-alone trials the same number of times as the experimental group given CS–UCS pairings, but the stimuli are presented in a random fashion (see Schneiderman and Gormezano, 1964). An examination of the responses occurring on CS trials (excluding responses in the alpha latency range) yields a summative measure of pseudoconditioned and spontaneous responses, or possibly some synergistic action of both stimuli. However, if pseudoconditioned responses are expected to fall in the latency range of alpha responses, then no procedures presently exist for distinguishing these responses from those resulting from sensitization. One potential difficulty with the random control-group procedure is that the perfectly negative correlation existing between presentation of the CS and presentation of the UCS on any trial may serve to underestimate nonassociative responses to the CS by its having acquired inhibitory properties through differentiation (Rescorla, 1967). The possibility of such an outcome, however, has only been demonstrated for fear mediated behavior (Rescorla and LoLordo, 1965).

Instructions and Set

Investigators studying classical conditioning in human *S*s have found it necessary to provide instructions prior to the experimental operations. In the absence of instructions *S* may adopt self-instructions that may facilitate or interfere with the acquisition or resistance to extinction of CRs. There is ample evidence to indicate that what is said to S is an important determinant in classical conditioning of not only skeletal (Fishbein and Gormezano, 1966; Lindley and Moyer, 1961; Gormezano and Moore, 1962), but also of autonomic responses (Cook and Harris, 1937; Grings, 1960; Hill, 1967). The problem is generally handled by presenting S with instructions designed to provide a "neutral" set, or by deliberately deceiving him as to the purpose of the experiment. However, S faced with "neutral" instructions is generally faced with an ambiguous situation in which no criteria are provided to permit him to determine whether or not his behavior is in compliance with the instructions. In the absence of objective criteria it can be reasonably expected that Ss will provide some type of self-instructions that will increase the variability of behavior among Ss as well as to possibly affect the behavior in a direction consistent or inconsistent with the objectives of the investigator.

Investigators in human classical conditioning have generally recognized the problem inherent in the use of "neutral" instructions. Alternative approaches have involved employing facilitative or inhibitory instructions in which S is instructed to attempt to make or refrain from making the response under observation (Miller, 1939; Norris and Grant, 1948; Gormezano and Moore, 1962). Under such instructions there is evidence to suggest that there is a reduction in the variability of performance among the Ss. It should be recognized that efforts to control self-instructional factors in classical conditioning should not be construed to mean that set and perceptual factors are artifactual contributors to the classical conditioning paradigm. That human Ss undergo set and perceptual modifications during repeated presentations of the CS and UCS should be well recognized. Grings and his associates (see Grings, 1965) have in fact been engaged in a series of studies manipulating set by repetitive stimulus sequences. Their experiments have

been designed around a "perceptual disparity test" in which following the repeated sequencing of two stimuli, the first stimulus is then followed by a different stimulus. The magnitude of GSRs made by Ss to the "unexpected" stimulus relative to controls on the disparity trial is taken as an index of the strength of the set. The program has been directed at determining the variables affecting this measure of Ss set.

Even when the investigator has exercised as much care as possible in formulating his instructions to S to obtain compliance and to reduce the variability in performance among Ss, he is still faced with the formidable task of establishing criteria for determining when Ss are not complying with instructions. An investigator who attempts to infer the failure of Ss to comply by examination of the response system under observation, as through examination of the rate of acquisition or form of the CRs (that is, latency, amplitude, duration, and recruitment), must be recognized as one who is relying, in part, upon some theoretical preconception of what constitutes the conditioning process. The effect of such procedures is, at best, the generating of empirical outcomes restricted in their generality to particular theoretical predispositions. On the other hand, certain classes of behavior outside of the response measure under observation may be usefully employed as criteria for eliminating Ss for failure to comply with instructions. Thus, Ss who block out sensory input by falling asleep, closing their eyes, plugging up their ears, removing a noxious source of stimulation, or otherwise disturbing the preparation would be readily recognized as demonstrating a failure to comply with instructions.

An issue of theoretical importance regarding instructional variables is whether this factor influences learning or whether it merely modulates performance. Fishbein (1967a) found that the facilitating effects of "voluntary blink" instructions transfer to reacquisition of the eyelid CR under "neutral" instructions following extinction, and inhibitory instructions led to a similar long-lasting decremental effect upon re-acquisition. Although not conclusive, these long-term influences of prior instructions suggest an influence on learning. A second issue revolves about the question of whether the laws of conditioning differ under inhibiting, neutral, or facilitating sets. For example, a concern that data from Ss who may adopt a facilitating set would obscure parametric relationships between measures of CR strength and independent variables has, in part, led some investigators to devise dependent variable criteria for inferentially identifying so-called voluntary responders (Spence and Ross, 1959; Hartman and Ross, 1961). Spence and his associates (see Spence, 1964) have dis-carded the data of these Ss, whereas Grant and his co-workers (see Grant, 1965) have treated these data separately. In some in-stances this breakdown supports the view that parametric relations in the two sets of data are fundamentally different (Spence and Ross, 1959; Hartman, Grant, and Ross, 1960). However, in view of the severe methodological and theoretical difficulties inherent in such an *a posteriori* classifica-tion of Ss (Gormezano, 1965, 1966), the direct experimental manipulation of in-structions would offer a methodologically sounder means of approaching this ques-tion. To this point, the results of several experiments suggest that processes govern-ing human eyelid conditioning, at least, are in fact similar under a variety of instruc-tions (Gormezano and Moore, 1962; Fishbein, 1967a, 1967b).

Infrahuman Organisms

One reason that may be advanced for regarding classical conditioning as a simple form of learning is that acquisition of CRs has been purportedly demonstrated in organisms as low on the phylogenetic scale as the planarian (see Jacobson, 1963). However, the level of conditioning ob-served in planaria has not been particularly impressive (Baxter and Kimmel, 1963), and Jensen (1965) has seriously questioned whether conditioning has been demon-strated at all. Another factor is that classical conditioning may be carried out without the elaborate pretraining frequently re-quired in other types of learning situations. At the human level classical conditioning may be carried out without instructions, although as indicated instruction is an important determinant of performance. This apparent advantage of classical con-ditioning over most other learning tech-niques should not obscure the fact that to obtain "compliance" of infrahuman organ-isms to the conditioning paradigm is one of the most taxing demands upon the ingenuity of the investigator. If the stimulating or recording equipment re-quires attachment to S, precautions must be exercised to prevent the organism from disturbing the preparation. One approach involves attaching the equipment on a portion of Ss body surface which is inaccessible to manipulation by him. Thus, for example, Shapiro and Miller (1965) have reported a preparation for recording salivary secretions of a polyethelene tube which emerges from the back of the dog's neck. The dog cannot readily dislodge it with his paws, and as such, the preparation requires the use of minimum restraints and can in fact permit free movement of the dog within the experimental chamber. When the preparation is not inaccessible, or gross skeletal movements interfere with the recording of the response, restraining devices are necessary to immobilize (assure "compliance" of) S. However, the investi-gator must attempt to construct a restrain-ing device which minimizes struggling behavior, and must frequently employ adaptation sessions. If S were to persist in resisting the restraints the competing be-havior can be expected to markedly impair the rate of conditioning. That rats, cats, and pigs vigoriously resist restraints may be one of the reasons for their minimal employment in classical conditioning research. In any event, their employment requires extensive adaptation to the apparatus. On the other hand, sheep and rabbits appear to adapt readily to restraints and it may be expected that they will be increasingly employed in classical conditioning.

Conditioned Stimuli

Any environmental change which the organism can detect may be employed as a CS. Various thermal, tactual, olfactory, and proprioceptive stimuli have been employed, but presumably because of the greater instrumentation demands for presenting such stimuli, visual and auditory CSs have been most commonly employed. Investigators employing infrahuman Ss appear to prefer intermittent stimuli. Thus, Pavlov (1927) tended to employ extensively intermittent CSs such as rotating disks, a metronome, and bubbling water, and there is evidence to indicate that an intermittent, as opposed to a continuous CS, results in a faster rate of conditioning (Papsdorf, Fishbein, and Gormezano, 1964). Investigators have often noted that acquisition is slower to a visual CS than to an auditory CS, even when these stimuli have been psychophysically equated for intensity (Marlatt, Lilie, Selvidge, Sipes, and Gormezano, 1966). It is not clear, however, whether any differences in acquisition can be attributed to differential neural encoding of the two sense modalities, or to the differential receptor orientation required for a spatially restricted visual stimulus.

Studies of the effects of the combination of two or more CSs, representing different sense modalities, on classical conditioning was initiated in America by Razran (1939), and only recently has this problem begun to receive systematic study by American investigators (Grings and O'Donnell, 1956; Wickens, 1965). Razran (1939, 1965) has presented a brief history of the development of compound CS conditioning research in Pavlov's laboratory and its elaboration by Russian investigators.

Essentially, compound CS conditioning research involves two different reinforcement histories. One procedure is that in which each stimulus of the compound has been previously paired with the same or different UCS before being presented in combination. The other involves compounds in which the two or more stimuli have only been paired with the UCS in combination. Within these two procedures, variations exist with regard to the temporal arrangements of the stimuli within the compound. One variation involves the sequential presentation of the stimuli, in which one component may terminate with the onset of the other, or they may terminate simultaneously. A second temporal variation involves the simultaneous onset and offset of all the stimuli in the compound. In general, these various stimulus compounds, relative to unimodal CSs, operate to enhance the rate and level of conditioning. At a later point, we will consider the effects of stimulus compounds in more detail.

Numerous investigations have been conducted in the Russian laboratories employing stimulation of the internal organs as the CS (Razran, 1961). This type of procedure is known as interoceptive conditioning. The most typical stimuli are distensions of the lumen of a viscus through rubber balloons inflated with air or water. Stimulation of the viscus through its distension is then varied with respect to rate of onset, and area stimulated. Other forms of stimulation involve jets of air or water as tactile stimuli, electrical stimulation, and chemical irrigation of the viscus. Of particular interest is the observation with human Ss of successful conditioning to these stimuli in the absence of any verbally stated awareness of the stimulus. Although such findings would appear to be of considerable theoretical importance, the surgical and operative techniques employed have appeared as formidable obstacles to the investigation of interoceptive conditioning by American investigators.

The converging interests of psychologists and physiologists to the area of the neurophysiology of learning has led, in recent years, to increased employment of electrical stimulation to various areas of the brain as the CS. The pioneer studies in this area were made feasible by Loucks' technique for brain stimulation of chronic preparations (Loucks, 1934). The technique employed a coil, buried just beneath the skin, from which insulated wires led to an electrode implanted in cortical tissue. When the primary coil of an inductorium was laid over the skin, adjacent to the coil, the induced current was conducted to the electrodes. Since then, enormous advances have been made in electrical stimulation techniques, as evidenced by a complete volume on electrical brain stimulation edited by Sheer (1961). The results indicate clearly there is no intrinsic property of electrical stimulation of any of the brain structures which precludes their serving as effective CSs for acquisition of a CR (Nielson, Knight, and Porter, 1962). What is not known as yet is the effectiveness of these CSs, relative to external stimuli.

Unconditioned Stimuli

Although the UCSs are generally selected with reference to the response system to be conditioned, a number of UCSs can be found for evoking any one response. Thus, the galvanic skin response (GSR), for example, can be elicited by stimulation of any sense modality if it is sufficiently intense. Electric shock is most commonly employed, however, because it appears to be less susceptible to adaptation effects.

Similarly, the salivary reflex can be elicited by mechanical or chemical stimulation of the oral cavity, particularly of the tongue. Of the wide variety of stimuli that can be employed, irrigation of the oral cavity with acid and alkaline solutions or dried meat powder are most commonly employed, because of the relative persistence of the response with repeated presentation of such stimuli.

As with the CS, a variety of interoceptive stimuli have been employed as UCSs by Russian investigators for conditioning of visceral responses such as micturition through stimulation of the bladder (Razran, 1961). Several studies also show that electrical stimulation of cortical tissue in any part of the sensory system normally activated by an external UCS, up to and including the cortex, will suffice for effective conditioning of the response evoked (Galambos and Morgan, 1960). There are also some studies to suggest the successful conditioning of motor responses following their elicitation by electrical stimulation of motor areas in the brain (Brogden and Gantt, 1942; Doty and Giurgea, 1961).

Once the UCS has been selected, consideration must be given to such parameters as the intensity and duration of the stimulus. One fundamental concern is that the intensity of the UCS employed be sufficient to mitigate the possibly rapid adaptation of the UCS, while at the same time not employing so intense a stimulus (particularly in classical defense conditioning) as to preclude the relative quiescence of the subject. American investigators generally prefer to present the UCS for only a brief duration. Presumably their thinking has been governed by the assumption that by employing brief stimulation one reduces the possibility that occurrence of the UCR or CR can modify the sensory consequences of the UCS, and thereby possibly contribute an instrumental component to the experiment.

Empirical Relationships

In this chapter we will examine some of the major facts of classical conditioning and relate this knowledge to existing behavior theory. A detailed examination of the role of classical conditioning as a theoretical device and of the theories dealing specifically with it will occupy part of the next chapter. Here we are concerned with the contribution research in classical conditioning has made to the development of learning theory, especially those S-R positions such as Hull-Spence which have evolved from Pavlov's findings.

The accumulation of empirical relationships from which the English-speaking theorist must draw his insights is at least partially circumscribed by the fact that most of these derive from research limited to human Ss and to one of two responses, the eyeblink or the GSR. Examples of human and infrahuman conditioning which employ other responses, such as salivation or heart rate, have not until recently contributed very much to our store of parametric relationships, even though their contribution in other ways has been great. Moreover, interest in many of the once popular skeletal responses, such as leg flexion, knee jerk, and finger withdrawal,

has eroded under the criticism that only autonomic responses provide a suitable prototype for the valid study of classical conditioning. Finally, the mountainous literature in instrumental and operant conditioning contains few facts which bear directly on classical conditioning, with instrumental avoidance conditioning paradigms as possible exceptions in that they presumably provide a means of investigating conditioned fear. It is still true that the theoretical burden of classical conditioning, relative to that of instrumental conditioning, is out of proportion to the pooled knowledge from the two areas.

The recent renewal of interest in what might be termed the comparative psychology of classical conditioning is thus overdue. Fortunately, many investigators are now using infrahumans in experiments which have familiar counterparts in the human literature. This comparative approach has been most apparent in eyelid, GSR, and heart-rate conditioning, and it is in these areas where the need to check the generality and limitations of our laws is most acute. It is to be expected that our faith in present knowledge will be shaken, perhaps fundamentally, and indications of this are already at hand, as we shall see.

Mindful of the high likelihood that our facts and theories will ultimately require extensive and fundamental revision in light of the rapidly accelerating output of the animal laboratories, there is good reason to retain our present beliefs a bit longer. We must be careful not to afford a greater validity to results obtained with rabbits, cats, or dogs simply because they appear to lack "contamination" from complex or cognitive processes. Although there may be good arguments against this conservatism, and although it may be true that animal experimentation often offers a wider range of experimental manipulation and smaller individual differences (less "error" variance), the very newness of large-scale animal work in classical conditioning suggests that at this writing it would be unwise to embrace findings which appear to be at odds with those based on extensive research with humans. And it would be even more foolish to always interject "verbal or cognitive mediation" to explain away a discrepancy. After all, we have only recently attained a stage of maturity in human eyelid and GSR conditioning where replication and agreement between laboratories is commonplace, and this came about only through tedious controversy and compromise, on the one hand, and a reasonable standardization of methodologies, on the other.

Comforted that substantial developments are on the horizon, but that present information and theories are not yet obsolescent, we have divided this chapter into four principal parts: (1) temporal parameters, including CS–UCS interval and intertrial interval (ITI); (2) manipulations of the UCS, including UCS-intensity and duration and their role in conditioning and performance; (3) manipulations of the CS, including CS intensity and compounding; and (4) schedules of reinforcement, including acquisition, extinction, and differentiation.

Temporal Relationships

Interstimulus Interval (ISI)

Although Pavlov (1927) did not direct his experimental program to a detailing of the functional relationship between ISI and ease of conditioning, he did regard CRs established at an ISI of 5 sec. (or less) to be basic to the formation of CRs at more extended ISIs. Thus, to establish a long-trace CR in Pavlov's laboratory CRs were first established at an ISI of about 5 sec., and then on each successive day of training the UCS was postponed by 5 sec. until the desired interval was attained. To account for the occurrence of CRs in the time gap between CS offset and UCS onset, Pavlov postulated that the effective stimulus for the CR was neither the onset nor offset of the external CS, but was instead the neural aftereffects of the excitation caused by the CS. These neural aftereffects he called the stimulus trace.

Because Pavlov considered conditioning at CS–UCS intervals up to 5 sec. to be "simultaneous," it is commonly assumed that he found no important differences in ease of conditioning at ISIs from 0 to 5 sec. Whether or not this assumption is warranted, it soon became clear to early American investigators that little or no conditioning occurred at ISIs close to zero. This fact, coupled with Pavlov's observations of conditioning under long-trace procedures, created a problem for American learning theorists who adopted the commonsense notion of contiguity of the CS and UCS as a basis for the association of events in classical conditioning. Thus, the CS–UCS interval problem became one of explaining why separation of the CS and UCS is superior to contiguity. Accordingly, Guthrie (1933, 1935) postulated that the "true" CS is not the external CS, but the proprioceptive stimuli arising from the S's (postural and orienting) responses to the CS. To obtain conditioning Guthrie assumed that these proprioceptive stimuli must always be coincident with the UCR, and hence the most favorable interval for securing simultaneity of the "true" (proprioceptive) CS and UCR is one where the CS precedes the UCS by some small interval.

Optimal ISI. Although Guthrie's concept of proprioceptive stimuli could explain why forward CS–UCS intervals would be superior to an ISI of zero, the theory could not readily account for the possible superiority of a particular ISI (that is, optimal interval). On the other hand, Hull (1943, 1952), by extending Pavlov's notion of the stimulus trace, attempted to account for the frequently reported observation that an ISI of around 500 msec. appeared to be more effective than either shorter or longer intervals. Specifically, he postulated that the frequency (that is, intensity) of the neural stimulus trace, initiated by the external CS, undergoes a relatively rapid phase of recruitment, reaching a maximum frequency at 450 msec. and then subsides. Then, according to Hull, because of stimulus-intensity dynamism, conditioning would be most effective if the UCS is applied when the stimulus trace is at its maximum, whereas conditioning becomes progressively less effective when the UCS is applied at the time of the lesser trace intensities of the recruitment or subsidient phase. From these concepts Hull deduced that the function relating ISI and response probability would have approximately the same form as the stimulus trace, both being concave-down functions with maxima at 450 msec. Hull also employed the stimulus-trace formulation to account for the anticipatory character of the CR by contending that CRs conditioned to one point on a phase of the stimulus trace (determined by the specific ISI employed) generalize to other points on that phase and to points on the opposite phase, particularly from the subsidient to the recruitment phase.

Hull's assertion that the optimal interval for conditioning is approximately 500 msec. rested upon a variety of conditioning experiments, including the instrumental avoidance finger-withdrawal studies of Wolfle (1930, 1932), the instrumental avoidance leg-flexion study with rats of Kappauf and Schlosberg (1937), and classical eyelid conditioning investigations of Reynolds (1945), who employed a trace, and Kimble (1947), who used a delayed procedure. Although examination of Table 7-1 will indicate that the majority of studies reported optima at about 500 msec., it also reveals less agreement on the existence of this optimal interval than had been assumed by Hull. Thus, early ISI studies which disagreed with Hull's postulated optimum were Bernstein's (1934) human eyelid conditioning investigations and Wolfle's (1932) finger-withdrawal experiment, both of which reported an optimum of approximately 300 msec. More recent human conditioning studies have reported optimal conditioning at intervals ranging from 250 msec. for eyelid conditioning (McAllister, 1953) to 1,500 msec. for conditioning pupillary dilation (Gerrall and Woodward, 1958). Infrahuman studies have ranged from an optimum of 200 msec. for conditioning the rabbit's nictitating membrane response (Smith and Gormezano, 1965a) to 2,000 msec. for conditioning "bracing" (gross body movements) CRs in fish (Noble, Gruender, and Meyer, 1959) and rhesus monkeys (Noble and Harding, 1963).

The considerable variation in ISI functions has served to bring into serious question Hull's assumption of an invariant optimal interval. Many investigators now appear disposed to the notion that no single optimal interval exists and have begun to direct their experimental and theoretical efforts to isolating the factors responsible for the diversity of ISI functions. Thus, the observation of Adams, Hardesty, and Noble (cited by Noble and Adams, 1963), that the optimal ISI in the earthworm appears to be at least as long as

Table 7-1   Summary of Human and Infrahuman Studies Reporting an Optimum ISI

Investigator	Organism	Response	ISIs sampled (in msec.)	Optimum ISI
Bernstein (1934)	Human	Eyeblink	−900, −500, 100, 250, 300, 500, 1,000, 1,500	300
Bierbaum (1959)	Human	GSR	−3,000, 0, 500, 3,000, 5,000	3,000
Boice and Denny (1959)	Rat	Licking	500, 1,000, 2,000, 4,000, 6,000	2,000
Ebel and Prokasy (1963)	Human	Eyeblink	200, 500, 800	500
Fitzwater and Thrush (1956)	Human	Finger-withdrawal	0, 100, 200, 300, 400, 600	400
Gerall and Woodward (1958)	Human	Pupillary dilation	125, 500, 1,500, 2,500	1,500
Hansche and Grant (1960)	Human	Eyeblink	190, 390, 590, 790	390
Jones (1961)	Human	GSR and Finger-withdrawal	20, 235, 440, 660, 860, 1,045, 1,245	440 (GSR) 235 (Finger-withdrawal)
Kappauf and Schlosberg (1937)	Rat	Respiration	333, 666, 1,000, 2,000, 4,000	666
McAdam, Knott, and Chiorini (1965)	Cat	Leg flexion	250, 500, 1,000, 2,000	500
McAllister (1953)	Human	Eyeblink	100, 250, 450, 700, 2,500	250
Moeller (1954)	Human	GSR	250, 450, 1,000, 2,500	450
Noble and Adams	Fish (Mollienisia)	Body Movement	500, 2,000, 4,000	2,000
Noble, Greunder, and Meyer (1959)	Fish (Mollienisia)	Body Movement	500, 1,000, 1,500, 2,000, 3,000, 4,000	2,000
Noble and Harding (1963)	Rhesus monkey	Body	500, 1,000, 2,000, 4,000	2,000
Prokasy, Fawcett, and Hall (1962)	Human	GSR	0, 500, 1,000, 3,000, 5,000	500
Reynolds (1945)	Human	Eyeblink	250, 450, 1,150, 2,250	450
Smith and Gormezano (1965)	Rabbit	Nictitating membrane	−50, 0, 100, 200, 400, 800	200
Sproner and Kellogg (1947)	Human	Finger-withdrawal	−500, −250, 0, 500, 1,000, 1,500	500
White and Schlosberg (1952)	Human	GSR	0, 250, 500, 1,000, 2,000, 4,000	500
Wolfle (1930)	Human	Finger-withdrawal (avoidance)	−500, −250, 0, 250, 500, 750, 1,000, 1,250, 1,500	500
Wolfle (1932)	Human	Finger-withdrawal (avoidance)	−2,000, −1,000, −600, −200, 0, 200, 300, 400, 600, 1,000, 2,000, 3,000	300

4 sec. has prompted Noble and Adams to suggest that species differences in speed of neural transmission is responsible. According to this notion, the slower speed of neural transmission in inframammalians leads to the optimal ISI being longer than in mammals. Although species differences in neural transmission speed undoubtedly play a role, a factor that has come to receive considerable attention as an important determinant of ISI functions is the E's choice of response system.

Response-system Effects. The ISI values found to produce effective conditioning of autonomic responses have generally been longer than those found for skeletal responses. Ellison (1964), for example, has reported salivary conditioning at a 16-sec. ISI, Church and Black (1958) cardiac conditioning at a 20-sec. interval, and Kamin CER conditioning (presumably involving the autonomically mediated fear response) at a 3-min. ISI. On the other hand, there is little evidence of effective conditioning of skeletal responses beyond ISIs of 5 to 10 sec. (Fishbein and LeBlanc, 1967; McAllister, 1953; Schneiderman and Gormezano, 1964; Spooner and Kellogg, 1947). Ross (1961) has emphasized the skeletal-autonomic dichotomy even more sharply. He contends that skeletal responses have an optimal ISI of approximately 500 msec. and an upper ISI boundary value for conditioning of about 2,000 msec., whereas adequate autonomic conditioning occurs at ISIs in excess of 2,000 msec., with little evidence of conditioning at the presumed skeletal optimum of 500 msec.

Ross's (1961) contentions would appear to be seriously questioned by GSR conditioning studies reporting optimal ISIs of about 500 msec. (Moeller, 1954; Prokasy, Fawcett, and Hall, 1962; White and Schlosberg, 1952). Moeller (1954) has suggested that the conditioned GSR is merely an innate accompaniment of a skeletal "bracing" response that has been conditioned to the CS, whereas Smith (1954) has gone even further by proposing that all autonomic conditioning is merely an artifact of skeletal responding. According to such reasoning ISI functions for autonomic responses would simply be those existing for the skeletal response system mediating the autonomic behavior. However, Kimmel and Davidov (1967), taking concurrent measurement of muscle action potentials during conditioning of the GSR, failed to find evidence of skeletal mediation of the GSR. In view of recent methodological work (Leonard and Winokur, 1963; Prokasy and Ebel, 1967; Stewart, Stern, Winokur and Fredman, 1961) it is also likely that GSR studies reporting optimal ISIs of 500 msec. have been based on the inclusion of alpha (reflex) responses to the CS that have been maximally sensitized at that interval. Furthermore, the obtaining of heart-rate and salivary conditioning at ISIs longer than those found effective in skeletal conditioning, and evidence of heart rate (Black, 1965; Black, Carlson, and Solomon, 1962) and pupillary conditioning (Gerall and Obrist, 1962) when skeletal responses were precluded by paralyzing drugs, have all served to question seriously the extent to which differences in ISI functions can be attributed entirely to an autonomic-skeletal dichotomy. Investigators have thus looked to other differences among response systems.

Hilgard and Marquis (1940) were apparently the first to suggest that ISI effects may be related to the latency of the response system. They suggested that the optimal intervals for conditioning are those which are somewhat greater than the average CR latency of the particular response. This prediction was derived from their assumption that classical conditioning involves a gradient of reinforcement mechanism, such that CRs which are initiated closest in time to UCS onset are maximally reinforced. Long-latency response systems (for example, salivary) would be expected to have optima at ISIs longer than those of short-latency responses (for example, eyelid), because too short an interval would preclude the occurrence of their CRs before UCS onset.

The gradient of reinforcement interpretation of ISI effects has been theoretically attractive to a number of investigators (Boneau, 1958; Kimmel, 1965; Prokasy, 1965). However, one of the major difficulties of the Hilgard and Marquis formulation is its failure to account for the initial occurrence of the CR. Jones (1962), recognizing this problem, has presented an analysis of ISI effects in terms of contiguity and reinforcement gradients. Briefly, her analysis rests on the interpretation that when the ISI is varied two important temporal relationships are affected, the CS–UCS contiguity and CR–UCS reinforcement gradients. These contiguity and reinforcement gradients are assumed to be bidirectional and equal in their effects such that a temporal disparity in the backward direction (that is, UCR–CS or UCS–CR) will have the same effect as the occurrence of this disparity in the forward direction. Furthermore, the observed level of conditioning is presumed to be determined by the summation of these gradients.

Because in the Jones formulation the effective temporal gradients are dependent upon the latency of the CR and UCR, the implication (as with Hilgard and Marquis) is that no single ISI value can be chosen which is optimal for all response systems. Of interest is her delineation of how CRs are initiated and maintained. According to the theory, unless the temporal proximity of the CS and UCR is arranged to fall within the effective (unspecified) range of the contiguity gradient, CRs will never occur. However, once CRs are established the CR–UCS reinforcement gradient begins to play a role and increases in importance until over the course of training the effects of the contiguity gradient on response strength become negligible by comparison. Because the CR–UCS gradi-

ent is assumed to operate chiefly during the later stages of training, the theory would appear to predict that CR latency would either remain fixed or move toward UCS onset as the probability of CR occurrence increases. On the other hand, the frequent observation that for a given ISI CR latencies decrease over the course of training (Ebel and Prokasy, 1963; Gormezano, Schneiderman, Deaux, and Fuentes, 1962; Schneiderman and Gormezano, 1964; Suboski, 1967) is inconsistent with Jones' formulations or for that matter with any extant gradient of reinforcement interpretation of CC. Decreases in CR latency operate to *decrease* rather than increase the effects of a presumed reinforcement gradient. Although there are other implications of the theory that may be questioned, one of particular interest is the expectation that effective backward conditioning can be obtained. We will defer consideration of this problem to a later point.

In retrospect it is, perhaps, surprising that for over twenty years, one of the main problems students of classical conditioning have centered on is the determination of the "optimal" ISI. Granting that for these many years the search of numerous investigators has been generated by the simple assumption that the same two events are associated at different ISIs, with variation only in the degree to which they have been associated, the fact remains that the results of these studies have not been as "fruitless" as some investigators have indicated (see Bitterman, 1965). Out of these studies has come the clear recognition that there is probably no invariant optimal ISI and that no present theoretical view encompasses all the empirical data on fixed ISI effects. One consequence has been a renewed interest in the effects of shifting the ISI within blocks of acquisition trials. As might be expected, Pavlov (1927) was the first to concern himself with ISI shifts, but as we shall see the current impetus has come from formulations (see Boneau, 1958; Prokasy, 1965) proposing that the response characteristics of classically conditioned responses, like those of instrumentally conditioned responses, are "shaped" by the reinforcement contingencies in the situation.

ISI SHIFTS. Pavlov (1927) observed that if over the course of training the ISI was gradually increased from a relatively short (for example, 5 sec.) to a long ISI (for example, 2 min.), there occurred a progressive delay in CR latency to the point where it just anticipated UCS onset. On the other hand, Pavlov noted that if the shift from short to long ISI was done suddenly (that is, without training at intermediate ISI values), a number of trials elapsed in which no CRs occurred, but eventually CRs would begin to appear just prior to UCS onset. The observed delay in CR latency under both shift procedures Pavlov called inhibition of delay and considered it to be the result of inhibitory processes similar to that acquired by the CS in experimental extinction (1927, pp. 99–100).

The phenomenon of inhibition of delay would appear to be consistent with theoretical formulations advocating the presence of a CR–UCS temporal reinforcement gradient. However, of particular relevance to the validity of such formulations is the question of whether the phenomenon of inhibition of delay is typical of the development of CRs of Ss trained throughout at long ISIs or whether it is uniquely determined by the employment of an ISI shift procedure. A number of human and infrahuman eyelid conditioning studies (Ebel and Prokasy, 1963; Prokasy and Papsdorf, 1965; Schneiderman, 1966; Schneiderman and Gormezano, 1964) have revealed that for groups trained throughout at long (as well as short) ISIs, CR latency decreased over trials, whereas groups trained with progressive increases in the ISI (Ebel and Prokasy, 1963; Prokasy and Papsdorf, 1965) demonstrated proportional increases in CR latency. Although there has been a reported instance of inhibition of delay

under a fixed ISI procedure for GSR conditioning (Kimmel, 1965), Pavlov himself noted that, "On continuing the experiments with the chosen interval of time the secretion progressively increases, and at the same time its commencement shifts further along towards the beginning of the conditioned stimulus . . ." (1927, p. 89). Thus, even by Pavlov's account it would appear that inhibition of delay, defined as an increase in CR latency over trials, is dependent upon a successive ISI shift procedure.

Ellison (1964) and Colavita (1965), on the basis of their salivary conditioning studies with dogs, have suggested that the definition of inhibition of delay be expanded to include instances where there is no withholding of the CR with training *per se*, but where there is a progressive increase in the temporal locus of maximum salivary flow toward the point of UCS application. Ellison, for example, employing fixed ISI conditions of 8 and 16 sec. and interspersing CS-alone test trials, found that over trials the peak amplitude of the salivary response moved away from CS onset toward the point of UCS application, and he called this trend "inhibition of delay." However, it is questionable whether such a peak amplitude shift can be considered compatible with the usual interpretation given to the phenomenon of inhibition of delay. Smith (1966), in conditioning the nictitating membrane response (that is, third eyelid) in rabbits at ISIs of 125, 250, 500, or 1,000 msec. for ten daily sessions of 110 trials per day, observed that although over the course of training the temporal locus of the peak amplitude of CRs in all groups increased back toward the point of UCS application, there was also a concurrent *decrease* in CR latency. Because the theoretical significance of the phenomenon of inhibition of delay has been the notion that the earlier segments of the CS acquire inhibitory properties that act to delay initiation of the CR, Smith's observations make the suggestions of Ellison and Colavita appear untenable.

Although a shift in the temporal locus of the peak amplitude of the CR appears incompatible with an inhibition-of-delay interpretation, it is not necessarily incompatible with a response-shaping analysis of classical conditioning. Prokasy (1965), the most articulate proponent of response shaping, has argued that in instrumental conditioning paradigms E can manipulate quite precisely some specified topographical characteristic of the response by making the reinforcing event contingent upon its occurrence (for example, duration), whereas in classical conditioning there is no behavioral criterion for presentation of the UCS and whether or not there is "reinforcement" when the UCS is delivered depends upon what S does in the situation. According to such an interpretation, then, a shift in the temporal locus of peak amplitude of CRs toward the point of UCS application is the result of differential reinforcement (shaping) of a topographical characteristic of the CR that maximizes the reinforcement available in the situation (for example, maximum salivary flow at a point just prior to application of an acid UCS is presumed to reduce the noxiousness of the acid by diluting it, hence this component of the response becomes strengthened). Considered in more general terms, the response-shaping hypothesis assumes that the reinforcing event in classical conditioning is the overlap of the CR and UCS with topographical characteristics of the CR established at a particular ISI, reflecting differential reinforcement of those components that maximize the reinforcement inherent in such overlap.

Logan (1956) had earlier utilized the construct of response differentiation to illustrate how a quantitative theory of instrumental learning based upon reinforcement of specific characteristics of a response can be developed. For example, a bar-press response of specified duration may be reinforced while responses of other durations are not. The response so established is considered as a distinct micromolar response rather than merely a gradation of the same molar response. Similarly, the response-shaping analysis of classical conditioning assumes, for example, that CRs of different latencies are different responses; those CRs that overlap the UCS increase in response strength, whereas CRs that do not would tend to extinguish. One implication of so considering CRs of different latencies (or other topographical characteristics) as different responses is that once they are established at a particular ISI a shift in the ISI should lead to their undergoing extinction while responses appropriate to the new ISI are established. Boneau (1958), employing the human eyelid conditioning situation, was the first to provide detailed information on this point.

In the Boneau study a group was trained for fifty trials at an ISI of 0.5 sec. and was then divided into two subgroups to receive another 100 trials at an ISI of 1.0 or 1.5 sec. In addition, two control groups were run that received all 150 training trials at an ISI of either 1.0 or 1.5 sec. The percentage CR acquisition curves following the ISI shift in the two subgroups were then compared with the acquisition curves of the respective controls. Figure 7-1 presents the results of such a comparison for the 0.5–1.0 shift and 1.0 sec. control group. The similarity in acquisition functions for these groups (as well as for the 0.5–1.5 shift and 1.5 sec. control group) led Boneau to conclude that previous conditioning at the shorter ISI had no effect on percentage CR acquisition at the longer interval. These findings also led him to infer that the increase in CR latency observed after the ISI shift was produced not by the CR gradually sliding through the interval toward the point of UCS application, but by the extinction of short-latency CRs and the *independent* acquisition of new long-latency CRs.

According to the response-shaping (or micromolar) analysis of ISI shift effects, evidence of the kind provided by Boneau to support the notion of independence of performance at one ISI from performance demonstrated at a previous ISI will depend upon the parameters employed. When the ISI shift is made in one large step as in the Boneau study, it would be assumed that there is little opportunity for the previously acquired short-latency responses to be reinforced (that is, CR–UCS overlap), and hence, they will undergo extinction while long-latency CRs are being acquired at the new ISI. On the other hand, when the shift from a short to long ISI is made in relatively small increments, the rate of extinction of previously established short-latency CRs would be expected to be retarded by the occasional reinforcement of responses of more sustained duration. Accordingly, one would expect a gradual increase in CR latency and duration and little change in CR frequency.

Prokasy, Ebel, and Thompson (1963) have provided evidence on this point. Three groups were run in a human eyelid conditioning study: one group (Group 6–25) received training at an ISI of 630 msec. for 300 trials and was then switched to an ISI of 2,497 msec. for sixty trials; another (Group 25) received an ISI of 2,497 msec. for all 360 trials; and the third (Group E) received ISIs of 630 msec. for forty trials, 791 msec. for forty trials, 996 msec. for fifty trials, 1,246 msec. for fifty trials, 1,570 msec. for sixty trials, 1,977 msec. for sixty trials, and 2,497 msec. for the last sixty trials. The percentage CR curves of these groups are presented in blocks of twenty training trials in Figure 7-2. As can be seen, Group E maintained a high level of responding throughout the successive shifts in ISI, illustrating how under such a procedure eyelid CRs can be acquired and maintained at a usually ineffective terminal ISI value. Group 25 responded on an average of just under 30 per cent for the last 300 trials, whereas Group 6–25, upon being switched to an ISI of 2,497 msec., demonstrated a drop from an 80 per cent level of responding to one just above that of Group 25. Although, as expected, Group E demonstrated a progressive increase in CR latency with each successive increase in ISI, it was a later analysis (Prokasy, 1965, p. 219) which revealed that following each shift the responses were also of longer duration.

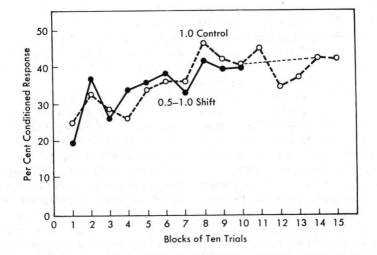

Figure 7-1. Comparison of responses for 0.5–1.0 Shift Group and 1.0 Control Group. (Reprinted with permission from Boneau, C. A. The interstimulus interval and the latency of the conditioned eyelid response. *J. exp. Psychol.*, 1958, **56**, 464–472.)

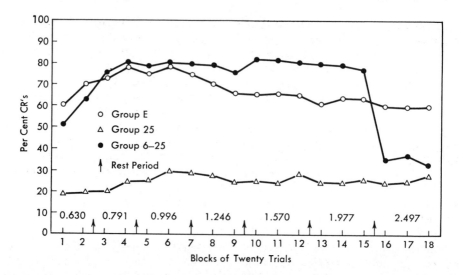

Figure 7-2. Percentage of conditioned responses as a function of blocks of twenty training trials. The arrows indicate the points at which brief rest periods of 30–50 sec. were introduced; the numerical values between the arrows indicate ISI, in sec., for Group E. (Reprinted with permission from Prokasy, W. F., Ebel, H. C., and Thompson, D. D. Response shaping at long interstimulus intervals in classical eyelid conditioning. *J. exp. Psychol.*, 1963, **66**, 138–141.)

Because in the response-shaping analysis performance changes associated with ISI shifts would appear to depend upon factors affecting the rates of extinction of "old" responses and acquisition of "new" responses, learning-rate parameters associated with species differences may be expected to be an important contributor to the rate of change. Gormezano and his associates have repeatedly observed that the rates of acquisition and extinction of the eyelid and nictitating membrane response of the rabbit are substantially lower than that in human eyelid conditioning (Gormezano, Schneiderman, Deaux, and Fuentes, 1962; Schneiderman and Gormezano, 1964; Smith and Gormezano, 1965).

Prokasy and Papsdorf (1965), paralleling the procedures employed in the Prokasy, Ebel, and Thompson study, investigated the effects of ISI shifts on conditioning of the nictitating membrane response. Group I received twenty-two seventy-one-trial sessions at an ISI of 2,500 msec.; Group II received seventeen sessions at an ISI of 400 msec., followed by two sessions each,

at successive ISIs of 650, 900, 1,200, 1,500, 1,800, and 2,150 msec., and the final five sessions at 2,500 msec. The particularly relevant finding was the observation that in contrast to the human eyelid conditioning study, the group shifted from a 400- to a 2,500-msec. ISI demonstrated a slow and modest decrease in the percentage of CRs and never declined to the level of responding to the 2,500-msec. control condition.

Consistent with the response-shaping hypothesis, the results of a nictitating membrane conditioning study by Leonard and Theios (1967) support the notion that the slow decline in responding observed in the Prokasy and Papsdorf investigation was due to the gradual extinction of short and concurrent acquisition of long-latency CRs. In their study the performance of rabbits trained for 120 trials was compared with that of two control groups receiving all their training at either the 250- or 1,000-msec. ISI. The percentage CR curve of the shift group revealed that when any response occurring throughout the 1,000-msec. postshift interval was scored as a CR there was (as in the Prokasy and Papsdorf study) only a small response decrement following the shift. However, examination of the latency distribution of CRs over successive thirds of the 100 postshift trials (see Figure 7-3) revealed a gradual decrease in "old" (that is, CRs with latencies under 250 msec.) and an increase in "new" responses (that is, CRs with latencies over 250 msec.).

The preceding ISI shift studies strongly support the notion that a learned time discrimination may be a major component of what Ss learn in the classical conditioning situation. Specifically, the time discrimination hypothesis assumes that a CR must overlap the UCS for reinforcement to occur, and that an important part of what Ss learn is when to make the response.

Ebel and Prokasy (1963) have proposed that the time discrimination hypothesis may provide an interpretation of ISI conditioning functions. They have suggested that

the function relating CR frequency and ISI reflects the relative difficulty of the temporal discrimination required for maximizing the CR–UCS reinforcement contingency. According to Ebel and Prokasy, then, the increase in CR latency usually observed with increases in fixed ISI values reflects response shaping that maximizes the reinforcement through CR–UCS overlap, whereas the increase in variability of response latencies as ISI is lengthened reflects the increased difficulty of the temporal discrimination problem of responding to overlap the UCS.

The time discrimination hypothesis has also been invoked as an explanatory mechanism to account for the diversity of ISI functions observed among response systems. Specifically, Boneau (1958) and Schneiderman (1964, 1966) have suggested that if strength of conditioning is a function of the ease with which a particular ISI permits a CR to overlap the UCS, then

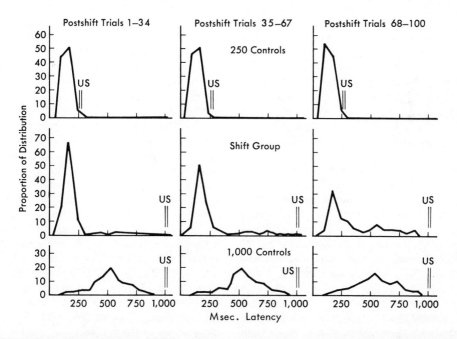

Figure 7-3. Distributions of CRs of various latencies over successive thirds of 100 postshift trials for shift groups (250 to 1,000 msec.) and two control groups. (Reprinted with permission from Leonard, D. W., and Theios, J. Classical eyelid conditioning in the rabbit under prolonged single alternating conditions of reinforcement. *J. comp. physiol. Psychol.*, 1967, **63**, 355–358.)

response systems whose functional characteristics permit sustained duration of the CR, will tend to have higher probabilities of such an overlap, and thus require a less precise temporal discrimination. The consequence is that long-duration response systems (for example, salivary, heart rate) would be expected to condition over a more extended range of ISIs than short-duration response systems (for example, eyelid, finger withdrawal, leg flexion).

Although response shaping and temporal discrimination mechanisms appear relevant to ISI effects, based as they are on the assumption of a CR–UCS reinforcement contingency, these mechanisms do not readily account for the initial occurrence of the CR. Perhaps the revising of Jones' (1962) two-process theory of CR–UCS contiguity and CR–UCS reinforcement to include response-shaping and temporal-discrimination mechanisms would provide the most attractive theoretical account of ISI effects. Under such a revision initial occurrence of the CR would be determined by the CS–UCR contiguity process, whereas response shaping and temporal discrimination mechanisms would be assumed to contribute to the CR–UCS reinforcement process. However, as consideration of backward conditioning will reveal, aspects of Jones' CS–UCR contiguity formulation also appear to be in need of revision.

Backward Conditioning. At one time Pavlov (1927, p. 27) regarded backward conditioning as impossible; later he revised his opinion (Pavlov, 1928, p. 381), holding that although backward conditioning is possible, the response established by this procedure is, at best, weak and unstable. Hull (1929), emphasizing as did Pavlov (1927) the biological utility arising from the organism being able to react to signals presented prior to the UCS, concluded that conditioning would not occur in the backward paradigm. Although there were early reports of successful backward conditioning of the eyelid (Bernstein, 1934; Switzer,

1930) and finger-withdrawal response (Wolfle, 1930, 1932), later studies in which a pseudoconditioning control group was run (Grether, 1938; Harlow, 1939; Fitzwater and Reisman, 1952) indicated that backward ISIs did not produce effects significantly different from those attributable to pseudoconditioning. It was Spooner and Kellogg (1947), however, on the basis of their finger-withdrawal study, who most clearly articulated the notion that forward and backward conditioning are fundamentally different processes, with the latter being a form of pseudoconditioning. Such a conclusion is consistent with the Darwinian biological utility formulations of Pavlov and Hull. There are several theoretical positions (Guthrie, 1933, 1935; Jones, 1962), however, in which there is assumed to be no qualitative difference in forward and backward temporal arrangements, and perhaps it is because of them that an interest in backward conditioning has persisted.

In Guthrie's (1933, 1935) formulations conditioning depends simply upon the coincidence of internal movement-produced cues, arising from the organism's movements to the external CS, and the UCR. Forward conditioning is postulated to be more effective than backward conditioning because the CS initiates a movement series of indefinite length and in the forward procedure any phase of the movement series can act to provide the proprioceptive cues coincident with the UCR. In contrast, because successful backward conditioning also depends on the UCR occurring in the presence of CS-produced movement cues, under a long backward ISI the UCR may no longer be present and hence no conditioning will occur. Even under a short backward ISI, if the UCR has a short latency, the UCR may be over before the movement-produced cues arise, and again no conditioning would occur. Thus, for Guthrie backward conditioning is theoretically possible; it is simply that the range of backward ISIs which would assure contiguity of movement-produced cues and the

UCR are more restricted than that required for forward conditioning.

Jones' (1962) two-process theory of classical conditioning also assumes that backward conditioning simply emerges as a special case of ISI effects, rather than differing qualitatively from forward conditioning. Recall that this theory views conditioning as involving the two conceptually independent processes of contiguity and reinforcement. In the contiguity process it is assumed that the closer in time (irrespective of order) the CS and UCR, the greater is the increment per trial in the capacity of the CS to evoke the CR. Once the contiguity process has caused some CRs to occur, the reinforcement process then begins to play its role such that the closer in time the CR is to the UCS (irrespective of order) the greater the increment per trial in the CR-evoking capacity of the CS. The summative effects of these two processes are assumed to determine observed response probability on any particular trial. It is in the early trials of training, however, when contiguity is the major contributor to change in response probability, that backward presentation of the CS and UCS is assumed to have its maximum effect. Because the UCR always has some finite latency from UCS onset, the closest temporal proximity of the CS and UCR would be achieved when the UCS precedes the CS by exactly the UCR latency. The CS and UCR would then occur simultaneously, and on the basis of the contiguity process alone the fastest initial conditioning would be expected under such a backward temporal arrangement. However, once CRs have begun to occur the reinforcement process is assumed to alter the dominant role of contiguity.

Champion and Jones (1961) have provided some evidence in support of backward conditioning occurring early in GSR training. They observed a slightly greater increase in GSR amplitude following a single backward-conditioning trial at a 750-msec. ISI than following a single forward-conditioning trial at a 500-msec. ISI or a pseudoconditioning control trial. Additional support has been provided by the GSR data of Champion (1962) and Trapold, Homzie, and Rutledge (1964). In the Champion study a faster initial rise in the GSR conditioning function was observed when the UCS preceded the CS by 1,200 msec. rather than when it preceded it by 2,800 msec. or followed it by 400 msec.; and in the study by Trapold et al. a greater increase in GSR amplitude occurred following a single conditioning trial at a 1,500-msec. backward ISI than for a 40-msec. backward interval. However, in the Champion study concurrent training of the eyelid response and in the Trapold et al. study concurrent training of the eyelid and finger-withdrawal response failed to reveal evidence of backward conditioning of these response systems.

These latter findings, in conjunction with the findings of earlier backward conditioning studies, would appear to restrict the generality of Jones' theoretical expectations of backward conditioning. Whether the theory only describes what happens in GSR conditioning or is applicable to other response systems not yet investigated (for example, heart rate, pupillary dilation, and so on) remains an empirical problem. On the other hand, the question can be raised as to whether backward conditioning has in fact been unequivocally demonstrated for the GSR. In both the Champion and Trapold et al. studies the purported evidence for backward conditioning of the GSR is seriously questioned by their failure to include a pseudoconditioning control group. Furthermore, although Champion and Jones (1961) reported a strikingly superior GSR performance curve for a 750-msec. backward ISI group, this control group differed in a number of parameters (for example, more variable UCS durations, greater number of CS exposures, and so on) not dictated by the pseudoconditioning procedure itself. Hence, substantive evidence for backward conditioning of even the GSR is still lacking.

Intertrial Interval (ITI)

Although it has long been recognized that learning is facilitated when trials are spaced rather than massed, the most powerful effects of trial distribution have appeared in such relatively complex learning situations as verbal and motor learning with human Ss, and serial maze learning with animal Ss. However, the theoretical formulations of Hull (1943, 1952) as related to time-dependent processes in learning and in particular those of Estes (1955a; 1955b; 1959, pp. 424–29), have recently generated considerable interest in the effects of ITI in classical conditioning. Broadly conceived, Hull's constructs of reactive inhibition (I_r) and conditioned inhibition $(_sI_r)$ localize the effects of time-dependent processes primarily within the organism, whereas Estes' stimulus-fluctuation model attributes time-dependent processes to variation in the external stimulus environment. Because the classical-conditioning paradigm is commonly regarded as a learning situation permitting the investigation of a "simple" response under a high degree of stimulus control, it has come to be considered as an ideal paradigm in which to assess these alternative theoretical formulations of ITI effects.

Postasymptotic Performance. Hovland (1936), in extinguishing the classically conditioned GSR in groups of Ss given eight or twenty-four conditioning trials, reported an initial rise in the extinction performance curve for the twenty-four-trial acquisition group. This initial rise Hovland attributed to the aftereffects of *inhibition of reinforcement*, a term coined by him to suggest that under conditions of massed reinforcement, a sufficient number of trials will eventually lead to a decrement in the strength of the conditioned response. Although Estes' stimulus fluctuation model has not addressed itself to this problem, Hull (1943, pp. 189–91) formalized the "inhibition of reinforcement" notion into

one of the corollaries of his system. In general, this corollary predicts that continued massed reinforcements (that is, relatively short ITIs) produce enough I_r (reactive inhibition built up with each reponse evocation) to offset eventually the effects of reinforcement, thus resulting in a gradual performance decrement over extended training. Critical to the prediction of a performance decrement is the assumption of inhibition building up each time a response is made without adequate time for this "fatigue" effect to dissipate between trials.

Although many secondary sources (Bugelski, 1956, pp. 166, 287, 349; Deese, 1958, p. 53) assume that postasymptotic decrements in performance occur over extended training, a critical review of the literature by Prokasy (1960) led him to conclude that only two instances of an acquisition performance decrement related to massed reinforced trials have appeared in the classical-conditioning literature. In both instances the reported decrements are based on the data of one S: one dog in the salivary conditioning preparation (Pavlov, 1927) and one human S in classical eyelid conditioning (Hilgard, 1933). Aside from the limited generality of these two findings, Prokasy's critique suggests that few studies have employed a sufficient number of postasymptotic trials to reveal possible decrements. More recently, however, a number of eyelid conditioning studies have appeared utilizing procedures wherein hundreds of conditioning trials have been given within or across sessions (Ebel and Prokasy, 1963; Krauss and Prokasy, 1963; Papsdorf, Prokasy, and Gormezano, 1964; Prokasy, Ebel, and Thompson, 1963; Prokasy and Whaley, 1963; Runquist and Muir, 1965).

Of these studies, only three have reported a progressive postasymptotic decrement (Papsdorf, Prokasy, and Gormezano, 1964; Prokasy and Whaley, 1963; Runquist and Muir, 1965). However, despite their apparent reliability, the evidence for the general occurrence of postasymptotic decrements is not particularly compelling because even in these studies the average decrease was not large. The largest reported decrement was 15 per cent, observed over the last four of twenty conditioning sessions of seventy trials per session in conditioning of the nictitating membrane response of the rabbit to a corneal air puff (Papsdorf, Prokasy, and Gormezano, 1964). That this decrement is probably not due to the building up of an inhibitory process, but instead to S's adaptation to the corneal puff, is indicated by other nictitating membrane studies involving para-orbital shock as the reinforcer in which no intrasession decrements have been observed when even shorter ITIs and more conditioning trials within and across days have been employed (Coleman, Patterson, and Gormezano, 1966). In summary, then, little evidence exists for post-asymptotic decrements attributable to "inhibition of reinforcement."

Acquisition. Although several classical-conditioning studies (Baron, 1952; Vandermeer and Amsel, 1952) have failed to find a relationship between ITI and acquisition performance, the majority of studies (Humphreys, 1940; Reynolds, 1945; Spence and Norris, 1950; Prokasy, Grant, and Myers, 1958) have found superior performance under longer ITIs. In the Spence and Norris (1950) study, four groups of Ss received eyelid conditioning training at average ITIs of 9, 15, 30, or 90 sec. The results indicated that at least for the shortest and longest ITI values, performance varied directly with length of the ITI. Prokasy, Grant, and Myers (1958), employing three average ITIs of 15, 45, and 135 sec., also observed the same ordered effect.

The fact that in classical conditioning response probability increases more rapidly in acquisition with spaced than with massed trials can be accounted for either by Hull's or Estes' formulation of time-dependent processes. Hull's construct of reactive inhibition (1952, p. 9) yields this result

because reducing the time between trials also reduces the amount of time available or the dissipation of response-produced inhibition, with the consequence of a reduction in overall response probability. Estes' stimulus-fluctuation model provides a similar prediction based on the fluctuation of stimulus elements in and out of a population of elements conceived to be available for sampling and conditioning on a particular trial. However, different predictions follow from these formulations when they are applied to response probability following individual ITI values.

In the usual study of ITI effects different groups of Ss are trained at different average ITIs, but for any one group there is usually some variation in the exact interval to minimize any possible temporal conditioning (for example, for an ITI of 20 sec., a range of ITI values of 5 to 30 sec. with an average of 20 sec. may be employed). Thus, if a set of ITI values, say, 5, 10, 15, 20, 25, and 30 sec., is given for many trials in a random order, it is possible by regrouping the data of each S to obtain response probabilities separately for trials following each ITI value. Because of the depressing influence of reactive inhibition, Hull's formulation should predict an increase in response probability going from 5 to 30 sec. On the other hand, Estes' stimulus-fluctuation model assumes a time-dependent correlation between the sample of elements drawn on successive trials, such that the correlation decreases with increasing time between trials. The result of this initially high, but decreasing correlation, should be a decrease in response probability following an increase in each ITI value.

Prokasy and his associates have performed several eyelid conditioning experiments concerned with assessing response probabilities following variations in ITI values within individual Ss. Prokasy and Whaley (1961), in a study involving an average ITI of 17.5 sec. and 679 trials administered in seven sessions, found no correlation between response probability and various ITI values (5, 10, 15, 20, 25, and 30 sec.). Prokasy and Whaley (1963), consistent with Hull's formulation, found a slight, though reliable, positive relationship between response probability and length of individual ITI values. On the other hand, Kraus and Prokasy (1963), in support of the Estes model, found a higher response probability following a 5-sec. ITI than a 50-sec. ITI when just these two values were randomly ordered within Ss. No differences, however, were observed for another group of Ss given only 5- and 30-sec. ITIs. Subsequently, Prokasy (1965) employing average ITIs shorter than those in his previous investigations, again observed a positive correlation between response probability and length of the immediately preceding ITI value. However, examination of response probability following the first of two successive occurrences of extreme ITI values for an average ITI condition (for example, 2- and 14-sec. ITIs for an 8-sec. ITI condition) revealed a higher response probability for the second of two successive 2-sec. ITIs than for the second of two successive 14-sec. ITIs. This finding is consistent with Estes' stimulus-fluctuation model.

Although radically different predictions follow from the formulations of Hull and Estes when applied to the sequence of different ITIs analyzed within Ss during acquisition, the results of the experiments of Prokasy and his associates have not provided unambiguous support for either formulation of time-dependent effects. Prokasy (1965) has suggested that much of the effects of ITI observed in within-Ss designs may be accounted for by Ss having acquired temporal cues on the basis of the distribution of trials. According to Prokasy, the acquisition of such temporal cues is determined by such factors as the discriminability of the particular ITI values employed, the likelihood of particular ITI values succeeding themselves, and the amount of redundancy in the temporal distribution.

Extinction and Spontaneous Recovery. The general fact of extinction is that following acquisition training an extended series of nonreinforced CS presentations leads to a weakening of the CR. On the other hand, after the CR has been weakened or eliminated by extinction, a period of rest (usually removal from the conditioning situation) followed by another extinction session may reveal that in the early trials at least, the response has recovered. The recovery of an extinguished CR in a second extinction series following a rest interval is referred to as spontaneous recovery. Although extinction has been studied as a function of the ITI employed in acquisition, we will only concern ourselves with the effects of ITI variation in extinction on the course of extinction and spontaneous recovery.

One of the earliest investigations of ITI effects in extinction was that reported by Pavlov (1927, p. 52). He observed that for ITIs of 2, 4, or 8 min. between successive nonreinforced presentations of the CS, extinction of the salivary responses was complete in 15, 20, and 54 min. respectively, whereas for a 16-min. ITI, extinction was incomplete after two hours. Pavlov concluded from these data that the shorter the ITI the more quickly will the response be extinguished. However, Pavlov's data do not in fact provide support for this conclusion; if the data are examined in terms of the number of CS trials required for extinction (obtained by dividing the ITI into the total time required for extinction), there is little difference. Furthermore, recent studies (Porter, 1939; Reynolds, 1945; Grant, Schipper, and Ross, 1952; Howat and Grant, 1958; Beeman, Hartman, and Grant, 1960) investigating the role of ITI in extinction have not yielded consistent findings. In conditioning the eyelid response Porter (1939), Grant, Schipper, and Ross (1952), and Beeman, Hartman, and Grant (1960) were unable to find that the distribution of extinction trials significantly affected resistance to extinction. Reynolds (1945) observed greater resistance to extinction under spaced trials, whereas just the reverse was observed by Howat and Grant (1960).

In the Howat and Grant (1958) study all Ss received acquisition trials with a random ITI averaging 35 sec. until they gave eight CRs in ten successive trials. After each S had reached criterion extinction was instituted at a massed or spaced ITI to a criterion of five consecutive trials on which no CR occurred. The Ss in the massed group were given extinction trials with an average ITI of 7.5 sec. and those in the spaced group an average ITI of 35 sec. Interestingly enough, the manner in which the spaced group demonstrated less resistance to extinction was precisely as would be predicted by Estes' stimulus-fluctuation model (1955b) and contrary to that of Hull (1943, 1952). According to Hull, massing extinction trials does not permit response-produced inhibition (I_r) to dissipate, and hence accelerates response decrements in extinction. The Estes theory would hold that although in the early extinction trials the decrements would be more rapid under massed trials, extinction would later be more rapid under spaced trials (1955b, p. 376). The Howat and Grant (1958) study observed this cross-over.

As regards the role of ITI in extinction upon spontaneous recovery, both the formulations of Hull and Estes would predict that when extinction is carried out to a criterion, spontaneous recovery would be greater under massed extinction conditions. For Hullian theory this is derived from the greater reactive inhibition presumed to develop under massed extinction and its dissipation in the rest interval prior to testing for spontaneous recovery. The Estes theory would hold that because of stimulus fluctuation massing extinction trials permits fewer of the conditioned stimulus elements to be available for extinction. During the spontaneous recovery period following massed extinction trials, however, more CS elements diffuse into the population available for extinction. Of the

classical-conditioning studies concerned with the effect of distribution of extinction trials on spontaneous recovery (Howat and Grant, 1958; Beeman, Hartman, and Grant, 1960), the results have not been encouraging to either theory; there was no discernible effect of massed or spaced distribution of extinction trials on spontaneous recovery.

Manipulations of the UCS

In considering the effects of intensity and duration of the UCS in classical conditioning brief consideration must be given to theoretical formulations that have provided the major impetus for research in this area. The principal formulations have been contiguity and effect theories of conditioning. In the contiguity formulation (Guthrie, 1935; Estes, 1959) the role of the UCS is presumed to assure the occurrence of the response (UCR) in the presence of the CS such that if the UCS occurs in the appropriate temporal relationship with the CS, the response becomes conditioned to the CS. For contiguity theory manipulations of the UCS are assumed to effect conditioning by varying the vigor (for example, amplitude, duration) of the UCR. On the other hand, although effect theories hold that contiguity is an essential condition, they contend that in addition to the UCS providing contiguity of the CS and UCR, the UCS must have motivational properties. Hence, a basic difference between contiguity and effect theory is whether one or two properties of the UCS are deemed essential for conditioning.

Although effect theorists agree that the UCS must have motivational properties differences exist as to the proposed mechanisms by which the motivational properties of the UCS operate to effect conditioning. Hull (1943, 1952), consistent with his analysis of instrumental conditioning, has held to a drive-reduction interpretation which assumes that onset or offset of a UCS is drive-reducing, thus, these events occurring in close temporal proximity to the UCR strengthen the associative bond of the UCR to the CS. According to this formulation, in classical reward conditioning UCS onset is the drive-reducing (reinforcing) event, and in classical defense conditioning it is UCS offset. Alternately, Spence (1956) has offered what may be termed a general-effect interpretation in which it is recognized that the UCS must have motivational properties, but no special hypothesis (such as drive reduction) is proposed as to the mechanism by which the UCS is reinforcing. Another effect type of formulation has stressed the presumed adaptive effects of the CR on the UCS, and essentially assigns a drive-reducing role to the CR (Schlosberg, 1937; Hilgard and Marquis, 1940; Prokasy, 1965). In this formulation the CRs are assumed to be acquired and maintained through drive reduction in a manner similar to that advocated for instrumental conditioning. In classical defense conditioning the CRs are presumed to attenuate the aversive properties of the UCS (for example, an eyeblink CR that overlaps the presentation of an air puff UCS precludes the UCS from falling on the more sensitive cornea), whereas in classical reward conditioning the CRs are assumed to potentiate the appetitive properties of the UCS (for example, the secretion of salivary CRs prior to presentation of food, facilitates the mastication and swallowing of the food UCS).

UCS Intensity. Although Pavlov (1927) recognized that hunger was a variable influencing appetitive salivary conditioning, little systematic attention has been given to assessing the effects of manipulating the intensive properties of the UCS (for example, extent of deprivation, amount of food, and so on) in classical reward conditioning. The few studies that have been conducted indicate that strength of salivary conditioning is an increasing function of amount of food (Gantt, 1938); conditioned licking in rats to a squirt of water is an increasing function of water need (DeBold, Miller, and Jensen, 1965) as is conditioned jawing (swallowing) in rabbits (Smith, DiLollo, and Gormezano, 1966; Coleman, Patterson, and Gormezano, 1966). A positive relationship between UCS intensity and CR frequency has also been amply demonstrated in a variety of classical defense conditioning studies (Passey, 1948; Dykman and Gantt, 1951; Spence, 1953; Prokasy, Grant, and Myers, 1958; Gormezano and Moore, 1962). Theoretically, this positive relationship provides no differential support for either contiguity or effect theory because both would predict the same functional relationship. However, effect theorists, and in particular those operating within a Hullian framework, have had to concern themselves with a number of implications of the observed empirical relationship of UCS intensity and CR frequency in classical defense conditioning.

According to the Hullian view, the development of the associative factor, habit strength (H), of a classically conditioned response is a positive function of the occurrence and intensity of the UCS. This assumption, taken in conjunction with the additional assumption that drive level (D) in classical defense conditioning, at least, is also a function of the intensity of the UCS, implies that the differences in performance level obtained with different intensities of the UCS reflect differences in both H and D. This implication derives from the Hullian interpretation that CR frequency is a multiplicative function of H and D, that is $R = H \times D$. One problem in testing this formulation for classical defense conditioning is the devising of experimental means for separating out the effects of UCS intensity and H and D. Another difficulty is the specification of the source of drive on any particular conditioning trial. Because CRs occur prior to the application of the UCS, appeal cannot be made to the UCS on that particular trial as the source of drive. Spence and his associates (Spence, 1953; Spence, 1958; Spence, Haggard, and Ross, 1958a, 1958b; Trapold and Spence, 1960; Spence and Tandler, 1963) have addressed themselves to these problems in an elegant series of human eyelid conditioning investigations.

In order to understand the logic of these experiments, it is first necessary to consider Spence's specification of the source of drive in classical aversive conditioning. In a theoretical paper Spence (1958) proposed that drive level, D, is a function of the magnitude or strength of a hypothetical response mechanism, r_e, considered to be a persisting emotional response in the organism aroused by an aversive UCS. More specifically, the UCS is assumed to arouse the hypothetical emotional response (r_e), and its effects are assumed to persist at least until the following conditioning trial. The assumption is also made that the level of this hypothetical emotional activity is fairly constant from trial to trial, and that the degree of arousal of r_e is determined by the intensity of the aversive UCS. Hence, the application of a noxious UCS increases the level of r_e, and therefore the level of D. In this manner the source of drive on any given conditioning trial is a function of the level of r_e generated by presentation of the UCS on the preceding conditioning trial(s).

Given that the source of drive has been specified, the experimental problem for testing Hull-Spence theory remains that of separating out the effects of UCS intensity on H and D. Spence, Haggard, and Ross (1958a) in the first of a series of studies, attempted to accomplish this separation by employing an experimental procedure in which the level of drive of Ss in all groups was equated while at the same time providing for differential amounts of reinforcement (that is, different UCS intensities) between groups on conditioning trials. In their experiment, Ss in a low-reinforcement group received a weak air puff on fifty conditioning trials, whereas a strong air puff was always presented on fifty trials in which no CS was presented, and hence no conditioning could occur on these trials. For a high-reinforcement group the conditions were reversed, the strong puff being presented on the conditioning trials and the weak puff being presented on trials in which no CS was presented. A control group also was run in which a weak puff was presented on both the fifty conditioning trials and fifty UCS-alone trials. The order of presentation of the fifty paired (conditioning) trials and fifty UCS-alone trials was given in a prearranged irregular order in which the number of each type of trial was equalized in blocks of four trials for all three groups. Figure 7-4 presents the results of the experiment and demonstrates the superiority of the high-reinforcement group (Group H) over the low-reinforcement group (Group L), despite the presumed equality of drive in these two groups. That the low-reinforcement group was superior to the control group (Group LL), which received a weak puff on both types of trials, was interpreted as due to the greater drive provided by the presentation of the strong puff on the fifty UCS-alone trials.

The results of the Spence, Haggard, and Ross (1958a) study support the proposition that UCS intensity is positively related to habit strength (H) over and above its effect on drive (D), because in the two experimental groups D had presumably been equated. Additional support for this proposition was provided by a second experiment reported in the same paper in which the procedural modification was the presenting of "nonreinforced" UCS presentations at an ISI of 2,650 msec., an interval presumed to be too long to produce conditioning. Further support was provided by additional eyelid conditioning studies involving a differential conditioning procedure (Spence, Haggard, and Ross, 1958b; Spence and Tandler, 1963). In the Spence, Haggard, and Ross (1958b) differential eyelid conditioning study all Ss were

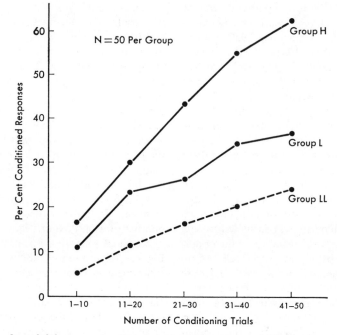

Figure 7-4. Acquisition curves showing the percentage of CRs in successive blocks of ten conditioning trials. (Reprinted with permission from Spence, K. W., Haggard, D. F., and Ross, L. E. UCS intensity and the associative (habit) strength of the eyelid CR. *J. exp. Psychol.*, 1958, **55**, 404–411.)

conditioned to two different conditioned stimuli (light and tone). Half of the *S*s had the light paired with a strong air puff UCS and the tone paired with a weak air puff. In the case of the other half of the *S*s the relations were reversed, the tone being paired with the strong UCS and the light with the weak UCS. The results presented in Figure 7-5 indicate that conditioning was superior to the conditioned stimuli paired with the strong air puff (2 lb. UCS). Spence and Tandler (1963) in another differential conditioning study also attempted to equate drive level, while at the same time varying the reinforcing property of the UCS. Thus, in the case of a high-reinforcement group the positive CS was always paired at an effective CS–UCS conditioning interval (500 msec.) with a strong air puff (2 lb. UCS), whereas the negative CS was followed at a long, ineffective CS–UCS conditioning interval

(2,500 msec.) with a weak UCS (0.33 lb. UCS). For the low-reinforcement group the relation of the two different UCSs to the two CSs was reversed. The results indicated that *S*s in the high-reinforcement group gave a higher percentage of CRs to the positive CS than did those in the low-reinforcement group and also demonstrated a better discrimination (that is, a greater difference in response frequency to the positive and negative CS). The better performance of the high-reinforcement group was interpreted as indicating that a higher level of habit strength (H) was developed in this group than in the low-reinforcement group because the drive levels of these two groups were presumably equalized.

The preceding studies of Spence and his associates have provided substantial support for the formulation that UCS intensity affects habit strength over and above its effects on drive level. Another aspect of Hull-Spence theory related to UCS intensity effects is the notion that habit strength, once accrued, is relatively permanent and cannot directly be reduced. An eyelid conditioning study by Trapold and Spence (1960) concerned itself with verifying this aspect of the theory by assessing the effects of shifts in UCS intensity on habit and drive. The experiment consisted of two phases with *S*s in all groups receiving a total of 260 trials, 130 randomly distributed conditioning trials of paired presentation of the CS and UCS (at an ISI of 500 msec.), and 130 randomly distributed trials involving presentation of only the UCS. In the first phase, which lasted for 180 trials (ninety paired conditioning trials and ninety UCS alone trials), two groups (Groups A and B) received identical conditions. For these groups the CS was always paired with a strong puff, a weak puff always being presented alone. For a third group (Group C) the conditions were reversed, the weak puff was always paired with the CS and the strong puff was always presented alone. In the second phase, consisting of eighty additional trials (forty paired conditioning trials and forty UCS-alone trials), Group A was switched to the reverse of its conditions of the first phase, the weak puff now being paired with the CS, and the strong puff being presented alone. Similarly, Group C was also switched to the reverse of its first phase conditions, whereas Group B was switched to receiving the weak puff on both the paired and unpaired trials. The results presented in Figure 7-6 reveal that Groups A and B, which had received the same treatment up to the point of switching conditions, attained almost identical performance. In contrast, Group C, which had the weak air puff on paired trials, reached an appreciably lower performance level. Following the shift (indicated by the vertical

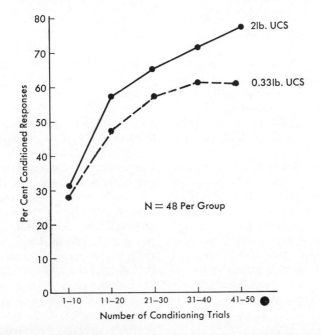

Figure 7-5. Percentage of CRs in blocks of ten trials made to CS paired with 2-lb. UCS and 0.33-lb. UCS. (Reprinted with permission from Spence, K. E., Haggard, D. F., and Ross, L. E. Intrasubject conditioning as a function of the intensity of the unconditioned stimulus. *Science*, 1958, **128**, 774–775.)

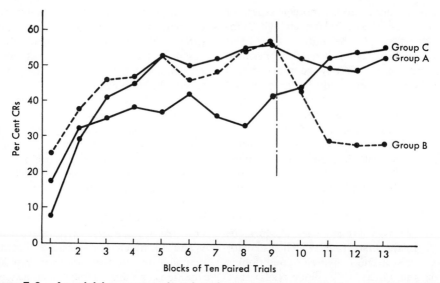

Figure 7-6. Acquisition curves showing the percentage of CRs in successive blocks of ten paired conditioning trials. The vertical line shows the point at which the shift was made. (Reprinted with permission from Trapold, M. A., and Spence, K. W. Performance changes in eyelid conditioning as related to the motivational and reinforcing properties of the UCS. *J. exp. Psychol.*, 1960, **59**, 209–213.)

line on the graph) Group B dropped quite rapidly in performance, a decrement which was interpreted by the authors as caused by a lowered drive. Conversely, Group C increased in response frequency to a level approximating the preshift performance of Groups A and B, indicating that further learning was taking place, as should happen, according to the authors, if UCS intensity affects habit strength. Although Group A showed a slight decrease over trials, it maintained a relatively stable level of performance following the shift. Recalling that in this group the Ss had been shifted from a strong to a weak puff on paired trials while now receiving strong puffs on UCS-alone trials, the stable level of responding was taken as strong confirmation of the hypothesis that habit strength is relatively permanent so long as drive is maintained.

UCS Duration. Whereas the work of Spence and his associates has been directed at supporting Spence's general interpreta-

tion, the drive-reduction hypothesis of Hull (1943) and Miller (1951) attempts to provide a more specific account of UCS intensity effects. According to this view, the cessation of a strongly aversive UCS provides greater drive reduction, and hence a greater increment of habit strength per trial, than does termination of a mildly aversive UCS. One implication of this hypothesis is that the greater the temporal interval between the occurrence of the UCR and offset of the aversive UCS, the poorer the conditioning. In most classical defense conditioning studies the noxious UCS is presented only briefly (for example, 50 to 100 msec.), with the consequence that the UCR, which generally occurs shortly after the onset of the UCS, is followed almost immediately (according to drive-reduction theory) by the reinforcing event, termination of the UCS. Differential predictions would be made by drive-reduction theory, however, if delay of UCS offset were manipulated by increasing the duration of the UCS. The few studies manipulating

UCS duration in classical defense conditioning have been concerned with testing this implication of drive-reduction theory.

Bitterman, Reed, and Krauskopf (1952), employing a differential conditioning design, conditioned the GSR of each S to two CSs, one with a short-shock UCS (500 msec.) and the other with a long-shock UCS (3,000 msec.). The Ss did not differ with regard to differences in drive level that might be associated with UCS duration. The results of the experiment, however, revealed no difference in responding to the stimulus paired with the short or long shock. Coppock and Chambers (1959), in another GSR conditioning study involving groups conditioned at one of three shock UCS durations of 500, 3,000, and 15,000 msec., also found no differences in GSR conditioning. Wegner and Zeaman (1958), extracting data from a series of previously conducted heart-rate conditioning studies in human Ss, compared strength of conditioning for shock-UCS durations of 100, 2,000, 6,000, and 15,000 msec. and found no differences. Runquist and Spence (1959), in four independent experiments deviating slightly from one another in procedure, compared eyelid conditioning performance of Ss receiving a 50 msec. or 1,000 msec. UCS air puff. The first two studies differed in the location and intensity of the UCS. In the first experiment, the UCS was a 1-lb. puff delivered to the cornea of the Ss right eye, whereas in the second experiment, the UCS was 8.3-lb. air puff delivered to the side of S's head, about 2 cm. from the cornea of the right eye. The purpose of the second study was to prevent the UCR (eyelid closure) from reducing the noxiousness of the UCS. The third and fourth studies were replications of the first two, with one exception. In the first two studies the CS duration was 550 msec. for both groups. In the last two studies the CS was extended to terminate 50 msec. after UCS offset for both UCS durations. Despite these precautions only a slight and statistically nonsignificant superiority was observed for the short UCS condition in each of the four separate studies. Nevertheless, the authors, by considering the statistical probability of four independent studies having outcomes in the same predicted direction, were led to conclude that increasing the duration of the UCS lowers conditioning performance.

Although the deduction from drive-reduction theory to the effect of UCS duration in classical aversive conditioning would appear to be straightforward, the essentially negative findings have led several investigators (Wegner and Zeaman, 1958; Runquist and Spence, 1959) to suggest possible sources of confounding that would operate to reduce or eliminate the effects of delaying reinforcement. One factor suggested (Runquist and Spence, 1959) is that the drive level produced by a long UCS duration may be greater than that produced by a short duration UCS, and if so, this factor would tend to reduce any differences in performance caused by differential delay. Secondly, even if the overall drive level were equated, as was the case in the differential conditioning study of Bitterman, Reed, and Krauskopf (1952), there could still be differential drive reduction, with the greater drive reduction occurring with the cessation of the long (presumably higher-drive-producing) UCS. Hence, if habit strength is related to the amount of drive reduction (Hull, 1943), the greater habit strength produced with a long UCS would counteract the performance decrement produced by the delay. Third, if there is a rapid subjective adaptation during the early part of a prolonged shock or air puff, it might produce the major part of drive reduction. Thus, an effect of this nature shortly after UCS onset could make the length of time to UCS offset quite irrelevant to the timing of the drive reduction. From the point of view of drive-reduction theorists, then, these possible confoundings have been offered as precluding the manipulation of UCS duration as a simple experimental test of the theory.

Manipulations of the CS

Chapter 6 reviewed the variety of stimuli which can serve as the CS in classical conditioning. Where E can control the CS, as is the case in most experimental investigations, he is usually careful to select a stimulus which is dynamic or phasic with respect to background stimulation and which is intense enough to compel S's attention, but not so intense as to aggravate alpha responding or to elicit defensive reactions. It is also important that the CS remain relatively invariant over a series of trials in order to minimize processes which tend to inhibit conditioning. In experiments on stimulus generalization, differential conditioning, and compound conditioning the *perceptual* aspects of the situation become extremely important, and the contrasts and blendings of stimulus components, whether they are presented singly or as compounds, exert a powerful control over performance. The foregoing simple-sounding observations certainly apply to instances of learning beyond classical conditioning. These principles generally hold whenever behavior is under the control of some stimulus provided by E, and for this reason results of manipulation of the CS in classical conditioning situations have been readily assimilated into a more general learning or behavior theory.

CS Intensity. Pavlov's designation of the CS as a "neutral" stimulus probably led early investigators to the conclusion that just about any suprathreshold stimulus, provided it is not too strong, could serve as an adequate CS, and there is little in Pavlov's lectures or writings to counteract this view. However, when we examine Pavlov's theory of cerebral physiology and the so-called law of strength, it will become apparent that the absolute and relative intensity of the CS is theoretically very important in the elaboration of a CR. At the behavioral level, though, it long seemed as if CS intensity was one of the least

important determiners of conditioning, and as a matter of fact, straightforward evidence that conditioning is directly related to CS intensity was unavailable until very recently.

Just what is meant by CS intensity? Does it influence the association process or does it merely *energize* or enhance the CR as a performance factor? In answer to the first question, at one time CS intensity was equated with the absolute physical intensity or energy of stimulation contiguous with the US, but recent evidence suggests that CS intensity is more appropriately defined as the *degree of stimulus change* relative to the background or intertrial level. The former, more simplistic view, originated from Hovland's (1937) discovery that stimulus generalization is greater when the test stimulus is stronger than the CS than if the roles of the two stimuli are reversed. This, together with some related experiments in instrumental conditioning, led Hull to elevate stimulus intensity to the status of an intervening variable in his behavior system (Hull, 1952). According to Hull's theory, stimulus-intensity dynamism, denoted V, is a performance factor which presumably combines multiplicatively with habit and drive to determine performance or strength of the CR. V is presumably a monotonic increasing function of CS energy. Hull's notion that CS intensity facilitates or energizes the CR, but does not affect the strength of conditioning, was quickly supported by two studies by Grant and Schneider (1948, 1949). These utilized a factorial design to separate the possible dual role of CS intensity. One study employed the eyelid response and the other the GSR, and both showed that the facilitating effects of CS intensity did not transfer from acquisition to extinction. The only serious contradiction to this view comes from a study by Kimmel, Hill, and Morrow (1962) in GSR conditioning which does report significant main effects in extinction related to CS intensity in acquisition. However, in agreement with Beecroft's (1966, p. 80) assessment, we feel that Hull's view of CS intensity as a performance factor has yet to be seriously challenged.

The idea that CS-intensity is best defined in terms of stimulus change evolved from tests of an alternative to V theory proposed by Perkins (1953) and Logan (1954). The Perkins-Logan theory, alternatively known as the "generalization" or "differential conditioning" hypothesis (Champion, 1962), maintains that CR strength is related to intensity only insofar as an intense CS differs from weaker inhibitory background stimuli along a psychophysical dimension. Inhibition presumably accrues to the background through nonreinforcement of generalized CRs. This inhibition, in turn, generalizes to the CS with decreasing effect as a function of the distance between the background and CS. Thus, a strong CS on a weak background will yield a stronger CR than will a medium CS on the same background. The theory also predicts that (1) if the background or intertrial stimulus is quite intense, the *weakest* CS will yield the strongest CR (Kamin, 1965), (2) stimulus offset is just as effective as stimulus onset as a CS (Hansche and Grant, 1960; Logan and Wagner, 1962), and (3) offset of a strong intertrial stimulus is a more effective CS than offset of a weak intertrial stimulus (Champion, 1962; Mattson and Moore, 1964).

The studies cited verify these predictions. Mattson and Moore (1964), in a human eyelid conditioning experiment, actually found the *offset* of a loud intertrial tone to yield better performance than its onset. This was thought to have been due to a higher drive level induced by the longer exposure to the loud tone in the offset conditions. Others have suggested that absolute stimulus intensity may facilitate conditioning through its effect on drive (Beecroft, 1966; Grice, Masters, and Kohfeld, 1966).

The stimulus offset experiments do not disprove Hull's V theory. Nor do they offer indisputable support for the Perkins-Logan hypothesis, because a simple redefinition of V in terms of stimulus change can handle the relevant data. Moore and Newman (1966) have demonstrated that an intertrial stimulus can have an inhibitory influence on human eyelid conditioning, as required by the Perkins-Logan theory, but records of intertrial blinking failed to reveal evidence of generalized CRs to the intertrial stimulus or of differential conditioning between the two stimuli. Evidence of generalization should have been revealed in higher intertrial blink rates when the intertrial stimulus and the CS were highly similar, and evidence for differential conditioning might have been seen as a rise in intertrial blink rate early in conditioning followed by a later decrease as generalized CRs were enveloped by deepening inhibition. Neither of these predictions materialized. Blink rates during the intertrial interval are unaffected by proximity of the CS and remain invariant over trials (Mattson and Moore, 1964).

More damaging evidence against the Perkins-Logan theory is a study by Grice, Masters, and Kohfeld (1966) in which human Ss underwent eyelid conditioning to CSs consisting merely of a *transition* in the intensity of a tone from one level to another. The transitions were either up or down and in steps of varying size. Besides introducing a novel conditioning paradigm, this procedure is interesting in that no one level of intensity was *consistently* the CS or the intertrial stimulus. Hence, the observed advantage of large transitions over small ones (all transitions were clearly detectable) cannot be accounted for by inhibition emanating from some fixed point on the intensity continuum. Instead, the results of this study suggest a dynamogenic property of stimulus change *per se*, supporting some sort of modified V theory. One potential difficulty with this study is that each trial was initiated by a buzzer of unspecified intensity and duration which served as a "ready" signal. Because this particular stimulus was constant and because the inhibitory effect of ready signals is well documented (Turner, 1966), we can only hope that this experiment will be repeated without this complicating factor.

An earlier series of studies in Grice's laboratory demonstrated that CS intensity effects are more pronounced in within-Ss designs than in those experiments, such as Walker's (1960), in which each S experiences only one level of CS intensity. Walker did obtain a reliable CS intensity effect, but most of the variance involved short latency CRs which were thought to be *voluntary*. A follow-up to Walker's study (Beck, 1963) was pivotal in varying CS-intensity within-Ss and in demonstrating a strong CS-intensity effect even when trials containing short latency (presumably voluntary) CRs were discarded from the data. The magnitude of the CS-intensity effect in Beck's study was more dramatic than that usually observed in between-groups designs. To account for this, Beck suggested that Ss' *adaptation level* for stimulus intensity, presumably lying between the two CS intensities employed in her study, aggravated their differences through the "bipolarity" principle (Helson, 1959). In short, Beck observed what would appear to be a perceptual contrast effect between the two CSs.

The existence of contrast was conclusively demonstrated by Grice and Hunter (1964) in an eyelid conditioning experiment which directly compared between- and within-Ss variation of CS intensity. Two groups of Ss were conditioned for 100 trials with either a loud (100 db. SPL) tone or soft (50 db. SPL) tone CS; a third group received 50 conditioning trials with each tone. In the latter group the order of presentation of each tone was random. As can be seen in Figure 7-7 the resulting contrast was quite dramatic and cannot be readily accounted for by a V theory or by the Perkins-Logan hypothesis. Grice and Hunter, like Beck,

urge adaptation-level theory as an alternative, at least where within-Ss designs are employed.

Lipkin and Moore (1966) found that CS-intensity and ISI interact in eyelid *trace* conditioning. Specifically, the CS-intensity effect was greater with a 0.5-sec. ISI than a 2-sec. ISI, and although this finding can be easily integrated into virtually any extant theoretical treatment, it is interesting to speculate on the possibility that the interaction does not occur in delay conditioning. Should this be the case, new life would be given to the notion that the absolute intensity contiguous with the UCS combines, perhaps only in a minimal way, with stimulus change to determine the total intensity effect. In support of this possibility, Kamin's (1965) work with CS intensity in conditioned suppression (CER) in rats illustrates quite clearly that a *moderate* increase in intensity is a more effective CS in a delay paradigm than is a decrease of the same magnitude. (*Gross* changes from background, either up or down, are equally effective and lead to extremely rapid conditioning and complete asymptotic suppression.) In the first case, it is unclear if the advantage was due to the direction of change itself or to the level of stimulus energy contiguous with the electric shock UCS. The second alternative was partially supported in an independent experiment which showed that *offset* of a low level of stimulus energy could serve as an effective CS in a *trace* paradigm, even though the same level of stimulus had proved to be ineffective in the usual onset trace procedure. Here it is unclear whether the superiority of the offset procedure was actually due to the higher level of stimulation acting in contiguity with the UCS or to some cumulative effect occurring mainly between trials. As previously noted, high levels of intertrial stimulation facilitate eyelid conditioning, presumably by way of a drive or arousal mechanism (Mattson and Moore, 1964; Grice, Masters, and Kohfeld, 1966), and the same mechanism

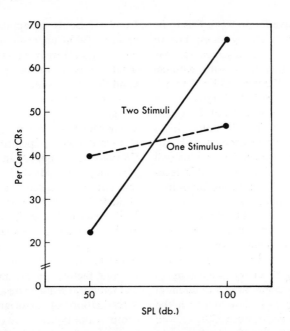

Figure 7-7. Percentage CRs during last sixty trials to the loud and soft tones under the one- and two-stimulus conditions. (Reprinted with permission from Grice, C. R., and Hunter, J. J. Stimulus intensity effects depend upon the type of experimental design. *Psychol. Rev.*, 1964, **71**, 247–256.)

may operate for the CER with even lower levels of stimulation.

In GSR conditioning, the problem of CR definition becomes critical in assessing the role of CS intensity. Because the magnitude of the GSR is directly related to the strength of the eliciting stimulus, separating out the effect of CS intensity on conditioning is a major methodological problem. These problems were nicely handled in a study by Prokasy and Ebel (1967) which suggests rather strongly that the facilitating effect of CS intensity is limited to responses occurring in the interval immediately after CS onset. These responses were described as resembling alpha responses in eyelid conditioning in that they were found to decrease in frequency over trials and to be enhanced through pairing of the CS with the UCS, just as a previously extinguished orienting response is reinstated when the CS takes on signal value (Sokolov, 1963). Responses occurring later in the CS–US

interval, thought to be unmistakably conditioned GSRs, were not influenced by CS intensity in this study.

The possibility that the alpha GSR *interferes* with conditioning has been noted by several investigators (for example, Kimmel, Hill, and Morrow, 1962), and this has reinforced Razran's (1957) notion that the weakest suprathreshold stimulus rather than the strongest is a more effective CS, at least for those responses which are components of the orienting response. Razran reviews the Soviet literature favoring the view that a weak CS paired with a strong UCS is most favorable for conditioning. Kamin (1965) criticizes this literature as consisting mainly of experiments in which *S*s were conditioned to a CS of moderate intensity and then tested with a stimulus of a different intensity. The procedure may introduce generalization decrements which spuriously reduce the effectiveness of stronger stimuli. As we have seen, few western studies have found weak CSs to be more effective than strong ones, but in GSR conditioning the discrepancy has been more dramatic, what with Kimmel and his associates (Kimmel, 1959; Kimmel, Hill, and Morrow, 1962) finding favorable evidence, whereas Hovland (1937), Grant and Schneider (1949), and Champion (1962) report evidence more in keeping with, for example, Hull's V theory. The conflict will no doubt be resolved when suitable techniques are developed to separate conditioning from alpha responding.

An experiment by Lockhart (1965) presents the most compelling evidence in support of the dominance ratio notion. Arguing that a legitimate test requires that the CS and UCS lie in the same sensory modality, he ran human Ss in a differential GSR conditioning situation in which the reinforced and nonreinforced CSs, as well as the UCS, consisted of electric shock. The electrodes delivering CS+, CS−, and the UCS were attached to different portions of the Ss calves, and the ratio of shock intensity between the CSs and the UCS was 1:3, 2:3, and 3:3 for three groups of Ss. The duration of all shocks was a constant 0.3 sec., and the CS-US interval was 0.5 or 10 sec. for different groups. The differential conditioning procedure served to control efficiently for sensitization and the *absolute* effects of CS intensity. In agreement with the theory, the results showed quite clearly that the magnitude of GSR discrimination (CR+ − CR−) was greatest in the 1:3 group and decreased linearly through the 2:3 and 3:3 conditions.

This discussion seems to leave us with roughly four useful principles: (1) CS intensity defined as stimulus change is a performance factor which possesses a dynamogenic property like Hull's intervening variable V; (2) absolute stimulus intensity also energizes performance, but to a lesser extent, possibly through its effect on drive; (3) CS intensity effects are exaggerated when one S experiences more than one level of intensity and principles

from Helson's adaptation-level theory seem useful in understanding this contrast effect; and (4) weak suprathreshold stimuli would appear to be most effective in conditioning responses which are components of the orienting reflex.

Compound CSs. Whenever the pattern of stimulation which operationally defines the CS consists of more than one component, each subject to independent variation, then this pattern is called a compound CS. A good deal of investigation has been directed at discovering those factors which determine the relative associative strength of the components of a compound CS. Intensity of a component is one rather obvious factor, sensory modality another, and temporal sequencing a third.

Evaluation of associative strength of components typically involves one of two basic transfer designs. The first consists of giving an equal number of conditioning trials to each component and then testing the compound. The second consists of training to a compound, and then testing the individual components. There are three possible outcomes of such experiments, and all three have been discussed by Hull (1943) and observed at one time or another in the laboratory (see Beecroft, 1966).

For simplicity, consider a compound consisting of only two components, The strength of the CR to this compound may *exceed* the strength of the CR to the strongest component when tested singly, in which case we say that "'summation'" has been demonstrated. The term *summation* here is not meant to imply algebraic addition of CR strengths. Instead, CR strength to the compound is more accurately predicted by Hull's "physiological addition" in which the number of reinforced trials to each component are added together and entered into the equation relating strength of conditioning to number of reinforcements (Hull, 1943, p. 178). Because this function is assumed to be a negatively accelerated growth curve, algebraic summation cannot occur (see Figure 7-7, p. 159).

When the compound elicits a CR of strength *less than* the strength of the strongest component, we say that "interaction" has been demonstrated. It is sometimes useful to distinguish between two types of interaction. The first is *averaging* and refers to those cases in which the strength of the CR to the compound falls somewhere between that of the weakest and strongest components. What might be termed *strong interaction*, then, refers to those cases where the compound elicits a response weaker than the weakest component. Interaction most often occurs when the two components lie in the same sense modality. A mixture of colored light, for example, may produce an effect bearing little resemblance to either monochromatic component.

Finally, the strength of the CR to the compound might *equal* that of the strongest component, in which case we might say that the stronger component "overshadows" the weaker. Hull (1943) indicated five factors which contribute to the strength of a component and hence its ability to overshadow other elements of the compound. A strong component would be: (1) dynamic or intermittent, (2) intense, (3) in a favorable sensory mode, such as audition, (4) relatively rare in the previous experiences of S (and therefore not associated with too many possible conflicting responses), and (5) conditioned to some strongly emotional reaction.

Of course, the reinforcement history of a component determines its contribution to a compound. Grings and his associates have demonstrated summation when reinforced components are combined, interaction when conditioned and nonreinforced components are mixed together, and minimal CR strength to compounds consisting only of nonreinforced components (Grings and Kimmel, 1959).

Recent work on the CER in rats by Kamin and his associates (Kamin, 1966) indicates that the order in which components and compounds are conditioned can be a crucial factor in determining the strength of the CR to components on later test trials. Kamin found that if an asymptotic CER is established to a one-component CS (CS_1) and if further reinforced trials are given to a compound consisting of CS_1 + CS_2, then a single test trial to CS_2 fails to reveal any evidence of conditioning. However, with a more sensitive "savings" measure, it became clear that the interpolated compound conditioning does facilitate acquisition of the CER to CS_2 to some degree, but the improvement is evidently limited to the first compound trial with the later trials contributing little or nothing to associative strength. Kamin speculated that the conditioning is limited to the first trial because it is only on this trial that generalization-decrements or external inhibition temporarily reduced the strength of the CER below an asymptotic level. Thus, it would appear that mere contiguity of a stimulus with UCS will not lead to conditioning unless the pairings occur over a series of trials during which suppression is something less than asymptotic. This idea was supported in related experiments which show that CS_2 becomes a very effective CS during the compound conditioning phase when it is paired with a weak CS_1, a stimulus too weak to produce complete suppression on preliminary conditioning trials.

Razran (1965) has summarized Russian research on compound stimulus conditioning which suggests that the components of a reinforced compound CS may fail to elicit a CR even though these same components can be conditioned separately. An even more surprising demonstration consists of an apparent failure of nonreinforcement of a previously conditioned component to reduce the strength of the CR to a compound. In an experiment originally reported in 1906, Palladin added a thermal stimulus to a tactile CS for salivation in dogs. He then reinforced the compound, and when tested alone, the thermal stimulus failed to elicit a CR. This result agrees with what one might expect on the basis of Kamin's experiments with a similar experimental design. Palladin then extinguished the CR to the tactile CS and found that this did not reduce the effectiveness of the compound. This and other studies reviewed by Razran illustrate what he refers to as configural conditioning. The point is that the compound CS acts as a unitary configuration (gestalt) which can be conditioned independent of its components. An even more dramatic instance of configurational conditioning is provided by a 1912 experiment by Platonov. Here human Ss received extensive overtraining of the plantar reflex to a bell and light compound. Platonov found that with extended overtraining the components gradually lost their effectiveness whereas the compound maintained its strength. The loss of conditioning seemed to be due to the overtraining and not to any differential reinforcement of the compound and non-reinforcement of the components. Additional evidence of configural conditioning through overtraining, with a variety of other responses and with infrahuman Ss, was obtained in the laboratories of Beritov and Voronin (Razran, 1965).

Wickens (1965) has recently tried to reproduce the Russian finding that CR strength to components drops out through overtraining. Shock was paired with a simultaneous compound consisting of a light and a tone. The Ss were cats, and conditioning was assessed by simultaneous recording of GSR, respiration, and paw withdrawal. With a 0.5-sec. CS-US interval, the compound was superior to components, but these failed to lose their strength even with extended overtraining. With an ISI of 2 sec., however, the components did show a significant decrease in strength, thus at least partially replicating the Russian experiments. Such discrepancies as there are may stem from the fact that the components were preconditioned and then extinguished in the Wickens experiment so that their strength at the beginning of compound conditioning would be equal.

Complex Compounds. In the previous section we reviewed some of the results and theoretical notions arising from a paradigm which is often called simultaneous compound conditioning. In this section we will treat some varieties of compound conditioning in which the temporal distribution of components within the compound can vary. The typical trace conditioning paradigm might be considered a rudimentary form of complex conditioning having two successive components; onset-offset or offset-onset.

Razran (1965) summarizes a 1918 study by Beritov in which a successive compound CS consisting of two components was conditioned to a paw withdrawal response in dogs. Intermittent tests to each component revealed that the CR was first established to the second component of the compound, but that later on in training both components elicited the CR with equal strength. Nevertheless, CRs to the second component were facilitated by application of the first. This led Beritov to conclude that associations or connections are formed not only between each component and the analyzer of the UCS, but between those of the first and second components as well. Research done in the laboratories of Beritov and Voronin suggests that components closest in time to the UCS are more enduring in that they are more difficult to dislodge through differential reinforcement and they drop out more slowly with extended overtraining to the successive compound.

Wickens (1965) has assessed the degree of conditioning to components in two kinds of complex conditioning paradigms. In one, the onset of the two components occurred simultaneously but one component was terminated by a CR (finger withdrawal); the other persisted for a short time past the scheduled shock UCS. In agreement with studies using a single component CS in both classical and instrumental conditioning, the component interrupted by the CR appeared to be more strongly conditioned than the component with delayed offset (Wickens, Cross, and Morgan, 1959).

What is the relative strength of the two components when they have differential onset times and simultaneous offset? If the second component has a more favorable ISI with respect to the UCS than the first, then we might expect that it would be the dominant cue. The situation is not this simple, as an experiment by Wickens, Born, and Wickens (1963) illustrates. In this experiment cats received GSR conditioning to a compound in which the onset of the *second* component always preceded the shock UCS by 0.55 sec. The CS_1-CS_2 interval was 0.15, 0.5, or 0.7 sec. All animals were conditioned and tested under each of these three conditions. Results indicated that CS_2 did not differ significantly from the compound *except* where the CS_1-CS_2 interval was 0.5 sec. Here CS_1 alone was as potent as the compound and CR strength to CS_2 alone was greatly diminished. In this study, as in earlier experiments with human Ss, the strength of CS_1 fell away as the CS_1-CS_2 interval either increased or decreased from a value of 0.5 sec. It seems quite evident that some sort of sensory conditioning can occur whereby the first component comes to evoke the sensory effect of the compound, provided the CS_1-CS_2 interval is favorable. Disallowing backward associations, CS_1 becomes more effective than CS_2 simply because it can evoke an effect closer to the actual pattern of stimulation paired with shock during conditioning trials. Why is it that CS_2 can lose its effectiveness when the CS_1-CS_2 interval is favorable for sensory conditioning but not when the interval is unfavorable? Wickens suggests that in this case the two components do not form an integrated compound, hence CS_2 can retain its strength independent of CS_1.

A sensory preconditioning experiment by Wickens and Cross (1963) suggests that it is not necessary to reinforce CS_2 in order for CS_1 to become conditioned to the sensory consequences of CS_2. In this study CS_1 and CS_2 were repeatedly paired at a variety of ISIs *prior* to conditioning a GSR to CS_2 with shock. Tests to CS_1 alone in extinction revealed the same sort of gradient of CS_1 strength evident in the earlier compound conditioning experiments.

CS Intermittency. We have noted that intermittency of the dynamic characteristics of the CS was postulated by Hull (1943) as being important in determining the effectiveness of a CS or of one of its components. An experiment by Papsdorf, Fishbein, and Gormezano (1964) directly compared the acquisition of the classically conditioned nictitating-membrane response in rabbits to a continuous tonal CS and an intermittent pulsed tone. Although differences were not striking, the intermittent tone was the more effective CS. The factors which contribute to this superiority remain largely unexplored.

Reinforcement Schedules

In this section we will discuss the effects of schedule of reinforcement on acquisition, extinction, and differentiation. Although most research in this area has been carried out with the eyelid CR in human Ss, some interesting contrasts are available from recent comparative studies.

Acquisition. Eyelid conditioning experiments with human Ss have typically found acquisition performance to be directly related to probability of reinforcement (for example, Hartman and Grant, 1960). The theoretically interesting question is whether partial reinforcement merely results in a slower rate of conditioning or in attainment of a lower asymptotic level of performance. Most of the available human studies have simply not involved enough training to provide an unequivocal answer to this question, but extrapolation from most of the published conditioning curves suggests that lower asymptotes are the rule. Particularly strong evidence for this comes from an experiment by Ross (1959) in which a shift from a continuous to a 50 per cent intermittent schedule was found to produce an immediate decrement in performance, even though the shift occurred after performance had stabilized at a high level. Following the shift, performance quickly fell to the level of a group which had received partial reinforcement from the beginning of acquisition and once again stabilized, but at the lower level. This reduced performance could not be attributed to a reduction in the density of UCS occurrences because the UCS was presented on nonreinforced trials, but at a delayed interval (2.4 sec.) unfavorable for conditioning. Does the same sort of rapid post-asymptotic decrement occur when the UCS is withheld on nonreinforced trials rather than merely delayed? This is a fair question in light of Moore and Gormezano's (1963) finding that UCS delay in human eyelid conditioning leads to lower levels of performance than UCS omission, and thus the rapid decrement in the Ross study may very well have been due to the unusually effective inhibitory properties of delayed UCS. The answer to this question would appear to be yes. Runquist (1963) also reports rapid decrements of CR performance when Ss were shifted from a continuous to a 50 per cent partial reinforcement schedule in which the UCS was completely omitted on nonreinforced trials. As in the Ross study, performance following the shift fell to the level of Ss who had received partial reinforcement from the beginning of acquisition. Thus, the existence of a relatively stable, long-term detrimental effect of nonreinforcement seems reasonably well documented, at least for normal adults in eyelid conditioning.

Ross, Koski, and Yeager (1964) compared eyelid conditioning in severely retarded young adults with a sample of college students as a function of reinforcement schedule. The normal Ss showed a typical partial reinforcement decrement even when conditioned during a distracting (if not absorbing) motion picture. Performance under the two reinforcement schedules did not differ for retardates even though they attained a respectable level of about 70 per cent CRs. Experiments with the conditioned nictitating-membrane response in rabbits (Coleman and Gormezano, 1966) indicate that animals conditioned with 50 per cent random reinforcement attain the same high performance level as do continuously reinforced animals, and similar results for the rabbit eyelid response had been reported earlier by Thomas and Wagner (1964). It is tempting to attribute this difference in eyelid conditioning between normal adults, on the one hand, and retardates and rabbits, on the other, to some complex psychological processes available only to sophisticated humans. Kimble (1967) has suggested that normal college-going Ss tend to resist attempts to manipulate their behavior, and certain procedures in eyelid conditioning such as inhibitory instructions, the use of ready signals, or partial reinforcement tend to aggravate this resistance. The S experiencing partial reinforcement, for example, presumably feels "tricked" by the E, and this immediately triggers an inhibitory set, a kind of "voluntary nonresponding," which would not be expected in animals or retardates. Kimble makes the interesting prediction that the inhibitory set triggered by partial reinforcement might actually be strengthened by increasing the noxiousness of the UCS. Speaking figuratively, a nonreinforced trial following a stronger UCS is a "dirtier trick" and the greater antagonism which results simply makes the S more determined not to respond. Such an inverted effect of UCS intensity under partial reinforcement has been reported by Runquist (1963). Runquist himself attributed the effect to a disproportionately large number of high-anxiety Ss in the partially reinforced group which received the weaker UCS. This could have produced higher responding in this group despite the less favorable UCS, but Kimble's hypothesis still seems to merit further investigation.

It is obviously necessary to exercise the utmost discretion in invoking "attitudes" or other observed processes to account for a particular datum. Postexperiment questionnaires, such as those developed by Kimble (1967), do not provide an entirely adequate check on whether a given attitudinal posture actually antedates a particular level of performance. It is true that questionnaire data obtained in conjunction with conditioning protocols are often illuminating, and the Ss ratings of their "degree of resistance" to the experiment might account for a good deal of the variance in an experiment. Nevertheless, direct experimental manipulation of attitudinal factors is a necessary adjunct in testing theories such as Kimble's. What would happen, for example, if Ss were specifically told, before the experiment, that the stimulus serving as the CS would not always be followed by the UCS? If they no longer feel "tricked" by a nonreinforced trial, the partial reinforcement decrement might indeed vanish.

The remaining comparative literature is somewhat divided on the question of asymptotic performance decrements under partial reinforcement. Those studies in classical conditioning which contrast continuous with 50 per cent random reinforcement are listed in Table 7-2. The aim of most of these studies was to detect a partial reinforcement effect in extinction (PRE) and for this reason acquisition training was often not extensive enough to reveal a clear-cut leveling-off of conditioning curves. There are perils in forming conclusions from such listings (for example, Gardner, 1966), but Table 7-2 does suggest that although worms and rodents do not

differ in acquisition under the two schedules, goldfish, dogs, and possibly pigeons do! If nothing else, these studies emphasize the fact that performance decrements under partial reinforcement in humans need not be attributed to such distinctly human factors as "voluntary nonresponding."

Extinction. Much has been made of the role of cognitive factors in human eyelid conditioning, and the same type of emphasis has been apparent in recent theoretical treatments of extinction by Spence (1966). The slower rate of extinction following partial reinforcement (PRE) by normal adults in eyelid conditioning is presumably caused by a failure to discriminate the onset of extinction. The comparatively rapid extinction following continuous reinforcement is brought about by the combined effects of ease of discrimination of the onset of extinction, on the one hand, and an inhibitory set not to respond based on this discrimination, on the other. The inhibitory set is presumably based on the Ss' hypothesis or expectancy that reinforcements are no longer forthcoming. This discrimination-expectancy hypothesis, as applied to eyelid conditioning, was first proposed by Humphreys (1939) in the original experimental demonstration of the PRE. In support of this hypothesis, Spence (1966) cites those experiments in Table 7-1 which demonstrate slow extinction rates in animals and no PRE. Also cited are numerous studies carried out in Spence's own laboratory which show that rate of extinction in human eyelid conditioning is a good deal slower when conditioning procedures are masked by a distracting probability learning task. One of these experiments was actually able to reverse the typical PRE. Bridger and Mandel (1965) have offered independent support for the discrimination hypothesis by demonstrating virtually immediate extinction of the conditioned GSR in Ss informed of the procedural change between acquisition and extinction (for example, shock

Table 7–2   Comparative Studies Contrasting 100 Per Cent and 50 Per Cent Random Reinforcement in Acquisition and Extinction

Species	Response	Author and Publication Year	Acquisition: $100\% > 50\%$?	Extinction: $50\% > 100\%$?
Planaria	Movement	Kimmel and Yaremko (1966)	No	Yes
Earthworm	Withdrawal	Wyers, Peek, and Herz (1964)	No	Yes
Goldfish	Activity	Gonzalez, Longo, and Bitterman (1961)	Yes	No
		Berger, Yarczower, and Bitterman (1965)	Yes	Yes[a]
Pigeon	Movement	Longo, Milstein, and Bitterman (1962)	Yes	No
	Activity	Slivka and Bitterman (1966)	No	Yes[a]
Rat	Cardiac	Fitzgerald, Vardaris, and Brown (1966)	No	—
	Startle	Wagner, Siegel, and Fein (1967)	Yes	No
	CER	Wagner, Siegel, and Fein (1967)	No	Yes
		Brimer and Dockrill (1966)	No	Yes
		Hilton (1967)	No	Yes
Rabbit	Eyeblink	Thomas and Wagner (1964)	No	No
	Nictitating membrane	Coleman and Gormezano (1966)	No	Yes
Dog	Salivation	Fitzgerald (1963)	Yes	Yes
		Wagner, Siegel, Thomas, and Ellison (1964)	Yes	Yes[a]
	Cardiac	Fitzgerald, Vardaris, and Teyler (1966)	Yes	Yes

NOTE: The superscript a indicates that the PRE appeared as a significant Schedule X Trials interaction rather than a main effect.

electrodes were removed) whereas a typical PRE was observed in two groups not so informed.

The evidence is therefore very compelling that an inhibitory set arising from discrimination of the onset of extinction can account for PREs in human conditioning. But what about the remaining comparative studies, not cited in Spence's paper, which do report PREs of one kind or another? Some of these PREs might be explained away as involving inappropriate assessment of the extinction process (Anderson, 1963), but enough remain to suggest the necessity of an alternative explanation of PREs in classical conditioning which is general enough to cut across species. A discrimination-expectancy factor, although sufficient to account for PREs in human conditioning, may not be necessary. We see little reason why a simpler notion, also based on the discriminability between acquisition and extinction, cannot account for the human literature as well as those experiments with infrahumans which have found PREs.

There are any number of forms such a theory might take, but the basic idea is quite familiar, namely that the greater the overall stimulus change between acquisition and extinction, the greater will be the transfer or generalization decrement, and hence the greater the loss in CR strength during extinction. Accordingly, PREs occur because extinction procedures are more similar to a partial than continuous reinforcement. Furthermore, there is no need for "cognitive factors" in this interpretation if we assume that procedures such as masking tasks or special instructions prior to extinction merely serve to mediate the similarity or distinctiveness between the two phases of the experiment (Grice, 1965). Clearly, this generalized discrimination hypothesis will not suffice as a means of predicting extinction performance or a PRE. We need to take into account the fact that the amount of acquisition training and the level of conditioning attained in acquisition are somehow *directly* related to resistance to extinction. As Grant and Schipper (1952) have indicated, these two processes work against each other in such a way that the greatest resistance to extinction is obtained with intermediate to high partial schedules whereas low partial schedules, which are more similar to extinction, simply do not yield enough CR strength to hold up very long in extinction. One of the nicest illustrations of the Grant and Schipper two-process theory of extinction is provided by an instrumental conditioning study by Bacon (1962) in which the amount o training rats received in a runway was covarieg with probability of reinforcement. In that experiment, *mean* running speed in extinction was (1) directly related to percentage of reinforcement for groups which received only ten training trials, (2) an inverted U-shaped function following thirty trials, and (3) a decreasing function after 100 or more trials. The *rate* of decrease in running speed over extinction trials was inversely related to percentage of reinforcement for all levels of amount of training.

Coleman and Gormezano (1966), investigating the nictitating-membrane CR in the rabbit, obtained the PRE only when extinction was begun *immediately* on reaching the performance asymptote. By contrast, the PRE was greatly diminished

or disappeared entirely when partial and continuously reinforced groups received the same number of acquisition trials and hence differential amounts of overtraining. Scheuer (1967), using the conditioned-suppression (CER) paradigm, reported a reversal of the PRE when all rats received the same number of CS presentations and attained the same high performance criterion in acquisition. It thus appears as though the extent of postasymptotic overtraining rather than the number of acquisition trials is the more critical factor covarying with reinforced schedule in determining resistance to extinction in some situations. As long as extensive overtraining is avoided, a PRE *in some form* should be obtained even though the continuous and partial schedules lead to different performance asymptotes. The potential importance of other factors in determining the occurrence of PREs cannot be minimized. Nevertheless, a simplistic but useful working hypothesis is that the divergence of outcomes in Table 7-2 can be attributed to a failure to achieve asymptotic levels of conditioning in those experiments reporting PRE and extensive overtraining or differential overtraining in those experiments which fail to observe a PRE.

Patterned Reinforcement Schedules. Partial reinforcement schedules in which reinforced and nonreinforced trials form an alternating pattern are of interest in that they provide another means of assessing the role of higher processes in conditioning. The question of interest is whether Ss utilize the added redundancy provided by patterned schedules so as to bring their performance in acquisition and extinction in line with known reinforcement contingencies. The answer to this question for human eyelid conditioning appears to be no (Hartman and Grant, 1962). Unless specifically instructed as to the reinforcement pattern, Ss receiving a double alternation schedule were indistinguishable in their performance from Ss conditioned under a 50 per cent random schedule. There was no evidence of Ss who were unaided by instruction or other means learning the pattern in the sense of responding with higher probability on reinforced than nonreinforced trials. In this respect humans and rabbits do not appear to differ. Leonard and Theios (1967) found no evidence of pattern learning with prolonged single alternation conditioning of the nictitating-membrane response. Finally, both the double alternation and random reinforcement groups in the Hartman and Grant experiment yielded about the same degree of PRE with respect to a continuously reinforced group. Like the Bridger and Mandel (1965) study in GSR conditioning, Hartman and Grant found that Ss are able to bring their performance in line with the reinforcement pattern if they are specifically informed about the reinforcement contingencies in acquisition or extinction. But Ss evidently do not readily discriminate these contingencies on their own. This observation emphasizes anew the need for caution in accepting those hypotheses about the effects of partial reinforcement which appeal to "inevitable" cognitive factors as a *sine qua non* in human conditioning. Cognitive factors when directly manipulated by E clearly affect conditioning in predictable ways. But observation of this same mode of respond-ing does not justify *a posteriori* inferences implicating the same or any cognitive factors.

Reinforcement Schedules in Differential Conditioning. We have indicated that performance in simple eyelid conditioning is directly related to reinforcement probability. This same relationship might be expected to hold in differential conditioning where the probability of reinforcement to CS_1 (π_1) and CS_2 (π_2) are varied independently such that CS_1 is the more frequently reinforced stimulus. If this were the case, the degree of differentiation between CS_1 and CS_2 should be directly related to the difference between π_1 and π_2. Newman (1966) found this to be the case in human differential eyelid conditioning *only* when π_2 was equal to zero. When CS_2 was paired with the UCS as little as 25 per cent of the time differentiation did not occur at all and responding to CS_1 for all values of π_1 was significantly reduced below the level of performance attained when π_2 was equal to zero. This strong interaction cannot be readily understood in terms of straight-forward conditioning principles. It will be interesting to see whether this breakdown of differentiation can be counteracted by increasing the distinctiveness of CS_1 and CS_2.

Beyond the Basic Parameters

The empirical relationships discussed in the previous chapter and those to be considered in the present chapter will have far from exhausted all of the phenomena subsumed under the term *classical conditioning*. In the previous chapter attention was given to the empirical effects and theoretical significance of some of the most fundamental parameters of classical conditioning, whereas in the present chapter we have selected for consideration three areas of research that may be regarded as dealing with more complex relationships. These are (1) the efforts of primarily Russian investigators to systematically follow-up the initial observations and speculations of Pavlov on semantic (or second signaling system) conditioning, interoceptive conditioning, and the orienting reflex; (2) classical-conditioning studies that have been regarded as having significant bearing on the nature of the associations formed in learning and the conditions necessary for the formation of such associations; and (3) studies generated by formulations that have extended conditioning concepts and laws to instrumental conditioning situations.

Empirical Extensions of Pavlov's Formulations

Semantic Conditioning

For Pavlov, the adaptation of man to his environment rested on three principal mechanisms. The first and most primitive mechanism of adaptation was assumed to be provided by unconditioned responses. A second and more broadly adaptive mechanism was assumed to be provided by the development of CRs; and because these CRs were interpreted as elicited by sensory stimuli signaling the occurrence of biologically significant events, Pavlov regarded the paradigm as involving the *first signaling system*. With the introduction of the mechanism of speech in man, Pavlov proposed an additional adaptive mechanism. Speech now provided a *second signaling system*, in which words were assumed to bear the same relationship to sensory conditioned stimuli as do sensory conditioned stimuli to unconditioned stimuli (that is, a higher-order conditioning relationship).

Although Pavlov believed the second

169

signaling system to be established through higher-order conditioning, he did not regard it as merely a case of simple higher-order conditioning, but rather as the basis of abstraction (that is, concept formation) unique to humans. Furthermore, Pavlov considered the development of the second signaling system (speech) as taking over some of the functions of the first signaling system. Consequently, early Russian investigators bent their efforts to the developmental study in children of the transfer of CRs from sensory stimuli to their word designation (object-word transfer). Later, Russian investigators expanded their efforts to include the study of word-object transfer, and began to refer to the transfer of CRs from one signal system to the other as "dynamic transmission" of CRs. However, the study of word-word CR transfer and the transfer of CRs between larger verbal units originated in this country with the study by Razran (1939). Razran also introduced the term *semantic conditioning* to refer to conditioning studies in which verbal stimuli are employed as CSs.

All of the standard conditioning preparations have been employed in the investigation of semantic conditioning (for example, GSR, salivation, eyeblink, heart rate, and so on), but Russian investigations, particularly those conducted with children, have involved the extensive use of the Ivanov-Smolensky anticipatory instructed conditioning preparation. The Ivanov-Smolensky preparation is often referred to in the Russian literature as the "motor method of speech reinforcement," and in the original method (see Chapter 6) Ss were instructed, prior to conditioning, to press a rubber bulb in response to a sound stimulus which was regularly preceded by some neutral CS. Currently, most Russian studies do not employ preliminary instructions, but simply present a CS followed approximately 2 sec. later by the spoken word *press*. This UCS produces the UCR of bulb squeezing. Once bulb-squeezing CRs occur to the CS, one of two reinforcement procedures are employed. Either E continues to present the UCS *press* or he shifts S to an instrumental conditioning paradigm by giving the spoken word *good* to every occurrence of the CR and discontinues the administration of the UCS (*press*).

Object-Word, Object-Object, and Word-Object Transfer. In the research to be considered here, a CR is established to a nonverbal stimulus and tests are then made for generalization to verbal stimuli (object-word transfer) and nonverbal stimuli (object-object transfer), or a CR is established to a verbal stimulus and tested for generalization to nonverbal stimuli (word-object) transfer. Although most of the Russian research reports have been relatively inaccessible, an edited volume by Ivanov-Smolensky (1956), available in English, presents a series of papers by their major contributors to semantic conditioning research. In one study reported by Naroditskaya (1956), the motor method of speech reinforcement was employed to reinforce positively a green light (by the word *press*) and to reinforce negatively a green light (by the words *do not press*) for subjects five to twelve years of age. The amount of CR transfer was then tested to related words (for example, *grass, sky, sea, leaf,* and so on) and to unrelated words. It was found that there was an increasing amount of CR transfer to related words with an increase in age.

In another study employing the Ivanov-Smolensky procedure, Korbatov (1956) studied both object-word and word-object CR transfer in four groups of children ages four to six, seven to eight, and fifteen to sixteen. Conditioning was conducted to objects or words and generalization tests were then made to the other signaling system after three, five, ten, twenty, or thirty CRs were made to the training CS. As in the findings of Naroditskaya, there was more CR transfer from the object to its verbal representation with increasing age of *S*s. For all age groups combined, there was more CR transfer from objects to words than from words to objects, but as the number of CRs to the original CS increased beyond five to ten CRs, the amount of transfer decreased.

Although Russian studies typically report more CR transfer from objects to words (see Hartman, 1965), American investigators typically report more CR transfer from words to objects. Thus, Branca (1957), employing the conditioned galvanic skin response (GSR), found significant CR transfer from words to objects, but no significant CR transfer from objects to words. Similarly, Keller (1943) conditioned the GSR to a picture of a boy scout hat and found no significant CR transfer to the word *hat* when compared to the control words *duck* and *ball*. He did find, however, significant CR transfer to the picture of a fireman's hat (that is, object-object transfer). A source of the divergent Russian and American findings may well be the degree of language development, because the majority of Russian studies involve children and the American studies adults.

Word-Word Transfer. Studies of word-word CR transfer may be classified into three categories: (1) transfer to synonyms, antonyms, and homonyms; (2) transfer within words or sentences of a general class (for example, rural words, political slogans, and so on); and (3) transfer to words related to the CS on the basis of free-association norms or by preconditioning manipulations of the associative connection of stimuli to the CS. The pioneer work on the transfer of CRs from words to synonyms and homonyms was the study by Razran (1939a). The CS words, *style, urn, freeze,* and *surf,* were flashed on a screen for three adult *S*s while they were consuming bits of food, chewing gum, or sucking lollipops. These eating periods lasted three min. during which each CS was flashed on the screen fifteen times.

Tests for generalization were begun after the second conditioning session, during which *S*s' salivation to the generalization stimuli was determined by the weighing of rolls of dental cotton inserted under *S*'s tongue for periods of 1 min. The mean amount of salivation to the generalization words *stile, fashion, earn, vase, frieze, chill, serf,* and *wave* revealed greater responding to synonyms than to homonyms. From these results Razran concluded that conditioning to verbal stimuli involves the conditioning to the "meaning" of the word rather than to its visual and auditory properties. Employing the same procedure, Razran (1949) conditioned salivation to three-word sentences consisting of a subject, a copula, and a predicate and tested for the generalization of CRs where certain parts of the sentences were changed. Statements employed as the CS were "Poverty is degrading," "Wealth is uplifting," "Poverty is uplifting," "Poverty is not degrading," and so on. Generalization of CRs to statements having total agreement in meaning was greatest; however, when the copulas were reversed (for example, "Poverty is not uplifting") there was less generalization than when the entire meaning was altered. Razran's word-word and sentence-sentence CR-transfer studies have not only instigated American research in this area, but also appear to have stimulated the research activities of Russian investigators (see Razran, 1961).

In an interesting study, Phillips (1958) examined the generalization of a conditioned GSR along an experimentally produced dimension of verbal similarity. To produce a gradient of verbal similarity she employed the procedure of establishing associative connections between five Turkish words (unfamiliar to *S*s, thus essentially meaningless) and five different shades of gray cards (varying on a continuum from light to dark), by means of paired presentations of the words and gray cards. Thus, *S*s were trained to respond with a particular Turkish word to a particular shade of gray, and to point to the proper shade of gray when the word was presented. Phillips expected that this training regime would establish the meaning of these words along a brightness dimension. In the second phase of the experiment, S's GSR was conditioned to the Turkish word associated previously with the darkest gray, and the amount of generalization of CRs to the other four Turkish words was then determined. In general, the amount of responding to these words was found to be a decreasing function of their distance from the CS on the brightness dimension.

Evaluation of Semantic Conditioning. In primary stimulus generalization a CR established to a CS will be elicited by other stimuli along the same physical dimension with the strength of the CR decreasing with distance of the test stimulus from the training CS. In the illustrative studies considered previously, it is obvious that something other than physical similarity must be invoked to account for the generalization of CRs. Although the majority of American investigators view semantic generalization as involving the transfer of meaning, it was Cofer and Foley (1942) who first attempted to apply conditioning principles to an analysis of the equivalence of meaning of verbal stimuli and objects as revealed in semantic conditioning research and in linguistic behavior in general.

It is clear that semantic generalization would not take place for Ss who did not know the meaning of the words or who saw no conceptual identity or similarity in the stimulus objects. Consequently, the explanatory problem to which Cofer and Foley addressed themselves was to the preconditioning basis of equivalence of verbal stimuli and objects. Following the theoretical analysis of Hull (1939), Cofer and Foley assumed that stimuli are similar in meaning or conceptual identity only to the degree to which they have been previously conditioned to the same or similar response. Thus, in their analysis they assumed that prior to semantic conditioning, stimuli schematized as CS_1 ... CS_n by their pairing with a UCS has led to the conditioning of some CR (r_g). Later, during semantic conditioning of CS_1 to some response r_y, each CS_1 presentation elicits r_g and its proprioceptive stimulation, s_g. Hence, r_y becomes conditioned not only to CS_1 but also to s_g. Now, when CS_2 ... CS_n are each presented alone for generalization testing, they will each elicit r_g, whose stimuli, s_g, will in turn elicit r_y. Although Cofer and Foley were the first to relate the various studies on semantic conditioning to some common mediating mechanism (that is, r_g–s_g), the application of mediating mechanisms has been substantially extended by Osgood (1953) and Mowrer (1960) to more complex linguistic behavior.

Despite the potential importance of semantic conditioning research to the understanding of linguistic behavior, the general body of research has not been impressive. The Russian practice of reporting individual protocols for only a small proportion of Ss in the experiment gives the impression of greater stability to their research than probably exists. Furthermore, most studies have only attempted to demonstrate the phenomenon of semantic conditioning rather than to determine precise quantitative relations. Although studies using the Ivanov-Smolensky procedure appear to show the most orderly results, American investigators have not been familiar with this technique and have most commonly employed the GSR. Unfornately, the methodological difficulties of employing the GSR, particularly in the absence of controls for sensitization and pseudoconditioning, makes the evidence for either conditioning or generalization effects in the majority of studies equivocal (see Feather, 1965). Hopefully, more methodologically sophisticated studies will be conducted in the future.

The Orienting Response

Pavlov observed that "investigative reflexes" of dogs seemed to be an unavoidable part of the procedure employed in his investigations of conditioning. In some instances this behavior, which we now call the orienting response (OR), clearly facilitated the formation of the CR, but when the eliciting stimulus was irrelevant to the conditioning task the OR seemed to interfere with the CR. From these anecdotal observations the OR has grown into an autonomous research topic which encompasses a good deal of contemporary work on autonomic conditioning as well as such topics as attention and arousal (Lynn, 1966).

The OR consists of a loosely knit pattern of autonomic, skeletal, and neuroelectrical reactions all of which presumably indicate the reception and processing of information. The eliciting stimulus for the OR might be a CS, UCS, or any other salient exteroceptive or interoceptive stimulus. It is generally agreed that stimuli which elicit ORs are either novel or biologically important because of their signal value or intensity. ORs of one kind or another have been observed in all classes of vertebrates and in six-week-old human infants (Lynn, 1966).

Perhaps the most precise and widely accepted definition of the OR has been given by Sokolov (1963). According to him a given reaction may be a component of the OR if it is nonspecific with respect to both the quality and intensity of the stimulus, and if it recovers from extinction (that is, habituation) through any modification of the eliciting stimulus. The components of the OR include the following:

Changes in sense organs:
1. Pupillary dilation.
2. Sensory thresholds at the receptor momentarily lowered.

Changes in orientation of sense organs:
1. Eyelids open wide and head turns toward the source stimulation.
2. Pricking up the ears, sniffing, and so on, depending upon the organism.

Changes in general skeletal musculature:
1. Ongoing activity is temporarily arrested.
2. Respiration deepens and slows.
3. Increase in EMG and muscle tone.

Changes in the central nervous system:
1. Alpha blocking of EEG.
2. Slower waves replaced by alpha.
3. Faster waves (beta and gamma) do not change during an OR.

Vegetative changes:
1. Blood vessels in the limbs contract while those in the head dilate.
2. GSR (skin conductance response) occurs.
3. Heart rate changes depending upon the law of initial value, generally a deceleration.

These reactions are in many instances the same as those which accompany a startle response insofar as the sympathetic nervous system is mobilized by the eliciting stimulus. In addition, the EEG component is essentially identical to what Western investigators call the *activation pattern*. For these reasons the definition of the OR also necessitates a reference to the role of each component in receiving, processing, and mobilizing the organism for dealing with the potentially important eliciting stimulus. Thus, the OR makes the organism more receptive to stimuli by increasing the exposure of sense organs and lowering thresholds. The increased cranial blood supply presumably aids information processing; the increased muscle tonus and the EMG and EEG activity represent the mobilization of body resources. The deepening and slowing of respiration maintains the oxygen level of the blood while lowering the "masking" effect of normal fast respiration and heart rate.

Some components of the OR to a given eliciting stimulus may actually be conditioned responses. If the eliciting stimulus had been paired with another stimulus which unconditionally evoked the reaction, then the new stimulus can acquire the capability of eliciting the same reaction. All components of the OR undergo extinction or habituation upon repeated, monotonous application of the eliciting stimulus, but if the stimulus changes in any way or if its rate of presentation is altered, the OR will temporarily recover its strength (disinhibition). Whenever the eliciting stimulus acquires signal value—for example, when it is a CS—the OR extinguishes only after the CR becomes well established. In more complex discrimination tasks the OR may never extinguish.

The OR in either its conditioned or unconditioned forms differs in several important respects from adaptive and defensive reactions. Adaptive reactions act in the opposite direction from the OR by tending to restore the organism to an optimal general level of excitability or activation. In general, the OR marks the onset of a stimulus, but if the stimulus persists the OR is replaced by adaptation. The best example of this involves the photochemical reactions of the retina. They act to lower the threshold for light intensity as a component of the OR but produce light adaptation with continued application of a bright stimulus, thereby raising the intensity difference threshold. Defensive reactions are also incompatible with the OR in that these tend to remove the organism from the source of stimulation. The best component for distinguishing between the OR and a defensive reaction is presumably the cranial vascular response. In a defensive reaction the cranial vessels constrict instead of dilate, as in the OR.

There are two dimensions which characterize the OR: a phasic-tonic dimension and a generalized-local dimension. The widespread arousal reaction, which perseverates for some time after the eliciting stimulus is removed, characterizes the initial presentations of the stimulus. This is the tonic-generalized phase of the OR. With further repetitions of the stimulus the generalized-tonic OR gives way to the

localized-phasic reactions which are largely confined to the primary sensory system of the eliciting stimulus.

The interrelationship between the OR and conditioning can best be illustrated in the following prototype experiment in which cortical EEGs are taken concurrently with behavioral conditioning of some response such as anticipatory limb flexion to shock. When the CS is first presented alone it produces a widespread desynchronization (alpha blocking or "activation" pattern) as part of the generalized OR. This widespread activity to the CS quickly subsides with repetitive nonreinforced presentations, but a local desynchronization persists for a much longer time in the primary afferent pathways of the CS and in its cortical projection area. If the CS is of at least moderate intensity this local OR may never become completely habituated. As soon as the CS and UCS are paired, widespread alpha blocking to the CS occurs once again (disinhibition), but repeated presentation of the paired stimuli soon leads to a recession of activity to the CS analyzer. Just before the behavioral CR emerges, the CS again elicits the generalized OR much as if the desynchronization itself becomes conditioned. This phase is probably most appropriately viewed as another instance of disinhibition of the habituated generalized OR produced by the emerging signal value of the CS. Once the behavioral response becomes well established, EEG activation to the CS occurs primarily in the cortical areas subserving the UCS, and the generalized OR once again undergoes habituation.

Opinion is divided as to whether the OR is essential for conditioning. Electrophysiological correlates of conditioning like those previously described are not essential for conditioning because some pharmacological agents which eliminate EEG activation do not interfere with acquisition of a behavioral CR. But conditioning with all components of the OR eliminated would seem to be impossible to realize experimentally. Other writers have cited conditioning without awareness as not involving ORs, but there is little direct evidence to support this viewpoint.

Interoceptive Conditioning

Interoceptive conditioning represents an extension of Pavlovian principles and techniques to situations in which the CS, UCS, or both are applied directly to internal organs. Most of this work was initiated by one of Pavlov's students, K. M. Bykov, whose 1943 book (Bykov and Gantt, 1957) remains the most authoritative source available in English, although Russian research in this field has increased at least ten fold since that time (Razran, 1961). In a typical interoceptive conditioning experiment, a dog is prepared with a gastric fistula fitted with inflow and outflow tubes into the stomach. These enable E to induce noiselessly a flow of water or some other solution over the receptors of the gastric mucosa. The flow of solution is systematically paired with some UCS such as electric shock for leg flexion or food for salivation. After a few pairings the internal flow will elicit the leg flexion or salivation. Compared with exteroceptive conditioning the CRs remain unstable for a long period of time, and if they are extinguished "below zero" they cannot be reinstated. In other preparations the CS might consist of changes in gastric pressure induced by swallowed balloons. This type of mechanical stimulation can also be applied to the intestines, the bladder, and other organs. Slight modifications of the atmosphere, such as the addition of 0.2 per cent CO_2, has served as an effective CS for defensive conditioning in dogs (Pogrebkova, 1966). As with many exteroceptive CRs, an extended series of reinforced trials with interoceptive CSs results in an increase of the latent period and diminution of the CR and UCR, that is, inhibition of delay (Mikushkin, 1961).

Differentiation based on interoceptive CSs has been established using a variety of stimulus dimensions and organs. Differential CRs have been established to differences in the temperature and chemical composition of fluids passed through the stomach or intestinal loops, to differences in mechanical pressure, and to induced changes in blood pressure. The differential inhibitor in such experiments seems to be quite labile and easily loses its inhibitory control, compared with exteroceptive inhibitory cues (Shapovalova, 1966).

Interoceptive conditioning has been successfully demonstrated in human Ss, but such experiments are obviously limited to patient populations. Diuresis seems to be particularly easy to condition in man. Excessive fluid intake in one context will establish an association whereby both the urge to urinate and the need become conditioned to that situation (Hofer and Hinkle, 1964).

The principal impact of interoceptive conditioning on Western psychological theorizing has been to alter our views of the role of conscious awareness in learning and conditioning. As presented by Razran (1961), interoceptive conditioning seems to involve stimulation which is below the threshold of awareness. Kimble (1962) has cited interoceptive conditioning literature as illustrating the fact that conditioning can occur without awareness of the CS, and Lynn (1966) refers to Razran's paper in support of his contention that the orienting response is not essential for conditioning. In point of fact, there is little direct evidence on the question of awareness in interoceptive conditioning or whether it can occur without orienting reactions to the CS. The following observations by Bykov (Bykov and Gantt, 1957) would seem to counter such intriguing, but possibly premature assertions:

It is important to note that during the action of an interoceptive conditional stimulus, an orientating reaction on the part of the animal is invariably observed. A new stimulus connecting the cerebral cortex with the animal's *milieu intérieur* calls forth a typical orienting reflex. This phenomenon is especially manifest when a conditional reflex ·to an interoceptive stimulus is being formed. The animal seems to be in search of some new message whose meaning has not yet been determined and this search is manifested either by general restlessness or by a special reaction that causes the animal to turn its head toward the point at which the interoceptive stimulation is being projected on the skin. [pp. 276–77]

Learning Theory and Classical Conditioning

Learning theories fall into two major categories: S-R (stimulus-response) theories and S-S (stimulus-stimulus) or cognitive theories. The central issue which has traditionally divided these systematic positions is whether the hypothetical changes presumed to take place in learning involve the formation of associations between stimuli (S-S associations) or stimuli and responses (S-R associations). Another major theoretical issue is whether contiguity alone or contiguity and reinforcement (that is, some equivalent of reward or punishment) is a necessary condition for learning to occur. It is the research in classical conditioning that bears on these theoretical issues on which we will now focus our attention.

S-R vs. S-S Associations

The essential notions underlying S-R formulations of learning were initially articulated in the S-R bond theory of Thorndike (1898, 1913). The S-R position has since come to include such diverse members as Guthrie (1935), Hull (1943, 1952), and Skinner (1938). Alternately, the essential ideas of S-S theory have been best exemplified in the extensive writings of Tolman (for example, 1932; 1934; 1937;

1945; 1959); it has also included such diverse members as Birch and Bitterman (1949), Maier and Schneirla (1942), Woodworth (1948, 1949), and Zener (1937). Among the classical-conditioning experiments designed to "settle" the issues implicit in the S-S and S-R positions, the most common forms of experimental attack have consisted of attempts to demonstrate the presence of preparatory set factors; sensory preconditioning; and conditioning without peripheral mechanisms. The occurrence of these phenomena has been generally interpreted as a source of embarrassment to the S-R position and consequently strenuous efforts have been made to reconcile these phenomena to the S-R point of view (Kimble, 1961).

Preparatory Set and Perceptual Disparity

The S-S position interprets the modifications that take place in learning as involving the perception of relationships among stimuli, cognitive (central) functions, and the anticipation of consequences. The clearest acceptance of an expectancy interpretation of classical conditioning was made by Zener (1937). Zener interpreted the functional character of the CR as a preparatory response for receipt of the UCS-to-come, and in support of this interpretation, drew upon his detailed observations of the concomitant behavior of dogs during salivary conditioning. He noted that the responses to the CS often differed from those occurring to the UCS and interpreted these deviations in the "complex of CRs" from the "complex of UCRs" as indicating that CRs operate as behaviors appropriate not to the *presence* of the UCS, but to the *expectation* that the UCS will appear. Unfortunately, in the hands of Zener, as well as such writers as Maier and Schneirla (1942), Woodworth (1948, 1949), and Schlosberg (1937), the origin of the "preparatory"

CRs has remained unexplained. To call a CR a preparatory or expectation response does not provide an explanation for the occurrence of CRs. It is only recently, with Grings' (1960, 1965) development of the perceptual disparity concept, that experimental operations have been offered for measuring the strength and course of development of a preparatory or expectation response.

To appreciate Grings' conceptual contribution it must be recognized that, in general, S-S theorists have failed to define many of the cognitive-perceptual variables of their theories operationally; and such failures have served to limit the possibility of specifying relations in classical conditioning presumably derivable from these theories, at the empirical level. Furthermore, although S-R psychologists have become concerned with the possible presence of cognitive-perceptual variables in classical conditioning, they have generally regarded these variables as sources of confounding to be controlled. Thus, Spence (1963) in his concern with extending the "laws" of conditioning from lower, nonverbal organisms to human Ss, devised a guessing-game "masking" procedure to control cognitive-perceptual factors in human classical conditioning. Similarly, Razran (1955a, 1965) has advocated restricting the use of the term *classical conditioning* to those operations in which S's perception of the relationship among stimuli has been excluded; and in his own research activities Razran (1939a, 1949, 1955) has employed the technique of providing instructions designed to mislead Ss on the nature of the experiment.

Grings (1960) proposed that the strength of preparatory set (that is, expectancy) established during classical conditioning could be estimated from a perceptual disparity situation in which a *perceptual disparity trial* is defined as one in which the CS is followed by a UCS different from that previously paired with the CS. Differences in the magnitude of the UCR on disparity and nondisparity trials are then taken as the measure of the strength of the preparatory set. The magnitude of the disparity response is assumed to be an inverse function of the degree to which the second stimulus (the UCS) is in accord with past experience. Accordingly, Grings and his associates have conducted experiments directed at determining the magnitude of the disparity response as a function of the *direction* of the disparity (that is, whether the UCS on the disparity trial is weaker or stronger than the UCS previously paired with the CS) and the amount of disparity (as measured on some scale of stimulus difference).

A study by Grings, Dossett, and Honnard (1959) is illustrative. In this investigation twenty-four Ss were assigned to each of two reinforcement schedules (67 per cent or 100 per cent) for GSR conditioning to two CSs (colored lights), each reinforced by a 50-db. tone UCS for eight trials followed by a single disparity trial. Within each reinforcement schedule the Ss were divided into four subgroups of six Ss each to receive a tone UCS on the disparity trial of either 30, 70, 90, or 110 db. Hence, there resulted four different degrees of discrepancy from the original tone UCS of − 20 db., 20 db., 40 db., and 60 db. The greater the amount of discrepancy between anticipated and actual stimulation the greater was the GSR elicited by the actual stimulus, and discrepancies in an upward direction appeared to yield larger disparity responses than discrepancies in a downward direction. In addition, the effects of these variables appeared to be a function of the number of reinforcements as well as the percentage of reinforcements employed.

On the basis of preliminary investigations, Grings (1960) has also hypothesized that the magnitude of the disparity response is a function of the number of CS-UCS pairings. Grings assumes that preparatory set factors are stabilized by repeated CS-UCS pairings and as long as no irregularities in the sequencing occur, S, in adopting an appropriate "set" for the receipt of the UCS, may show a curve of adaptation of his CRs and UCRs with increased CS-UCS pairings. He further assumes that the strength of preparatory set factors increases with pairings. Consequently, because the magnitude of the disparity response is taken as evidence of the strength of the preparatory set, Grings suggests that the disparity response may reveal a different and perhaps better estimate of the course of development of preparatory set than the CR.

An important implication of such formulations is that the reduction in the magnitude of CRs with increased pairings, as is commonly observed in GSR conditioning (see Kimmel, 1959), may be a function of changes in the strength and stability of the preparatory set. In support of these formulations Grings, Carlin, and Appley (1962) have reported an investigation in which word stimuli serving as the CS were appropriately reinforced at a 5-sec. interstimulus interval (ISI) during acquisition of the GSR, that is, the words *cool breeze* were followed by brief stimulation from an electric fan, the words *soft music* by a brief presentation of orchestral music, and so on. After fourteen or forty-nine reinforcements of these words a previously reinforced or neutral word was introduced in a test series in which a disparity trial (for example, the CS *soft music* followed by stimulation from an electric fan) was also included. According to Grings' formulations, the CR to the CS *loud tone*, for example, would become less with more pairings because of "adaptation" resulting from the establishment of an appropriate "set" to the receipt of an actual tone as the UCS. For the same reason the UCR to the tone would be expected to demonstrate "adaptation." On the other hand, the magnitude of the disparity response to the tone following another CS (for example, *green light*) would be expected to increase with the greater number of pairings of *green light* and onset of a green

light. The effects of number of reinforcements in the Grings *et al.* study on both the conditioned GSR (that is, anticipatory CRs) and magnitude of the disparity response supported Grings' predictions, the CRs showing a significant decrease in magnitude and the disparity response showing an increase from fourteen to forty-nine reinforcements.

Sensory Preconditioning

The basic paradigm characterizing the phenomenon of sensory preconditioning (SPC) involves three successive phases. In the first, termed the preconditioning (PC) phase, the initially neutral stimuli, CS_1 and CS_2, are paired together. In the second or conditioning phase, CS_1 is then repeatedly paired with a UCS until a CR is established. In the third or test phase, CS_2 is presented alone and if the CR occurs, SPC is said to have been demonstrated. Although the second phase may involve either classical or instrumental conditioning procedures, it is the first or PC phase which has led to its inclusion into the general class of classical-conditioning paradigms, because no instrumental contingency is operative during this stage.

The first successful demonstration of SPC is generally credited to Brogden (1939), who also applied the name *sensory preconditioning* to the phenomenon. Eight dogs were given 200 PC trials consisting of simultaneous presentation of a light and sound of a bell. These Ss were then divided into two groups of four dogs each. One group was given paired presentation of the sound of the bell and shock to the foot-pad for leg flexion conditioning, whereas the other group received light-shock pairings. Two control groups of four dogs each did not receive the preconditioning phase of pairing bell and light, but were treated the same in all other respects as the experimental groups. In the test stage, the mean number of flexion responses to the stimulus never directly paired with the UCS was significantly greater for the experimental groups. Although Brogden offered no hypothesis regarding the nature of the phenomenon, sensory preconditioning has since been regarded as highly significant to one of the fundamental issues of the psychology of learning. To the question of whether the modification that takes place in learning involves a central, cognitive event (S-S associations) or whether some overt behavior must be involved (S-R associations), the demonstration of preconditioning made it appear that the simple contiguity of purely sensory events (S-S associations) is sufficient for learning.

Definitive research in sensory preconditioning must of necessity incorporate controls for a form of stimulus generalization known as cross-modal generalization and for the possible differential effects produced by unequal familiarity with the test stimuli on the part of control as opposed to experimental Ss. Many of the later studies by Brogden and his colleagues (Siedel, 1959) employed controls in which CS_1 and CS_2 were presented equally often in the first stage, but unpaired. This procedure insures equal familiarity with the CSs for experimental and control groups. The question of cross-model generalization requires a control group in which CS_2 is not introduced until the test phase. When familiarity and cross-modal generalization are suitably controlled the size of the SPC effect is greatly attenuated but not completely eliminated.

Peripheral Mechanisms

The principal polemic in learning theory between the S-S (centralist) and S-R (peripheralist) positions generated a good deal of interest on the part of physiological psychologists in the possibility of demonstrating behavioral conditioning in preparations in which normal peripheral sensory or motor systems are by-passed or rendered inoperative. Since the 1930's an intriguing literature has accumulated bearing more or less directly on this issue, and offering a confusing tangle of conflicting findings. But this picture has now been brought into reasonably good focus and each of the specific questions and answers appears to be at hand. There have been two principal lines of research: one employs curare so as to block motor involvement in conditioning and another employs brain stimulation as either the CS or UCS so as to by-pass primary sensory pathways from peripheral receptors. The curare literature can be further broken down into at least two separate, but related, issues. One concerns the role of skeletal activity in classical autonomic conditioning. The other relates to the question of whether a motor response can be conditioned while blocked by curare.

Black and his associates (Black, 1965; Black and Lang, 1964; Black, Carlson, and Solomon, 1962) have demonstrated rather convincingly that autonomic conditioning can proceed in the curarized state. Smith (1954) has suggested that autonomic CRs may be artifacts of concomitant skeletal activity associated with the CS. For example, heart-rate changes during cardiac conditioning might arise from respiratory changes, glandular secretions might be mediated by changes in tonus or postural adjustments, the conditioned GSR may reflect nothing more than a tensing of the skeletal muscles in anticipation of shock, and so on. The issue was fundamentally important for learning theory because if Smith's hypothesis were correct, one could accept the simplistic notion that there is only one kind of learning and it is basically instrumental in nature. The Black experiments showed that heart-rate changes were easily conditioned and differentiated in dogs paralyzed with tubocurarine. Smith (1964) questioned whether total paralysis had been achieved in these experiments and thus whether skeletal mediation could be unequivocally ruled out. Black (1965) and

Black and Lang (1964) countered by showing that EMG patterns from curarized dogs were not correlated with simple cardiac conditioning and differentiation.

The question of whether it is possible to condition *skeletal* responses under curare also appears to have been resolved affirmatively. A superlative review of the literature in this area may be found in Solomon and Turner's (1962) experimental report. These investigators trained dogs to press a panel to avoid shock in the presence of a cue (light offset). The CS-UCS interval was 10 sec. and all dogs learned to a criterion of at least twenty consecutive avoidance trials. The dogs were then tested for sensitization to the two tones to be used as CS+ and CS− in the second phase of the study. In this phase all animals were paralyzed with tubocurarine and given differential conditioning in which one tone (CS+) was always paired with shock and the other (CS−) never reinforced. The ISI was 10 sec., as in preliminary avoidance training, and the UCS was a 4-ma shock applied for 5 sec. (which is quite severe). Two days after the curare-conditioning session, the dogs were tested on the panel press avoidance to the original cue, the CS+ tone, and CS−. These were presented according to sequences designed to minimize bias, and the shock was never administered in this phase of the experiment. The results showed that panel presses to CS+ were more reliable, vigorous, and had shorter latency than responses to CS−. Thus, the animals were able to transfer classical conditioning under a curare drug to appropriate performance of a skeletal response.

Earlier unsuccessful attempts to demonstrate transfer from curarized to normal states in both autonomic and motor conditioning were mainly the result of amnesia or "dissociation" induced as a side effect of raw curare. Flaxedil and tubocurarine are among the synthesized curares which do not induce dissociation. These forms were not available to investigators during the period of most active experimentation during the 1930's and 1940's. Of interest in the Solomon and Turner (1962) study is the fact that no overt skeletal responses could occur during curare conditioning. Therefore differential peripheral skeletal responses (and their associative feedback) could not have been a factor in mediating the effects of the differential classical conditioning training on discriminative instrumental responding. For classical aversive conditioning at least, formulations which restrict themselves to skeletal responses and their correlated proprioceptive feedback, as mediators of instrumental conditioning, would be inadequate. One possibility, of course, is that autonomic CRs and their correlated feedback are the effective mediators (see Solomon and Turner, 1962). Whether the modulating effects of classical appetitive conditioning on instrumental responding can also be obtained in the absence of skeletal responding remains an empirical question.

Attempts to employ direct electrical stimulation of the brain (ESB) as a CS, thereby short-circuiting peripheral pathways, were successful from the beginning. A series of experiments by Loucks in the 1930's established this fact, and the work of Doty and his collaborators (Doty, 1961) has confirmed and extended the early findings. Doty's group showed that subcortical as well as cortical stimulation can successfully serve as a CS for a conditioned leg flexion in dogs. They have also demonstrated differential conditioning of ESB's at two different sites and stimulus generalization between peripheral and central CSs. More recently, Doty (1965) has shown that ESB of virtually any site in the brain of a monkey can control lever-press avoidance behavior. Such stimulus control does not arise indirectly from "peripheral" receptors. The principal sources for such feedback would be proprioceptive cues from possible motor components of the CS or interoceptive cues from vascular, meningeal, or visceral receptors. All of these possibilities have been virtually eliminated by Loucks and Doty.

Loucks (1935) also attempted conditioning in dogs using electrical stimulation of motor cortex as the UCS. The idea was to establish a motor CR based solely on the contiguous relationship between the CS and whatever reaction was elicited by the cortical UCS. In this way the motivational systems which normally accompany a motor reflex are presumably eliminated. The importance of the motivational factor in defensive conditioning with peripherally applied stimuli can be illustrated by the fact that in rabbits good eyelid and nictitating-membrane conditioning requires a direct threat to the eye by the UCS. Application of the electric shock to points several centimeters from the eye yield good UCRs, but very little conditioning. It therefore does not seem too surprising that Louck's attempt to establish motor conditioning based solely upon S-R contiguity failed.

Doty and Giurgea (1961) apparently succeeded where Loucks had failed by employing intertrial intervals of 3 to 5 min. compared with the relatively massed trials (30 to 60 sec.) employed by Loucks. The UCS in these studies presumably affects only those structures essential for association and those efferent pathways serving the elicited response. The UCR might be lifting a paw or turning the head in a stereotyped manner. Meningeal pain, positive reward effects from "leakage" into the hypothalamus, or other affective aspects of the UCS were ruled out as possible sources of motivation for these responses. Nor was there any evidence that the motor CRs were merely postural adjustments which enabled the animal to maintain his equilibrium to the anticipated UCS. It would appear, then, that stimulus substitution is sufficient for classical conditioning and that motivational factors might be dispensed with as unessential.

Doty and Giurgea's demonstration of classical conditioning based on direct stimulation of motor cortex has been confirmed by Wagner, Thomas, and Norton (1967), but these investigators found evidence that a motivational factor may exist in this preparation after all. In one of their experiments, two dogs were trained to press either of two panels for food and, at intervals of 3, 4, or 5 min., cortical stimulation which elicited a hind-leg UCR. Presses on one panel at these times would result in presentation of the UCR alone after a 1-sec. delay. Presses on the other panel produced a 1-sec. train of clicks which served as a CS. At the end of preliminary training for food on the two panels, both dogs showed a preference for the right panel. When stimulation was introduced with the CS-UCS on the left and the UCS alone on the right, the Ss showed an unmistakable shift in preference to the left panel. Even after several reversals of the CS-UCS or UCS contingency the dogs continued to prefer whichever panel provided the CS. Thus, dogs receiving cortical stimulation are not neutral with respect to the conditioning situation. Wagner, Thomas, and Norton contend that the CS permits postural adjustments which reduce the presumed noxiousness of the UCS. This is not to say that the CR is a preparatory postural adjustment rather than a copy of the UCR, only that a parallel motivational component involving postural adjustments probably exists in the situation. Thus, although all sources of motivation cannot be ruled out of the cortical stimulation experiments, neither is it possible to infer a causal relationship between these motivational factors and the classical conditioning.

Classical Conditioning and Instrumental Learning

Mediation of Instrumental Learning

Theoretically, any instrumental learning situation has within it the conditions for the development of classically conditioned responses. The reinforcing event (for example, food), although response contingent, occurs in a specific situation; and because these situational stimuli are regularly associated with reinforcement in the manner of classical conditioning, CRs may concurrently develop. Learning theorists have given formal recognition to the possibility of CR accompaniments of instrumental conditioning by such concepts as secondary reinforcement, secondary drive, and incentive motivation. In the application of these concepts to instrumental conditioning it is assumed that two different learning processes are involved. One process consists of the acquisition of the specific instrumental response, whereas the second consists of the acquisition of collateral CRs conditioned to situational stimuli and/or proprioceptive stimuli arising from the organism's instrumental responses. It is then assumed that these CRs modulate the instrumental response tendency by their action as either *motivators* (that is, incentive motivators and secondary drives) or *reinforcers* (that is, secondary reinforcers) of the instrumental response.

Perhaps the most extensively employed two-process account of instrumental *reward* conditioning is that proposed by Spence (1956). Briefly, the theory assumes that in an instrumental runway situation, for example, stimulus cues in the goal box and cues from the alley preceding the goal box become classically conditioned to components of the goal response. The goal response, designated as R_g, is regarded as the UCR to the reinforcing event (for example, presentation of food or water) and consists of consummatory activity (for example, eating food or drinking water). The CR components of R_g, designated as r_g, and referred to as the fractional anticipatory goal response, may consist of such responses as salivating, chewing, licking, and swallowing. Over the course of extended training and through stimulus generalization (in the manner of

stimulus trace accounts of interstimulus interval effects), stimuli at earlier points in the runway are assumed to acquire the capacity to elicit r_g.

The theory also assumes that the incentive motivation construct, K, is determined by the strength of r_g, and that K has a multiplicative relationship with the associative learning factor H (see Chapter 4 for a more extended treatment). Hence, the Spence formulation assumes that the collateral CR, r_g, interacts in a motivational fashion with the habit strength of the instrumental response to affect its overt occurrence. On the other hand, other formulations (Konorski, 1948) have emphasized the rewarding function of collateral CRs, by assuming that an increase in salivary flow, for example, reflects a reinforcing state of affairs for instrumental responses that precede the salivary flow.

Starting with the initial formulations of Mowrer (1947) and Miller (1948), two-process formulations of instrumental *aversive* conditioning have invoked a classically conditioned "fear" response as both the motivating and reinforcing mechanism for instrumental avoidance behavior (see Chapter 5). Specifically, these formulations have assumed that an aversive stimulus (for example, shock) elicits an unconditioned "fear" response, which, following the laws of classical conditioning, becomes conditioned to the CS preceding the aversive stimulus. Furthermore, the stimulus consequences of the conditioned "fear" response are assumed to have drive properties which when reduced can operate to reinforce a contingent response. Thus, the proprioceptive feedback from the conditioned "fear" response, to environmentally produced cues (for example, tone or light) preceding the aversive event is postulated to instigate or motivate the instrumental response that avoids the UCS. In turn, the instrumental avoidance response by terminating the cue is reinforced by the reduction in the conditioned "fear" response and its stimulus consequence.

A similar analysis is applied to the passive avoidance (punishment) paradigm. The proprioceptive feedback from the conditioned "fear" response to response-produced cues of a to-be-punished instrumental response, is assumed to provide a secondary drive state whose termination by the cessation of the instrumental response (that is, passive avoidance) provides the reinforcement for such cessation.

Concurrent Measurement. To explore the hypothesis that instrumentally conditioned responses are mediated by CRs, some Es have employed the procedure of concurrently measuring the instrumental response and one or more of the response systems elicited as UCRs to the reinforcing event (for example, food or shock). Under the specific hypothesis that CRs operate as instigators or motivators of the instrumental response, CRs would be expected to precede the instrumental response, whereas CRs acting as reinforcers would be expected to follow the instrumental response. Consequently, a number of these Es have also attempted to examine the temporal sequence of instrumental responses and CRs.

As noted by Rescorla and Solomon (1967), Konorski and Miller (1930) were apparently the first investigators to direct attention to the possible mediation by classically conditioned responses of instrumental reward behavior. Employing dogs in a discriminative instrumental paw-movement response for food reinforcement and concurrently recording salivary flow, they observed that the instrumental response consistently preceded an increase in salivary flow. In more recent work involving dogs in an operant lever-press response for food reinforcement and the recording of salivary flow (Shapiro, 1961; Kintsch and Witte, 1962; Williams, 1965), Es have observed similar sequential relationships under two types of reinforcement schedules (fixed ratio and fixed interval). On the other hand,

Shapiro (1962) observed that under another reinforcement schedule (differential reinforcement of low rates) bursts of salivation preceded the instrumental response. Thus, the sequence of salivary flow and instrumental response appears to depend upon the type of reinforcement schedule used (see Shapiro and Miller, 1965).

Miller and De Bold (1965) employed rats in a discriminated bar-press situation, using water reinforcement delivered via a fistula into the rat's oral cavity, and concurrently recorded the licking response. They observed that although the probability of licking was greater just prior to a barpress it was maximal following a nonreinforced barpress. Deaux and Patten (1964) have also provided some data suggestive of the possible mediation by collateral CRs of instrumental runway behavior. These Es ran rats to water reinforcement while a measure was taken of anticipatory licking (CRs) in the runway and consummatory licking to delivery of water reinforcement in the goal box. They observed that anticipatory licking in the runway increased as the animals approached the goal box. Furthermore, across days of training the animals revealed an increase in the rate of licking concomitant with an increase in the speed of running.

In the instrumental aversive conditioning situation, heart-rate change has been the most extensively employed index of the presumed mediating fear response. Typically, during acquisition of an instrumental avoidance response, dogs have revealed an increase in heart rate to the discriminative stimulus prior to the acquisition of the avoidance response (Gantt and Dykman, 1957; Black, 1959). Considering asymptotic performance, Soltysik (1960) has reported an increase in the heart rate of dogs preceding the avoidance response and a decrease following the response. On the other hand, Bersh, Notterman, and Schoenfeld (1956) have observed that with continued avoidance training at asymptote, human Ss fail to show heart-rate change to the discriminative stimulus. Rescorla and Solomon (1967) have noted that in extinction the relationship of heart-rate change to the instrumental response has also been contradictory. Thus, Gantt and Dykman (1957) found that the instrumental response extinguished long before the heart-rate CR, whereas Soltysik (1960) observed trial-by-trial correspondence of the instrumental response and heart-rate CR, and Black (1959) found more rapid extinction of the heart-rate CR than of the instrumental response.

The contradictory observations on the order of CRs and instrumental responses would appear to weaken the validity of the theoretical notion that peripheral CRs operate as mediators of responses in the instrumental learning situation. It is possible, of course, that the concurrent measurement of a complex of CRs may reveal more ordered relationships to the instrumental response. However, different sequential orderings of CRs and instrumental responses can arise from simply employing different response criteria (see Shapiro and Miller, 1965; Williams, 1965). Furthermore, the correlational nature of the data precludes the specifying of a causal relationship between CRs and instrumental responses. Consequently, the results of concomitant measurement research has the logical difficulty of being unable to reject the hypothesis that CRs are interesting but nonetheless inconsequential concomitants of the instrumental learning situation.

Rescorla and Solomon (1967) have suggested that a theoretical conception which considers some "central state" to be conditioned by classical-conditioning operations would lead to a more effective research strategy for investigating the interrelationship of classical and instrumental conditioning. According to their formulation, considering a conditioned "central state" as the mediator of overt CRs and instrumental responses would lead to the research strategy of first submitting Ss to classical-conditioning training

and then determining the interacting effects of such training on instrumental learning. Although such classical-instrumental transfer designs have been most extensively investigated by Solomon and his associates, the majority of earlier as well as most recent investigations have received their theoretical impetus from the assumption that the procedures required to provide a neutral stimulus with secondary reinforcing or acquired drive properties are those of classical conditioning (Hull, 1943; Miller, 1951; Mowrer, 1960a). Accordingly, classical-instrumental transfer designs have been traditionally employed to determine the possible motivating and/or reinforcing effects of a CS (that is, a stimulus paired with primary reinforcers by classical-conditioning operations) on already established, or to-be-established, instrumental responses.

Classical Appetitive Transfer Designs. The motivating effects of a CS, following appetitive classical-conditioning operations, on instrumental reward responses was revealed in the pioneer studies of Estes (1943, 1948). Estes (1943) first conditioned the bar-press response of rats on a partial reinforcement schedule for food reinforcement and then, removing the bar, he interpolated thirty "CS-UCS" trials in which a 60-sec. tone was followed by the delivery of food into a magazine. To determine the motivating effects of the CS, Estes introduced two 10-min. presentations of the tone in extinction for the experimental group whereas the control group received no tone. The effect of the tone was to produce an elevation in the rate of bar pressing. In a second study Estes (1948) showed that a similar motivating effect of the CS can be obtained if the pairing of tone and food occurs prior to the establishment of the conditioned barpress.

The Estes transfer paradigm has also been extended to a determination of the motivating effects of CSs, following differential classical conditioning, on instrumen-

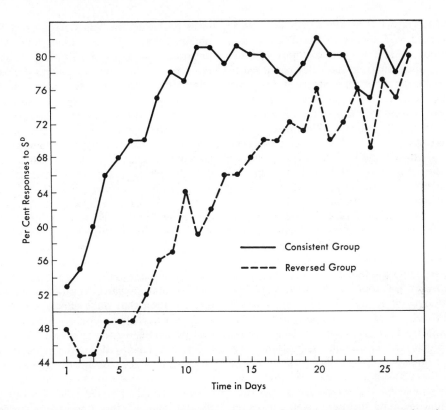

Figure 8-1. Group average discrimination scores plotted against successive days of training. (Reprinted with permission from Bower, G., and Grusec, T. Effect of prior Pavlovian discrimination training upon learning an operant discrimination. *J. exp. Anal. Behav.*, 1964, **7**, 401–404.)

tal conditioning. Thus, Morse and Skinner (1958), using pigeons, paired food presentation with one color (CS+) and presented another color (CS−) without reinforcement. The CS+ and CS− were then introduced alternately into the extinction phase of a key-peck response which had previously been reinforced in the presence of a white light. They observed many more responses during CS+ than during CS−. Bower and Grusec (1964) further assessed the effects of differential classical conditioning by determining the effects of such training on subsequent instrumental discrimination training. The Ss were first trained to bar-press for water reinforcement and then the lever was removed for differential classical-conditioning training in which CS+ was

paired with the availability of water in the magazine and CS− was presented in the absence of water. The Ss were then divided into two groups for instrumental discrimination training where the CS+ and CS− occurred in alternate 1-min. periods. For one group (consistent group), bar pressing was reinforced in the presence of CS+, whereas bar pressing was not reinforced in the presence of CS−. For the other group (reversed group), the discriminative role of the stimuli were reversed, with bar pressing reinforced in the presence of CS− and not reinforced in the presence of CS+. The consistent group revealed a large and sustained superiority in discriminative responding, as shown in Fig. 8–1.

Trapold and his associates (Trapold,

1966; Trapold, Carlson, and Myers, 1965; Trapold and Fairlis, 1965; Trapold and Odom, 1965; Trapold and Winokur, 1967) have also employed the Estes paradigm to explore the motivating effects of a number of appetitive, classical-conditioning manipulations upon instrumental reward conditioning. Particularly illustrative is the study conducted by Trapold and Winokur (1967) to test the implications of Spence's (1956) classical-conditioning account of incentive motivation (K) and its role in instrumental conditioning. On the assumption that pairings of a stimulus with a positive reinforcing event leads to the classical conditioning of r_g, and consequently, the development of some value of K, these Es tested and obtained confirmation of four predictions: (1) conditioning of r_g through pairing of a CS with delivery of food in a magazine in the manner of classical conditioning would facilitate the subsequent acquisition of a discriminative operant bar-press response to the CS; (2) extinction of r_g through nonreinforced presentations of the CS, would facilitate the subsequent extinction of a discriminative instrumental bar-press response to the CS; (3) conditioning the r_g response through reinforced presentation of another stimulus, CS[1], would facilitate subsequent generalized responding of the instrumental response from the CS to CS[1]; and (4) generalized instrumental responses from the CS to CS[1] would be decreased if preceded by the nonreinforced presentation of CS[1].

In studies concerned with assessing the secondary reinforcing effects of a classical appetitive CS on instrumental reward conditioning, the occurrence of the CS is made response contingent either in acquisition or during extinction of an instrumental response. For example, Bersh (1951) gave 160 paired presentations of a light and food pellet for each of six groups of rats at interstimulus intervals of 0, 0.5, 1, 2, 4, and 10 sec. Subsequently, the lever was introduced in the Skinner box with each bar-press producing the light CS for 1 sec. The obtained curve, based upon total bar-presses for a fixed one and one-half hour test period, indicated a maximum secondary reinforcing effect for Ss trained at an interstimulus interval between 0 and 2 sec. Other investigators have similarly employed the transfer paradigm to determine the effects on secondary reinforcement of the manipulation during the classical conditioning phase of such variables as amount of primary reinforcement (Butter and Thomas, 1958), reinforcement schedule (Fox and King, 1961), drive level (Estes, 1949), and brain-shock reward (Stein, 1958).

Although classical appetitive transfer studies provide support for the motivating and reinforcing effects of the CS on instrumental reward conditioning, the interpretation that these effects are mediated by classically conditioning responses may be seriously questioned in view of the procedures employed. In the majority of these studies the Ss must make instrumental approach responses to the magazine to obtain food or water reinforcement. It could be argued that once the approach response develops, the situation approximates the classical-conditioning paradigm because the CS consistently precedes reinforcement whereas the approach response alone cannot produce the reinforcement. On the other hand, the possibility exists that the motivating or reinforcing effects of the CS on instrumental conditioning may be mediated by conditioned instrumental approach responses. At the present time, there is no empirical basis for arguing that one or the other of these two classes of responses is more important to the transfer. What is needed are studies employing classical-conditioning preparations (for example, salivary) in which an attempt is made to minimize the occurrence of instrumental behavior changes during the classical-conditioning manipulations.

Classical Aversive Transfer Designs. Experiments have shown that when a CS has been paired with an aversive UCS, the introduction of the CS in an instrumental learning situation where the evocation of a new instrumental response terminates the CS, can lead to the acquisition of the response (Brown and Jacobs, 1949; Gwin, 1949; Kalish, 1954; Miller, 1951). Because the capacity of the CS to function as a reinforcer is one of the common criteria employed in identifying motivational variables (see Brown, 1961; Miller, 1951), these studies have been interpreted as support for both the acquired motivation and secondary reinforcing effects of the CS.

The investigation of Brown and Jacobs (1949) is illustrative. *E*s subjected an experimental group of eight rats to the pairing of a CS (tone and light) with shock for twenty-two trials at a CS-UCS interval of 3 sec. in one side of a two-compartment shuttle box, whereas a control group of eight rats received just CS presentations. To test for the drive and consequent reinforcing effects of the CS, the door between the two compartments was raised and the *S*s received forty instrumental conditioning trials in which they could terminate the CS by jumping a hurdle to the other compartment. The results indicated a significant decrease in the latency of the hurdle jumps for the experimental group whereas the performance of the controls became progressively worse. The hurdle-jumping performance of the experimental group has been interpreted as being instigated by the occurrence of a conditioned "fear" response with CS offset.

Another line of experimental inquiry traditionally regarded as involving classical-instrumental transfer has been that concerned with the effects on operant reward behavior of a CS paired with an aversive UCS. Starting from the report of Estes and Skinner (1941), a number of investigations have been conducted to reveal that introduction of a CS, previously paired with shock, may serve to suppress an on-going bar-press response for food reinforcement. Hunt and Brady (1951), as well as Estes and Skinner, have interpreted the suppression of the on-going bar-press response as being largely the result of the CS eliciting an incompatible conditioned emotional response (CER). The degree of behavioral suppression for such classical conditioning manipulations as CS and UCS intensity (Kamin and Brimer, 1963), interstimulus interval (Kamin, 1965), and reinforcement schedule (Brimer and Dockrill, 1966) reveals the effects of these variables to parallel those reported in the salivary conditioning experiments of Pavlov. The results of the CER paradigm would appear to contradict the enhancing effects obtained with other transfer paradigms. However, if one concedes that the ability to suppress on-going responses is one of the criteria for identifying a stimulus as having motivational properties (see Brown, 1961), then the CER paradigm poses no particular problem of interpretation. The one difficulty is that most investigators have employed the CER technique by introducing CS-UCS pairings within the bar-pressing situation and not by instituting separate classical conditioning training. Although suppression occurs under both transfer and nontransfer procedures, there are data which suggest that classical-conditioning manipulations operate differently in the two situations. For example, Wagner, Siegel, and Fein (1967) observed that a partial reinforcement effect appeared under the nontransfer procedure, but failed to appear under the transfer procedure of presenting CS-UCS pairings separate from the bar-pressing situation. Consequently, the proposition that there are parallel effects of classical-conditioning manipulations on the acquired drive properties of the CS in the CER paradigm and the salivary conditioning experiments of Pavlov must be accepted with caution.

The transfer paradigm has also been extended to an analysis of the effects of classical aversive conditioning on instrumental aversive conditioning. The Solomon and Turner (1962) investigation, discussed earlier, falls into this category. Rescorla and LoLordo (1965) trained dogs to jump a barrier, separating the two sides of a shuttle box, to avoid shock. An unsignaled (Sidman) avoidance procedure was used. If S did not jump the barrier, a shock was delivered to the grid floor every 10 sec.; whereas if S jumped, the shock was postponed for 30 sec. After the dogs learned to perform the avoidance response at a stable rate they were given alternate classical-conditioning and instrumental avoidance conditioning sessions. During classical-conditioning sessions the dogs were confined to one compartment of the shuttlebox and given differential classical-conditioning trials to auditory CSs. For one experiment, CS duration was 5 sec. and for CS+ trials shock was presented at a CS-UCS interval of 5 sec. whereas CS− trials were presented alone. A single test session was then given in which the dogs performed the avoidance response under extinction conditions (that is, no shocks were delivered). During this session the tones were presented sixty times each in random order, independent of S's behavior. The CS+ trials resulted in a large increase and CS− trials a large decrease in the baseline jumping rate. Hence, CS+ presentations revealed acquired motivating properties and CS− trials acquired inhibitory properties.

Employing the same transfer paradigms, Rescorla (1967) observed another form of acquired inhibition. Once the dogs had attained a stable jumping rate, they were subjected on alternate days to long-delay classical conditioning in which a tone CS was paired with shock at an interstimulus interval of 30 sec. Later, when the dogs performed the avoidance response in extinction conditions, the 30-sec. tone was presented randomly throughout the session. Rescorla found that the onset of the tone produced a decrease in jumping rate below the baseline, and the rate thereafter increased until, at about 20 sec. after CS onset, the jumping rate went above baseline, and continued to increase steadily to the end of the 30-sec. interval. Here, then, Rescorla observed both inhibitory and facilitating effects of the CS in a temporal pattern analogous to Pavlov's inhibition of delay.

Solomon and Turner (1962), in a more complex variant of the classical aversive-instrumental aversive transfer paradigm, employed the technique of completely paralyzing their Ss during the classical-conditioning phase. Specifically, dogs were trained to panel-press, in the presence of a discriminative visual stimulus (CS_o), to avoid shock. After the dogs were reliably pressing the panel in the presence of CS_o, they were totally paralyzed by d-tubocurarine and subjected to differential classical conditioning to tone CS_s. A 15-sec. CS+ tone was paired with shock at a CS-UCS interval of 10 sec. and shock duration of 5 sec., whereas CS− was presented alone for 15 sec. Following a random sequence of ninety-nine differential conditioning trials, the dogs were given forty-eight hours to recover from the various physiological effects of curarization. They were then returned to the panel-press avoidance situation where CS_o, CS+, and CS− stimuli were presented under extinction conditions. The dogs revealed a retention of their avoidance response to CS_o, but in addition, they showed reliable panel-pressing responses in the presence of CS+, and little responding in the presence of CS−. Of interest in this study is the fact that no overt skeletal responses could occur during curare conditioning. Therefore, differential peripheral skeletal responses (and their associative feedback) could not have been a factor in mediating the effects of the differential classical-conditioning training on discriminative instrumental responding. For classical aversive conditioning, at least, formulations which restrict themselves to skeletal responses and their correlated proprioceptive feedback, as mediators of instrumental conditioning, would be inadequate. One possibility, of course, is that autonomic CRs and their correlated feedback are the effective mediators (see Solomon and Turner, 1962). Whether the modulating effects of classical appetitive conditioning on instrumental responding can also be obtained in the absence of skeletal responding remains an empirical question.

Glossary

analyzer. (1) The cortical projection area of a stimulus. (2) The entire functional system involved in processing the information in a given stimulus.

anticipatory instructed conditioning (Grant). A conditioning procedure in which the UCS consists of a command or signal for the performance of some arbitrarily preselected motor response.

alpha response. The original response to the CS. It differs from the orienting response in being specific to modality and intensity of the CS.

backward conditioning. Any conditioning paradigm in which the UCS precedes the CS.

beta response (Grant). In eyelid conditioning with visual CSs, a response of short latency which develops during dark adaptation.

centralist. One who holds that the central nervous system is sufficient for all conditioning. Essentially equivalent to S-S theory.

classical defense conditioning. Any conditioning procedure which employs an aversive stimulus as the UCS.

classical reward conditioning (also called, *appetitive conditioning*). Any conditioning procedure which employs a positive reinforcer as the UCS.

complex CS. A compound CS in which the onset of component stimuli occur in sequence rather than simultaneously.

compound CS. A CS consisting of two or more stimulus components.

concentration (Pavlov). The focusing of excitation or inhibition within a relatively small cortical area.

conditioned emotional response (*CER;* also called *conditioned suppression*). When a CS is paired with a noxious stimulus, such as unavoidable shock, it attains the power to interrupt ongoing operant behavior. The extent of this interruption is measured as the rate of responding to the CS divided by this quantity plus the pretrial rate.

conditioned response (*CR*). A response which develops as a result of paired presentations of a conditioned stimulus and reinforcement.

conditioned stimulus (*CS*). An original indifferent or neutral stimulus which comes to evoke a CR through conditioning.

conditioning (also called *classical conditioning*). (1) The procedures which lead to establishment of a CR. (2) The process of CR formation, also known as *acquisition*.

delay conditioning. A conditioning paradigm in which the CS precedes the UCS and stays on at least until the onset of the UCS.

differentiation (also called *differential conditioning*). In conditioning, the procedures and processes of discrimination training consisting of successive presentations of a reinforced and nonreinforced stimulus denoted CS + and CS − respectively.

disinhibition. The disruption of an inhibitory process by a distracting stimulus.

dominant focus. In Pavlov's theory, the cortical site having the greatest concentration of excitation or inhibition. Ordinarily it resides within the UCS analyzer.

EEG. Electroencephalogram, an oscillographic recording of action currents from the brain.

EMG. Electromyogram, an oscillographic recording of action currents from a muscle.

excitation. One of two hypothetical processes (with inhibition) which determines CR strength. Excitation is associated with high response strength.

external inhibition. The transient suppression of CR strength produced by a distracting stimulus.

extinction. In classical conditioning, a series of nonreinforced trials following acquisition.

galvanic skin responses (GSR). A change in the electrical properties of the skin associated with bioelectrical activity of sweat glands and epidermis. A GSR can be elicited by virtually any stimulus and is thought to be a component of the orienting response.

induction (Pavlov). The enhancement of an excitatory or inhibitory process through its opposite. For example, in positive induction CR strength is augmented following presentation of a nonreinforced or inhibitory stimulus.

inhibition. The opposite of excitation. Inhibition is associated with low CR strength.

inhibition of delay. The suppressing of CR strength during the interstimulus interval.

interoceptive conditioning. Any conditioning procedure in which the CS is applied to interoceptors.

interstimulus interval (ISI). Time separating the onset of the CS from the onset of the UCS.

intertrial interval (ITI). Average time between CS presentations; usually measured from onset to onset.

irradiation (Pavlov). The cortical spread of excitation or inhibition which according to Pavlov's theory is one of the basic mechanisms for CR formation (with *induction* and *concentration*) and which is the basis for stimulus generalization.

nonreinforcement. In classical conditioning, a trial on which the UCS is withheld.

orienting response (also called *orienting reflex, investigatory reflex*). A complex of autonomic and motor reactions elicited by novel stimuli.

paradigm. In conditioning, a model of the temporal sequences and duration of CS and UCS; the structure of a reinforced trial.

perceptual disparity response (Grings). An enhanced GSR produced by unexpected stimuli. It might be viewed as a component of the orienting response.

peripheralist. One who holds that the peripheral nervous system is essential for *conditioning* of peripheral response systems. Essentially equivalent to S-R theory.

pseudoconditioning. Augmentation of a response resembling a CR by repeated UCS presentations.

reinforcement. In classical conditioning, a trial consisting of paired presentation of the CS and UCS.

sensitization. Augmentation of the alpha response by the UCS.

sensory preconditioning (also called *sensory conditioning*). Any procedure in which two neutral stimuli are paired as in conditioning and in which the strength of their association is assessed by transfer designs in which an observable CR is attached to one of the training stimuli and tested with the other.

simultaneous conditioning. A conditioning paradigm in which the CS and UCS are presented simultaneously. Pavlov referred to a delay conditioning paradigm with a short interval of delay as simultaneous conditioning.

spontaneous recovery. The reappearance of an extinguished CR following an interpolated "rest" period.

S-R theory. The view that the connection formed in conditioning is a direct one between the sensory system of the CS and the motor system of the UCR. Essentially equivalent to the peripheralistic philosophy.

S-S theory. The view that the connection formed in conditioning is a direct one between the sensory systems of the CS and UCS. Essentially equivalent to the centralistic philosophy.

stimulus substitution. The view that conditioning imbues the CS with the properties of the UCS. This implies that the CR topographically resembles the UCR, and, in fact, that the two are fundamentally equivalent.

temporal conditioning. A conditioning paradigm in which the UCS is presented at a fixed interval with no other stimulus. The trace of the preceding UCS is the only CS.

trace conditioning. A conditioning paradigm in which the CS terminates at a fixed interval (the trace interval) before UCS onset.

trial. In classical conditioning, a single presentation of the CS with or without the UCS.

unconditioned response (UCR). In conditioning, the original response elicited by the UCS.

unconditioned stimulus (UCS). In conditioning, the stimulus which elicits the UCR and which reinforces CR formation.

References

Anderson, N. H. Comparison of different populations: Resistance to extinction and transfer. *Psychol. Rev.*, 1963, **70**, 162–179.

Babkin, B. P. *Pavlov: A biography.* Chicago: University of Chicago Press, 1949.

Bacon, W. E. Partial reinforcement extinction effect following different amounts of training. *J. comp. physiol. Psychol.*, 1962, **55**, 998–1003.

Baron, M. R. The effect of longer intertrial intervals on the limit of eyelid conditioning. *J. exp. psychol.*, 1952, **44**, 438–441.

Baxter, R., & Kimmel, H. D. Conditioning and extinction in the planarian. *Amer. J. Psychol.*, 1963, **76**, 665–669.

Beck, S. B. Eyelid conditioning as a function of CS intensity, UCS intensity, and manifest anxiety scale score. *J. exp. Psychol.*, 1963, **66**, 429–438.

Beecroft, R. S. *Classical conditioning.* Goleta, Calif.: Psychonomic Press, 1966.

Beeman, E. V., Hartman, T. F., & Grant, D. A. Influence of intertrial interval during extinction on spontaneous recovery of conditioned eyelid responses. *J. exp. Psychol.*, 1960, **59**, 279–280.

Berger, B. D., Yarczower, M., & Bitterman, M. E. Effect of partial reinforcement on the extinction of a classically conditioned response in the goldfish. *J. comp. physiol. Psychol.*, 1965, **59**, 399–405.

Bernstein, A. L. Temporal factors in the formation of conditioned eyelid reactions in human subjects. *J. Gen. Psychol.*, 1934, **10**, 173–197.

Bersh, P. J. The influence of two variables upon the establishment of a secondary reinforcer for operant responses. *J. exp. Psychol.*, 1951, **41**, 62–73.

Bersh, P. J., Notterman, J. M., & Schoenfeld, W. N. Extinction of a human cardiac-response during avoidance-conditioning. *Amer. J. Psychol.*, 1956, **59**, 244–251.

Bierbaum, W. B. The temporal gradient in GSR conditioning. *J. Gen. Psychol.*, 1958, **59**, 97–103.

Birch, H. G., & Bitterman, M. E. Reinforcement and learning: The process of sensory integration. *Psychol. Rev.*, 1949, **46**, 292–308.

Bitterman, M. E. The CS-US interval in classical and avoidance conditioning. In W. F. Prokasy (Ed.), *Classical conditioning: A symposium.* New York: Appleton-Century-Crofts, 1965. Pp. 1–19.

Bitterman, M. E., Reed, P., & Krauskopf, J. Effect of duration of the unconditioned stimulus on conditioning and extinction. *Amer. J. Psychol.*, 1952, **65**, 257–262.

Black, A. H. Heart rate changes during avoidance in dogs. *Canad. J. Psychol.*, 1959, **13**, 229–242.

Black, A. H. Cardiac conditioning in curarized dogs: The relationship between heart rate and skeletal behavior. In W. F. Prokasy (Ed.), *Classical conditioning: A symposium.* New York: Appleton-Century-Crofts, 1965. P. 20–47.

Black, A. H., Carlson, N. J., & Solomon, R. L. Exploratory studies of the conditioning of autonomic responses in curarized dogs. *Psychol. Monogr.*, 1962, **76**, No. 548.

Black, A. H., & Lang, W. M. Cardiac conditioning and skeletal responding in curarized dogs. *Psychol. Rev.*, 1964, **71**, 80–85.

Boice, R., & Denny, M. R. The conditioned licking response in rats as a function of the CS-UCS interval. *Psychon. Sci.*, 1965, **3**, 93–94.

Boneau, C. A. The interstimulus interval and the latency of the conditioned eyelid response. *J. exp. Psychol.*, 1958, **56**, 464–472.

Bower, G. H., & Grusec, T. Effect of prior Pavlovian discrimination training upon learning an operant discrimination. *J. exp. Anal. Behav.*, 1964, **7**, 401–404.

Branca, A. A. Semantic generalization at the level of the conditioning experiment. *Amer. J. Psychol.*, 1957, **70**, 541–549.

Bridger, W. H., & Mandel, I. J. Abolition of the PRE by instructions in GSR conditioning. *J. exp. Psychol.*, 1965, **69**, 476–482.

Briggs, M. H., & Kitto, G. B. The molecular basis of memory and learning. *Psychol. Rev.*, 1962, **69**, 537–541.

Brimer, C. J., & Dockrill, F. J. Partial reinforcement and the CER. *Psychon. Sci.*, 1966, **5**, 185–186.

Brogden, W. J. Sensory preconditioning. *J. exp. Psychol.*, 1939, **25**, 323–332.

Brogden, W. J., & Gantt, W. H. Intraneural conditioning. Cerebellar conditioned reflexes. *Archives of Neurology and Psychiatry*, 1942, **48**, 437–455.

Brown, J. S. *The motivation of behavior.* New York: McGraw-Hill, 1961.

Brown, J. S., & Jacobs, A. The role of fear in the motivation and acquisition of responses. *J. exp. Psychol.*, 1949, **39**, 747–759.

Butter, C. M., & Thomas, D. R. Secondary reinforcement as a function of the amount of primary reinforcement. *J. comp. physiol. Psychol.*, 1958, **51**, 346–348.

Bugelski, B. R. *Psychology of learning.* New York: Holt, Rinehart, and Winston, 1956.

Bykov, K. M., & Gantt, W. H. (Ed.), *The cerebral cortex and the internal organs.* New York: Chemical, 1957.

Champion, R. A. Stimulus-intensity effects in response evocation. *Psychol. Rev.*, 1962a, **69**, 428–449.

Champion, R. A. Stimulus response contiguity in classical aversive conditioning. *J. exp. Psychol.*, 1962b, **64**, 35–39.

Champion, R A., & Jones, J. E. Forward, backward, and pseudoconditioning of the GSR. *J. exp. Psychol.*, 1961, **62**, 58–61.

Church, R. M., & Black, A. H. Conditioned heart rate and CS-US interval. *J. comp. physiol. Psychol.*, 1958, **51**, 478–482.

Cofer, C. N., & Foley, J. P., Jr. Mediated generalization and the interpretation of verbal behavior: I. Prolegomena. *Psychol. Rev.*, 1942, **49**, 513–540.

Colavita, F. B. Dual function of the US in classical salivary conditioning. *J. comp. physiol. Psychol.*, 1965, **60**, 218–222.

Coleman, S. R., & Gormezano, I. Resistance to extinction of the conditioned nictitating membrane response: Effects of amount of acquisition training, and amount of asymptotic overtraining. Paper read at The Psychonomic Society, St. Louis, 1966.

Coleman, S. R., Patterson, M. M., & Gormezano, I. Conditioned jaw movement in the rabbit: Deprivation procedure and saccharin concentration. *Psychon. Sci.*, 1966, **6**, 38–40.

Cook, S. W., & Harris, R. E. The verbal conditioning of the galvanic skin reflex. *J. exp. Psychol.*, 1937, **21**, 202–210.

Coppock, H. W., & Chambers, R. M. GSR conditioning: An illustration of useless distinctions between "type" of conditioning. *Psychol. Rep.*, 1959, **6**, 171–177.

Deaux, E. B., & Patten, R. L. Measurement of the anticipatory goal response in instrumental runway conditioning. *Psychon. Sci.*, 1964, **1**, 357–358.

DeBold, R. C., Miller, N. E., & Jensen, D. D. Effect of strength of drive determined by new technique for appetitive classical conditioning of rats. *J. comp. physiol. Psychol.*, 1965, **59**, 102–108.

Deese, J. *Psychology of learning.* (2nd ed.) New York: McGraw-Hill, 1958.

Doty, R. W. Conditioned reflexes formed and evoked by brain stimulation. In D. E. Sheer (Ed.), *Electrical stimulation of the brain.* Austin: Univer. Texas Press, 1961.

Doty, R. W. Conditioned reflexes elicited by electrical stimulation of the brain in Macaques. *J. of Neurophysiol.*, 1965, **28**, 623–640.

Doty, R. W., & Giurgea, C. Conditioned reflexes established by coupling electrical excitation of two cortical areas. In J. F. Delafresnaye, A. Fessard, R. W. Gerard, & J. Konorski (Eds.), *Brain, mechanisms and learning.* Oxford: Blackwell Scientific, 1961.

Dykman, R. A., & Gantt, W. H. The parasympathetic component of unlearned and acquired cardiac responses. *J. comp. physiol. Psychol.*, 1959, **52**, 163–167.

Ebel, H. C., & Prokasy, W. F. Classical eyelid conditioning as a function of sustained and shifted interstimulus intervals. *J. exp. Psychol.*, 1963, **65**, 52–58.

Ellison, G. D. Differential salivary conditioning to traces. *J. comp. physiol. Psychol.*, 1964, **57**, 373–380.

Estes, W. K. Discriminative conditioning. I. A discriminative property of conditioned anticipation. *J. exp. Psychol.*, 1943, **32**, 150–155.

Estes, W. K. Discriminative conditioning. II. Effects of a Pavlovian conditioned stimulus upon a subsequently established operant response. *J. exp. Psychol.*, 1948, **38**, 173–177.

Estes, W. K. A study of motivating conditions necessary for secondary reinforcement. *J. exp. Psychol.*, 1949, **39**, 306–310.

Estes, W. K. Toward a statistical theory of learning. *Psychol. Rev.*, 1950, **57**, 94–107.

Estes, W. K. Statistical theory of distributional phenomena in learning. *Psychol. Rev.*, 1955a, **62**, 369–377.

Estes, W. K. Statistical theory of spontaneous recovery and regression. *Psychol. Rev.*, 1955b, **62**, 145–154.

Estes, W. K. The statistical approach to learning theory. In S. Koch (Ed.), *Psychology: A study of a science.* Vol. II. New York: McGraw-Hill, 1959. Pp. 380–491.

Estes, W. K., & Skinner, B. F. Some quantitative properties of anxiety. *J. exp. Psychol.*, 1941, **29**, 390–400.

Fearing, F. *Reflex action: A study of the history of physiological psychology.* New York: Hafner Publishing Co., 1930.

Feather, B. W. Semantic generalization of classically conditioned responses: A review. *Psychol. Bull.*, 1965, **63**, 425–441.

Fishbein, H. D. Effects of differential instructions, differential feedback, and UCS intensity on the conditioned eyelid response. *J. exp. Psychol.*, 1967a, **75**, 56–63.

Fishbein, H. D. Effects of differential instructions and number of acquisition trials on extinction and reacquisition of the conditioned eyelid response. *J. exp. Psychol.*, 1967b, **75**, 126–127.

Fishbein, H. D., & Gormezano, I. Effects of differential instructions, differential payoffs, and the presence or absence of feedback on the percentage, latency, and amplitude of the conditioned eyelid response. *J. exp. Psychol.*, 1966, **71**, 533–538.

Fishbein, H. D., & LeBlanc, M. Human eyelid conditioning as a function of interstimulus interval. *J. exp. Psychol.*, 1967, **75**, 130–133.

Fitzgerald, R. D. Effects of partial reinforcement with acid on the classically conditioned salivary response in dogs. *J. comp. physiol. Psychol.*, 1963, **56**, 1056–1060.

Fitzgerald, R. D., Vardaris, R. M., & Brown, J. S. Classical conditioning of heart rate deceleration in the rat with continuous and partial reinforcement. *Psychon. Sci.*, 1966, **6**, 437–438.

Fitzgerald, R. D., Vardaris, R. M., & Teyler, T. J. Effects of partial reinforcement followed by continuous reinforcement on classically conditioned heart-rate in the dog. *J. comp. physiol. Psychol.*, 1966, **62**, 483–486.

Fitzwater, M. E., & Reisman, M. N. Comparisons of forward, simultaneous, backward and pseudoconditioning. *J. exp. Psychol.*, 1952, **44**, 211–215.

Fitzwater, M. E., & Thrush, R. S. Acquisition of conditioned response as a function of forward temporal contiguity. *J. exp. Psychol.*, 1956, **51**, 59–62.

Fox, R. E., & King, R. A. The effects of reinforcement scheduling on the strength of a secondary reinforcer. *J. comp. physiol. Psychol.*, 1961, **54**, 266–269.

Galambos, R., & Morgan, C. T. The neural basis of learning. In J. Field, H. W. Magoun, & V. E. Hall (Eds.), *Handbook of physiology.* Vol. 3. Washington, D.C.: American Physiological Society, 1960.

Gantt, W. H. The nervous secretion of saliva: The relation of the conditioned reflex to the intensity of the unconditioned stimulus. *Amer. J. Physiol.*, 1938, **123**, 74–75.

Gantt, W. H., & Dykman, R. A. Experimental psychogenic tachycardia. In P. H. Hock, & J. Zubin (Eds.), *Experimental psychopathology.* New York: Grune & Stratton, 1957.

Gardner, R. A. On box score methodology as illustrated by three reviews of over-training reversal effects. *Psychol. Bull.*, 1966, **66**, 416–418.

Gerall, A. A., & Obrist, P. A. Classical conditioning of the pupillary dilation response of normal and curarized cats. *J. comp. physiol. Psychol.*, 1962, **55**, 386–491.

Gerall, A. A., & Woodward, J. K. Conditioning of the human pupillary dilation response as a function of the CS-UCS interval. *J. exp. Psychol.*, 1958, **55**, 501–507.

Gonzalez, R. C., Longo, N., & Bitterman, M. E. Classical conditioning in the fish: Exploratory studies of partial reinforcement. *J. comp. physiol. Psychol.*, 1961, **54**, 452–456.

Gormezano, I. Yoked comparisons of classical and instrumental conditioning of the eyelid response; and an addendum on "voluntary responders." In W. F. Prokasy (Ed.), *Classical conditioning: A symposium.* New York: Appleton-Century-Crofts, 1965. Pp. 48–70.

Gormezano, I. Classical conditioning. In J. B. Sidowski (Ed.), *Experimental methods and instrumentation in psychology.* New York: McGraw-Hill, 1966. Pp. 385–420.

Gormezano, I., & Moore, J. W. Effects of instructional set and UCS intensity on the latency, percentage, and form of the eyelid response. *J. exp. Psychol.*, 1962, **63**, 487–494.

Gormezano, I., Schneiderman, N., Deaux, E. B., & Fuentes, I. Nictitating membrane: Classical conditioning and extinction in the albino rabbit. *Sci.*, 1962, **138**, 33–34.

Grant, D. A. Classical and instrumental conditioning. In A. W. Melton (Ed.), *Categories of human learning.* New York: Academic Press, 1964. Pp. 1–31.

Grant, D. A., & Schipper, L. M. The acquisition and extinction of conditioned eyelid responses as a function of the percentage of fixed-ratio reinforcement. *J. exp. Psychol.*, 1952, **43**, 313–320.

Grant, D. A., Schipper, L. M., & Ross, B. M. Effect of intertrial interval during acquisition on extinction of the conditioned eyelid response following partial reinforcement. *J. exp. Psychol.*, 1952, **44**, 203–210.

Grant, D. A., & Schneider, D. E. Intensity of the conditioned stimulus and strength of conditioning. I. The conditioned eyelid response to light. *J. exp. Psychol.*, 1948, **38**, 690–696.

Grant, D. A., & Schneider, D. E. Intensity of the conditioned stimulus and strength of conditioning: II. The conditioned galvanic skin response to an auditory stimulus. *J. exp. Psychol.*, 1949, **39**, 35–40.

Grether, W. F. Pseudo-conditioning without paired stimulation encountered in attempted backward conditioning. *J. comp. Psychol.*, 1938, **25**, 91–96.

Grice, G. R. Do responses evoke responses? *Amer. Psychologist*, 1965, **20**, 282–294.

Grice, G. R., & Hunter, J. J. Stimulus intensity effects depend upon the type of experimental design. *Psychol. Rev.*, 1964, **71**, 247–256.

Grice, G. R., Masters, L., & Kohfeld, D. L. Classical conditioning without discrimination training: A test of the generalization theory of CS intensity effects. *J. exp. Psychol.*, 1966, **72**, 510–513.

Grings, W. W. Preparatory set variables related to classical conditioning of autonomic responses. *Psychol. Rev.*, 1960, **67**, 243–252.

Grings, W. W. Verbal-perceptual factors in the conditioning of autonomic responses. In W. F. Prokasy (Ed.), *Classical conditioning: A symposium.* New York: Appleton-Century-Crofts, 1965. Pp. 71–89.

Grings, W. W., Carlin, S., & Appley, M. H. Set, suggestion, and conditioning. *J. exp. Psychol.*, 1962, **63**, 417–422.

Grings, W. W., Dossett, W. F., & Honnard, R. R. Conditioned GSR in perceptual disparity situations. *Amer. Psychologist*, 1959, **14**, 393.

Grings, W. W., & Kimmel, H. D. Compound stimulus transfer for different sense modalities. *Psychol. Rep.*, 1959, **5**, 253–260.

Grings, W. W., & O'Donnell, D. E. Magnitude of response to compounds of discriminated stimuli. *J. exp. Psychol.*, 1956, **52**, 354–359.

Guthrie, E. R. Conditioning as a principle

of learning. *Psychol. Rev.*, 1930, **37**, 412–418.

Guthrie, E. R. Association as a function of time interval. *Psychol. Rev.*, 1933, **40**, 355–367.

Guthrie, E. R. *The psychology of learning.* New York: Harper & Row, 1935.

Gwinn, G. T. The effects of punishment on acts motivated by fear. *J. exp. Psychol.*, 1949, **39**, 260–269.

Hansche, W. J., & Grant, D. A. Onset versus termination of a stimulus as the CS in eyelid conditioning. *J. exp. Psychol.* 1960, **59**, 19–26.

Harlow, H. F. Forward conditioning, backward conditioning, and pseudo-conditioning in the goldfish. *J. gènet. Psychol.*, 1939, **55**, 49–58.

Harlow, H. F., & Stagner, R. Effect of complete striate muscle paralysis upon the learning process. *J. exp. Psychol.*, 1933, **16**, 283–294.

Hartman, T. F. Dynamic transmission, elective generalization, and semantic conditioning. In W. F. Prokasy (Ed.), *Classical conditioning.* New York: Appleton-Century-Crofts, Inc., 1965. Pp. 90–106.

Hartman, T. F., & Grant, D. A. Effect of intermittent reinforcement on acquisition, extinction, and spontaneous recovery of the conditioned eyelid response. *J. exp. Psychol.*, 1960, **60**, 89–96.

Hartman, T. F., & Grant, D. A. Effects of pattern of reinforcement and verbal information on acquisition, extinction, and spontaneous recovery of the eyelid CR. *J. exp. Psychol.*, 1962, **63**, 217–226.

Hartman, T. F., Grant, D. A., & Ross, L. E. An investigation of the latency of "instructed voluntary" eyelid responses. *Psychol. Rep.*, 1960, **7**, 305–311.

Hartman, T. F., & Ross, L. E. An alternative criterion for the elimination of "voluntary" responses in eyelid conditioning. *J. exp. Psychol.*, 1961, **61**, 334–338.

Helson, H. Adaptation level theory. In S. Koch (Ed.), *Psychology: A study of a science. Vol. I. Sensory, perceptual, and physiological formulations.* New York: McGraw-Hill, 1959.

Hilgard, E. R. Modification of reflexes and conditioned reactions. *J. gen. Psychol.*, 1933, **9**, 210–215.

Hilgard, E. R., & Bower, G. H. *Theories of learning.* (3rd ed.) New York: Appleton-Century-Crofts, 1966.

Hilgard, E. R., & Marquis, D. G. *Conditioning and learning.* New York: Appleton-Century-Crofts, 1940.

Hill, F. A. Effects of instructions and subject's need for approval on the conditioned galvanic skin response. *J. exp. Psychol.*, 1967, **73**, 461–467.

Hilton, A. Partial reinforcement of a conditioned emotional response. Paper presented at the meeting of the Eastern Psychological Association, Boston, 1967.

Hofer, M. A., & Hinkle, L. E. Conditioned diuresis in man: Effects of altered environment, subjective state, and conditioning experience. *Psychosom. Med.*, 1964, **26**, 108–124.

Howat, H. G., & Grant, D. A. Influence of intertrial interval during extinction on spontaneous recovery of conditioned eyelid responses. *J. exp. Psychol.*, 1958, **56**, 11–15.

Hovland, C. I. "Inhibition of reinforcement" and phenomena of experimental extinction. *Proceedings of the National Academy of Science*, Washington, 1936, **22**, 430–433.

Hovland, C. I. The generalization of conditioned responses. II. The sensory generalization of conditioned responses with varying intensities of tone. *J. genet. Psychol.*, 1937, **51**, 279–291.

Howat, H. G., & Grant, D. A. Influence of intertrial interval during extinction on spontaneous recovery of conditioned eyelid responses. *J. exp. Psychol.*, 1958, **56**, 11–15.

Hull, C. L. A functional interpretation of the conditioned reflex. *Psychol. Rev.*, 1929, **36**, 498–511.

Hull, C. L. Mind, mechanism, and adaptive behavior. *Psychol. Rev.*, 1937, **44**, 1–32.

Hull, C. L. The problem of stimulus equivalence in behavior theory. *Psychol. Rev.*, 1939, **46**, 9–30.

Hull, C. L. *Principles of behavior.* New York: Appleton-Century-Crofts, 1943.

Hull, C. L. *A behavior system.* New Haven: Yale University Press, 1952.

Humphreys, L. G. The effect of random

alternation of reinforcement on the acquisition and extinction of conditioned eyelid reactions. *J. exp. Psychol.*, 1939, **25**, 141–158.

Humphreys, L. G. Distributed practice in the development of the conditioned eyelid reaction. *J. gen. Psychol.*, 1940, **22**, 379–385.

Hunt, H. F., & Brady, J. V. Some effects of electroconvulsive shock on conditioned emotional response (anxiety). *J. comp. physiol. Psychol.*, 1951, **44**, 88–98.

Ivanov-Smolensky, A. G. Metodika issledovaniya uslovnykh refleksov u cheloveka (Methods of investigation of conditioned reflexes in man). Moscow: Medgiz (Medical State Press), 1933.

Ivanov-Smolensky, A. G. (Ed.) *Works of the institute of higher nervous activity: Pathophysiological series.* Vol. 2. Moscow: Academy of Sciences of the USSR, 1956.

Jacobson, A. L. Learning in flatworms and annelids. *Psychol. Bull.*, 1963, **60**, 74–94.

Jensen, D. D. Paramecia, planaria, and pseudolearning. *Animal Behavior*, 1965, Supplement I, 9–20.

Jones, J. E. The CS-UCS interval in conditioning short- and long-latency responses. *J. exp. Psychol.*, 1961, **62**, 612–617.

Jones J. E. Contiguity and reinforcement in relation to CS-UCS intervals in classical aversive conditioning. *Psychol. Rev.*, 1962, **69**, 176–186.

Kalish, H. I. Strength of fear as a function of the number of acquisition and extinction trials. *J. exp. Psychol.*, 1954, **55**, 637–644.

Kamin, L. J. Unpublished research. 1966.

Kamin, L. J. Temporal and intensity characteristics of the conditioned stimulus. In W. F. Prokasy (Ed.), *Classical conditioning: A symposium.* New York: Appleton-Century-Crofts, 1965. Pp. 118–147.

Kamin, L. J., & Brimer, C. J. The effects of intensity of conditioned and unconditioned stimuli on a conditioned emotional response. *Canad. J. Psychol.*, 1963, **17**, 194–200.

Kamin, L. J., & Schaub, R. E. Effects of conditioned stimulus intensity on the conditioned emotional response. *J. comp. physiol. Psychol.*, 1963, **56**, 502–507.

Kandel, E. R., & Tauc, L. Heterosynaptic facilitation in neurones of the abdominal ganglion of *Aplysia Depilans. J. Physiol.*, 1965, **181**, 1–27.

Kappauf, W. E., & Schlosberg, H. Conditioned responses in the white rat. III. Conditioning as a function of the length of the period of delay. *J. genet. Psychol.*, 1937, **50**, 27–45.

Keller, M. Mediated generalization: The generalization of a conditioned galvanic response established to a pictured object. *Amer. J. Psychol.*, 1943, **56**, 438–448.

Kellogg, W. N. Is "spinal conditioning" conditioning? *J. exp. Psychol.*, 1947, **37**, 263–265.

Kellogg, W. N., Deese, J., Pronko, N. H., & Feinberg, M. An attempt to condition the chronic spinal dog. *J. exp. Psychol.*, 1947, **37**, 99–117.

Kimble, G. A. Conditioning as a function of the time between conditioned and unconditioned stimuli. *J. exp. Psychol.*, 1947, **37**, 1–15.

Kimble, G. A. *Hilgard and Marquis' conditioning and learning.* New York: Appleton-Century-Crofts, 1961.

Kimble, G. A. Classical conditioning and the problem of awareness. *Journal of Personality Supplement*, 1962, **30**, 27–45.

Kimble, G. A. Attitudinal factors in eyelid conditioning. In G. A. Kimble (Ed.), *Foundations of conditioning and learning.* New York: Appleton-Century-Crofts, 1967.

Kimmel, H. D. Amount of conditioning and intensity of conditioned stimulus. *J. exp. Psychol.*, 1959, **58**, 283–288.

Kimmel, H. D. The relationship between direction and amount of stimulus change and amount of perceptual disparity response. *J. exp. Psychol.*, 1960, **59**, 68–72.

Kimmel, H. D. Instrumental inhibitory factors in classical conditioning. In W. F. Prokasy (Ed.), *Classical conditioning: A symposium.* New York: Appleton-Century-Crofts, 1965. Pp. 148–171.

Kimmel, H. D., & Davidov, W. Classical GSR conditioning with concomitant EMG measurement. *J. exp. Psychol.*, 1967, **74**, 67–74.

Kimmel, H. D., Hill, F. A., & Morrow, M. C. Strength of GSR and avoidance conditioning as a function of CS intensity. *Psychol. Rep.*, 1962, **11**, 103–109.

Kimmel, H. D., & Yaremko, R. M. Effect of partial reinforcement on acquisition and extinction of classical conditioning in the Planarian. *J. comp. physiol. Psychol.*, 1966, **61**, 299–301.

Kintsch, W., & Witte, R. S. Concurrent conditioning of bar press and salivation responses. *J. comp. physiol. Psychol.*, 1962, **55**, 963–968.

Konorski, J. *Conditioned reflexes and neuron organization.* Cambridge: Cambridge University Press, 1948.

Konorski, J., & Miller, S. Méthode d'examen de l'analysateur moteur par les réactions salivomatrices. *Compte Rendu Hebdomadaire des Seances et Mémoires de la Societé de Biologie*, 1930, **104**, 907–910.

Korbatov, B. M. Study of the dynamic transmission of a conditioned connection from one cortical signal system into the other. In A. G. Ivanov-Smolensky (Ed.), *Works of the institute of higher nervous activity: Pathophysiological series.* Vol. 2. Moscow: Academy of Sciences of the USSR, 1956.

Kraus, H. H., & Prokasy, W. F. On intertrial interval discrimination in classical conditioning. *Psychol. Rep.*, 1963, **12**, 138.

Leonard, C., & Winokur, G. Conditioning versus sensitization in the galvanic skin response. *J. comp. physiol. Psychol.*, 1963, **56**, 169–170.

Leonard, D. W., & Theios, J. Effect of CS-US interval shift on classical conditioning of the nictitating membrane in the rabbit. *J. comp. physiol. Psychol.*, 1967, **63**, 355–358.

Lindley, R. H., & Moyer, K. E. Effects of instructions on the extinction of a conditioned finger-withdrawal response. *J. exp. Psychol.*, 1961, **61**, 82–88.

Lipkin, S. G., & Moore, J. W. Eyelid trace conditioning, CS intensity, CS-UCS interval, and a correction for "spontaneous" blinking. *J. exp. Psychol.*, 1966, **72**, 216–220.

Lockhart, R. A. Dominance and contiguity as interactive determinants of GSR discrimination conditioning. Paper read at the meeting of the Psychonomic Society, Chicago, October, 1965.

Logan, F. A. A note on stimulus intensity dynamism (V). *Psychol. Rev.*, 1954, **61**, 77–80.

Logan, F. A. A micromolar approach to behavior theory. *Psychol. Rev.*, 1956, **63**, 63–73.

Logan, F. A., & Wagner, A. R. Direction of change in CS in eyelid conditioning. *J. exp. Psychol.*, 1962, **64**, 325–326.

Longo, N., Milstein, S., & Bitterman, M. E. Classical conditioning in the pigeon: Exploratory studies of partial reinforcement. *J. comp. physiol. Phychol.*, 1962, **55**, 983–986.

Loucks, R. B. A technique for faradic stimulation of tissues beneath the integument in the absence of conductors penetrating the skin. *J. comp. Psychol.*, 1934, **18**, 305–313.

Marlatt, G. A., Lilie, D., Selvidge, B. D., Sipes, M. D., & Gormezano, I. Cross-modal generalization to tone and light in human eyelid conditioning. *Psychon. Sci.*, 1966, **5**, 59–60.

Martin, I. A further attempt at delayed GSR conditioning. *Brit. J. Psychol.*, 1963, **54**, 359–368.

Mattson, M., & Moore, J. W. Intertrial responding and CS intensity on classical eyelid conditioning. *J. exp. Psychol.*, 1964, **68**, 396–401.

McAdam, D., Knott, J. R., & Chiorini, J. Classical conditioning in the cat as a function of the CS-US interval. *Psychon. Sci.*, 1965, **3**, 89–90.

McAllister, W. R. Eyelid conditioning as a function of the CS-UCS interval. *J. exp. Psychol.*, 1953, **45**, 417–422.

Mikushkin, M. K. On changes in the magnitude of an interoceptive conditioned reflex with systematic application of the conditioned stimulus. *J. Higher nerv. Activ.*, 1961, **11**, 303–305.

Miller, J. The effect of facilitatory and inhibitory attitudes on eyelid conditioning. Ph.D. dissertation, Yale University, 1939.

Miller, N. E. Studies of fear as an acquirable drive: I. Fear as motivation and fear reduction as reinforcement in the learning of new responses. *J. exp. Psychol.*, 1948, **38**, 89–101.

Miller, N. E. Learnable drives and rewards. In S. S. Stevens (Ed.), *Handbook of experimental psychology.* New York: Wiley, 1951.

Miller, N. E., & DeBold, R. C. Classically conditioned tongue-licking and operant bar pressing recorded simultaneously in the rat. *J. comp. physiol. Psychol.,* 1965, **59,** 109–111.

Moeller, G. The CS-UCS interval in GSR conditioning. *J. exp. Psychol.,* 1954, **48,** 162–166.

Moore, J. W., & Gormezano, I. Effects of omitted versus delayed UCS on classical conditioning under partial reinforcement. *J. exp. Psychol.,* 1963, **65,** 248–257.

Moore, J. W., & Newman, F. L. Intertrial stimuli and generalization of the conditioned eyelid response. *J. exp. Psychol.,* 1966, **71,** 414–419.

Morgan, C. T. The psychophysiology of learning. In S. S. Stevens (Ed.), *Handbook of experimental psychology.* New York: Wiley, 1951. Pp. 758–788.

Morse, W. E., & Skinner, B. F. Some factors involved in stimulus control of operant behavior. *J. exp. Anal. Behav.,* 1958, **1,** 103–107.

Mowrer, O. H. On the dual nature of learning—a re-interpretation of "conditioning" and "problem-solving." *Harvard educ. Rev.,* 1947, **17,** 102–148.

Mowrer, O. H. *Learning theory and behavior.* New York: Wiley, 1960a.

Mowrer, O. H. *Learning theory and the symbolic processes.* New York: Wiley, 1960b.

Muir, W. R., & Runquist, W. N. Extended differential conditioning of the classically conditioned eyeblink reflex. *Psychon. Sci.,* 1965, **3,** 581–582.

Naroditskaya, G. D. A study of the question of the phenomenon of the so-called secondary excitation in the cerebral cortex of children. In A. G. Ivanov-Smolensky (Ed.), *Works of the institute of higher nervous activity: Pathophysiological series.* Vol. 2. Moscow: Academy of Sciences of the USSR, 1956.

Newman, F. L. Differential eyelid conditioning as a function of the probability of reinforcement. *J. exp. Psychol.,* 1967, **75,** 412–417.

Nielson, H. C., Knight, J. M., & Porter, P. B. Subcortical conditioning, generalization and transfer. *J. comp. physiol. Psychol.,* 1962, **55,** 168–173.

Noble, M., & Adams, C. K. The effect of length of CS-US interval as a function of body temperature in a cold-blooded animal. *J. gen. Psychol.,* 1963, **69,** 197–201.

Noble, M., Gruender, A., & Meyer, D. R. Conditioning in fish (Molienisia Sp.) as a function of the interval between CS and US. *J. comp. physiol Psychol.,* 1959, **52,** 236–239.

Noble, M., & Harding, G. E. Conditioning in rhesus monkeys as a function of the interval between CS and US. *J. comp. physiol. Psychol.,* 1963, **56,** 220–224.

Norris, E. B., & Grant, D. A. Eyelid conditioning as affected by verbally induced inhibitory set and counter reinforcemen-. *Amer. J. Psychol.,* 1948, **61,** 37–49.

Osgood, C. E. *Method and theory in experimental psychology.* New York: Oxford University Press, 1953.

Papsdorf, J. D., Fishbein, H. D., & Gormezano, I. A comparison of an intermittent versus continuouⵝ CS in classical conditioning of the nictitating membrane response of the rabbit. *Psychon. Sci.,* 1964, **1,** 305–306.

Papsdorf, J. D., Gormezano, I., & Prokasy, W. F. Intertrial interval and UCS intensity effects on the acquisition and extinction of the classically conditioned nictitating membrane of the rabbit. Paper read at the meeting of the Midwestern Psychological Association, St. Louis, May 1964.

Passey, G. E. The influence of intensity of unconditioned stimulus upon acquisition of a conditioned response. *J. exp. Psychol.,* 1948, **38,** 320–428.

Pavlov, I. P. *The work of the digestive glands.* (Translated by W. H. Thompson). London: Charles Griffen, 1902.

Pavlov, I. P. The scientific investigation of the psychical facilities or processes in the higher animals. *Sci.,* 1906, **24,** 613–619.

Pavlov, I. P. *Conditioned reflexes.* (Translated by G. V. Anrep). London: Oxford University Press, 1927.

Pavlov, I. P. *Lectures on conditioned reflexes.* (Translated by W. H. Gantt). New York: International, 1928.

Perkins, C. C., Jr. The relation between conditioned stimulus intensity and response strength. *J. exp. Psychol.*, 1953, **46**, 225–231.

Phillips, L. W. Mediated verbal similarity as a determinant of the generalization of a conditioned GSR. *J. exp. Psychol.*, 1958, **55**, 56–61.

Pogrebkova, A. V. The role of conditioning in subthreshold stimulation of the respiratory system. *Rep. Acad. Sci. USSR*, 1966, **167**, 241–244.

Porter, J. M., Jr. Experimental extinction as a function of the interval between successive nonreinforced elicitations. *J. gen. Psychol.*, 1939, **20**, 109–134.

Prokasy, W. F. Postasymptotic performance decrements during massed reinforcements. *Psychol. Bull.*, 1960, **57**, 237–247.

Prokasy, W. F. Classical eyelid conditioning: Experimenter operations, task demands, and response shaping. In W. F. Prokasy (Ed.), *Classical conditioning: A symposium.* New York: Appleton-Century-Crofts, 1965. Pp. 208–225. (a).

Prokasy, W. F. Stimulus fluctuation, reactive inhibition, and time between trials in classical eyelid conditioning. *J. exp. Psychol.*, 1965, **70**, 464–472. (b).

Prokasy, W. F., & Ebel, H. C. Three components of the classically conditioned GSR in human subjects. *J. exp. Psychol.*, 1967, **73**, 247–256.

Prokasy, W. F., Ebel, H. C., & Thompson, D. D. Response shaping at long interstimulus intervals in classical eyelid conditioning. *J. exp. Psychol.*, 1963, **66**, 138–142.

Prokasy, W. F., Fawcett, J. T., & Hall, J. F. Recruitment, latency, magnitude, and amplitude of the GSR as a function of interstimulus interval. *J. exp. Psychol.*, 1962, **64**, 513–518.

Prokasy, W. F., Grant, D. A., & Meyers, N. A. Eyelid conditioning as a function of unconditioned stimulus intensity and intertrial interval. *J. exp. Psychol.*, 1958, **55**, 242–246.

Prokasy, W. F., & Papsdorf, J. D. Effects of increasing the interstimulus interval during classical conditioning of the albino rabbit. *J. comp. physiol. Psychol.*, 1965, **60**, 249–252.

Prokasy, W. F., & Whaley, F. L. Intertrial interval range shift in classical eyelid conditioning. *Psychol. Rep.*, 1963, **12**, 55–58.

Prosser, C. L., & Hunter, W. S. The extinction of startle responses and spinal reflexes in the white rat. *Amer. J. Physiol.*, 1936, **117**, 609–618.

Razran, G. A quantitative study of meaning by a conditioned salivary technique (semantic conditioning). *Sci.*, 1939a, **90**, 89–91.

Razran, G. Studies in configural conditioning: I. Historical and preliminary experimentation. *J. gen. Psychol.*, 1939b, **21**, 307–330.

Razran, G. Attitudinal determinants of conditioning and generalization of conditioning. *J. exp. Psychol.*, 1949, **39**, 820–829.

Razran, G. Conditioning and perception. *Psychol. Rev.*, 1955a, **62**, 83–95.

Razran, G. Partial reinforcement of salivary CRS in adult human subjects: Preliminary study. *Psychol. Rep.*, 1955b, **1**, 409–416.

Razran, G. The dominance-contiguity theory of the acquisition of classical conditioning. *Psychol. Bull.*, 1957, **54**, 1–46.

Razran, G. The observable unconscious and the inferable conscious in current Soviet psychophysiology: Interoceptive conditioning, semantic conditioning, and the orienting reflex. *Psychol. Rev.*, 1961, **68**, 81–147.

Razran, G. Empirical codifications and specific theoretical implications of compound-stimulus conditioning: Perception. In W. F. Prokasy (Ed.), *Classical conditioning: A symposium.* New York: Appleton-Century-Crofts, 1965. Pp. 226–248.

Rescorla, R. A. Inhibition of delay in Pavlovian fear conditioning. *J. comp. physiol. Psychol.*, 1967a, **64**, 114–120.

Rescorla, R. A. Pavlovian conditioning and its proper control procedures. *Psychol. Rev.*, 1967b, **74**, 71–80.

Rescorla, R. A., & LoLordo, V. M. Inhibition of avoidance behavior. *J. comp. physiol. Psychol.*, 1965, **59**, 406–412.

Rescorla, R. A., & Solomon, R. L. Two-process learning theory: Relationships between Pavlovian conditioning and instrumental learning. *Psychol. Rev.*, 1967, **74**, 151–182.

Reynolds, B. The acquisition of a trace conditioned response as a function of the magnitude of the stimulus trace. *J. exp. Psychol.*, 1945a, **35**, 15–30.

Reynolds, B. Extinction of trace conditioned responses as a function of the spacing of trials during the acquisition and extinction series. *J. exp. Psychol.*, 1945b, **35**, 81–95.

Ross, L. E. The decremental effects of partial reinforcement during acquisition of the conditioned eyelid response. *J. exp. Psychol.*, 1959, **57**, 74–82.

Ross, L. E. Conditioned fear as a function of CS-UCS and probe stimulus intervals. *J. exp. Psychol.*, 1961, **61**, 265–273.

Ross, L. E., Koski, C. H., & Yaeger, J. Classical eyelid conditioning of the severely retarded: Partial reinforcement effects. *Psychon. Sci.*, 1964, **1**, 253–254.

Runquist, W. N. Performance in eyelid conditioning following changes in reinforcement schedule. *J. exp. Psychol.*, 1963, **65**, 616–617.

Runquist, W. N., & Muir, W. R. Intrasession decrements in the performance of the classically conditioned eyelid reflex. *J. exp. Psychol.*, 1965, **70**, 520–525.

Runquist, W. N., & Spence, K. W. Performance in eyelid conditioning as a function of UCS duration. *J. exp. Psychol.*, 1959, **57**, 249–252.

Scheuer, C. Resistance to extinction of the conditioned emotional response (CER) as a function of shock-reinforcement acquisition schedules. Paper read at the meeting of the Midwestern Psychological Association, Chicago, May 1967.

Schlosberg, H. A study of the conditioned patellar reflex. *J. exp. Psychol.*, 1928, **11**, 468–494.

Schlosberg, H. The relationship between success and the laws of conditioning. *Psychol. Rev.*, 1937, **44**, 379–394.

Schneiderman, N. *The CS-US interval function of the nictitating membrane response of the rabbit as a function of delayed and trace conditioning procedures.* (Doctoral dissertation, Indiana University), Ann Arbor, Mich.: University Microfilms, 1964.

Schneiderman, N. Interstimulus interval function of the nictitating membrane response of the rabbit under delay versus trace conditioning. *J. comp. physiol. Psychol.*, 1966, **62**, 397–402.

Schneiderman, N., & Gormezano, I. Conditioning of the nictitating membrane of the rabbit as a function of CS-US interval. *J. comp. physiol. Psychol.*, 1964, **57**, 188–195.

Sechenov, I. M. *Reflexes of the brain.* (Refleksy golovnogo mozga, St. Petersburg, 1863). Translated from the Russian by S. Belsky. Cambridge: M.I.T. Press, 1965.

Seidel, R. J. A review of sensory preconditioning. *Psychol. Bull.*, 1959, **56**, 58–73.

Shapiro, M. M. Salivary conditioning in dogs during fixed-interval reinforcement contingent upon lever pressing. *J. exp. Anal. Behav.*, 1961, **4**, 361–364.

Shapiro, M. M. Temporal relationship between salivation and lever pressing with differential reinforcement of low rates. *J. comp. physiol. Psychol.*, 1962, **55**, 567–571.

Shapiro, M. M., & Miller, T. M. On the relationship between conditioned and discriminative stimuli and between instrumental and consummatory responses. In W. F. Prokasy (Ed.), *Classical conditioning: A symposium.* New York: Appleton-Century-Crofts, 1965. Pp. 269–301.

Shapovalova, K. B. Action of several functional tests on interoceptive conditioned reflexes from the mechanoceptors of the small intestine. *J. higher nerv. Activ.*, 1966, **16**, 795–804.

Sheer, D. D. (Ed.) *Electrical stimulation of the brain.* Austin: Univ. Texas Press, 1961.

Shurrager, P. S., & Culler, E. Conditioning in the spinal dog. *J. exp. Psychol.*, 1940, **26**, 133–159.

Shurrager, P. S., & Shurrager, H. C. The rate of learning measured at a single synapse. *J. exp. Psychol.*, 1946, **36**, 347–354.

Slivka, R. M., & Bitterman, M. E. Classical appetitive conditioning in the pigeon: Partial reinforcement. *Psychon. Sci.*, 1966, **4**, 181–182.

Smith, K. Conditioning as an artifact. *Psychol. Rev.*, 1954, **61**, 217–225.

Smith, K. Curare drugs and total paralysis. *Psychol. Rev.*, 1964, **71**, 77–79.

Smith, M. C. *Classical conditioning of the nictitating membrane response of the rabbit as a function of CS-US interval and US intensity.* Unpublished doctoral dissertation, Indiana University, 1966.

Smith, M. C., DiLollo, V., & Gormezano, I. Conditioned jaw movement in the rabbit. *J. comp. physiol. Psychol.*, 1966, **62**, 479–483.

Smith, M. C., & Gormezano, I. Conditioning of the nictitating membrane response of the rabbit as a function of backward, simultaneous and forward CS-UCS intervals. Paper presented at the meeting of the Psychonomic Society, Chicago, 1965a.

Smith, M. C., & Gormezano, I. Effects of alternating classical conditioning and extinction sessions on the conditioned nictitating membrane response of the rabbit. *Psychon. Sci.*, 1965b, **3**, 91–92.

Smith, S., & Guthrie, E. R. *General psychology in terms of behavior.* New York: Appleton-Century-Crofts, 1921.

Sokolov, E. N. Higher nervous functions: The orienting reflex. *Ann. Rev. Physiol.*, 1963, **25**, 545–580.

Solomon, R. L., & Turner, L. H. Discriminative classical conditioning in dogs paralyzed by curare can later control discriminative avoidance responses in the normal state. *Psychol. Rev.*, 1962, **69**, 202–219.

Soltysik, S. Studies on the avoidance conditioning: II. Differentiation and extinction of avoidance reflexes. *Acta Biol. Exper.*, 1960, **20**, 171–182.

Spence, K. W. Learning and performance in eyelid conditioning as a function of the intensity of the UCS. *J. exp. Psychol.*, 1953, **45**, 57–63.

Spence, K. W. *Behavior theory and conditioning.* New Haven: Yale Univer. Press, 1956.

Spence, K. W. A theory of emotionally based drive (D) and its relation to the performance in simple learning situations. *Amer. Psychol.*, 1958, **13**, 131–141.

Spence, K. W. Anxiety (Drive) level and performance in eyelid conditioning. *Psychol. Bull.*, 1964, **61**, 129–139.

Spence, K. W. Cognitive and drive factors in the extinction of the conditioned eyeblink in human subjects. *Psychol. Rev.*, 1966, **73**, 445–458.

Spence, K. W., Haggard, D. F., & Ross, L. E. UCS intensity and the associative (habit) strength of the eyelid CR. *J. exp. Psychol.*, 1958a, **55**, 404–411.

Spence, K. W., Haggard, D. F., & Ross, L. E. Intrasubject conditioning as a function of the intensity of the unconditioned stimulus. *Sci.*, 1958b, **128**, 774–775.

Spence, K. W., & Norris, E. B. Eyelid conditioning as a function of the intertrial interval. *J. exp. Psychol.*, 1950, **40**, 716–720.

Spence, K. W., & Ross, L. E. A methodological study of the form and latency of eyelid responses in conditioning. *J. exp. Psychol.*, 1959, **58**, 376–381.

Spence, K. W., & Tandler, B. F. Differential eyelid conditioning under equated drive as a function of the reinforcing UCS. *J. exp. Psychol.*, 1963, **65**, 35–38.

Spooner, A., & Kellogg, W. N. The backward conditioning curve. *Amer. J. Psychol.*, 1947, **60**, 321–334.

Stein, L. Secondary reinforcement established with subcortical stimulation. *Sci.*, 1958, **127**, 466–467.

Stewart, M. A., Stern, J. A., Winokur, G., & Fredman, S. An analysis of GSR conditioning. *Psychol. Rev.*, 1961, **68**, 60–67.

Suboski, M. D. UCS intensity and the latency of the classically conditioned eyelid response. *J. exp. Psychol.*, 1967, **74**, 31–35.

Switzer, S. A. Backward conditioning of the lid reflex. *J. exp. Psychol.*, 1930, **13**, 76–97.

Theios, J., & Brelsford, J. W. A Markov model for classical conditioning: Application to eye-blink conditioning in rabbits. *Psychol. Rev.*, 1966, **73**, 393–408.

Thomas, E., & Wagner, A. R. Partial reinforcement of the classically conditioned eyelid response in the rabbit. *J. comp. physiol. Psychol.*, 1964, **58**, 157–158.

Thorndike, E. L. *Animal intelligence.*

Macmillan: New York & London, 1898.

Thorndike, E. L. *Educational Psychology*, Vol. II. *The psychology of learning*. New York Teachers College, Columbia University, 1913.

Tolman, E. C. *Purposive behavior in animals and men*. New York: Appleton-Century-Crofts. 1932.

Tolman, E. C. Theories of learning. In F. A. Moss (Ed.), *Comparative psychology*. Englewood Cliffs N.J.: Prentice-Hall, 1934. Pp. 367–408.

Tolman, E. C. The acquisition of string-pulling by rats—conditioned response or sign-gestalt? *Psychol. Rev.*, 1937, **44**, 195–211.

Tolman, E. C. A stimulus-expectancy need-cathexis psychology. *Sci.*, 1945, **101**, 160–166.

Tolman, E. C. Principles of purposive behavior. In S. Koch (Ed.), *Psychology: A Study of a science*. Vol. 2. New York: McGraw-Hill, 1959. Pp. 92–157.

Trapold, M. A., Carlson, J. G., & Myers, W. A. The effect of non-contingent fixed- and variable-interval reinforcement upon subsequent acquisition of the fixed-interval scallop *Psychon. Sci.*, 1965, **2**, 261–262.

Trapold, M. A., & Fairlie, J. Transfer of discrimination learning based upon contingent and noncontingent training procedures. *Psychol. Rep.*, 1965, **17**, 239–246.

Trapold, M. A., Homzie, M., & Rutledge, E. Backward conditioning and UCR latency. *J. exp. Psychol.*, 1964, **67**, 387–391.

Trapold, M. A., & Odom, P. B. Transfer of a discrimination and a discrimination reversal between two manipulandum-defined responses. *Psychol. Rep.*, 1965, **16**, 1213–1221.

Trapold, M. A. Reversal of an operant discrimination by non-contingent discrimination reversal training. *Psychon. Sci.*, 1966, **4**, 247–248.

Trapold, M. A., & Spence, K. W. Performance changes in eyelid conditioning as related to the motivational and reinforcing properties of the UCS. *J. exp. Psychol.*, 1960, **59**, 209–213.

Trapold, M. A., & Winokur, S. Transfer from classical conditioning and extinction to acquisition, extinction, and stim-ulus generalization of a positively reinforced instrumental response. *J. exp. Psychol.*, 1967, **73**, 517–525.

Turner, B. B. Effects of a ready signal upon eyelid conditioning. *J. exp. Psychol.*, 1966, **72**, 11–14.

Vandermeer, S., & Amsel, A. Work and rest factors in eyelid conditioning. *J. exp. Psychol.*, 1952, **43**, 261–266.

Wagner, A. R., Siegel, L. S., & Fein, G. G. Extinction of conditioned fear as a function of percentage of reinforcement. *J. comp. physiol. Psychol.*, 1967, **63**, 160–164.

Wagner, A. R., Siegel, S., Thomas, E., & Ellison, G. D. Reinforcement history and the extinction of the classical reward response. *J. comp. physiol. Psychol.*, 1964, **58**, 354–358.

Wagner, A. R., Thomas, E., & Norton, T. Conditioning with electrical stimulation of motor cortex: Evidence of a possible source of motivation. *J. comp. physiol. Psychol.*, 1967, **64**, 191–200.

Walker, E. G. Eyelid conditioning as a function of intensity of conditioned and unconditioned stimuli. *J. exp. Psychol.*, 1960, **59**, 303–311.

Watson, J. B. The place of the conditioned-reflex in psychology. *Psychol. Rev.*, 1916, **23**, 89–116.

Watson, J. B. *Behaviorism*. New York: Norton, 1925.

Wegner, N., & Zeaman, D. Strength of cardiac CR's with varying unconditioned stimulus durations. *Psychol. Rev.*, 1958, **65**, 238–241.

White, C. T., & Schlosberg, H. Degrees of conditioning of the GSR as a function of the period of delay. *J. exp. Psychol.*, 1952, **43**, 357–362.

Wickens, D. D. Colloquium presented at the University of Massachusetts, 1965.

Wickens, D. D. Compound conditioning in humans and cats. In W. F. Prokasy (Ed.), *Classical conditioning: A symposium*. New York: Appleton-Century-Crofts, 1965. Pp. 323–339.

Wickens, D. D., Born, D. G., & Wickens, C. D. Response strength to a compound conditioned stimulus and its elements as a function of the element interstimulus interval. *J. comp. physiol. Pyschol.*, 1963, **56**, 727–731.

Wickens, D. D., & Cross, H. A. Resistance to extinction as a function of temporal relations during sensory preconditioning. *J. exp. Psychol.*, 1963, **65**, 206–211.

Wickens, D. D., Cross, H. A., & Morgan, R. M. CS termination and the response strength acquired by elements of a stimulus complex. *J. exp. Psychol.*, 1959, **58**, 363–368.

Williams, D. R. Classical conditioning and incentive motivation. In W. F. Prokasy (Ed.), *Classical conditioning*. New York: Appleton-Century-Crofts, 1965. Pp. 340–357.

Wolfle, H. M. Time factors in conditioning finger-withdrawal. *J. gen. Psychol.*, 1930, **4**, 372–378.

Wolfle, H. M. Conditioning as a function of the interval between conditioned and the original stimulus. *J. gen. Psychol.*, 1932, **7**, 80–103.

Woodworth, R. S. Reinforcement of perception. *Amer. J. Psychol.*, 1947, **60**, 119–124.

Wyers, E. J., Peeke, H. V. S., & Herz, M. J. Partial reinforcement and resistance to extinction in the earthworm. *J. comp. physiol. Psychol.*, 1964, **57**, 113–116.

Yerkes, R. M., & Morgulis, S. The method of Pavlov in animal psychology. *Psychol. Bull.*, 1909, **6**, 257–273.

Zener, K. The significance of behavior accompanying conditioned salivary secretion for theories of the conditioned response. *Amer. J. Psychol.*, 1937, **50**, 384–403.

Suggested Readings

Babkin, B. P. *Pavlov: A biography*. Chicago: University of Chicago Press, 1949. A useful biography of Pavlov.

Beecroft, R. S. *Classical conditioning*. Goleta: Psychonomic Press, 1966. A comprehensive review of the recent western research literature on conditioning.

Gormezano, I. Classical conditioning. In Sidowski, J. B. (Ed.), *Experimental methods and instrumentation in psychology*. New York: McGraw-Hill, 1966. A detailed review of the methods of eyelid, GSR, and salivary conditioning.

Grant, D. A. Classical and operant conditioning. In Melton, A. W. (Ed.), *Categories of human learning*. New York: Academic Press, 1964. A taxonomy of classical and instrumental conditioning procedures.

Hilgard, E. R., & Bower, G. H. *Theories of learning*. (3rd ed.) New York: Appleton-Century-Crofts, 1966. Contains a review of Pavlovian concepts and a brief summary of neurophysiological factors in learning.

Kimble, G. A. *Hilgard and Marquis' conditioning and learning*. (2nd ed.) New York: Appleton-Century-Crofts, 1961. Offers a balanced discussion of the place of classical conditioning within the psychology of learning.

Prokasy, W. F. (Ed.) *Classical conditioning*. New York: Appleton-Century-Crofts, 1965. An in-depth review of research in several American conditioning laboratories.

IV

Stimulus Generalization

Harry I. Kalish

State University of New York,
Stony Brook

Method and Theory[1]

Stimulus generalization and discrimination are more frequently encountered in discussions of the principles of conditioning and theories of learning than any other of the behavioral phenomena. The reason for this is not that processes in generalization or discrimination are any more readily understood, but probably because, as Guttman (1956) has pointed out, both phenomena are useful as explanatory concepts and thus help to extend the scope of conditioning theory to more complex and derived behavior such as concept formation, transfer of training, and transposition.

There is little doubt that stimulus generalization is an extremely important and useful element in models of conditioning and learning, but its utility is in rather striking contrast to the lack of information which exists concerning the conditions which affect the establishment of the gradient and the variables which determine its characteristics. In fact, the use of stimulus generalization as a concept has probably added to

its status as a fundamental and "irreducible" part of behavior, perhaps prematurely, and helped to obscure the possibility that generalization itself may be the complex result of the interaction between subtle consequences of reinforced and nonreinforced responding in discrimination and processes basic to the neurophysiology of the organism, both of which are dimly understood at present.

This latter possibility has gained some support lately from studies which have swung away from an examination of the parameters of generalization toward a consideration of the relationship between generalization and discrimination (Guttman and Kalish, 1956) and the conditions which produce a gradient of responses (Jenkins and Harrison, 1960, 1962). These experiments and a large number of others reported in the following chapters no longer leave us secure in the feeling that generalization is a phenomenon in its own right which accompanies the conditioning of a response to a specific stimulus. They have also served to revive the old arguments about the theory of generalization which placed Lashley in opposition to Pavlov and Hull in his assertion that

[1] These chapters and part of the research contained in them was made possible by grants MH-1002, M-1459, MH-06096 from the National Institute of Mental Health, USPHS, and HD-00935 from the National Institute of Child Health and Human Development.

generalization is an epiphenomenon re- sulting from processes involved in dis- crimination behavior.

This debate between Lashley and Wade (1946) and Hull (1947) concerning the properties of the generalization process provides us with a convenient and system- atic method for organizing and presenting the mass of diverse and otherwise unrelated experiments in the area of stimulus general- ization. It should be stated at the outset that the issues involved in the debate will not be resolved by the presentation of the experi- mental evidence. A consideration of the studies in the light of the theoretical issues, however, may serve to encourage new in- sights, stimulate further research, and per- haps even result in a reformulation of the old ways of thinking about stimulus gener- alization and discrimination.

This first chapter will be devoted to the definition and experimental procedures used in the study of stimulus generalization. It will also contain a discussion of the theoret- ical issues and provide the framework for the subsequent chapters. Chapter 10 will review those studies which appear to affirm the point of view that generalization is an epiphenomenon of more basic processes involved in discrimination (Lashley and Wade, 1946; Stevens, 1965). Chapter 11 will be concerned with the experiments which appear to urge the necessity for a consideration of generalization as an in- trinsic part of behavior accompanying the conditioning process (Hull, 1947; Brown, Bilodeau, and Baron, 1951). The final chap- ter will consider mediated generalization, the common elements theory, and the neuro- physiological evidence as alternative inter- pretations of the generalization process.

Although these chapters are primarily concerned with stimulus generalization, it would be difficult, if not impossible, to dis- cuss the problem of generalization without simultaneously considering the subject of discrimination. In fact, given the current state of affairs in this area, such an omission would be a tacit assumption that generaliza- tion is a phenomenon separate and distinct from the behavior involved in discrimina- tion—a belief which would be difficult to defend in view of the experimental evidence. The idea that generalization represents a fundamental process in behavior probably first emerged from Pavlov's (1927) neuro- physiological theory of generalization (ir- radiation), but a great amount of the recent effort in this area is directed toward an analysis of the relationship between gener- alization and discrimination prompted largely by the belief that the same under- lying processes are involved in both. In view of this, material on discrimination will be introduced wherever it is relevant to the discussion, but no attempt will be made to organize the vast amount of literature on the subject.

Definition

Generalization and discrimination are perhaps two of the most important prin- ciples of behavior issuing from the work of Pavlov (1927) and his associates. Both phenomena are important elements in vir- tually all theores of behavior (Estes, 1950, 1959; Guthrie, 1935; Hull, 1939–1952; Spence, 1936–1956; Tolman, 1959), and both have been employed as constructs in the explanation of more complex behavior, such as verbal learning (Gibson, 1940, 1941, 1942), concept formation (Buss, 1950; Kalish and Haber, 1962), and psycho- pathology (Miller, 1948; Mednick, 1958; Rodnick and Garmezy, 1957).

Although the experimental methods have been modified since the early studies of Anrep (1923) and Pavlov (1927)—especially with the introduction of operant tech- niques—the definition and description of generalization and discrimination (dif- ferentiation) remain essentially unchanged, a tribute to the meticulousness of the early investigators and to the basic stability of the phenomena, both of which tend to be rare events in psychological research.

Stimulus generalization, as a behavioral phenomenon distinct from speculations of the generalization process, occurs when responses conditioned to one stimulus can also be elicited by other stimuli on the same dimension. Under these circumstances a *gradient* of responses is usually obtained in which the amplitude or frequency of response decreases with increased differences (psychological or physical) between the CS and the test stimuli. (For reasons which will become apparent in a later section no distinction will be made between primary and secondary generalization.)

The absolute amount of generalization, that is, the extent to which other stimuli can evoke the response associated with the CS, will depend, among other things, upon the characteristics of the stimulus dimension. If the stimuli form a continuum with an underlying attribute such as size, brightness, wavelength, and so on, the slope of the gradient as measured from a line parallel to the abscissa and intersecting the point on the ordinate corresponding to CS response strength will vary from 90 degrees (complete generalization) to 0 degrees (complete discrimination), depending upon both the conditions of training prior to generalization testing and the method of generalization testing. Anrep's (1923) early study with dogs yielded a falling positively accelerated gradient of magnitude of salivary CR to vibro-tactile stimuli spaced several inches apart on the skin and Pavlov (1927) obtained the same results with dogs using the salivary response and several stimulus dimensions such as frequency of metronome, tone, and light. In his discussion of "generalization of stimuli" Pavlov concluded that "if a tone . . . is established as a conditioned stimulus, many other tones *spontaneously acquire similar properties* [italics ours], such properties diminishing proportionally to the intervals of these tones from the CS" (1927, p. 113). In general, the paradigm for the generalization experiment involves conditioning (or a substitute such as verbal instructions in experiments with human Ss) to one stimulus and testing, usually under conditions of nonreinforcement with other stimuli on the same continuum. The test stimuli are presented in random order and a gradient is formed by combining the results of several tests to each stimulus.

Basically, all studies designated as generalization experiments involve training to one stimulus, successive (*stimuli presented in sequence*) *presentation of stimuli during testing, and no differential reinforcement during training or testing.* Discrimination training, on the other hand, is generally characterized by successive or simultaneous (stimuli presented in pairs) presentation of stimuli with differential reinforcement. The purpose of discrimination training, in contrast to generalization, is to narrow the response class to one stimulus value. (A note on terminology. The terms *generalization decrement* or *generalization gradient* will be used synonymously with *generalization slope*. Although the word *decrement* may imply a theoretical position suggesting that the formation of the generalization gradient is a result of a differential decrease in responding to the peripheral stimuli caused by discrimination, no such meaning is intended. One could just as easily subscribe to the viewpoint that the generalization gradient represents a differential increase in response to the test stimuli as a result of conditioning.)

The concept of stimulus generalization assumes that a class of stimuli becomes conditioned to a given response as a result of training; the concept of response generalization makes a similar assumption about classes of response. Certain experiments have demonstrated that responses similar to the conditioned response can be elicited more readily by the CS under certain conditions (Wickens, 1948; Antonitis, 1951).

With few exceptions, most of the early studies in stimulus generalization were designed to explore the possibility of obtaining gradients with varying species, stimulus dimensions and dependent variables. Razran (1949) has reviewed approximately sixty-four experiments conducted in Pavlov's laboratory in which gradients were obtained from dogs using magnitude of salivary response. Moreover, Razran (1949) has obtained similar results with human Ss using spatial light patterns, color, and musical intervals as stimulus dimensions and magnitude of salivary response as the criterion measure. The studies reviewed by Mednick and Freedman (1960) and Kimble (1961, p. 330–331) indicate that a generalization gradient can be obtained for virtually any sense modality and with any stimulus dimension having ordinal properties. (This statement will be examined in more detail later in view of the studies on mediated generalization.)

The consistency with which gradients are obtained under a large number of varying conditions indicates that it is a stable phenomenon basic to the functioning of virtually all human and infrahuman organisms. Pavlov regarded generalization as an exceedingly important element in the survival of the organism and suggested that animals must develop "accessory reflexes" or "generalization of stimuli" to compensate for the inconstancy of "natural stimuli" (1927, p. 113). Hull later elaborated this point of view in the *stimulus learning* and *stimulus evocation paradoxes*: "Since stimuli are not exactly repeated, how can more than one reinforcement occur? But even if the superthreshold bond should be established it becomes a mystery how it could ever evoke a reaction in a time of need, since the exact stimulus would probably never be encountered" (1943, p. 194–95).

Experimental Methods

Although the experimental procedure for most current studies of generalization conforms to the description given above—with reinforced training to one stimulus followed by nonreinforced testing to several stimuli —most of the early experiments in generalization followed the methods of classical conditioning used to test for the appearance of a conditioned response (CR). Accordingly, several reinforced trials to the conditioned stimulus (CS) are alternated with a nonreinforced test trial to the generalized or peripheral stimuli and the gradient is obtained from an analysis of the strength of the CR on these trials (method of contrasts —Pavlov, 1927).

Anrep (1923) reports that, although generalization of the salivary response in dogs occurs with either simultaneous (CS and UCS overlap) or trace (CS and UCS separated by some time period) conditioning to a tactile stimulus, the characteristics of the generalized response appear to differ. In simultaneous conditioning (Coopalov in Anrep, 1927, p. 407) generalization is fairly widespread immediately after training and can be evoked by stimulation to any part of the skin. With further reinforced trials, however, the sensitive area diminishes to a relatively small part of the skin surrounding the spot originally stimulated. Generalized responses resulting from trace conditioning, on the other hand, can be evoked by stimulation applied to any part of the skin throughout the entire course of conditioning. There are, moreover, differences in generalization between trace reflexes with a long latent period (relatively long period between termination of the CS and onset of the UCS) and those with a short period. Although trace reflexes with a short latent period are confined largely to the receptor organ originally involved in establishing the response (the skin in the case of tactile conditioning), a stimulus applied to any receptor organ following long trace conditioning will also elicit the CR. In addition, Anrep observes that, "the longer the pause the wider is the irradiation" (1923, p. 408). Unfortunately, subsequent studies in generalization have not explored these interesting differences.

The methods introduced by the early

Russian investigators in the study of generalization were also used by Bass and Hull (1934, classical short-trace conditioning) and Grant and Dittmer (1940, classical simultaneous conditioning) to obtain a generalization gradient for the galvanic skin response (GSR) in human *S*s. Because differential reinforcement to the CS continued throughout the course of the experiment in these methods, the primary difference between a study in generalization and one in discrimination is apparently based on the number of differing stimuli presented during the test trials. If one stimulus is consistently substituted for the CS on test trials, the experiment resembles a discrimination study. If several stimuli are presented on different test trials the result is a generalization study. Ultimately, however, the outcome of the experiment was the same in both instances under these conditions; discrimination learning occurred and the response was gradually confined to the CS. These results did much to encourage the belief that generalization is a fundamental process which always precedes differentiation.

Hovland (1937a, b) recognized the presence of differential reinforcement in the studies of Anrep, and Bass and Hull speculated that the nature of the generalization function is distorted by the inability to separate the effects of "initial generalization and ultimate differentiation" (1937a, p. 137). He avoided differential reinforcement in his studies of the generalized galvanic skin response to a tonal intensity dimension for human *S*s and introduced a procedure which has generally been accepted as the prototype for most generalization experiments. Instead of alternating reinforced and nonreinforced trials during conditioning (classical short-trace) and generalization testing, Hovland first established a substantial conditioned response (GSR) to one stimulus intensity. The test for generalization consisted of random presentations of the test stimuli and the original CS during extinction. The gradient

was formed from an average of the two test trials to each of the four test stimuli. Because no differential reinforcement was involved, Hovland concluded that the generalization gradient obtained by him represented "true initial generalization" (1937a, p. 135). We shall see later (conditions of generalization testing) that the question of a "true" generalization gradient subsequently occupied the attention of a number of investigators.

In addition to the studies already mentioned, generalization gradients have been obtained for both classical short-trace conditioning with humans (Humphreys, 1939; Littman, 1949; Wickens, Schroder, and Snide, 1954) and classical simultaneous conditioning with animals (Beritoff, 1924; Britt, 1935) and humans (Eisen, 1954; Grant and Schiller, 1953; Hake, Grant, and Hornseth, 1948; Razran, 1949).

Instrumental conditioning with both animal and human subjects has also been employed in generalization studies. In an early experiment Gibson (1939) instructed *S*s to respond verbally when only one of several vibrators arranged in two rows horizontally and vertically across the back was activated. The frequency of false positive responses to vibrators other than the one established as the CS was regarded as generalized responding. Axelrod and Kankolenski (1967) combined a discriminative stimulus in the form of stimulation to electrodes imbedded along the side of a rat with a bar-pressing response for water. A generalization gradient of bar-pressing responses emerged when regions other than the training site were stimulated.

Voluntary responding and the use of verbal instructions with human *S*s to substitute for the establishment of a CR as in animals have become increasingly prevalent in recent experiments (Andreas, 1954; Buss, 1950; Duncan, 1951; Eriksen, 1954; Rosenbaum, 1953). Brown, Bilodeau, and Baron (1951), for example, obtained an orderly generalization gradient for a visual-spatial dimension with a method resembling

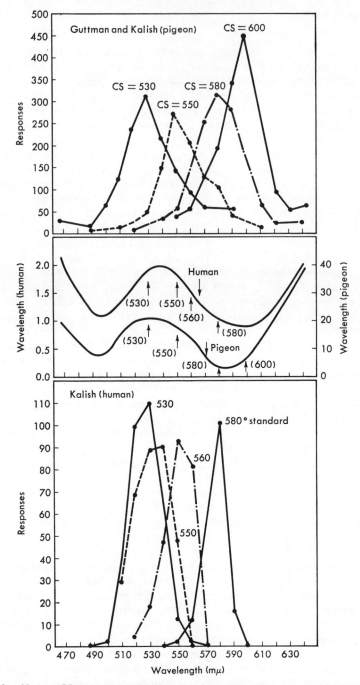

Figure 9-1. Upper: Mean generalization gradients for pigeon (Guttman and Kalish, 1956). Middle: Hue discrimination as a function of wavelength for pigeons (Hamilton and Coleman, 1933) and humans (Geldard, 1953). Lower: Generalization gradients of total responses for humans (Kalish, 1958). (Reprinted with permission from Kalish, H. I. The relationship between discriminability and stimulus generalization: A re-evaluation. *J. exp. Psychol.*, 1958, **55**, 637–644.)

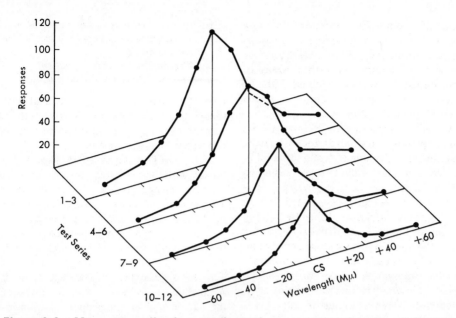

Figure 9-2. Mean generalization gradients for successive fourths of first test. (Reprinted with permission from Guttman, N., and Kalish, H. I. Discriminability and stimulus generalization. *J. exp. Psychol.*, 1956, **51**, 79–88.)

Gibson's (1939). *S*s were told to respond as rapidly as possible to the center of several lights arranged in an arc in front of them. After a number of training trials to the center light, test trials to the peripheral lights (including the center light) were introduced and generalization gradients were derived from the frequency of response to all stimuli. Several methods were devised to overcome the objections inherent in this procedure that the instructions to the *S*s are phrased to condone false reactions and that the gradient is ultimately based on the decline of reaction time to peripheral visual stimulation. Among these was a horse-race technique (Brown, Clarke, and Stein, 1958) in which the lights on the visual-spatial dimension were associated with different win frequencies known only to the experimenter (center lamp 80 per cent, peripheral lamps 20 per cent) and *S* was instructed to guess whether a given lamp (horse) will win or lose. Increases in the frequency of win guesses above the established 20 per cent base for lamps nearest

the center were interpreted as instances of generalization. Bass (1958) obtained the same results using a nonspatial dimension of silhouette density.

Generalization gradients have also been established for the color continuum (spectral wavelength) using human *S*s tested by the method of single stimuli (Kalish, 1958). The method, which is similar to those already described, involves preliminary familiarization with a standard color and a series of tests in which the *S*s are instructed to select the standard from among a number of colors displayed in random sequence (Guilford, 1936).

The gradient for animal *S*s using instrumental conditioning is substantially similar to that obtained for humans. One of the chief difficulties with both the classical and instrumental procedures described previously, however, is that the response to the CS must be maintained through differential reinforcement or it becomes labile, extinguishing rapidly when the reinforcement is removed. This makes it difficult, if not impossible, to investigate some of the more complex problems in generalization requiring the manipulation of variables during the course of generalization testing. Many of these difficulties were eliminated with the introduction of operant techniques in the study of generalization.

A method suggested by Skinner (1950) and adopted by Guttman and Kalish (1956, 1958) made it possible to test a large number of stimulus values over sustained periods during extinction, because of a high rate of response generated during training. This was accomplished by training S (a pigeon) to peck at a disk displaying the CS by the method of successive approximations. After several days of training on a variable interval schedule during which 60-sec. stimulus-on intervals were alternated with 10-sec. stimulus-off intervals, a response rate of approximately fifty per minute was attained. In the generalization tests following training, nonreinforced responses to each of the selected test stimulus values as well as the CS were sampled for successive 30-sec. periods. The resulting generalization gradients, consisting of mean number of responses to the CS and each peripheral stimulus, are shown in the upper graph of Figure 9-1. In this particular study four different groups of animals were trained with the spectral wavelength values 530, 550, 580, and 600 mμ and tested with a range of stimuli 60 mμ on either side of the CS. The advantages of this method can be seen in the family of curves for successive fourths of the generalization test in Figure 9-2. Such prolonged responding makes it possible to assess the effects of variables inserted during the formation of the generalization gradients.

Concepts and Controversies

There are two fundamental issues in stimulus generalization which seem to be basic to all theoretical formulations of the generalization process:

1. *How can stimuli acquire control over behavior without ever having been involved in the original conditioning?*
2. *Why does an ordered gradient of responses appear under certain circumstances?*

One of the earliest attempts to deal with these issues appears in Pavlov's (1927) account of the generalization process in his conceptual nervous system.

A study by Krasnogorsky (1911) provided Pavlov with the evidence necessary to create a neurological analogue of generalization. Tactile stimulators were arranged along the hind leg of a dog. The first, placed directly over the paw, was never reinforced, whereas the remainder, separated by distances of 3, 9, 15, and 22 cms., were always reinforced with food whenever they were presented. According to Pavlov, "Stimulation over the paw was given the properties of an inhibitory stimulus, while stimulations at the four upper places were given positive conditioned properties" (1927, p. 153). When regions to which the stimulators were affixed were subsequently tested, Krasnogorsky found that, although the initial response to all four stimulators was approximately five drops of saliva, the amount of responding to these stimuli was reduced proportionally with the introduction of the inhibitory stimulus above the paw. Pavlov states:

The significance of this experiment is clear. The different sensory places on the skin must be regarded as projecting themselves upon corresponding areas in the cortex of the hemispheres. Therefore, it is reasonable" to suppose that the inhibitory process initiated in a definite point of the cortex by the tactile stimulation of the inhibitory place *irradiates* into the surrounding region, giving a smaller inhibitory effect with increase in distance from the inhibitory point and becoming indistinguishable at the more distant points. [Pavlov, 1927, p. 154.]

On the basis of these experiments Pavlov established the cortical analogue of generalization: *Irradiation of excitation and in-*

hibition denoting a diminishing wavelike spread of excitatory or inhibitory energy across the sensory cortex from the point of conditioning.

Several investigators have questioned the adequacy of this hypothesis. Loucks (1933) rejected the irradiation hypothesis on the basis of success in conditioning decorticate dogs and substituted the term *generalization* for *irradiation* to distinguish the observable gradient obtained by Bass and Hull (1934) from the brain state hypothesized by Pavlov. Gradients for intensity dimensions (Hovland 1937b; Grice and Hunter, 1964) which depend upon frequency of discharge also contradict the spatial properties inherent in the irradiation hypothesis.

Two direct tests were made of the Pavlovian hypothesis. In one (Bass and Hull, 1934), generalization gradients for the GSR were obtained by stimulating the region between the calf and shoulder. If, as Pavlov had supposed, generalization results from spread of excitation across the cortex, stimulation of the area between the waist and buttocks should yield a gradient with an inversion because the sensory projection of this area on the cortex in man is interrupted by projections from the thigh, calf, and foot. No such inversion was found. In a second test, Grant and Dittmer (1940) showed that tactile stimulation of 4-in. steps along the medial line of the back in human *S*s will produce a somewhat steeper gradient for the GSR than 1-in. steps along the finger. These differences are not in the expected direction, because the cortical projections for the hand are much larger than that for the back and, according to the authors, "hand irradiation taking place over a large cortical area would suffer greater decrement between successive points than back irradiation . . ." (1940, p. 308). Grant and Dittmer also point out that *S*'s inability to discriminate any except the two most extreme points on the back was reflected in an inversion for the gradient in this region, suggesting *some sort of theory of generalization based on discrimination.*

The various complex stimulus dimensions such as rate of flashing light and time which have been used in recent experiments are not easily explained in terms of the relatively simple anatomical counterparts proposed by Pavlov. (Thompson has suggested a neurophysiological theory of generalization based on common neuronal interconnections which attempts to answer the objections raised previously. This theory is discussed in Chapter 12, pp. 281–284.) In discussing the Pavlovian hypothesis, Guttman asserts that, "Generalization is not a process but the name of a category for which the word *transfer* could be used with equal accuracy. If cortical irradiation were a fact, it would explain both generalization and transfer" (1963, p. 152).

The idea of the stimulus generalization gradient as a fundamental process *sui generis* accompanying conditioning probably emerged from Pavlov's irradiation hypothesis and has persisted in many theoretical considerations of generalization. Some of the earliest non-neurological speculations concerning the generalization process embodied the view that the generalization gradient is the result of associative connections formed during conditioning to elements of the CS complex common to both the CS and the test stimuli (Thorndike, 1913; Guthrie, 1930, 1935). This interpretation of generalization has recently been revived and is an important factor in many mathematical models of learning (Estes, 1950, 1959) and generalization (Bush and Mosteller, 1951; Restle, 1964) and also serves as the basis for mediated generalization (Osgood, 1962). A detailed discussion of mediated generalization and the common elements explanation is reserved for Chapter 12 (p. 276).

Unlike the irradiation hypothesis, the common elements interpretation of generalization does not require a concept of "transfer of excitation" in order to explain the acquisition of stimulus control of behavior because the elements of the test stimulus are already present during conditioning. Hull acknowledged that Guthrie's (1930) "common afferent molecules" might eventually serve as the model for all primary stimulus generalization, but in the absence of any proof on the molecular level (see Thompson, 1965) he preferred to direct his attention to a molar analysis of generalization based on empirical relationships (Hull, 1943, p. 191).

Although Hull rejected the idea of irradiation as a neural explanation of the generalization process, his statements regarding generalization have often been regarded, perhaps mistakenly, as functional equivalents of Pavlovian irradiation (Lashley and Wade, 1946; Guttman, 1963). Thus, for example, according to Hull, the gradient derives from a process where, "the reaction involved in original conditioning becomes connected with a considerable zone of stimuli other than but adjacent to, the stimulus conventionally involved in the original conditioning . . ." (1943, p. 183), with the result that "the receptors of normal higher organisms appear to yield afferent generalization continua for all physical stimulus dimensions to which they respond at all" (1943, p. 188). It is essentially this latter view of the generalization gradient as an indigenous part of receptor mechanisms and CNS responding which stimulated the controversy between Lashley and Wade (1946) and Hull (1947).

Hull (1943) defined primary stimulus generalization as the growth of habit strength to peripheral stimuli, on the one hand, and used the jnd as a parameter in the equation describing the generalization gradient, on the other. The first part of the definition assumes that the peripheral stimuli become connected to the response associated with the CS as a result of conditioning. The second part implies that the basis for the generalization gradient is the unit of discrimination used to denote the difference limen. In other words, excitation becomes connected with a considerable zone of stimuli *during conditioning*, but the extent of this connection which is reflected in the

shape of the gradient is presumably also affected by the discriminability of the stimulus dimension (jnd)—a measure which can only be determined from the *S*'s response *after testing*. Because it seems hardly likely that the growth of associative strength is governed by the discriminability of the stimulus dimension, especially because only one stimulus is present during training, two separate processes appear to be required. Part of the generalization gradient is determined by "connections" established during conditioning, whereas another part is influenced by the characteristics of the stimulus dimension during generalization testing.

A similar situation is found in other descriptions of the generalization process. Shephard, for example, combines the idea of "diffusion of trace elements" during conditioning with stimulus dissimilarity as a measure of "psychological distance" (1958, p. 247). The same idea is also prevalent in Schlosberg and Solomon (1943) and Brown, Bilodeau, and Baron (1951).

The belief that the generalization gradient reflects processes other than that involved in *S*'s inability to distinguish between the CS and the test stimuli during generalization testing has stimulated a search for the "true initial gradient" (Hovland, 1937a) or the "primary" (Grice and Saltz, 1950) or "true" (Kling, 1952) generalization gradient.

Lashley and Wade (1946) questioned the basis of Hull's explanation for the generalization gradient as part of their broader criticism of the conditioning-excitation model applied to the interpretation of learning in general. Generalization gradients, they maintained, represent imperfect discrimination due to "failure of association" to the CS. A *gradient* of responses is not formed until the organism experiences the stimulus dimension through an act of comparison. The core of Lashley's position with respect to generalization is contained in three statements:

1. "The phenomenon of stimulus generalization represents a failure of association."

2. "The dimensions of a stimulus series are determined by comparison of two or more stimuli and do not exist for the organism until established by differential training."

3. "Differentiation of conditioned reflexes involves the redirection of attention to new aspects of the stimuli and the formation of new associations. . . ." [Lashley and Wade, 1946, p. 74.]

The latter statement is especially significant in view of the importance currently being attached to the role of *attention* in the interpretation of generalization, as we shall subsequently see (Reynolds, 1961c; Guttman, 1963; Ganz, 1964; Boneau and Honig, 1964).

Although the position taken by Lashley and Wade (1946) has sometimes been interpreted as a declaration that empirical gradients of generalization do not exist, a communication from Lashley to Hull (Hull, 1947, footnote 3, p. 129) indicates otherwise. Lashley did not question the graded series of responses obtained by Pavlov and Anrep. Instead, he proposed an alternative to the generalization gradient which eliminated the assumption that associative strength accrues to the test stimuli by virtue of conditioning to the CS. A gradient is an indication that the *S* has already "attended to" the stimulus dimension.

Hull (1947) argued that because neither simultaneity nor close succession of stimuli was involved in obtaining the gradient, an act of comparison could not conceivably occur. For Lashley, however, the comparison was between a trace or nervous patterning which is left as a result of training and rearoused in later trials: "The comparison may be between this trace and the later stimuli (between a memory image and a stimulus . . .)" (Hull, 1947, pp. 129–130). Lashley's proposal reduces generalization to a discrimination process involving an act of comparison and establishes a neural event (trace) as a logical necessity to substitute for the absence of an overt comparison stimulus.

The positions taken by Lashley and Wade (1946) and Hull (1947) can be summarized as follows:

Hull: Generalization gradients are natural consequences of responding to stimulus dimensions and reflect "afferent generalization continua." Generalization gradients are established as a result of conditioning to one stimulus. The use of the jnd embraces the possibility that the formation of such gradients is also influenced by the sensitivity of the receptor mechanism.

Lashley and Wade: Gradients of generalization do exist as empirical phenomena, but they are artifacts of imperfect discrimination, caused in large measure by the organism's inability to redirect attention to new aspects of the stimuli. The *S*'s lack of familiarity with the stimulus dimension produces complete generalization, that is, nondifferential responding to all stimuli. The gradient ultimately emerges only after differential responding has been elicited through differential reinforcement.

Razran (1949) has taken a position somewhat similar to that of Lashley and Wade. In a summary article he considers four views of stimulus generalization—corticophysiological (Pavlov-Bekhterev), physicobehavioral (Hull-Spence), failure of association-transposition (Lashley-Wade), and categorizing-rating (Razran)—and concludes that both the first and second are in disagreement with the evidence. Razran also distinguishes between "pseudo-generalization" which, he believes, is the equivalent of Lashley and Wade's "failure of association," where circumstances prevent the organism from noting the distinguishing characteristics of the CS, and "true generalization" which requires *S* to "categorize or rate the new stimulus on some sort of crude similarity-dissimilarity scale" during the actual generalization testing. Because rating would require something similar to an act of comparison, Razran's position does not appear to be appreciably different from that of Lashley and Wade.

The interpretation of the generalization

gradient as a twofold process involving growth of associative strength to the peripheral stimuli as well as sensitivity of receptor mechanisms appears to have been anticipated in an earlier study by Schlosberg and Solomon (1943), who utilized the generalization gradient to predict response latency of rats in a successive discrimination ("single-stimulus type") task. The results of the experiment persuaded the investigators to make a distinction between "primary stimulus generalization" and "gradient of response strength." The former corresponds to measures of similarity typical of psychophysical procedures and "probably determined by receptors and their associated neural mechanisms," whereas the latter is "due to the spread of the effects of punishment and reward along the primary gradient of generalization" (1943, p. 30). They were also led to conclude that the primary generalization gradient for response latencies is a straight line in logarithmic units upon which a superimposed gradient of response strength is developed (1943, p. 38).

A similar view was espoused by Brown, Bilodeau, and Baron (1951) in the study, described earlier, designed to test the assumption that generalization gradients could be derived from a spatial continuum. After distinguishing between the empirical gradient and its theoretical explanation, the authors contrasted the view of the generalization gradient as a measure of discriminative thresholds (Lashley and Wade, 1946) with the belief that positive associative strengths are developed to the test stimuli during conditioning (Hull, 1947). Although they agree with the proposition that some component of the generalization gradient can be attributed to the same processes affecting psychophysical judgments (Schlosberg and Solomon's

"primary stimulus generalization"), they object to the idea that generalization can be explained entirely in these terms. According to the authors, it might be more profitable to conceive of psychophysical studies and generalization experiments as two ends of the same continuum ". . . arranged according to the degree to which their procedures permit the appearance of empirical generalization" (1951, p. 60). At one end, the absence of differential reinforcement results in large difference limens and marked generalization (relatively flatter gradients). At the other, where differential reinforcement or its functional equivalent (like instructions to Ss) occurs, generalization is minimal and yields smaller difference limens and relatively steep gradients. Thus, Brown, Bilodeau, and Baron (1951) conceptualize generalization in terms of increments in associative response strength following conditioning. The extent of generalization, that is, slope of the generalization gradient, is influenced by those factors affecting the sensitivity of the receptor mechanism. The generalization gradient at any given moment, therefore, is the result of *"generalized associative strength and fluctuations in receptor-neural thresholds"* (Brown, Bilodeau, and Baron, 1951) [italics ours]. Kimble (1961) also suggests that processes in addition to those involving discrimination are necessary to account adequately for generalization, and more recently, Schumsky (1964) has conducted a study which purports to demonstrate the relevance of both a discrimination and generalization component. It has been pointed out that the choice of either interpretation of generalization, the necessity for both or the emergence of still a third, will ultimately depend upon their "predictive and subsumptive powers" (Brown, Bilodeau, and Baron, 1951, p. 60).

Generalization as an Epiphenomenon

Generalization and Maturation

Bindra, among others, has suggested that "a final answer to this question of primary stimulus generalization would require an experiment in which animals are reared without any sense modality until the time of the experiment. Such a procedure would guarantee that a discriminated dimension has not been established before the animal is subjected to experimentation" (1959, p. 199).

Conditions of stimulus deprivation were approximated by Peterson (1962), who suggested that the traditional gradient of stimulus generalization would not be obtained if the stimulus environment were controlled to preclude differential reinforcement of responding. To accomplish this, Peterson raised four Peking ducklings from the time they were hatched in a monochromatic environment illuminated by a sodium lamp (589 mμ). During this time the birds were trained to peck at a key illuminated by 589 mμ in order to obtain water, of which they were deprived. Two other control Ss were raised in an environment illuminated by 200-watt tungsten filament lamps. Subsequent generalization

testing of both groups over a range of stimuli from 490 to 650 mμ yielded a flat generalization function (complete generalization) to all stimuli for the group raised in a uniform environment (589 mμ) and the customary gradient for the control group (Figure 10-1). In a second experiment two ducklings were raised in a monochromatic environment under conditions identical to those in the first experiment. The ducklings were then subjected to discrimination training in which 610 mμ was reinforced after a pause of forty-five sec. while the training stimulus (589 mμ) continued to receive reinforcement after a fixed number of responses. Under these conditions the response to 610 mμ decreased, indicating that differential responding was possible with appropriate discrimination training. A replication of Peterson's work by Terrace (1965, personal communication) yielded strikingly similar results. The gradient for ducklings raised in a monochromatic environment remained essentially flat even after as many as six separate test sequences for each test stimulus. Differential reinforcement for 589 mμ positive and 630 mμ negative resulted in a steep gradient and the appearance of the "peak shift" phenomenon (see p. 246).

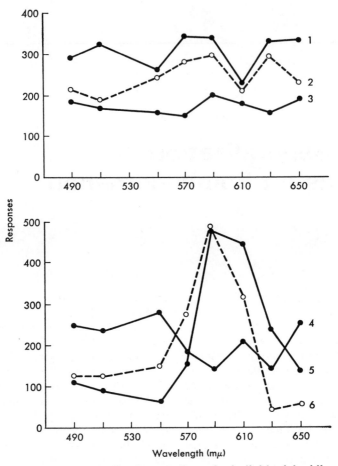

Figure 10-1. Stimulus generalization gradients for individual ducklings. Birds 1 to 4 were raised in a monochromatic environment; birds 5 and 6 were not. (Reprinted with permission from Peterson, N. Effect of monochromatic rearing on the control of responding by wavelength. *Science*, 1962, **136**, 774–775.)

Tracy (1968) has recently presented evidence from a series of three studies suggesting that the results of Peterson's experiment must be interpreted with some degree of caution. In repeating Peterson's work with a larger group of birds, Tracy also found that ducklings reared in white light produced steeper generalization gradients than those raised in monochromatic sodium-vapor illumination. In contrast to Peterson, however, gradients with slopes significantly different from zero were obtained from the sodium-vapor group. A second experiment revealed that increased stimulus control, and hence steeper gradients, could be obtained by training the sodium-vapor group to 589 or 630 mμ prior to generalization testing. The final experiment in the series indicated that ducklings show an innate color preference in the green region. This finding further complicates the analysis and interpretation of visual wavelength gradients following stimulus deprivation because of the possible confounding of color preference and generalized reinforcement. It may also suggest, however, that greater significance should be attached to the relatively flat gradients in Peterson's study, because these were obtained despite the bias of color preference. In any event, the discovery of a color preference emphasizes the necessity for using Ss other than ducklings.

Differences in experimental procedure may well account for the inconsistencies between Tracy's and Peterson's studies. As Tracy pointed out, Peterson used a sodium-vapor light to illuminate both the environment in which the Ss were raised and the response key, whereas Tracy used interference filters to illuminate the response key during generalization testing. Interference filters generally have a relatively wider band pass than sodium-vapor lamps, exposing the ducklings to less precise wavelength control during generalization testing. In addition, Peterson's Ss were isolated in a small refrigerator, whereas Ss in Tracy's study were housed in cages in a relatively large room where they had an opportunity to acquire both intensity and form discriminations as a result of the experimenter's activity during feeding, watering, and handling. Such discriminations on one continuum have been shown to influence the course of generalization on another (Honig 1965a).

A study conducted by Cofoid and Honig (1961) demonstrated that gradients obtained from neonate chicks during imprinting were considerably flatter for the spectral wavelength dimension than the equivalent gradient for the pecking response in pigeons. Similar results were obtained by Ganz and Riesen (1962), who raised two groups of four infant monkeys (*moraca mulatta*) in visually controlled environments. One group was raised in complete darkness from birth, whereas the second was raised under normal conditions. The second group was then placed in darkness and both groups received monocular stimulation of the right eye with a monochromatic stimulus (either 449, 509, 567, or 631 mμ) while seated in a specially constructed chair. Key pressing during a dark period delayed the onset of the reinforced monochromatic light for a period of 15 sec. Ss continued to be reinforced for responding to the CS during generalization testing when other stimuli ranging from 449 to 631 mμ in approximately thirty steps were also presented. The gradient for the group raised in darkness from birth was flat and comparable to the deprived group in Peterson's and Terrace's studies. On the subsequent tests, and under conditions of continued differential reinforcement, however, a gradient emerged. The authors also point out that the gradient appeared to be a combination of two processes, consisting of decreased responding to the generalized stimuli and increased responding to S+, the positive stimulus. Comparable distortions in the generalization gradient were also reported for human adults who recovered their sight after being congenitally deprived (Ganz, 1966). Ganz (1966) interprets non-differential responding to changes in the stimulus after vision has been restored as an indication of "shallow generalization" and suggests that the "mechanism" which orders the stimuli along a dimension innately is attenuated by the effects of early stimulus deprivation.

Studies in human generalization have also demonstrated the importance of maturation as a variable in generalization. Reiss (1946), for example, found increased generalization along a dimension of homonyms for children compared to adults. Mednick and Lehtinen (1957) reported similar results for a spatial dimension; London (1958) observed a tendency for broader generalization gradients among younger children and Landau (1965) obtained completely flat gradients for children aged three and a half to four and a half years on a dimension of line orientation. Mental age rather than chronological age has been isolated as an important factor in the relationship between maturation and stimulus generalization. Tempone (1965) found that frequency of response for three groups of eight-year-old children to test stimuli along a spatial dimension (Brown,

Bilodeau, and Baron, 1951; Mednick and Lehtinen, 1957) increased with decreases in MA scores from 10.9 years through 8.7 years to 6.6 years, resulting in flatter gradients for lower MA scores. Latency measures, on the other hand, were not found to be related to MA. Tempone's results are contrary to the finding of Arnhof and Loy (1957) who used young adults (eighteen to twenty-two years) and a relatively attentuated range of intelligence (101–135). Maturational factors were also shown to be important in transposition behavior. Older children who were capable of verbalizing the relationship between the two training stimuli showed successful discrimination of stimulus pairs (complete transposition) remote from the training stimuli. Younger children and those incapable of verbalizing the difference in the original discrimination operated largely on a chance basis (Kuenne, 1946).

It is not entirely clear from the previously cited evidence whether experience with the environment in the form of differential reinforcement alone or some combination of maturational factors and specific sensory experience is necessary to produce the generalization gradient. In the case of Peterson (1962), Ganz and Riesen (1962), and Terrace (1965), relatively flat generalization was obtained from young animal *S*s after stimulus deprivation. The same was true of human adults whose sight was restored after a period of blindness. In both situations, however, a generalization gradient was obtained following differential training. Flat generalization functions, on the other hand, are frequently found for children who, it is assumed, have had ample experience with many stimulus dimensions under conditions of differential reinforcement. These differences between young animals and children suggest that a specific maturational level must be reached before differential training produces a gradient of generalization. Recent neurophysiological evidence raises the possibility that the central nervous system in cats is structured to

produce a generalization gradient in the auditory dimension (Thompson, 1965). But these results were obtained from mature cats. Whether this is the result of the development of physiological factors, specific differential training on a sensory dimension, or both, is still largely a matter of conjecture.

Conditions of Generalization Training and Testing: A Search for the Controlling Stimulus

Stimuli acquire the ability to control behavior when variations in the stimulus properties produce corresponding changes in behavior. Under these conditions *S* is also said to be "attending" to the stimulus dimension (Skinner, 1953). Presumably, this is what Lashley and Wade (1946) meant when they maintained that the generalization gradient occurs only after a "relevant dimension" is established for the organism through differential conditioning. According to Lashley and Wade (1946) and Lashley (1942), two conditions must be satisfied in order to transform the flat generalization function denoting absence of stimulus control to a response gradient. (1) Differential training must occur to two values on a given dimension and (2) *S*'s attention must be redirected to new aspects, qualities or attributes of the stimulus complex. Ostensibly, neither of these conditions prevail in the traditional generalization experiment because only one stimulus is present during generalization training. Yet generalization gradients are obtained under these circumstances. A number of recent experiments have shown that, in fact, subtle sources of differential reinforcement are involved during generalization training which may account for the formation of a gradient.

One of the first experiments to deal with unrecognized sources of differential training in producing the generalization gradient showed that a relatively flat generalization function was obtained for the pigeon when the auditory frequency used as the CS was continuously present while S was being reinforced on a variable interval schedule (Jenkins and Harrison, 1960; see Figure 10-2). More pronounced bidirectional gradients (Figure 10-3) were obtained, however, when periods of silence were alternated with presentations of tone; a condition which approximated the stimulus-on, stimulus-off periods used by Guttman and Kalish (1956). Jenkins and Harrison suggest that differential training may, in fact, be the basis for most gradients of generalization. Where explicit sources of differential reinforcement are not apparent the discrimination conditions may be present between the stimulus and its surround (stimulus contrast). Both Perkins (1953) and Brown (1965) have also suggested this as a possibility, and Ray (1967) has recently shown that sharper gradients result following differential reinforcement along a dimension in contrast to training on a single stimulus.

Heinemann and Rudolph (1963) lend a great deal of support to this speculation. They hypothesized that cues, in addition to the relevant stimulus, acquire stimulus control over behavior through inadvertent differential reinforcement. Three groups of pigeons were trained to peck at a disk (response key) surrounded by concentric gray rings of varying widths. The first was trained to a narrow gray ring (1.75 in.) terminating in a black background, the second to a wider gray ring (5.25 in.) and the last to the response key surrounded completely by a gray background. Generalization tests consisted of presentations of the response key with the luminance of the gray used during training (10.1 ft.-L.) and both a darker (1.5 ft.-L.) and lighter (15.4 ft.-L.) shade. The group trained with a narrow gray band showed a relatively steep generalization gradient around the original training stimulus. The group with a completely gray background during training yielded a horizontal function, and the remaining group was midway between the other two. The authors suggest that differential reinforcement occurred when the pigeons trained to peck with the narrow ring often pecked at the black wall for which no reinforcement was received. In effect, this group received differential reinforcement for a brightness dimension— white key and gray background reinforced,

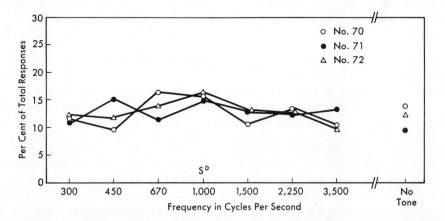

Figure 10-2. Generalization gradients following *nondifferential* **training with a 1,000-cps tone as S^D. Individual gradients are based on the means of three generalization tests.** (Reprinted with permission from Jenkins, H. M., and Harrison, R. H. Effect of discrimination training on auditory generalization. *J. exp. Psychol.*, 1960, **59**, 246–253.)

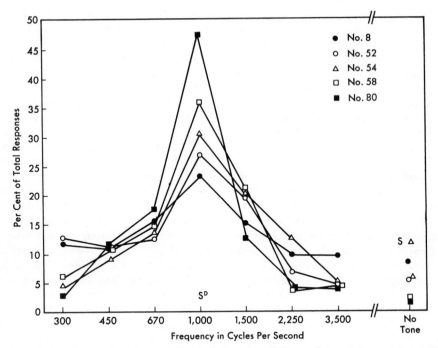

Figure 10-3. Generalization gradients following differential training with a 1,000-cps tone as S^D; no tone as S delta. Individual gradients are based on the means of three generalization tests. (Reprinted with permission from Jenkins, H. M., and Harrison, R. H. Effect of discrimination training on auditory generalization. *J. exp. Psychol.*, 1960, **59**, 246–253.)

black background not reinforced. When brightness was changed during generalization testing, a response decrement occurred. For the groups with a completely gray background no such differential reinforcement took place.

In a complementary study, Boneau and Honig (1964) manipulated a stimulus complex consisting of monochromatic light and a vertical line to determine whether generalization gradients can be obtained from stimuli which have been made "irrelevant" by a conditional discrimination during generalization training. A group of pigeons was trained on a conditional discrimination problem during which they were reinforced for pecking at a vertical line when the background was illuminated with a given spectral value (550 mμ). Another stimulus (570 mμ) served to indicate that reinforcement was available only with the vertical line absent. A generalization gradient was obtained when tests were conducted on a dimension of angular orientation with a background illumination of 550 mμ, but the gradient was initially flat and emerged only after several generalization tests. The function for angular orientation with 570 mμ as a background, on the other hand, was flat throughout all the tests. Further tests along the wavelength dimension yielded two gradients with maxima and minima at those values associated with positive and negative reinforcement during training. Boneau and Honig (1964) also suggest that although the dimension of angular orientation was "destroyed" by conditional discrimination, a gradient for length of line might have been obtained if tests were conducted. This would have been consistent with the assumption that a continuum between presence and absence of line was established by the conditions of the experiment.

Newman and Baron (1965) also explored the effects of differential training involving two dimensions on the formation of the generalization gradient. In this study pigeons were trained to peck at a white vertical line on a green background. Following initial training with continuous reinforcement, Ss were assigned to four groups and given conditional discrimination training similar to that used by Boneau and Honig (1964). During this phase of the experiment the white vertical line on a green background originally used as the training stimulus continued to be the reinforced stimulus for all groups. The nonreinforced stimulus for each group was as follows: Group I, green background with vertical line absent; Group II, red background with vertical line absent; Group III, no $S-$; Group IV, red background with vertical line present. The generalization tests were conducted after conditional discrimination on a dimension of angularity with the green background. Only Group I yielded a reliable generalization gradient. The generalization function for the remaining groups was completely flat. The authors conclude that control of behavior is demonstrated by the appearance of a gradient after differential training and that, apparently, a reliable generalization gradient for line orientation can only be obtained after differential training to presence-absence of the vertical line.

This interpretation is not supported by the results of a study by Butter and Guttman (1957), who found a gradient for angular orientation without differential training. Newman and Baron point out, however, that unlike the conditions in their experiment Butter and Guttman alternated nonreinforced blackout periods with stimulus presentations—a condition which produces a gradient for the tonal dimension (Jenkins and Harrison, 1960). Newman and Baron also suggest that some dimensions (for example, line orientation, tonal frequency) may require differential training before S can "attend" to the dimension. Others (for example, spectral wavelength, light intensity) seem to require little or no differential training possibly as a result of pre-experimental differential training or innate factors. In this respect it is instructive to note that although the conditions for Group IV (vertical line, green background-reinforced; vertical line, red background-nonreinforced) in the Newman and Baron study were essentially similar to the conditional discrimination in the Boneau and Honig study (vertical line, 550-mμ reinforced; vertical line, 570-mμ nonreinforced), Newman and Baron failed to obtain a gradient for line orientation. Because the major difference between these two experiments was the presentation of blackout periods during generalization testing in the Boneau and Honig study, it would appear that blackout periods constitute an important source of differential reinforcement in generalization experiments. However, Switalski, Lyons, and Thomas (1966) have succeeded in generating wavelength gradients without the use of blackouts, which no longer appear to be a major source of variance equivalent to the tone-off periods in the Jenkins and Harrison (1960) study.

The difficulty involved in the interpretation of the stimulus dimension actually controlling the behavior is illustrated in an experiment by Landau (1965) which bears a marked similarity to the study just described (Boneau and Honig, 1964). Prior to generalization testing, Ss in Landau's study (children ranging in age from three and a half to four and a half years and college students) were given discrimination training (stimuli presented both successively and simultaneously) in which $S+$ was a line oriented 90 degrees (vertical) on a white background and $S-$ was the white background with line absent. S was required to respond to the positive stimulus by saying "yes" if he thought it belonged to the training concept and "no" if he did not.

Later generalization tests on the dimension of angular orientation revealed a flat function for the children, along with the usual decrement for the college students. Landau concludes from this that the two groups of Ss learned something different during the pregeneralization training sessions. If we examine the results of this experiment in the light of Boneau and Honig's analysis, it is highly probable that the dimension of angular tilt was made irrelevant for the children by virtue of discrimination training to a "line present-line absent" dimension. Thus, a gradient for length of line might have been obtained for the children if the proper tests were conducted. The differences in performance between college students and children suggests that this interpretation may be appropriate only for young children and infrahuman Ss.

Heinemann, Chase, and Mandell (1968) have used the conditional discrimination procedure to demonstrate that the formation of a generalization gradient and, therefore, stimulus control can be made contingent on the presence of a stimulus which has been associated with differential reinforcement. Prior to generalization testing, pigeons were reinforced for pecking a right-hand red disk in the presence of a 1,000-hz tone and a left-hand red disk in the presence of a 300-hz tone. When both keys were illuminated by a green color only the right-hand key was reinforced regardless of the tone present. During generalization testing with other frequencies, a gradient of responses to the disk that was correct for the 1,000-hz tone was formed around 1,000 hz only when the red disk was available. When the green disk was present only flat generalization functions were obtained. The authors concluded from this that, under the influence of the green stimulus and no prior discrimination training, tone became a nonrelevant dimension and failed to command S's "attention."

A number of studies have also shown that the elements of a compound stimulus made up of stimuli from two separate dimensions can each independently acquire stimulus control of behavior. Fink and Patton (1953) found that the slope of the generalization decrement of an instrumental drinking response in rats increased as the number of components along the generalization testing dimension was altered. White (1958) also showed greater generalization decrement in children when stimuli were varied in two dimensions rather than one dimension alone. Butter and Guttman (1957) and Butter (1963) obtained a generalization gradient for both spectral wavelength and angular orientation of line when pigeons were trained with a standard stimulus consisting of a vertical line at 90 degrees through which a 550-mμ band of light was transmitted. Butter (1963) also found that the animals showed a greater generalization decrement to stimuli varied in two dimensions rather than a single dimension. Two gradients were obtained by Bloomberg (1962) for a visual and auditory dimension when pigeons were trained to a conditioned stimulus consisting of a 1,000-hz tone and a spectral wavelength value of 580 mμ. Similar results were found by Healey (1965) for rats on a compound dimension of spot size and tone and Chase (1966) for pigeons using a dimension of tone and line orientation.

The experiments just described (Guttman, 1963; Heinemann and Rudolph, 1963; Boneau and Honig, 1964; Newman and Baron, 1965; Heinemann, Chase, and Mandell, 1968) as well as those of Reynolds (1961a, b) and Mackintosh (1965) place a great deal of emphasis on the role of differential reinforcement and attention in the generalization phenomenon. Ganz (1966), for example, regards the study by Heinemann and Rudolph (1963) as a reaffirmation of Lashley's view that the stimulus dimension does not exist for the organism until differential reinforcement directs attention toward specific attributes and away from others. Newman and Baron (1965) come to somewhat the same conclusion in their study with pigeons in which a generalization gradient to line orientation was obtained only after differential training to presence or absence of a vertical line on a green surround, and the experiment by Heinemann, Chase, and Mandell (1968) was an explicit effort to demonstrate that discriminative control of attention could be achieved through conditional discrimination. In a similar vein, Guttman (1963) points out that the establishment of a tone-off, tone-on discrimination in the Jenkins and Harrison (1960) study was probably responsible for producing a generalization gradient in contrast to training with tone continuously present.

The idea expressed in these studies is, of course, similar to that proposed by Lashley to explain generalization, namely, that differential reinforcement leads to attention which, in turn, leads to stimulus control. The relationship between variations in the stimulus and corresponding changes in behavior characterized by the generalization gradient provides an instance of the formation of stimulus control of behavior, and the generalization gradient is often used as a probe in studies of attention. There has been a tendency to use "attention" as a mediating concept in the recent discrimination and generalization literature. It should be noted, however, that the term adds very little to our understanding of generalization. Skinner defines *attention* solely in terms of the behavior represented by the discriminative reaction—for example, a pigeon strikes a key when a light is flickering and does not strike it when the light is still (1953, p. 124)—and, as such, the word conveys no more meaning than is expressed in the operational definition of stimulus control.

Although at first glance differential reinforcement and stimulus contrast are compelling explanations of the generalization gradient, especially in view of the evidence just presented, they do not explain why an ordered gradient appears. The result of reinforcing one stimulus and withholding reinforcement for another should be completely differential responding. Differential reinforcement does not provide a satisfactory explanation of the fact that other stimuli on the continuum, which have never been involved in discrimination training, evoke responses as well, and that, moreover, these responses show a systematic decrement if the stimuli lie on the continuum somewhere between the two which have been used as discriminanda. It would appear that the concept of generalization of inhibition must also be invoked to explain the gradient, but results from the study by Heinemann, Chase, and Mandell (1968) complicate matters still further. In their experiment a generalization gradient appeared only when a red stimulus, previously associated with discrimination training, was present during generalization testing. Under the circumstances it appears as if the red stimulus acted as a signal for the pigeon to begin making discriminal responses while the green stimulus elicited no such behavior. Such a demonstration makes it difficult to appeal to a gradient of inhibition to account for generalization, because the red signal would have to initiate an inhibitory process, and lends support to a discrimination interpretation of the generalization process.

Variations in the conditions of generalization testing have also been used to test Lashley's hypothesis concerning the formation of generalization gradients. Usually these tests are conducted under one of four conditions: (1) random nonreinforced trials to pairs of stimuli after conditioning (Honig, 1962); (2) nonreinforced trials randomly interspersed among conditioning trials (Pavlov, 1927); (3) random nonreinforced trials to the entire range of selected stimuli after conditioning (Guttman and Kalish, 1956); and (4) extinction to only one stimulus per group after conditioning (Kalish and Haber, 1963). The first condition provides maximum opportunity for discrimination to occur based on the presence of a comparison stimulus, whereas each subsequent condition reduces

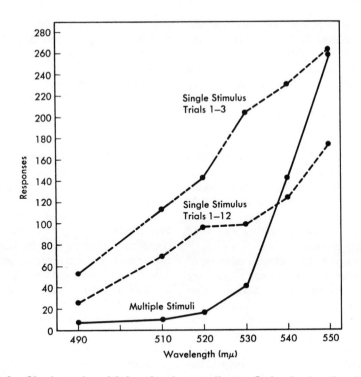

Figure 10-4. Single and multiple stimulus gradients. *S*s in single stimulus groups were extinguished to one wavelength. *S*s in multiple stimulus groups sampled all wavelengths during extinction. (Reprinted with permission from Kalish, H .I., and Haber, A. Generalization: I. Generalization gradients from single and multiple stimulus points. II. Generalization of inhibition. *J. exp. Psychol.*, 1963, **65**, 176–181.)

this likelihood by making comparison stimuli less available.

The last of the conditions for generalization testing listed previously is usually regarded as a more direct test of Lashley's view because comparison stimuli (overt) are eliminated almost entirely during testing. Although gradients have been obtained under this condition using either rate of extinction or frequency of response to a single test stimulus, the results have been far from uniform (Grice and Saltz, 1950; Kling, 1952; Grant and Schiller, 1953; Wickens, Schroder, and Snide, 1954; Margolius, 1955; Kalish and Haber, 1963; Tosti and Ellis, 1964; Hiss and Thomas, 1963). Using the human GSR and visual stimuli (a rectangle of light of varying size), Grant and Schiller (1953) obtained an

orderly generalization gradient from first trial extinction data which disappeared in the subsequent analysis of five trial averages. Wickens, Schroder, and Snide (1954) repeated the same procedure with auditory stimuli and found that, contrary to Grant and Schiller (1953), the gradient did not emerge until after several extinction trials. Tosti and Ellis (1964) also found a generalization gradient for a voluntary response in humans to size of rectangle.

Hull (1950) attributed the failure to obtain a gradient on the first trial to the presence of stimuli which had acquired habit loading during conditioning. He assumed that the gradient was systematically flatter on the first trial because these alleged secondary stimuli increased resistance to extinction, thus preventing the gradient from "emerging." Because responses to the secondary stimuli extinguish at a much faster rate, the gradient should occur somewhere after the initial extinction trials. To test this assumption, Wickens, Schroder, and Snide (1954) presented a click with the CS (tone) during the conditioning trials. The gradient obtained under these conditions was compared with one in which no such extraneous stimulus was present. The gradients in both instances were similar and did not support Hull's analysis. The most frequent result in generalization testing indicates that the gradient is relatively flat during the early trials becoming progressively steeper with continued generalization testing (Littman, 1949; Kalish and Haber, 1963; Friedman and Guttman, 1965).

Because none of the experiments with single stimulus values described previously utilized a comparison group, Kalish and Haber (1963) designed a study to compare generalization gradients obtained from tests to a single stimulus with the gradient following tests to all the selected test values. The method used to train and test the pigeons followed that of Guttman and Kalish (1956). Instead of being exposed to the entire range of stimulus values, however, separate groups of Ss were extinguished to one test stimulus. The resulting gradient, properly adjusted for number of responses, was compared to an equivalent gradient (Guttman and Kalish, 1956) generated from responses to all the selected peripheral stimuli. A comparison of the two gradients in Figure 10-4 indicates that the multiple stimulus gradient is concave, the result of an increase in response differences between the conditioned stimulus and the test values. The single stimulus gradient is linear by comparison. These findings suggest that the increase in discrimination for the multiple stimulus gradient probably resulted from S's continued sampling over the stimulus dimension. The evidence from the single stimulus generalization studies indicates that gener-

alization gradients can be obtained even when the conditions for comparison are markedly reduced. But the differences between the single and multiple gradient emphasize the importance of the context in which the stimulus appears in determining the form of the gradient. Marsh (1967) has demonstrated a similar phenomenon (Figure 10-5, p. 234). Support for this view is contained in a study conducted by Ganz (1963). Monkeys were first trained to press a key differentially to two monochromatic stimuli 150 mμ apart in wavelength. One stimulus (S+) was reinforced on a VI fifteen-second schedule, whereas the other (S−) was presented with a fifteen-second delay of reinforcement. Prior to tests for generalization the animals were exposed to repeated presentations of stimuli from the spectral wavelength continuum and it was found that simple exposure to stimuli 20 mμ above and below S^Δ increased the response rate to SD during generalization testing. This increase in the differences between the training stimulus and the exposure stimuli is similar to the increase in the differences between the training stimulus and the test stimulus for the multiple stimulus gradient in the Kalish and Haber (1963) study.

Ganz (1963) concludes that the form of the generalization gradient is determined, in large part, by the same successive contrast effects proposed by Helson (1947, 1959) in his adaptation-level theory. In essence, the response to any stimulus is determined by the position of the stimulus within a series after a reference level has been established. This reference level, which is the adaptation level (AL) derived from the weighted log mean of all stimuli in the test series as well as S's past experience with the stimulus dimension, determines (and predicts) S's response to the test stimuli because all the test stimuli are presumably judged with respect to AL. The reference level is also subject to fluctuations depending upon the nature of the experience with the stimulus dimension. If the subject is exposed to stimuli on the low end of the dimension prior to testing over the entire range, the AL will be determined by this experience and will, in turn, alter the judgment of the entire stimulus dimension (Helson, 1959, pp. 592–595). Blue and Hegge (1965) conducted an experiment (described in detail in the section on generalization and transposition) which lends a great deal of credibility to the idea that the AL shifts to accommodate the scale. The form of a generalization gradient for rats on a loudness dimension was preserved when the entire dimension was shifted 45 db. The stimulus (55 db.) which was formerly the modal stimulus on the first dimension elicited the fewest number of responses on the altered scale, while the stimulus 45 db. removed became the new modal stimulus. All the intervening stimuli maintained the relationship they had on the unaltered scale. Grice and Hunter (1964) have proposed a similar explanation for the effects of stimulus intensity on the generalization gradient.

Stimulus-Intensity Generalization

The role of stimulus contrast has also been recently emphasized in studies dealing with the phenomenon of stimulus-intensity dynamism, which often occurs when a dimension is scaled in terms of magnitude of physical energy (brightness, loudness, and so on) and S is trained to one of the relatively weaker stimuli. Under these conditions the resultant gradient is steeper on the side of the training stimulus toward decreasing magnitude and relatively flatter in the other direction (Hovland, 1937b; Hull, 1949; Grice and Saltz, 1950; Brush, Bush, Jenkins, John, and Whiting, 1952; Fink and Patton, 1953; Miller and Green, 1954; Spiker, 1956b; Razran, 1949).

Hull (1949) brought stimulus-intensity dynamism into his behavior system by creating a stimulus-intensity component (V) of reaction potential which enters into multiplicative relations with habit strength and manifests itself in greater responding or reduced latency to the more intense stimuli. Hull's interpretation of stimulus-intensity effects was based primarily on three studies reported by him (1947, 1949, 1952) using rats in a black-white discrimination procedure. The studies conducted by Spence, Hays, and Antoinetti all demonstrated that discrimination training with a white card as the positive stimulus resulted in fewer errors and lower response latency than with a black stimulus positive.

Both Perkins (1953) and Logan (1954) independently questioned the necessity for a separate dynamism construct to explain increased responding with increases in stimulus intensity. Instead, they devised an explanation of intensity effects from the principles of discrimination learning. Assumptions were made that in experiments employing a brightness dimension, for example, a gradient of excitation is generated at the intensity value used as the CS and a gradient of inhibition at the background intensity present during the intertrial intervals. Because the background illumination is on the same dimension as the CS, although lower on the scale, the gradient of inhibition generated to this value during periods of nonreinforcement, when the CS is not present, will have its maximum somewhere below the CS. Accordingly, the net excitatory strength (excitation minus inhibition) will be lower for stimulus values below the CS and higher for values above the CS. Obviously this explanation regards the asymmetrical generalization gradient in terms of a response decrement to stimulus values of decreasing magnitude below the CS rather than increases in response to values above the CS explicit in Hull's dynamism formulation. This reinterpretation of intensity effects proposed by Perkins and Logan also introduced the notion that responding may be largely determined by contextual stimulus conditions, an idea which we have already seen introduced to account for generalization itself (generalization training and testing, p. 222).

In order to test this proposed explanation of intensity effects, Bragiel and Perkins (1954) replicated the study by Hays (Hull, 1947). Although the background intensity was not indicated in Hays' study, Bragiel and Perkins assumed it must have been black if increased responsiveness to the white card reported in the study is to be interpreted in terms of a gradient of inhibition to the black stimulus. By varying the background intensity under four conditions (W-W, white stimulus-white background; W-B, white stimulus-black background; B-B, black stimulus-black background; B-W, black stimulus-white background) in a Lashley jump discrimination task, Bragiel and Perkins (1954) demonstrated a decrease in jump latency for both of the groups with contrasting stimulus conditions relative to the other groups. Johnsgard (1957) found substantially similar results with variations in reflectance against a background of medium intensity. Rats running to a goal box containing the stimulus cards showed an increase in running speed when the luminance of the stimulus card differed from the background luminance in either direction. These results are predictable because the gradient of inhibition generated at the medium intensity value used as the background stimulus would reduce the net excitatory strength only in the region of medium intensity without affecting the more remote stimuli in either direction.

Results contrary to the customary intensity effects for stimuli of increasing magnitude are also deducible from the Perkins-Logan explanation. Thus, for example, in experiments where the background stimulus is more intense than the reinforced stimulus, inhibition generalizes to the more intense stimulus values producing a decrement in response to these stimuli. In the case of generalization, the gradient would be steeper in the direction

of increasing magnitude. In his review of the literature Gray reports that such results have been obtained in both discrimination and generalization studies and concludes that the following conditions must be satisfied to obtain stimulus intensity effects in general (1965, p. 193):

1. Stimulus intensity must be redefined as the degree of contrast in intensity between positive and negative stimuli.
2. Behavior should be measured during reinforced responding rather than during extinction.
3. Discrimination training is necessary for the appearance of intensity effects and must be explicitly introduced where it is not already a part of the experimental procedure (classical conditioning with alternate presence and absence of the CS as opposed to operant conditioning).

Conditions (1) and (3), which may be deduced from the Perkins-Logan explanation of the intensity effect, suggest that the effect is a special case of generalization and discrimination rather than a phenomenon in its own right (Gray, 1965, p. 193).

In citing (2) as a condition for stimulus intensity effects, Gray has responded to a number of experiments which have failed to demonstrate intensity effects with all the other conditions satisfied. Exceptions to intensity generalization have been found by Blough (1959) and Olson and King (1962) among others. They observed relatively flat functions on a brightness dimension for pigeons with a tendency toward higher rates of responding at lower luminosities. These studies showed gradients of generalization during extinction and after generalization training. Farmer, Schoenfeld, and Harris (1966), who succeeded in obtaining a generalization gradient from latency measures for the white rat along a brightness dimension, also failed to observe the occurrence of intensity effects.

Two experiments recently conducted by Grice and Hunter (1964) and Grice, Masters, and Kohfeld (1966) have demonstrated certain limitations in the Perkins-Logan explanation of intensity effects. The first of these experiments (Grice and Hunter, 1964) showed that the intensity effect can be increased if a "frame of reference" is established during conditioning. They found that the difference in per cent CR of a conditioned eyelid response for trials 41—100 was greater for a group of *S*s conditioned to random presentations of two loudness levels (50 and 100 db.) than for two groups of *S*s each conditioned separately to only one level (50 or 100 db.) prior to these trials. An additional experiment using reaction time showed similar results. According to Grice and Hunter, these experiments provide a source of embarrassment to Perkins and Logan because of the *increase* in response which occurs to the 100-db. tone solely as a result of *S*'s exposure to both the 50- and 100-db. tone during conditioning and in spite of the ensuing reduction in number of reinforced presentations to the 100-db. tone. The explanation proposed by Perkins and Logan predicts a decrease in absolute responding to the more intense stimulus with the addition of a weaker stimulus.

In a more direct test of the Perkins-Logan proposal, Grice, Masters, and Kohfeld (1966) designed an eyelid conditioning experiment in which the CS consisted of a change in stimulus intensity from one of three conditions (stimulus-off, 50 db., and 100 db.) to one of the remaining two stimulus values. (In a second experiment 70 db. was substituted for 50 db.) Thus, each of the three intensity values served as the intertrial background stimuli one third of the time during the experiment. Under these conditions, with no consistent background intensity as a point of origin for the gradient of inhibition, intensity effects should not occur. The experimental procedures yielded intensity effects despite the absence of an inhibitory gradient, and analysis of the results also revealed that these intensity effects depended upon the *amount of stimulus change* rather than its direction.

Because the explanation of the intensity

effects obtained in both experiments appears to demand a variable in the form of stimulus contrast, Grice and Hunter (1964) utilized Helson's (1959) adaptation level (AL) to account for the results. Their interpretation assumes that the dynamogenic potency of a stimulus, that is, its ability to evoke greater responding, depends upon the extent of its departure from the AL established during training. In the case of single stimulus training, AL should be somewhere near the stimulus value used as the CS (50 or 100 db.). Grice and Hunter say:

This would lead to the prediction of minimal intensity effects since, irrespective of absolute intensity, departure from AL would be small. . . . In the two stimulus situation . . . the AL might be expected to lie between two values. With the weak stimulus below AL and the strong above, an exaggerated intensity effect would be expected. [1964, p. 252.]

Grice and Hunter's (1964) interpretations of intensity effects in terms of stimulus contrast was substantiated as a result of a study by Murray and Kohfeld (1965) in which intensity dynamism was predicted from adaptation-level theory but not Hullian theory. Human *S*s were given an initial series of "adaptation trials" to a 1,000-cycle tone of either 100 db., 40 db., or silence during which no responses were elicited. In the test trials following adaptation, each *S* in the three adaptation groups was required to press a key in response to random presentations of the 1,000-cycle tone at 40-, 50-, 80-, and 100-db. levels. Three gradients of reaction time were obtained from the test trials. Reaction time was fastest at all levels of signal intensity for the group adapted to 40 db., slowest for the group adapted to 100 db., and intermediate for *S*s adapted to silence. These results conformed to the prediction made by the authors that the expected reaction time would be fastest for the 40-db. group because the test signals were above AL

(40 db.), slowest for the 100-db. group with test signals below AL (100 db.), and intermediate for the silence group whose AL was assumed to be near the geometric mean of the test trial intensities (70 db.). It should be recognized that these results were predicted without any appeal to discrimination training involving either generalization gradients of excitation or inhibition.

The successful use of stimulus contrast and adaptation level to account for the results of these experiments strongly increases the possibility that S's response in both the generalization and stimulus-intensity studies is controlled, at least in part, by stimulus differences.

Generalization and Variations in the Stimulus Dimension

A direct test of the hypothesis that the generalization gradient is determined principally by the characteristics of the stimulus dimension was made in the study by Guttman and Kalish (1956) described previously. This hypothesis (inverse hypothesis) assumes that absolute generalization increases (that is, the gradient becomes flatter) as discrimination decreases and that the organism's inability to respond differentially to changes in the stimulus dimension (discriminability) is the basis for stimulus generalization. We have already noted a similar assumption implicit in Hull's (1943) description of the generalization gradient as a decreasing exponential function on a jnd scale, in Schlosberg and Solomon's (1943) proposal that generalization gradients are straight lines on an equal-appearing interval scale, and in the view that generalization represents a failure of association proposed by Lashley and Wade (1946).

To test this hypothesis an independent measure of S's sensitivity to a given stimulus dimension is necessary. For their study,

Guttman and Kalish (1956) selected wavelength of light as a stimulus dimension having a known discriminability function. In it, also, the difference limen ($\Delta\gamma$) is not constant over the spectrum (λ). The discriminability function (Figure 9-1), derived from an experiment with pigeons by Hamilton and Coleman (1933), is similar in form to a function for humans obtained by Geldard (1953) and provides a number of differential predictions concerning the shape of the gradient depending upon the particular region from which the CS values are selected.

Where delta lambda is small, the gradient should be sharp; where delta lambda is large, the gradient should be relatively flat; and if the CS is fixed at a value where delta lambda is either increasing or decreasing, the generalization gradient should show a corresponding asymmetry. [Guttman and Kalish, 1956, p. 79.]

Contrary to expectation, the gradients were uniform and failed to conform to the predictions made from the discriminability function (upper graph, Figure 9-1).

One of the several factors invoked to account for the lack of correspondence between discriminability and generalization was the absence of brightness control over the region of the spectrum used. Blough (1958, 1961) showed, however, that the effect of brightness variation, although substantial in other respects, could not be used to explain the uniformity among the gradients. Subsequent studies by Ganz and Riesen (1962) and Ganz (1926) with primates and Yarczower and Bitterman (1965) with fish were successful in demonstrating that the slope of the generalization gradient does relate to the discriminability function.

An explanation of the inability to find the expected relationship between generalization and discriminability in the Guttman and Kalish (1956) study has recently been provided by Marsh (1967). Using the same methods employed by Guttman and Kalish (1956), Marsh (1967) trained two groups of pigeons to 520 and 590 mμ, respectively. These groups were then divided on the basis of the number of test stimuli (2, 3, or 4) used during generalization testing. Figure 10-5a indicates that the initial difference between the gradients, when two test stimuli, were used, related to the differences in the discriminability function for these stimuli, thus supporting the inverse hypothesis. As the number of test stimuli increased, however, the two gradients became more uniform (Figure 10-5b and c). Marsh also showed that the difference in the slope between the two gradients in Figure 10-5a is approximately 4 to 1, which is roughly equivalent to the differences in the relative size of the jnd found by Hamilton and Coleman (1933) in the regions of 520 and 590 mμ (middle graph, Figure 9-1). When these two gradients are plotted on a jnd abscissa as in Figure 10-6a, the slope differences disappear as expected, whereas the differences between gradients with 3 and 4 test stimuli (Figure 10-6b and c) become more pronounced. These findings strongly suggest that the relationship between generalization and discriminability was evidently obscured by the use of a larger number of test stimuli in the Guttman and Kalish (1956) study.

The results of Marsh's (1967) experiment are strikingly similar to those from studies in which the generalization gradient is obtained by extinguishing Ss to only one test stimulus during the generalization test series (p. 229). The gradients obtained under these conditions are generally flatter when compared to gradients in which Ss are permitted to sample a larger number of stimuli (Kalish and Haber, 1963, Figure 10-4). How does the addition of test stimuli operate to alter the gradient and produce changes in the discriminability-generalization relationship? Ganz (1962) has proposed an explanation similar to that involved in the discrimination model devised by Spence (1937) using the algebraic summation of generalized excitation and inhibition. The generalization test series during extinction produces a gradient of inhibition along the jnd scale which acts to cancel the effect of generalized excitation. When stimuli are equally spaced along the wavelength continuum, as they most generally are in generalization studies, the net effect is to make all gradients appear uniform despite the difference in jnd steps at different regions on the continuum.

Although this explanation appears adequate on rational grounds, the results of

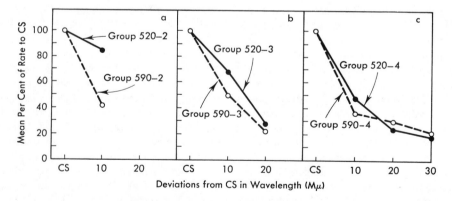

Figure 10-5a, b, c. Relative generalization gradients in the 520-mμ and 590-mμ groups as a function of the number of test stimuli and distance in wavelength. (Reprinted with permission from Marsh, G. D. Inverse relationship between discriminability and stimulus generalization as a function of number of test stimuli. *J. comp. physiol. Psychol.* 1967, **64**, 284–289.)

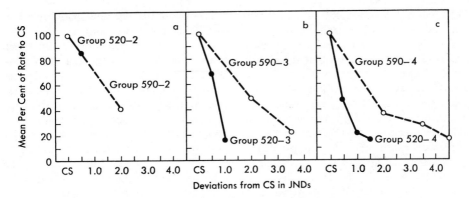

Figure 10-6a, b, c. Relative generalization gradients in the 520-mμ and 590-mμ groups as a function of the number of test stimuli and distance in jnd; jnd abscissa derived from Hamilton and Coleman, 1933. (Reprinted with permission from Marsh, G. D. Inverse relationship between discriminability and stimulus generalization as a function of number of test stimuli. *J. comp. physiol. Psychol.* 1967, **64**, 284–289.)

several experiments do not support it. In the first place, Ganz's hypothesis presupposes that the gradient of inhibition is the "mirror image" of the gradient of excitation. The experimental evidence indicates, however, that the mirror-image hypothesis is an oversimplification (Hanson, 1959; Honig, Thomas, and Guttman, 1959; Kalish and Haber, 1963). When pigeons are trained to a CS, extinguished to one stimulus on the continuum, and tested over a range of values, the resulting generalization gradient reveals that (1) only stimuli nearest the CS have any inhibitory effect, and (2) the greatest inhibitory effect is on the CS (Figure 10-8, 10-9: pp. 243–244). It is also difficult to explain why Ganz (1962) obtained support for the inverse hypothesis with four test stimuli whereas Marsh (1967) did not.

Marsh's (1967) experiment, as well as those described in the section on the conditions of generalization testing and training (p. 222), shows that there are serious methodological and semantic problems involved in the consideration of generalization and discrimination as separate phenomena. If the simple addition of stimuli beyond the CS and one other test stimulus during the test series is all that distinguishes discrimination from generalization, then the focus on the discontinuity of the two phenomena is clearly in error and a desirable parsimony can be achieved by deciding that both involve the same fundamental processes. Such a decision at this point, however, would be premature. As we shall see (Chapter 11), Marsh's data as well as the single-stimulus studies (Kalish and Haber, 1963) may be explained in terms of generalization of inhibition.

Honig and Shaw (1962) have speculated that "although the slope of the gradient may indicate relative sensory distances on both sides of a training stimulus, the gradient as such is by no means adequate for scaling, since the relationship between response rate and sensory distance is not known" (1962, p. 2). In an experiment designed to obtain a more substantial measure of sensory distances in the pigeon, Honig and Shaw (1962) employed the method of bisection of stimulus intervals in a procedure involving explicit discrimination training. *S*s were required to peck at a left key on a variable interval schedule whenever 490 and 590 mμ were displayed and at the right key for 530 and 630 mμ. After a training period the test stimuli consisting of 10-mμ intervals between the discriminative stimuli (for example, 490, 500,

510, and 520 between 490 and 530 mμ) were introduced while training was continued. Because the discriminability function (Figure 9-1) indicates that the size of the jnd increases between 490 and 530 mμ and decreases between 590 and 530 mμ and "the bisection of a sensory interval divides it into parts containing equal numbers of jnds, the bisection of 490–530 mμ should be displaced toward 490 from the physically intermediate point of 510 mμ. Similarly, the bisection point should be displaced above 560 mμ for the 530–590 interval, and below 610 mμ for the 590–630 interval" (Honig and Shaw, 1962, p. 4). Using a procedure devised by Luce and Edwards (1957) for deriving subjective scales, Honig and Shaw (1962) estimated the predicted bisection points for the pigeon from the discriminability function in Figure 9-1 (Hamilton and Coleman, 1933) and compared these with the obtained bisection points derived by dividing the sum of the percentage of responses to the discriminative stimuli comprising the interval in half. At 490–630 mμ, where the jnd differences and the anticipated displacement is small, the predicted value is 508 mμ. In all three replications the comparable obtained displacement was in the opposite direction (510, 514, 521 mμ). For the 530–590 mμ interval the obtained bisections were 561, 552, and 569 mμ, and the expected displacement was 758 mμ. The expected bisection of 602 mμ was obtained in all three instances for the 590–630-mμ interval. Although the predicted results were not obtained except in one instance, the procedure introduced by Honig and Shaw (1962) is noteworthy because it provides a more direct method to test the discriminability-generalization hypothesis.

Honig (1965) is also pursuing the possibility that gradients of stimulus differences may yield further answers to questions concerning the psychophysical behavior of animals because such derived gradients make it possible to compare different stimulus dimensions.

The absence of the anticipated relationship between generalization and discriminability for the pigeon raised questions concerning the existence of a similar relationship in human behavior. In an attempt to provide an answer to this question, Kalish (1958) devised a method for obtaining generalization gradients with human Ss based on a modification of the psychophysical procedures involved in the method of single stimuli, a variant of the constant methods (Guilford, 1936, p. 205). The principal difference between this procedure and that employed with animal Ss was that the human Ss were instructed to identify a color (standard) from among a number of colors (variable) presented to them in succession after the standard was displayed for a minute prior to the beginning of the series. It was assumed that the initial period of familiarization with the standard is analogous to conditioning before generalization testing with animals (Guttman and Kalish, 1956). The standard stimulus for the group of Ss in one experiment was 530 mμ and for the second experiment with the same group, 560 mμ. The second group received 580 and 600 mμ as the standard stimuli. The four generalization gradients formed around each standard stimulus in the lower group of Figure 9-1 were obtained by summing the number of instances each variable stimulus was incorrectly identified as the standard. Both the appearance of the gradients and the statistical analysis indicate that the shape and breadth of the gradients correspond remarkably well to expectations from the discriminability function. Where stimulus changes ($\Delta\gamma$) are relatively small (580 mμ), the gradient is narrow, suggesting heightened discriminability. At 530 mμ the gradient is broader although the asymmetry is not in the expected direction. In those cases where large numbers of stimulus changes ($\Delta\gamma$) occur on one side of the standard as opposed to the other, the gradients are asymmetrical in the expected direction (550 and 560 mμ).

Similar results were obtained by Thomas and Mitchell (1962) in an attempt to determine whether the instructions given *S*s (Kalish, 1958) were instrumental in producing the variations in the shape of the gradients. Although the effect of instructions was found to be negligible, *S*s appeared to exhibit a "regression" in response to subjectively primary colors red, yellow, green, and blue during the course of generalization testing. Thomas and De Capito (1966) explored the "regression" hypothesis by requiring *S* to label the standard (490 mμ) prior to generalization testing. *S*s who labeled the standard *green* responded more to longer wavelengths (greener) and less to shorter wavelengths (bluer) than those *S*s labeling the standard *blue*. Most of these experiments suggest that certain generalization tasks for human *S*s, quite probably those requiring voluntary judgmental processes, are accomplished, at least in part, through verbal mediation (Caronite, Levis, and Thomas, 1963).

The method of single stimuli was subsequently used to test Phillip's (1952) conclusions that the shape of the gradient is also a function of the location of the original or standard stimulus within the generalization test series. Thomas (1961) and Thomas and Jones (1962) confirmed these results by an experiment in which human *S*s trained to a spectral wavelength of 525 mμ were required to select the standard from among randomly presented series of test stimuli. Although the standard occupied a differential ordinal position in each of the test series (ranging from the highest to the lowest value), the modal number of "same" responses occurred away from the standard and toward the center of the series. A similar "centering tendency" behavior was observed by Ganz (1963), with animals; Gewirtz, Jones, and Waerneryd (1956) and Grice and Hunter (1964), with humans; and more recently, by Helson and Avant (1967) in a replication of Thomas and Jones' study using white squares as stimuli. The shift in the perceived value of the original stimulus toward the center of the distribution is a logical extension of Helson's adaptation-level theory as Thomas (1961) points out, because the theory assumes that the stimulus context in which the standard occurs is used as a frame of reference to judge the standard.

Another striking example of the "centering effect" is found in an experiment by Fishbein, Shackney, and Sinclair (1965) in their attempt to show that stimulus generalization is the basis for the serial position effect in verbal learning. *S*s were required to learn a paired-associates task in which the stimulus terms were six circles of varying size each associated with a particular letter of the alphabet. Stimulus presentations were randomized and the list learned until all twelve pairs were correctly anticipated. An analysis of the mean number of errors to each stimulus revealed a distribution characteristic of the serial position effect found in serial learning. A gradient of errors was formed, the least number of errors occurring to the smallest and largest stimuli and the largest number to the central stimulus. To explain these results in terms of backward and forward associations, it would be necessary to assume that some ordinal dimension analogous to the position of items in serial learning is established by *S* during learning. Conceivably, this could be accomplished by a procedure in which *S*s "dimensionalize" the stimuli by establishing reference stimuli on both ends of the continuum (anchoring effects). Once the reference stimuli are established the effects are similar to those found in serial learning.

Hiss and Thomas (1963) and Thomas and Hiss (1963) employed the method of single stimuli to investigate Mednick and Freedman's (1960) hypothesis that the generalization decrement is related to the number of stimulus units separating the test stimulus from the standard and is independent of the relative position of the stimulus within the series. The first part of the hypothesis was substantiated, because the generalization decrement (slope of the gradient) appeared to increase with increases in the number of intervening stimuli, but generalization was also shown to be a joint function of the physical size of the stimulus as well as the number of intervening stimuli. As the size of the stimulus unit decreased (that is, as the physical difference between stimuli decreased), the slope of the generalization decreased—a finding that is consonant with the idea that discriminability ultimately determines the generalization decrement. Further work on this subject has led to the conclusion that both the number and ordinal position of stimulus units determine the shape of the generalization gradient (Thomas and Bistey, 1964; Marsh, 1965).

The phenomenon of octave generalization provides an interesting exception to the rule that the absolute number of responses on the generalization gradient varies inversely with the magnitude of the stimulus difference. In at least two instances, Humphreys (1939), with human Ss, and Blackwell and Schlosberg (1943), with rats, the response of a tone one octave removed from the CS showed an abrupt rise instead of the continuing decrement characteristic of the generalization gradient. In effect, the generalization test yielded a psychophysical function which disclosed that two stimuli are "subjectively similar" independent of their location on the physical scale.

The difference between human and animal Ss is quite clearly indicated in two studies which failed to confirm the units hypothesis. In a study by Friedman (1963) generalization gradients for a spectral wavelength dimension contradicted the units hypothesis and showed that the pigeon's response is primarily determined by the distance in wavelength between the training and testing stimuli rather than the number of intervening stimuli. The same results were obtained by Muntz (1965) for the octopus when these animals were trained to attack a white 2.25-in. square and tested with 0.75-, 1.5-, 2.25-, 3.25-, and 4.75-in. squares. Muntz concluded that the units hypothesis did not apply and that "stimulus generalization is a good measure of discriminability of stimuli for these animals" (1965, p. 144). In view of the differences in results between animal and human Ss, it may be profitable to explore the possibility that the human generalization gradient obtained from tasks requiring nonvoluntary responses, and thus, no verbal mediation, is similar to the generalization gradients obtained from animal Ss.

In addition to their value as examples of the generalization phenomenon, the studies cited previously, as well as those conducted by Brown, Bilodeau, and Baron (1951); Brown, Clarke, and Stein (1958); and Bass (1958) have served to bring the question of generalization and discrimination into much sharper relief by suggesting the presence of a discrimination component in generalization, by showing that the generalization gradient is markedly influenced by those factors affecting discriminability, and by emphasizing the similarities in method between psychophysical procedures and the operations employed to obtain gradients.

Among these factors the similarity in method appears to be interesting very largely because of the traditional link between psychometric functions and the idea of comparative judgments. The use of the method of single stimuli (Guilford, 1936, p. 166; Kalish, 1958), which is a special case of the constant methods, has stressed this relationship between psychometric functions and generalization gradients. In the method of single stimuli, for example, Ss are customarily given an initial practice period with the standard to establish an "absolute impression of its weight" (Guilford, 1936, p. 205). The distribution of judgments during the testing period shows a somewhat lower precision than that obtained by the usual constant methods, but a distribution tends to form around the standard regardless of whether it is inserted during the test series or not. The customary responses obtained from *S*s—proportions of heavier or lighter, greater or less judgments—form ogives which are known as psychometric functions. Stevens asserts that the "generalization gradients of the animal trainers is the psychometric function of the weight lifters," and maintains further that the gradient of generalization is, in essence, a "poikilitic" function describing the amount of scatter or variation which results when an observer is asked to sort stimuli into one kind or another, for example, greater or less (1965, p. 25). For Stevens, the generalization procedure is a test of the organism's ability to detect relative differences for a given stimulus dimension.

Shephard (1965) has entertained the possibility that scales of "psychological space" may be derived from an analysis of generalization gradients which reduces them to a uniform shape. The ordinates of generalization gradients from the same stimulus continuum (Guttman and Kalish, 1956) are given unit height by computing the ratio of the number of responses for a test stimulus to the number of responses for the training stimulus. Shephard argues that if a "preferred psychological scale" emerges from such a transformation of the physical scale the result may be a significant "underlying psychological space" (1965, p. 96). It is, of course, interesting to note that psychophysicists have dealt with generalizationlike phenomena in their search for psychological scales, but the necessity for a concept of generalization did not emerge until Pavlov (1927) conducted psychophysical experiments with animals and interpreted the results in terms of neurophysiological irradiation processes.

Summation of Generalization

Hull (1939) made several specific predictions concerning the effect of overlapping gradients of generalization resulting from training to two stimulus values on the same dimension consistent with his view of generalization as gradients of associative strength. According to Hull, overlapping gradients will summate exponentially to produce gradients of greater response strength than would ordinarily occur from training to each stimulus value separately.

Evidence of summation has been observed in certain experiments, but indications of the summated generalization gradients proposed by Hull (1939, 1943) have not been found. Bilodeau, Brown, and Meryman (1956) reported summation in an experiment with human *S*s using the spatial generalization technique. However, the phenomenon was confined to the region between the two training stimuli. A tendency toward summation in the central region was also found in a study with pigeons (Kalish and Guttman, 1956), but the authors suggest that these cannot be regarded as instances of Hullian summation because the total gradient remained unaffected. An additional study (Kalish and Guttman, 1959) was designed specifically to test the Hullian hypothesis by training animals to three stimulus values close together on the spectral wavelength dimension (10 mμ apart) on the grounds that the almost total overlap of the three gradients would provide an unequivocal test of the hypothesis. In this instance there was no evidence of summation and the results could be explained in terms of three individual gradients erected at the three different training values.

Two experiments with human *S*s (Carterette, 1961; La Berge and Martin, 1964) and one with pigeons (Hoffman, Selekman, and Fleshler, 1966) report summation effects, but these were also confined largely to the central region between the two training stimuli. The bulk of the evidence seems to suggest that some form of summation does occur, but not in the manner specified by Hull (1939).

Generalization, Discrimination, and Transposition

Generalization, discrimination, and transposition are linked through two sources: the experimental procedures used to define them and the attempts which have been made to reduce both discrimination and transposition to the interaction of generalization processes.

Distinctions among the three phenomena appear to represent subtle differences in experimental procedure for the most part. Whether behavior is designated generalization, discrimination, or transposition depends, very largely, on the particular combinations of training and testing procedures chosen by E. If S is reinforced for responding to one or several stimulus values on a given dimension and tested (usually under conditions of nonreinforcement) with other values on the same dimension either singly (successive presentation of individual stimuli) or in pairs (simultaneous presentation of two or more stimuli), the resultant behavior is called generalization. Continuous differential training (one stimulus reinforced, the other nonreinforced) to two or more stimuli to a predetermined criterion of correct and incorrect responses, results in discrimination. (It should be recalled that in the original procedure for generating gradients which Pavlov called the "method of contrasts," Ss continued to receive reinforcement to the training stimulus during generalization testing.) Transposition involves differential training to two or three stimuli (usually one positive stimulus flanked by two negative stimuli—the intermediate size problem) on the same dimension either successively or simultaneously, and testing to two or three stimulus values either under conditions of reinforcement or nonreinforcement.

The idea that generalization gradients of excitation and inhibition are fundamental to discrimination learning was originally developed by Spence (1936) and Hull (1939,

1943) and later extended to transposition behavior by Spence (1937, 1941, 1942). Both theories incorporate the same basic assumptions, although as we shall see later Spence's is more elaborate and consistent with the experimental results.

The assumptions involved in Hull's discrimination learning theory involving generalization are as follows:

1. Generalization of excitation and inhibition (extinction) are established as a result of reinforcement and nonreinforcement during discrimination learning.
2. The gradient of inhibition (extinction) is lower in magnitude than that of excitation.
3. Both gradients summate algebraically.
4. The resultant response to any stimulus on the dimension is determined by the resultant gradient which combines the net effects of excitatory and inhibitory strength. [Hull, 1943.]

The question which inevitably arises from the Spence-Hull theory of discrimination learning concerns the validity of the presumed relationship between generalization and discrimination. Whether discrimination learning is fundamentally determined by the joint interaction of gradients of excitation and inhibition depends in part upon two criteria: (1) the extent to which gradients of excitation and inhibition conform to either Hull or Spence's expectation after discrimination learning has occurred (the effect of discrimination on generalization), and (2) the extent to which the course of discrimination learning can be predicted from systematic variations in the gradients of excitation and inhibition.

The Effect of Discrimination on Generalization

One of the most important aspects of Spence (1936) and Hull's (1952) discrimination theory concerns the characteristics of the postdiscrimination gradient. Any change in the shape of the hypothetical gradients of inhibition and/or excitation will materially alter the kind of prediction which can be made from the theory. Because virtually no information on this subject existed prior to Spence's work, the gradients used to predict both discrimination and transposition were largely hypothetical. Several later attempts to obtain postdiscrimination gradients (Antoinetti in Hull, 1952; Passey and Herman, 1955) provided only limited information. Antoinetti (Hull, 1952) obtained zero slope for the generalization gradient after training rats in a black-white discrimination, and Passey and Herman (1955) found the same results with a similar apparatus and procedure. Lawrence (1955) also pointed out that considerable modification must be made in the assumption underlying the generalization model as formulated by Spence to account for the results of a transfer of discrimination study with rats in which the performance of a gradual transition group was superior to that of a difficult discrimination group.

Hanson, who was the first to apply the operant methods used by Guttman and Kalish (1956) to study the effects of discrimination on generalization, summarized the expected changes in the gradient following discrimination training according to Spence (1936, 1937, 1942). A generalization gradient obtained after discrimination training with two stimuli on the same dimension should show the following characteristics:

a. The postdiscrimination gradient will be steeper than a (comparable) generalization gradient in the region of $S-$.

b. If complete discrimination is developed, the value of the postdiscrimination gradient will be zero at $S-$.

c. The mode of the postdiscrimination gradient will be displaced away from $S-$ in relation to the mode of the (control) generalization gradient.

d. The magnitude of this displacement will increase as the $S+$, $S-$ difference is reduced.

e. The maximum heights of the post-

discrimination gradients will be reduced as the $S+$, $S-$ difference is reduced.

f. The postdiscrimination gradient will be a fractional part of the (control) generalization gradient and will nowhere exceed it. [Hanson, 1959, pp. 321–322.]

Hanson trained pigeons in a successive discrimination task with 550 mμ positive $(S+)$ and, depending upon the group, either 555, 560, 565, or 590 mμ negative $(S-)$. An analysis of the postdiscrimination gradients in Figure 10-7 revealed that, although many of the qualitative elements of Spence's expectations were supported, the predictions contained in (e) and (f) were not. It is apparent from the gradients in Figure 10-7 that although they display the anticipated displacement away from the negative stimulus, the frequency of response to the new modal stimulus is greatly increased ("peak shift," Guttman, 1963) instead of being reduced as Spence had anticipated.

Although the deductions from Spence's theory of discrimination and transposition are somewhat independent of the exact shape of the gradients of excitation and inhibition, their limits appear to be fixed by the nature of the predictions. Bilateral, symmetrical gradients of inhibition and excitation are necessary in order to be consistent with the experimental findings, but most of the studies have failed to yield gradients which even approximate the required form. According to Hanson's (1959) analysis, for example, a number of improbable assumptions must be made to reconcile both the uniformity and increased height of the postdiscrimination gradients with excitation-inhibition theory. The underlying gradients of excitation for the 555 mμ $(550+, 555-)$ and 590 mμ $(550+, 590-)$ gradients in Figure 10-7, for example, would have to be approximately double the area of the control gradient $(550+)$ to account for the empirical gradients by algebraic summation of excitatory and inhibitory strengths. *Furthermore, and what is perhaps more important, the hypothetical gradients of inhibition resulting from this*

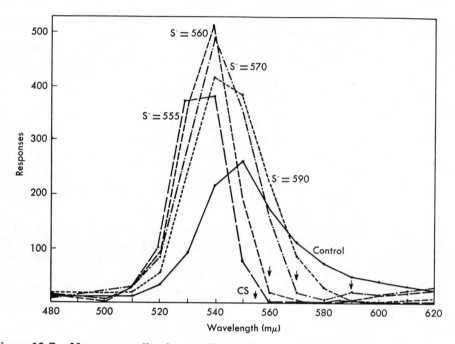

Figure 10-7.   Mean generalization gradients of a control group and four discrimination groups, identified by the respective values of the negative stimulus (S⁻). Arrows indicate the positions of the negative stimuli. (Reprinted with permission from Hanson, H. M. Effects of discrimination training on stimulus generalization. *J. exp. Psychol.*, 1959, **58**, 321–334.)

analysis would be asymmetrical with maximum inhibitory strength occurring at the CS value rather than the negative stimuli.

Evidence to support Hanson's (1959) findings is also contained in studies by Honig, Thomas, and Guttman (1959) and Kalish and Haber (1963). In each of these studies generalization gradients were obtained after several groups of pigeons were trained to a CS of 550 mμ and extinguished in the presence of one stimulus value on the spectral wavelength continuum. In the case of Honig, Thomas, and Guttman (1959) one group was extinguished at 570 mμ, whereas in the experiment conducted by Kalish and Haber (1963; Figure 10-8) six groups were extinguished at 540, 530, 520, 510, and 490 mμ, respectively. In both studies, the hypothetical gradients of inhibition necessary to explain the post-extinction excitation gradients did not have

their peaks at the nonreinforced stimulus used during training. Instead, the modal values for the hypothetical gradients of inhibition were displaced toward the training stimulus (S+), with maximum inhibitory strength occurring to this value. These results are shown in Figure 10-9. The bidirectional gradients in the lower halves of the panels in Figure 10-9 were derived by using the 550-mμ gradient from the Guttman-Kalish study (Figure 9-1, p. 212) as a model for the predicted gradient. Both the height and slope of the inhibition gradient were assumed to be equivalent to the height and slope of the 550-mμ excitation gradient at the corresponding extinction point. The predicted gradients in the upper halves of Figure 10-9 were obtained by calculating the difference between the Guttman-Kalish 550-mμ gradient and the expected gradient of inhibition at each stimulus value. The actual gradients obtained after extinction in the upper halves of Figure 10-9 are similar to the Guttman-Kalish gradient for the groups extinguished at 490, 510, and 520 mμ. The gradients obtained from 530, 540, and 550 mμ, on the other hand, are significantly different from the predicted gradients. The unidirectional gradients in the lower halves of Figure 10-9 are gradients of inhibition obtained by calculating the difference between the expected and obtained gradients of excitation in the upper half of the graphs. It is apparent from comparing these gradients of inhibition with the predicted bidirectional gra-

dients that the maximum decrement for 530 and 540 mμ occurs at the training stimulus instead of at the point of extinction. Kalish and Haber (1963) did find, on the other hand, that the heights of the post-extinction gradients were diminished as the difference between the S+ and S− was decreased, precisely as Spence had predicted (Figure 10-8).

Results similar to those just described were also found by Sloane (1964) for stimulus generalization gradients obtained along a light flicker continuum. Because successive discrimination training and generalization testing were given to the

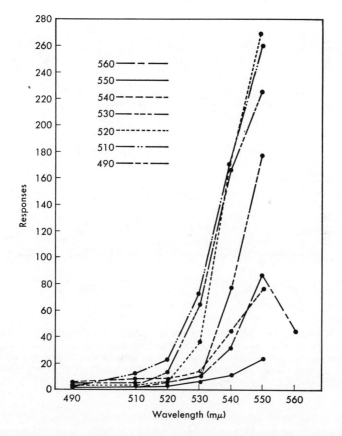

Figure 10-8. Generalization gradients obtained following extinction to one stimulus value after conditioning. Each of the seven groups of Ss was extinguished to one of the stimulus values listed in the body of the graph. (Reprinted with permission from Kalish, H. I., and Haber, A. Generalization: I. Generalization gradients from single and multiple stimulus points. II. Generalization of inhibition. *J. exp. Psychol.*, 1963, **65**, 176–181.)

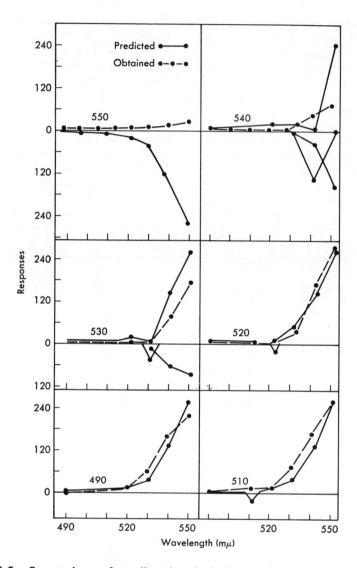

Figure 10-9. Comparison of predicted and obtained gradients of inhibition and excitation. Bidirectional curves in lower half are predicted gradient of inhibition. Unidirectional curves are obtained gradients of inhibition. (Reprinted with permission from Kalish, H. I., and Haber, A. Generalization: I. Generalization gradients from single and multiple stimulus points. II. Generalization of inhibition. *J. exp. Psychol.*, 1963, **65**, 176–181.)

same pigeons in contrast to the use of individual groups in the Kalish and Haber experiment (1963), the results are not directly comparable to the previously described experiment. In the experiment conducted by Sloane, pigeons initially

trained to discriminate between two light flicker values were subsequently given additional S− stimuli. Generalization tests conducted after the introduction of each additional S− value revealed that changes in the generalization gradients were marked by successive flattening on the side of the continuum from which the S— values were introduced without any significant effect on the responding to S+. When the stimulus value closest to S+ was presented as S—, however, the modal response shifted from S+ to the stimulus one step removed. (This phenomenon is the "peak shift" found by Hanson and is reserved for later discussion. See p. 246.) Sloane concluded from these results that the postdiscrimination gradients could not be explained in terms of the algebraic summation of gradients of excitation and extinction.

Honig (1965) has also shown that the gradient for pigeons is steepened substantially by prior discrimination training. One group received successive discrimination training to white and pink lights. The same lights were randomly correlated with reinforcement for a second group. Generalization tests were subsequently conducted after training to a vertical line on a white background and steeper gradients were obtained for the group receiving prior discrimination training.

We have already seen how difficult it is to specify the characteristics of a gradient of inhibition necessary to account for the changes in the postdiscrimination gradient. Terrace (1963b, 1964, 1966a) has added substantially to this difficulty by showing that discrimination learning can occur without errors under certain conditions and that, therefore, the concept of a gradient of inhibition may be superfluous in models of discrimination learning. He has shown that pigeons can be trained to discriminate between two spectral wavelength values (green and red) without errors if responses to S— are kept to an absolute minimum in the early stages of discrimination training. This is accomplished by increasing the discriminability of the non-reinforced stimulus ("fading in"), introducing it for relatively brief periods early in discrimination training and progressively changing both the duration and characteristics of S— during the course of train-

ing. Thus, in the "early progressive" group discrimination training began 30 sec. after conditioning to the red stimulus and S— was progressively changed from a dark key of 5 sec. duration to a fully bright green key of 3 min. duration. Under these conditions no response to S— occurred in contrast to the "late constant" group in which S— was introduced in full strength after a large number of conditioning trials had already occurred to S+. The technique of fading in the S— stimulus to achieve errorless discrimination was also used by Terrace (1966c) to demonstrate that the peak shift (see p. 246) and stimulus control of inhibition (see p. 235) result only when S generates errors during discrimination learning by responding to S—.

A number of studies outside of the area of operant conditioning have also shown that discrimination training can substantially affect the characteristics of the generalization gradient. Reinhold and Perkins (1955), for example, demonstrated that discrimination training along one dimension (black-smooth reinforced; black-rough nonreinforced) for rats in a straight alley maze served to steepen the generalization gradient along a second dimension (black-smooth; white-smooth) when compared with the appropriate controls. The authors attribute these results to the development of a set to discriminate, analogous to the development of learning sets. The generalization gradient along the second dimension containing the novel stimulus became flatter as the difficulty of discrimination along the first dimension increased, or as the difference between S+ and S— was reduced (Perkins, Hershberger, and Weyant, 1959). These results were also reproduced with human Ss who received discrimination training along a loudness (intensity) dimension with a 1,000-hz tone and generalization training on a tonal continuum. The procedure required Ss to judge the tones initially to establish an equal loudness dimension, but both discrimination and generalization testing were conducted with a bar-pressing technique which required a specific rate of response to actuate a reinforcement light. The generalization gradients for groups receiving discrimination training on the intensity dimension were considerably steeper than the gradients for those groups without prior training (Hoving, 1963). In a study of cross-modal generalization, Thompson (1959) found that instrumental shock-avoidance training to light in cats decreased both absolute and relative generalization to a tone dimension.

According to Switalski, Lyons, and Thomas (1966), the characteristic steepening of the generalization gradient has been observed after three types of discrimination training: "intradimensional," in which the same dimension is used for both discrimination training and generalization testing (Hanson, 1959; Thomas, 1962); "interdimensional," in which the nonreinforced (S^Δ) condition consists of either the absence of a positive stimulus on the same dimension or a stimulus on another dimension "orthogonal" to the first (Honig, Boneau, Burstein, and Pennypacker, 1963; Jenkins and Harrison, 1960, 1962); and "extradimensional," involving discrimination training on one dimension and generalization testing on another, irrelevant dimension (Perkins, Hershberger, and Weyant, 1959; Reinhold and Perkins, 1955). Three explanations have also been proposed to account for the observed effect in generalization. Steepening of the gradient following intradimensional discrimination has been related to the algebraic summation of hypothetical gradients of excitation and inhibition, as we have already seen (Spence, 1937). Other interpretations for inter- and extradimensional training have been suggested by Reinhold and Perkins (1955), who proposed that training on one dimension increases the set to discriminate on any dimension and Restle (1955) and Jenkins and Harrison (1960) who expressed a similar, but more precise view that the control over responding by extraneous cues is reduced in generalization because of their association with nonreinforced periods during discrimination training.

If discrimination training prior to generalization testing acts to steepen the generalization gradient in the manner proposed by either of the preceding explanations, nondifferential (equal) reinforcement to two different stimuli should flatten the gradient by reducing the set to discriminate or by decreasing control of the original training stimulus through the introduction of an additional, extraneous stimulus. Support for this hypothesis was found by Switalski, Lyons, and Thomas (1966) when flattened gradients were obtained from pigeons on a spectral wavelength dimension following interdimensional nondifferential training.

The increase in response to a displaced modal stimulus in the postdiscrimination generalization gradient can readily be seen in Figure 10-7, which shows the results of Hanson's (1959) study. This phenomenon, which has come to be known as the *peak shift*, is a consistent finding in operant conditioning studies using two discriminative stimuli prior to generalization testing (Honig, Thomas, and Guttman, 1959; Guttman, 1959; Thomas, Ost, and Thomas, 1960; Honig, 1962; Terrace, 1964). It also occurs in a modified form (increased responding to adjacent stimuli) in those instances in which the discriminative stimuli consist of a positive stimulus bounded by two negative stimuli (Hanson, 1961) and a negative stimulus bounded by two positive stimuli (Thomas and Williams, 1963). Pierrel and Sherman (1960), using rats and a dimension of auditory intensity, also succeeded in producing a displacement of the maximum response to stimuli beyond $S+$ and in the direction opposite to the negative stimulus ($S-$) after successive discrimination training. Increases in the amount of successive discrimination training with the discriminative stimuli at the extreme ends of the dimension also resulted in an increase in the slope of the generalization gradient and a decrease in the variability (Sherman and Pierrel, 1961; Pierrel, Sherman, and Fischman, 1963). Kimble (1961) has suggested that the increase in response following generalization testing is analogous to Pavlov's "positive induction," which defines the increase in responding to the positive stimulus following a series of nonreinforced trials.

Guttman (1963) has interpreted the peak shift as an indication that S is responding on a relational rather than an absolute basis. He cites the absence of a peak shift after simultaneous discrimination (Honig, 1962) as evidence that the potency of the negative stimulus is diminished when the opportunity for choice is permitted. More direct evidence to support this assertation of relational responding comes from a study by Guttman (1959) in which pigeons were reinforced at one level (one per min.) in the presence of 550 mμ and at a lower level (one per 5 min.) for 570 mμ. Generalization testing after this treatment did not produce a summated gradient or one which reflected the differential rates of reinforcement to the two stimulus values. Instead, there was a shift in maximum responding away from the stimulus associated with low-level reinforcement and beyond 550 mμ, characteristic of the peak shift. *In effect, the stimulus paired with low-level reinforcement assumed all the functional properties of the negative stimulus in Hanson's study* (1959). Dickson and Thomas (1963) replicated Guttman's study with duration rather than frequency of reinforcement as the independent variable and failed to obtain the peak shift. Yarczower, Dickson, and Gollub (1965) also failed to obtain the peak shift when they used a tandem schedule of reinforcement which generated equal response rates in the training stimuli despite the dissimilar frequencies of reinforcement. Terrace (1964) has added another important facet to the peak shift phenomenon by demonstrating that it does not occur when $S-$ is introduced gradually with low intensity during spectral wavelength dis-

crimination training and discrimination develops without large amounts of responding to the negative stimulus. He concludes that $S-$ may function as an aversive stimulus with the displacement representing a shift away from the aversive $S-$.

Friedman and Guttman (1965) have systematically explored some of the conditions underlying the postdiscrimination gradient following Reynolds' (1961a, b) assertion that the observed rate of increase to $S+$ generally obtained during discrimination training (behavioral contrast) is sufficient to account for both the height and the displaced peak of the postdiscrimination gradient, and that the rate increase to $S+$ occurs independently of the nature of $S-$ used during discrimination training. Using several variations of discrimination procedures with wavelength of light as a positive stimulus dimension and patterns (cross or shadow) as a negative stimulus, Friedman and Guttman found the following relationships:

1. Initial rate of responding to $S+$ during generalization testing is similar to $S+$ during discrimination training.
2. Initial rate to the displaced stimulus on the postdiscrimination gradient exceeds the rate to $S+$ during discrimination training.
3. Shifts in the postdiscrimination gradient (peak shift) will occur without increases in $S+$ during hue discrimination training if the increase to $S+$ has been established to a prior pattern discrimination.
4. Discrimination training with hue as $S+$ and pattern as $S-$ results in a shifted gradient for hue after separate extinction to one peripheral wavelength stimulus. In this case, however, there was a marked reduction in the overall gradient despite the relative increase at the displaced stimulus. The greatest relative decrease in responding occurred to the stimulus used as $S-$.
5. Discrimination training with time-out (interspersed blackout trials) as the negative stimulus does not produce the peak shift or increase to $S+$ after extinction to a peripheral stimulus despite the rate increase

to S+ during discrimination training. The same is also true of extended VI training.

From the results of Friedman and Guttman it would appear that although rate increase to S+ as a result of discrimination training is a necessary condition, it is not a sufficient condition to produce these changes in the postdiscrimination gradient. Contrary to Reynolds' assumption, some aspect of the discrimination procedure itself, notably that concerned with the characteristics of the negative stimulus, is also important. Yarczower, Dickson, and Gollub (1966) have recently challenged the supposition that behavioral contrast is either a necessary or sufficient condition to produce the postdiscrimination peak shift. In a series of experiments with pigeons on a spectral wavelength dimension, behavior contrast was eliminated during discrimination training through the use of tandem schedules of reinforcement. One group was given a *mult tand* VI 30 sec. DRL 4 sec. reinforcement schedule for S+ (550 mμ) and nonreinforcement for the negative stimulus (570 mμ). This schedule had the effect of markedly reducing the number of responses and eliminating the increase in response rate to S+ customarily found when S− is introduced. Despite the absence of behavioral contrast, generalization tests to seven test stimuli (520 to 580 in 10-mμ steps) yielded a shift in the modal point of the gradient from 550 to 540 mμ. The authors have concluded from this and other studies that the peak shift will occur despite the absence of behavioral contrast during discrimination training if S+ and S− are alternated in some way during discrimination with a resultant reduction in S− responding.

All of the studies concerned with the postdiscrimination gradient appear to agree that some form of discrimination learning prior to tests for generalization is necessary to produce the unique changes in the gradient described by the peak shift. It is instructive to note, however, that not all extinction and/or discrimination proce-

dures lead to such changes. Neither of the studies by Honig, Thomas, and Guttman (1959) or Kalish and Haber (1963) produced peak shifts in the generalization gradient after individual groups were extinguished to one stimulus on the spectral wavelength dimension following training to 500 mμ. Honig (1962), as another example, found no evidence for the postdiscrimination shift following *simultaneous* discrimination training with pigeons on a hue dimension, and although Terrace (1964) obtained the peak shift following successive discrimination training, the phenomenon failed to appear when S− was introduced gradually during discrimination training and discrimination learning proceeded without a large amount of responding to S− (1966c). This finding is specially interesting because it indicates, along with Friedman and Guttman (1965), *that some amount of responding to S− is a necessary factor in the postdiscrimination shift in addition to increases in S+ and successive discrimination learning.*

The nature of S− and the conditions for its presentation appear to be substantial variables in determining the form of the postdiscrimination gradient. The peak shift phenomenon does not appear when S− is introduced in extinction sessions, after training (Honig, Thomas, and Guttman, 1959; Kalish and Haber, 1963; Hearst and Poppen, 1965); when S− consists of blackout trials interspersed among the training trials (Friedman and Guttman, 1965); or when the negative stimulus has been paired with shock (Hoffman and Fleshler, 1964). These facts do not appear to be consistent with Terrace's (1964) conjecture that the peak shift represents an emotional response on the part of the pigeon and a shift away from an aversive S−. Under the circumstances one would have to assume that the emotional response to S− can only occur when it is presented in close context with S+ because the studies cited previously failed to obtain the shift when S− was presented separately.

An alternate hypothesis is that under conditions of simultaneous discrimination training, S has an opportunity to reduce the number of responses to S− and any of the inhibitory potential associated with it. This opportunity is not present in successive discrimination learning because only one alternative (either S+ or S−) is present. If this hypothesis is correct, it might be possible to demonstrate the postdiscrimination shift in the gradient early in simultaneous discrimination training when S− still elicits responses. Pierrel and Sherman (1960) have reported results which appear to have some relevance to this speculation. They trained rats to discriminate between different auditory intensities. Early in training the highest rate of responding occurred at the extreme of the intensity continuum furthest from S−. With continued discrimination training, however, the peak of the gradient shifted back to S+. It should also be noted, however, that Terrace (1966a) has used this same study to support the "emotional" hypothesis by suggesting that the shift back to S+ after prolonged training was caused by a decrease in emotionality, and by demonstrating in a subsequent experiment (1966b) that both behavioral contrast and the peak shift disappeared during extended discrimination training prior to generalization testing.

In summary, the increase and displacement of the modal response away from S+ during generalization testing following discrimination training appears to be due to the following conditions (1) successive rather than simultaneous discrimination training prior to generalization testing, (2) the alternation of S+ and S− in some fashion during discrimination training, (3) responding to S− during discrimination training, and (4) a reduction in response to S− during training.

In the face of the evidence just presented it is difficult to maintain that the form of the postdiscrimination generalization gradients of excitation or inhibition resemble those predicted by Spence or Hull. The evidence against a bilaterally symmetrical gradient of inhibition appears to be convincing and the concept seems to be unnecessary to predict the development of discrimination, at least in certain cases (Terrace, 1963b). What about the need for a gradient of excitation? This question can be explored in an examination of the second criterion; the extent to which the course of discrimination learning can be predicted from systematic variations in the gradient of excitation.

The Effect of Generalization on Discrimination

Discrimination is facilitated when the amount of similarity between stimuli is decreased. The finding that appears most consistently in the literature is that discrimination becomes more difficult if the *similarity* of the stimuli *is* increased (MacCaslin, 1954; Bevan and Saugstad, 1955). In some instances, changes in discrimination performance or in the performance of the discrimination-contingent task (verbal learning) were explained in terms of changes in the generalization gradient (Gibson, 1940, 1941, 1942; Spiker, 1956c; Kalish and Haber, 1962). No attempts were made until recently, however, to vary the slope of the generalization gradient systematically and *use* the differences between gradients to generate predictions in a discrimination task (Haber and Kalish, 1963; Kalish and Haber, 1965).

We have already seen that in order to predict behavior in discrimination, Spence (1937) resorted to the use of two hypothetical gradients and the net excitatory potential at the reinforced and nonreinforced stimuli. Virtually the same purpose is achieved in two discrimination studies (Haber and Kalish, 1963; Kalish and Haber, 1965) by using the differences in response strength between two selected stimuli on a generalization gradient to predict both the ratio of discrimination and the rate of discrimination formation. In the

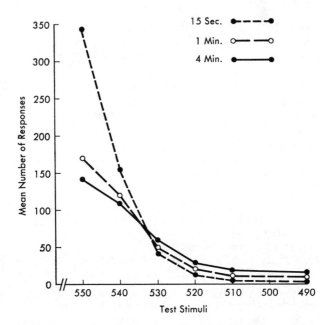

Figure 10-10. Stimulus generalization gradients following training to 550 mµ on VI 15-sec., 1-min., and 4-min. schedules. (Reprinted with permission from Haber, A., and Kalish, H. I. Prediction of discrimination from generalization after variations in schedule of reinforcement. *Science*, 1963, **142**, 412–413. Copyright 1963 by the American Association for the Advancement of Science.)

first study (Haber and Kalish, 1963), three different generalization gradients were obtained from three groups of pigeons under differing schedules of variable interval reinforcement (15/sec. 1/min. and 4/min.) for a spectral wavelength continuum ranging from 490 to 550 mµ in 10-mµ steps (Figure 10-10). Several different groups of pigeons, trained to 550 mµ with reinforcement schedules identical to the first groups, were then given successive discrimination training to either 550+, 540−, or 540+, 530−. In each case the ratios of response to 540/550 and 530/540 computed from the generalization gradients conformed to the same ratios obtained from discrimination training. Number of trials to reach a discrimination criterion also decreased with decreases in the magnitude of the response ratios. This experiment was repeated with substantially the same results for a series of three deprivation schedules (Kalish and Haber, 1965). Jaynes (1958) reported a similar finding for an imprinting study. Discrimination

among the various stimuli used for imprinting occurred more rapidly for birds who had shown a greater generalization decrement previously.

The experiments just described indicate that the course of discrimination learning is, in part, a function of the differences between stimuli as reflected in the slope of the generalization gradient. Thus, the generalization gradient itself was used to predict discrimination formation on the basis of relative response differences between two stimuli and without recourse to hypothetical gradients of inhibition. This view of the relationship between generalization and discrimination places greater emphasis on relative differences among stimuli as the important factor determining the formation of generalization and discrimination.

Generalization and Transposition

Spence (1936, 1937, 1942) maintained that both the principles of discrimination and

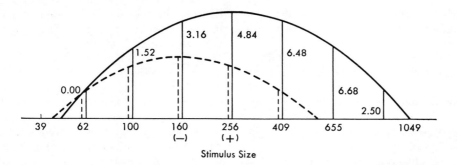

Figure 10-11. Hypothetical overlapping gradients of excitation (solid line) and inhibition (dashed line). (Adapted with permission from Spence, K. W. The differential response in animals to stimuli varying within a single dimension. *Psychol. Rev.*, 1937, **44**, 430–444.)

transposition can be deduced from a model which assumes that generalization is fundamental to both. As in the case of Hull, the model (Figure 10-11) postulates that gradients of excitation and inhibition are established to both positive and negative stimuli as a result of conditioning and extinction during discrimination training. Discrimination or transposition behavior is subsequently determined by the net response strength (excitation minus inhibition) at various points on the stimulus dimension resulting from the algebraic summation of overlapping generalization gradients.

Spence's model has been singularly successful in predicting both transposition of a response (transfer of a discrimination) to stimuli varying within a single dimension and transposition reversal. This is clearly illustrated in Figure 10-11, which shows the hypothetical overlapping gradients when Ss are reinforced for responding to 256 cm.[2] as the positive stimulus and 160 cm.[2] as the negative stimulus. Because the response occurs to the stimulus with the greatest effective excitatory potential, subsequent tests with 256 cm.[2] (excitatory potential equal to 4.8) and 409 cm.[2] (excitatory potential equal to 6.5) should result in a greater proportion of response (transposition) to 409 cm.[2] and, by the same token, greater responding to 655 when the

stimulus pair 409 and 655 cm.[2] are presented. Transposition reversal, on the other hand (response to the smaller of the two stimuli), should occur to the stimulus pair 655 and 1,049 cm.[2] because of the greater excitatory potential (6.7) associated with the smaller stimulus.

These predictions have been confirmed by many studies (Spence, 1936; Kuenne, 1946; Kendler, 1950; Alberts and Ehrenfreund, 1951; Honig, 1962), but the model has also been shown to have limited usefulness. Herbert and Krantz (1965) summarized the difficulties encountered by the model beyond the successful prediction of simple transposition. Developmental studies of transposition, for example, have done much to support the view that, at least under some conditions, transposition behavior is determined by the relationships among stimuli rather than absolute stimulus values. Kuenne (1946) and Alberts and Ehrenfreund (1951) demonstrated that transposition reversal was eliminated for children of higher MA levels, with transposition responses presumably mediated by verbal control. Analysis of the responses disclosed that the children were verbalizing "larger or smaller than" relationships among the stimuli and were thus achieving total transposition to all stimuli, even those remote from the training pair. Most of the developmental studies appear to indicate that Spence's model is only applicable to nonverbal human and infrahuman subjects.

Even with these restrictions, however, the model appears to have serious limitations. Lawrence and De Rivera (1954) obtained support for a relational view in an experiment with rats described subsequently in detail. More recently, Blue and Hegge (1965) showed transposition for an entire stimulus dimension which is difficult to reconcile in terms of Spence's model. Rats initially reinforced for bar pressing to a 55-db. tone were given generalization tests to stimuli ranging from 15 to 50 db. in 5-db. steps. Reinforcement to the 55-db. tone continued throughout generalization testing. On the eighth day of training all the stimuli were increased in intensity by 45 db., altering the range of the continuum to 60–100 db. Generalization tests conducted for the new continuum revealed complete transposition in which the entire gradient was shifted 45 db. with the new modal response at 100 db. Although the gradient for the first hour of training on the new continuum was somewhat higher than the comparable gradients for days six and seven, the gradient for the fourth hour of training was similar in virtually all respects to the other gradient.

A second area of difficulty has to do with an analysis of the stimulus controlling behavior and is encountered in two types of studies—those dealing with differences in transposition behavior as a function of the type of discrimination training prior to transposition testing, and those in which stimulus contrast is an important factor. In the first group of studies Baker and Lawrence (1951), among others, have shown that a relational rather than absolute view of discrimination and transposition can be employed to account for the higher rate of transposition for animals trained under simultaneous as opposed to successive discrimination conditions prior to transposition testing. The rationale here is that successive discrimination training

destroys the relationship between stimuli inherent in presenting both stimuli simultaneously, that is, giving the animal an opportunity to observe both stimuli together. Thompson (1955) and Riley, Ring, and Thomas (1960) demonstrated this by experiments in which both stimuli were made available on each learning trial, but the animals were prevented from comparing both in the case of successive discrimination. When a comparison was possible the amount of transposition increased.

The presence of contrast and background effects in the stimulus used for both training and testing also reduces the effectiveness of Spence's model in predicting stimulus preference during transposition testing. Lawrence and De Rivera (1954) indicated that transposition is predominantly a function of stimulus contrast when S is given a choice of responding to either the relationship between two stimuli or their absolute values in terms of hypothetical excitatory potential. Rats were trained on a Lashley jumping stand to jump left if the top half of a card affixed to each of two doors was darker gray (5,6,7) than the bottom half (4), and right if the top half was lighter (1,2,3). Subsequent transposition tests revealed that the rats preserved the stimulus relationship learned during discrimination training and continued to jump right or left depending upon whether the stimulus in the upper half was lighter or darker than the bottom stimulus regardless of the shade of gray. Additional evidence to support the supposition that transposition behavior is governed largely by S's response to stimulus contrast, comes from an experiment (Riley, 1958) in which the transposition reversal effect was eliminated by varying the relationship of the stimulus to its background. Riley (1958) observed that the decline in transposition and transposition reversal following the presentation of remote pairs of stimuli might be attributed to the difference between the stimulus and its surround rather than to any change in response strength associated with the absolute value of a stimulus through generalization. Using a brightness task with rats similar to Kendler (1950), Riley demonstrated that when the ratio of the stimulus to its surround is controlled to approximately the ratio used during training, transposition reversal does not occur. To be consistent with these results, the absolute hypothesis would require a reformulation of the stimulus dimension underlying the gradients of excitation and inhibition in terms of the relative differences between stimuli.

In 1953, James proposed a formulation of transposition based on Helson's adaptation level theory (1959; see also Zeiler, 1963) which represents a departure from either the absolute or relational interpretation of the transposition phenomenon. James' proposal utilizes the notion that in the process of training a response to one of two stimuli, a neutral point corresponding to Helson's adaptation level (AL), is established. This neutral point is analogous to the standard stimulus in psychophysics and has the effect of initially "anchoring" the subsequent transposition responses. James further assumes that S learns to avoid stimuli less intense than the neutral point and approach those which lie above it. From these assumptions it follows that perfect transposition will be predicted on the *first* transposition test if the test stimuli fall on either side of the training AL. If both test stimuli fall on one side of the AL the responses will be randomly distributed. The response preference will gradually change in the direction of the critical stimulus when, following a third assumption, subsequent transposition tests and the introduction of new stimuli shift the AL in the appropriate direction. James' analysis of previous transposition experiments using a revised adaptation-level procedure indicates substantial agreement between the observations in the experiment and predictions made from the AL formulation.

The intermediate size problem poses a third area of difficulty for Spence's discrimination-transposition model. The hypothetical values contained in Figure 10-11 suggest that a S trained to 160 cm.^{2} as the positive stimulus and 100 and 256 cm.^{2} as the negative stimuli should continue to respond to 160 cm.^{2} when the stimulus constellation 160, 256, and 409 cm.^{2} is presented in a transposition test and that no transposition should occur. This is because the two hypothetical gradients of inhibition generated at the nonreinforced stimuli (100 and 256) will leave the greatest net excitatory strength at the training stimulus. Although Spence (1942) confirmed this hypothesis in his study, some of the evidence reported by Herbert and Krantz (1965) indicates that transposition to the intermediate member of the stimulus configuration does occur. This finding tends to support the position that S responds on the basis of the relationship learned during pretransposition discrimination training. For the most part, however, the results have been largely equivocal, favoring one or the other position as transposition occurs or fails to occur.

Zeiler (1963) has proposed a ratio theory of intermediate size discrimination using the basic postulates in Helson's adaptation-level theory (1959) which appears to predict both the occurrence and nonoccurrence of transposition for the intermediate size problem. Although the theory has certain basic similarities to James' (1953) formulation with respect to the use of AL as a standard, it eliminates some of the awkward assumptions and is more consistent with the idea that stimulus equivalence (stimulus generalization) is the basis for transposition behavior. James, it will be recalled, assumed that S approaches stimuli above and avoids stimuli below AL. Zeiler points out that even if this assumption were extended to the intermediate size problem by supposing that S learns to approach the stimulus that is at the AL and avoid stimuli above and below it, "transposition could occur only when the intermediate stimulus of the test set is precisely at the neutral point and systematic response to a non-intermediate test stimulus could occur only if that stimulus were exactly at the AL" (1963, p. 517). Zeiler's theory, on the other hand, avoids the cumbersome assumption that S approaches stimuli above AL and avoids stimuli below it. The theory rests on the notion of stimulus equivalence and ultimately on stimulus generalization because S's response during transposition testing is determined by the similarity between St/AL_t (the stimulus/AL ratio during testing) and S/AL (the ratio formed during training).

Herbert and Krantz (1965) have illustrated Zeiler's use of the AL by the following example. To calculate the AL value and the subsequent training ratio, assume that S is reinforced during pre-transposition training to the intermediate value of a series of stimuli differing in size; 4, 5.6, and 42.2 in.² From the AL formula

$$\log \text{training AL} = \log Xi/n \qquad [1]$$

a log training value is determined to be 9.8 in.² Because the training ratio is equal to the area of the positive stimulus/AL, this value becomes S/AL or 0.57. If the test series consists of three stimuli 4, 5.6, and 7.8 in.² the log test AL is given by the formula

$$\log \text{test AL} = y(\log Xi/n) - x(\log \text{training AL}) \qquad [2]$$

For purposes of illustration x and y are taken to be 0.40 and 0.60. In actual use, however, these constants were determined by Zeiler (1963) by an inspection of the data from several experiments previously conducted by other investigators. The values used in Zeiler's own studies (1963) with children from which predictions were made, were obtained from a similar study by Stevenson and Bitterman (1955). The log test AL, which is determined to be 7.0 in.², is used to calculate the test ratio for each test stimulus by Test Stimulus/Test AL (St/ALt). For the three test stimuli these values are 4/7.0, or 0.57; 5.6/7.0, or

0.80; and 7.8/7.0, or 1.11. Because S's response is determined by the similarity between the training ratio (0.57) and the test ratio, the 4-in.² test stimulus with a test ratio equal to the training ratio (0.57) should elicit the greatest number of responses. As Herbert and Krantz point out, this expectation is contrary to that of Spence and the relational theorists because it predicts response preference for a previously nonreinforced stimulus (4 in.²) with the previously reinforced stimulus (5.6) present. Spence would have predicted a response preference for the previously reinforced stimulus (5.6 in.²) and the relational approach would have made the same prediction because this value is the intermediate value and S has learned to respond to intermediate values during training (1965, p. 281). Zeiler's (1963) predictions were substantiated by an analysis of the first-trial transposition data from several studies conducted by other Es as well as in a series of experiments designed by the author himself.

A recent study by Zeiler and Gardner (1966) provides additional evidence that the ratio theory of size discrimination can explain the transposition behavior of children. In a previous experiment, Zeiler (1963) found that the behavior of children below the age of six was characterized by transposition at one step (for example, training to set 2–3–4, testing to set 3–4–5) from the training stimulus, choice of the test set most similar in size to the positive training stimulus two steps from the training stimulus, and random choice with larger step differences. Adults, on the other hand, chose the test stimulus one step removed from the training stimulus on the basis of absolute size and showed complete transposition thereafter to test sets five steps removed from the training stimulus (Zeiler, 1964). The Zeiler and Gardner study (1966) was devised as an attempt to supply the missing link between the transposition behavior of children below the age of six and adults. Transposition training and testing were conducted with children seven and eight years of age along a dimension of size and squares. Zeiler and Gardner found a decreasing gradient of transposition with transposition reversal as the distance between the training and test set was increased. The data failed to support either Kuenne's (1946) hypothesis that transposition in older children is based on relational principles mediated by verbalization or Spence's (1942) notion of preference in terms of absolute stimulus properties. According to the authors, the stimulus choice of seven- and eight-year-old children appears to be determined by similarity of stimulus ratios and, ultimately, the range of stimulus equivalence on a training-test ratio dimension.

Another exceedingly important aspect of Zeiler's theory follows from the assumption that S's response preference is determined by the similarity between the training and test ratio and concerns the distribution of responses to all stimuli in the test stimulus configuration. If this assumption is correct, the number of responses to any test stimulus will decrease as the similarity between the test ratio involving the stimulus and the training ratio decreases. In effect, the theory makes it possible to predict the relative proportion of responses to all stimuli within the test set. These conclusions have also been demonstrated in Zeiler's (1963) studies and serve to support his position that stimulus generalization (in this instance a generalization gradient of responses to a ratio continuum) is an important, if not fundamental, element in transposition behavior.

The generality of the ratio theory of size discrimination has recently been questioned by Zeiler (1965) in a study of the intermediate size problem with animals as Ss. In this study, pigeons were initially trained to respond to the middle-sized member of a set of three white disks of varying dimensions. In the subsequent transposition tests the birds were found to

prefer those members of the sets of three stimuli most similar to the stimulus reinforced during training. Thus, if the pigeons were reinforced for responding to stimulus 4 in the set 2–4–6 and were given 1–3–5 and 3–5–7 as test sets, the preference for stimulus 3 would indicate that the animal's behavior was being controlled by the absolute rather than the relational properties of the stimulus. As Zeiler (1965) points out, the ratio theory of size discrimination explains transposition on the basis of similarity between the training and test sets. In the current study, however, pigeons transferred the response on the basis of the absolute properties of the stimulus regardless of the similarity between the training and test sets.

Although no theory appears to account satisfactorily for the diverse findings in transposition, the evidence from Spence and Zeiler emphasizes the importance of stimulus generalization and the role it must ultimately play in any theoretical consideration of discrimination and transposition behavior. The exact nature of this role is still somewhat obscure, although, from the evidence presented by James (1953), Lawrence and De Rivera (1954), Riley (1958), Zeiler (1963), and Terrace (1963b), the concept of a generalization gradient of inhibition appears to be considerably less important.

The increasing use of adaptation-level theory to explain the results of transposition (as well as stimulus contrast effects) is an interesting and significant innovation despite the somewhat *post hoc* procedure of calculating the constants in the determination of the log test AL (equation 2) from previous experiments. Nevertheless, the view of transposition and generalization which emerges from Zeiler's use of adaptation-level theory is of special interest because of its similarity to the theoretical formulation of Lashley and Wade (1946). According to Zeiler (1963), stimulus generalization is a special case of stimulus equivalence which, in principle, is analyzable in terms of stimulus/AL ratios. This means that a "frame of reference" (AL) is established from S's past and present experience with the stimulus dimension, and that the test stimuli vary as a function of their presentation within this context. In effect, if the organism has had no previous experience with a stimulus dimension, "the test sets are not on the same *psychological continuum* although they vary on the same *physical dimension*" (Zeiler, 1963, p. 530), and because S has no standard against which the test stimuli are to be judged, differential responding cannot occur. Experience with a stimulus dimension consistently alters the frame of reference and hence the nature of the response to other stimuli on the continuum. This view is reminiscent of Lashley's assertion that the dimensions of a stimulus are not determined until the organism experiences differential reinforcement. The concept of AL may be, in effect, the long sought for "trace" which is a necessary element in Lashley's notion of generalization.

The definition of AL as the weighted log mean of the series of stimuli (plus the residual AL from past experience) is an interesting development because it appears to bring generalization, discrimination, and transposition much closer to the operations involved in the determination of psychophysical functions.

The studies presented in this chapter were used primarily to support the argument that the generalization gradient is not simply the accrual of response strength to stimuli on the same continuum as a result of conditioning. Most of the experiments seem to indicate that some reference stimulus or anchor point is necessary to explain the generalization phenomenon. This is largely evident in the increasing use of adaptation-level theory (Helson, 1947, 1948, 1959) as an interpretative device and in the focus on "attention" as an important factor in the processes by which stimuli come to control behavior. The

findings which emerge from a review of the literature to support these assertions are as follows:

1. The generalization function for stimulus deprived and immature organisms is generally flat, but a generalization *gradient* is elicited when the organism "experiences" the stimulus dimension through differential reinforcement (Cofoid and Honig, 1961; Peterson, 1962; Ganz and Riesen, 1962; Terrace, 1964).

2. Differential reinforcement may be a factor in the establishment of all generalization gradients (Jenkins and Harrison, 1958, 1960). The complexity of the stimulus in generalization training as well as conditions for testing and training increases the likelihood that differential training takes place (Heinemann and Rudolph, 1963; Boneau and Honig, 1964; Newman and Baron, 1965; Heinemann, Chase, and Mandell, 1968).

3. The context or frame of reference in which the test stimulus appears is important in determining the form of the generalization gradient. Generalization testing with only one stimulus alters the gradient from a concave to a linear form (Kalish and Haber, 1963). The presence of an anchor or comparison stimulus affects discriminability resulting in an increase in the slope of the generalization gradient (Ganz, 1963; Grice and Hunter, 1964).

4. Variations in the stimulus dimension which affect discrimination also affect the slope of the generalization gradient (Kalish, 1958; Ganz, 1962; Marsh, 1967). Increases in physical difference between stimuli, as well as number of stimulus units, affect slope of the gradient. (Thomas *et al.* 1959–65; Friedman, 1963.)

5. Hypothetical gradients of excitation and inhibition are not the best models for predicting discrimination and transposition behavior. Evidence indicates that the organism may respond on a relational basis (in terms of a relationship learned during discrimination training, Lawrence *et al.* 1950–55; Riley, 1958; Blue and Hegge, 1965; or in terms of relative differences between a standard and the test stimulus, Zeiler, 1963).

6. The postdiscrimination gradient dif-

fers in many respects from the form predicted using algebraically summated gradients of excitation and inhibition. Gradients of excitation following successive discrimination training display a peak shift (Hanson, 1959) and inferred gradients of inhibition are markedly asymmetrical with the maximum not at the point of extinction (Honig, Thomas, and Guttman, 1959; Kalish and Haber, 1963).

7. Discrimination training prior to generalization testing alters the form of the generalization gradient in both the same and different dimensions (Reinhold and Perkins, 1955; Hoving, 1963).

8. The course of discrimination learning can be predicted from an analysis of response differences on the generalization gradient (Honig, 1962; Haber and Kalish, 1963; Kalish and Haber, 1965) and without the necessity for a hypothetical gradient of inhibition (Terrace, 1963b).

CHAPTER 11

Generalization as a Fundamental Phenomenon

The studies to be considered in this chapter make it difficult to reconcile generalization as a mere epiphenomenon dependent upon such factors in discrimination as differential reinforcement, attention, or AL level. These studies indicate that changes take place in the shape of the generalization gradient when associative or motivational variables are introduced during generalization training; changes which affect the rate of response to the test stimuli even though the stimuli do not appear to have been involved in differential reinforcement.

The Effect of Training and Reinforcement Variables

In order to assess properly the nature of the changes in the generalization gradient resulting from increases in number of training or conditioning trials, a distinction must be made between absolute and relative generalization, the two criterion measures which have been employed in such studies. The hypothetical gradients in Figure 11-1 will help to understand these criterion measures and to interpret the

results of the studies to be discussed. Absolute generalization refers to the height of the gradient in responses for all stimulus values. The gradient labeled B in Figure 11-1, which is intended to be parallel to A, shows an additive increase in absolute generalization since a constant added to each point on gradient A will generate B. Gradient C, which differs from A and B in height and slope, reflects an increase in both absolute level of responding and in response differences between stimuli on the continuum. Although gradient C in Figure 11-1 was obtained by multiplying each point on A or B by a constant, such changes in slope resulting from experimental procedures are more often both additive and multiplicative.

Two methods for expressing relative generalization appear in the research literature. The first converts the number of responses at each stimulus value to a per cent of total response over the entire gradient (Rgs/Rtotal). The second employs a ratio of number of responses at the generalized stimuli to the number at the conditioned stimulus (Rgs/Rcs). The rationale governing the use of either measure has not been clearly demonstrated although both have been used to determine

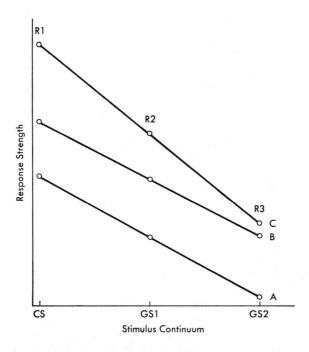

R1

R2

R3

C
B

A

Response Strength

CS   GS1   GS2

Stimulus Continuum

Figure 11-1. Hypothetical Gradients of Generalization. CS designates the training stimulus. GS1 and GS2 are the generalized test stimuli.

whether the difference between two gradients can be reduced to a multiplicative constant or for ascertaining slope differences. If the relationship is multiplicative, the slope differences between two gradients should disappear when the gradients are converted to relative measures (Hearst and Koresko, 1968).

Increases in both the height and slope of absolute generalization appear to be a uniform finding in virtually all studies concerned with number of training trials or number of reinforcements despite differences in stimulus dimension, subject species and conditions of generalization testing. Pavlov (Razran, 1949) and Beritoff (1924) were among the first to report this relationship with the salivary response in dogs and a tone continuum. Similar results have also been reported under the following conditions: tone, human *S*s, GSR (Hovland, 1937d); combinations of tone, buzzer, and colored lights, salivary re-

sponse, human *S*s (Razran, 1949); size dimension, runway performance, rats (Margolius, 1955); colored filters, lever pulling, children (Spiker, 1956b); tone, shock-avoidance, cats (Thompson, 1958); tilt of line, disk pecking, pigeons (Hearst and Koresko, 1967). Decreases in relative generalization, in the studies where such measures have been used (Hovland, 1937d; Margolius, 1955; Thompson, 1958; Hearst and Koresko, 1967), serve to confirm the steepening of the generalization gradient with increased number of training trials.

Although slope increases do result from increased training trials, most of the studies indicate that the gradient first exhibits an overall change in height (additive) and relatively little slope change with fewer numbers of training trials. As the number of training trials is increased, slope differences begin to appear. Gibson (1942) has used this finding to explain interference in paired-associate learning. In her study, increases in absolute generalization early in learning resulted in pronounced interference and poorer performance. As learning progressed, however, increases in the slope of the gradient were accompanied by a reduction in the number of errors.

The effect of variations in schedule of reinforcement has also been investigated, but the results are difficult to interpret in view of the fact that number and schedule of reinforcements are not independent. Humphreys (1939) and Wickens, Schroder, and Snide (1954) reported flattened gradients for "intermittent" reinforcement in human *S*s with GSR as the response measure, but these results have not been confirmed in the studies with animals (Guttman and Kalish, 1956; Haber and Kalish, 1963 (Figure 10-10); Hearst, Koresko, and Poppen, 1964). The study by Hearst, Koresko, and Poppen (1964) suggests that, at least in certain cases, schedule of reinforcement may have properties which are independent of number of reinforcements. These conclusions were based on observations of a relatively flat gradient for pigeons trained on a DRL schedule (differential reinforcement of low rates of responding) compared to those trained on a VI schedule with mean number of reinforcements appreciably similar for both schedules. The explanation for the flattened gradient offered by the authors is that discriminative control during VI training is predominantly exteroceptive and becomes interoceptive when the schedule is shifted to DRL. Because the DRL schedule emphasizes temporal discrimination involving proprioceptive feedback and an increased reliance on internal cues, the reduction of control by external cues (the training stimulus) results in a flattening of the generalization gradient. On the basis of this hypothesis, Thomas and Switalski (1966) designed an experiment to compare differences in stimulus generalization following training with VI and VR (variable ratio) schedules. The increased proprioceptive (internal) control generated by the

VR schedule led to a flattened gradient of generalization as in the Hearst, Koresko, and Poppen study.

The absolute measures and slope differences of generalization gradients convey two different meanings in the interpretation of the generalization process, according to Brown (1965). If the absolute frequency of response to each test stimulus is used as a criterion measure, increases in the frequency of response are synonymous with increased generalization and consistent with the idea that the generalization gradient is an index of "generalized habit strength." Slope differences, on the other hand, reflect differences between the CS and the test stimuli during generalization testing. Hence, the slope of the generalization gradient can be construed as an index of discriminability.

Brown (1965) has used the distinction between slope and absolute differences in generalization as the basis for an argument against the inverse hypothesis (Guttman and Kalish, 1956; Kalish, 1958) which equates generalization with "failure to discriminate" and is a derivative of the Lashley-Wade point of view. The hypothesis states, in effect, that generalization and discrimination are two sides of the same coin. Generalization (absolute) increases to the extent that discrimination decreases. Brown (1965) has argued, rather convincingly, that although these two measures do not appear to be independent, it is in principle possible to obtain an increase in absolute generalization without affecting the slope of the generalization gradient (gradients A and B, Figure 11-1). In this case, absolute generalization has increased while discriminability (differences in response between the CS and the test stimuli) remains constant. In effect, *S*'s response has changed independently of any change in discrimination, and this, according to Brown, suggests the possibility that generalization involves a process separate from discriminability.

We have noted that two changes take

place in the generalization gradient following an increase in the number of reinforced trials to the training stimulus: an increase in the amount of responding to all test stimuli (increase in absolute generalization) and an increase in the discriminability of the test stimuli (decrease in slope). If the discriminability of stimuli on a dimension is affected by changes in slope, a discrimination task involving these stimuli should also reflect these changes.

Such changes in discrimination learning were observed by Haber and Kalish (1963) in a study described previously. In the first of two experiments, three groups of pigeons were trained to respond to a spectral wavelength of 550 mμ on differing VI schedules of reinforcement (four per min., one per min., and one per 15 sec.). Increases in the slope of the generalization gradients for a range of stimuli from 490 to 550 mμ in 10-mμ steps were directly related to increases in the number of reinforcements to the training stimulus (Figure 10-10). The gradient for the 15-sec. group had a steeper slope between the stimulus values 550–540 and 540–530 than the gradient for the other two groups. This suggested that Ss trained to 550 mμ on a 15-sec. VI schedule prior to discrimination learning would reach a discrimination criterion more rapidly than the groups trained under less favorable schedules when either 550+, 540− or 540+, 530− are used as discriminative stimuli.

In a second experiment three groups of pigeons were trained to 550 mμ with a different schedule of reinforcement for each group. After ten days, the pigeons were divided into six groups and given successive discrimination training on one of two sets of discriminative stimuli: either 550+, 540− or 540+, 530− under the same schedule of reinforcement (VI 1). Thus, the six groups were distinguished by the schedule of reinforcement prior to discrimination training and the discriminative stimuli employed during discrimination training, Ratios of responses obtained

from the generalization gradients in the first experiment were used to predict both the ratio of responses and number of trials to a criterion during discrimination learning. In virtually all cases, the rate of discrimination formation was related to the response differences between stimuli on the generalization gradient. When these differences were large, the discrimination criterion was attained rapidly. *In effect, continued reinforced responding to the training stimulus led to increased discriminability along a stimulus dimension without any change in the distance of the physical units on the scale or any explicit discrimination training.*

Marsh (1967) has added to the generality of these findings by demonstrating that number of correct responses to a discrimination learning criterion is similarly related to the slope of the generalization gradient determined by the region of the spectrum at which training occurred (Figure 10-5). Gynther (1957) has also shown that pretraining with the positive stimulus prior to discrimination learning leads to more rapid attainment of the discrimination criterion.

An increase in the absolute height of the generalization gradient with greater number of reinforced trials to the CS appears to support the view that response strength "accrues" to the peripheral stimuli as a result of conditioning. The simultaneous increase in the slope of the gradient, on the other hand, also suggests that increases in discriminability are occurring although, as Thompson (1958) has observed, it is difficult to understand why increased discrimination occurs in the absence of explicit discrimination training. It should be understood, however, that failure to demonstrate discrimination training does not rule out the possibility that such differential training does occur. As many of the previous experiments disclosed (Jenkins and Harrison, 1960; Heinemann and Rudolph, 1963; Boneau and Honig, 1964), Ss are conditioned in an exceedingly complex environment and under conditions which may promote subtle sources of differential training. These studies increase the likelihood that now undisclosed conditions of differential reinforcement may ultimately play a greater role in explaining the generalization phenomenon. Estes (1950) proposed a solution to this problem (see Chapter 15 on mediated generalization) in his formulation of the generalization process which, as Mednick and Freedman (1960) observed, is similar to Lashley's (1942) "failure of association" hypothesis. According to Estes, only a certain number of elements of a stimulus complex are associated with the response on any given trial. Increasing the number of training trials increases the probability that the S begins to attend to the "relevant" stimulus elements in the CS and thus the likelihood that these will be distinguished from other elements in the test stimuli during generalization testing. Attention to more of the relevant stimulus elements and the corresponding change in discriminability should result in a steeper gradient with a larger number of training trials to the CS. Mednick and Freedman (1960) state that this explanation is not supported because the literature shows absolute rather than relative changes in generalization with increased training trials. The previously cited evidence indicates otherwise and supports Estes' interpretation.

The results obtained by Terrace (1963b) in the studies on errorless discrimination learning do not appear to support Estes' interpretation nor are they consistent with the findings of Haber and Kalish (1963). In Terrace's study discrimination training was more rapid when S− was introduced early (early constant group) rather than late (late constant group) in training after the pigeon had received relatively fewer training trials to S+. This would suggest that the underlying gradient for the early group is steeper than the gradient for the late group and that the effect of increases in number of training trials is to increase

the absolute number of responses to the peripheral stimuli and flatten the gradient.

The Effect of Motivational Variables

The manipulation of motivational variables appears to have the same meaning for the interpretation of the generalization process as variations in number of reinforced trials. Marked changes take place in the shape of the generalization gradient with the introduction of motivational variables during generalization training or testing and in the absence of explicit discrimination training which are difficult to reconcile in terms of a "failure of association hypothesis."

For the most part, studies in this area were designed to test Hull's (1943) assumption that the function relating generalization gradients at varying levels of motivation (D) is multiplicative (gradients B and C in Figure 11-1). As a result, experiments employing a number of different variables ranging from hunger and thirst (Brown, 1942, 1948; Rosenbaum, 1951) through electric shock (Rosenbaum, 1953) and anxiety (Wenar, 1953; Fager and Knopf, 1958) to schizophrenia (Garmezy, 1952; Rodnick and Garmezy, 1957; Broen, Storms, and Goldberg, 1963) have been classified as motivational largely because of theoretical expectations. [An alternative hypothesis utilizing an additive constant was also proposed by Miller (1944).]

Increases in drive level under hunger, thirst, and shock have generally resulted in increased responsiveness (absolute generalization) to the peripheral stimuli and, in some cases, to the standard stimulus itself. Some experiments have also approximated the multiplicative relationship proposed by Hull (1943). Brown (1942) found both increases in steepness of the gradient and increases in the absolute levels of response for the high drive condition with variation in number of hours of deprivation prior to generalization testing for rats in a straight alley maze. Rosenbaum (1951) did not find Brown's results in a study of temporal generalization under two degrees of hunger drive with rats, but a subsequent experiment with shock to human Ss indicated an increase in absolute generalization and an increase in slope when time scores were transformed to speed measures. These results were replicated in a study with rats (Brown, 1948; Rosenbaum, 1953). Coate (1964) also found a similar relationship in the post-discrimination gradient for rats deprived of water and trained to press a lever. Differences in the prediscrimination gradients, however, did not reflect the effect of water deprivation because all the gradients were uniformly flat. Newman (1955) and Porter (1962) found tendencies for converging gradients in studies specifically designed to test Hull's (1943, 1952) and Spence's (1956) assumptions concerning the effects of drive on generalization. Neither Newman's (1955) study with rats in a runway nor Porter's (1962) experiment with human eyelid conditioning and air puff intensity yielded statistically significant results. A later study by Kalish and Haber (1965) using percentage body weight loss in pigeons as an index of deprivation produced an interaction between drive and generalization for the wavelength continuum.

Although the preceding results suggest that the multiplicative relationship between drive and stimulus generalization is tenable, there have been some notable exceptions. Murray and Miller (1952) reported results within the context of approach-avoidance theory suggesting that the multiplicative relationship holds between fear (as a learnable drive) and pain (as a primary drive), but not between varying levels of pain-produced drive. Increases in generalization gradients for pain appeared to be additive at the higher levels of pain with some indication that a multiplicative constant was necessary only between the

low and high levels. Another study (Miller and Kraeling, 1952) indicated that the gradients for an aversive drive (fear) were steeper than those for hunger. Bersh, Notterman, and Schoenfeld (1956) also demonstrated additive generalization gradients for the conditioned heart response in man with a tonal stimulus dimension and a weak (20 volts) and strong (28 volts) shock as the UCS.

The conclusions in the study by Murray and Miller (1952) that generalization gradients for varying drive levels are not adequately described by a simple multiplicative constant have also been supported in several other studies dealing with both animal and human Ss. As higher levels of drive are attained, a ceiling effect begins to appear which limits the response to the CS at the same time that responses to the adjacent stimuli continue to increase. This flattening of the gradient at extreme drive levels is apparent in an experiment with pigeons conducted by Thomas and King (1959; see Figure 11-2.) The gradients for a spectral hue dimension exhibited both the multiplicative and additive relationships with decreases in body weight from 90 to 70 per cent of *ad libitum* feeding weight. With a further decrease to 60 per cent, however, responses to the CS (550 mμ) decreased below that of the 70 per cent groups while responses to the peripheral stimuli continued to increase. The gradients obtained by Jenkins, Pascal, and Walker (1958) for pigeons on a dimension of spot size exhibited the same characteristics although decreases in response to the CS did not occur.

Flattened gradients have been consistently found for stress situations with humans (Hilgard, Jones, and Kaplan, 1951; Wenar, 1953; Eriksen, 1954; Mednick, 1957; M. T. Mednick, 1957) and animals (Sidman, 1958, 1961; Hearst, 1965) and for the performance of pathological groups (Bender and Schilder, 1930; Garmezy, 1952; Dunn, 1954; Rodnick and Garmezy, 1957) or organically

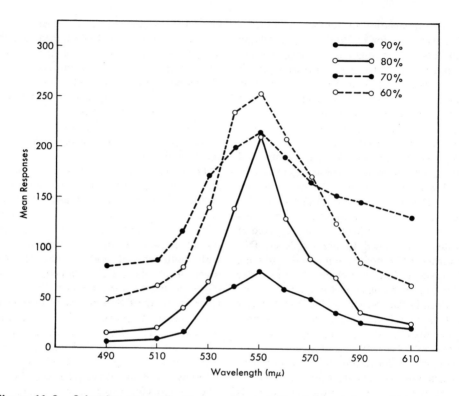

Figure 11-2. Stimulus generalization gradients following training to 550 mμ after weight loss. Figures in body of graph indicate percentage of ad libitum feeding weight employed during training and testing. (Reprinted with permission from Thomas, D. R., and King, R. A. Stimulus generalization as a function of level of motivation. *J. exp. Psychol.,* 1959, **57**, 323–328.)

impaired *S*s (Mednick, 1955; Kirschner, 1964). A recent experiment by Buss and Daniel (1967) with chronic schizophrenics proves to be an exception to these findings because the *E*s showed no difference between the pathological groups and normal controls in extent of generalization on a length of line dimension.

Most of these investigators, including Dollard and Miller (1950) and Mednick (1958), have also suggested that impaired functioning, especially in discrimination learning, is related to the flattening of the gradient with increased drive. But because the multiplicative relationship proposed by Hull and Spence predicts increased discriminability with higher drive levels, some modification in the theory was apparently

necessary. Recognizing this, Broen and Storms (Broen and Storms, 1961; Broen, Storms, and Schenck, 1961; Broen, Storms, and Goldberg, 1963) introduced a change in the theory in the form of a reaction potential ceiling which occurs at or somewhat below maximum drive. Thus, although low levels of drive act to facilitate the dominant responses at the CS or training stimulus, additional increases in drive serve to diminish the dominant response to the CS at the same time that these responses continue to increase to the peripheral stimuli, producing a flat generalization gradient.

Deductions made from the modified theory were tested in two experiments, the first of which utilized psychiatric patients with higher than normal levels of anxiety (MMPI scores) (Broen, Storms, and Goldberg, 1963, Exp. 1). Drive level was further varied by induced muscular tension (hand dynamometer). Generalization scores, measured in terms of left-right lever movements to stimuli varying along a size dimension, supported the authors' supposition that increases in drive would serve to flatten the gradient. A second study (Broen, Storms, and Goldberg, 1963, Exp. 2) was conducted using "neutral" stimuli (that is, stimuli ostensibly without symbolic meaning) similar to those employed by Dunn (1954). Schizophrenic patients used as *S*s were required to press a lever to the left for the standard stimulus (house and tree) and to the right for the test stimuli, which varied from the standard only in the angle of the lower left branch. Drive was varied through induced dynamometer tension as in the first study and, although no gradient is reported, the number of dominant responses to the training stimulus showed a decrement for both drive levels. Although the intent of these experiments was to demonstrate decreased discrimination as a function of increased drive, no explicit discrimination training was given. Instead, decreases in discrimination were inferred from changes in the generalization gradient on the assumption that generalization and discrimination are inverse processes.

The assumption of an inverse relationship between generalization and discrimination is frequently made in studies dealing with anxiety and pathology because impairment in discrimination is usually attributed to a flat generalization gradient. But as in the case of Broen, Storms, and Goldberg (1963), no inverse relationship between discrimination and generalization had ever been directly demonstrated. In fact, evidence suggesting that increases in drive may have no effect on discrimination was reported by Dinsmoor (1952), who found that the increase in responding to a negative stimulus in a discrimination task

was part of an overall increase in response level. Using rats under varying degrees of hunger in a bar-pressing study, Dinsmoor (1952) showed that the rates of responding to S+ and S− remained proportional with increases in drive.

Contrary evidence indicating that an increase in drive does result in poorer discrimination learning under certain conditions was obtained in a study by Kalish and Haber (1965). In an experiment similar to one already described (Haber and Kalish, 1963) several groups of pigeons were trained to 550 mμ under varying degrees of deprivation (70, 80, and 90 per cent of weight during *ad libitum* feeding) with VI 1 reinforcement. Systematic differences in the generalization gradient were obtained under these conditions when the animals were tested on a range of stimuli from 490–550 mμ (Figure 11-3). Six different groups of animals were trained under the same deprivation conditions and then shifted to a successive discrimination task with 550+, 540− or 540+, 530− as the discriminative stimuli. Ratios of response to 540/550 mμ and 530/540 mμ, obtained from the generalization gradients, were successfully used to predict identical ratios as well as trials to a discrimination criterion for successive discrimination training. Moreover, the rate of responses to S+ and S− during discrimination were not found to be proportional as Dinsmoor had indicated.

Certain other interesting facts are apparent from an examination of the gradient in Figure 11-3. Impaired performance in discrimination learning does not always occur under conditions of increased drive. The performance for the 70 per cent group with 540+ and 530− was clearly superior to the other groups, which is consistent with the large response difference between these two stimuli on the generalization gradient. The 70 per cent group with 550+ and 540−, on the other hand, showed poorest discrimination learning. Thus, differential predictions concerning

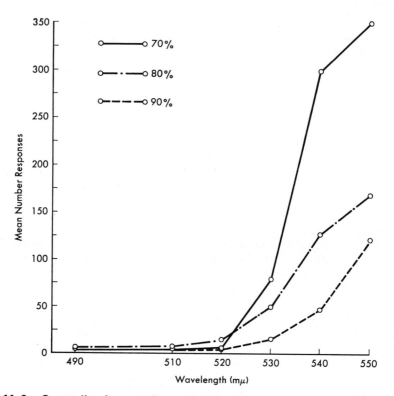

Figure 11-3. Generalization gradient obtained after training to 550 mμ under varying degrees of weight loss. (Reprinted with permission from Kalish, H. I., and Haber, A. The prediction of discrimination from generalization following variations in deprivation level. *J. comp. physiol Psychol.*, 1965, **60**, 125–128.)

discrimination behavior were made for two groups of *S*s each with the *same drive level* but with differing discriminative stimuli. These results may explain why in certain instances an increase in drive may result in improved discrimination whereas in others opposing results are obtained. Kimble has considered the possibility that differences in discrimination learning under differing drive states may be due to differences in the generalization gradient (1961, p. 372).

It should also be noted that increases or decreases in discrimination with increased drive may well be a function of the experimental conditions (see Chapter 4). In maze problems where response differences are used as dicrimination criteria, no change in discrimination is indicated. In such a situation *S* is not likely to begin making

errors as a result of increased drive. By the same token, increased drive will probably not affect simultaneous discrimination because *S* has a choice and no response inhibition is involved. In successive discrimination, however, the opportunity for decreased discrimination is present because S— is presented by itself on some trials. A similar explanation was used to account for the "peak shift."

Drive Stimulus Generalization

The question of the effect of drive on stimulus generalization also raises interesting methodological problems which are unique to drive as an independent variable. Because all generalization experiments require training to a CS prior to generalization testing, a variation in drive between the testing and training condition imposes an additional difficulty on the interpretation of changes in the shape of the gradient. This question has been treated directly (Estes, 1958; Thomas and King, 1959) as a problem in generalization and perception (Zajonc and Dorfman, 1964; Zajonc and Cross, 1965) and indirectly (Meehl and MacCorquodale, 1953; Yamaguchi, 1952) as a problem in the generalization of drive stimuli.

Unlike drives, which refer to a set of observable antecedent events such as deprivation, drive stimuli consist of interoceptive responses which are assumed to be unique to either specific drive states (hunger, thirst, and so on) or to varying degrees of the same drive. Kimble (1961) cites the experiments by Heathers and Arakelian (1942) and Elliot (1929) as evidence for a generalization gradient along a dimension of drive stimulus intensity. In the case of Heathers and Arakelian (1942) extinction of a bar-pressing response was found to be more rapid if two extinction sessions were conducted with the same degree of hunger drive. Elliot (1929) showed that a maze learning response was disrupted when the drive was changed from thirst to hunger during learning. The implications of these studies is that qualitative or quantitative changes in the drive state will lead to a relative loss in response strength presumably because of an equivalent change in part of the drive stimulus complex to which the response has been conditioned (Hull, 1951, p. 90; Kimble, 1961, pp. 420–521). This, of course, is analogous to varying the stimulus dimension in generalization testing. According to Hull (1943) generalization gradients for drive stimulus intensity should also show the asymmetry found in stimulus intensity gradients because the reduction in response from changes in drive stimuli accompanying shifts from low to high drive are offset by the increase in response in high drive states.

Moreover, Meehl and MacCorquodale (1953) suggest that the drive stimulus gradient would be steeper on the low-drive side (S trained on low drive, tested on high).

Yamaguchi (1952) conducted a study to test the hypothesis that the principle of stimulus intensity generalization applies to the concept of drive stimulus. Several groups of rats, trained to press a bar at one drive level were tested at several other levels, including the level used in training. The group trained at 3 and tested at 3, 24, 48, and 72 hrs. hunger showed a relatively flat gradient, whereas the groups trained at 72 hrs. exhibited a steeper gradient. The gradients for the other groups varied in steepness between the two extreme groups. *In addition, and with only one exception, the shortest latencies were found when the drive level was the same during training and testing.* The flat gradient for the group following training with low and testing with high levels of drive suggests that generalization occurs on a dimension of drive stimuli and that the gradient is also asymmetrical. Evidently, a flat generalization gradient represents the net result of a response decrement caused by changes in drive stimulus and the increase in response associated with increases in drive.

What are the implications of Yamaguchi's (1952) study for the problem of drive shift during generalization training and testing? Apparently, training with high and testing with low drive levels should result in gradients whose absolute level of response diminishes with decreases in drive (gradients A and B in Figure 11-1). Moreover, the overall level of response for these gradients will be lower than the level for the Ss trained and tested with the same drive. In effect, the absolute generalization gradient for a group trained at 48 hrs. deprivation (or its equivalent) and shifted to 24 hrs. during testing should be below that of a group trained and tested at 24 hrs. This follows from the supposition that the change in drive stimuli from 48 to

24 hrs. deprivation produces a decrement in responding which does not occur when the drive stimuli are constant throughout training and testing.

The relatively flat gradient obtained by Yamaguchi for groups trained low and tested high suggests that the generalization gradients for these groups would be quite similar to each other. As the difference between the training drive and the test drive is increased the response decrement caused by changes in drive stimuli also increases, but these reductions in response are combined with the increasing response from increased drive. Thus, the generalization gradient for *S*s trained and tested at 3 hrs. hunger should not differ from the gradient for *S*s trained at 3 and tested at 72 hrs. hunger.

Estes' (1958) speculations concerning the effects of variations in drive on generalization during testing and training are also based on a drive stimulus concept. The predictions made by Estes (1958), however, imply that the differential effects of drive stimuli can never really be determined because they are completely confounded with the effects of variation in magnitude of drive itself. For example, Estes suggests that the form of the gradient for training and testing with low drive is the same as that for training with high and testing with low drive. Similarly, the gradient for training with low drive and testing with high drive resembles that for training and testing with high drive. Under the circumstances the effects of drive stimuli appear to be negligible because the same predictions could be made solely from a consideration of the drive state present during generalization testing. According to Estes, the generalization gradient appears to vary with the level of drive during testing and is independent of drive during training.

Studies of the effects of shift in drive from generalization training to testing have been relatively infrequent. In a study by Thomas and King (1959, Exp. 2) two groups of pigeons from a previous experiment

concerning the effects of deprivation on generalization (Thomas and King, 1959, Exp. 1) were each trained on a spectral wavelength dimension with 550 mµ as the CS under 80 per cent *ad libitum* feeding weight. One group was shifted to 70 per cent whereas the other remained at 80 per cent during generalization testing. A third group was trained at 70 per cent and tested at the same level. The results disclosed that the gradients for the 80–70 per cent drive shift and the 70–70 per cent groups were markedly similar, from which the authors concluded that the slope of the generalization gradient is a function of drive level during testing and unaffected by drive level during training. These conclusions appear to be unwarranted, however, in view of the analysis of Yamaguchi's data which suggests that the effects of variations in drive and drive stimuli interact. The predicted gradient for *S*s trained low and shifted to higher levels of drive (80–70 per cent in Thomas and King) should be similar to the gradient obtained for no drive shift for the reasons already discussed. The appropriate group for which differential predictions could be made (trained high and tested low) was not included in the experiment.

Zajonc and Dorfman (1964) regard the subject of the effects of drive stimulus on generalization as part of the more general problem of sensory interaction effects in perception. This follows from their view that drive has energizing as well as perceptual effects and that drive stimuli can be construed as *extraneous stimuli*. The question of the relationship between drive stimuli and generalization, then, is reduced to an exercise in the interaction of two stimulus dimensions; the sensory dimension to which *S* is being conditioned (the eliciting stimuli) and a dimension consisting of differences in drive stimuli produced by variations in drive (the extraneous stimuli). They point out that the failure in behavior theory to distinguish between stimulation and perception distorts the kind of deductions that can be made and illustrate this by an analysis of Hull's (1951, 1952) and Estes' (1958) predictions concerning the effects of drive shift on the generalization gradient.

The basis for Zajonc and Dorfman's (1964) views is derived, very largely, from what is known about the perceptual consequences of variations in sensory thresholds in the presence of extraneous stimuli. The results of the sensory interaction literature indicate that simultaneous stimulation by an extraneous stimulus results in a lowering of sensory thresholds and an overestimation or underestimation of stimulus magnitudes. In contrast to both Estes and Hull, Zajonc and Dorfman predict a lateral displacement of the generalization gradient following drive shift. These predictions are developed from the following assumptions concerning the effects of extraneous stimuli:

1. Stimuli on a known continuum A are overestimated when judged in the presence of an extraneous stimulus B1. Stimulus B2 of higher magnitude then B1 will increase the effect of overestimation.

2. Performance to the original CS on continuum A will show a reduction as the amount of extraneous stimulation is increased.

3. The effect of extraneous stimulation on stimuli less intense than the CS would be to make these more similar to the CS. Because the amount of extraneous stimulation increases the degree of overestimation, the generalized response to CS-A, CS-2A, and so on, will be greater in the presence of B2 than B1.

4. The effect of extraneous stimulation on stimuli more intense than the CS would be to decrease the similarity of these stimuli to the CS. In this case, responses to the CS would be weaker with B1 present.

5. As a result of the reasoning involved in 1–4, a lateral displacement of the generalization gradient toward lesser stimulus intensities with the modal response shifting to CS-A is anticipated following a shift in drive (Zajonc and Dorfman, 1964, pp. 273–277).

An initial experiment was conducted to test the hypothesis of lateral displacement as a consequence of extraneous stimulation (Dorfman, 1961). In this study Dorfman used a generalization procedure similar to that developed by Brown, Clarke, and Stein (1958) with human Ss. The eliciting or generalization stimuli were slight electric shocks and the extraneous stimuli a tone of 45 and 96 db. The response "win" was associated with the -0.20 log milliamp. shock and "lose" to shocks of the lowest and highest intensities. The three training stimuli were presented individually with either the 45- or 96-db. extraneous stimulus during a series of nineteen training trials. [It should be noted that the training conditions are similar to the discrimination conditions used to obtain the "peak shift," that is, a positive stimulus bounded by two negative stimuli (Hanson, 1961; see p. 241).] The generalization tests consisted of nonreinforced presentations of the seven shock stimuli with either 45 or 96 db. present. The data for generalization indicate a lateral displacement of the generalization gradient when the extraneous stimulation was changed from training to test.

Two experiments were subsequently conducted with drive as the extraneous variable. The first with human Ss (Platz, 1962) employed experimental conditions of training and testing similar to Dorfman's (1961) with high and low shock as the extraneous drive dimension and loudness as the eliciting dimension. The second experiment with pigeons (Zajonc and Cross, 1965) used body weight loss (70 and 90 per cent of *ad libitum* feeding weight) as the extraneous drive stimulus and diameter of an illuminated spot as the eliciting stimulus. Both experiments showed the predicted lateral shift in the generalization gradient with the displacement toward larger stimuli when the drive level was raised and toward the smaller stimuli when it was lowered.

The experiments by Zajonc *et al.* appear

to be an extraordinary solution to the drive shift-generalization problem. Although, as Zajonc and Dorfman (1964) point out, Estes (1958) maintained that the significant aspect of drive is its stimulus element, his predictions of changes in the gradient drive shift were restricted to either a flattening or steepening of the gradient under the appropriate drive shift conditions. The work of Zajonc et al. places more emphasis on the perceptual rather than energizing functions of the drive state.

Some comment on the unusual experimental conditions employed in the experiments by Zajonc et al. appears to be necessary in view of the results obtained in studies concerned with the "peak shift" described previously. (Hanson, 1961; Thomas and Williams, 1963). In the studies described by Zajonc, and in particular the pigeon study conducted by Zajonc and Cross (1965) which is the most appropriate for comparison, Ss were given discrimination training with one stimulus as S+ flanked by two negative stimuli prior to shifts in the extraneous stimulus and generalization testing. In Hanson's (1961) study, where a similar training method was used, the generalization test disclosed a marked increase in response to the CS (550 mμ) and the peripheral stimulus 540 mμ and a reduction in response to all other test stimuli. Hanson, it appears, obtained an effect remotely similar to Zajonc and Cross without the presence of extraneous stimulation. It should also be noted that if only one training stimulus is used in generalization training prior to drive shift and generalization testing, as in Thomas and King's (1959) experiment, the lateral displacement phenomenon does not appear despite the presence of extraneous stimulation in the form of drive shift.

Apparently some assessment must be made of the effects of discrimination training per se prior to generalization testing.

Generalization of Inhibition

An inhibitory process to explain the effects of nonreinforced responding has become generally accepted in the study of behavior since Pavlov (1927) used it to account for extinction and the related phenomena of spontaneous recovery and disinhibition. The supposition that inhibitory control could be transferred to other stimuli, however, emerged from his experiments in conditioned inhibition and generalization of inhibition. In this group of studies, Pavlov (1927) demonstrated that a positive stimulus S1 lost its effectiveness if it occurred within the stimulus complex S1S2 which was never reinforced. When S2 was subsequently presented with another positive stimulus S3, which had been conditioned to evoke the salivary response, the response was reduced to zero presumably because of the presence of the "conditioned inhibitor" S2 (Pavlov, 1927, p. 77). Although these results were interpreted in terms of transfer of inhibitory control from S− to S+, they do not preclude the possibility that S− acquired the properties of a discriminative stimulus and that the S, then, had merely learned that S− in any context means: stop responding. Jenkins (1965) has aptly noted that the central problem in studies of inhibition is "to distinguish the presence of an inhibitory effect from the reduction of an excitatory effect" (1965, p. 56), a particularly difficult distinction in view of the fact that inhibition is generally inferred from a reduction in excitation. In fact, Skinner regards inhibition merely as a decrement in excitation.

A more persuasive set of circumstances for the concept of inhibitory transfer appeared in Krasnagorsky's experiments which served as the basis for the irradiation hypothesis (Pavlov, 1927, p. 154). Generalization of extinction effects was obtained when four of five regions on a dog's leg were stimulated with reinforcement whereas the fifth received no reinforcement. Unlike the studies of conditioned inhibition described previously, in which S+ and S− appeared in the same stimulus configuration, the positive stimuli in Krasnogorsky's experiments were linked to S− only through a dimension of spatial proximity. Nevertheless, salivary responses to the positive stimuli were diminished as a result of nonreinforcement to S−. It was logical, therefore, for Pavlov to assume that because the positive and negative stimuli were never presented together, reduction in responding to the positive stimuli was accomplished by some other means, namely transfer of inhibitory control.

Subsequent studies of the generalization of extinction used Krasnogorsky's methods with some modifications to reduce the effects of confounding caused by alternate presentations of both positive and negative stimuli. Bass and Hull (1934), for example, using the GSR as a criterion measure, reinforced several areas on the backs of human Ss with tactile stimulation. After an equal number of reinforcements to all stimuli, one region was stimulated for several trials without reinforcement. Tests to the other areas revealed that the reduction in response varied inversely with distance from S−. Following the same procedure, Hovland (1937a, 1937b) first established a GSR response in equal strength to four auditory stimuli. Extinction to both the highest and lowest tones for two different groups of the Ss resulted in a gradient of extinction effect during generalization testing.

Kling (1952) pointed out that the classical procedures used by Bass and Hull (1934) and Hovland (1937a, 1937b) required pre-extinction trials as tests for strength of conditioning during which the UCR was omitted. Under the circumstances, the gradient would also reflect the effects of discrimination training as well as extinction. To avoid this, Kling (1952) used an instrumental running response and independent groups of rats. Each group was trained to respond to two white circles of different size which were systematically varied among the different groups. Decrease in response to one circle of a pair, after the other was extinguished, was found to be related to difference in circle size. As this difference increased, the generalized effects of nonreinforcement became less pronounced. Further refinements in method were introduced by Honig (1961), who used the procedure employed by Guttman and Kalish (1956) to establish high and equal rates of responding to seven wavelength values. Pigeons used as Ss generated a gradient of extinction effects after the center stimulus (570 mµ) was extinguished and tests for generalization were conducted among the other stimuli. The same results were obtained when shock instead of nonreinforcement was associated with the central stimulus (Honig and Slivka, 1964).

Support for an inhibitory effect has generally come from experiments such as those previously described in which "indirect" methods for generating gradients of extinction have been employed and absence of responding accepted as evidence for stimulus control of inhibition. The problem, as Jenkins has noted, is to distinguish the presence of an inhibitory effect from the absence or reduction of an excitatory effect (1965, p. 56). He further asserts that in order to demonstrate inhibitory control, the inhibitory stimulus should control the tendency not to respond in the same manner that an excitatory stimulus controls responding; that is, variations in the inhibitory stimulus should result in corresponding changes in the tendency not to respond. Jenkins' (1965) analysis of discrimination learning led him to conclude that such pure instances of inhibitory control can only be demonstrated if S− is varied independently of S+ so that changes in the distance between S− and the test stimuli do not entail corresponding changes in the distance between S+ and S−. In the usual discrimination procedure both S+ and S−

are taken from the same stimulus dimension. Under these circumstances the interpretation of any change in the frequency of responding may be attributed to a change in the distance between the test stimulus and S+ or to a change in the distance between the test stimulus and S−. This confounded effect could be avoided by selecting S+ and S− from different stimulus dimensions. If the excitatory response is controlled by a stimulus from another dimension, control of the inhibitory response (not responding) could be demonstrated by changing the properties of the negative stimulus to produce an increase in responding.

Experiments conducted by Jenkins and Harrison (1962); Honig, Boneau, Burstein, and Pennypacker (1963); and Terrace (1966c) satisfied the conditions described previously. In the first study (Jenkins and Harrison) the dimension containing the negative stimulus values ranged from an auditory frequency of 300 to 3,500 hz, whereas the positive stimulus was taken from an "orthogonal" dimension. In the first phase, the pigeons were trained to discriminate between absence of tone as S+ and 1,000 hz as S−; in the second, both 300 and 3,500 hz were the negative stimuli and S+ was again absence of tone; in the last phase white noise was S+ and 1,000 hz the negative stimulus. Generalization tests to the negative dimension after discrimination training revealed broad and shallow gradients in which frequency of responding increased as the test stimuli deviated from the value originally used as S−. The same general procedure used by Honig, Boneau, Burstein, and Pennypacker yielded an unmistakable gradient on a dimension of angular orientation after training to discriminative stimuli consisting of a blank key as S+ and a vertical line as S−. The pigeon's response increased as the vertical line was changed toward the horizontal. Terrace's pigeons learned to discriminate between a white vertical line on a dark background as S+ and a mono-

chromatic circle of light as S− either with or without responses to S− (errorless discrimination training). Only the group who learned to discriminate with errors to S− exhibited an increase in responding as the distance between S− and the test stimuli increased during generalization testing. Responding for the errorless training group was completely flat across the entire test dimension. The results of these three experiments indicate that inhibition can be brought under stimulus control producing a gradient of inhibitory control analogous to that for excitation.

Jenkins has correctly observed that S− and S+ must come from different stimulus dimensions in order to demonstrate unequivocally that stimuli can acquire inhibitory control. When the two stimuli are from the same dimension, however, as in most cases of discrimination learning, stimulus control of inhibition must be demonstrated indirectly by calculating the net difference between gradients in which no extinction has occurred and those in which the responses to one of several stimuli have undergone extinction.

Changes in the generalization gradient following successive discrimination training clearly indicate that gradients of excitation are influenced by gradients of inhibition when the discriminative stimuli are taken from the same dimension. This phenomenon has already been explored in a discussion of the peak shift in Chapter 10. Hanson's study (1959), among others, suggests that S learns more than just cessation of responding to S−, because the shape of the postdiscrimination gradient indicates that responses to all test stimuli to the right of S− in the direction away from S+ were reduced almost to zero and the frequency of responding to test stimuli intervening between S+ and S− was also markedly reduced (Figure 10-7). Generalization gradients obtained after Ss have been trained to one stimulus and extinguished to another on the same dimension also support the idea that the tendency not-to-respond which accrues to S— as a result of nonreinforcement acts to reduce responding to other stimuli in close proximity. Honig, Thomas, and Guttman (1959), and Friedman and Guttman (1965) trained pigeons to 550 mμ and extinguished the response to 570 mμ prior to generalization testing. The gradient obtained during tests for generalization showed reduced responding to 550 mμ as well as all the stimuli intervening between 550 and 570 mμ. Kalish and Haber (1963) reported the same results when several groups of pigeons were trained to 550 mμ and extinguished to 540, 530, 520, 510, and 490 mμ, respectively. It was also shown that the influence of extinction effects on 550 mμ, the training stimulus, was largely confined to a region approximately 20 mμ from 550 because extinction to stimuli beyond 530 mμ produced no discernible changes in the gradient as a whole (Figure 10-9).

The nature of inhibitory control and its influence on stimuli adjacent to the nonreinforced stimulus raises serious doubts concerning the adequacy of differential reinforcement and discrimination as sole explanations of the generalization process. In dealing with generalization of inhibition we are confronted with more than the idea that the generalization decrement is the result of S's dimensionalization of the stimulus continuum. We have already seen that the shape of the generalization gradient following discrimination training is jointly determined by the amount of inhibitory and excitatory control resulting from reinforced and nonreinforced responding during discrimination training. This clearly suggests that some process is involved which serves to reduce the amount of responding to the test stimuli simply by virtue of nonreinforced responding to S— and that the extent of reduction in response is directly related to the amount of nonreinforced responding to S—. Where there are no errors and, hence, no nonreinforced responding as in the case of Terrace's errorless discrimination training

(1963b, 1964, 1966c), inhibition has a negligible influence on the course of discrimination learning, presumably because none has accumulated to S—. Marsh's study (1967) also serves to illustrate this point. Figure 10-5 shows that as the number of test stimuli for Group 520 increases from one to three, the generalization gradient becomes steeper, suggesting that the addition of more test stimuli increases both the total amount of nonreinforced responding and the magnitude of inhibitory potential. A similar interpretation can be used to explain the steeper gradients in multiple versus single stimulus generalization (Kalish and Haber, 1963; Figure 10-4).

Although postdiscrimination gradients do not conform to Hull's or Spence's models as we have seen from a discussion of the effect of discrimination on generalization, a theory based on the difference between gradients of excitation and inhibition will probably prove to be useful in explaining discrimination training. It is also true, however, that the hypothetical gradient of inhibition will not simply be the "mirror-image" of the gradient of excitation, especially since some of the more recent studies concerned with generalization of inhibition have produced broad and shallow gradients (Jenkins and Harrison, 1962; Terrace, 1966c).

Hypothetical gradients of excitation and inhibition have been used to accurately predict the course of discrimination learning. Gynther (1957), for example, conducted a series of experiments with human Ss in which expectations of performance were based on the assumption that generalization gradients of excitation and inhibition were similar in form, the gradient of inhibition being somewhat lower in magnitude. Discrimination learning was also assumed to be the result of the algebraic summation of these two gradients.

In the first of these studies, a group given 50 straightforward eyelid conditioning trials to a light followed by an airpuff as the UCS, showed a progressively larger mean percentage of conditioned eyelid responses than a group given the same number of reinforced trials with an equal number of nonreinforced trials to a light approximately 2 in. from the positive stimulus. These results, as well as an increase in response to S−, were attributed to the generalized effects of inhibition and excitation to the negative and positive stimuli. In a second study the ratio of reinforced to nonreinforced trials was increased with the expectation that a drop in the inhibitory gradient would result in a higher level of response to S+. This, in turn, would raise the gradient of excitation and increase the response to S−. The results of the experiment confirmed these predictions.

Several other deductions were made and subjected to experimental verification. An increase in discrimination performance was obtained after one of the stimulus lights was covered with a red filter and made more discriminable. Finally, the level of response to S+ was shown to be lower with partial (combined reinforced and nonreinforced trials) rather than continuous reinforcement, indicating that inhibitory potential develops during the nonreinforced trials and transfers to S+.

Although the empirical form of the postdiscrimination gradient necessary to predict the results obtained by Gynther (1957) has not been found (Hanson, 1959), Hoffman and Fleshler (1964) reported gradients following discrimination training with an aversive stimulus (shock to pigeons) which approximate the postdiscrimination gradient predicted by Hull and Spence. The only exception was the failure to find a reduction to S+ during generalization testing. This result should have been obtained in order to substantiate Spence's supposition that the gradient of inhibition generated at S− extends to the positive stimulus. It should be especially noted that in both instances where results consistent with Hull and Spence's theory were found, an aversive stimulus was used as S− (air puff, Gynther; shock, Hoffman and Fleshler). The peak shift, on the other hand, tends to appear in those experiments in which the negative stimulus is associated with nonreinforcement. Differences in the properties of inhibition associated with pain and nonreinforcement may be a major source of variability in these studies.

The effects of delayed generalization testing after training are markedly different from the effects of extinction. Perkins and Weyant (1958) reported that the generalization gradient for rats trained on a runway were flatter after a delay of one week was introduced between generalization training and testing. The control tests were conducted immediately after training. A study by Thomas and Lopez (1962) confirmed these results with pigeons on a spectral wavelength dimension, but, in addition, *showed that the reduction in response was confined largely to the training stimulus without any apparent effect on the peripheral stimuli.* When the pigeon is given a series of extinction trials to the CS prior to generalization testing, however, reduction in responding occurs to both the CS and the test stimuli (Hearst and Poppen, 1965). The almost inescapable conclusion from these studies is that continued nonreinforced responding results in a negative state (inhibition) which transfers to other stimuli on the same dimension. The same situation does not prevail when testing is delayed and several days intervene between conditioning and tests for generalization.

In Chapter 10 we were primarily concerned with evidence supporting the generalization gradient as an epiphenomenon of processes involved in discrimination training while in the present chapter attempts were made to support the hypothesis that the generalization gradient involves fundamental processes in addition to those involved in discrimination. One of the interesting distinctions between the two chapters is that in Chapter 10 virtually all the generalization studies dealt with comparisons within a single generalization gradient whereas those in the current chapter focused on between-gradient comparisons. Brown (1965) has made the point that it is the between-gradient comparisons which validate the idea that changes can occur between gradients without affecting the discriminability of the stimulus continuum. The studies in this chapter appear to support this view. It is interesting to note, however, that the studies conducted by Zajonc et al. have introduced the supposition that changes in motivational variables such as those in drive shift may be construed as changes in perceptual elements.

Alternative Explanations

The basic problem in stimulus generalization, we have already noted, is twofold: (1) the acquisition of control by stimuli not involved in the original conditioning, and (2) the formation of a gradient of response. Hull (1943) resolved the first problem by assuming that the responses become connected to a range of stimuli during conditioning. Although he was not explicit on the second problem, the appearance of the jnd as a parameter suggests that the discriminability of the stimulus dimension was also involved in determining the characteristics of the gradient. Lashley and Wade (1946) never addressed themselves specifically to the first problem and regarded the gradient as an artifact of imperfect discrimination. The literature review contained in Chapters 10 and 11 appears to provide evidence for a dual process of generalization, one in which the gradient represents a combination of basic receptor functioning, modified by the characteristics of the stimulus continuum, and the conditions of generalization training. As we shall subsequently see, the non-neurophysiological explanations to be presented in this chapter answer the two main questions posed previously by making generalization part of the initial associative process occurring during conditioning.

Mediated Generalization

Mediated generalization, which grows out of Guthrie's (1935) explanation of transfer and stimulus generalization and Hull's (1939) treatment of "secondary generalization," has been regarded by some (Dollard and Miller, 1950; Osgood, 1953) as the basis for all generalization. Guthrie (1935) initially proposed that all generalization occurred because common or identical stimulus elements evoked similar proprioceptive responses. Hull (1939) proposed a similar explanation, but restricted it to the situation in which differing stimuli associated with a common response become *functionally equivalent* in evoking further responses. If, for example, SA and SE, two nonsimilar stimuli, are both associated with R1, and SA is further associated with R2, SB will also come to evoke R2. The assumption is made that both SA and SB have been made functionally equivalent through association with R1. This scheme has also been used to explain the phenomenon of sensory preconditioning, in which an association between two sensory events is established by merely pairing the two events. As in mediated generalization, the two sensory stimuli become functionally equivalent during pairing through a common mediating event. Unlike mediated generalization, however, the mediating event is presumed to be an interoceptive response evoked by one of the stimuli. Thus, if a light S1 and tone S2 are presented simultaneously, the tone becomes associated with the interoceptive stimuli elicited by the light. When S1 and its internally aroused stimuli are conditioned to a specific response, S2 also evokes the response because of its association with the same interoceptive stimuli. Like Guthrie, Hull (1939) asserted that these mediated responses are implicit and function as "pure stimulus acts," their primary purpose being to produce stimuli for further responses—"cue-producing responses" (Dollard and Miller, 1950). Unlike Guthrie, however, he described this process as "secondary generalization" to distinguish it from primary generalization. Secondary generalization produces "generalizationlike" effects, whereas primary generalization occurs on the basis of physical similarity among stimuli.

The method used in most experiments illustrating mediated generalization (Lumsdaine, 1939; Grice, 1965) involves the association of two stimuli with a common response, conditioning one of the stimuli to a different response, and demonstrating that the second stimulus can evoke the CR in the absence of explicit conditioning. Using this paradigm, Grice and Davis (1958) trained Ss to push a lever in the presence of two tones only one of which was reinforced by an air puff to the eye. For a third tone, Ss were required to push a lever in the opposite direction. More CR's were given to the tone requiring the same motor response as the CS than to the other tone. In a series of subsequent studies these same investigators attempted to demonstrate mediated generalization

where the mediation response was made implicit (an important element in the cue-response theory) by substituting a set to respond, thoughts about responding, or spoken words for the motor response. These conditions did not result in mediated generalization unless the experiment was so arranged that the mediated response produced the UCR. A detailed analysis of the results and further experimentation in which the temporal interval between the mediated response and the UCR was made optimal for conditioning did not support the response-produced cue theory (Grice, 1965).

Substantial generalization gradients have been obtained, on the other hand, for unrelated stimuli after they have been associated with a dimension of similarity. This method involves (1) establishing S-R(s) connections between two sets of stimuli—an ordered and unordered set (usually in a paired-associate paradigm). (2) using a single stimulus from the unordered set as the CS in the formation of a CR (for example, GSR), and (3) demonstrating that a generalization gradient for the CR can be obtained from the set of unrelated stimuli. In some instances unrelated words were associated with lists of synonyms, antonyms, and homophones (Cofer, Janis, and Rowell, 1943; Foley and Cofer, 1943), in other instances, nonsense syllables were associated with a well-established sensory dimension such as brightness (Phillips, 1958). The discriminability of such derived dimensions can also be increased or decreased to the extent that these dimensions are associated with mediating responses of varying discriminability (Richards, 1965).

Osgood (1953) has based his interpretation of the generalization gradient on the mediation hypothesis. In fact, he has gone further than this in suggesting the possibility that primary stimulus generalization is a special case of the acquired equivalence of cues. Hull (1939), as we have already seen, regarded mediated transfer

as a process producing pseudogeneraliza-
tion effects, but Osgood notes that "Hull
has not explored the possibility that all
generalization phenomena may fit this
paradigm rendering superfluous a generalization principle *per se* . . ." (1953, p. 359).

Osgood's reduction of primary stimulus
generalization to the process involved in
the acquired equivalence of cues is accomplished by way of three important assumptions: (1) the central neural effects of
physical stimulation are innately organized
along continua, (2) the earliest perceptual
learning involves establishment of distinctive mediating responses to patterns of
stimuli, and (3) the probability of two
stimuli being associated with a common
(mediating) response varies inversely with
the physical difference between them
(1953, pp. 359–60). All three assumptions
are necessary to explain why stimuli
never present during conditioning can
elicit the CR. The third assumption
accounts for the graded series of responses
by equating probability of association to
the mediated response with the strength of
a response. Thus, if a stimulus on a
continuum removed from the CS has a
certain degree of probability of being
associated with the CS, this also determines
its capacity to evoke the CR.

The validity of Osgood's hypothesis
depends almost completely on a demonstration that transfer on the basis of
acquired mediational responses and stimuli
is possible. One of the chief difficulties
with the mediation hypothesis, however, is
that although the rationale for acquired
equivalence of cues has been demonstrated
with the use of overt responses as mediators, the evidence for implicit mediational
processes is virtually nonexistent (Grice,
1965). But even if implicit responses could
be established as mediators, the antecedent events leading to differing response
probabilities and ultimately to the generalization gradient would still have to be
established (assumption 2).

Whereas Osgood (1953) emphasizes the
role of implicit mediators from Guthrie's
explanation of generalization, Estes (1959)
and Bush and Mosteller (1951) focus
completely on the idea of common stimulus
elements. This interpretation of generalization eliminates several cumbersome
assumptions including the view that differential associative connections between
similar stimuli and a common mediating
response are established during the
organism's early perceptual learning experiences. Estes' (1959) explanation also
eliminates the necessity to account for the
evocation of responses by stimuli never
involved in the original conditioning
because all the relevant stimuli are associated with the CR during conditioning.
These stimuli are present during generalization training as elements of the stimulus
complex which form the CS. The gradient
is subsequently formed because the original number of common stimulus elements
associated with the response is also reduced as the physical difference between
stimuli is increased. This follows from
Estes' view that the change in the probability of a response is a function of
changes in the stimulus compound determined by the ratio of the number of
stimuli on any given trial to the total
number available. Because Estes is dealing
with a dimension of similarity in stimulus
generalization, this ratio becomes the
number of common elements on any given
test trial to the total number of common
elements.

Although the common-elements view of
stimulus generalization solves the two
basic problems in the interpretation of
generalization, it encounters several other
difficulties which are equally serious. In the
first place, no independent definition of
common elements is available where the
stimulus continuum cannot be analyzed
into components. According to Estes, the
number of elements a test stimulus has in
common with the CS is ultimately determined by *S*'s response to that stimulus
(Estes, 1959, p. 465). This definition of

common elements is not consistent, however, with his general definition of an "empirical independent variable" as a stimulus "which is describable in physical terms without reference to the behavior of the organism" (1959, p. 455). In effect, the definition of common elements is circular because the gradient is explained in terms of the similarity of the stimulus dimension which is determined from S's response.

Secondly, the effect of motivational variables on the number and distribution of elements is not explicit and no predictions concerning the change in the generalization gradient with changes in drive can be derived from common elements alone. Finally, the observations of Thomas and Hiss (1963), Hiss and Thomas (1963), and Marsh (1967) indicate that the ordinal position of the test stimulus is an important factor in determining the shape of the gradient. This is contrary to the common-elements view, which suggests that the response to any stimulus on the continuum is predetermined by the number of elements the stimulus has in common with the CS and is independent of its relative position on the scale (that is, not affected by the number of stimuli on the test series which intervene between the stimulus and the CS).

The Neurophysiology of Generalization

Neurophysiological equivalents of generalization and discrimination have been explored through CNS recording (John and Killam, 1959; Thompson, 1965), extirpation, cortical mapping (Thompson, 1965), and lesions (Butter, Mishkin, and Rosvold, 1965; Randall, 1965).

The neurophysiological work of John and Killam (1959) and John (1960, 1963) involving electrophysiological recordings during avoidance and appetitive conditioning in the cat bears an interesting relationship to the mediation hypothesis and may be the equivalent of the trace response for which Lashley was searching (p. 217). Animals were prepared by implantation of electrodes in the cortical visual and auditory areas as well as such related structures as the lateral geniculate body, superior colliculus, and mesencephalic reticular formation. They were then exposed to twenty 15-sec. periods of flicker (10-sec. flashes from a fluorescent tube) daily for twenty days during the familiarization period. Following familiarization, a conditioned avoidance reaction consisting of hurdle jumping was established to paired presentations of the 10-sec. flicker followed 15 sec. later by intermittent shocks. When a criterion of 100 per cent conditioned avoidance reactions was achieved, several tests were conducted from which the following findings were derived. The description of the preceding experimental procedure is illustrative of one of the methods used by John and Killam. Experiments were also conducted using lever pressing under appetitive conditions. The conclusions listed below are abstracted from both situations:

1. Establishment of a "representational system." As a result of repeated experiences (conditioning or familiarization) a general representational system is established in the central nervous system which is both specific to the sensory system and general with respect to the region of the reticular formation, intralaminar and association nuclei of the thalamus, hypothalamus, and the rhinencephalon.

This representational system reflects certain attributes of the stimulus configuration. For example, in the presentation of a temporal stimulus such as flicker, a corresponding rate is established as a representational system. Cats trained to perform an avoidance response to a ten per sec. flickering light displayed a twenty per sec. response in the visual cortex and related structures.

2. Increased stability of the representational response and higher amplitude occur

when the overt response is brought under stimulus control.

3. The presentation of a stimulus on the same dimension, but not involved in the original conditioning, evokes the original representational response. An animal trained to a ten per sec. CS with a corresponding twenty per sec. representational response *will continue to display the twenty per sec. response to a six per sec. flicker.*

4. Continued presentation of the six per sec. flicker (nonreinforced) alters the uniformity with which the representational response appears in the nonspecific regions. When discrimination training is instituted and the number of overt errors decreased, a more stable and marked representational response can be observed in the specific as well as nonspecific regions. After generalization testing, and prior to complete discrimination, the waveform in several regions (visual cortex, mesencephalic reticular formation) becomes a composite (algebraic summation) of the separate waveforms for the training and the test stimulus.

5. Errors of omission: After the cats failed to depress the lever during the ten per sec. SD, a five to six per sec. representational system corresponding to the six per sec. flicker is observed in the various structures.

6. Errors of commission: If S pressed the lever during the presentation of a six per sec. flicker, the representational rate corresponding to the ten per sec. flicker was observed.

7. Variations in drive level appeared to alter the relative ease of activation of these systems.

8. The presentation of a ten per sec. flicker during satiation which resulted in a cessation of bar-pressing was also accompanied by a predominantly six per sec. representational response.

9. Acquisition of two differential conditioned responses—two flicker rates of different frequencies—produced two distinct representational systems established in nonspecific structures.

10. John concludes from this that memory appears to be analogous to the congruence between the dominant pattern of activity arising in nonspecific systems, and the pattern of activity in the specific sensory system reflecting the present stimulus configurations impinging on the organism.

The work of John and Killam (1959) and John (1961, 1963) presents a very striking illustration of the extent to which both the generalization and discrimination can be reduced to a *unitary process* corresponding to the arousal and extinction of representational responses in the nervous system. The process, abstracted from the findings described previously, appears to be as follows:

1. Representational neural responses (systems) occur as a function of both reinforced and nonreinforced presentation of stimuli. (Apparently the value of continued reinforcement is to stabilize the response; this view is somewhat similar to Guthrie's assumptions regarding the function of reinforcement in learning.)

2. The presentation of a stimulus other than the CS produces the response associated with the CS. The stability and, therefore, the strength of the representational response decreases with continued presentation of the test stimulus. Decreases in absolute frequency of responding correspond to the instability of the representational system. "*Generalized responding*" thus becomes the initiation of the representational system associated with the CS by some stimulus similar to the CS. Overtly, the response associated with the CS is evoked by the test stimulus.

The analogue between the neural process and overt generalization is not complete, however, because John and Killam have not explored systematic changes in either the latency or frequency of the representational system with changes in the physical similarity of the test stimuli.

Deductions from John's observations suggest that the establishment of a generalization gradient in the overt response should be directly related to the length of time necessary to disrupt the representational system established by training to the CS and to institute a representational system corresponding to the test stimulus. In effect, the duration of the representational system should be an inverse function of stimulus similarity; the nearer the test stimulus is to the CS the greater the duration of the system. The curve describing the relationship between duration of the representational system and stimulus similarity should be similar to the generalization gradient.

3. Continued presentation of the test stimulus produces changes in the representational system until that system corresponds to the configuration of the test stimulus. When this point is reached, S no longer produces the overt response associated with the CS. With continued presentation, "discrimination" is achieved.

Thus, for the most part, both generalization and discrimination can be regarded as overt counterparts of continuous modifications in the representational system produced by nonreinforced presentations of the test stimuli. Administration of differential reinforcement, as in the case of the discrimination experiment (where the CS is positive), serves to increase the stability of the representational system in related cortical and subcortical structures. This process makes it increasingly difficult for the nonreinforced stimulus to alter the representational system.

The effect of changes in drive level on the representational system reported by John (1961) is also worth noting for its usefulness in explaining the effects of drive on generalization. According to John (1961), increases in drive resulted in increased ease of activation of the representational system. This would suggest that with increases in drive the representational response associated with the CS would be evoked more easily and perhaps more frequently by the test stimuli, an assumption which corresponds to the flattened gradients of generalization found with increased motivation.

Thompson (1965) has proposed a more elaborate neurophysiological theory of generalization which appears to comple-

ment the representational system of John (1961). In a series of earlier studies, Thompson (1958, 1962) had already established the importance of the sensory cortex in generalization and discrimination behavior by demonstrating that bilateral removal of the auditory cortex in the cat resulted in flat generalization, that is, the total absence of a gradient. An additional finding that is significantly related to the discussions in Chapters 10 and 11 and that Thompson interprets as a refutation of the "failure to discriminate hypothesis" is the observation that animals who demonstrate a flat gradient with lesions in the auditory cortex can subsequently "learn frequency discriminations rapidly and with normal preoperative differential thresholds" (1965, p. 155). Unfortunately, no attempt was made to obtain a generalization gradient from the prepared animal after discrimination training was completed. Because we have already noted that such training usually results in a generalization gradient (Jenkins and Harrison, 1958, 1962), it would have been instructive to test for the presence of a gradient.

The fundamental model in Thompson's proposal is a synaptic relay mechanism in which a given number of afferent or input neurons are interconnected with each other through output neurons which are common to them. Thus, activation of any single input neuron will excite both output neurons which are unique to the activated neuron and other output neurons. The response is ultimately determined by the number of excited common neurons. The analogy between Thompson's model and the common-elements hypothesis is apparent. In either case the generalization gradient is a function of the number of elements common to both the training and test stimulus. Stimuli furthest from the training stimulus would, by definition, excite fewer cortical elements in common with the training stimulus and, hence, reduce probability of evoking the response associated with the training stimulus. Increases in similarity between the training and test stimulus also increases the number of common cortical elements stimulated and the probability of response (see also Wolpe, 1952).

Thompson's theory suggests the generalization process at the synaptic level, which may conceivably be the neural mechanism underlying the evoked potentials in the representational system reported by John (1961). Under the circumstances, the ability of a test stimulus to evoke the representational system analogous to the training stimulus and maintain it for longer periods may depend upon the number of output neurons common to the afferent neurons associated with the test and training stimuli.

Thompson (1965) cites the studies by Hind *et al.* (1961) as neurophysiological evidence to support the idea of common cortical elements. The activity of single neurons, analyzed by Hind with the use of microelectrodes, revealed that cells in the auditory cortex of the cat respond in terms of "best frequencies" such that the threshold for a particular cell at one frequency was considerably lower than at other frequencies. Hind also found that although cells differed in terms of their best frequencies, the range or bandwidth never exceeded three octaves, with a linear relationship between best frequency and distance along the auditory cortex. Thompson devised a behavior test of the cortical-elements hypothesis on the basis of Hind's results; in this he predicted a linear generalization gradient with a total range not to exceed three octaves. Cats were trained in an instrumental shock avoidance task to respond to a 250-hz tone. Five subgroups were subsequently extinguished to one of the following frequencies: 250, 500, 1,000, 2,000, or 8,000 hz. Total number of responses on the first day revealed a generalization gradient which fell to zero at 2,000 hz—a distance of three octaves from the training stimulus. The gradient was not linear when plotted on the geometric frequency scale. When Thompson transformed the scale, however, to correspond to the arithmetic "best-frequency" scale along the auditory cortex determined from Hind's data, the mean number of responses for the test tones all fell on a straight line. Thompson also presents evidence to indicate that the removal of the auditory cortex results in a flat generalization response. These results are expected in view of the fact that the auditory association area which remains after ablation is not tonotopic, that is, does not respond differentially to tonal frequencies.

Although Thompson's theory is a spatial-neural theory, the locus of excitation is not confined to the cortex as in the case of the irradiation hypothesis (Pavlov, 1927). Under the circumstances, Loucks' (1933) objection to the irradiation hypothesis on the grounds that conditioning can be demonstrated in the decorticate dog is not applicable. But because the theory is a spatial theory similar to the irradiation hypothesis, Thompson has found it necessary to reconcile the same inconsistencies. Following Mednick and Freedman (1960), Thompson considers the following contradictions:

1. Lack of correspondence between generalization gradients obtained on the surface of the skin and the projection of the skin surface on the cortex. Grant and Dittmer (1940), it will be recalled (Chapter 9, p. 215), anticipated a steeper gradient following stimulation of 4-in. steps along the back as opposed to 1-in. steps along the hand on the grounds that the projection of the hand area on the cortex is considerably larger than the back, according to the observations of Penfield and Boldrey (Grant and Dittmer, 1940, p. 301). Failure to obtain the steeper gradient for the hand led to the conclusion that the cortical irradiation hypothesis was invalid. Thompson (1965) points out that according to recent neuroanatomical findings, the ratio of the total cortical area activated for hand

stimulation relative to back stimulation is approximately 7 to 1. Apparently, therefore, the physical distance between stimulus points on the back must be at least seven times greater than that for the hand in order to generate gradients of equal steepness and, as a consequence, the ratio of 4 to 1 used by Grant and Dittmer should result in a steeper gradient for the back.

2. The smooth generalization gradients obtained from stimulation of the skin surface are not consistent with the distorted representations of the body area on the cortex. In stimulating the region between the back and buttocks, Bass and Hull (1934) found no inversion in the gradient for the GSR despite the fact that in man the sensory cortex between these two regions is interrupted by an intervening area representing the thigh, calf, and foot. Thompson (1965) argues that this interpretation is valid only if excitation on the cortex is assumed to spread in a wavelike form. In Thompson's hypothesis, smooth gradients are possible because overlap of excitation on the cortex is a function of neuronal interconnections at all levels. Thus, if two areas on the brain corresponding to a body site are separated by a third representing a different region, it would not be necessary to stimulate the intervening area to obtain a smooth gradient.

3. Octave generalization is not possible with a cortex organized along spatial lines. This objection is answered by the empirical demonstration that some cells in the auditory cortex have more than one best frequency. These best frequencies have been found to be octave multiples on the fundamental frequency.

4. Intensity generalization is not possible because stimulus intensity is not reflected in the activity of a single neuron. Evidence from Hind *et al.* (1961) indicates that the bandwidth of a cell increases as the intensity of the stimulus is increased. Moreover, new elements are activated only when a weak stimulus is introduced. Training to a strong stimulus will result in a steeper gradient when testing occurs to weak stimuli, according to Thompson (1965).

It is obvious from a review of the generalization literature that no theory of generalization can reconcile the extraordinarily diverse findings at the present time. Advocates of a discrimination interpretation of generalization (that is, failure of discrimination) have attempted to demonstrate that generalization is an epiphenomenon which depends upon more fundamental processes involved in establishing sensory dimensions in general. Those who espouse a "spread of associative strength" hypothesis regard the *generalization gradient* as a derivative of conditioning and, hence, a fundamental process, at least on the molar level of behavior.

The neurophysiological evidence reported by John (1961) and Thompson (1965) strongly suggests that the cortex (as well as other parts of the CNS) is structured so that the generalization gradient occurs naturally as a result of conditioning to one stimulus. But these are the cortical properties of mature animals, for the most part. Has the cortex and the CNS in general always been organized in this manner? Studies with both stimulus-deprived and immature organisms suggest otherwise. The gradients obtained under these circumstances are relatively flat, resembling the gradient Thompson (1965) obtained when the auditory cortex was removed, leaving only the nontonotopic auditory association area. Apparently, a comprehensive theory of stimulus generalization must also include the possibility that a given amount of sensory experience is necessary to produce a gradient of responses or that the generalization gradient emerges as a result of cortical development, or both.

A detailed analysis of the implications for generalization contained in the mediation hypothesis and the neurophysiological models of John and Thompson is beyond the scope of these chapters. The possibility that such an analysis may provide greater

subsumptive and predictive powers, however, should make such a laborious task worthwhile.

Glossary

absolute generalization. Strength of response to each test stimulus.

attention. The control exerted by a discriminative stimulus. "A pigeon is attending to a light if it consistently makes the correct discriminative reaction—if it strikes the key when the light is flickering and does not strike it when the light is still" (Skinner, 1953, p. 124).

behavioral contrast. An increase in response to S+ accompanying a decrease in the strength of response to S− during discrimination training. Originally referred to as "induction" by Pavlov and "contrast" by Skinner.

discrimination. Behavior resulting from differential reinforcement of two stimuli from the same or different dimensions presented either successively (S1 followed by S2) or simultaneously (S1 and S2 presented together). Responses to the positive stimulus (S+) are reinforced while those to the negative stimulus (S−) are not. Responding is ultimately elicited largely by the positive stimulus. Per cent of total responses to S+ and S− is usually employed as an arbitrary criterion to denote the establishment of discriminative behavior. The definition given here refers to a situation in which S must either respond or inhibit responding, depending upon the conditions of stimulus presentation. Other types of discrimination training may employ procedures in which S must choose between two alternative responses, each associated with a different stimulus.

discriminability. A measure of the sensitivity of the organism to stimulus differences. Usually characterized by a function describing the magnitude of stimulus change (or difference) for a given stimulus necessary to evoke response, called DL (difference limen) in psychophysics.

drive stimulus generalization. Generalization based upon changes in the stimuli

accompanying shifts in the level of drive. Usually demonstrated by increases or decreases in the slope of the generalization gradient with shifts in drive level from generalization training to testing. Changes in the internal cues associated with specific drive state (drive stimuli) are assumed to be responsible for the changes.

generalization decrement. Slope of the generalization gradient characterized by a decrease in response strength to the test stimuli when compared to response strength at the CS. Also a more general term describing loss in response strength caused by changing stimuli from trial to trial.

generalization gradient. A gradient of responses resulting from the generalization process. The amplitude or frequency of response to stimuli on the same dimension as the CS decreases with an increase in the difference between the CS and the test stimuli.

generalization of extinction. The behavioral phenomenon which occurs when the effects of nonreinforcement or punishment associated with a given stimulus act to reduce responses to other stimuli on the same dimension. Extinction effects are usually determined by calculating the net difference between a gradient of excitation and a gradient in which responses to one or several of the stimuli has undergone extinction. (See also *stimulus control of inhibition*.)

peripheral or adjacent stimuli. Stimulus values on the same dimension as the CS used as test stimulus.

primary stimulus generalization (Hull). Generalization gradient which results from training and testing on a dimension of physical similarity (for example, brightness, spectral wavelength, loudness, and so on).

relative generalization. Ratio of number of responses at each of the peripheral stimulus values to the number of responses at the CS (RTS/RCS). This has also been expressed as the percentage of the total response to each stimulus.

stimulus control. A stimulus achieves control of behavior when variations in the stimulus produce corresponding changes in behavior. *Stimulus control of inhibition.* In order to demonstrate inhibitory control uncontaminated by excitation, S− and S+ are chosen from different dimensions in discrimination learning. (See also *generalization of extinction.*)

stimulus generalization. The behavioral phenomenon which indicates that responses conditioned to one of several stimuli can also be elicited by other stimuli on the same dimension.

simultaneous discrimination. Discrimination training in which S+ and S− (the discriminative stimuli) are both presented together.

stimulus-intensity generalization (stimulus-intensity dynamism). Decreases in the slope of the generalization gradient (increases in absolute generalization) caused by increases in energy levels associated with stimuli on a given dimension (for example, loudness, brightness, and so on).

successive discrimination. Discrimination training in which presentations of S+ and S− are presented singly according to some predetermined arrangement.

summation of generalization. Generalization gradients resulting from the reinforcement of two stimuli on the same dimension. To demonstrate summation, the response to the overlapping stimulus values must be greater than the response to two single stimulus gradients erected at the reinforced stimulus values.

secondary generalization (Hull) (also called *mediated generalization* and *pseudo-generalization*). The behavior which follows when two dissimilar stimuli become functionally equivalent (acquired equivalence of cues). Operation entails association of Sa and Sb with R1 and the further association of Sb and R2 with the demonstration that Sa will elicit R2 in the absence of explicit conditioning.

transposition. Generalization of discrimination. Occurs when a discrimination to two stimuli on a given dimension is transferred to other pairs of stimuli on the same dimension. The relationship of the two stimuli is preserved so that S reinforced for responding to the larger of two stimuli during discrimination training will continue to respond to the larger of selected pairs of stimuli during testing.

transposition reversal. Occurs when the response to test pairs of stimuli after discrimination training is reversed and the original relationship is no longer preserved. For example, instead of responding to the larger of the two stimuli, response preference is for the smaller stimulus.

References

Alberts, E., & Ehrenfreund, S. Transposition in children as a function of age. *J. exp. Psychol.*, 1951, **41**, 30–38.

Andreas, B. G. Empirical gradients of generalization in a perceptual-motor task. *J. exp. Psychol.*, 1954, **48**, 119–122.

Anrep, G. V. The irradiation of conditioned reflexes. *Proc. Roy. Soc.*, Ser. B, 1923, **94**, 404–425.

Antonitis, J. J. Response variability in the white rat during conditioning. *J. exp. Psychol.*, 1951, **42**, 273–281.

Arnhoff, F. N., & Loy, D. L. Relationship between two measures of stimulus generalization, influence of intelligence on performance. *Psychol. Rep.*, 1957, **3**, 465–470.

Axelrod, S., & Kankolenski, P. F. Somesthetic spatial generalization in individual rats. *Psychon. Sci.*, 1967, **7**, 101–102.

Baker, R. A., & Lawrence, D. H. The differential effects of simultaneous and successive stimuli presentation on transposition. *J. comp. physiol. Psychol.*, 1951, **44**, 378–382.

Bass, B. Gradients in response percentages as indices of non-spatial generalization. *J. exp. Psychol.*, 1958, **56**, 178–281.

Bass, M. J., & Hull, C. L. The irradiation

of a tactile conditioned reflex in man. *J. comp. Psychol.*, 1934, **17**, 47–65.

Bender, L., & Schilder, P. Unconditioned reactions to pain in schizophrenia. *Amer. J. Psychiat.*, 1930, **10**, 365–384.

Beritoff, J. S. On the fundamental nervous processes in the cortex of the cerebral hemispheres. I. The principle stages of the development of the individual reflex: Its generalization and differentiation. *Brain*, 1924, **47**, 109–148.

Bersh, P. J., Notterman, J. M., & Schoenfeld, W. N. Generalization to varying tone frequencies as a function of intensity of unconditioned stimulus. Air. Univ. School of Aviation Medicine, 1956, U.S.A.F., Randolph AFB, Texas, p. 4.

Bevan, W., & Saugstad, P. Breadth of experience, ease of discrimination, and efficiency of generalization. *Brit. J. Psychol.*, 1955, **46**, 14–19.

Bilodeau, E. A., Brown, J. S., & Meryman, J. J. The summation of generalized reactive tendencies. *J. exp. Psychol.*, 1956, **51**, 293–298.

Bindra, D. *Motivation*. New York: 1959, Ronald Press.

Blackwell, H. R., & Schlosberg, H. Octave generalization, pitch discrimination and loudness thresholds in the white rat. *J. exp. Psychol.*, 1943, **33**, 407–419.

Bloomberg, L. I. Stimulus generalization along two dimensions within two modalities. Unpublished doctoral dissertation, Adelphi Univer., 1962.

Blough, D. S. A method for obtaining psychophysical thresholds from the pigeon. *J. exp. Anal. Behav.*, 1958, **1**, 31–43.

Blough, D. S. Generalization and preference on a stimulus-intensity continuum. *J. exp. Anal. Behav.*, 1959, **2**, 307–315.

Blough, D. S. Experiments in animal psychophysics. *Scient. Amer.*, 1961, **205**, 113–122.

Blue, S., & Hegge, F. W. Transposition of a stimulus generalization gradient along an auditory intensity continuum. *Psychon. Sci.*, 1965, **3**, 201–202.

Boneau, C. A., & Honig, W. K. Opposed generalization gradients based upon conditional discrimination training. *J. exp. Psychol.*, 1964, **68**, 89–93.

Bragiel, R. M., & Perkins, C. C., Jr. Con-

ditioned stimulus intensity and response speed. *J. exp. Psychol.*, 1954, **47**, 437–441.

Britt, S. H. Tonal sensitivity in the white rat. *J. comp. Psychol.*, 1935, **19**, 243–264.

Broen, W. E., Jr., & Storms, L. H. A reaction potential ceiling and response decrements in complex situation. *Psychol. Rev.*, 1961, **68**, 405–415.

Broen, W. E., Jr., Storms, L. H., & Shenck, H. H., Jr. Inappropriate behavior as a function of the energizing effect of drive. *J. Pers.*, 1961, **29**, 489–498.

Broen, W. E., Jr., Storms, L. H., & Goldberg, D. H. Decreased discrimination as a function of increased drive. *J. abnorm. soc. Psychol.*, 1963, **67**, 266–273.

Brown, J. S. The generalization of approach responses as a function of stimulus intensity and strength of motivation. *J. comp. Psychol.*, 1942, **33**, 209–226.

Brown, J. S. Gradients of approach and avoidance responses and their relation to level of motivation. *J. comp. physiol. Psychol.*, 1948, **41**, 450–466.

Brown, J. S., Bilodeau, E. A., & Baron, M. R. Bidirectional gradients in the strength of a generalized voluntary response to stimuli on a visual spatial dimension. *J. exp. Psychol.*, 1951, **41**, 52–61.

Brown, J. S., Clarke, F. R., & Stein, L. A new technique for studying spatial generalization with voluntary responses. *J. exp. Psychol.*, 1958, **55**, 359–362.

Brown, J. S. Generalization and discrimination. In D. Mostofsky (Ed.), *Stimulus generalization*. Stanford, Calif.: Stanford Univer. Press, 1965.

Brush, F. R., Bush, R. R., Jenkins, W. O., John, W. F., & Whiting, J. W. M. Stimulus generalization after extinction and punishment: An experimental study of displacement. *J. abnorm. soc. Psychol.*, 1952, **47**, 633–640.

Bush, R. R., & Mosteller, F. A model for stimulus generalization and discrimination. *Psychol. Rev.*, 1951, **58**, 413–423.

Buss, A. H. A study of concept formation as a function of reinforcement and stimulus generalization. *J. exp. Psychol.*, 1950, **40**, 494–503.

Buss, A. H., & Daniel, E. F. Stimulus generalization and schizophrenia. *J. abn. Psychol.*, 1967, **72**, 50–53.

Butter, C. M. Stimulus generalization along one and two dimensions in pigeons. *J. exp. Psychol.*, 1963, **65**, 339–346.

Butter, C. M., & Guttman, N. Stimulus generalization and discrimination along the dimension of angular orientation. *Amer. Psychologist*, 1957, **12**, 449 (Abstract).

Butter, C. M., Mishkin, M., & Rosvold, H. E. Stimulus generalization in monkeys with inferatemporal lesions and lateral occipital lesions. In D. Mostofsky (Ed.), *Stimulus generalization*. Stanford, Calif.: Stanford Univer. Press, 1965.

Caronite, S. C., Levis, D. J., & Thomas, D. R. Color naming and color generalization. Paper presented at Midwestern Psychol. Assn., May, 1963.

Caronite, S. C., & Thomas, D. R. Stimulus generalization of a positive conditioned reinforcer: III. The new learning method. *J. exp. Psychol.*, 1966, **71**, 385–388.

Carterette, T. S. An application of stimulus theory to summated generalization. *J. exp. Psychol.*, 1961, **62**, 448–455.

Chase, S. The effect of discrimination training on the development of stimulus control by single dimensions of a compound stimulus. Unpublished doctoral dissertation, City Univer. of N.Y., 1966.

Coate, W. B. Effect of deprivation on postdiscrimination stimulus generalization in the rat. *J. comp. physiol. Psychol.*, 1964, **57**, 134–138.

Cofer, C. N., Janis, M., & Rowell, M. M. Mediated generalization and the interpretation of verbal behavior: III. Experimental study of antonym gradients. *J. exp. Psychol.*, 1943, **32**, 266–269.

Cofoid, D. A., & Honig, W. K. Stimulus generalization of imprinting. *Science*, 1961, **134**, 1692–1694.

Dickson, J. F., Jr., & Thomas, D. R. Operant discrimination learning and stimulus generalization as a function of reward exposure. *J. comp. physiol. Psychol.*, 1963, **56**, 829–833.

Dinsmoor, J. A. The effect of hunger on discriminated responding. *J. abn. soc. Psychol.*, 1952, **47**, 67–72.

Dollard, J., & Miller, N. E. *Personality and psychotherapy*. New York: McGraw-Hill, 1950.

Dorfman, D. D. Some effect of drive on the perceived intensity of a stimulus. Unpublished doctoral dissertation, University of Michigan, 1961.

Duncan, C. R. Stimulus generalization and spread of effect. *Amer. J. Psychol.*, 1951, **64**, 585–590.

Dunn, W. L. Visual discrimination of schizophrenic subjects as a function of stimulus meaning. *J. Pers.*, 1954, **25**, 48–64.

Eisen, N. H. The influence of set on semantic generalization. *J. abn. soc. Psychol.*, 1954, **49**, 491–496.

Elliot, M. H. The effect of change in drive on maze performance. *Univ. Calif. Publ. Psychol.*, 1929, **4**, 185–188.

Eriksen, C. W. Some personality correlates of stimulus generalization under stress. *J. abnorm. soc. Psychol.*, 1954, **49**, 561–565.

Estes, W. K. Toward a statistical theory of learning. *Psychol. Rev.*, 1950, **57**, 94–107.

Estes, W. K. Stimulus-response theory of drive. In M. R. Jones (Ed.) *Nebraska symposium on motivation*: Vol. VI. Lincoln: Univer. Nebraska Press, 1958.

Estes, W. K. The statistical approach to learning theory. In S. Koch (Ed.) *Psychology: A study of a science* (Vol. 2). New York: McGraw-Hill, 1959.

Fager, R. E., & Knopf, I. J. Relationship of manifest anxiety to stimulus generalization. *J. abn. soc. Psychol.*, 1958, **57**, 125–126.

Farmer, J., Schoenfeld, W. N., & Harris, A. H. Generalization gradients from "reaction time" on latencies of the white rat to visual brightness. *Psychon. Sci.*, 1966, **4**, 23–24.

Fink, J. B., & Davis, R. C. Generalization of a muscle action potential response to tonal duration. *J. exp. Psychol.*, 1951, **42**, 403–408.

Fink, J. B., & Patton, R. M. Decrement of a learned drinking response accompanying changes in several stimulus characteristics. *J. comp. physiol. Psychol.*, 1953, **46**, 23–27.

Fishbein, H. D., Shackney, C., & Sinclair, D. A stimulus generalization explanation of the serial position effect. *Psychon. Sci.*, 1965, **3**, 563–564.

Foley, J. P., & Cofer, C. N. Mediated generalization and the interpretation of verbal behavior: II. Experimental study of certain homophone and synonym gradients., *J. exp. Psychol.*, 1943, **32**, 168–175.

Frick, G. C. An analysis of operant discrimination. *J. Psychol.*, 1948, **26**, 93–123.

Friedman, H. Wavelength generalization as a function of spacing of test stimuli. *J. exp. Psychol.*, 1963, **65**, 334–338.

Friedman, H., & Guttman, N. Further analysis of the various effects of discrimination training upon stimulus generalization. In D. Mostofsky (Ed.), *Stimulus generalization.* Stanford, Calif.: Stanford Univer. Press, 1965.

Ganz, L. Hue generalization and hue discrimination in *Macaca Mulatta. J. exp. Psychol.*, 1962, **64**, 142–150.

Ganz, L. Effect of an anchor stimulus on the stimulus generalization gradient. *J. exp. Psychol.*, 1963, **65**, 270–279.

Ganz, L. An analysis of generalization behavior in the stimulus deprived organism. In G. Newton and S. Levine (Eds.), *Early experience and behavior.* Springfield, Ill.: Charles C. Thomas, 1968.

Ganz, L., & Riesen, A. H. Stimulus generalization to hue in the darkreared macaque. *J. comp. physiol. Psychol.*, 1962, **55**, 92–99.

Garmezy, N. Stimulus differentiation by schizophrenic and normal subjects under conditions of reward and punishment. *J. Pers.*, 1952, **20**, 253–276.

Geldard, F. A. *The human senses.* New York: Wiley, 1953.

Gewirtz, J. L., Jones, L. V., & Waerneryd, K. Stimulus units and range of experienced stimuli as determinants of generalization discrimination gradients. *J. exp. Psychol.*, 1956, **52**, 51–57.

Gibson, E. J. Sensory generalization with voluntary reactions. *J. exp. Psychol.*, 1939, **24**, 237–253.

Gibson, E. J. A systematic application of the concepts of generalization and differentiation to verbal learning. *Psychol. Rev.*, 1940, **47**, 196–229.

Gibson, E. J. Retroactive inhibition as a function of degree of generalization between tasks. *J. exp. Psychol.*, 1941, **28**, 93–115.

Gibson, E. J. Intra-list generalization as a factor in verbal learning. *J. exp. Psychol.*, 1942, **30**, 185–200.

Gibson, E. J. A re-examination of generalization. *Psychol. Rev.*, 1959, **66**, 340–342.

Grandine, L., & Harlow, H. F. Generalization of the characteristics of a single learned stimulus by monkeys. *J. comp. physiol. Psychol.*, 1948, **41**, 327–339.

Grant, D. A., & Dittmer, D. G. An experimental investigation of Pavlov's cortical irradiation hypothesis. *J. exp. Psychol.*, 1940, **26**, 299–310.

Grant, D. A., & Schiller, J. J. Generalization of the conditioned galvanic skin response to visual stimuli. *J. exp. Psychol.*, 1953, **46**, 309–313.

Gray, J. A. Stimulus intensity dynamism. *Psychol. Bull.*, 1965, **63**, 180–196.

Grice, G. R. The acquisition of a visual discrimination habit following response to a single stimulus. *J. exp. Psychol.*, 1948, **38**, 633–642.

Grice, G. R. Investigations of response-mediated generalization. In D. Mostofsky (Ed.), *Stimulus Generalization.* Stanford, Calif.: Stanford Univer. Press, 1965.

Grice, G. R., & Davis, J. D. Mediated stimulus equivalence and distinctiveness in human conditioning. *J. exp. Psychol.*, 1958, **55**, 565–571.

Grice, G. R., & Hunter, J. J. Stimulus intensity effects depend upon the type of experimental design. *Psychol. Rev.*, 1964, **71**, 247–256.

Grice, G. R., Masters, L., & Kohfeld, D. L. Classical conditioning without discrimination training: A test of the generalization theory of CS intensity effects. *J. exp. Psychol.*, 1966, **72**, 510–513.

Grice, G. R., & Saltz, E. The generalization of an instrumental response to stimuli varying in the size dimension. *J. exp. Psychol.*, 1950, **40**, 702–708.

Guilford, J. P. *Psychometric methods.* New York: McGraw-Hill, 1936.

Guthrie, E. R. Conditioning as a principle of learning. *Psychol. Rev.*, 1930, **37**, 412–428.

Guthrie, E. R. *The Psychology of Learning,* New York: Harper & Row, 1935.

Guttman, N. The pigeon and the Spectrum

and other perplexities. *Psychol. Rep.*, 1956, **2**, 449–460.

Guttman, N. Generalization gradients around stimuli associated with different reinforcement schedules. *J. exp. Psychol.*, 1959, **58**, 335–340.

Guttman, N. Laws of behavior and facts of perception. In S. Koch (Ed.), *Psychology: A study of a Science*, (Vol. 5) New York: McGraw-Hill, 1963.

Guttman, N., & Kalish, H. I. Discriminability and stimulus generalization. *J. exp. Psychol.*, 1956, **51**, 79–88.

Guttman, N., & Kalish, H. I. Experiments in discrimination. *Sci. Amer.*, 1958, **198**, 77–82.

Gynther, M. D. Differential eyelid conditioning as a function of stimulus similarity and strength of response to the CS. *J. exp. Psychol.*, 1957, **53**, 408–416.

Haber, A., & Kalish, H. I. Prediction of discrimination from generalization after variations in schedule of reinforcement. *Science*, 1963, **142**, 412–413.

Hake, H. W., Grant, D. A., & Hornseth, J. P. Generalization and discrimination in the conditioned eyelid response to sound stimuli. *Amer. Psychologist*, 1948, **3**, 361 (Abstract).

Hamilton, W. F., & Coleman, T. B. Trichromatic vision in the pigeon as illustrated by the spectral hue discrimination curve. *J. comp. Psychol.*, 1933, **15**, 183–191.

Hanson, H. M. Effects of discrimination training on stimulus generalization. *J. exp. Psychol.*, 1959, **58**, 321–334.

Hanson, H. M. Stimulus generalization following three-stimulus discrimination training. *J. comp. physiol. Psychol.*, 1961, **54**, 181–185.

Harlow, H. F. The formation of learning sets. *Psychol. Rev.*, 1949, **56**, 51–65.

Healey, A. F. Compound stimuli, drive strength and primary stimulus generalization. *J. exp. Psychol.*, 1965, **69**, 536–538.

Hearst, E. Approach, avoidance and stimulus generalization. In D. Mostofsky (Ed.), *Stimulus generalization*. Stanford, Calif.: Stanford Univer. Press, 1965.

Hearst, E., & Koresko, M. B. Stimulus generalization and amount of prior training on variable-interval reinforcement.

J. comp. physiol. Psychol., 1968, **66**, 133–138.

Hearst, E., Koresko, M. B., & Poppen, R. Stimulus generalization and the response-reinforcement contingency. *J. exp. Anal. Behav.*, 1964, **7**, 369–380.

Hearst, E., & Poppen, R. Steepened generalization gradients after massed extinction to the CS. *Psychon. Sci.*, 1965, **2**, 83–84.

Heathers, G. L., & Arakelian, P. The relationship between strength of drive and rate of extinction of bar-pressing reaction in the rat. *J. gen. Psychol.*, 1942, **24**, 243–248.

Heinemann, E. G., & Rudolph, R. L. The effect of discriminative training on the gradient of stimulus generalization. *Amer. J. Psychol.*, 1963, **76**, 653–658.

Heinemann, E. G., Chase, S., & Mandell, C. Discrimination control of "attention." *Science*, 1968, **160**, 553–554.

Helson, H. Adaptation-level as a frame of reference for prediction of psychophysical data. *Amer. J. Psychol.*, 1947, 60, 1–29.

Helson, H. Adaptation-level as a basis for a quantitative theory of frames of reference. *Psychol. Rev.*, 1948, **55**, 297–313.

Helson, H. Adaptation level theory. In S. Koch (Ed.), *Psychology: A study of a science*. Vol. 1. New York: McGraw-Hill, 1959, pp 565–621.

Helson, H., & Avant, L. L. Stimulus generalization as a function of contextual stimuli. *J. exp. Psychol.*, 1967, **73**, 565–567.

Herbert, J. A., & Krantz, D. L. Transposition: A re-evaluation. *Psychol. Bull.*, 1965, **63**, 244–257.

Hilgard, E. R., Jones, L. V., & Kaplan, S. J. Conditioned discrimination as related to anxiety. *J. exp. Psychol.*, 1951, **42**, 94–99.

Hind, J. E., Rose, J. E., Davies, P. W., Woolsey, C. N., Benjamin, R. M., Welker, W. I., & Thompson, R. F. Unit activity in the auditory cortex. In G. L. Rasmussen & W. F. Windle (Eds.), *Neural mechanisms of the auditory and vestibular mechanisms*. Springfield, Ill.: C. C. Thomas, 1961.

Hiss, R. H., & Thomas, D. R. Stimulus generalization as a function of testing procedure and response measure. *J. exp. Psychol.*, 1963, **65**, 587–592.

Hoffman, H. S., & Fleshler, M. Stimulus aspects of aversive controls: stimulus generalization of conditional suppression following discrimination training. *J. exp. Anal. Behav.*, 1964, **7**, 233–239.

Hoffman, H. S., Selekman, W. L., & Fleshler, M. Stimulus factors in aversive controls: Conditioned suppression after equal training on two stimuli. *J. exp. Anal. Behav.*, 1966, **9**, 649–653.

Honig, W. K. Generalization of extinction on the spectral continuum. *Psychol. Rec.*, 1961, **11**, 269–278.

Honig, W. K. Prediction of preference, transposition, and transposition-reversal from the generalization gradient. *J. exp. Psychol.*, 1962, **64**, 239–248.

Honig, W. K. Discrimination generalization, and transfer on the basis of stimulus differences. In D. Mostofsky (Ed.), *Stimulus generalization*. Stanford, Calif.: Stanford Univer. Press, 1965.

Honig, W. K. The effects of irrelevant discrimination training on the slope of a generalization gradient. Paper presented at Eastern Psychol. Assn., April, 1965.

Honig, W. K., Boneau, C. A., Burstein, K. R., & Pennypacker, H. S. Positive and negative generalization gradients obtained after equivalent training conditions. *J. comp. physiol. Psychol.*, 1963, **56**, 111–116.

Honig, W. K., & Shaw, J. The bisection of spectral intervals by pigeons: a first attempt. Unpublished manuscript, 1962.

Honig, W. K., & Slivka, R. M. Stimulus generalization of the effects of punishment. *J. exp. Anal. Behav.*, 1964, **7**, 21–25.

Honig, W. K., Thomas, D. R., & Guttman, N. Differential effects of continuous extinction and discrimination training on the generalization gradient. *J. exp. Psychol.*, 1959, **58**, 145–152.

Hoving, K. L. Influence of type of discrimination training on generalization. *J. exp. Psychol.*, 1963, **66**, 514–520.

Hovland, C. I. The generalization of conditioned responses: I. The sensory generalization of conditioned responses with varying frequencies of tone. *J. gen. Psychol.*, 1937a, **17**, 125–148.

Hovland, C. I. The generalization of conditioned responses. II. The sensory generalization of conditioned responses with varying intensities of tone. *J. genet. Psychol.*, 1937b, **51**, 279–291.

Hovland, C. I. The generalization of conditioned responses. III. Extinction, spontaneous recovery, and disinhibition of conditioned and of generalized responses. 1937c, *J. exp. Psychol.*, **21**, 47–62.

Hovland, C. I. The generalization of conditioned responses: IV. The effects of varying amounts of reinforcement upon the degree of generalization of conditioned responses. *J. exp. Psychol.*, 1937d, **21**, 261–276.

Hull, C. L. The problem of stimulus equivalence in behavior theory. *Psychol. Rev.*, 1939, **46**, 9–30.

Hull, C. L. *Principles of behavior.* New York: Appleton-Century-Crofts, 1943.

Hull, C. L. The problem of primary stimulus generalization. *Psychol. Rev.*, 1947, **54**, 120–134.

Hull, C. L. Stimulus intensity dynamism (V) and stimulus generalization. *Psychol. Rev.*, 1949, **56**, 67–76.

Hull, C. L. Simple qualitative discrimination learning. *Psychol. Rev.*, 1950, **57**, 303–313.

Hull, C. L. *Essentials of Behavior.* New Haven: Yale Univer. Press, 1951.

Hull, C. L. *A Behavior System.* New Haven: Yale Univer. Press, 1952.

Humphreys, L. G. Generalization as a function of method of reinforcement. *J. exp. Psychol.*, 1939, **25**, 361–372.

James, H. An application of Helson's theory of adaptation level to the problem of transposition. *Psychol. Rev.*, 1953, **60**, 345–352.

Jaynes, J. Imprinting: The interaction of learned and innate behavior: I. Development and generalization. *J. comp. physiol. Psychol.*, 1956, **49**, 201–206.

Jaynes, J. Imprinting: The interaction of learned and innate behavior: IV. Generalization and emergent discrimination. *J. comp. physiol. Psychol.*, 1958, **51**, 238–242.

Jenkins, H. M. Generalization gradients and the concept of inhibition. In D. Mostofsky (Ed.), *Stimulus Generaliza-*

tion. Stanford, Calif.: Stanford Univer. Press, 1965.

Jenkins, H. M., & Harrison, R. H. Auditory generalization in the pigeon, 1958. Washington: Air Research and Development Command. TN No. 58–443: Astia Document No. 158248.

Jenkins, H. M., & Harrison, R. H. Effect of discrimination training on auditory generalization. *J. exp. Psychol.*, 1960, **59**, 246–253.

Jenkins, H. M., & Harrison, R. H. Generalization gradients of inhibition following auditory discrimination training. *J. exp. Anal. Behav.*, 1962, **5**, 435–441.

Jenkins, W. O., Pascal, G. R., & Walker, R. W., Jr. Deprivation and generalization. *J. exp. Psychol.*, 1958, **56**, 274–277.

John, E. R. Some speculations on the psychophysiology of mind. In J. Scher (Ed.), *Toward a definition of mind.* New York: The Free Press, 1960.

John, E. R. High nervous functions (brain functions and learning). *Ann. Rev. Physiol.* Stanford, Calif.: Annual Reviews, Inc., 1961.

John, E. R. Neural mechanisms of decision making. In Fields, W. S. & Abbott, W. (Eds.), *Information storage and neural control.* Springfield, Ill.: C. C. Thomas, 1963.

John, E. R., & Killam, K. F. Electrophysiological correlates of avoidance conditioning in the cat, *J. pharm. exp. Therap.*, 1959, **125**, 252–274.

John, E. R., & Killam, K. F. Studies o electrical activity of brain during differential conditioning in cats. In J. Wortis (Ed.), *Recent Advances in Biological Psychiatry.* New York: Grune and Stratton, 1960.

Johnsgard, K. W. The role of contrast in stimulus intensity dynamism (V). *J. exp. Psychol.*, 1957, **53**, 173–179.

Kalish, H. I. The relationship between discriminability and stimulus generalization: A re-evaluation. *J. exp. Psychol.*, 1958, **55**, 637–644.

Kalish, H. I., & Guttman, N. Stimulus generalization after equal training on two stimuli. *J. exp. Psychol.*, 1957, **53**, 139–144.

Kalish, H. I., & Guttman, N. Stimulus generalization after training on three stimuli: a test of the summation hypothesis. *J. exp. Psychol.*, 1959, **57**, 268–272.

Kalish, H. I., & Haber, A. Generality of stimulus generalization. *Psychol. Rep.*, 1962, **11**, 741–746.

Kalish, H. I., & Haber, A. Generalization: I. generalization gradients from single and multiple stimulus points. II. Generalization of inhibition. *J. exp. Psychol.*, 1963, **65**, 176–181.

Kalish, H. I., & Haber, A. The prediction of discrimination from generalization following variations in deprivation level. *J. comp. physiol. Psychol.*, 1965, **60**, 125–128.

Kendler, Tracy S. An experimental investigation of transposition as a function of the difference between training and test stimuli. *J. exp. Psychol.*, 1950, **40**, 552–562.

Kimble, G. H. *Hilgard and Marquis' Conditioning and Learning.* New York: Appleton-Century-Crofts, 1961.

Kirschner, D. Differences in gradients of stimulus generalization as a function of "abstract" and "concrete" attitude. *J. consult. Psychol.*, 1964, **28**, 160–164.

Kling, J. W. Generalization of extinction of an instrumental response to stimuli varying in the size dimension. *J. exp. Psychol.*, 1952, **44**, 339–346.

Krasnogorsky, N. I. Studies upon central inhibition and upon the localization of the tactile and motor analyzers in the cortex of the dog. Thesis, Petrograd, 1911. In I. P. Pavlov, *Conditioned reflexes.* Oxford Univer. Press, 1927.

Kuenne, Margaret R. Experimental investigation of the relation of language to transposition behavior in young children. *J. exp. Psychol.*, 1946, **36**, 471–490.

LaBerge, D., & Martin, D. R. An analysis of summated generalization. *J. exp. Psychol.*, 1964, **68**, 71–79.

Landau, J. A developmental investigation of stimulus generalization. Unpublished doctoral dissertation, 1965, City Univer. of N.Y.

Lashley, K. S. An examination of the "continuity theory" as applied to discriminative learning. *J. gen. Psychol.*, 1942, **26**, 241–265.

Lashley, K. S., & Wade, M. The Pavlovian theory of generalization. *Psychol. Rev.*, 1946, **53**, 72–87.

Lawrence, D. H. Acquired distinctiveness of cues: II. Selective association in a constant stimulus situation. *J. exp. Psychol.*, 1950, **40**, 175–188.

Lawrence, D. H. The applicability of generalization gradients to the transfer of a discrimination. *J. gen. Psychol.*, 1955, **52**, 37–48.

Lawrence, D. H., & De Rivera, J. Evidence for relational transposition. *J. comp. physiol. Psychol.*, 1954, **47**, 471–475.

Littman, R. A. Conditioned generalization of the galvanic skin response to tones. *J. exp. Psychol.*, 1949, **39**, 868–882.

Logan, F. W. A note on stimulus intensity dynamism (V). *Psychol. Rev.*, 1954, **61**, 77–80.

London, P. Developmental aspects of discrimination in relation to adjustment. *Genet. Psychol. Monogr.*, 1958, **57**, 293–336.

Loucks, R. B. An appraisal of Pavlov's systematization of behavior from the experimental standpoint. *J. comp. Psychol.*, 1933, **15**, 1–47.

Luce, R. D., & Edwards, W. The derivation of subjective scales from just noticeable differences. *Psychol. Rev.*, 1957, **64**, 153–181.

Lumsdaine, A. A. Conditioned eyelid responses as mediating generalized conditioned finger reactions. *Psychol. Bull.*, 1939, **36**, 650.

MacCaslin, E. F. Successive and simultaneous discrimination as a function of stimulus-similarity. *Amer. J. Psychol.*, 1954, **67**, 308–314.

Mackintosh, N. J. Selective attention in animal discrimination learning. *Psychol. Bull.*, 1965, **64**, 124–150.

Margolius, G. Stimulus generalization of an instrumental response as a function of the number of reinforced trials. *J. exp. Psychol.*, 1955, **49**, 105–111.

Marsh, G. D. The inverse relationship between discriminability and stimulus generalization as a function of the number of test stimuli. *J. comp. physiol. Psychol.*, 1967, **64**, 284–289.

Mednick, M. T. Mediated generalization and the incubation effect as a function of

manifest anxiety. *J. abnorm. soc. Psychol.*, 1957, **55**, 315–321.

Mednick, S. A. Distortions in the gradient of stimulus generalization related to cortical brain damage and schizophrenia. *J. abnorm. soc. Psychol.*, 1955, **51**, 536–542.

Mednick, S. A. Generalization as a function of manifest anxiety and adaptation to psychological experiments. *J. consult. Psychol.*, 1957, **21**, 491–494.

Mednick, S. A. A learning theory approach to research in schizophrenia. *Psychol. Bull.*, 1958, **55**, 316–327.

Mednick, S. A., & Freedman, J. L. Stimulus generalization. *Psychol. Bull.*, 1960, **57**, 169–200.

Mednick, S. A., & Lehtinen, L. F. Stimulus generalization as a function of age in children. *J. exp. Psychol.*, 1957, **53**, 180–183.

Meehl, P. E., & MacCorquodale, K. Drive conditioning as a factor in latent learning. *J. exp. Psychol.*, 1953, **45**, 20–24.

Miller, N. E. Experimental studies of conflict. In J. McV. Hunt. (Ed.), *Personality and the behavior disorders*. New York: Ronald Press, 1944.

Miller, N. E. Theory and experiment relating psychoanalytic displacement to stimulus-response generalization. *J. abnorm. soc. Psychol.*, 1948, **43**, 155–178.

Miller, N. E., & Kraeling, Doris. Displacement: Greater generalization of approach than avoidance in generalized approach-avoidance conflict. *J. exp. Psychol.*, 1952, **43**, 217–221.

Miller, W. C., & Greene, J. E. Generalization of an avoidance response to varying intensities of sound. *J. comp. physiol. Psychol.*, 1954, **47**, 136–139.

Murray, E. J., & Miller, N. E. Displacement: Steeper gradient of generalization of avoidance than of approach with age of habit controlled. *J. exp. Psychol.*, 1952, **43**, 222–226.

Murray, H. G., & Kohfeld, D. L. Role of adaptation level in stimulus intensity dynamism. *Psychon. Sci.*, 1965, **3**, 439–440.

Muntz, W. R. A. Stimulus generalization and the "units hypothesis" in Octopus. *J. comp. physiol. Psychol.*, 1965, **59**, 144–146.

Newman, F. L., & Baron, M. R. Stimulus generalization along the dimension of angularity. *J. comp. physiol. Psychol.*, 1965, **60**, 59–63.

Newman, J. R. Stimulus generalization of an instrumental response as a function of drive strength. Unpublished doctoral dissertation. Univer. of Illinois, 1955.

Newman, J. R., & Grice, R. G. Stimulus generalization as a function of drive level and the relation between two measures of response strength. *J. exp. Psychol.*, 1965, **69**, 357–362.

Olson, G., & King, R. A. Supplementary report: stimulus generalization gradients along a luminosity continuum. *J. exp. Psychol.*, 1962, **63**, 414–415.

Osgood, C. E. *Method and theory in experimental psychology.* New York: Oxford Univer. Press, 1953.

Passey, G. E., & Herman, P. N. The shape of the discrimination gradient for two intracontinuum stimulus separations. *J. exp. Psychol.*, 1955, **49**, 273–277.

Pavlov, I. P. *Conditioned reflexes.* New York: Oxford Univer. Press, 1927.

Perkins, C. C., Jr. The relation between conditioned stimulus intensity and response strength. *J. exp. Psychol.*, 1953, **46**, 225–231.

Perkins, C. C., Jr., Hershberger, W. A., & Weyant, R. G. Difficulty of a discrimination as a determiner of subsequent generalization along another dimension. *J. exp. Psychol.*, 1959, **57**, 181–185.

Perkins, C. C., Jr., & Weyant, R. G. The interval between training and test trials as a determiner of the slope of generalization gradients. *J. comp. physiol. Psychol.*, 1958, **51**, 596–600.

Peterson, N. Effect of monochromatic rearing on the control of responding by wavelength. *Science*, 1962, **136**, 774–775.

Phillip, B. R. Effect of length of series upon generalization and central tendency in discrimination of a series of stimuli. *Canad. J. Psychol.*, 1952, **6**, 173–178.

Phillips, L. W. Mediated verbal similarity as a determinant of the generalization of a conditioned GSR. *J. exp. Psychol.*, 1958, **55**, 56–61.

Pierrel, R., & Sherman, J. G. Generalization of auditory intensity following dis-crimination training. *J. exp. Anal. Behav.*, 1960, **3**, 313–322.

Pierrel, R., Sherman, J. G., & Fischman, M. W. Generalization as a function of small amounts of discrimination training. *J. exp. Anal. Behav.*, 1963, **6**, 545–548.

Platz, A. Some effects of conditioned fear on stimulus generalization. Unpublished doctoral dissertation, Univer. of Michigan, 1962.

Porter, J. J. Stimulus generalization as a function of UCS intensity in eyelid conditioning. *J. exp. Psychol.*, 1962, **64**, 311–313.

Prokasy, W. J., & Hull, J. F. Primary stimulus generalization. *Psychol. Rev.*, 1963, **70**, 310–322.

Raben, M. W. The white rat's discrimination of differences in intensity of illumination measured by a running response. *J. comp. physiol. Psychol.*, 1949, **42**, 254–272.

Randall, W. L. Generalization after frequency discrimination in cats with central nervous system lesions. In D. Mostofsky (Ed.), *Stimulus generalization.* Stanford, Calif.: Stanford Univer. Press, 1965.

Ray, B. A. The course of acquisition of a line-tilt discrimination by Rhesus monkeys. *J. exp. Anal. Behav.*, 1967, **10**, 17–33.

Razran, G. H. S. Stimulus generalization of conditioned responses. *Psychol. Bull.*, 1949, **46**, 337–365.

Reinhold, D. B., & Perkins, C. C., Jr. Stimulus generalization following different methods of training. *J. exp. Psychol.*, 1955, **49**, 423–427.

Reiss, B. F. Genetic changes in semantic conditioning. *J. exp. Psychol.*, 1946, **36**, 143–152.

Restle, F. A. Theory of discrimination learning. *Psychol. Rev.*, 1955, **62**, 11–19.

Restle, F. A cognitive interpretation of intensity effects in stimulus generalization. *Psychol. Rev.*, 1964, **71**, 514–516.

Reynolds, G. S. Behavioral contrast. *J. exp. Anal. Behav.*, 1961a, **4**, 57–71.

Reynolds, G. S. Contrast, generalization, and the process of discrimination. *J. exp. Anal. Behav.*, 1961b, **4**, 289–294.

Reynolds, G. S. Attention in the pigeon. *J. exp. Anal. Behav.*, 1961c, **4**, 203–208.

Richard, J. F. Influence of response discriminability on stimulus discriminability. *J. exp. Psychol.*, 1965, **69**, 30–34.

Riley, D. A. The nature of the effective stimulus in animal discrimination learning: transposition reconsidered. *Psychol. Rev.*, 1958, **65**, 1–7.

Riley, D. A., Ring, K., & Thomas, J. The effect of stimulus comparison on discrimination learning and transposition. *J. comp. physiol. Psychol.*, 1960, **54**, 415–421.

Rodnick, E. H., & Garmezy, N. An experimental approach to the study of motivation in schizophrenia. In M. R. Jones (Ed.), *Nebraska Symposium in Motivation*, Vol. V. Lincoln: Univer. Nebraska Press, 1957.

Rosenbaum, G. Temporal gradients of response strength with two levels of motivation. *J. exp. Psychol.*, 1951, **41**, 261–267.

Rosenbaum, G. Stimulus generalization as a function of level of experimentally induced anxiety. *J. exp. Psychol.*, 1953, **45**, 35–43.

Schilder, P. The psychology of schizophrenia. *Psychoanal. Rev.*, 1939, **26**, 380–398.

Schlosberg, H., & Solomon, R. L. Latency of response in a choice discrimination. *J. exp. Psychol.*, 1943, **33**, 22–39.

Schumsky, D. A. Relationship between generalization and discrimination: Training and the definition of response. *J. exp. Psychol.*, 1964, **68**, 470–476.

Shepard, R. N. Stimulus and response generalization: Deduction of the generalization gradient from a trace model. *Psychol. Rev.*, 1958, **65**, 242–256.

Shepard, R. N. Approximation to uniform gradients of generalization by monotone transformations of the scale. In D. Mostofsky (Ed.), *Stimulus Generalization*. Stanford, Calif.: Stanford Univer. Press, 1965.

Sherman, J. G., & Pierrel, R. Generalization of auditory intensity as a function of amount of discrimination training. *J. exp. Anal. Behav.*, 1961, **4**, 237–241.

Sidman, M. By-products of aversive control *J. exp. Anal. Behav.*, 1958, **1**, 265–280.

Sidman, M. Stimulus generalization in an avoidance situation. *J. exp. Anal. Behav.*, 1961, **4**, 157–169.

Skinner, B. F. Are theories of learning necessary? *Psychol. Rev.*, 1950, **44**, 430–444.

Skinner, B. F. *Science and human behavior.* New York: Macmillan, 1953.

Sloane, H. N., Jr. Stimulus generalization along a light flicker rate continuum after discrimination training with several S−'s. *J. exp. Anal. Behav.*, 1964, **7**, 217–221.

Spence, K. W. The nature of discrimination learning in animals. *Psychol. Rev.*, 1936, **43**, 427–449.

Spence, K. W. The differential response in animals to stimuli varying within a single dimension. *Psychol. Rev.*, 1937, **44**, 430–444.

Spence, K. W. Failure of transposition in size-discrimination of chimpanzees. *Amer. J. Psychol.*, 1941, **54**, 223–229.

Spence, K. W. The basis of solution by chimpanzees of the intermediate size problem. *J. exp. Psychol.*, 1942, **31**, 257–271.

Spence, K. W. *Behavior theory and conditioning.* New Haven: Yale Univer. Press, 1956.

Spiker, C. C. The effects of number of reinforcements on the strength of a generalized instrumental response. *Child Developm.*, 1956a, **27**, 37–44.

Spiker, C. C. The stimulus generalization gradient as a function of the intensity of stimulus lights. *Child Developm.*, 1956b, **27**, 85–97.

Spiker, C. C. Effects of stimulus similarity on discrimination learning. *J. exp. Psychol.*, 1956c, **51**, 393–395.

Stevens, S. S. On the uses of poikilitic functions. In D. Mostofsky (Ed.), *Stimulus generalization.* Stanford, Calif.: Stanford Univer. Press, 1965.

Stevenson, H. W., & Bitterman, M. E. The distance-effect in the transposition of intermediate size by children. *Amer. J. Psychol.*, 1955, **68**, 274–279.

Storms, L. H., & Broen, W. E., Jr. Drive theories and stimulus generalization. *Psychol. Rev.*, 1966, **73**, 113–127.

Switalski, R. W., Lyons, J., & Thomas, D. R. The effects of inter-dimensional training on stimulus generalization. *J. exp. Psychol.*, 1966, **72**, 661–666.

Tempone, V. J. Stimulus generalization as

a function of mental age. *Child Development*, 1965, **36**, 229–235.

Terrace, H. S. Errorless transfer of a discrimination across two continua. *J. exp. Anal. Behav.*, 1963a, **6**, 223–232.

Terrace, H. S. Discrimination learning without errors. *J. exp. Anal. Behav.*, 1963b, **6**, 1–27.

Terrace, H. S. Wavelength generalization after discrimination learning with and without errors. *Science*, 1964, **144**, 78–80.

Terrace, H. S. Stimulus control. In W. K. Honig (Ed.), *Operant behavior: Areas of research and application*. New York: Appleton-Century-Crofts, 1966a.

Terrace, H. S. Behavioral contrast and the peak shift: Effect of extended discrimination training. *J. exp. Anal. Behav.*, 1966b, **9**, 613–617.

Terrace, H. S. Discrimination learning and inhibition. *Science*, 1966c, **154**, 1677–1680.

Thomas, D. R. Stimulus generalization as a problem viewed in perception. *Amer. Psychologist*, 1961, **16**, 430 (Abstract).

Thomas, D. R. The effects of drive and discrimination training on stimulus generalization. *J. exp. Psychol.*, 1962, **64**, 24–28.

Thomas, D. R., & Bistey, G. Stimulus generalization as a function of the number and range of generalization test stimuli. *J. exp. Psychol.*, 1964, **68**, 599–602.

Thomas, D. R., & Caronite, S. C. Stimulus generalization of a positive conditioned reinforcer: II. The effects of discrimination training. *J. exp. Psychol.* 1964, **68**, 402–406.

Thomas, D. R., & De Capito, A. The role of stimulus labeling in stimulus generalization. *J. exp. Psychol.*, 1966, **71**, 913–915.

Thomas, D. R., & Hiss, N. H. A test of the units hypothesis employing wavelength generalization in human subjects. *J. exp. Psychol.*, 1963, **65**, 59–62.

Thomas, D. R., & Jones, C. G. Stimulus generalization as a function of the frame of reference. *J. exp. Psychol.*, 1962, **64**, 77–80.

Thomas, D. R., & King, R. A. Stimulus generalization as a function of level of motivation. *J. exp. Psychol.*, 1959, **57**, 323–328.

Thomas, D. R., & Lopez, L. J. The effects of delayed testing on generalization slope. *J. exp. Psychol.*, 1962, **55**, 541–544.

Thomas, D. R., & Mitchell, K. The role of instructions and stimulus categorizing in a measure of stimulus generalization. *J. exp. Anal. Behav.*, 1962, **5**, 275–381.

Thomas, D. R., Ost, J., & Thomas, Doris H. Stimulus generalization as a function of the time between training and testing procedures. *J. exp. Anal. Behav.*, 1960, **3**, 9–14.

Thomas, D. R., & Switalski, R. W. Comparison of stimulus generalization following variable-ratio and variable interval training. *J. exp. Psychol.*, 1966, **71**, 236–240.

Thomas, D. R., & Williams, J. L. Stimulus generalization of a positive conditioned reinforcer. *Science*, 1963, **141**, 172–173.

Thompson, R. Transposition in the white rat as a function of stimulus comparison. *J. exp. Psychol.*, 1955, **50**, 185–190.

Thompson, R. F. Primary stimulus generalization as a function of acquisition level in the cat. *J. comp physiol. Psychol.*, 1958, **51**, 601-606.

Thompson, R. F. Effect of acquisition level upon the magnitude of stimulus generalization across sensory modality. *J. comp. physiol. Psychol.*, 1959, **52**, 183–185.

Thompson, R. F. Role of cerebral cortex in stimulus generalization. *J. comp. physiol. Psychol.*, 1962, **55**, 279–287.

Thompson, R. F. The neural basis of stimulus generalization. In D. Mostofsky (Ed.), *Stimulus generalization*. Stanford, Calif.: Stanford Univer. Press, 1965.

Thorndike, E. L. *Educational psychology*. II. *The psychology of learning*. New York: Teachers College, Columbia Univer., 1913.

Tolman, E. C. Principles of purposive behavior. In S. Koch (Ed.), *Psychology: A study of a science* (Vol. 2). New York: McGraw-Hill, 1959.

Tosti, D. T., & Ellis, H. C. Stimulus generalization in the absence of discrimination factors. *J. exp. Psychol.*, 1964, **68**, 595–598.

Tracy, W. K. Generalization and preference on the wavelength continuum following monochromatic rearing of ducklings. Unpublished doctoral dissertation. Columbia Univer. 1968.

Wenar, C. Reaction time as a function of manifest anxiety and stimulus intensity. *J. abnorm. soc. Psychol.*, 1953, **48**, 129–134.

White, S. W. Generalization of an instrumental response with variations in two attributes of the CS. *J. exp. Psychol.*, 1958, **56**, 339–343.

Wickens, D. D. Stimulus identity as related to response specificity and response generalization. *J. exp. Psychol.*, 1948, **38**, 389–394.

Wickens, D. D., Schroder, H. M., & Snide, J. D. Primary stimulus generalization of the GSR under two conditions. *J. exp. Psychol.*, 1954, **47**, 52–56.

Wolpe, J. Primary stimulus generalization: A neuro-physiological view. *Psychol. Rev.*, 1952, **59**, 8–10.

Yamaguchi, H. G. Gradients of drive stimulus (SD) intensity generalization. *J. exp. Psychol.*, 1952, **43**, 298–304.

Yarczower, M., & Bitterman, M. E. Stimulus generalization in the goldfish. In D.

Mostofsky (Ed.), *Stimulus generalization*. Stanford, Calif.: Stanford Univer. Press, 1965.

Yarczower, M., Dickson, J. F., & Gollub, L. R. Some effects on generalization gradients of tandem schedules. *J. exp. Anal. Behav.*, 1966, **9**, 631–639.

Zajonc, R. B., & Cross, D. J. Stimulus generalization as a function of drive shift. *J. exp. Psychol.*, 1965, **69**, 363–368.

Zajonc, R. B., & Dorfman, D. D. Perception, drive, and behavior theory. *Psychol. Rev.*, 1964, **71**, 273–290.

Zeiler, M. D. The ratio of intermediate size discrimination. *Psychol. Rev.*, 1963, **70**, 516–533.

Zeiler, M. D. Transposition in adults with simultaneous and successive stimulus presentation. *J. exp. Psychol.*, 1964, **68**, 103–107.

Zeiler, M. D. Solution of the intermediate size problem by pigeons. *J. exp. Anal. Behav.*, 1965, **8**, 263–268.

Zeiler, M. D., & Gardner, A. M. Intermediate size discrimination in seven and eight-year-old children. *J. exp. Psychol.*, 1966, **71**, 203–207.

Suggested Readings

Guttman, N. Laws of behavior and facts of perception. In S. Koch (Ed.), *Psychology: A study of a science* (Vol. 5). New York: McGraw-Hill, 1963. A provocative and penetrating discussion of the role of perception in behavior. Stimulus generalization is used as a medium to develop the theme that concepts from both behavioral and sensory-perceptual traditions are necessary to understand complex behavior.

Guttman, N., & Kalish, H. I. Experiments on discrimination. *Scient. Amer.*, 1958, **198**, 77–82. A popularized version of the role of stimulus generalization in behavior from Pavlov to operant conditioning. Describes some of the first work done in generalization on a wavelength continuum with pigeons and discusses the discriminability hypothesis.

Kimble, G. A. *Hilgard and Marquis' conditioning and learning.* New York: Appleton-Century-Crofts, 1961. The

most recent and thorough discussion of generalization and discrimination. Develops the distinction between "failure to discriminate" and "spread of association" hypotheses with an impartial selection of experimental evidence. Deals with virtually every subject related to stimulus generalization and relates generalization to discrimination learning.

Mostofsky, D. (Ed.). *Stimulus generalization.* Stanford, Calif.: Stanford Univer. Press, 1965. A collection of the most recent experimental and theoretical work in the area of stimulus generalization and discrimination by most of the investigators working in the area. An invaluable reference source and an excellent reservoir of research ideas.

Osgood, C. E. *Method and theory in experimental psychology.* New York: Oxford Univer. Press, 1953. An excellent, although now somewhat dated, account of the problems in stimulus generalization and discrimination. Analysis of the Lashley-Hull controversy in stimulus generalization, discrimination, and the continuity-noncontinuity issue. Detailed treatment of mediated generalization and the mediation hypothesis in general by an able proponent.

Terrace, H. S. Stimulus control. In W. K. Honig (Ed.), *Operant behavior: Areas of research and application.* Appleton-Century-Crofts, 1966. An interpretation of stimulus generalization experiments as a method for determining the extent to which stimulus dimensions exert control over behavior. Describes most of the recent work in the operant study of generalization and discrimination.

V

Verbal Learning

Charles N. Cofer

Pennsylvania State University

13

Introduction, Conceptions, Methods, and a Controversy

This section is concerned with the experimental study of verbal learning, that is, with the *acquisition* of verbal habits or associations. We will not deal with the development of language in children, except incidentally; the study of retention (or its obverse, forgetting) and the transfer of learning from one set of verbal materials and skills to others will not receive focused attention in this section, as retention and transfer are treated elsewhere in this book.

It seems clear that the factor which has given a distinctive character to the study of verbal learning derives from its historical background. This background is in the philosophical tradition known as British associationism, some of the main adherents of which were Thomas Hobbes, John Locke, George Berkeley, David Hume, Thomas Brown, James Mill and his son John Stuart, and Alexander Bain. Other names could be mentioned, in France as in England, but the list just given includes most of the major figures.

Central to the conceptions of the British associationists was the hypothesis that the mind's knowledge arises from *experience*. There were no innate ideas, in other words, and experience with the world was seen as requisite to the formation of simple ideas.

The latter, however, could be linked together into more complex units by *association*, and association was also regarded as the factor which led from one idea to another, as in a train of thought.

Aside from analyses of their own experiences (introspections), the British associationist philosophers did not study the formation of associations among ideas or the factors responsible for the sequences of ideas in the stream of thought. They did suggest *laws* of *association* but did little to subject them to possible verification or disproof. It remained for Hermann Ebbinghous (1850–1909), a German psychologist, to invent a way to study associations and to carry out experiments concerning the factors involved in the formation (and retention) of associations.

The British associationists spoke of ideas as if they were discrete units, capable of being linked with other units into more complex units. What Ebbinghaus (1885) accomplished included the invention of the nonsense syllable, a unit composed of a vowel between two consonants (sometimes referred to as a CVC) which did not form a word. Because they presumably had no meaning and were of equal size, they could be considered equivalent to one another and afforded Ebbinghaus a large pool of materials with which he could study association among ideas, each syllable, perhaps, being the equivalent of an idea. Ebbinghaus' pioneering and classical work established methods and set many of the problems which have engaged the attention of many investigators ever since.

The characteristic investigation of verbal learning may be described as follows. A list of nonsense syllables (or of other discrete items such as words) is presented one at a time to the learner. His attempt is to master the list so that he may recite it. Of interest have been the variables which influence the acquisition of such lists and which are related to its retention or to its transfer effects on other lists. We shall be concerned in this section with acquisition, and at this juncture it is advisable to distinguish among the terms *acquisition*, *retention*, and *transfer*.

Acquisition, Retention, and Transfer

In order to study learning, we must provide, first of all, that the materials be presented to the learner. Let us take as an example the pair DAX-WUB. We wish *S* to learn that when he sees or hears DAX he is to respond with the nonsense syllable WUB. Instructing him that this is what he is to do, we then present the pair to him, visually or orally. But how are we to know whether he has learned the pair? Simply presenting it will not do as evidence for learning, as at any given presentation *S* may not have perceived, for one reason or another, one or both of the pair members. If the presentation has not registered we cannot expect that the pair will have been learned. Even if the pair has registered, however, one presentation might not be enough to effect learning, especially if several pairs are presented together or one after another. Clearly then we need a method for *testing* whether learning has occurred.

There are several methods for making such tests, and we will describe them later. One is that, some time after the presentation, we present the stimulus (DAX) and ask the learner to give the response that goes with it. If he does so, we can say that he learned WUB as a response to DAX during the presentation, as it is highly unlikely that he would respond to DAX in this way without the presentation. But note that some time has elapsed between the presentation of the pair and of the stimulus member alone; although this time may be very short (for example, one second), nevertheless the evidence for learning is obtained *subsequent* to the presentation. And this is true of all tests for learning. There seems to be no way to assess whether learning is occurring or has occurred without doing so after the acquisition period has ended.

The importance of this discussion lies in the fact that a subsequent test measures not only what was acquired during the presentation but also *what was retained* during the interval between the presentation and the test. This interval may be called the *retention interval* (or *forgetting interval*, as retention may not be perfect). We have said that in verbal learning both acquisition and retention are problems of interest and importance, but we have just seen that acquisition cannot be studied without involving retention. How may this paradox be resolved?

The only answer that we can give is to indicate that a convention has grown up among students of questions concerning acquisition and retention which distinguishes these two processes in terms of the focus of interest. When one is interested in the events which occur in a presentation (or in a series of presentations—trials), he is said to be studying acquisition. When his interest focuses, however, on the interval, or on events occurring during the interval, he is studying retention (Melton, 1963, p. 3). It is also true, for the most part, although there are important exceptions, that short retention intervals characterize studies of acquisition, whereas longer intervals characterize retention. Likewise, the retention intervals which occur between the trials necessary for *S* to master a task (for example, to be able to reproduce a list of nonsense syllables without error) are included in the acquisition process; retention intervals which occur after mastery has been achieved or practice has ceased are usually employed to study retention or forgetting (McGeoch and Irion, 1952, p. 6). Despite these distinctions of convention, which should become clearer as we proceed, there will be instances whose classification will not be easy.

We have also listed *transfer* as a term to be distinguished from *acquisition* and *retention*. In general, *transfer* refers to the influence learning one task has on the learning of another one. For example, if one learns to read Latin will this have an influence on later learning to read French or German or Sanskrit? Or, having learned one list of nonsense syllables, will *S* learn a second list in the same time or number of presentations as he would had he not learned the first list? Transfer can appear in three forms: the acquisition of the second task may be facilitated (positive transfer) by the learning of the first task; or, second task learning may be impeded by the learning of task one (negative transfer); or there may be no determinate effect of the learning of the first task on the acquisition of the second one (usually called zero transfer). But it should be evident that for positive or negative transfer to occur, first task effects must still be present at the time of second task learning, that is, the first task must be *retained*. So transfer depends on retention; the two processes are not independent. On occasion, transfer has been used as a *measure* of retention.

In most of the tasks studied in human learning, moreover, it is likely that there is transfer (positive or negative). To learn a list of nonsense syllables by the usual procedures, for example, one must be able to read or understand visually presented or spoken letters or syllables. Reading letters or understanding speech sounds is possible only if habits of reading and speech *transfer* to the nonsense-syllable learning situation. If words or sentences are to be used in learning, the very fact that *S* can distinguish words from nonsense syllables or sentences from random strings of words presumes *transfer* from prior linguistic experience to the learning situation. It follows that most of the experiments in verbal learning which concern the process of acquisition do so by studying acquisition against the background of massive transfer (which may be either positive or negative) arising from prior linguistic experience. It is not possible to begin adult verbal learning at zero. Except in the human infant, it is almost impossible to conceive a verbal learning task which can be isolated from such transfer effects. Even in very young infants, there are many vocalizations which seem to appear natively. When observations are made of these sounds, it appears that their variety is much greater than that present in the language community into which the child is born (McCarthy, 1946, p. 492). It is tempting to conclude that even during language acquisition in the infant, there is transfer from his native vocalizations to the learning of the language of his caretakers. Although this transfer in the infant is probably positive, it is possible that the transfer may be greater to some languages than to others. We do not know.

We see, then, that when we study the learning of verbal materials, we necessarily involve retention and transfer as well. By adopting certain conventions we distinguish acquisition from retention. We always study verbal learning against a background of transfer. So long as we can hold the amount of transfer constant, however, the effects of a number of variables on the learning process can be assessed. Or, alternatively, we may vary the amount of transfer systematically and determine its effects on acquisition. Although transfer as such is treated elsewhere in this book, many of the variables usually considered as affecting acquisition may be given an interpretation in terms of transfer. We will see instances of such interpretations later.

Verbal Learning Experiments

Let us look at several common situations in which verbal learning is studied. Two purposes can be served by a general description. To begin with, we can become familiar with the kinds of problems experiments are designed to investigate. Secondly, we can acquaint ourselves with the methods and materials commonly employed. In the process of serving these purposes we will identify and introduce many of the topics to be treated in later chapters of this section.

The example given in the earlier discussion used a single item, DAX-WUB, to illustrate the relationships of learning and retention. This item is an instance of a *paired associate*, that is, an association is to be formed between two members of the pair. Verbal learning experiments do not, however, usually study the acquisition of associations by means of a single pair. Typically, a list of such pairs is arranged, and *S*'s task is to learn all the pairs.

The *method of paired associates (PA) learning* proceeds as follows in the case of the *anticipation technique*. For illustration we shall use this list of five pairs: DAX WUB, GEX CAG, MIB VOB, DIJ BUP, KOQ TEF. Often a much longer list would be employed.

First, the stimulus member, GEX, of the first pair would be presented alone for an interval (say, 2 sec.) and would be joined, for another interval (again, say, 2 sec.), by the response member, CAG. Then the stimulus member of the next pair (MIB) would be presented for its interval and then the pair (MIB VOB) for its interval. Similarly, the other three pairs would be presented in their turn. The first run through

the list serves, of course, to acquaint or to *familiarize S* with the pairs, and it is often called a familiarization or study trial. This trial is followed by *anticipation trials*.

The trial after the familiarization trial is the first anticipation trial. For it, the order of presentation of the pairs is typically altered from the one used in the familiarization trial, and several orders of the pairs would be used during the anticipation trials that follow. These variations in order are employed to assure that *S* will learn only the pairs, not the serial sequence of the items in the list. If the order of the items is always the same, serial learning, which we will consider shortly, would occur.

In the anticipation trials, *S* is asked, on presentation of the stimulus member of the pair, to give the response term that goes with it. For example, if DIJ BUP is now the first pair, DIJ will occur and *S* is to anticipate the appearance of BUP by giving it. A correct response is recorded if the anticipation is right and occurs in time. A failure to respond or a response that is wrong is scored as an error. (The actual erroneous response is usually recorded, as information on errors is often useful.)

Anticipation trials continue until *S* reaches what is called a *criterion of learning*. Many possible criteria may be imagined, but one that is commonly employed is to continue trials until *S*, on one trial, correctly anticipates all the responses. This might mean that some responses had been correctly anticipated several times, others never, and still others sometimes correctly and sometimes incorrectly on earlier trials. But on the criterion trial (that is, the one on which the criterion is reached) all of the responses are correctly anticipated on presentation of their appropriate stimuli. Other criteria of mastery may be employed, depending on the investigator's decision. For example, two or more successive perfect trials may be required (a rather stringent criterion) or, alternatively, anticipation trials may be continued to the one on which four of the five responses are

Table **13-1**   Hypothetical Record of Paired-Associate Learning*

Trial	DAX WUB	GEX CAG	MIB VOB	DIJ BUP	KOQ TEF	Total +
1	+	CAB	−	TEF	−	1
2	−	WUB	−	PUX	−	0
3	+	+	−	−	TEL	2
4	+	−	−	+	−	2
5	+	−	−	+	+	3
6	+	+	−	+	+	4
7	+	−	+	+	+	4
8	+	+	+	+	+	5
Total Correct	7	3	2	5	4	21

* + indicates correct responses, − an omission or failure to respond. Items appearing in the body of the table are incorrect responses and are either misplaced responses or intrusions from outside the list. Data are for anticipation trials to a criterion of one perfect trial. The order of the pairs at the top is used for convenience, as order varies from trial to trial.

correctly anticipated (a not so stringent criterion).

Each presentation of all the pairs constitutes a *trial*. If learning is carried to a fairly stringent criterion, it may be useful to look at the data in another way. That is, we may wish to know how many trials were required to reach several criteria, for example, two of five correct anticipations, three of five, four of five, one perfect trial. From the record, also, one can determine how many correct responses and errors occurred in any given trial and, in sum, for all trials. Or one can make the same counts for single items. There are many ways of studying the data obtained from this relatively simple procedure. The hypothetical record shown in Table 13-1 for the list we have been using provides an illustration. Note that a criterion of two of five correct is reached on trial 3 and one of three of five correct on trial five, whereas learning to the criterion of one perfect trial occurred on the eighth trial.

Paired associates learning, as we have described it, is a very commonly used method. A variant of it, the *recall technique*, will be described later. Several features of the method can be varied. It can be used with words and nonsense units other than CVCs, as well as with larger units, such as phrases or even sentences. The exposure intervals can be altered. We spoke of a 2-sec stimulus and a 2-sec. pair exposure, that is, a 2-2 rate. Either or both of these intervals can be lengthened or shortened. The response term may be omitted on some trials. The effects of these and other variations on characteristics of acquisition will be considered later. Unmentioned in our discussion is that there is usually another interval, the one between trials, called the intertrial interval. This is subject to variation but often is fixed in a given experiment at from 6 to 30 sec.

Another popular procedure is the *method of serial anticipation learning*. In this case the five pairs we have used before can be considered as a 10-item list. For example, the first item could be DAX, the second WUB, the next GEX, the fourth CAG, and so on, to TEF. Again, as a given item is presented, S is asked to anticipate the next one before it is given. Thus, seeing DAX, he is to respond with WUB, seeing WUB with GEX, and then with CAG, and so on. A trial is usually begun by presenting a neutral symbol, for example, a row of asterisks (to which the response DAX will be given before DAX appears), and there is an interval after each trial. From trial to trial, however, the order is fixed, as it is not in typical PA learning. Our comments about criteria and the recording of responses in the case of PA learning apply to serial anticipation also. A table showing the performance over trials for one S in serial anticipation learning would look much like Table 13-1, but there would be a column for each item, rather than one for each pair. There would thus be twice as many responses for a ten-item serial list as for a five pair list.

The exposure interval for each item is often 2 sec., but this, as well as the intertrial interval, is subject to variation. Other materials than CVCs can be used. A method of analysis of data, not readily possible with PA learning in which the pairs occupy different serial positions from trial to trial, is to analyze correct responses or errors over learning or over a single trial with reference to the *serial position of an item*. For serial learning, we can ask, does the fifth or sixth item behave the same way during learning as, for example, the first or last item?

Both serial learning and paired associates learning typically involve the exposure of a small amount of material for a fixed period of time. Other methods are not so restricted. Before considering them, we should mention that devices to present material for PA and serial learning are usually employed. Sometimes these materials are presented by using cards with the items typed on them, and for many problems this procedure is satisfactory. However, for precise control, especially of exposure intervals, devices such as the *memory drum* have been developed. Such a device is essentially composed of a drum which rotates behind a window or an exposure aperture. Material to be learned is typed on paper or on a tape and the paper or tape is attached to the drum in such a way that the typed material is visible to the learner through the window. The drum (driven by an electric motor) does not rotate continuously but moves

periodically. The duration of its rest is the exposure interval, and it is then that the S looks at the material to be learned. Shutters for the windows, which can be opened or closed, provide for further control over what is exposed and for how long. Slide projectors, film strips, card changers, and other kinds of equipment may be used instead of a memory drum, but to be maximally useful such devices must provide for control of exposure and interexposure intervals.

Paired associates and serial anticipation methods are used for many of the problems studied in experiments on verbal learning. However, there are others which have wide use. Among these is the *method of complete presentation*. This consists of giving the entire group of items—nonsense syllables, words, a list of sentences, a prose selection, a poem—to S for a study period. The learner is free to use the allotted time period as he chooses in his effort to learn the material. Consequently, there is no control over how much attention is devoted to any item. (All of the materials listed a moment ago could, of course, be presented in well-controlled fashions. Large amounts of materials, such as stories, however, tend to be given by means of complete presentation.)

Immediately after the study interval, some measure, in studies of acquisition rather than retention, is undertaken. The S may be asked to *reproduce* or *recall* what he has studied or to recall and *reconstruct* the order of the items he examined. (The items may also be given the S, so that he does not have to produce them, with the instruction to put them in order or into proper relation to one another.) Another possibility is to ask the learner to select the items he has just seen from a larger group in which they are included. This is a *recognition* procedure. Thus, if during the study period, ten words were shown, S might, at test, be asked to identify these ten from among a larger group, say twenty items. Of course, reproduction, reconstruction, and recognition could be used with paired associates and serial anticipation methods. They usually are not so employed, but the anticipation interval constitutes for these two methods the equivalent of a reproduction or recall procedure.

A method similar to complete presentation is the one known as *free learning* (Ekstrand and Underwood, 1963) or *free recall*. In this case, a list of items is presented one at a time while *S* looks or listens. During presentation, however, *S* works under the instruction that, after presentation, he will be asked to recall the items *in any order in which they occur to him*.

There is one procedure, developed relatively recently but widely used, which studies the acquisition and retention of a single item. This method, described by Peterson and Peterson (1959), provides for the presentation of one CVC, one word, one pair, or whatever, for 1 sec. or slightly longer; if a retention interval is used, it is filled by requiring *S* to count backward by 3s or 4s from a number given to him. Most of the work with the technique has been devoted to the study of forgetting, which, in this situation, occurs very quickly. There is no evident reason, however, why the Petersons' procedure could not be adapted to the study of acquisition.

We have now sketched major and typical ways of studying verbal learning experimentally. We have only hinted at the many variables that have been studied, however, but they will concern us in the next chapters. It is worthwhile noting, also, that many changes have been rung on the methods we have described and that students of verbal learning have been inventive in designing techniques for the study of problems not tractable to more ordinary methods.

Are Associations Formed Gradually?

In what has been said so far, there is an implicit assumption about the character of verbal learning. This assumption is that repeated presentations, or trials, are necessary, in the typical case, for associations to be formed. We can designate work predicated on this assumption as the *incremental view*. But there is an alternative which holds that associations are either formed or not formed on a particular presentation. This position we will call the *all-or-none* view. Let us examine these views a little more thoroughly.

Incremental View. The incremental view asserts that maximal associative strength is ordinarily achieved gradually. That is, each presentation contributes an increment of association strength and over a series of presentations of trials these increments summate. There can be cases, however, in which an association will seemingly be formed on one trial, as in the instance of DAX WUB in Table 13-1. That this occurs is because of unusual conditions; perhaps there was already some associative strength between these CVCs before the first presentation or perhaps the item was in an unusually favorable position to acquire and to manifest associative strength. If it was the first one in the list, it would have advantages over the others.

In the opposite case, where many trials are necessary for a correct response (MIB VOB in Table 13-1), the argument holds that increments of association are being added throughout the incorrect trials. Unfavorable conditions, such as the presence of a competing response which must be eliminated or interference from other items in the list, could be the reason that it takes so long for the increasing association to manifest itself. Some notion of a *threshold* is often invoked. That is, association strength must reach a certain level before the response mediated by the association can be given. A number of increments must be added, over a series of trials, to the association before it reaches threshold strength.

Common experience seems often to support the incremental view. Many of us

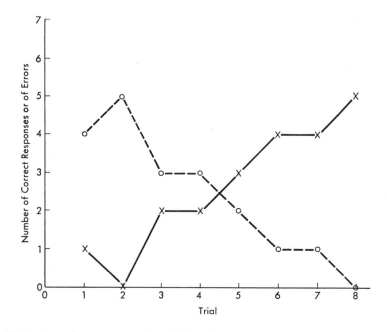

Figure 13-1. Learning curves plotted from the data of the hypothetical *S* shown in Table 1. The solid curve is for correct responses, the broken curve for errors (including omissions). The irregularity of these curves is characteristic of curves plotted for individual *S*s.

would subscribe to the adage that practice makes perfect, on the basis of our own experience. Support seems to come also from learning curves. Figure 13-1 displays such a curve, plotted in two ways from the data of Table 13-1 for the five-item PA list. The solid curve gives the number of correct responses per trial, the dashed curve the number of errors (including omissions) per trial. It may be seen that learning, measured by either the increase in correct responses or the decrease in errors, proceeds gradually. Figure 13-2 presents more idealized curves of the same kind. These curves are often said to describe the formation of a single association as well as the learning of a list. Both curves in each figure are negatively accelerated, that is, their rate of rise or fall slows down as trials increase.

Another finding supports the notion that repetition strengthens associations. This is the evidence that retention (see section on retention and transfer) is improved when

the material in question has been *over-learned*, that is, given practice beyond that required for a single correct trial.

The argument for incremental formation of associations based on the shape of the learning curve has, however, been challenged (see Estes, 1956). The data in Figure 13-1 are taken from the performance of *one* hypothetical *S* in learning five items. Other learning curves (for example, Figure 13-2) are plotted from data obtained from several *S*s, each one learning a number of items. The point in question is whether curves based on several items or on several *S*s and several items can be used to portray the acquisition of a *single item*. It is possible to generate a negatively accelerated curve (for a group of *S*s) even when each item is learned at one trial and is never failed again. Summary scores across items for the several individual trials give us a negatively accelerated curve. Yet each item has shown a change *only once*—from the last trial on which it was wrong to the first trial on which it is correct. So far as the nature of the learning of associations is concerned then, the evidence yielded by the negative acceleration of learning curves for groups of items or for groups of *S*s is indeterminate.

All-or-None View. From the considerations just summarized, it follows that the individual item must be the unit to be examined to determine whether or not associations are formed gradually. Before looking at relevant evidence, it is in order to state a view that contrasts with the incremental one. A number of writers have espoused an all-or-none view of the learning process. We shall here consider the formulation of Estes (1960) as representative.

The basic statement of this viewpoint is simple: If an association is formed at all on a given trial, it reaches maximal strength at that time, that is, it develops either full

or no associative strength; the association is all or none.

This assertion may be illustrated and compared with the incremental view by means of an example. Let us take the case of four *S*s learning a paired associate item. After the first presentation, the probability of the occurrence of the correct response is 0.25. To the incremental view this means that each person has learned the association to some extent, that is, to a probability of 0.25, although only one person actually gives the correct response. To the all-or-none theorist, however, the situation is different: for three of the *S*s no change in associative strength has accompanied the reinforcement—the probability of the correct response is still zero, as it was before the presentation. In the remaining *S*, the probability has changed from zero to 1—the association has been fully formed. It follows, then, from the all-or-none view, that trials in which the correct response does not

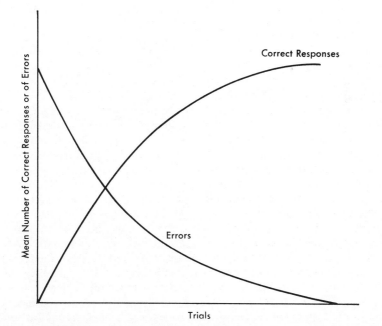

Figure 13-2. Idealized learning curves, the rising one for correct responses, the falling one for errors. Such curves are negatively accelerated, that is, their rate of change diminishes as we go from trial 1 to the final trial.

actually occur do not contribute to the formation of the association; for incremental theory, however, they do. Further, if a second test is introduced without additional presentations, the all-or-none view predicts retention of the correct response by the S who gave it on the first test and, of course, that the other Ss cannot give the correct response on the second test (except through guessing). The incremental view, on the other hand, conceives that any of the four Ss can give the response correctly on the second test or that the one who gave it correctly on the first test can fail to do so on the second test. This follows because associative strength is seen to vary in time; if it varies upward it may be strong enough to lead to the response; if it varies downward, it may become too weak to lead to the response. But the most important point is that all Ss, on the presentation, will acquire some increment in the associative strength.

Estes applies his arguments to several learning situations, including paired associate learning. We will consider some of the experiments which have figured in the resulting controversy, so far as verbal learning is concerned.

In the first experiment, reported by Estes, Hopkins, and Crothers (1960), CCCs were paired with the numbers 1 through 8. One minute after a single presentation of the eight items, there was a test trial, consisting of the presentation of the eight stimuli alone. A second presentation trial followed, in which four of the pairs were shown to each S, and then a second test trial in which all the stimuli were presented.

Analysis was made of the fate on the second test trial of the items which were correct (C_1) or incorrect (N_1) on the first test trial and which were given only one presentation. Seventy-one per cent of the items correct on trial 1 were correct on trial 2 ($C_2 : C_1$) and only 9 per cent of the items incorrect on trial 1 were correct on trial 2 ($C_2 : N_1$). The latter figure is less than could have been expected by guessing and is

clearly contrary to expectation based on incremental theory. The 71 per cent value indicates that some forgetting had occurred.

The question arises whether the items correct after a single presentation are much easier than those not correct. If such a difference is present, then a conclusion concerning the theoretical question is not possible, despite the difference between 71 and 9 per cent. Estes found that of the items incorrect after the first presentation, 46 per cent were correct ($C_2 : N_1$) after the second presentation. This compares favorably with the proportion of all items correct after one presentation (49 per cent). Hence, he concludes that item difficulty is not a factor in his results. Postman (1963b, p. 307) points out, however, that the two percentage figures can be interpreted to indicate differences in item difficulty. The 49 per cent correct is obtained following one presentation of eight items; the 46 per cent is obtained after the (second) presentation of *only four* items, a condition more favorable to learning than an eight-item list. This is a persuasive argument and leaves Estes' support for the all-or-none view of learning in doubt. Easy items benefit more from repeated presentations than difficult items (Postman, 1963b, p. 311, Fig. 8-2).

Schwartz (1963) tested the effect of failures on the first test trial by means of the following design. All of her Ss had a presentation and then a test trial on a list of eighteen number-word pairs. There was then a second study trial followed by two more test trials. For the control group, the items in the list failed on the first test were the same throughout. For the experimental group, however, these items were altered following the first test by interchanging response members for all failed items. (An equal number of response members were interchanged in the two groups for items correct on the first test.) If the presentation of the failed items had no effect on learning, the two groups should not differ on subsequent tests (after the second presentation).

If some increment had been added to association, however, with the items failed on the first test, the experimental group should be inferior to the control group on the later tests. This is what Schwartz found on the two test trials following the second presentation: the control group did significantly better than the experimental group, despite the fact that item difficulty favored the experimental group. Evidently some associative strength was developed for the pairs failed after one presentation.

Another major argument concerns the effect of multiple presentations. Although more correct responses will occur after several than after a single presentation, Estes suggests that this means that additional responses are being learned rather than that already formed associations are being strengthened. He reports evidence (Estes, Hopkins, and Crothers, 1960) consistent with this view for one versus two presentations. However, several other experiments, involving several more presentations, have found effects on retention consistent with an incremental view (Jones, 1962; Postman, 1963b; Seidel, 1963; Williams, 1962). There is evidence in the experiments by Williams (1962) and by Eimas and Zeaman (1963) that latencies decrease over trials in situations patterned after Estes' experiments even when probability of recall does not change. If decline in latency is an index of growing associative strength, as most investigators believe, this finding is clearly contrary to the notion that all of the association is formed on one trial.

The evidence we have presented does not support, very well, the claims of all-or-none theory and seems to fit better with those of incremental theory. An important consequence of this controversy, however, is to direct the attention of investigators to the individual item as opposed to the exclusive concern with means for groups of items. This reorientation can lead to augmented understanding of the processes involved in verbal learning. Further, Estes (1964) has indicated the utility of the all-or-none

assumption in guiding research into learning processes and believes that it is unwise to give it up in view of its fruitfulness and of the good fits of the data to expectations derived from models which assume it.

Tulving (1964, p. 221) has suggested another source of evidence that learning occurs in a single trial. We have mentioned the short-term memory experiments in which, after the presentation of a single item (for example, a paired associate), S is required to recall it following a filled interval. When the recall is immediate, however, there is no forgetting (see Melton, 1963). It may be argued then, as Tulving does, that learning occurs on a single trial and that failures of retention, occurring later, are due to factors acting during the retention interval rather than at the time of acquisition. (Tulving does not preclude the possibility that further presentations may make the item more resistant to forgetting, however.)

This argument is an interesting and plausible one, and the evidence in its favor is clear-cut. Its major limitation, however, lies in the following question: Do the items which are equally recalled have the same degree of learning (Underwood, 1964b)?

Degree of Learning

It is obvious that if items are equally recalled at a given time, we must discover means other than immediate recall to find out whether they were equally learned. One possibility is to test them for retention later: If they differ in recallability and if all other conditions are equal, then they must have been unequally learned (though equally recalled) to begin with. Another way is to determine their latencies, that is, the time S takes to give them when presented with suitable stimuli. Latency is assumed to be inversely related to associative strength, that is, the shorter latencies occur for the stronger associations.

Underwood (1964b, pp. 118–119) has reported data for paired associate learning of eight nonsense syllable-adjective pairs. If, during learning, an item had been correctly anticipated eight, nine, ten, or eleven times, the probability that it would be correctly anticipated on the next trial was almost 1.0, that is, almost 100 per cent. However, after twenty-four hours, the per cent recall of these same items showed differences (Underwood, 1964b, p. 118, Fig. 2). Thus for one list, the per cents hovered around 80 per cent after twenty-four hours for items which had been correctly anticipated during learning eight or nine times; the per cent of recall after twenty-four hours approximated 95 per cent for items correctly anticipated ten or eleven times. These results show quite different effects in retention after twenty-four hours for items all of which were at virtually the 100 per cent level during learning. (Even more striking differences were found for a more difficult list.) Clearly, items which are equally recalled at one time may be recalled differentially later. Direct evidence of differential item recall following perfect recall at an immediate test in the short-term memory situation is not available to the writer. It is reasonable to suppose that, as in the case of Underwood's findings, there would be differences. Such differences would invalidate the evidence used by Tulving in favor of one-trial learning (although it would not invalidate his quantitative analysis of acquisition curves in free recall learning). As noted previously however, Tulving has indicated that repetition may enhance the resistance to forgetting of an item. This could be interpreted as involving the strengthening of associations by repetition.

Murdock (1961), in a short-term memory experiment, found essentially no difference in the per cent of immediate recall for one-syllable words (mean, 0.98) and for three-word triads (mean, 0.93). Yet the latencies for these two kinds of items were 1.13 and 1.63 sec., a significant difference (Underwood, 1964b, p. 128); recall over retention intervals from 3 to 18 sec. showed the word triads to be markedly inferior to words. The latency difference is consistent with the differential recalls over the 3- to 18-sec. intervals, but the small difference at immediate recall in per cent recalled is not. Latency differences may index different association strengths. If so, Murdock's latency data for immediate recall show that words and word triads differed, despite their approximately equal percentages of recall. This information also opposes the notion that perfect immediate recall in short-term memory necessarily means that all items have been learned to the same degree.

The problem of assessing degree of learning is a difficult one but, aside from the considerations just discussed, has its major importance in the area of retention and forgetting. Underwood (1964b) has discussed the problem thoroughly and offered suggestions for its solution.

Criteria of Learning

On an earlier page, it was mentioned that mastery in a learning task may be defined by various criteria: one perfect trial, two successive perfect trials, six correct responses out of eight possibilities, and so on. Weitz (1961) has pointed out that one's conclusions from an investigation may vary as a function of the criterion of learning he employs.

Cramer and Cofer (1960) conducted an experiment in which S learned two paired associate lists in succession. The stimuli of the two lists were the same, the responses differed, and the investigators were interested in the effects of relationships between the responses on the learnability of the second list. For example, one pair in the two lists was GEX-Justice (List 1) and GEX-Peace (List 2), and another pairing was WUB-Tobacco (List 1) and WUB-Butter (List 2). Interest lay in whether the associative and meaning relations common to Justice and Peace would facilitate the learning of the pairs in the second list in which such relations were present as compared to pairs in the second list whose response members did not have such relations to response members of the first list (Butter-Tobacco). Cramer and Cofer found a facilitating effect, limited to the first two trials (of the eight they gave) in second-list learning.

Weitz reanalyzed these data using various criteria so far as second-list learning is concerned. He found that as criteria varied so did the conclusion to which the data led. The conclusions of the investigators were not challenged, because the criterion they had used was sensitive to the differences in which they were interested. Had they chosen other criteria, however, they might have reached different and perhaps erroneous vice versa.

Weitz' analysis suggests that the criterion of learning must be chosen with care and, further, that enough data should be collected so that a variety of criteria may be applied to them. Application of multiple criteria may indicate conditions under which differences are and are not found and knowledge of these conditions can be important, both theoretically and practically. Weitz tentatively suggests the generalization that in easy tasks maximal differences will be shown by stringent criteria, and vice versa.

CHAPTER

14

Characteristics of Materials

The materials used in experiments on verbal learning vary in a number of ways. These variations have profound effects on the rate of learning, and interpretations of these effects have many implications for our conceptions of verbal learning processes. A broad classification of the differences among these materials would group single or discrete items, such as nonsense syllables or words, or pairs of nonsense syllables or words, together and connected material, such as prose or poetry, in another class. The differentiation here may rest on the conception that the single item is unrelated to others. This is assuredly not true (Deese, 1961, p. 11), as we shall see, but the differentiation is adequate insofar as the *E* may frequently present one, or a pair, of the single items at a time whereas with connected material he almost always must present a string of items.

Ebbinghaus (1885), as we have said, invented the nonsense syllable. He wished to rule out meaning, relations to other items, and connectedness in order to study the basic associative processes without the influence of these factors. He also hoped that nonsense syllables would be equal units, one being as easy or as difficult to

learn as the other. He had doubts himself as to whether the nonsense syllable actually met these goals very well, and as Deese (1961, p. 14) has observed, later research has justified these doubts.

Characteristics of material will be discussed under two broad headings: single or discrete items, and connected materials. As the methods for evaluating the characteristics of these classes of material differ, our discussion of the two will not be around parallel topics.

Single or Discrete Items

To learn a list of ten or twelve meaningful, common words seems to us to be a much easier task than to learn ten or twelve CVCs or CCCs, and Davis' (1930) data support this expectation. Serial learning of twelve three-letter words was accomplished in an average of 3.7 trials, whereas twelve CVCs required 9.8 trials. Lyon (1914, Plates I, III, V, VII) found that 200 words of poetry could be learned in ten min. whereas 200 nonsense syllables required ninety-three minutes. These differences in learning rates represent meaningfulness, at least in part:

314

the advantage shown by poetry arises from other factors as well, as discussed subsequently.

There are a number of ways in which discrete units may vary. Some of the more prominent ways include association value, meaningfulness, familiarity, pronunciability. These terms may denote distinct variables but it is possible that some one fundamental variable underlies them all. Research with these variables has been concerned not only with defining them operationally, with determining their relations to one another, with discovering their influence on learning, but also with what is their basic character.

Association Value and Meaningfulness

Even nonsense syllables show variation in one or the other of these properties. In 1928 Glaze reported calibrations of the *association value* (*a*-value) of 2,019 such syllables. He presented each syllable visually to a S for from 2 to 3 sec. and also spelled it. The S was to say, in a few words, what, if anything, the syllable meant to him or whether the syllable meant something even if he could not verbalize what that something was. Glaze used fifteen Ss and for each syllable determined the percentage of Ss who had an association (verbalized or unverbalized) to the syllable. Thus, for a syllable with 100 per cent association value (for example, FEL, RAV) all Ss had an association; for syllables with 0 per cent association value (for example, QOB, ZIL), no S thought of anything. Other more or less comparable calibrations were made by Hull (1933) and by Krueger (1934) for nonsense syllables (CVCs) and for consonant syllables (CCCs) by Witmer (1935). McGeoch (1930) had S first study lists of ten items for 2 min., then recall the items immediately. Only 5.09 syllables at 0 per cent were recalled, and the number increased as association value increased; for 100

per cent association value syllables 7.35 items were recalled.

The term *meaningfulness*, or *m*, was introduced by Noble (1952) to denote measurements achieved by another association method. This is the *production method*. In this procedure, S is asked to give as many different associations to a stimulus word as he can in a 1-min. interval. The stimulus word is presented a number of times in order that the associations obtained be made to it rather than to S's prior response or responses. The mean number of associations so obtained for a stimulus is its meaningfulness score or *m* value. The stimuli Noble first used were dissyllables (two-syllable units some of which were real words and some of which were nonsense words). Items with low *m* values are Gojey (0.99) and Neglan (1.04), with intermediate values are Zenith (4.44) and Yeoman (4.60), and with high values are Army (9.43) and kitchen (9.61). Recalibrations of these same dissyllables with other Ss and by other investigators have indicated that they are highly reliable (Noble, 1963, p. 85).

A number of experiments (Noble, 1963, p. 91; Underwood and Schulz, 1960, pp. 27–31) have varied association value or *m*-value in serial learning. All of them show that as *a*-value or *m*-value increases, rate of learning also increases. Underwood and Schulz indicate (1960, p. 31) that differences in serial learning rates of the order of 3 to 1 may be associated with maximum differences in the *a*- or *m*-values of the materials.

In paired-associate learning, too, *m* is related to the rate of learning. Pairs both of whose members have high *m*-values are learned more rapidly than pairs both of whose members have low *m*-values when the items are dissyllables (Kimble and Dufort, 1955; Noble and McNeely, 1957) or nonsense syllables (Mandler and Huttenlocher, 1956; see also Underwood and Schulz, 1960, pp. 34–35).

One can vary independently, of course, the *m*-value of the stimulus and the response members of the pair in paired-associate

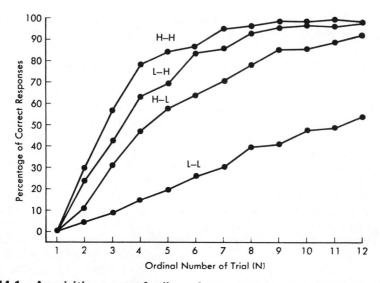

Figure 14-1. Acquisition curves for lists of ten paired associates, showing percentage of correct responses in relation to trials. Meaningfulness (*m*) was varied. The curve marked H-H indicates high *m* for both the stimulus and the response term, the one marked H-L indicates high stimulus *m* and low response *m*, and so on. (Reprinted with permission from Cieutat, V. J., Stockwell, F. E., and Noble, C. E. The interaction of ability and amount of practice with stimulus and response meaningfulness (*m*, *m'*) in paired-associate learning. *J. exp. Psychol.*, 1958, **56**, 193–202.)

learning. When this is done, learning rate is affected much more by response *m* than by stimulus *m* (Underwood and Schulz, 1960, pp. 35–42), for both nonsense syllables and dissyllables. A fairly typical set of results is shown in Figure 14-1, taken from the experiment by Cieutat, Stockwell, and Noble (1958).

The results of all these experiments are clear: *m* is a significant factor in both serial anticipation and in paired associate learning and has its most pronounced effect in the latter case when the response member rather than the stimulus member varies in *m*.

It is possible to substitute a scaling method for the production method; scaling procedures are easier to use than the production method, and their use would thus have advantages over the production method. Noble (1963) obtained ratings designed to estimate the relative number of associations a stimulus would elicit on a five-point scale. The correlation of these ratings with production method scores for dissyllabic nouns

was 0.918 (Noble, 1963, p. 86) and another scale which calls for comparative judgments of number of associations correlates with production scores for CVCs at values ranging from 0.71 to 0.91. The latter value was obtained with a sample of twenty-one CVCs ranging over the entire spectrum of *m* (Noble, 1963b, pp. 86–87). Although these correlations are high, there is, when scaled meaningfulness is plotted against *m* based on the production method, some curvilinearity in the relationship of the two variables, as Figure 14-2 shows. Nevertheless, it seems likely that rated *m* can be used in the place of production *m* in the assessment of the meaningfulness of verbal materials (Underwood and Schulz, 1960, pp. 15–25).

Why does *m* relate, as it does, to learning scores? There are several ways in which this question has been answered (see Goss, 1963). First, it can be argued that measures of *m* actually reflect the influence of other variables, such as frequency or familiarity or pronunciability. This is an answer to which we shall return following the discussion of these other parameters.

A second possible answer has been the associative probability hypothesis (Underwood and Schulz, 1960, pp. 45–49) or the grapnel hypothesis (Glanzer, 1962, p. 34). Measures of *m* relate to the number of associations which a unit possesses. If units are to be linked, then with high *m* there is an augmented probability that associations in one unit will be identical to or otherwise related (associative probability) to those of another unit; or, in Glanzer's figure of speech, the more hooks there are on the grapnel of one unit the more likely it is that one of them will attach itself to the other unit. This interpretation runs into a number of difficulties, as both Glanzer and Underwood and Schulz have pointed out. One difficulty is the interference paradox (Underwood and Schulz 1960, p. 46). The more associations each unit has (the higher the *m*) the more possibilities there are for interference arising from the associations with desired learning. Postman (1963a) has point-

ed to some ways in which the interference paradox may be overcome, but it is still premature to accept unequivocally the associative probability hypothesis as an explanation for the effects of *m*.

A third answer may be mentioned, and it will apply to familiarity and pronunciability as well as to *m*. This answer involves the notion that verbal units must be put together (Mandler, 1954), that is, integrated or "unitized," before they can be learned or associated with one another; *m* value would enter here if it can be assumed that high-*m* items already possess complete or partial integration at the start of list-learning, whereas low-*m* items do not. (Goss, 1963, puts this another way when he says that high-*m* units elicit quicker and more stable "recognition responses" than low-*m* units.)

To illustrate the notion of response integration, consider the two nonsense syllables LAT and XOK. LAT has the highest and XOK the lowest *m* value in Mandler's (1955, p. 664) set of 100 CVCs. LAT is a frequently encountered string of letters,

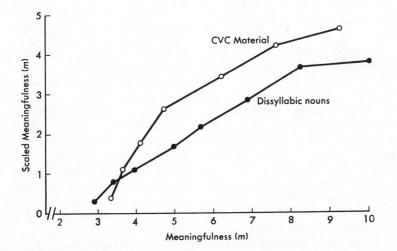

Figure 14-2. Relationship between rated or scaled meaningfulness (*m′*) and production method *m̄* for CVC material and dissyllabic nouns. (Reprinted with permission from Noble, C. E. Meaningfulness and familiarity. In C. N. Cofer, and B. S. Musgrave, (Eds.), *Verbal behavior and learning: Problems and processes.* New York: McGraw-Hill, 1963, pp. 76–119.)

appearing in such words as *late, later, latter, latex, latch, latent, lateral, lathe, Latin, latitude,* and *latrine,* to name just some of the words in which LAT enters as the first three letters. XOK, however, occurs with little or no frequency. It seems likely that having seen LAT once or twice, the *S* would then easily remember it as a unit; seeing it only briefly or glancingly, he would still know what it is and be able to say it quickly and easily or to spell it readily. With XOK, on the other hand, *S* might require several more trials to have the comparable facility with it. If what has been said is true, we can say that LAT is a better organized, integrated or more unitary item than is XOK at the beginning of learning. Put another way, we could say that it would require *S* very little time to remember the letters *L, A, T* and to put them in proper order. These processes would require more time in the case of XOK. (These differences may not appear obvious for these two syllables treated alone. Consider, however, the following list of six syllables: VOJ, ZEG, MON, NIY, QIJ, MAB. MAB and MON, high-*m* syllables, would certainly be easier to recall as units than VOJ, ZEG, NIY, and QIJ, low-*m* syllables.)

If a high-*m* unit possesses unity or integration earlier than a low-*m* unit, then it can begin to enter into association with other units sooner than low-*m* units. In PA learning, for example, LAT could be associated *as a unit* with its stimulus at an early trial, while at that same trial *S* may still be learning, in the case of XOK, that X is followed by O and O by K.

The foregoing discussion implies a two-stage process in verbal learning: unit formation or integration and association of units with one another. Such a two-stage analysis has been made by a number of writers, including Underwood and Schulz (1960, pp. 92–94), whose views have been summarized in what has just been said. As they have been mainly concerned with PA learning they have emphasized response integration;

the term used here, *unit integration,* means the same thing without being tied to the response member in PA learning.

Response or unit integration can account for some of the effects which *m* has on learning but *m* is probably also involved in the associative stage (Underwood and Schulz, 1960, pp. 304–305). Detailed working out of the nature of this influence remains to be accomplished (Postman, 1963a).

The two-stage conception in verbal learning can accommodate a good deal of the effect of *m* but it can also incorporate, as we shall see, the effects of other variables like pronunciability and frequency. It is possible that the effects of *m* are not independent of these other variables, as we suggested earlier. To these other variables and their relationships with *m* we turn now.

Familiarity and Frequency

An item which is meaningful will, in the typical case, also be familiar. The converse is not always true, that is, a familiar item is not necessarily a meaningful one (Noble, 1963, p. 99). It is necessary, in dealing with verbal items, to determine whether familiarity affects their learning and whether the effects of *m* can, perhaps, be reduced to familiarity.

Familiarity, as used here, refers to ratings or judgments which *S*s make of materials presented to them. Familiarity is presumably related to the relative frequencies with which the materials have been experienced, so that frequency is the factor which underlies familiarity. Frequency counts have been made for letters, bigrams, trigrams, and words and may be used to select materials of varying frequencies for experimental purposes or for validation of ratings of familiarity. The frequency factor can also be manipulated in the laboratory.

When *S*s judge the familiarity of dissyllables, the correlation (curvilinear) of their judgments with the *m* values for the corresponding items is 0.92 (Noble, 1963, p. 100).

There is evidence that when *S*s judge familiarity or frequency their judgments do have some validity, that is, they are related to the actual frequencies of the units employed. This has been shown for single letters (Attneave, 1953), words (Howes, 1954; Noble, 1963, p. 89), and for bigrams and trigrams (Underwood and Schulz, 1960, pp. 52–56). It is possible, then, that the relation of *m* to learning is really caused by frequency, as *m* and familiarity judgments (which reflect frequency) are so highly correlated. Do frequency and familiarity relate to learning?

Hall (1954) presented lists of twenty words each to *S*s five times and then asked for recalls. The words in the four lists varied in the frequency of occurrence in printed English according to the counts made by Thorndike and Lorge (1944). The most frequent words occurred from fifty to one hundred times per million printed words, and the least frequent once per million. There was a regular increase in recall scores from the less to the more frequent words (12.04 words for the least and 15.04 words for the highest-frequency word lists). Although significant, these differences are small. Deese (1960) and others have verified these findings. Deese, however, was able to show that the relation of recall scores to word frequency is probably due not directly to the frequency of words as such, but to the fact that there are more interword associations among highly frequent than among infrequent words. (Interword associations will be considered in detail in a later section.) If words are associated, the occurrence of one of them is apt to cause *S* to think or "remember" another one. This would increase his recall score for words which are interassociated, as high-frequency words apparently are in the natural language. (High-frequency words yield more associations by the production method than low-frequency words—Underwood, 1959, p. 113; Cofer and Shevitz, 1952.)

So far as words are concerned, high-frequency words are learned more readily by the serial anticipation method than low-frequency words, but three-letter words are learned more rapidly than nonword trigrams which occur with the same frequency in printed English (Underwood and Postman, 1960; Postman, 1961). In paired-associate learning, acquisition was faster when the response terms were high-frequency words (for example, *moment*, *dinner*, *table*) than when they were medium-frequency (for example, *fetish*, *hermit*, *relic*), or low-frequency words (for example, *abbess*, *prefix*, *tenure*). When word frequency varied on the stimulus side, however, learning rate increased between low-frequency and medium-frequency words and declined for high-frequency words. This curvilinear effect is probably due to interword associations (for example, *country* and *doctor* were high-frequency stimuli and may be interassociated).

Word frequency, then, is a variable that is related to rate of learning in free recall, serial, and paired-associate learning. Words are learned faster than trigrams of equal frequency of occurrence in the language. At least some of the effects of word frequency, however, can be attributed to the fact that high-frequency words are interassociated. As will be brought out later, the effect of word associations need not be a facilitative one on learning. Whether facilitation will occur will depend on characteristics of what the task requires *S* to learn.

The effect of frequency in the case of nonwords has also been investigated. Underwood and Schulz (1960, pp. 163–167) studied PA learning with lists in which the stimuli were two-digit numbers and the responses were single letters which varied in frequency of occurrence in printed English. Over fifteen trials high-frequency letters (such as *A*, *O*, and *T*) yielded from eight to eleven correct responses; low-frequency letters (like *V*, *Y*, and *Z*) were correctly anticipated six or seven times. There were exceptions to an exact parallelism between frequency and ease of learning but the general relationship when letters of

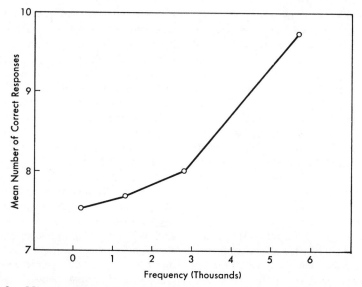

Figure 14-3. **Mean number of correct responses made over fifteen trials of paired-associate learning by thirty-six** *S*s **learning digit-letter pairs. The letters varied in frequency of occurrence in printed English.** (Reprinted with permission from Underwood, B. J., and Schulz, R. W. *Meaningfulness and verbal learning*. Chicago: J. B. Lippincott, 1960.)

similar frequencies are grouped together is regular, as Fig. 14-3 shows.

A similar but much less regular relationship exists between learning rate of bigrams (two-letter sequences) and the frequency of occurrence of bigrams in printed English (Underwood and Schulz, 1960, p. 167–169). Further, when trigrams are used as responses in PA learning, the relationship between learning rate and frequency of occurrence of the the trigrams in English words drops virtually to zero (Underwood and Schulz, 1960, p. 148, pp. 169–173). In serial learning, however, lists composed of high-frequency trigrams are learned somewhat more rapidly than lists made up of low-frequency trigrams (Underwood and Schulz, 1960, pp. 157–161). The interpretation of this finding, as will be seen, is not clear.

The breakdown of the relation between frequency and learning is not complete. As we have seen, the frequency of individual letters and of words relates to learning, although associative factors may be involved in the latter case. In addition, for poorly

integrated units (for example, low-*m* CCCs), letter frequency enters. If, for a poorly integrated CCC, one sums the frequencies in English of each of its letters, learning rate correlates well with the sum of the letter frequencies (Underwood and Schulz, 1960, p. 279). In this instance, however, another factor, the pronunciability of the units, also correlates with learning. Pronunciability also correlates with learning in the case of trigrams in which frequency fails to predict learning. Is pronunciability the basic variable?

We shall consider this question in the next section. Before doing so, however, we will discuss two other ways in which the frequency variable has been manipulated.

Generated Values. To develop materials for learning experiments, Underwood and Schulz (1960, Chapter 9) first collected association data for single letters and for bigrams. In the former case, *S* was asked to give a letter which, to him, most naturally followed the letter presented to him. When 2 letters (bigrams) were presented to *S*, he was asked to write a third letter which seemed to follow the two naturally. Association frequencies were tabulated, revealing such findings as that, among 273 Ss, sixty-one respond to the letter A with the letter T, fifty with the letter B, eleven with the letter R, none with the letter G. To the bigram AA, 127 of the Ss responded with A, twenty-two with T, twelve with U, and none with X or Y. The bigram BF gave no very high-frequency response, the highest being T, which occurred twenty-eight times. The remaining responses were distributed over all the letters, the smallest occurrence being one—for H and Q. (Underwood and Schulz, 1960, present these associative data completely in their Appendix F, pp. 374–428.) Having established these associations, Underwood and Schulz (1960, Chapter 10) could construct trigrams having specific "generated values" (GVs). Let us start with the letter S. We can choose three letters which vary in the frequencies of their occurrences as responses to S, 0 (110), T (50), and B (0). We thus have the bigrams SO, ST, and SB. We can then, for each bigram, choose three letters varying in frequency as responses to each bigram, thus constructing three trigrams. For SO, we might choose T (50), leading to the (word) trigram SOT, or B (33), yielding SOB, or Y (0), yielding SOY. Or, in the case of SB we might choose M (0), giving us the trigram SBM. The trigrams so constructed have different generated values based on the associative responses previously obtained. Thus,

$$S + O = 110 + T\ (50) = SOT = 160$$
$$S + O = 110 + B\ (33) = SOB = 143$$
$$S + O = 110 + Y\ (0)\ = SOY = 110$$
$$S + B = 0 + SB + M\ (0) = SBM = 0$$

Trigrams made up in this way, varying in generated values, were used as stimuli or as responses in PA learning, paired with the numbers 2 through 9. When they were responses, the trigrams AND (GV, 120) and BUG (GV, 53) were correctly anticipated on the average 19.06 times in twenty

trials; HFG (GV, 43), however, was anticipated correctly only 6.17 times. The correlations between GV and learning (over several lists) are high, ranging from 0.67 to 0.89. However, learning also correlates well with the pronunciability of these items, the range being from 0.61 to 0.97; the one correlation below 0.87 occurred for a list which included the trigram XYZ. This trigram is rated as very difficult to pronounce, but its GV is 116. Alphabetical sequences, like XYZ, upset the relationship between rated pronunciability and learning. When trigrams including alphabetical sequences are removed, the correlation for all remaining items between pronunciability and learning is 0.91, whereas for these items GV correlates only 0.78 with learning. Except for alphabetical sequences, GVs, based on frequency, do not do as well in predicting learning of response term trigrams as pronunciability.

When the trigrams are stimuli in PA learning, the same relations with learning hold, but the correlations are not as high. None of the correlations between GV and learning is higher than 0.82, and they range down to 0.39; the r's between pronunciability and learning range from 0.62 to 0.99, and only three are above 0.80. Figure 14-4 shows number of correct responses made in twenty trials as a function of GV and pronunciability for trigrams as stimuli and as responses. It is clear that these predictors have much more importance for *response* trigrams than for stimulus trigrams.

Manipulated Frequency. Frequency of experience can be manipulated in the laboratory, and when this is done the procedure is usually referred to as familiarization. Various methods have been used to accomplish familiarization, and they have in common that S sees or hears each item and makes a reaction to it, by saying or spelling it. Varying amounts of familiarization may be provided.

Noble (1954) found that familiarization training increased the ratings of familiarity

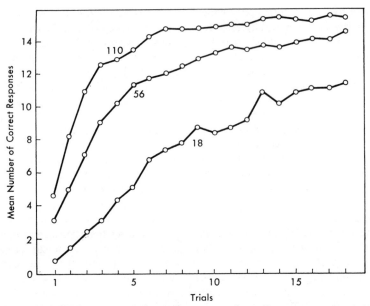

Figure 14-4. Acquisition curves for paired-associate lists over twenty trials for lists with trigram responses; the trigrams represent generated values of 110, 56, and 18. (Reprinted with permission from *Meaningfulness and verbal learning* by Underwood and Schulz, published by J. B. Lippincott Company. Copyright © 1960 by J. B. Lippincott Company.

made for low-*m* dissyllables by *S*s who had not known, during familiarization trials, that they would be asked to rate the items later. Noble (1955), in another experiment, gave zero, one, two, three, four, five, ten, and twenty trials of familiarization in which *S*s pronounced the items; then *S*s learned a serial list. Rate of learning was increased by the higher levels of familiarization training. Similar results for serial learning have been reported by Hovland and Kurtz (1952), by Riley and Phillips (1959), and by Underwood and Schulz (1960, pp. 113–119) for nonsense syllables.

For paired-associate learning, the results reported conflict. Gannon and Noble (1961) found with dissyllables that stimulus familiarization (twenty trials) facilitates PA learning but that response familiarization (also twenty trials) has no effect. In their procedure, the dissyllables were pronounced during both the familiarization and the PA phases of the experiment. Underwood and Schulz (1960, Chapter 6, Experiments 1, 2,

and 4) used nonsense syllables and had their *S*s spell the items during both familiarization and PA learning. They found facilitation of PA learning when the response terms had been familiarized but found either a decrement in or no effect on learning after stimulus term familiarization.

Schulz and Tucker (1962a) used Gannon and Noble's dissyllables and familiarized the dissyllables which were the stimulus terms in PA learning. Number of correct responses made during PA learning increased as a function of number of stimulus familiarization trials (zero, twenty, or sixty trials) when the dissyllables were pronounced during PA learning, thus confirming Gannon and Noble, but went down under instructions not to pronounce them, a result in keeping with some of the results obtained by Underwood and Schulz. In a second experiment, Schulz and Tucker (1962b) used a 4-sec. anticipation interval during PA learning; they used a 4:2 rate. Here there were no differences in rate of learning with familiarization trials for either the pronounce or the do-not-pronounce conditions. Schulz and Tucker believe that practice at pronouncing the dissyllables during familiarization reduced the time required to say them during PA learning. At a 2-2 rate the more of this practice there is, the more quickly S can say the stimulus term and thus have more time in which to anticipate the response. At the 4-2 rate, this advantage of much familiarization is lost, presumably because the 4-sec. interval is enough time to say either familiarized or unfamiliarized dissyllables and still have time to give the response term.

If this interpretation is correct (and there can be dispute about it, see Cofer and Musgrave, 1963, pp. 106–08, 156), perhaps the effects of familiarity-frequency can be reduced to pronunciability. We turn now to this variable, which we have mentioned several times.

Pronunciability

The factor of pronunciability has been identified by Underwood and Schulz (1960) as a very potent one in verbal learning. It is defined by Ss' ratings on a nine-point scale of how easy or difficult it is to pronounce a combination of letters, such as trigrams. To make the ratings, S is instructed to say the items to himself and then to check a point on a rating scale which he thinks is appropriate to each item.

Pronunciability correlates well (0.78) with ratings of the number of associations nonsense syllables would elicit (Underwood and Schulz, 1960, p. 25) and with actual learning for trigrams (for example, 0.76 to 0.95 in one experiment, and 0.81, 0.21, and 0.52 in another), even where frequency fails as a predictor. Correlations between pronunciability and learning vary, as the values just noted indicate, but pronunciability does especially well in predicting learning for items that are relatively easy to pronounce including words (Underwood

and Postman, 1960, p. 80); very difficult items are not predicted consistently as well. At any rate, for trigrams varying between poorly and well-integrated ones, Underwood and Schulz (1960, p. 196) conclude that association value, printed frequency, and m are not fundamental variables in predicting learning so far as response terms in the PA situation are concerned. In their view, a-value, f and m-value display the relations with learning that they do because they are often closely correlated with pronunciability. Frequency, however, for words and for single letters is a predictive variable, and for very poorly integrated units (chiefly, CCCs) summed letter frequency works fairly well.

There is still a question whether pronunciability is or may be based on some kind of frequency. Underwood and Schulz (1960, p. 257, pp. 290–292) suggest that emitted frequency (that is, the frequency with which syllables and words occur in oral speech) may underlie pronunciability and its relationships with other variables. R. C. Johnson (1962) has challenged the emphasis put on pronunciability by Underwood and Schulz. He reanalyzed the data of two of their experiments by first separating the three-letter words, the trigrams which occur as syllables in English (as judged by college students), and the trigrams which are nonsyllables. Then, for each of these sets of items, he compared learning scores for those above and below the median for the set in pronunciability. The differences in learning scores for items thus differentiated by pronunciability were very small. Pronunciability did, however, differentiate the words from syllables and the syllables from nonsyllables. Learning rates were highest for the words as a group, then the syllables, and last the nonsyllables.

Summary

There is no question that *meaningfulness* (either *a* or *m* value), *frequency* and *famili-*

arity, and *pronunciability*, under many conditions, are excellent predictors of the rate of verbal learning. This point may have been obscured in the preceding discussion. Our concern has been to identify the one variable which is perhaps the fundamental one and which underlies the others. So far as the response integration stage in verbal learning is concerned, we are still uncertain as to what the most basic variable is. It is probably frequency of some kind, as Underwood and Schulz indicate when they say that pronunciability may depend on emitted (rather than printed) frequency or when Johnson suggests that three-letter words are experienced more frequently than syllables, which, in turn, occur more frequently than nonsyllables. The easy learning manifested by alphabetical sequences (for example, ABC, XYZ) or common initials (for example, IBM, TWA, IOU) suggests the role of frequency.

Associations may help in the second, or hook-up stage of verbal learning. In this case, *m*- or *a*-value may play a role which is independent of its relations to frequency and pronunciability. R. C. Johnson (1962) used a kind of production method with the trigrams identified as syllables (in which pronunciability made no difference to learning). This method, which required *S*s to write down in 20 sec. as many words as they could think of which contained the syllabic sound, yielded values which correlated between 0.48 and 0.75 with learning scores for the syllables in three of Underwood and Schulz's experiments. Presumably, these correlations indicate the role of the associations in the hook-up stage of learning.

Interitem Association Relations

We have mentioned several times that words are often interassociated and that this fact has implications for verbal learning. What are interword associations, how are they measured, and what may be their effects?

Perhaps the simplest way to describe what interword associations are is to discuss word-association procedures. Suppose one were to say to another person, "I am going to show you a word. When you see the word, please tell me (or write down) the first word other than the word I show you that you think of or that comes to

Table **14-1**   Single Word Free-Association Responses

Response	Male Frequency	Female Frequency	Total Frequency
Chair	325	366	691
Food	35	24	59
Desk	17	16	33
Top	20	10	30
Cloth	16	13	29
Eat	15	8	23
Leg	9	2	11
Dish	2	6	8
Legs	4	3	7
Wood	2	5	7
Kitchen	4	2	6
Fork	0	5	5
Spoon	4	1	5

*S*s were 500 male and 500 female students at the University of Minnesota. Responses were to the stimulus word *Table* (from Palermo and Jenkins, 1964a, pp. 297–298).

Responses occurring with a total frequency of 4: Brown, Dinner, Dishes, Salt
Responses occurring with a total frequency of 3: Flat, Plate, Set, Table, Cloth
Responses occurring with a total frequency of 2: Chairs, Dark, Eating, Floor, Maple, Round, Tennis
Responses occurring with a total frequency of 1: Big, Book, Large, Silverware, Sit

mind." This is an example of word-association procedure, and it would yield single-word, free associations; the associations are free in the sense that no restraints are put upon the respondent. (In controlled association, on the other hand, *S* is restricted to certain kinds of responses, such as opposites or synonyms of the stimulus word.)

Typically, a series of stimulus words is presented to a group of *S*s, each one of which responds to each stimulus under instructions like those just given. For many

Table **14-2**   Interitem Associative Matrix for Fifteen High-frequency Associates of *Butterfly**

	Moth	Insect	Wing	Bird	Fly	Yellow	Net	Pretty	Flowers	Bug	Cocoon	Color	Stomach	Blue	Bees	Average
Moth		2	2		10				2	10						
Insect	4				18					48					2	
Wing				50	24											
Bird			6		30									2		
Fly		10		8						18						
Yellow									3			11		16		
Net	2	2		2												
Pretty																
Flowers						2						2		2	2	
Bug	2	36		2	4										4	
Cocoon	16	6		4						10						
Color														20		
Stomach																
Blue												10				
Bees				15					5							
	24	56	8	81	86	2	0	0	10	86	0	23	0	40	8	28.3

* Reprinted with permission from J. Deese, From the isolated verbal unit to connected discourse. In C. N. Cofer (Ed.). *Verbal learning and verbal behavior.* New York: McGraw-Hill, 1961, p. 18.

stimulus words, particularly frequent nouns and adjectives, adults yield distributions of responses to each stimulus word. Table 14-1 shows such a distribution, taken from Palermo and Jenkins' (1964a) norms for the stimulus word *table*. Inspection of Table 14-1 reveals that the word *chair* occurs with great frequency (69.1 per cent) but that many other responses occur also. The responses, ordered as they are in Table 14-1, form an associative hierarchy to the stimulus word, and the most frequent response (*chair*) is called the primary response.

It turns out, in some instances, that

associations obtained in this way are bi-directional. Thus, *table* elicits the response *chair* and, when *chair* is used as the stimulus word, it elicits *table* as its primary response (total frequency, 428). Other responses, occurring both to *table* and to *chair* are (in college students): *brown, cloth, desk, floor, leg, legs, set, sit, wood.*

It is probable that the vast majority of words, at least those that are known to us, elicit associations, although the variety of responses and the characteristics of their hierarchies may differ considerably from those exhibited for *table* in Table 14-1. Further, some sets of words can be found which are highly associated with one another. Table 14-2, taken from Deese (1961, p. 18), shows interassociations for fifteen words; these associations are limited to the elicitation of one word in the table by any other word also in the table. Other kinds of relations are shown in Table 14-3, taken from Marshall and Cofer (1963, p. 411), for four stimulus words, *oak, pine, hand,* and *glove. Oak* does not elicit *pine* or conversely, but the two words are associatively linked through *tree, forest, shade,* and *wood. Hand* elicits *glove* and

glove elicits *hand,* and these two words are additionally linked by the common responses *finger, hold,* and *warm.*

The examples given in Tables 14-2 and 14-3 show how words may be associatively related. (That words can have no associative relations is clear in Table 14-3; neither *oak* nor *pine* elicits any responses in common with *hand* or *glove.*) Such associative relations may be treated quantitatively (see Garskoff and Houston, 1963; Marshall and Cofer, 1963; Pollio, 1963). Quantitative indices of associative relation vary from simple measures (like the probability with which one word elicits another) to more complex expressions. Two of the somewhat more complex procedures, the Index of Interitem Associative Strength (IIAS) (Deese, 1959) and the Mutual Relatedness (MR) Index (Bousfield, Whitmarsh, and Berkowitz, 1960; Marshall and Cofer, 1963) may be described with reference to Tables 14-2 and 14-3.

Table 14-2 shows for each word in the left-hand column the percentage of *S*s who responded to it with the words in the row at the top. Thus, when *moth* was stimulus, 2 per cent responded with *insect,* 2 per cent

Table **14-3**   Computation of the MF or MR Index for Two Pairs of Words*

| | Stimuli | | | | | Stimuli | | |
	Oak	Pine	R_c‡			Hand	Glove	R_c‡
Oak	(102)†	0	0		Hand	(102)†	53	53
Pine	0	(102)†	0		Glove	17	(102)†	17
Tree	88	70	70		Finger	20	5	5
Forest	1	2	1		Hold	2	1	1
Shade	2	1	1		Warm	1	1	1
Wood	2	5	2					
Sum R_c			74					77

$$\text{MR index} = \frac{R_c}{R_t} = \frac{74}{204} = 0.363 \qquad \text{MR index} = \frac{R_c}{R_t} = \frac{77}{204} = 0.377$$

* These indices were calculated from single response free association. (The words in the columns are responses whose frequencies are entered under their stimuli). Norms collected from 102 students at Brooklyn College.
† Implicit responses.
‡ R_c stands for the responses common to the two stimuli.
Reprinted with permission from Marshall, G. R., & Cofer, C. N. Associative indices as measures of word relatedness: A summary and comparison of ten methods. *J. verb. Learn. verb. Behav.,* 1963, **1,** 408–421.

with *wing*, 10 per cent with *fly*, and so on. Empty cells mean that the word at the head of the column was not given as a response to the stimulus word for that row. To compute IIAS, the entries in the columns are summed, giving the values 24, 56, 8, and so on. In turn, the column sums are totaled, and this total is divided by the number of columns. Many sets of words, of course, have no interitem associative relations and hence IIAS is zero. The value 28.3 is a fairly high one among sets for which IIAS has been computed, but sets with values as high as 48 have been reported (Marshall and Cofer, 1963, p. 416).

The values listed in Table 14–3 for *oak* and *pine* and for *hand* and *glove* are limited to those responses which both of the stimuli in the two cases elicit. Thus, *tree*, *forest*, *shade*, and *wood* are elicited by both *oak* and *pine* and may be regarded as responses in common, or R_c. The MR index is computed by taking the lower of the two values for each R_c and summing them. The lower value is taken because the responses in excess of the lower value are not in common; thus, for the response *wood*, the value 2 is taken, rather than 5, because the latter value means that *wood* occurred as a response to *pine* three more times than it did to *oak*. Hence, the three responses are not in common between the words. The lower values for the common responses are summed and divided by the number of Ss responding. In Table 14-3, the data are for 102 Ss responding to *oak* and also to *pine*. The denominator is, therefore, 204.

The procedure is the same for *hand* and *glove* as it is for *oak* and *pine* with one exception. *Oak* and *pine* do not elicit each other as associates, whereas *hand* and *glove* do. It is assumed that on seeing the word, all Ss say it to themselves. (They are prevented by the instructions from saying or writing it as an association.) If this is true for *hand*, for example, one can count as common responses the value 53, which is the frequency with which *hand* occurs as a response to *glove*. In other respects, the

computation of MR for this pair is the same as it is for the pair *oak–pine*.

We have now discussed what word associations are and how they may be measured. What of their effects?

The presence of interitem associations facilitates *free* learning or recall, that is, lists of words with high IIAS values are recalled better than lists with low values; Deese (1959) found a correlation of 0.88 between recall scores and IIAS values in this situation. Likewise, as MR increases, word recall increases (Marshall, 1963), as Figure 14-5 shows. In addition, items that are interassociated tend to be recalled together even though at presentation they were separated. Jenkins, Mink, and Russell (1958) made up a list of words by using word-association stimuli and words (one for each stimulus) which were free associates of the stimuli. These S-R pairs were scrambled at presentation. In the recalls of the list, however, the Ss tended to recall the two members of the pair together, that is, to *cluster* them. Such associative clustering occurred more frequently when the response member in the pair was a high-frequency than when it was a low-frequency associate of the stimulus term. Characteristics of the free recall of words then, that is, its amount and its organization as indicated by clustering, are closely related to the pre-existing associations among the words.

It seems reasonable that paired-associate learning of pairs which have interword associations should be easier than learning of pairs not having such free associations. With adults, however, differences in learning of pairs in which the associative connections of the pair members vary have failed to occur, except when the associative difference is very large (Cofer, 1961, pp. 194–195). With children, on the other hand, smaller differences in the associative connection between pair members are reflected in paired-associate learning, the pairs with the stronger connections being easier to learn (Wicklund, Palermo, and Jenkins, 1964).

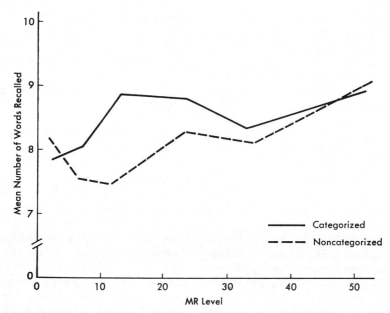

Figure 14-5. Mean number of words recalled from six pairs whose members were categorized and six pairs whose members were not categorized as a function of the MR level of the pairs. (Reprinted from Marshall, G. R. The organization of verbal material in free recall: The effects of patterns of associative overlap on clustering. Ph. D. dissertation, New York University, 1963.)

With adults, Postman (1962) used the paired-associate method with pairs in which the response members were primary free-association responses to the stimuli with which they were paired and with pairs in which the responses had been given by only two of 1,000 Ss in free association to the stimuli. The stimuli varied in their Thorndike-Lorge frequencies. For high-frequency stimuli, Postman found no difference in learning scores between the pairs in which the responses were primaries and the pairs in which the responses were low-frequency associates (2/1,000). However, with low-frequency stimuli, the pairs including the primaries were learned faster than the ones including the low-frequency associates. Martin (1964) has reported similar findings.

Associative strength can facilitate paired-associate learning in a somewhat different way. Suppose that a word, such as *stem*, elicits as its primary associate another word,

flower. *Flower*, as a stimulus, elicits as its primary the word *smell*. *Stem* does not elicit *smell* as an associate, nor does *smell* elicit *stem*. The question, however, is whether the learning of a pair like *stem–smell* will be facilitated by the indirect linkage between these two words, as compared to the learning of a pair of unassociated words which have equal Thorndike-Lorge frequencies.

Palermo and Jenkins (1964b), with fifth-grade children, have replicated and extended an experiment with adults reported by Jarrett and Scheibe (1963). The latter investigators had found that directly associated pairs, like *stem–flower*, were learned more quickly than the indirectly related pairs, like *stem–smell*. Pairs of the latter kind, however, were learned faster than control pairs, such as *stem–joy*. Palermo and Jenkins studied two situations. In one, the A-B list, the normative associative strength between the stimulus (A) and its response (B) was varied, from 0.05 to 0.45. The other situation was provided by list A-C. We can illustrate the setup of this list by an example. *Black* elicits the free association *dark* thirty-six times in 100 (0.36) fifth-grade *S*s; *dark* elicits *light*, similarly, forty-one times (0.41). *Black* does not elicit *light* and *light* does not elicit *black*. One can estimate, however, the indirect or mediated association between *black* and *light* by multiplying the two probability values already mentioned (0.36 × ±0.41), yielding a value of 0.15. Palermo and Jenkins set up a number of A-C pairs in which the product of the two associative tendencies varied from 0.01 to 0.20. Both kinds of pairs, A-B and A-C, were learned more rapidly than control pairs. In addition the strength of the connection affected learning whether it was direct (A-B) or indirect (A-C). This is indicated by the rank order correlation of −0.76 between number of errors during learning and associative strength for the twenty-four pairs of both types. (See also Houston, 1964.) These studies, like those on free-recall learning, indicate that interword association influences learning in the PA case. The effects with adults are not so strong in PA learning as they are in free-recall learning and are not as marked as they are in children. What these differences may mean will be discussed in more detail later in this section.

The effects of interword associations have also been studied in serial anticipation learning. Weingartner (1963) used two lists of sixteen words, each one of which was composed of fifteen free associates to the stimulus *butterfly* (and it included *butterfly*). We will speak only of this list. The interword associations of these sixteen words had been factor-analyzed by Deese (1962a). The results of this analysis showed that the associations to the sixteen words arranged the words into four groups, each group being highly interrelated in an associative sense. The groups were: *moth, butterfly, insect, bug; bird, wing, bees, fly; blue, color,*

sky, yellow; sunshine, summer, garden, spring. One of the arrangements in which Weingartner presented this list for serial learning was the one just indicated, so that the interword associative relations were preserved within each group. In another arrangement, the sixteen words were randomized so that the associative groupings or structures were disrupted. The question was the following: Would the list with the associative structure intact be learned more readily than the randomized list in serial learning? The answer is clear; the list with associative structure was learned to criterion in an average of nine trials, whereas the randomized list required 15.2 trials, a highly significant difference. (Space prevents us from describing other arrangements studied by Weingartner.)

Weingartner does not report on a control list of unrelated words, so we cannot say whether the difference just described is due to the facilitating effects of the intact associations or to interference arising from the disruption of the associative structures. Probably both effects are operating. It is clear that interword associations can interfere with learning when what is to be learned is incompatible with the nature of the associations. Coleman (1963) had his *S*s learn paired associates connected by the word *is*—for example, *Doughnut is crusty.* For each of the nouns he employed as stimuli (for example, *doughnut*), Coleman obtained continued associations restricted to adjectives. For a given *S* and a given stimulus, Coleman was then able to select an associate which occurred early in the association period and one that occurred later. The ones occurring early can be considered as stronger than the ones occurring later, and it is also true that for the early ones there are fewer other and stronger associations than there are for the later ones. Suppose with *doughnut* as the stimulus the following adjective associations are given in sequence: *round, sweet, sugary, powdery, crusty. Round* is the strongest associate, as it is given first, and *crusty* is the weakest.

Sweet is preceded by one stronger associate, but *crusty* is preceded by four stronger associates. Would the pairs *doughnut–round*, or *doughnut–sweet*, be learned more rapidly than *doughnut–crusty*? Coleman's findings provide an affirmative answer to this question and also indicate that a large proportion of extralist intrusions for a given pair consists of the occurrence of an associate which is stronger than the response to be learned in relation to that stimulus. This suggests that the stronger associations *interfered with* the learning of the pairs containing the weaker associates (see also Bilodeau, Fox, and Blick, 1963; Spence, 1963).

Pre-experimental interword associations, it may be concluded, have powerful effects in all the major situations employed to study learning of discrete verbal items— free recall, paired-associate learning, and serial anticipation learning. Whether the effects yield facilitation or interference is dependent on the task and on the relationship between what *S* is required to learn and what the pre-existing associations are.

Conceptual Relations

Words have many relationships to one another. Many of these may be designated as logical or conceptual. Thus, a word like *dog* fits into the class or category *animal*, along with other animal names such as *cat*, *lion*, *monkey*, *giraffe*, *donkey*, *zebra*, *aardvark*, and many others. A word like *smooth* has synonyms, like *even*, and opposites, like *rough*. It is also an adjective, whereas the animal names are nouns. Other words may represent parts of things designated by still other words; thus, *head*, *toe*, *feet*, *hand*, *finger*, *nose*, and so on, are all parts of the whole indicated by the word *body*. These are only a few of possible conceptual relations among words, but they will suffice to illustrate the possibilities.

A question that can be raised is whether the kinds of relations we have just described are significant to verbal learning. Will a pair composed of two synonyms be learned more readily than a pair composed of unrelated words?

Some research is available which can be used to answer this question. Before describing it, however, we must point to a possible confounding of logical relationships among words. Figure 14-6 shows a plot of data reported by Cofer (1957). The curve shows the extent of associative overlap between the members of pairs of words; the pair members vary in the extent to which they are judged to be synonyms of one another (Haagen, 1949). Highly synonymous pair members, like *ancient–old* (high synonymity is indicated by the low numbers on the x-axis of the figure), have a high degree of associative overlap, whereas pair members like *kingly* and *sceptered*, which are rated as distant synonyms, have a low degree of associative relationship. Now if a pair like *ancient–old* is more quickly learned than the pair *kingly–sceptered*, shall we attribute the difference to the differing degrees of synonymity or the differing amounts of associative overlap? (In this example, the Thorndike-Lorge frequencies of the words in the two pairs also differ.) Ideally, the variables, confounded in the illustration, should be separated so that their individual contribution to learning may be assessed. Relatively few experiments, however, have made the separation. Conceptual relations have been studied chiefly in free-recall learning and in paired-associate learning.

Free Recall. Bousfield (1953) presented a randomized list of sixty words to his *S*s a single time. The list was composed of an equal number of words which could be classified into the mutually exclusive categories of vegetables, animals, professions, and men's first names. The recalls were scored both for words recalled and for clustering of words from the same category. The mean recall score was about 25, and there was evidence of pronounced

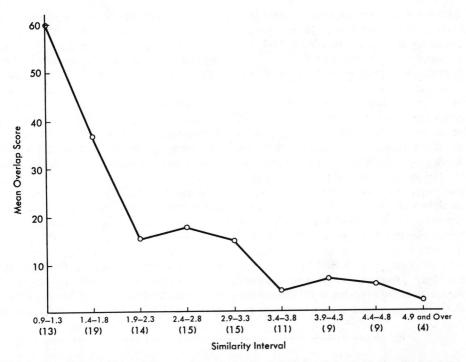

Figure 14-6. **Mean associative overlap scores (MR) for pairs of items judged for synonymity (similarity). Highly similar words received low ratings, less similar words high ratings. The numbers in parentheses along the abscissa indicate the number of pairs represented in the mean overlap score for the similarity interval.** (Reprinted with permission from Cofer, C. N. On some factors in the organizational characteristics of free recall. *Amer. Psychol.*, 1965b, **20**, 261–272.)

clustering in terms of the categories contained in the list. This experiment has been repeated with a variety of word lists by both Bousfield and by other investigators, with similar results. Bousfield has investigated a number of the variables involved in clustering, but space does not permit this work to be reviewed here. Underwood (1964a, pp. 63–65) has reported that the recall scores are higher for word lists which contain categorized words than for comparable lists without categorized words. Category relations, then, may facilitate total recall as well as provide a basis for the reorganization of materials in recall which clustering of related items seems to signify.

A possible interpretation of category clustering is that it is mediated in the sense

that *S*, identifying the categories and their names as he hears the randomly presented items, can during recall remember the categories and list items pertinent to them. This would account for clustering and also, perhaps, for the augmented recall. Cofer, Bruce, and Reicher (1966) have carried out a test of this formulation in the following experiment. They used two lists of words, one of which (HF) was composed of high-frequency associates of the category names employed, the other (LF) composed of low-frequency associations to the same names. Each list was presented randomly to an independent group of *S*s and also by means of a block presentation. In the latter procedure, all the items from one category were presented one after another, then the items from a second category, and so on.

Item exposure times were also varied under each of these conditions. Their data for clustering are shown in Figure 14-7 and for word recall in Figure 14-8.

Postexperimental inquiry revealed that Ss could correctly identify the categories contained in both the RF and LF lists following block presentation. If the S codes by means of category names, then clustering should be augmented more by block presentation for the LF list than for the HF list, as compared to clustering after random presentation. However, the results, as shown in Figure 14-7, do not support this expectation, as block presentation augments clustering slightly more in the HF list than in the LF list. One might expect also that word recall would be augmented by block presentation, because category names become available with this procedure. As Figure 14-8 shows, there was in-

creased recall after block presentation for the HF list but not for the LF list. Because their manipulations for augmenting clustering and recall via the category name affected the HF list more than the LF list, Cofer, Bruce, and Reicher interpret their findings in terms of associative factors rather than coding or category factors. Whether all findings of category clustering in Bousfield's situation can be reduced to associative factors must remain, however, an open question.

Marshall (1963) has studied clustering in the recall of *pairs* of words. In his lists, the pairs, which were separated at presentation, were of two types. In one, the pair members were instances of the same category (for example, *eagle*, *crow*) and in the other the pair members were not categorized (for example, *dream*, *night*). The associative overlap (MR), however, was the same for

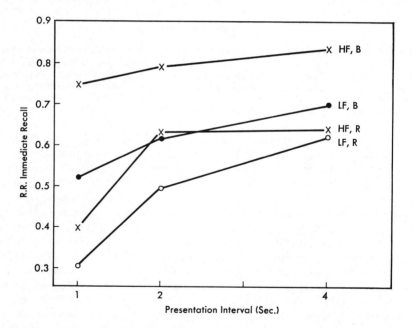

Figure 14-7. Mean ratio of repetition scores obtained from free recall of lists varying (H, L) in associative probability of the items as responses to the category names and varying in manner of presentation, that is, the items from the categories occurred randomly (R) or were blocked (B). Presentation interval for the items also varied, as shown on the abscissa. (Reprinted with permission from Cofer, C. N., Bruce, D. R., and Reicher, G. M. Clustering in free recall as a function of certain methodological variations. *J. exp. Psychol.*, 1966, **71**, 858–866.

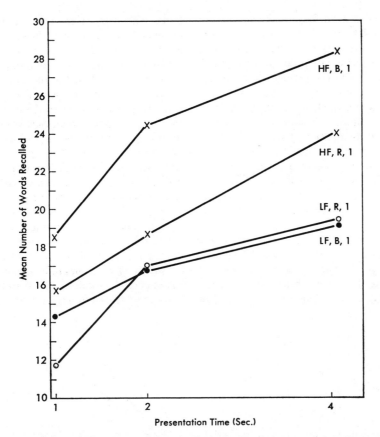

Figure 14-8. Mean number of words recalled for the same conditions as shown in Fig. 14-7. (Reprinted with permission from Cofer, C. N., Bruce, D. R., and Reicher, G. M. Clustering in free recall as a function of certain methodological variations. *J. exp. Psychol.*, 1966, **71**, 858–866.

the categorized pair members as for the noncategorized pair members. Figure 14-9 shows clustering and Figure 14-5 word recall for categorized and noncategorized pairs as a function of MR level. This evidence suggests that, at least at low to moderate MR levels, the factor of categorization augments clustering and the recall score in free recall.

Paired-Associate Learning. Rate of learning for pairs, equal in associative overlap (MR) but in some of which the pair members were categorized and in others of which they were not, has been studied in the writer's laboratory (Cofer, 1965a). Over

the first five trials of learning (after which the differences become small) in one experiment, the categorized pairs showed significantly more correct responses than the noncategorized pairs, as Figure 14-10 shows. In another experiment which employed different items, however, there was no difference in the rate of acquisition for categorized and noncategorized pairs.

A variation in the method of paired-associate learning, which resembles methods used in some studies of concept formation, is to require that one response be associated to more than one stimulus. Suppose, for example, that we have twenty-four stimuli and only six responses. We can then pair each response with four of the stimuli. In studies which have used this procedure, the relations among the stimuli with which a given response is paired are of interest. How will it affect learning if the stimuli with the common response are similar (for example, synonyms) or instances of some class (for example, animals)?

Richardson (1958) used sixteen-item lists in which there were sixteen stimuli and only four responses. The responses were nonsense syllables and the stimuli were words. In one list, the response VOM was associated separately with each of the words *sacred, divine, hallowed, holy*, all of which have similar meanings, and in another list VOM was associated with the words *perfect, dirty, removed, rising*, which are not similar; there were three other sets of four words in each list, each having one response. The

pairs with the same response were *not* presented consecutively during learning. More correct responses were shown during learning for the list containing sets of similar stimuli than for the other list. In another experiment (Richardson, 1960) three lists were compared. In one, a given response was paired with each word in a set of four synonyms, as in the experiment just described; in another a given response was paired with each of four examples of a class (for example, *pine, maple, walnut, elm*, each of which belongs to the class *tree*). In the third, the four words with which a response was paired contained a common property (for example, *barrel, doughnut, knob, balloon*, all of which are round). The list involving examples of a class was learned significantly more rapidly than the other lists; the list containing sets of synonyms

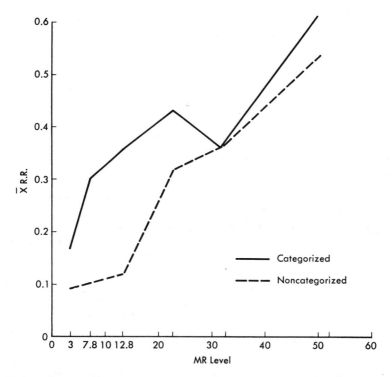

Figure 14-9.   Mean ratio of repetition ($\bar{x}$RR) scores as a function of MR level for free recall of pairs whose members were categorized or not categorized. (Reprinted from Marshall, G. R. The organization of verbal material in free recall: The effects of patterns of associative overlap on clustering. Ph.D. dissertation, New York University, 1963.)

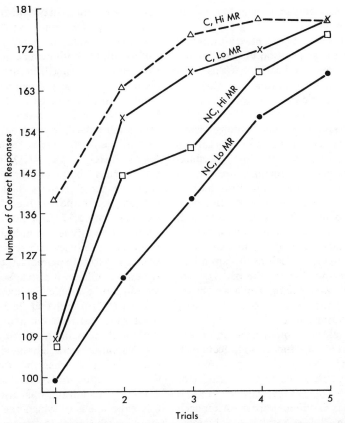

Figure 14-10. Mean number of correct responses during paired-associate learning of pairs whose members were from the same category (C) or not from the same category (NC) and whose members shared high associate overlap (high MR) or low associative overlaps (low MR). (Plotted from data reported by Cofer, C. N. Measures of associative overlap and paired associate learning. Technical Report No. 7, under Contract Nonr 656(30), the Pennsylvania State University, 1965a.)

was next but not significantly different from the third list.

It is not certain, from Richardson's work, whether the differences obtained reflect conceptual relations; it is possible that associative interrelations in the word sets would differ among the lists and account for the learning differences. Further investigation is needed to settle this problem.

Similarity Among Items

Verbal items may be similar to one another in a variety of ways, but the major aspects of similarity which have been studied are letter correspondences, meaning, and association. Among nonsense trigrams, similarity is varied by the number of letters two trigrams have in common. DAX and BUP are dissimilar because they have no letters in common; DUP is more similar to DAX than BUP is because of the common letter; DAP is even more similar than DUP, of course.

Similarity of meaning can be varied among words by manipulating the synonymity between items. Or, similarity can be manipulated by varying associative relations among items in a list. Words which are interassociated can be said to be associatively similar.

Interitem similarity can have a profound effect upon the acquisition of verbal materials. The evidence indicates that this effect is usually positive during the response learning phase and is often negative during the associative phase of verbal learning.

Evidence concerning the response learning phase comes, for the most part, from studies of free recall. In this procedure, specific associational linkages are not required; instead, S is asked to reproduce, in any order, a list of items which has been presented to him. We have already seen that interitem associational relations and common category membership of items appear to augment recall in this situation: both of these features of the material can be regarded as providing similarity among the items. Thus, in free recall, similarity augments performance.

Further evidence comes from an experiment reported by Underwood, Runquist, and Schulz (1959). One group of Ss was shown ten highly similar words (for example, *cheerful, sunny, carefree,* and so on) five times in different orders. After each presentation, a free recall was obtained. The other group went through the same procedure for a list of ten dissimilar words (for example, *spicy, rounded, hairy,* and so on). On the first three trials the numbers of responses correctly given for the highly similar list was considerably larger than it was for the low similar list. These two sets of words were also used in a paired-associate situation (with CVCs as stimuli), but the Ss were asked, at given trials, to give a free recall of the response terms. Again, after the early trials, more correct responses were given for the highly similar than for the low similar list. In actual paired-associate learning over fifteen trials, however, these findings were reversed, the low-similarity list occasioning more correct responses than the highly similar list. This reversal presumably reflects the influence of similarity on the associative phase of paired-

associate learning. In two other experiments (Underwood, Ekstrand, and Keppel, 1964), PA learning was compared for two lists, the stimuli for both being color names and the responses being trigrams. In the low-similarity list, the six trigrams were dissimilar, no letters being duplicated. In the highly similar list, however, the six trigrams were made up from only five letters, so that the items were very similar (XQV, XKH, KHQ, VHX, VKQ, HVK). Over fifteen trials, the mean number of correct responses per S given for the low-similarity list was 31.50 and for the high-similarity list was only 5.77. The power of the response similarity factor in learning is clear from the ratio of correct responses for the two lists: 5 to 1. In paired-associate learning stimulus similarity is also a factor in rate of learning; for example, Feldman and Underwood (1957) found that 28.53 trials were required to learn a seven-item list in which the stimuli were highly similar trigrams and the responses were unrelated words and only 15.13 trials when the stimuli (for the same response words) were dissimilar trigrams. A condition was also studied in this experiment in which the stimuli (trigrams) were similar to one another and the responses (words) were similar to one another also. This condition required the greatest number of trials for learning (34.20).

Parallel results appear for serial anticipation learning. Underwood and Toad (1951) compared the learning of a list of fourteen similar adjectives with that of a list of fourteen dissimilar adjectives. The similar adjectives required an average of 18.70 trials for learning, whereas the dissimilar adjectives took only 13.75 trials (Underwood and Toad, 1951, Table 1, p. 127). Underwood (1952) also compared the learning of lists of fourteen CVCs, in which three levels of similarity were arranged by means of repetitions of letters in the first or last position of the trigram. Again, considerably more trials were needed for learning the high-similarity trigrams than for the trigrams of intermediate similarity; in turn, the latter were more difficult to learn than dissimilar trigrams.

Horowitz (1961) has pointed out that these studies of interitem similarity in serial learning yield different results from those using free recall (Miller, 1958). To resolve this conflict, he studied two lists of twelve trigrams each, one made up from only four letters and the other from twelve different letters. With different groups of Ss, Horowitz then obtained free recalls for these lists and with other Ss provided the trigrams and asked the Ss to place them in the order in which they had been presented. Each of these procedures was carried out over ten trials. In the first five trials of free-recall learning, more of the highly similar than of the low-similarity trigrams were correctly recalled. However, the dissimilar trigrams achieved higher scores on a measure of ordering throughout learning as compared with the similar trigrams. This suggests that response learning was facilitated by similarity but that serial ordering (presumably involving associative learning) was impeded by similarity. Unusual features of Horowitz' high-similarity trigram list, however, may reduce the generality of this conclusion in the free-recall with trigrams (Underwood, Ekstrand, and Keppel, 1964, pp. 207–208).

Higa (1963) has made a study of paired-associate learning with words in which associative and semantic similarity was studied. Each list consisted of twelve trigram-word pairs. In one list the twelve response words included six pairs of antonym associates (for example, *dark*, *light*), in another of coordinates (for example, *apple*, *pear*), in a third of free associates (for example, *scissors*, *cut*), in a fourth of synonyms (for example, *fast*, *rapid*), and so on. A list in which the response words were unrelated served as the control. The finding was that lists the response members of which included antonyms, synonyms, or free associates were more difficult to learn than the control list. Presumably this is because of the interference among response members in these three lists which was not present in the control list. It is important to note that this experiment differs from those described in the sections on association and conceptual relations, where associative and category relations were said to facilitate PA learning. In those experiments the facilitation arose because the *stimulus and response* were linked associatively or conceptually. In Higa's experiment, however, it was the *responses in the list* (each paired with a different trigram) which were related in these ways.

We have seen from the work just reviewed that interitem similarity is a potent variable in verbal learning. In general, its influence seems to be facilitative of response learning but is negative for associative learning. This negative effect probably arises from the interference occurring because of confusions due to the similarity of stimuli, of responses or of both. This interference will be discussed elsewhere in this book, especially in the section on retention and transfer. We have emphasized here interitem similarity (or intralist similarity). In retention and transfer, interlist similarity will be emphasized as well.

Connected Materials

Many of the variables we have discussed with regard to single items and the relationships among them may be relevant to items which are connected, the case when words are found in passages of prose or in poems. However, most of the efforts to describe and to investigate the effects on learning of characteristics of connected materials have considered other problems. Chief of these have been the statistical structure and the grammatical features of connected material. We will consider these matters shortly.

One of the problems which has impeded work on the learning of connected materials, in contrast to discrete items, has been the scoring of the recalls. This has been a problem because Ss, in recalling a story for example, often alter the original wording by putting the materials in their own words. Or, in other instances, they alter the tense or the arrangement of modifiers, and the like. Although scoring in terms of "idea units" has been employed, thus permitting variations in language to be ignored, idea units are not entirely satisfactory for many purposes. King (1960), King and Schulz (1960), King and Yu (1962) have conducted several studies designed to throw light on this problem.

Basic to King's procedure is a criterion score. This score is obtained by having judges take a series of recalls and rank or otherwise compare them for accuracy against the original story itself. The result is a set of recalls scaled for accuracy in terms of the original; such scale values have been found to be highly reliable. Employing these scaled criterion values, King has then determined the relationships between them and various other ways of scoring the stories objectively. In his studies, King has found two kinds of scores which relate very well to the criterion values. One of these is a measure of the length of the recall, as indexed by number of words in the recall (without respect to accuracy) or the number of words in the recall that are identical to words in the original. The other kind of score is more complex, sometimes being reflected in the number of content words (words other than articles, conjunctions, prepositions, and so on) correctly reproduced from the story, the number of idea units present in the recall, or in other similar scores. The writer's impression is that this second kind of score has something to do with accurate reproduction of content. King has shown that, for some stories, sheer number of words in the recall is the best measure as compared with the scaled accuracy scores; for other stories, however, one of the content scores is to be preferred.

King's work, so far as it has gone, is encouraging in that it suggests that two relatively simple and objective kinds of scores can be used to evaluate the accuracy of recalls for complex materials such as stories. Most of the work to be reviewed next has employed somewhat cruder measures.

Redundancy. One feature of connected discourse is that it has a structure such that given the occurrence of one item the later occurrence of certain items is more likely than the occurrence of other items. This is to say that connected discourse is, to some extent, redundant.

For example, if a sentence begins, "The boy . . .," certain kinds of words are much more likely to follow than others. Thus verbs and conjunctions are much more probable than an article or another noun. If a conjunction follows, giving "The boy and . . .," another article and another noun are very likely, whereas verbs, another conjunction, or prepositions have almost no likelihood of occurrence. The context, then, given by one or more items, has a restrictive influence on what word classes can follow next. The context can limit not only what part of speech will follow but also the members of a given part of speech that will occur. Thus, if we are asked to add the next word to the following, "The boy and the . . .," most of us will not only add a noun but will also choose only a few of all the nouns that there are. *Girl*, *man*, and *dog* might be very likely additions, but *grass*, *shelf*, and *desk* would be unlikely.

Miller and Selfridge (1950) have inquired whether this redundant property of connected material is a factor in the long reported readiness with which connected material is learned as compared with the learning of unconnected items. To study the problem, they first devised several approximations to normal English text. They constructed "passages" of several lengths (10 to 50 words) at each level of approximation.

We can illustrate the procedure best by

starting with the construction of a second-order approximation to English. First, a common word, say *it*, is selected and presented to someone who is asked to use it in a sentence. Suppose he writes, "It is raining." We then take the word written next after the one we gave *S* and ask another person to use it in a sentence. In our example, *is* would be used next, and the second *S* might provide the sentence, "Is he going?" *He* would then be given to the third *S*, and he might provide the sentence, "He rode away." Continuing this process over enough people would give us a string of words of the desired length, each pair of which could be used in a sentence and each item of which had been chosen in the context of one other word. The string we have generated so far is composed of *is he rode*. Higher orders of approximation are developed by enlarging the contents determining the selection of the successive words. Two-word, three-word, four-word contexts would be used for third-, fourth-, and fifth-order approximations, respectively.

After they had obtained higher-order approximations, Miller and Selfridge scrambled words from them, and these scrambled strings were the first-order approximation. The zero-order approximation was obtained by randomly selecting words from the 30,000 commonest words listed by Thorndike and Lorge (1944). A sample of text was taken from contemporary fiction or biography.

Miller and Selfridge presented lists of this kind to *S*s who attempted to recall them. Figure 14-11 shows a plot of the per cent of words correctly recalled as a function of order of approximation for the four passage lengths employed. Order of approximation is clearly an important determiner of recall (as is list length); its effects are seen over a wider range of approximation for the longest list than for the shortest list, however.

Because all the words used were English words, and the major difference among the orders of approximation lay in their statistical structure or redundancy, it is clear that redundancy is a factor which can influence recall. Deese (1961, pp. 23–27) suggests that the higher orders permit *S*s to guess more accurately what must have been in the passage than do the lower orders. He has deleted words from passages at each of several orders of approximation and has asked *S*s to guess at the deleted words. Guessing scores increase, as order of approximation goes up, approximately as do recall scores. Deese's interpretation implies that *S*s do not necessarily recall more from the higher than from the lower orders of approximation but rather that they can more effectively use their language habits (based on the redundancy of the language) to fill in what must have been there in the higher orders than in the lower orders. This is certainly a distinct possibility, but it may also be that more is learned from the higher- than from the lower-order approximations.

Before leaving this topic, it will be of interest to give examples (from the ten-word sets) for some of the approximations (Miller and Selfridge, 1950, pp. 184–185):

zero-order: byway, consequence, handsomely, financier, bent, flux, cavalry, swiftness, weather-beaten, extent.

third-order: tall and thin boy is a biped is the beat.

seventh-order: recognize her abilities in music after he scolded him before.

Grammatical Organization. In speaking, in the last section, of the redundant features of connected material, we implied a more or less statistical character to this redundancy; that is, given a certain amount of material, the probabilities of what can or will follow are altered in comparison with what they would be given other amounts of material as context. However, connected material has features, for example, its grammar, which may confer on it an organization that is independent of this statistical structure, or, perhaps, which may help to explain or account for redundancy.

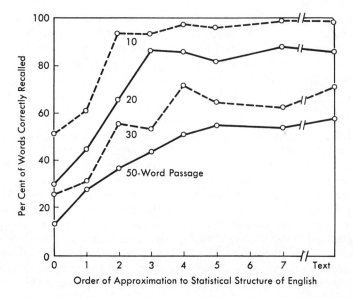

Figure 14-11. Percentage of words correctly recalled from passages of differing length and varying in order of approximation to the statistical structure of the English language. (Reprinted with permission from Miller, G. A., and Selfridge, J. Verbal context and the recall of meaningful material. *Amer. J. Psychol.*, 1950, **63**, 176–185.)

Epstein (1961, 1962) has reported experiments which cast light on this matter. He has compared the acquisition of a string of nonsense words under several conditions. In one, the seven items were presented, together with the article *the* and the preposition *in*. Thus:

the yig wur vum rix hum in jeg miv

In another, the same items were presented as a sentence (with initial capitalization and a terminal period) and with grammatical endings on the items. Thus,

The yigs wur vumly rixly hum in jegest miv.

Other conditions repeated the items in sentence form, but in a random sequence, or shifted the grammatical endings around among the nonsense stems.

These lists were learned by *S*s (the method of complete presentation) to a criterion of one perfect repetition. The "pure" items (the first example given above), required 7.56 trials, on the average, for learning, whereas the set with the gram-matical tags (the second example above) required 5.77 trials, a significant difference. This suggests that the grammatical tags facilitated learning.

Epstein has also compared the learning of nonsense sentences (for example, *cruel tables sang falling circles to empty bitter pencils*) with the learning of randomized strings composed of the same words. Only 3.50 trials were required to learn the meaningless sentences, but 5.94 trials were required for the same words in random order. It is highly unlikely that the sequences of specific items in either the sentences composed of nonsense words or of meaningful words has any prior likelihood of occurrence. Yet the addition of the endings in the first case and the imposition of grammatical order, in the second, have made these strings easier to learn. How generally this effect would occur is not known with certainty. Marks and Miller (1964) report data confirming Epstein's results with nonsense sentences.

Do parts of speech vary in their learnability? Glanzer (1962) studied paired-associate learning for word-nonsense syllable and nonsense-syllable-word pairs. When the words in the pairs were content words (nouns, adjectives, verbs, adverbs), the pairs were learned more readily than when the words were function words (prepositions, conjunctions, and pronouns). The nonsense-word pairs showed better learning than the word-nonsense pairs, a result in keeping with what we already know about the effects of m in PA learning. Nouns and adjectives were learned faster than adverbs and verbs, and nouns were consistently somewhat superior to adjectives. (All of the English words were at the AA level in the count of Thorndike and Lorge.) In an unpublished study, P. Welsh (1955) compared free recalls of adjectives and nouns of roughly comparable Thorndike-Lorge frequency over three trials of acquisition. Recall scores for the eight high-frequency nouns (7AA, 1A) for the three trials were 4.89, 6.43, and 7.15 as compared to the scores of the high-frequency adjectives (4AA, 4A) of 2.63, 4.46, and 6.13. The direction of this difference is the same as that reported by Glanzer.

In English, we usually place adjectives before nouns, whereas in other languages this is not always the case. Lambert and Paivio (1956) asked their Ss to learn two lists of twenty-eight words each. The lists were composed of seven groups of four words, each group containing one noun and three adjectives. The S learned one list with the items within groups arranged in noun-adjective order (for example, *bachelor bold respectable homely*) and the other list with the words within groups arranged in adjective-noun order (*pleasing vivid memorable melody*). The Ss, who were native speakers of English, required twenty-two trials and made 183 errors in learning the items in the A-N order but only 16.65 trials and 136 errors in the N-A order. Thus, the easier list contained items in an order contrary to that of ordinary English. This

finding may reveal the point that nouns and adjectives have different functions in language, the nouns serving as a sort of anchor around which adjectives are organized and therefore facilitating the learning and retention of adjectives in the N-A order (performance was better for nouns in the A-N than in the N-A order, however).

Grammatical structure is much more complicated than is perhaps implied in the discussion of grammatical tags, nonsense sentences composed of words, and parts of speech. There is some uncertainty as to how grammar may best be described and what psychological processes it involves in the user of a language. Current emphasis seems to be on the analysis of phrase structure or constituent structure and the transformation by sets of rules of sentences from a basic model (called a kernel) to various realized forms, such as simple, declarative sentences, interrogatives, passives, negatives, and so on (Miller, 1962). Implicit in these notions is the idea that a conception of the generation of sentences from one word to the next, in a left to right order, such as was implied in our discussion of redundancy, is much too simple (Chomsky, 1957).

Contemporary linguists find a description of language which conceives of an hierarchical structure in language to be a useful one. Consider the sentence *The tall boy saved the dying woman* (N. F. Johnson, 1964). This sentence, S, can be decomposed into a number of constituents. At the first level, S may be rewritten as a noun phrase (NP: The tall boy) and a verb phrase (VP: saved the dying woman). In turn, these constituents can be decomposed further, into their constituents. For example, the verb phrase contains the units, verb and noun phrase. Although the latter unit can be broken down further, the verb itself (saved) cannot be. What we end up with from an analysis of this kind is the string of words which make up the sentence but with the relationships of the words to one another laid out in a diagram sometimes

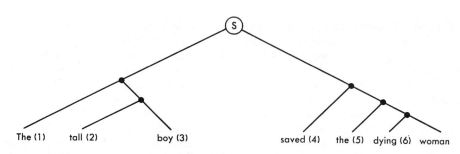

Figure 14-12. Tree diagram showing the constituent or phrase structure of the sentence, "The tall boy saved the dying woman." (Reprinted with permission from Johnson, N. F. Linguistic models and functional units of language behavior. In S. Rosenberg (Ed.), *Directions in psycholinguistics*. New York: Macmillan, 1965. Pp. 48.)

called a tree diagram or a phrase marker. Johnson (1964, Fig. 2) presents the diagram shown in Figure 14-12 for the foregoing sentence.

Diagrams such as this one carry the implication of a hierarchical organization. A further implication is that some words go together smoothly, in a unitary way, and others do not. In the example it is clear that *the dying woman* is a unit but that *saved the dying* is not. The idea, in brief, is that the words belong together in terms of the higher-order units (phrases) in which they have common membership.

Some sentences are ambiguous, and it will help us to see what is involved in this kind of analysis to describe one. The ambiguity arises from uncertainty as to what are the underlying units. In the sentence *They are eating apples*, the meaning is ambiguous, and the two possible implications of the sentence are seen in the two diagrams

of Fig. 14-13 (from Miller, 1962, Fig. 3). The ambiguity arises over whether eating is a part of the verb or a part of the predicate noun phrase. Without other information as to what is being said, we cannot decide on the appropriate constituent or phrase structure for this sentence.

Constituent or phrase structure analysis appears to afford a useful way to describe some features of language (but additional descriptive devices are necessary). However, the question can be raised whether this kind of analysis also has psychological reality, that is, do the linguistic levels or units revealed in a phrase marker function as units in the behavior of speakers, listeners, and learners?

N. F. Johnson (1964; see also Miller, 1962) has made a direct attempt to answer this question. Johnson's work is predicated on the assumption that if the linguistic units have psychological reality and if the

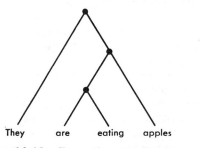
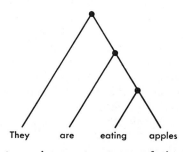

Figure 14-13. Tree diagram illustrating the two phrase structures of the ambiguous sentence, "They are eating apples." (Reprinted with permission from Miller, G. A. Some psychological studies of grammar. *Amer. Psychol.*, 1962, **17**, 748–762.)

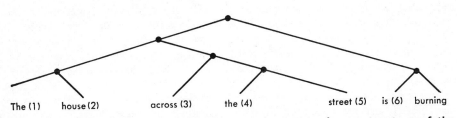

The (1)   house (2)   across (3)   the (4)   street (5)   is (6) burning

Figure 14-14. Tree diagram showing the constituent or phrase structure of the sentence, "The house across the street is burning." (Reprinted with permission from Johnson, N. F. Linguistic models and functional units of language behavior. In S. Rosenberg (Ed.), *Directions in Psycholinguistics*. New York: Macmillan, 1965. Pp. 48.)

linguistic units are present in material to be learned, then learning scores should vary in some way with the linguistic units.

Johnson tested these propositions in a learning experiment. There were eight pairs, composed of a digit (the stimulus) and a sentence (the response), for a given *S*, and thirteen trials were given with the anticipation method of P-A learning. Half of the *S*s learned sentences of the form *The tall boy saved the dying woman*, whose structure we have already indicated, and the other half learned sentences of the form *The house across the street is burning*, whose structure is as Figure 14-14 shows.

The *S*'s responses were scored for transitional errors; that is, given that a preceding word was correct what is the probability that the next item would be wrong? Thus, to give an example from the sentence on the burning house, if the word *The* is correct, what proportion of the time (over trials and *S*s) is an error made on *house*? If constituent structure is the only factor working, then in the sentence about the dying woman the main transition is between NP and VP, and Johnson could argue that errors across transition 3 should be greater than across the other transitions, as transition 3 is between constituent structures, whereas the other transitions occur within the two major units. In the sentence about the burning house, however, there are two transitions [(2) and (5)] between major units, and they should show more errors than the other transitions.

Johnson's data reveal that the highest

transitional error probabilities do, in fact, occur at transition 3 and at transitions 2 and 5 in the two sentences, respectively. This suggests the psychological reality of the phrase structure units, although other aspects of his data suggest to Johnson · that the complete pattern of transitional error probabilities, including those within phrases, requires a more detailed analysis. Johnson offers an analysis which suggests that the difficulty of any transition may be related to the number of levels within the phrase structure involved in its derivation. This hypothesis, together with other factors, can account fairly well for transitional error probabilities both within and between constituent units.

The psychological reality of the units arising in phrase structure analysis has so far been little investigated (see also, Mandler and Mandler, 1964), but as far as such investigations have gone it would appear that properties of connected materials, important to learning them, may be revealed by such analyses. Although some linguists do not see any need to go beyond constituent structure in the analysis of language, others do. Among these is Chomsky (1957), who has proposed conceptions referred to as transformational grammars.

A goal of linguists, according to Chomsky, is to devise a statement of the grammar of a language in terms of rules, which when applied will generate all of the grammatical sentences of the language (many of which have not perhaps been spoken) and no sentences which are ungrammatical. In addition, the system of rules should be as simple as possible. There are many sentences in a language like English which have structures very different from those we have considered so far. For example, there are questions, negations, passives, and a number of others. It may be possible to develop phrase structure analyses of many of these types of sentences, but Chomsky argues that it would be more parsimonious to develop a statement of a basic or kernel grammar and to derive the various kinds of sentences the language has from this grammar by means of a set of transformation rules. These rules would comprise a transformational grammar, which, with the phrase structure grammar (and also morphophonemic rules), provide for a complete grammar of a language.

In the space available, we cannot develop these ideas further here. However, several psychologists have been concerned with the question of whether the steps involved in a transitional grammar have psychological reality. In doing so, they have translated Chomsky's notions into terms permitting psychological study. (These translations have not always met with linguistic approval. See Bever, Fodor, and Weksel, 1965.) In essence, the translations involve the assertion that fewer transformational steps are involved in deriving a simple, affirmative, declarative sentence from the kernel than are involved in deriving sentences such as negatives, passives, passive negatives, and the like.

So far as acquisition of connected materials is concerned, the major study to date of the relative difficulty of different kinds of sentences was reported by Mehler (1963). Each of his Ss was given five presentations of a group of eight sentences, containing one example of each of eight types of sentences. The major findings were that the simple declarative sentences were learned more readily than the other kinds and that more of the errors of syntax that were made during the learning were in the direction of simplification of the syntactic structure than in the direction of making it more complex.

Summary. We have seen that connected material, unlike discrete items, has features such as redundancy and grammatical organization that are important to its acquisition. It has long been said that connected materials are easier to learn than unconnected materials containing the same number of items. The studies of redundancy and grammatical organization help to specify the reasons for this difference and to indicate the critical features of connected materials which make it easier to learn.

Many other factors may be mentioned in relation to the properties of materials which may affect their learnability. We can mention amount of material, its sensory qualities (for example, color, size), its emotionality, whether it can be grouped or organized, whether it permits rhythmical recitation, and so on. Such factors have not received the extensive study and analysis that, as we have seen, the variables reviewed here have been given. It is not at all certain whether the other factors are independent of those reviewed here. In any case, current research has been mainly concerned with those characteristics of materials which we have discussed. Reviews of the material on other characteristics may be found in McGeoch (1942) and McGeoch and Irion (1952).

Methods and Models

Now that we have examined in some detail the major ways in which verbal materials employed in the laboratory may vary, we can turn to a further consideration of the common procedures used in the study of verbal learning. We outlined the basic features of these methods in the first chapter of this section. We now summarize work directed to the understanding of the processes involved in the methods and to the description of certain methodological variation which have effects on acquisition.

Paired-Associate Learning

Variations in Procedure

Random Versus Serial Presentation. In Chapter 13, we mentioned that the sequence of the pairs is usually altered from trial to trial to prevent serial learning. Results of experiments in which constant serial order and varying serial order of the pairs have been compared have, in the main, found that acquisition is facilitated by the constant serial order (Battig, Brown, and Nelson, 1963). However, the differences are seldom large and are occasionally reversed

(Martin and Saltz, 1963). The advantage of constant serial presentation, when it occurs, arises, according to Battig *et al.*, not from the serial chaining of the response terms but from the association of the stimulus term, in the case of difficult associations, with serial-position cues.

Anticipation Versus Recall Procedures. Many, if not most, experiments on PA learning use the anticipation procedure, in which, during presentation of the stimulus term, S tries to give the response term before the latter appears in the aperture of the drum. This procedure is presumed to have the virtue of providing for immediate knowledge of results (or reinforcement). Alternative methods do not provide immediate knowledge of results. Nevertheless, these alternative procedures have been found to produce learning (Battig and Brackett, 1961; Cook and Spitzer, 1960; Lockhead, 1962) as rapidly as the anticipation procedure.

Battig and Brackett's procedure may be described to illustrate the essential point. In their *recall method*, each trial is composed of two parts. In the first part the pairs are presented, one by one, at a given exposure interval. In the second part the stimuli are presented, and S is asked to produce the response. In neither part of the trial does S anticipate (at least overtly) the response, and he receives no direct knowledge of results. Yet Battig and Brackett obtained more rapid learning for the recall than for the anticipation procedure. This finding has interesting implications for the role of knowledge of results and reinforcement in verbal learning, but the evidence indicates that it occurs under a restricted set of conditions.

Time Relations. There are two loci in PA learning where time may be varied. One is the presentation interval for the pairs (or of the stimulus alone or of the pair alone). The other is the intertrial interval. In a sense, either locus may be used in order to distribute practice, although the intertrial interval is more commonly employed in studies of distributed practice.

Bugelski (1962) presented the stimulus of his pairs for 2 sec., and the stimulus remained in view while the response, in different groups, was presented for 2, 4, 6, 8, or 15 additional sec. Each S learned eight pairs of nonsense syllables. Much faster learning was obtained for the long presentations than for the short ones, in terms of trials. However, when the exposure time of an item was multiplied by the number of trials it required for learning, thus yielding a value for total presentation time, a constant value was obtained. That is, an item presented for a long interval was learned in fewer trials than one presented for a short interval, but the total presentation time was equal. In this sense, distribution had no real effect on learning as represented by presentation time. Nodine (1963) varied the stimulus presentation interval and the pair presentation time independently of one another over intervals from 0.5 to 4 sec. Elongating either presentation time increased the rate of learning, more effect occurring with lengthened pair than stimulus presentation intervals. (No comparison can be made in Nodine's data for

total presentation time.) Bugelski and Nodine believe the effects of the lengthened intervals arise from attempts at mediation and rehearsal.

In motor-skills learning, pronounced effects on acquisition have been observed from spacing trials, that is, distributing practice by elongating the intertrial interval. Underwood (1961), however, has been able, in an extensive series of investigations with verbal materials, to obtain only small effects for distributed as compared to massed practice. Where it occurs, the advantage for distributed practice seems to arise during the response integration stage of learning and not during the associative stage of learning.

Processes and Models

Stimulus and Item Selection. What processes underlie paired-associate learning? We have already seen, in the previous chapter, the arguments and the evidence concerning a two-stage conception of verbal learning. In PA learning, of course, *response* integration has been said to be critical. However, there is additional information concerning the stimulus. Underwood, Ham, and Ekstrand (1962) investigated whether Ss use all the stimulus information available or whether they show a selection process so far as the stimulus is concerned. The investigators devised compound stimuli which were paired with single-digit numbers during acquisition. The stimuli for one group were trigrams (T) and in the other three-letter words (W) and, in each instance, the verbal unit was surrounded by a colored border (C). After acquisition each group was divided into three subgroups. One continued with the same material for additional trials (WC-WC, TC-TC), a second had additional trials with only the colors as stimuli (WC-C, TC-C), and the third with only the verbal units as stimuli (WC-W, TC-T). For the TC-C group there was very little change in performance as compared with the TC-TC group, suggesting that during original learning the colors, rather than the trigrams, had been serving as the effective or functional stimuli; the TC-T group showed a marked impairment in the first several trials without the colors, indicating that the trigrams had not been used much as stimuli when the colors were available. For the other groups, however, there was impairment for both WC-W and WC-C, as compared to the unchanged subgroup (WC-WC), the impairment being more pronounced for WC-C than for WC-W. This suggests that the words were somewhat more effective than the colors as functional stimuli, whereas the colors were more effective than the trigrams.

From this and other evidence it is clear that Ss may select what aspect of the stimulus they use in paired-associate learning (see Underwood, 1963) and that this selection may be based on meaningfulness (on the assumption that words are more meaningful than colors and that colors are more meaningful than trigrams). This is to say that the stimulus which the E sets up (the nominal stimulus) may not be the one to which S is responding (the functional stimulus). Stimulus selection in PA learning makes PA learning somewhat similar to concept formation (Underwood, 1963, p. 47).

We have already encountered the idea that Ss in verbal learning experiments are or may be selective with respect to the *pairs* they learn, or learn first, during PA procedures. In Chapter 13 we mentioned in connection with the purported demonstrations of one-trial learning that item selection on the basis of difficulty perhaps operated and that item selection made the results obtained difficult to interpret unequivocally. There are probably other bases on which items are selected and learned before other items are turned to and their learning attempted. Item selection and use of a functional rather than the nominal stimulus complicate the nature of PA learning and

must ultimately be taken into account by models of the process.

Reverse Associations. The fundamental interest of Es in paired associate learning is usually in the formation of associations in the direction S → R. The question can be asked, however, whether Ss learn anything about the reverse association, that is, R → S. A number of studies have provided evidence that the backward association is learned. For example, Jantz and Underwood (1958) studied the acquisition (S-R) of nonsense-syllable-word pairs and then tested for recall (R-S) of the nonsense syllables. Both the meaningfulness of the nonsense syllables and the number of trials of S-R learning were positively related to stimulus recall (R-S), a result also found for meaningfulness by Hunt (1959).

McGuire's Model. McGuire (1961) has attempted to integrate a number of processes involved in PA learning in a single formulation. Specifically, McGuire has spoken of three habits which must or may be learned in the case of a single pair. One is or may be an implicit mediating response which "represents" the stimulus. It represents that aspect of the stimulus which discriminates that stimulus from the other stimuli of the set. Thus, if BUK and DUK are two stimulus trigrams in a set, Ss need encode only the first letter to differentiate them. The work on stimulus selection suggests that Ss may do just this.

The representational response (r) is conceived by McGuire to be stimulus producing, so that it can be written as r → s. This stimulus produced by the r is what is actually associated with the response member of the pair, in McGuire's analysis, and this association is the second habit learned. The third habit involved is, where necessary, what we have elsewhere termed the integration of the response, that is, the assembling of the elements (such as C, Q, X) into a unit (CQX). The response thus may itself represent a chain of habits to be learned, although, in the case of well-integrated responses, this habit may be transferred to the PA task from prior learning. McGuire (1961, p. 336) conceptualizes the learning of a pair with a poorly integrated response as follows:

$$S \rightarrow r \rightarrow s \rightarrow Ra \rightarrow sa \rightarrow Rb \rightarrow sb \rightarrow Rc,$$

in the case of a three-element response (Ra, Rb, Rc) which must be integrated.

McGuire tested this formulation in the following experiment. Each S learned nine paired associates by the anticipation method. The stimuli were solid black circles of varying diameters, and in Set I differed by 0.14 cm. steps, in Set II by 0.07 cm. steps. Discrimination among stimuli therefore should be easier for Set I than for Set II. The responses were numbers, one set being the single digit 1 through 9, the other being three-digit numbers which began with a different integer from 1 to 9 and in which the second and third digits were assigned randomly. The single-digit numbers should be well integrated as responses, the three-digit numbers less so.

Stimulus discrimination was thus varied by means of the diameters of the circles and response integration by means of the one and three-digit numbers. McGuire arranged his instructions so that Ss would be likely to label the stimuli with numbers from 1 to 9; such labeling constitutes the representational response (r) indicated earlier. To vary the difficulty of learning the association between the labeling response ($r \rightarrow s$) and the response (single or three-digit numbers) McGuire arranged the responses in one of two ways. In one the smallest number (single-digit or first digit of the three-digit unit) was assigned to the smallest circle, and the other numbers were assigned to the circles in order of increasing size. The other arrangement was to assign the numbers to the circles randomly. Where there was a correspondence between the response number and circle size, S was so informed ahead of time, whereas in

the other cases the random pairing was described.

The difficulty of the $r \rightarrow s \rightarrow R$ habit was, then, varied by having the numbers ordered or random with respect to circle size. Together with the levels of stimulus discriminability and response integration, this experiment gets at all three components of McGuire's model.

McGuire's results show that all three of these components affected learning scores. By making certain assumptions, he derived quantitative estimates of the effects and the results obtained agree well with these estimates. We shall not go further in presenting the details of the estimates and the results as, to at least some extent, these are probably specific to McGuire's experiment.

Mediation Model. McGuire's labeling response is essentially a mediator, that is, it intervenes between and links the nominal stimulus and the response. Other writers have emphasized mediational processes in PA learning, however, without stressing the representational character of the mediator, so far as the nominal stimulus is concerned.

Underwood and Schulz (1960, pp. 296–300) report an experiment in which thirty-five Ss learned lists of eight low-m trigrams paired with responses which were common three-letter words. The Ss were asked how they tied together the members of the pairs. Of the 280 pairs involved (8 pairs × 35 Ss), the Ss reported for 205 of them that they used an association between some aspect of the stimulus and the response to put the pair members together. These associations had the character that they intervened between the stimulus and the response, or *mediated* the connection. For example, for the pair RZL-cat, one S reported that Z is the hissing sound of a cat and for RZL-boy another reported that RZL resembles lazy, and he used lazy to hook boy to RZL. Other, more complex mediators were reported. It is important to note, of course, that no such associations were reported for

27 per cent of the pairs (which were, however, learned), so that mediation through associations is not essential for learning pairs. It should also be made clear that the mediating associations being discussed here supply a chain: stimulus-association-response. It is not true that the response was already an association (in the sense of free association) to the stimulus (in Chapter 14 we discussed such cases).

A mediation model holds that, in PA learning, the hook-up stage involves mediating associations; if it is true that there were no associations for mediation when the *S*s did not report any such, then the mediation model cannot account for all of PA learning (see Underwood, 1964a, pp. 68–70), and it should be noted also that the responses in the experiment just summarized were high in *m*; low-*m* stimuli and responses might not yield as much evidence for mediating associations as was shown in this experiment. Nevertheless, mediating processes are probably widespread in PA learning (see Dallett, 1964a).

Free Recall and Free-Recall Learning

We discussed free recall in the last chapter, stressing (1) the predictability of recall scores from interitem associations, (2) associative and other kinds of clustering, and (3) the effects of interitem similarity on recall. Most of our discussion dealt with recalls obtained after a single presentation of a list. In the present section, we bring out certain other factors related to recall after one or more presentations and outline a model for free-recall learning.

Variations in Procedure

Murdock (1960a) has made an extensive study of free recall of lists made up of unrelated words drawn from a set of common English words. Using lists composed of 20, 30, 40, 50, 75, and 100 words and multiple trials, he finds that acquisition can be described according to the general equation,

$$R = c(1 - e^{-bn})$$

where R is the number of words recalled after each presentation, c is the upper limit or asymptote, b is the slope of the curve, and n is the number of presentations (e is the base of natural logarithms). The asymptote (c) turns out to be list length, and the equation fits the data reasonably well. In further work, Murdock was able to show that recall after one presentation is a function chiefly of total presentation time of the list. That is, recall would be essentially the same for the following condition: with list length given by the first number and presentation-time (sec.) by the second, presentation time is constant for the following lists: 20-3, 30-2, 40-1½, 60-1. Recalls for these four lists in fact were 9.3, 9.3, 9.6, and 8.4 words, differences which are not significant. Although there are undoubtedly limits to the prediction of number of items recalled from list presentation time, these results show the power of this factor.

In most experiments employing free recall, S is given virtually unlimited time in which to recall the items after a presentation. Ekstrand and Underwood (1963) have compared free recall under such unpaced conditions with scores obtained under paced recall. In paced recall, *S*s were cued to recall a word every 2 sec. Recall scores were uniformly and significantly higher under unpaced than under paced conditions, but the differences were not large. Unfortunately, total recall time was over twice as great for unpaced as for paced recall, and the disadvantage of paced recall might be much reduced had equivalent recall time been provided under paced recall conditions.

The free-recall procedure does not require that the order in which the items were presented be duplicated in recall. It is of some interest, however, to compare recalls for the same items when order is and is not a required feature of recall. In this comparison, interitem similarity is minimal, whereas our concern in Chapter 14, where we also made this comparison, was with the effects of interitem similarity on the two conditions of recall.

Waugh (1961) compared recalls of forty-eight-item lists over six trials under the following conditions: (1) serial recall, in which the items were to be recalled in their order of presentation; (2) free recall, in which the order of items at presentation varied on each trial; and (3) free recall, in which the order in which the items were presented was constant over the trials. The increase in number of items recalled in serial recall was linear with trials, but free recall, for both kinds of presentation, showed a negatively accelerated growth of recall scores with trials. On early trials, more words were recalled under free than under serial recall, but by the sixth trial this difference was reversed, and serial recall was superior, a finding confirmed by Dallett (1963). The linear learning curve for serial recall suggests the addition of a constant number of words to recall for each presentation, whereas free recall reveals a declining addition to recall with each presentation (negative acceleration). These curve forms may mean that different mechanisms are involved in free and serial recall, as studied by Waugh. There was no difference for free recall arising from varied and constant orders of presentation.

Serial Position Curves. In attempting to understand free recall, information concerning the order in which the items are recalled and the extent to which recall of items differs in accordance with their serial positions in the list as presented is of interest. Deese and Kaufman (1957) asked separate groups of Ss to make oral recalls of lists of either ten or thirty-two unrelated words. Each S heard and recalled ten individual lists one at a time at one list length. The

results show a pronounced tendency for the items presented last (end of list) to be recalled better than those presented in the middle of the list and those at the beginning of the list; recall was poorest for the items in the middle of the list. This result has been verified by Murdock (1962), who has presented an idealized curve which describes rather well serial position curves under these conditions (many lists for a given S) for free recall. It is shown in Figure 15-1. Deese and Kaufman also report a marked relationship between the frequency with which an item is recalled and the time of its occurrence in recall: the items recalled early are those most often recalled, those recalled late are least often recalled. In terms of Figure 15-1, this means that the end items are recalled first (recency), then the initial items, and last the middle items (see also Deese, 1957).

Deese and Kaufman (1957) also studied recalls for 100-word passages of prose, constructed in such a way that there were ten statements in each passage, and so that the serial position of the statements could be varied without change in meaning. The serial position curve for the recall of these passages was markedly different from that shown in Figure 15-1. For the passages, the best recall occurred for the first position (primacy), next the two end positions, and the intermediate positions declined regularly from each end to the sixth position, which showed the least recall. This curve, unlike that for free recall of unrelated words, is similar to that obtained for serial anticipation learning (see the relevant part of this chapter), although Ss who recalled the passages were not instructed explicitly to preserve the order of items in their recalls. Deese and Kaufman then studied free recall of passages of different approximations to English. In general, the serial position curves they obtained for zero and first-order passages resemble the one shown in Figure 15-1, whereas the curves for the higher-order approximations resemble the one described previously for the ten-

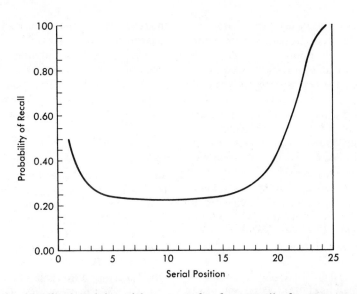

Figure 15-1.   Idealized serial position curve for free recall of a twenty-word list. (Reprinted with permission from Murdock, B. B., Jr. The serial position effect of free recall. *J. exp. Psychol.*, 1962, **64**, 482–488.)

statement passages. Clearly the sequential character of the higher order approximations (and of textual passages) reorganizes the way in which *S*s recall; the relationship here is between order in recall and position in the passage rather than between order in recall and frequency of recall. Instructions can also alter the character of recall (Deese, 1957). Introducing instructions for sequential recall after the list is presented changes the curve from one displaying a strong recency effect to one showing a strong primacy effect. These changes are further accentuated if instructions for sequential recall occur both before list presentation and before recall.

The data we have discussed come from recalls after a single presentation of a given list. Work with multiple presentations would have considerable interest (Dallett, 1963).

Number of Categories in a List. In the last chapter we spoke of category clustering and the recall of lists in which items are categorized as compared to lists in which items are not categorized. We now turn to a consideration of recall as a function of the number of categories into which the items of a list may be classified.

Mathews (1954) used lists composed of twenty-four names (for example, of poets and scientists) and found that recall increased as the number of categories represented in the list increased, up to six categories, which was the largest number of categories her lists contained. Bousfield and Cohen (1956) studied forty-item lists, with the items belonging to two, four, or eight categories, and found recall to increase with number of categories for naive but not for experienced *S*s (see also Cohen and Bousfield, 1956). Dallett (1964b) used twelve-item lists containing items from one to six categories. When the items from the same category were presented contiguously, recall was best for the four category list and dropped for the one with six categories; when the items were randomized, recall was best for a list with two categories and dropped for four- and six-category lists. In another experiment, Dallett gave his *S*s a listing of the categories involved before the list was presented, and *S*s retained the category list during list presentation and at recall. Under these conditions, recall did not drop for the six-category list under contiguous presentation and improved also for two and six-category lists under random presentation. (The list of categories did not help recall for random presentation of the four-category list.) With twenty-four-item lists, Dallett found recall to decline fairly consistently with the number of categories in the list (2 to 12) for both random and contiguous presentation arrangements. Dallett's findings do not agree with those obtained by Mathews and by Bousfield and Cohen, and the discrepancy is as yet unexplained.

Tulving's Model. Tulving (1964) has presented an analysis of the processes implicated in the acquisition of a list of words by free-recall learning. Tulving argues (see Chapter 13) that immediately after a word is presented it can be recalled at once. The fact that it may not be recalled in the recall of the entire list he attributes, then, not to a failure of its being learned but rather to its having been forgotten. There are two loci of forgetting for items, according to his analysis. One is *intratrial forgetting*, that is, forgetting that occurs between the presentation of the item and the time at which it is to be recalled. The other is intertrial forgetting; intertrial retention may be perfect on a given trial—the S remembers the item during the recall phase of the trial. However, he may have forgotten it by the recall phase of the *next* trial. This is *intertrial forgetting*. These two processes must be overcome if S is to learn the list. He may do so by augmenting intratrial and intertrial *retention*, which presumably increases because of processes incident to the repetition of the list. However, the evidence indicates that it is intertrial retention which changes. Tulving analyzed free-recall learning data for lists of unrelated words by measuring over pairs of trials (for example, trials 0 and 1, 1 and 2, 2 and 3) intratrial and intertrial retention. He found that

intertrial retention rises linearly with the logarithm of trials (n) and that intratrial retention declines slightly but linearly with trials (n). (There is reason to believe that its slope should be zero.) Summing these two components yields the equation:

$$P \text{ (performance} = a \log n + bn + c,$$
$$\text{where } a, b, \text{ and } c \text{ are constants.}$$

This equation was found to fit the obtained data closely and better than the exponential function suggested by Murdock (1960a).

Why does intertrial retention improve over trials? Tulving argues that this improvement arises from the fact that Ss organize the items of the list as they proceed from trial to trial. This "subjective organization" (Tulving, 1962) is seen in trial-to-trial analysis when two or more items recalled adjacently on one trial continue to be recalled on subsequent trials. The S is conceived to organize items into units or "chunks" (Miller, 1956) and the chunks can get larger as trials proceed. Tulving suggests that it is this subjective organizing process which permits items to be added to the recalls as trials continue and for mastery of the list to be achieved. Not all investigators of free recall agree with Tulving on this proposition. Carterette and Coleman (1963), for example, argue that knowledge of the items precedes their organization, the reverse of Tulving's position.

Serial Learning

As was pointed out in Chapter 13, Ebbinghaus (1885) used the method of serial learning in the first studies of verbal learning, and the method has been used widely in the investigation of a number of problems of human learning. Over the last decade or so, however, PA learning has come to equal or greater prominence than serial learning. One reason for this is the desire of investigators that the study of associative processes be conducted in a simple situation—in the individual pair. The usual procedures employed in PA learning have been thought to permit this more than does serial learning because the pairs in a PA list are relatively more independent of one another than the items are in a serial list. In addition, the position of an item in a serial list is an important condition of learning, one that is not present in ordinary PA learning. So for the study of minimal conditions of association, PA learning has come to be preferred.

However, serial learning still poses problems of interest in its own right. One of long standing is the mechanisms responsible for the serial-position curve itself. Another, which has come to light more recently, is the nature of the stimulus and of what is learned in serial learning. In connection with these problems, models of serial learning processes have developed. We turn to these problems and the models after first describing some variables which affect serial learning and some phenomena which characterize it.

Variables

We spoke in the last chapter of variations in serial learning performance as a function of the characteristics of materials. Here we shall speak essentially of procedural variations.

Time Relations. Item-presentation time may be varied in serial learning, and learning with the longer intervals usually requires a reduced number of trials to criterion (Hovland, 1938). However, in serial learning duration of item presentation is confounded with time for anticipation of the correct response, and weak responses (with longer latencies) might be recalled with longer exposure intervals but would not be recalled under short exposures. Although Hovland found that presentation time (trials × exposure duration) was roughly

constant for serial learning, paralleling Bugelski's (1962) findings with PA learning, his results are inconclusive because of the confounding just mentioned—weak responses may have latencies too long to be given under short exposures. Keppel and Rehula (1965) studied acquisition of a fourteen-adjective serial list under a 2-sec. or a 4-sec. item-presentation interval. After criterion (five out of fourteen or ten out of fourteen) was reached, half of each group was switched to the other rate, the other halves remaining at the original rates. There was also an alternation group in which alternate trials were at the short and long exposure intervals. During acquisition, Keppel and Rehula found that the long exposure groups reached criterion more rapidly than the short exposure groups, but that there were no differences when total presentation time was constant. Further, after the switch to the other exposure rate, performance appeared to be independent of the rate present during acquisition but was affected by the rate present after the switch. Parallel findings were obtained from the alternation group. Total presentation time, in serial as well as in PA and free-recall learning, rather than presentation interval, seems to be a temporal determinant of rate of learning.

Underwood (1961) has reviewed the evidence on variations in learning attributable to differences in the intertrial interval (distributed practice). Some facilitation of learning in the case of serial lists does occur under distribution, and he attributes the facilitation to the response integration stage of learning.

Phenomena

Two major phenomena in serial learning have received extensive treatment. One concerns the formation of remote associations. The other is the serial position effect. At one time, explanations of the serial position effect drew heavily on remote associations (see McGeoch and Irion, 1952, pp. 125-134). This seems no longer to be true, so that we can treat these topics separately.

Remote Associations. If items are presented in the invariant order 1, 2, 3, 4, 5, 6, 7 (with numbers standing for syllables or words), S may be said to form the correct associations, during learning, between items 1 and 2, 2 and 3, 3 and 4, and so on. These associations are termed direct, forward associations. However, S may also learn other associations, that is, between items 1 and 3, 1 and 4, 1 and 5, 2 and 4, 4 and 7, and so on. These are remote, forward associations, remote (at varying degrees of remoteness) because the items are not adjacent. In addition, it is conceivable that backward associations may also be formed, that is, $3 \rightarrow 1$, $5 \rightarrow 4$, and so on. It has long been believed that remote forward and backward association are formed and that, in general, the strength of such associations is a function of their degree of remoteness.

Slamecka (1964) has questioned whether the evidence in fact justifies the assertion that remote associations exist. Three methods have been used to demonstrate remote associations, and we will now describe each one, together with Slamecka's critique of it.

THE METHOD OF DERIVED LISTS. This was the method used by Ebbinghaus to study the question of remote associations. After a list had been learned, say one with items 1, 2, 3, 4, 5, 6, 7, a derived list (one degree forward remoteness) would be the items in order 1, 3, 5, 7, 2, 4, 6. Skipping more than one intervening item and using backward associations were other ways of setting up derived lists. Ebbinghaus found that learning of such lists was most rapid when the degree of remoteness was small and declined as remoteness increased; backward associations, by this method, appeared to be weaker than forward associations of comparable remoteness. Ebbinghaus' control was a random arrangement of items from the first list, and he computed for all of his derived lists (including the random

one) a savings score, that is, how many sec. learning time were saved in second-list learning as compared to first-list relearning. All of the derived lists showed greater savings than the random one. This result, which has been taken as evidence for remote associations, has also been interpreted as showing positive transfer arising from remote associations.

However, as Hakes and Young (1966) have observed, when suitable controls are instituted [as by Irion (1946)] the random list actually shows negative transfer, and the derivative lists show negative transfer as well, though less than the random lists. As Hakes and Young point out, negative transfer should be expected, as the strongest associations, when second-list learning begins, are the direct associations (for example, 1–2, 2–3), and they provide a source of interference with the learning of the associations in the derived lists. Such an argument, valid though it is, is not critical, however, to the question whether remote associations are formed.

Slamecka (1964) has argued that evidence of faster learning of derived lists does not establish the existence of remote associations. He points out that Ebbinghaus made use of the method of complete presentation and thus could have viewed nonadjacent associations in sequence during acquisition. Also, Ebbinghaus was his own S and knew the principle by which derived lists were constructed. Furthermore, Ebbinghaus read the lists in a rhythmical fashion, whereas rhythm is usually prevented in other investigations. Slamecka believes that the regular patterning involved in the relation of the derived lists to the first list (that is, 1–3–5 from 1–2–3–4–5) may permit S to mediate his performance on derived lists and thus to appear to learn them more rapidly than the first list. Slamecka reports three experiments which support his arguments and lead him to conclude that the method of derived lists does not demonstrate the existence of remote associations (see Bugelski, 1965; Slamecka, 1965).

THE ASSOCIATION METHOD. In this procedure, S first learns the serial list; then each item is presented to him, one at a time, and S is asked to respond by giving the first response (usually from the list) that occurs to him. It has often been reported (see McGeoch, 1936) that the number of associations decreases as degree of remoteness increases. Slamecka has argued that these findings result not from remote associations, but rather from the different availabilities of items arising from the serial positions they occupied in the serial list. This is to say that since midlist items are perhaps marginally learned they would not be as available as end-of-the-list items, which are better learned (reflecting the serial position curve). Slamecka reported an experiment in which no serial learning could occur at all but provided different frequencies of exposure (availabilities) for the several items used. Then, using an association test, he obtained results which resemble remote association gradients. Although Dallett (1965) and Bugelski (1965) have attacked this conclusion, Slamecka (1965) has provided satisfactory answers.

METHOD OF ANTICIPATORY AND PERSEVERATIVE ERRORS. If in learning a list one gives a response that is wrong where given but which would have been right later in the sequence, he has committed an anticipatory error; if he gives a response, wrong in that place but right at an earlier part of the sequence, he has made a perseverative error. Analysis of the patterns of such errors has revealed evidence often taken to demonstrate the existence of remote associations. Although more forward than backward associations occur under this method and although errors are inversely related to degree of remoteness, Slamecka (1964) has argued that these facts do not demonstrate the existence of remote associations. Rather, he asserts, these responses represent guessing on the part of S. Using this assumption, Slamecka was able to predict fairly well the pattern of errors in learning data (see Bugelski, 1965; Slamecka, 1965).

Slamecka has, thus, challenged the findings from each of the classical methods for demonstrating remote associations. As our discussion has indicated, we have accepted his challenges as well supported. If further work indicates that Slamecka is correct, then we can no longer say that remote associations are formed, in either direction, in serial learning. As we shall see, however, serial learning is complex and is poorly understood. At some future time, compelling evidence may require us once again to consider remote associations.

Serial Position Curve. As we have already said, serial learning yields a curve (see Figure 15-2), when errors or correct responses made over learning are plotted against the serial position each item occupied in the list during learning. This curve is referred to as the bow-shaped curve of serial position and has generally the features that the largest number of correct responses (and least errors) occurs at the first few positions (primacy), the next largest number of correct responses at the end of the list positions (recency), and the fewest correct responses (and most errors) in the middle items; the point of maximal difficulty is just beyond the middle of the list.

At one time it was believed that the effects of a number of variables (such as meaningfulness, distribution of practice, individual differences) had their major effects on the items in the middle of the list. McCrary and Hunter (1953), however, computed the *proportion* of errors (rather than the absolute number of errors) at each serial position and found that the resulting curve did not vary with these variables (see also Braun and Heymann, 1958). In other words, they concluded that these variables have their effects across all serial positions, rather than affecting differentially those in the middle. Since 1953, less concern has been apparent over the serial position curve as influenced by other variables, although Jensen (1962b) has shown difficulties with the McCrary-Hunter method and has

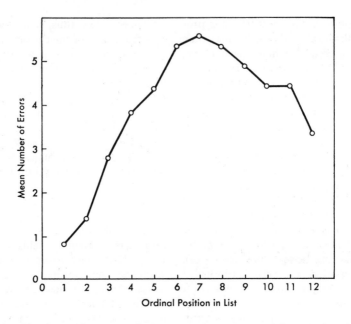

Figure 15-2. Number of errors made at each serial position during learning of the list by the method of serial anticipation. (From Hovland, C. I. Experimental studies in rote-learning theory. III. Distribution of practice with varying speeds of syllable presentation. *J. exp. Psychol.*, 1938, **23**, 172–190.)

proposed an alternative, and interest has shifted to attempts to explain the curve itself. The curve probably occurs with a variety of materials and in a number of conditions. Jensen (1962f), for example, has reported that spelling errors made by eighth graders (seven-letter words), tenth graders (nine-letter words), and junior-college freshmen (eleven-letter words) are distributed in terms of serial position of the letters much as are errors in a laboratory serial learning task. Serial position effects have been found in sentences (Mandler and Mandler, 1964), but the form of the curve varies from that of the bow-shaped curve in ways roughly corresponding to the structure of the material.

There are several unanswered problems concerning serial learning and a number of models have been proposed for it. Our discussion of explanations of the serial position curve can best be combined with these issues. First, however, we mention some experiments directly related to the serial position curve.

Glanzer and Peters (1962) compared serial position curves for six-CVC lists in two groups of Ss. In one, the list started with an asterisk (as is usual in this situation) and the last item was followed by a 6-sec. interval and then the asterisk. In the other group, Ss began the list from a middle syllable; the interval and the asterisk, then, were not related, for them, to the beginning and ending of the list. Glanzer and Peters plotted errors for both groups as a function of the serial position in the items in the first, or usual, group. There was no difference in the shapes of the serial position curves obtained. This suggests that temporal primacy (first items) or recency (last items) cannot account for the curve, as the first and last items were midlist items for the second group. In a second experiment, the intertrial interval was varied over five values from 0 to 16 sec. There were differences in the resulting serial position curves, that is, the curve tended to be flat when there was no interval and to be bow-shaped with intervals, especially the longer ones. The fact that more intertrial intervals were used here than by McCrary and Hunter (1953) and by Braun and Heymann (1958) makes the Glanzer-Peters experiment a more sensitive one so far as spacing is concerned. The writers suggest that the spacing leads to the initial learning of the first and last items of a list, which then serve as anchors to which other items are successively added (see Ribback and Underwood, 1950).

Jensen (1962c) has questioned whether serial learning in the usual sense is necessary at all for the serial position curve to appear. In an experiment directed to this point, Jensen presented nine colored geometric forms one at a time each in the center of a screen. The S had nine response buttons, arranged in a line in front of him from left to right. The task was to learn which button went with the which stimulus. Plotting per cent errors as a function of serial position of the response buttons yielded a serial position curve showing greatest difficulty for the middle response buttons. This curve is not an exact replica of the serial position curve obtained with serial anticipation learning, but it has common features. Thus, nonserial presentation of stimuli and a spatial arrangement of responses preserve some features of serial position curves.

Deese and Kresse (1952) made a careful study of the kinds of errors made during serial anticipation learning of twelve-item CVC lists. For over-all errors, they found the usual serial position curve. When they plotted intralist intrusions however, they found such errors to be symmetrically distributed around the middle item and when they plotted omissions they found them to increase from the first positions in the list to about the middle items and to remain constant thereafter. Combining these two curves for the different sorts of errors would produce the classical curve. Deese and Kresse suggested that the intralist intrusions represent interference, whereas the omissions might reflect the operation of memory span.

Memory span refers to the number of items which a person can reproduce correctly immediately after a single presentation. Jensen and Roden (1963) have studied the relation of memory span to the shape of serial position curves. They found that Ss with a high memory span learned the first part of a nine-item list more rapidly than Ss with a low memory span but that the two groups did not differ on positions 6 through 9. This difference produces a more skewed serial position curve for the former than for the latter Ss, and the degree of skewness (point of maximum difficulty toward the end of the list) increases with practice at serial learning (see Lepley, 1934) which Jensen and Roden suggest enlarges the memory span. They found greater skewness in the serial position curve for materials (letters) for which the memory span is larger than for materials (CVCs) for which the memory span is limited. Memory span, therefore, appears to have some relationship to the bow-shaped curve of serial position.

Another phenomenon, commonly seen in studies of serial learning (as well as in other learning situations), is known as the Von Restorff effect (see Wallace, 1965). This effect (Von Restorff, 1933) was obtained when an item, say a number, was inserted in a list composed of nine syllables (or vice versa). The isolated item, the number, was recalled better than the average of the homogeneous (or "crowded") items —the syllables. Another way of varying the homogeneity of the items is to use, for example, all syllables but to print one in red, the others in black. In serial learning, we should expect, if the isolated item is easier to learn than the crowded items, that there would be more correct responses or fewer errors for the item printed in red than for the same item at the same serial position printed in black. This is indeed what occurs.

The evidence indicates (Wallace, 1965, p. 417) that isolation facilitates learning of the isolated item alone, at the expense of other items. That is, the total list is no easier to learn when it contains an isolated item than when it does not, and there are no consistent effects on the items to either side of the isolated item. There are smaller effects when there is more than one isolated item. The effect seldom appears in incidental learning, and it is most pronounced when the meaningfulness of the homogeneous items is low (Rosen, Richardson, and Saltz, 1962). Jensen (1962e) found that the isolated item tends to be learned sooner than a control item in the same serial position but that it is not in fact any easier to learn, that is, it seems to be attended to and learned earlier than other items. This may give the isolated item an advantage in learning scores because it is learned first, not because it is actually an easy item.

Much of the work on the Von Restorff effect has involved theories concerning it. We shall not enter into these matters here as no satisfactory account has yet been developed. In serial learning, it appears that this effect, like the serial position curve, can best be treated in a general discussion of the nature of serial learning.

What Is Learned in Serial Learning?

For many years serial learning was conceived as a series or chain of associations. Take the sequence A–B–C–D–E–F. Except for the initial and terminal entries, each item can be conceived as both a stimulus and a response; B is a response to A and the stimulus for C, and so on. However, recent developments (Underwood, 1963) have made this conceptualization doubtful. It seems clear now that serial learning is complex. In serial learning the conception of a chain of associations, as we have said, implies a *double function* for most of the items, that is, each item is believed to serve both as a stimulus and as a response. Yet when in PA learning an item appears both

as a stimulus and as a response (for example, *use–eye, eye–hat, hat–jug*), learning becomes much more difficult than when this is not the case (Primoff, 1938; Young, 1961a). As serial learning usually is thought to occur faster than PA learning (Underwood, 1963, p. 41), and the double function situation makes PA learning very difficult, it can be questioned whether the double function conception is appropriate for serial learning.

In addition, transfer from serial learning to paired-associate learning, which would be expected on the serial association hypothesis, is usually found to be slight, and often limited, when found at all, to the early PA trials (Young, 1959, 1961b, 1962; Erickson, Ingram, and Young, 1963; Jensen and Rohwer, 1965). The converse case, that of transfer from PA learning to serial learning, typically produces positive transfer, but its magnitude is less than would be expected on the basis of the theoretical conception (Primoff, 1938; Young, 1959; Young, Milauckas, and Bryan, 1963; Jensen, 1962a). Horowitz and Izawa (1963) have found transfer in both of these situations, which varies with the internal associative structure (pre-experimental) of the lists. A wide range of materials and of variations of associative structures will be required to explicate the conditions under which transfer from serial to PA learning and vice versa occurs.

However, the difficulties with double-function PA lists and the amounts of transfer between serial and PA learning (in both directions) have led a number of writers to question the serial chaining conception of serial learning. In doing so, they have asked, what is the stimulus in serial learning (Underwood, 1963)? Young (1962), in one experiment, used as the stimulus for a response in PA learning the two items that had preceded the response in the prior serial list, thus suggesting a compound stimulus hypothesis in serial learning. However, he obtained no positive transfer in PA learning.

Another possibility, suggested, for example, in Woodworth (1938, pp. 33, 35), is that the *position* of items in the list is a key to serial learning. This idea is that the temporal or spatial position is somehow linked to the item itself. Asch, Hay, and Diamond (1960) have stressed spatial and perceptual cues generally as possibly involved in serial learning and have deplored the fact that for many years these cues were not emphasized.

Some illustrative findings may serve to clarify what is meant by the role of position. Young, Patterson, and Benson (1963) reasoned that if a given serial list is learned in one order (ABCDEFG) and then in the reverse order (GFEDCBA) serial position would be most constant for the middle items. Hence, if position is important to serial learning, these middle items should be learned readily in the backward list. The results of their experiment yielded some confirmation of this expectation. Young (1962) had Ss learn two serial lists in succession, with the even items in the first list being in the identical positions in the second list and with the odd items of the first list randomly rearranged in the second list. Second list learning was faster for the items occupying in the second list the positions they had held in the first list, as compared to the scrambled items, and the effect was most pronounced for the items in the middle of the list (see Keppel and Saufley, 1964). Young thinks that position is important for the learning of midlist items but that serial associations may have the important role so far as end items are concerned.

A difficulty with this interpretation is that when tests are made by asking Ss the positions items had held (Schulz, 1955) during learning, they are least accurate concerning the middle positions. Ebenholtz (1963a, b) has also suggested position as the basis for serial learning, and his proposals are the opposite of those of Young and therefore fit better with Schulz' observations. Ebenholtz (see also Winnick and Dornbush, 1963; Bowman and Thurlow, 1963) has

obtained evidence favoring position as a cue for serial learning.

Unfortunately, the record of experiments with respect to position is not unblighted with negative results. Rehula (1960, as cited in Underwood, 1963, pp. 45–46); Jensen and Blank (1962); Battig, Brown, and Schild (1964); and Jensen and Rohwer (1965) have all reported evidence contrary to the position interpretation. Clearly, we are still largely in the dark as to the stimulus in serial anticipation learning and as to the conceptualization of this learning process.

Models

Murdock (1960b) has proposed that a measure of stimulus distinctiveness which he has developed is related to the serial position curve. In the serial position case the measure involves finding the difference between the numerical value of the serial position of each stimulus and the values of the serial positions of all the other stimuli and summing them. This sum is the distinctiveness of the stimulus, and the sum of these distinctiveness values for all the stimuli in the set is the total distinctiveness in the set. We can then find the per cent (D per cent) of this total for each serial position, and this is Murdock's prediction for the proportion of errors or of correct responses made for that stimulus during serial learning. Murdock reports good agreement between predicted values and actual data reported by Bugelski (1950) for an eight-item serial list, although it is evident that there will be minor discrepancies (see Murdock's Table 5, p. 25) between his predicted values and those usually found in serial learning. It is to be noted that Murdock can predict the serial position curve simply on the basis of differences in serial positions of the items; no assumptions are made about processes involved or even that learning is involved.

Feigenbaum and Simon (1961), however, have achieved a somewhat better fit to Bugelski's data from their model of serial learning (see also Feigenbaum and Simon, 1962, 1963). Fundamentally, these authors assume that Ss have a technique or a strategy with which they approach serial learning tasks. As a result of the strategy, the characteristics of serial learning, especially the serial position curve, are generated. The strategy involves using certain items as "anchors," a suggestion made also by Glanzer and Peters (1962) and also utilized by Jensen (1962d). Some evidence that indicates variation in serial position curves perhaps consistent with strategies was reported by Krueger (1932). He had Ss learn lists of twelve pairs of unrelated nouns. All Ss were told to learn all the items, but one group simply to learn as fast as possible, one to learn the first and the last three pairs first, and one to learn the middle six pairs first. The results show that the serial position curves were markedly altered by the instructions in the two instructed groups. If instructions can be said to have induced strategies, then strategies alter serial position curves.

Feigenbaum and Simon (1962) suggest an information processing model of serial learning, in which it is assumed that the processing mechanism can do but one thing at a time and that this operation requires time. Further, they assume an immediate memory of limited size, so that serial learning must proceed in such a way as not to "strain" the capacity of this memory. In order to reduce the burden on this memory, S typically will choose certain items to work on first (the end items typically) and add the other items to these anchors one at a time in a regular sequence, that is, from the ends to the middle. (Of course if the list contains items which have features that could make them anchors—isolation, for example—the sequence may be altered.) By making assumptions about the sequence that Ss actually follow, Feigenbaum and Simon are able to derive a serial position curve which has properties closely similar to those actually found in serial learning.

Jensen's (1962d) model is similar in many respects to the foregoing one. He likewise suggests an orderly sequence in which items are learned, starting from an anchor point. He believes (as do Feigenbaum and Simon) that items are learned in an all-or-none fashion and that the connection of each item to others requires equal effort on the part of the S. The order in which items are learned is determined on the principle that it is easier to attach an adjacent unlearned item to a previously learned item than to do so with a nonadjacent item. The degree of skewness of the serial position curve will be a function of the memory span of the S and/or the length and type of item in the list (see preceding discussion).

It is perhaps too early to say whether the Jensen and Feigenbaum and Simon models, or others like them, will be found adequate to the study of serial learning and its phenomena. It is noteworthy, however, that these models do not make much use of concepts we have mentioned, such as position, serial associations, or remote associations. Both models seem to imply a stress on perceptual and attentional factors as responsible for the organization of the sequence in which items are processed. Neither is very explicit about the mechanisms by which items are added to anchor items, but both are yet in relatively undeveloped stages.

Incidental and Intentional Learning

For many years there has been interest in the extent to which intent to learn is essential to effective learning. Or, alternatively, the problem may be stated as the determination of the extent to which learning occurs without intention or plan. Do we learn things *incidentally*, as we perform other tasks or go about our business without attempting to learn this or that about them? These questions have engaged the attention of investigators for many years in a number of the situations in which learning is studied. Verbal learning is no exception.

The problem of whether incidental learning occurs or not is a very difficult one to solve. The reason is that to rule out all intent to learn, when learning occurs, is virtually impossible. We can give our *S*s instructions which do not require them to learn anything and which occupy them with some task whose performance seems plausible. If we are to test them for learning, of course, we must be sure that the relevant aspects of the task have been attended to. The difficulty is to rule out implicit efforts to learn the materials on the part of *S*s, who may decide and tell themselves to do so. Most of the putative demonstrations of incidental learning that have been reported suffer from this difficulty and perhaps all of them do.

Insofar as a solution to this situation has been achieved, it has consisted of defining intentional and incidental learning operationally by means of instructions and by discarding *S*s who admit to intentional learning during post experimental inquiry. Then the interest has been in determining whether variables known to be related to characteristics of intentional learning are related to incidental learning and, if so, whether in the same way.

Types of Incidental Learning Situation.
Postman (1964) has summarized the types of situations studied (see also McLaughlin, 1965). In Type I no instructions to learn are given, and *S* is exposed to the materials under some pretext. For example, he might be shown a list of words one at a time with the request that he rate them on some feature. Afterward, he could be asked to recall the words. In Type II, there are instructions to learn something but *S* is then asked about features or aspects of the materials to which the instructions have not directed his efforts to learn. Thus, *S* might be asked to learn pairs of nonsense syllables

which are printed in different colors. Later he might be asked which color was associated with which syllables. The color was irrelevant to the learning task but was intrinsic to the materials involved in it. This is one kind of Type II incidental learning, involving intrinsic components of the task. On the other hand, *S* may be shown a series of two-word pairs, one member of which he is to learn and the other of which he is to rate for phonetic similarity to the first (see Mechanic, 1962a). Then he may be asked to recall the items he had rated. In this case the items tested for incidental learning are *extrinsic* to the task of learning the other items, that is, they are not parts of the items which *S* is directed to learn.

Is "intent" the critical variable? To answer this question, one can manipulate various factors, holding the instructional differences constant, to determine whether performance can be made equal, despite the instructions. If such conditions can be found, then intent is perhaps not the critical variable but rather an interaction between instructions and other factors produce the differences which are often found for incidental and intentional learning. Several such conditions have been found.

Postman and Adams (1956) varied the orienting task (the procedure used to assure exposure of the materials to the incidental learners). The materials the learning of which was to be tested were (1) a list of twenty nonsense syllables varying widely in association value and (2) a list of thirty adjectives. One orienting task required *S* to give meaningful associations to the items on his list, whereas the other orienting task involved matching the list items with geometric figures (both tasks illustrate a Type I design). There were three groups for each list: one, an intentional group, learned the list items; a second performed the orienting task under the instruction also to learn the items; and the third, the incidental group, performed the orienting task without instructions to learn. Recall of the items was obtained from all groups.

Although the intentional learners performed better on the nonsense syllable list than the other groups for that task, the intentional group which performed the figure-matching task did not. It was almost identical in performance to the figure-matching incidental group and was actually inferior to the incidental group which provided associations to the nonsense syllables. These findings may mean that intentional learning was interfered with by the orienting task, but in any case, it is clear that there are conditions, here defined by the orienting tasks, under which incidental learners do as well as or better than intentional learners. With adjectives, intentional learners were always better than incidental learners, but materials differences have been found which do and which do not separate the two kinds of learning situations.

Postman, Adams, and Phillips (1955) used nonsense syllables of widely varying association value and, after presenting them a single time, asked for free recall. The incidental learning manipulation was Type I in character. For syllables of high association value, there was no recall difference between intentional and incidental learners but there was for syllables with low association value. Interestingly enough, when retention was tested by a recognition procedure (with other Ss) the incidental learners did not differ from the intentional learners, at any level of association value (see Eagle and Leiter, 1964).

There are other cases in which certain properties of material do not seem to affect incidental learners as they do intentional learners. Incidental learners do not remember "isolated" items better than crowded ones, as intentional learners do (Postman and Phillips, 1954). Intralist interference affects intentional learners more than incidental learners, the differences being more pronounced for serial anticipation learning than for free recall (Postman and Adams, 1957). Recall scores of intentional learners are augmented more by increasing approximations to the English language than are those of incidental learners (Postman and Adams, 1960).

In verbal learning the Type II kind of design has been used infrequently. Mechanic (1962a), following the preceding procedure, showed that the meaningfulness of the incidental items was related to the extent to which they were learned and further showed that the difference in learning for intentional and incidental learning was greater for low meaningful items than for high meaningful items, confirming work with the Type I situation. A parallel finding has been shown for another Type II situation (intrinsic) by Feldman and Underwood (1957) and by Jantz and Underwood (1958). These authors have suggested that R-S learning (see above) during instructed S-R learning qualifies as incidental learning. Recall of R-S pairs is related to the meaningfulness of the pairs as would be expected on the basis of work with Type I situations (Postman, Adams, and Phillips, 1955).

Results with Type II situations have not always been in agreement for verbal situations with findings in nonverbal situations (see Postman, 1964; McLaughlin, 1965; Mechanic, 1962b). It is possible to show, however, that the relative interference between the incidental and intentional components of the tasks in these situations can account for the differences obtained (Mechanic, 1962a).

Theory. Although there can be dispute about his point (McLaughlin, 1965), Postman (1964) has concluded that it is probably unnecessary to call upon "intent" or upon motivational variables to account for the differences between incidental and intentional learning, where they are obtained. What is learned, Postman argues, is dependent upon what responses the stimuli of the situation elicit. If differential responses occur to the materials, they will be learned without regard to intent. If differential responses are not made or if they are interfered with by other responses in the situation, learning will be poor, even with intent to learn. These conclusions derive from the facts of no difference for intentional and incidental learning with, for example, stimuli of high M and association value. Where differences do occur in the learning scores, then it may be presumed that the necessary differential responses have not been instigated in the incidental learning situation. Let there be no mistake, the instructions, in combination with characteristics of materials and other aspects of the situation, are important, but there seems little reason to appeal to *intent* as an explanatory factor.

Other Problems

As was the case in Chapter 14, our review of methods and models has highlighted areas of recent empirical and theoretical interest and has tended to slight other issues that have received attention in the literature. Among these problems are those dealing with the effects of recitation, sense modality used for learning, the whole-part problem (for a recent study see Postman and Goggin, 1964), rhythm, grouping, tension, guidance, and the comparison of logical and rote learning. These problems receive attention elsewhere (see McGeoch, 1942; McGeoch and Irion, 1952; Osgood, 1953; Woodworth and Schlosberg, 1954).

Current Status and Prospects

A close reading of Chapters 14 and 15 of the present section will suggest that the study of verbal learning has come a long way from the conceptions which seemed to underlie Ebbinghaus' initial experiments. For one thing, methods have changed and developed, and sophistication about them has greatly increased. Variables have been introduced and explored which had not been thought of eighty years ago. More important, however, are perhaps two conclusions to which the evidence reviewed seems to point.

One is that it is virtually impossible to design units which are independent of S's language skills and background. The prominence we have given to meaningfulness, familiarity, association value, pronunciability, interword associations, sequential organization, category membership, and grammatical structures makes this abundantly clear. Past experience with the language results in skills and habits which interact, in an inexorable way, with contemporary verbal learning tasks. That verbal units may not be independent is further brought out, for example, by the effects of item similarity and by the material on clustering in free recall.

It is also clear that S is not a passive actor

when he learns verbal material. He selects stimuli; he chooses certain items to work with first; he uses mnemonic devices and codes and mediates relations between items; and sometimes he reconstructs, on the basis of his linguistic knowledge, what he has learned without actually remembering much more than the substance of what he has studied. Sometimes these operations on the part of the learner are referred to as *strategies.*

A question that can be raised is whether the influence of language skills and the use of strategies introduce problems which cannot be investigated by means of the classical methods of verbal learning. One answer, of course, is that it is through these methods, at least in part, that the influence of these factors has been realized. Another question, however, is whether the true influence of language skills and strategies has not been long obscured by these traditional methods of study. Conventions of method often do have influences on the problems studied, the conclusions reached (see Underwood, 1957), and the kinds of data which an investigator examines. But the methods themselves reflect a conception of underlying processes, and it may be that such conceptions in verbal learning, involving, as they do, the notions that associations are formed gradually and that behavior is mediated by associations which are to some extent independent of one another have narrowed the range of processes to which the study of verbal learning has been oriented. Several writers have objected strenuously to the methods and conceptions of experimentation in classical verbal learning.

For example, Ausubel (1963) has distinguished (as have many writers) between the rote learning of lists studied in the laboratory and learning which occurs in the classroom. He refers to the latter as "meaningful verbal learning," stressing the learning of materials not by rote but in terms of relations among units and of relations with what has already been learned. Shepard (1963) has argued that evidence for stimulus selection and for the use of strategies makes an approach which emphasizes the connection of stimuli with responses inadequate. Miller (1963) has also argued that behavior is much too complex to be guided by simple S-R associations, and Mandler (1962) has attempted to show that complex structures, which do not function in terms of association, may emerge from associative processes.

Assertions of these kinds, of course, are not new, having appeared from time to time in the history of the study of verbal learning (see Bartlett, 1932). It is difficult to decide just what to make of them. Clearly, the kind of work we have reviewed has little direct application to learning as it occurs in the classroom or as it occurs elsewhere in life situations. On the other hand, study of learning in such situations is fraught with difficulties—control of variables, equation of past experience, and the like. Studies of schoolroom learning have yielded few conclusions that are clear-cut or that are not so general as to be virtually meaningless. In contrast, we can point to significant gains in information about the variables and processes involved in learning under the restricted conditions imposed by the kinds of materials and the sorts of variables introduced in the laboratory.

No ready solution to the conflict of views we have just summarized is apparent. Clearly, the problems studied in the laboratory and the processes identified there are restricted ones. There are perhaps many other problems and processes that should be studied. But the problem is, how? In the course of a conference, Mandler (in Cofer, 1961, pp. 79–80) spoke of a similar problem, one having to do with the relation of associative processes to grammatical knowledge. In part, he said, "I strongly believe that in the long run it will be the psychologists who have worked analytically in the field of verbal learning who are likely to develop the necessary techniques to provide a better understanding of these problems" (development and acquisition of syntactic structures). Further, he said that, while associationist concepts and verbal labels cannot handle the problem of syntactic structures, "the glib invocation of 'schemas,' 'structures,' or 'organizations' does not seem to contribute to an explanation or analysis of these phenomena." The writer believes that Mandler's remarks may be extended to cover many of the points raised in the last few paragraphs.

Individual Differences

In the study of verbal learning in the laboratory, the two greatest sources of clear-cut effects which we have discussed are meaningfulness (and its related variables) and interitem similarity. As every investigator must inevitably notice, however, there is a third factor whose effects on acquisition are very substantial. This variable is individual differences.

Individual differences refer to variations among people on many traits and characteristics. We are all familiar with variations in height, weight, ability, strength, appearance, and so on. And people vary in the rate at which they learn tasks in the laboratory such as those we have discussed. Even within a homogeneous group of male college freshmen and sophomores, one S will master a list of ten pairs of CVCs in eight trials whereas another will know only six of the pairs after twenty trials.

The fact of individual differences in verbal learning is evident, but the explanation of their influence is not. There is evidence that learning ability varies with age, and small sex differences are often reported, usually in favor of females. Measured intelligence is sometimes found to be related to laboratory learning and sometimes not. McGeoch and Irion (1952) have reviewed the evidence on these topics, and a recent discussion of individual differences in several varieties of learning situations is provided by Gagné (1966; see also, Noble, 1961b).

Despite the importance of individual differences as a source of variance in learning experiments, there is little information available as to just what they are and how they interact with the tasks employed. We saw in Chapter 15 that Jensen has stressed memory span in connection with the skewness of the bow-shaped curve of serial anticipation learning. It is fairly easy to understand this relation. A person who can retain many (for example, nine) items after a single presentation will show, for a list exceeding memory span (say, twelve items) in length, greater difficulty with items in later positions in the list than a person whose memory can contain only a few items (for example, five). Plenderleith and Postman (1956, 1957) devised a test situation which differentiated people on the basis of their ability to take multiple sets. People scoring high on this test showed more incidental learning than those whose scores were low. This study tells us not only how the individual differences relate to performance, but also verifies a conception of processes (multiple sets) involved in incidental learning. Investigations such as these and those of Jensen help us understand the way in which individual differences in learning arise and tie them to processes involved in the learning tasks themselves. Thus, they are much more informative and interesting than work which relates global traits, like personality constructs or intelligence, to learning.

But studies like these are few in number. Some questions can be asked which illustrate the kinds of factors which may be involved in the marked differences found in an apparently homogeneous group of Ss during verbal learning. Are there knowledges of letter frequencies, sequences, and combinations which facilitate response integration for some Ss? Are there factors of associative fluency which permit some Ss to mediate or code relationships more effectively than others do? Do Ss respond differentially to the time pacing of serial and paired-associate learning?

We have spoken of strategies, organization, and coding. Do Ss vary in these or in the effectiveness of such devices that they apply in learning situations? At the present time little is known about such processes or individual variations with respect to them. We know that with practice or training in verbal learning, Ss become more efficient in mastering the tasks they are assigned. Perhaps study of the ways in which variables influence learning scores in naive and practiced Ss and of the devices which naive and practiced Ss use in learning would help to answer some of these questions. [For further discussion of some of these problems, see Russell (1961) and Jenkins (1961).]

Verbal Learning and Other Influences

Verbal learning, involving as it does the verbal behavior of people, must have relationships to the science of language, linguistics. In addition, it has been of interest to workers concerned with computer simulation of intellectual processes and to model builders with a strong inclination to employ mathematics. In concluding this chapter, a few comments may be made concerning these influences.

Linguistics. Many of the topics treated in Chapter 14, including phrase structure and transformational grammars, are closely related to the science of linguistics. This discipline is concerned with the description of language (usually spoken) and has been instrumental in devising units (for example, phonemes, morphemes, constructions) in terms of which language may be analyzed. We did not do so, but some of our discussion of meaningfulness, association value, and pronunciability could have been considered in relation to linguistic units. Greenberg and Jenkins (1964) have shown that linguistic analysis of CVCs is a feasible way of describing characteristics which have significance to verbal learning.

The study of verbal learning and verbal behavior by psychologists has been enriched since about 1950, by linguistic concepts and, in some instances, by collaboration with linguists, and vice versa. Such interactions have led to the terms *psycholinguistics* and *psycholinguist* (see Osgood and Sebeok, 1954, 1965; Osgood, 1963). These terms do not designate a highly articulated discipline but rather denote investigations and investigators, influenced by both disciplines.

In general, linguists have taken their task as being the description of language and have made few attempts to theorize about behavioral processes involved in using the language. Miller (1962, 1965), however, a psychologist, has expressed the view that phrase structure and transformational grammars, developed by linguists, indicate that language users use rules and that the rules are organized hierarchically. He has been critical of the neglect of these matters by psychologists and says that psychologists, concerned as they have been with verbal learning, association, and referential meaning, have not come to grips with the important features of language use,

involving rules. He has been critical of conceptualizations employing concepts derived from conditioning or stressing associative habits and the like.

Skinner (1957) has presented an analysis of language based on the principles which have emerged in the study of operant conditioning, largely with animals. His approach is one to which Miller would perhaps apply his strictures. Certainly the review of Skinner's analysis, made by the linguist Chomsky (1959), shows that linguists, as represented by Chomsky, do not believe that much can be gained in the study of language by a conceptual analysis such as Skinner's.

Perhaps the most compelling argument used by linguists (and psychologists influenced by their work) in favor of the proposition that language users know rules and function in terms of them rather than in terms of associations is exemplified by the following. Suppose we give someone with a full knowledge of English the following sentence: "The boy *volvaps* the book." Most English speakers will have no trouble in using the nonsense word *volvap* in other contexts, after this single experience, and will inflect the word appropriately as a verb. Thus, forms such as *volvaping, volvaped, will volvap, has volvaped, has been volvaped,* and so on, will be used. This emphasis on rules (and the organization of language into a hierarchy of constituents, as suggested in Chapter 14) is not capable, at present, of being given simple (or complex) associative interpretations. The notion of rules has some kinship, as the reader may have discerned, to the idea of strategies mentioned already.

It seems quite clear that in the future, verbal learning will continue to be influenced by linguistics (and, perhaps, conversely). The challenge posed by the behavior of experienced speakers, such as that just given as an example, will force the student of verbal learning to evaluate his concepts and perhaps to alter and extend them. On the other hand, we may also expect that the rather sweeping assertions sometimes made concerning the rule-using capacities of the native speaker and concerning the insufficiency of associative conceptions to cope with such skills will be subjected to analytic laboratory investigation by the student of verbal learning.

Computer Simulation. Computer simulation of behavior is a way of evaluating conceptions and hypotheses about behavior. In essence, the process involves reducing the conceptions and hypotheses to a program which, fed into the computer, produces the consequences which the conceptions and hypotheses contain. To carry out an operation such as this, the theoretical ideas must be capable of explicit formulation, because a computer requires explicitness of statement in the instructions which are given to it. It is often valuable, of course, to make assertions explicit, as then we know precisely what they say and, in the process of explication, we often become aware of uncertainties, lack of exactness, inconsistencies, and so on.

We have already mentioned, in Chapter 15, some of the work of Feigenbaum and Simon on serial learning. Their work is carried out in the context of computer simulation. As the reader will recall, this work made use of notions like strategy, the selection of anchor items (based on perceptual properties of the items), and an all-or-none learning assumption. Efforts at computer simulation tend to use concepts like these, rather than those of stimulus and response, interference, and incremental habit growth. Although excellent fits between simulated and obtained outcomes are sometimes reported, the usefulness of this approach is still to be evaluated. We can anticipate that it will be an active area

of work in the future (see Feigenbaum and Simon, 1961, 1962, 1963; Shepard, 1963; Miller, 1963).

Mathematical Models. We mentioned, in Chapter 15, several attempts to develop models of paired-associate learning, free-recall learning, and serial learning. These efforts are representative of a number of developments of the last decade or so. We cannot enter into further discussion of these models here, but must be content to say that verbal learning seems to be especially congenial to developers of methematical models and to mention that frequently the concepts employed in these models do not resemble closely the processes and variables discussed in Chapters 14 and 15.

Conclusions

The matters taken up in this chapter illustrate problems and contemporary developments in the context of which the further course of verbal learning will take place. At the same time it seems clear that the topics treated in Chapters 14 and 15 are viable ones and that they will continue to receive much attention. In reading this section on verbal learning, the reader may have noticed that the vast majority of the references cited bear dates since 1955. This is mute testimony to the fact that work on verbal learning has been very active in the years since 1955. It is almost fair to say that verbal learning is a different field from what it was when McGeoch and Irion reviewed it in 1952. With the active research on the topics summarized in Chapters 14 and 15 and with the impact of the matters discussed in the present chapter, we may anticipate further drastic developments in the years ahead.

Glossary

association value. For a verbal unit, like a nonsense syllable, the proportion of Ss who report having an association to it

or who rate it as having many or few associations.
criterion of learning. The degree of mastery

to be reached in learning, which is set *E*. Learning may continue to such criteria as one perfect trial, three successive perfect trials, or mastery of some proportion of the items.

familiarization. Training in which items are practiced, as by pronouncing, writing or spelling them, but without associating an item with other items.

free recall. A recall trial in which items are to be reproduced in any order in which they occur to *S*. When multiple presentations and multiple free recalls are used, this technique is known as free-recall learning.

frequency-familiarity. The item which is frequent in experience is familiar, and conversely. Frequency is usually measured by counts of words, syllables, trigrams, bigrams, or single letters in printed sources. Familiarity is usually measured by ratings.

functional stimulus. That part or aspect of the stimulus presented (the nominal stimulus) which *S* actually uses as the cue for responses.

incidental learning. Any learning which occurs without explicit instruction to *S* that he is to learn anything or to learn some particular feature of the context or aspect of the stimulus or response.

interitem association. A relationship between two items such that one item elicits the other as a free associate and/or such that the items elicit other items in common as free associates.

meaningfulness (m). The extent to which an item elicits associates as measured by the production method or is rated has having many associates.

mediation. The linkage of two or more items by (usually) covert responses or other processes which they have in common.

method of complete presentation. A method which involves giving *S* the entire list, passage, or story he may study, within the time limit allowed, in any way he chooses.

nominal stimulus. The stimulus which is under the control of and is presented by the *E*. See *functional stimulus.*

nonsense syllable. A three-letter unit which is not a word composed of two consonants separated by a vowel. Also, consonant syllables which consist of three consonants.

overlearning. Continuation of practice beyond some criterion of learning or of mastery.

paired-associate learning. Technique by which associations are formed between members of a pair but not between either pair member and other items in the list. In the anticipation version, *S* sees first the stimulus member and is to respond with the response member of the pair before it comes into view. In the study-test or recall version, the pairs are presented one after another and then the stimuli are presented one by one and *S* recalls the response associated with each stimulus.

production method. A procedure for assessing meaningfulness, in which *S* gives as many associations to a stimulus as he can within a time period.

pronunciability. A procedure in which *S*s rate verbal units on how easy they are to pronounce.

recall. Any method in which *S* is required to reproduce an item "from memory."

recognition. A method in which *S* is asked to discriminate an item presented to him in the past from other items.

reconstruction. A method in which, typically, the items are provided *S* and he is asked to reproduce their serial order or some other feature of their original arrangement.

remote association. In serial learning, the possible associations formed, in either direction, between a given item and items that are not adjacent to it in the list.

serial anticipation learning. A method in which a list of items is presented one by one in a constant serial order and in which *S* on seeing one item is to respond by giving the one which follows.

serial position curve. The proportion of errors or of correct responses associated with the items as a function of their serial position in the list in serial anticipation learning.

serial (or ordered) recall. A recall task in which *S* is asked to reproduce the order of the items as well as the items themselves.

verbal discrimination learning. A technique in which two or more items are presented simultaneously or successively only one of which is correct. _S_'s task is to learn which one of the pair or the set of items is the correct one.

word association. The situation in which _S_ is presented with a verbal stimulus and asked to respond with the first response other than the stimulus which comes to his mind (free association) or is asked to respond with a response from a restricted class of responses (controlled association).

References

Asch, S. E., Hay, J., & Diamond, R. M. Perceptual organization in serial rote-learning. *Amer. J. Psychol*, 1960, **73**, 177–198.

Attneave, F. Psychological probability as a function of experienced frequency. *J. exp. Psychol.*, 1953, **46**, 81–86.

Ausubel, D. P. *The psychology of meaningful verbal learning.* New York: Grune and Stratton, 1963.

Bartlett, F. C. *Remembering.* Cambridge: Cambridge Univer. Press, 1932.

Battig, W. F., & Brackett, H. R. Comparison of anticipation and recall methods in paired-associate learning. *Psychol. Rep.*, 1961, **9**, 59–65.

Battig, W. F., Brown, S. C., & Nelson, O. Constant vs. Serial order in paired-associate learning. *Psychol. Rep.*, 1963, **12**, 695–721.

Battig, W. F., Brown, S. C., & Schild, M. E. Serial positions and sequential associations in serial learning. *J. exp. Psychol.*, 1964, **67**, 449–457.

Bever, T. G., Fodor, J. A., & Weksel, W. Theoretical notes on the acquisition of syntax: A critique of "contextual generalization." *Psychol. Rev.*, 1965, **72**, 467–482.

Bilodeau, E. A., Fox, P. W., & Blick, K. A. Stimulated verbal recall and analysis of sources of recall. *J. verb. Learn. verb. Behav.*, 1963, **2**, 422–428.

Bousfield, W. A. The occurrence of clustering in the recall of randomly arranged associates. *J. gen. Psychol.*, 1953, **49**, 229–240.

Bousfield, W. A., & Cohen, B. H. Clustering as a function of the number of word-categories in stimulus-word lists. *J. gen. Psychol.*, 1956, **54**, 95–106.

Bousfield, W. A., Whitmarsh, G. A., & Berkowitz, H. Partial response identities in associative clustering. *J. gen. Psychol.*, 1960, **63**, 233–238.

Bowman, R. E., & Thurlow, W. R. Determinants of the effect of position in serial learning. *Amer. J. Psychol.*, 1963, **76**, 436–445.

Braun, H. W., & Heymann, S. P. Meaningfulness of material, distribution of practice, and serial-position curves. *J. exp. Psychol.*, 1958, **56**, 146–150.

Bugelski, B. R. A remote association explanation of the relative difficulty of learning nonsense syllables in a serial list. *J. exp. Psychol.*, 1950, **40**, 336–348.

Bugelski, B. R. Presentation time, total time, and mediation in paired-associate learning. *J. exp. Psychol.*, 1962, **63**, 409–412.

Bugelski, B. R. In defense of remote associations. *Psychol. Rev.*, 1965, **72**, 169–174.

Carterette, E. C., & Coleman, E. A. Some comments on Tulving's subjective organization. Tech. Rep. No. 17, Contract Nonr 233(58), University of California, Los Angeles, 1963.

Chomsky, N. *Syntactic Structures.* The Hague: Mouton, 1957.

Chomsky, N. Review of verbal behavior, by B. F. Skinner. *Language*, 1959, **35**, 26–58.

Cieutat, V. J., Stockwell, F. E., & Noble, C. E. The interaction of ability and amount of practice with stimulus and response meaningfulness (m, m') in paired-associate learning. *J. exp. Psychol.*, 1958, **56**, 193–202.

Cofer, C. N. Associative commonality and rated similarity of certain words from Haagen's list. *Psychol. Rep.*, 1957, **3**, 603–606.

Cofer, C. N. (Ed.). *Verbal learning and verbal behavior.* New York: McGraw-Hill, 1961.

Cofer, C. N. Measures of associative overlap and paired associate learning. Technical Report No. 7, under Contract Nonr 656(30), The Pennsylvania State University, 1965a.

Cofer, C. N. On some factors in the organizational characteristics of free recall. *Amer. Psychol.*, 1965, **20**, 261–272b.

Cofer, C. N., Bruce, D. R., & Reicher, G. M. Clustering in free recall as a function of certain methodological variations. *J. exp. Psychol.*, 1966, **71**, 858–866.

Cofer, C. N., & Musgrave, B. S. (Eds.). *Verbal behavior and learning.* New York: McGraw-Hill, 1963.

Cofer, C. N., & Shevitz, R. Word-association as a function of word-frequency. *Amer. J. Psychol.*, 1951, **65**, 75–79.

Cohen, B. H., & Bousfield, W. A. The effects of a dual-level stimulus-word list in the occurrence of clustering recall. *J. gen. Psychol.*, 1956, **55**, 51–58.

Coleman, E. B. The association hierarchy as an indicator of extra-experimental interference. *J. verb. Learn. verb. Behav.*, 1963, **2**, 417–421.

Cook, J. O. & Spitzer, M. E. Prompting vs. confirmation in paired associate learning. *J. exp. Psychol.*, 1960, **59**, 275–276.

Cramer, P., & Cofer, C. N. The role of forward and reverse associations in transfer of training. *Amer. Psychol.*, 1960, **15**, 463.

Dallett, K. M. Practice effects in free and ordered recall. *J. exp. Psychol.*, 1963, **66**, 65–71.

Dallett, K. M. Implicit mediators in paired-associate learning. *J. verb. Learn. verb. Behav.*, 1964a, **3**, 209–214.

Dallett, K. M. Number of categories and category information in free recall. *J. exp. Psychol.*, 1964b, **68**, 1–12.

Dallett, K. M. In defense of remote associations. *Psychol. Rev.*, 1965, **72**, 164–168.

Davis, F. C. The relative reliability of words and nonsense syllables. *J. exp. Psychol.*, 1930, **13**, 221–234.

Deese, J. Serial organization in the recall of disconnected items. *Psychol. Rep.*, 1957, **3**, 577–582.

Deese, J. Influence of interitem associative strength upon immediate free recall. *Psychol. Rep.*, 1959, **5**, 305–312.

Deese, J. Frequency of usage and number of words in free recall: The role of association. *Psychol. Rep.*, 1960, **7**, 337–344.

Deese, J. From the isolated verbal unit to connected discourse. Chapter 2 in C. N. Cofer (Ed.). *Verbal learning and verbal behavior.* New York: McGraw-Hill, 1961. Pp. 11–31.

Deese, J., & Kaufman, R. A. Serial effects in recall of unorganized and sequentially organized verbal material. *J. exp. Psychol.*, 1957, **54**, 180–187.

Deese, J., & Kresse, F. H. An experimental analysis of the errors in rote serial learning. *J. exp. Psychol.*, 1952, **44**, 199–202.

Eagle, M., & Leiter, E. Recall and recognition in intentional and incidental learning. *J. exp. Psychol.*, 1964, **68**, 58–63.

Ebbinghaus, H. Ueber das Gedächtniss. Leipzig: Duncker and Humblot, 1885. (1913) H. Ruger & C. Bussenius (Trans.) New York: Teachers College (1964) Reprinted, New York: Dover Publications, Inc.

Ebenholtz, S. M. Position mediated transfer between serial learning and a spatial discrimination task. *J. exp. Psychol.*, 1963a, **65**, 603–608.

Ebenholtz, S. M. Serial learning: Position learning and sequential associations. *J. exp. Psychol.*, 1963b, **66**, 353–362.

Eimas, P. D., & Zeaman, D. Response speed changes in an Estes' paired-associate "miniature" experiment. *J. verb. Learn. verb. Behav.*, 1963, **1**, 384–388.

Ekstrand, B., & Underwood, B. J. Paced versus unpaced recall in free learning. *J. verb. Learn. verb. Behav.*, 1963, **2**, 288–290.

Epstein, W. The influence of syntactical structure on learning. *Amer. J. Psychol.*, 1961, **74**, 80–85.

Epstein, W. A further study of the influence of syntactical structure on learning. *Amer. J. Psychol.*, 1962, **75**, 121–126.

Erickson, C. C., Ingram, R. D., & Young, R. K. Paired-associate learning as a function of rate of presentation and prior serial learning. *Amer. J. Psychol.*, 1963, **76**, 458–463.

Estes, W. K. The problem of inference from curves based on group data. *Psychol. Bull.*, 1956, **53**, 134–140.

Estes, W. K. Learning theory and the new

"mental chemistry." *Psychol. Rev.*, 1960, **67**, 207–223.

Estes, W. K. All-or-none processes in learning and retention. *Amer. Psychol.*, 1964, **19**, 16–25.

Estes, W. K., Hopkins, B. L., & Crothers, E. J. All-or-none and conservation effects in the learning and retention of paired associates. *J. exp. Psychol.*, 1960, **60**, 329–339.

Feigenbaum, E. A., & Simon, H. A. Comment: The distinctiveness of stimuli. *Psychol. Rev.*, 1961, **68**, 285–288.

Feigenbaum, E. A., & Simon, H. A. A theory of the serial position effect. *Brit. J. Psychol.*, 1962, **53**, 307–321.

Feigenbaum, E. A., & Simon, H. A. Brief notes on the EPAM theory of verbal learning. In C. N. Cofer & B. S. Musgrave (Eds.), *Verbal behavior and learning*, New York: McGraw-Hill, 1963, pp. 333–335.

Feldman, S. M., & Underwood, B. J. Stimulus recall following paired-associate learning. *J. exp. Psychol.*, 1957, **53**, 11–15.

Gagné, R. M. (Ed.). Conference on learning and individual differences. Columbus: Merrill Books, 1966.

Gannon, D. R., & Noble, C. E. Familiarization (*n*) as a stimulus factor in paired-associate verbal learning. *J. exp. Psychol.*, 1961, **62**, 14–23.

Garskoff, B. E., & Houston, J. P. Measurement of verbal relatedness: An idiographic approach. *Psychol. Rev.*, 1963, **70**, 277–288.

Glanzer, M. Grammatical category: A rote learning and word association analysis. *J. verb. Learn. verb. Behav.*, 1962, **1**, 31–41.

Glanzer, M., & Peters, S. C. Re-examination of the serial position effect. *J. exp. Psychol.*, 1962, **64**, 258–266.

Glaze, J. A. The association value of nonsense syllables. *J. genet. Psychol.*, 1928, **35**, 255–269.

Goss, A. E. Comments on Professor Noble's paper. In C. N. Cofer & B. S. Musgrave (eds.), *Verbal behavior and learning: Problems and Processes.* New York: McGraw-Hill, 1963. Pp. 119–155.

Goss, A. E., & Sugarman, M. E. Paired associates learning with varying relative percentages of occurrence of alternative response members. *J. exp. Psychol.*, 1961, **62**, 24–34.

Greenberg, J. H., & Jenkins, J. J. Studies in the psychological correlates of the sound system of American English. *Word*, 1964, **20**, 157–177.

Haagen, C. H. Synonymity, vividness, familiarity, and association value ratings of 400 pairs of common adjectives. *J. Psychol.*, 1949, **27**, 453–463.

Hakes, D. T., & Young, R. K. On remote associations and the interpretation of derived-list experiments. *Psychol. Rev.*, 1966, **73**, 248–251.

Hall, J. F. Learning as a function of word-frequency. *Amer. J. Psychol.*, 1954, **67**, 138–140.

Higa, M. Interference effects of intralist word relationships in verbal learning. *J. verb. Learn. verb. Behav.*, 1963, **2**, 170–175.

Horowitz, L. M. Free recall and ordering of trigrams. *J. exp. Psychol.*, 1961, **62**, 51–57.

Horowitz, L. W., & Izawa, C. Comparison of serial and paired-associate learning. *J. exp. Psychol.*, 1963, **65**, 352–361.

Houston, J. P. Ease of verbal S-R learning as a function of the number of mediating associations. *J. verb. Learn. verb. Behav.*, 1964, **3**, 326–329.

Hovland, C. I. Experimental studies in rote-learning theory. III. Distribution of practice with varying speeds of syllable presentation. *J. exp. Psychol.*, 1938, **23**, 172–190.

Hovland, C. I., & Kurtz, K. H. Experimental studies in rote-learning theory: X. Prelearning syllable familiarization and the length-difficulty relationship. *J. exp. Psychol.*, 1952, **44**, 31–39.

Howes, D. On the interpretation of word frequency as a variable affecting speed of recognition. *J. exp. Psychol.*, 1954, **48**, 106–112.

Hull, C. L. The meaningfulness of 320 selected nonsense syllables. *Amer. J. Psychol.*, 1933, **45**, 730–734.

Hunt, R. G. Meaningfulness and articulation of stimulus and response in paired-associate learning and stimulus recall. *J. exp. Psychol.*, 1959, **57**, 262–267.

Irion, A. L. Retroactive inhibition as a

function of the relative serial positions of the original and interpolated items. *J. exp. Psychol.*, 1946, **36**, 262–270.

Jantz, E. M., & Underwood, B. J. R-S learning as a function of meaningfulness and degree of S-R learning. *J. exp. Psychol.*, 1958, **56**, 174–179.

Jarrett, R. F., & Scheibe, K. E. Association chains and paired-associate learning. *J. verb. Learn. verb. Behav.*, 1963, **1**, 264–268.

Jenkins, J. J. Comments on Professor Noble's paper. In C. N. Cofer (Ed.), *Verbal Learning and Verbal Behaviour* New York: McGraw-Hill, 1961. Pp. 146–150.

Jenkins, K. J., Mink, W. D., & Russell, W. A. Associative clustering as a function of verbal association strength. *Psychol. Rep.*, 1958, **4**, 127–136.

Jenkins, J. J., & Palermo, D. S. Mediation processes and the acquisition of linguistic structure. In U. Bellugi & R. Brown (Eds.), The acquisition of language. *Monogr. Soc. Res. Child Development*, 1964, **29**, No. 1 (Serial No. 92).

Jensen, A. R. Transfer between paired-associate and serial learning. *J. verb. Learn verb. Behav.*, 1962, **1**, 269–280.

Jensen, A. R. Is the serial-position curve invariant? *Brit. J. Psychol.*, 1962b, **53**, 159–166.

Jensen, A. R. Temporal and spatial effects of serial position. *Amer. J. Psychol.*, 1962c, **75**, 390–400.

Jensen, A. R. An Empirical theory of the serial-position effect. *J. Psychol.*, 1962d, **53**, 127–142.

Jensen, A. R. The Von Restorff isolation effect with minimal response learning. *J. exp. Psychol.*, 1962e, **64**, 123–125.

Jensen, A. R. Spelling errors and the serial-position effect. *J. educ. Psychol.*, 1962f, **53**, 105–109.

Jensen, A. R., & Blank, S. S. Association with ordinal position in serial rote-learning. *Canad. J. Psychol.*, 1962, **16**, 60–63.

Jensen, A. R., & Roden, A. Memory span and the skewness of the serial-position curve. *Brit. J. Psychol.*, 1963, **54**, 337–349.

Jensen, A. R., & Rohwer, W. D., Jr. What is learned in serial learning? *J. verb. Learn. verb. Behav.*, 1965, **4**, 61–72.

Johnson, N. F. A model of sentence generation: Paper presented at symposium on Psychological Aspects of Language Structure, meetings of American Psychological Association, Los Angeles, September, 1964.

Johnson, R. C. Reanalysis of "meaningfulness and verbal learning." *Psychol. Rev.*, 1962, **64**, 233–238.

Jones, J. E. All-or-none versus incremental learning. *Psychol. Rev.*, 1962, **69**, 156–160.

Keppel, G., & Rehula, R. J. Rate of presentation in serial learning. *J. exp. Psychol.*, 1965, **69**, 121–125.

Keppel, G., & Saufley, W. H., Jr. Serial position as a stimulus in serial learning. *J. verb. Learn. verb. Behav.*, 1964, **3**, 335–343.

Kimble, G. A., & Dufort, R. H. Meaningfulness and isolation as factors in verbal learning. *J. exp. Psychol.*, 1955, **50**, 361–368.

King. D. J. On the accuracy of written recall: A scaling and factor analytic study. *Psychol. Rec.*, 1960, **10**, 113–122.

King, D. J., & Schultz, D. P. Additional observations on scoring the accuracy of written recall. *Psychol. Rec.*, 1960, **10**, 203–204.

King, D. J., & Yu, K. C. The effect of reducing the variability of length of written recalls on the rank order scale values of the recalls. *Psychol. Rec.*, 1962, **12**, 39–44.

Krueger, W. C. F. Learning during attention. *J. exp. Psychol.*, 1932, **15**, 517–527.

Krueger, W. C. F. The relative difficulty of nonsense syllables. *J. exp. Psychol.*, 1934, **17**, 145–153.

Lambert, W., & Paivio, A. The influence of noun-adjective order on learning. *Canad. J. Psychol.*, 1956, **10**, 9–12.

Lepley, W. M. Serial reactions considered as conditional reactions. *Psychol. Monogr.*, 1934, **46**, No. 205.

Lockhead, G. R. Methods of presenting paired associates. *J. verb. Learn. verb. Behav.*, 1962, **1**, 62–65.

Lyon, D. O. The relation of length of material to time taken for learning and the optimum distribution of time. Part II. *J. educ. Psychol.*, 1914, **5**, 85–91.

McCarthy, D. Language development in

children. In L. Carmichael (Ed.), *Manual of child psychology*. New York: Wiley, 1946. Pp. 476–581.

McCrary, J. W., & Hunter, W. S. Serial position curves in verbal learning. *Science*, 1953, **117**, 131–134.

McGeoch, J. A. The influence of associative value upon the difficulty of nonsense-syllable lists. *J. genet. Psychol.*, 1930, **37**, 421–426.

McGeoch, J. A. The direction and extent of intra-serial associations at recall. *Amer. J. Psychol.*, 1936, **48**, 221–245.

McGeoch, J. A. *The psychology of human learning*. New York: Longmans, Green, 1942.

McGeoch, J. A., & Irion, A. L. *The Psychology of Human Learning* (2nd edition). New York: Longmans, Green, 1952.

McGuire, W. J. A multiprocess model for paired-associate learning. *J. exp. Psychol.*, 1961, **62**, 335–347.

McLaughlin, B. "Intentional" and "Incidental" learning in human subjects: The role of instructions to learn and motivation. *Psychol. Bull.*, 1965, **63**, 359–376.

Mandler, G. Response factors in human learning. *Psychol. Rev.*, 1954, **61**, 235–244.

Mandler, G. From association to structure. *Psychol. Rev.*, 1962, **69**, 514–527.

Mandler, G., & Huttenlocher, J. The relationship between associative frequency, associative ability and paired-associate learning. *Amer. J. Psychol.*, 1965, **59**, 424–428.

Mandler, G., & Mandler, J. M. Serial position effects in sentences. *J. verb. Learn. verb. Behav.*, 1964, **3**, 195–202.

Marks, L. E., & Miller, G. A. The role of semantic and syntactic constraints in the memorization of English sentences. *J. verb. Learn. verb. Behav.*, 1964, **3**, 1–5.

Marshall, G. R. The organization of verbal material in free recall: The effects of patterns of associative overlap on clustering. Ph.D. dissertation, New York Univ. 1963.

Marshall, G. R., & Cofer, C. N. Associative indices as measures of word relatedness: A summary and comparison of ten methods. *J. verb. Learn. verb. Behav.*, 1963, **1**, 408–421.

Martin, C. J., & Saltz, E. Serial versus random presentation of paired associates. *J. exp. Psychol.*, 1963, **65**, 609–615.

Martin, J. G. Associative strength and word frequency in paired-associate learning. *J. verb. Learn. verb. Behav.*, 1964, **3**, 317–320.

Mathews, R. Recall as a function of number of classificatory categories. *J. exp. Psychol.*, 1954, **47**, 241–247.

Mechanic, A. The distribution of recalled items in simultaneous intentional and incidental learning. *J. exp. Psychol.*, 1962a, **63**, 593–600.

Mechanic, A. Effects of orienting task, practice, and incentive on simultaneous incidental and intentional learning. *J. exp. Psychol.*, 1962b, **64**, 393–399.

Mehler, J. Some effects of grammatical transformations on the recall of English sentences. *J. verb. Learn. verb. Behav.* 1963, **3**, 346–351.

Melton, A. W. Implications of short-term memory for a general theory of memory. *J. verb. Learn. verb. Behav.*, 1963, **2**, 1–21.

Miller, G. A. The magic number seven, plus or minus two: Some limits on our capacity for processing information. *Psychol. Rev.*, 1956, **63**, 81–96.

Miller, G. A. Free recall of redundant strings of letters. *J. exp. Psychol.*, 1958, **56**, 485–491.

Miller, G. A. Some psychological studies of grammar. *Amer. Psychol.*, 1962, **17**, 748–762.

Miller, G. A. Comments on Professor Postman's paper. In C. N. Cofer & B. S. Musgrave (Eds.), *Verbal behavior and learning: Problems and processes*. New York: McGraw-Hill, 1963. Pp. 321–329.

Miller, G. A. Some preliminaries to psycholinguistics. *Amer. Psychol.*, 1965, **20**, 15–20.

Miller, G. A., & Selfrige, J. Verbal context and the recall of meaningful material. *Amer. J. Psychol.*, 1950, **63**, 176–185.

Murdock, B. B., Jr. The immediate retention of unrelated words. *J. exp. Psychol.*, 1960, **60**, 221–234.

Murdock, B. B., Jr. The distinctiveness of stimuli. *Psychol. Rev.*, 1960, **67**, 16–31.

Murdock, B. B., Jr. The retention of individual items. *J. exp. Psychol.*, 1961, **62**, 618–625.

Murdock, B. B., Jr. The serial position effect of free recall. *J. exp. Psychol.*, 1962, **64**, 482–488.

Noble, C. E. An analysis of meaning. *Psychol. Rev.*, 1952, **59**, 421–430.

Noble, C. E. The familiarity-frequency relationship. *J. exp. Psychol.*, 1954, **47**, 13–16.

Noble, C. E. The effect of familiarization upon serial verbal learning. *J. exp. Psychol.*, 1955, **49**, 333–338.

Noble, C. E. Measurements of association value (*a*), rated associations (*a'*), and scaled meaningfulness (*m'*) for the 2100 CVC combinations of the English alphabet. *Psychol. Rep.*, 1961a, **8**, 487–521.

Noble, C. E. Verbal learning and individual differences. In C. N. Cofer (Ed.), *Verbal learning and verbal behavior*. New York: McGraw-Hill, 1961b. Pp. 132–146.

Noble, C. E. Meaningfulness and familiarity. In C. N. Cofer, & B. S. Musgrave (Eds.), *Verbal behavior and learning: Problems and processes*. New York: McGraw-Hill, 1963. Pp. 76–119.

Noble, C. E., & McNeely, D. A. The role of meaningfulness (*m*) in paired-associate verbal learning. *J. exp. Psychol.*, 1957, **53**, 16–22.

Nodine, C. F. Stimulus durations and stimulus characteristics in paired-associates learning. *J. exp. Psychol.*, 1963, **66**, 100–106.

Osgood, C. E. *Method and theory in experimental psychology*, New York: Oxford Univer. Press, 1953.

Osgood, C. E. Psycholinguistics. In S. Koch (Ed.), *Psychology: A Study of a Science*, Study II. Vol. 6, *Investigations of man as socius: Their place in psychology and the social sciences*. New York: McGraw-Hill, 1963. Pp. 244–316.

Osgood, C. E., & Sebeok, T. A. Psycholinguistics: A survey of theory and research. *J. abnorm. Soc. Psychol.*, 1954, **49**, Suppl. to No. 4.

Osgood, C. E., & Sebeok, T. A. *Psycholinguistics: A survey of theory and research problems*, with *A survey of psycholinguistic research, 1954–64*, by A. R. Diebold, Jr., and *Psycholinguistics*, by G. A. Miller. Bloomington, Indiana: Indiana University Press, 1965.

Palermo, D. S., & Jenkins, J. J. *Word association norms: Grade school through college*. Minneapolis: Univ. Minnesota Press, 1964.

Palermo, D. S., & Jenkins, J. J. Paired-associate learning as a function of the strength of links in the associative chain. *J. verb. Learn. verb. Behav.*, 1964, **3**, 406–412.

Peterson, L. R., & Peterson, M. J. Short-term retention of individual verbal items. *J. exp. Psychol.*, 1959, **58**, 193–198.

Plenderleith, M., & Postman, L. Discriminative and verbal habit in incidental learning. *Amer. J. Psychol.*, 1956, **69**, 236–243.

Plenderleith, M., & Postman, L. Individual differences in intentional and incidental learning. *Brit. J. Psychol.*, 1957, **48**, 241–248.

Pollio, H. A Simple matrix analysis of associative structure. *J. verb. Learn. verb. Behav.*, 1963, **2**, 166–169.

Postman, L. Extra-experimental interference and the retention of words. *J. exp. Psychol.*, 1961, **61**, 97–110.

Postman, L. The effects of language habits on the acquisition and retention of verbal associations. *J. exp. Psychol.*, 1962, **64**, 7–19.

Postman, L. Does interference theory predict too much forgetting? *J. verb. Learn. verb. Behav.*, 1963, **2**, 40–48.

Postman, L. One-trial learning. In C. N. Cofer & B. S. Musgrave (Eds.), *Verbal behavior and learning: Problems and Processes*. New York: McGraw-Hill, 1963. Pp. 295–321.

Postman, L. Short-term memory and incidental learning. In A. W. Melton (Ed.), *Categories of human learning*. New York: Academic Press, 1964. Pp. 145–201.

Postman, L., & Adams, P. A. Studies in incidental learning: IV. The interaction of orienting tasks and stimulus materials. *J. exp. Psychol.*, 1956, **51**, 329–332.

Postman, L., & Adams, P. A. Studies in incidental learning: VI. Intraserial interference. *J. exp. Psychol.*, 1957, **54**, 153–167.

Postman, L., & Adams, P. A. Studies in incidental learning: VIII. The effects of contextual determination. *J. exp. Psychol.*, 1960, **59**, 153–164.

Postman, L., Adams, P. A., & Phillips, L. W. Studies in incidental learning: II. The effects of association value and of the method of testing. *J. exp. Psychol.*, 1955, **49**, 1–10.

Postman, L., & Goggin, J. Whole versus

part learning of serial lists as a function of meaningfulness and intra-list similarity. *J. exp. Psychol.*, 1964, **68**, 140–150.

Postman, L., & Phillips, L. W. Studies in incidental learning: I. The effects of crowding and isolation. *J. exp. Psychol.*, 1954, **48**, 48–56.

Primoff, E. Backward and forward association as an organizing act in serial and in paired associate learning. *J. gen. Psychol.*, 1938, **5**, 375–395.

Rehula, R. J. A test of two alternative hypotheses of the associations that develop in serial learning. Ph.D. dissertation, Northwestern University, 1960.

Ribback, A., & Underwood, B. J. An empirical explanation of the skewness of the bowed serial position curve. *J. exp. Psychol.*, 1950, **40**, 329–335.

Richardson, J. The relationship of stimulus similarity and number of responses. *J. exp. Psychol.*, 1958, **56**, 478–484.

Richardson, J. Association among stimuli and the learning of verbal concept lists. *J. exp. Psychol.*, 1960, **60**, 290–298.

Riley, D. A., & Phillips, L. W. The effects of syllable familiarization on rote learning, association value, and reminiscence. *J. exp. Psychol.*, 1959, **57**, 372–379.

Rosen, H., Richardson, D. H., & Saltz, E. Meaningfulness as a differentiation variable in the Von Restorff effect. *J. exp. Psychol.*, 1962, **64**, 327–328.

Russell, W. A. Assessment versus experimental acquisition of verbal habits. In C. N. Cofer (Ed.), *Verbal learning and verbal behavior.* New York: McGraw-Hill, 1961. Pp. 110–123.

Schulz, R. W., & Tucker, I. F. Supplementary report: stimulus familiarization in paired associate learning. *J. exp. Psychol.*, 1962a, **64**, 549–550.

Schulz, R. W., & Tucker, I. F. Stimulus familiarization and length of the anticipation interval in paired-associate learning. *Psychol. Rec.*, 1962b, **12**, 341–344.

Schulz, R. W. Generalization of serial position in rote serial learning. *J. exp. Psychol.*, 1955, **49**, 267–272.

Schulz, R. W., & Runquist, W. N. Learning and retention of paired adjectives as a function of percentage occurrence of response members. *J. exp. Psychol.*, 1960, **59**, 409–413.

Schwartz, M. Transfer from failed pairs as

a test of one-trial vs. incremental learning. *Amer. J. Psychol.*, 1963, **76**, 266–273.

Seidel, R. J. RTT Paridigm: No panacea for theories of associative learning. *Psychol. Rev.*, 1963, **70**, 565–572.

Shepard, R. N. Comments on Professor Underwood's paper. In C. N. Cofer & B. S. Musgrave (Eds.), *Verbal behavior and learning: Problems and processes.* New York: McGraw-Hill, 1963. Pp. 48–70.

Skinner, B. F. *Verbal Behavior.* New York: Appleton-Century-Crofts, 1957.

Slamecka, N. J. An inquiry into the doctrine of remote associations. *Psychol. Rev.*, 1964, **71**, 61–76.

Slamecka, N. J. In defense of a new approach to old phenomena. *Psychol. Rev.*, 1965, **72**, 242–246.

Spence, J. T. Associative interference on paired-associate lists from extra-experimental learning. *J. verb. Learn. verb. Behav.*, 1963, **2**, 329–338.

Thorndike, E. L., & Lorge, I. *The teacher's wordbook of 30,000 words.* New York: Bureau of Publications, Teachers College, Columbia University, 1944.

Tulving, E. Subjective organization in the free recall of unrelated words. *Psychol. Rev.*, 1962, **69**, 344–354.

Tulving, E. Intratrial and intertrial retention: Notes toward a theory of free recall verbal learning. *Psychol. Rev.*, 1964, **71**, 219–237.

Underwood, B. J. Studies of distributed practice: VII. Learning and retention of serial nonsense lists as a function of intralist similarity. *J. exp. Psychol.*, 1952, **44**, 80–87.

Underwood, B. J. Interference and forgetting. *Psychol. Rev.*, 1957, **64**, 49–60.

Underwood, B. J. Verbal learning in the educational process. *Harvard educ. Rev.*, 1959, **29**, 107–117.

Underwood, B. J. Ten years of massed practice on distributed practice. *Psychol. Rev.*, 1961, **68**, 229–247.

Underwood, B. J. Stimulus selection in verbal learning. In C. N. Cofer & B. S. Musgrave (Eds.), *Verbal behavior and learning.* New York: McGraw-Hill, 1963. Pp. 33–48.

Underwood, B. J. The representativeness of rote verbal learning. In A. W. Melton (Ed.), *Categories of human learning.* New

York: Academic Press, 1964. Pp. 47–78.

Underwood, B. J. Degree of learning and the measurement of retention. *J. verb. Learn. verb. Behav.*, 1964, **3**, 112–129.

Underwood, B. J., Ekstrand, B. R., & Keppel, G. Studies of distributed practice: XXIII. Variations in response-term interference. *J. exp. Psychol.*, 1964, **68**, 201–212.

Underwood, B. J., & Goad, D. Studies of distributed practice: I. The influence of intra-list similarity in serial learning. *J. exp. Psychol.*, 1951, **42**, 125–134.

Underwood, B. J., Ham, M., & Ekstrand, B. Cue selection in paired-associate learning. *J. exp. Psychol.*, 1962, **64**, 405–409.

Underwood, B. J., & Postman, L. Extra-experimental sources of interference in forgetting. *Psychol. Rev.*, 1960, **67**, 73–95.

Underwood, B. J., Runquist, W. N., & Schulz, R. W. Response learning in paired-associate lists as a function of intra-list similarity. *J. exp. Psychol.*, 1959, **58**, 70–78.

Underwood, B. J., & Schulz, R. W. *Meaningfulness and verbal learning.* Chicago: J. B. Lippincott, 1960.

Von Restorff, H. Ueber die Wirkung von Bereichsbildungen im Spurenfeld. *Psychol. Forsch.*, 1933, **18**, 299–342.

Voss, J. F., Thompson, C. P., & Keegan, J. H. Acquisition of probabilistic paired associates as a function of $S-R_1$, $S-R_2$ probability. *J. exp. Psychol.*, 1959, **58**, 390–399.

Wallace, W. P. Review of the historical, empirical, and theoretical status of the Von Restorff phenomenon. *Psychol. Bull.*, 1965, **63**, 410–424.

Waugh, N. C. Free versus serial recall. *J. exp. Psychol.*, 1961, **62**, 496–502.

Weingartner, H. Associative structure and serial learning. *J. verb. Learn. verb. Behav.*, 1963, **2**, 476–479.

Weitz, J. Criteria for criteria. *Amer. Psychologist*, 1961, **16**, 228–231.

Welsh, P. A preliminary study of the role of certain structural variables in learning. Unpublished ms., 1955.

Wicklund, D. A., Palermo, D. S., & Jenkins, J. J. The effects of associative strength and response hierarchy on paired-associate learning. *J. verb. Learn. verb. Behav.*, 1964, **3**, 413–420.

Williams, J. P. A test of the all-or-none hypothesis for verbal learning. *J. exp. Psychol.*, 1962, **64**, 158–165.

Winnick, W. A., & Dornbush, R. L. Role of positional cues in serial rote learning. *J. exp. Psychol.*, 1963, **66**, 419–421.

Witmer, L. R. The association value of three-place consonant syllables. *J. genet. Psychol.*, 1935, **47**, 337–360.

Woodworth, R. S. *Experimental psychology.* New York: Holt, Rinehart and Winston, 1938.

Woodworth, R. S., & Schlosberg, H. *Experimental Psychology.* Revised. New York: Holt, Rinehart and Winston, 1954.

Young, R. K. A comparison of two methods of learning serial associations. *Amer. J. Psychol.*, 1959, **72**, 554–559.

Young, R. K. Paired-associate learning when the same items occur as stimuli and responses. *J. exp. Psychol.*, 1961a, **61**, 315–318.

Young, R. K. The stimulus in serial verbal learning. *Amer. J. Psychol.*, 1961b, **74**, 517–528.

Young, R. K. Tests of three hypotheses about the effective stimulus in serial learning. *J. exp. Psychol.*, 1962, **63**, 307–313.

Young, R. K., Milauckas, E. W., & Bryan, J. D. Serial learning as a function of prior paired-associate training. *Amer. J. Psychol.*, 1963, **76**, 82–88.

Young, R. K., Patterson, J., & Benson, W. M. Backward serial learning, *J. verb. Learn. verb. Behav.*, 1963, **1**, 335–338.

Suggested Readings

Cofer, C. N. (Ed.). *Verbal learning and verbal behavior.* New York: McGraw-Hill, 1961. A report of a conference in which prepared papers supply authoritative reviews of such topics as free recall, meaning, individual differences and interference theory.

Cofer, C. N., & Musgrave, B. S. (Eds.). *Verbal behavior and learning: Problems and processes.* New York: McGraw-Hill,

1963. Another conference report, this one including papers on such topics as stimulus selection, recognition, meaningfulness and familiarity, mediated associations, one-trial learning, short-term memory, and the acquisition of language.

Deese, J. *The structure of associations of language and thought.* Baltimore: Johns Hopkins University Press, 1965. An original investigation of the structure of interword associations together with a review of the history of association theory and suggestions for new laws of association.

Dixon, T. R., & Horton, D. L. (Eds.). *Verbal behavior and general behavior theory.* Englewood Cliff , N.J.: Prentice-Hall, 1967. A volume based on a conference for which papers were prepared on most of the standard topics of verbal learning and retention, together with several having to do with controversial issues in psycholinguistics.

Goss, A. E., & Nodine, C. F. *Paired-associates learning: The role of meaningfulness, similarity, and familiarization.* New York: Academic Press, 1965. A review of the literature, together with the report of a number of original experiments, concerned with the topics indicated in the title and subtitle.

Kausler, D. H. (Ed.). *Readings in verbal learning: Contemporary theory and research.* New York: Wiley, 1966. A selection of recent papers in the field of verbal learning, many of which have been cited and discussed in the section on this topic.

Lenneberg, E. H. (Ed.). *New directions in the study of language.* Cambridge, Mass.: The M.I.T. Press, 1964. Contains papers presented at 17th International Congress of Psychology in 1963. Implications of biological perspective and linguistics are stressed, and there are treatments of the role of imitation in the acquisition of language.

Mandler, J. M., and Mandler, G. (Eds.). *Thinking: From association to gestalt.* New York: Wiley, 1964. A number of classical papers and other writings on association theory are reprinted here together with introductory commentaries by the authors.

Mandler, G. In *New directions in Psychology III.* New York: Holt, Rinehart, and Winston, 1967. An interpretation in verbal learning representing a point of view different in important respects from the one presented in this book.

Mandler, G. Organization and memory. In K. W. Spence and J. T. Spence (Eds.), *The psychology of learning and motivation: Advances in research and theory.* New York: Academic Press, 1967.

McGeoch, J. A., & Irion, A. W. *The Psychology of human learning,* 2nd. ed. New York: Longmans, Green, 1952. A comprehensive and authoritative review of the literature of human learning over the period 1885 to 1952.

Melton, A. W. (Ed.). *Categories of human learning.* New York: Academic Press, 1964. Contains a variety of papers on topics in human learning, including one on rote verbal learning and one on short-term memory and incidental learning.

Palermo, D. S., & Jenkins, J. J. *Word association norms: Grade school through college.* Minneapolis: University of Minnesota Press, 1964. An invaluable normative source which provides free associations to 200 stimuli obtained from *S*s over a wide age range.

Rosenberg, S. (Ed.). *Directions in psycholinguistics.* New York: Macmillan, 1965. Several papers which interrelate the fields of verbal learning and linguistics in connection with several problems.

Underwood, B. J., & Schulz, R. W. *Meaningfulness and verbal learning.* Philadelphia: Lippincott, 1960. Reviews the literature on meaningfulness and related variables with respect to verbal learning, reports sixteen original experiments, and attempts to uncover the basic variable which meaningfulness represents. An invaluable feature are its six appendices in which normative material is given for association or meaningfulness values for nonsense syllables, consonant syllables, disyllables, bigram and trigram frequencies, pronunciability ratings, and associations to single-letter and two-letter stimuli.

VI

Transfer and Retention

Henry C. Ellis

University of New Mexico

CHAPTER 17

Transfer: Nature, Measurement, and Fundamental Processes

The Nature of Transfer

Transfer of training is a concept that represents the net or overall effects of performance or experience with one type of task on performance with some subsequent task. Such net influence may take three possible forms: (1) performance on one task may aid or facilitate performance on a second task, which describes *positive transfer*; (2) performance on one task may interfere or inhibit performance on a second task, which describes *negative transfer*; and (3) there may be no effect of one task on another, in which case we have *zero transfer*. Zero transfer can occur either as a result of earlier performance having no effect on subsequent performance or as a result of combined effects of positive and negative transfer which cancel.

Defining Operations of Transfer. Although transfer has been described in a general way, it is best understood in terms of the way it is measured. Typically, transfer is inferred from the comparative performance of two groups, an experimental and a control, as shown below. The experimental group learns an initial task, Task A, and then learns a second task, Task B. The control group learns only Task B without experiencing the initial task.

Experimental Group:	Learn Task A	Learn Task B
Control Group:	—	Learn Task B

If positive transfer occurs from the learning of A to B, it is inferred from the superior performance of the experimental group on Task B as compared with the control group. For example, the experimental group might make fewer errors or more correct responses on Task B. In contrast, if the experimental group is inferior in performance on Task B, compared with the control group, we infer that negative transfer has occurred. In some fashion the learning of Task A has interfered with the subsequent learning of Task B. Finally, if the two groups perform the same on Task B, we have an instance of zero transfer.

It is assumed that the experimental and control groups are equivalent with respect to factors important in learning the tasks, such as intelligence and previous experience with related tasks; this is usually accomplished by either matching Ss on some relevant task prior to the transfer experiment or by assigning Ss at random to the experimental and control groups. A crucial feature of this design is the task given the control group during the period in which the experimental group learns Task A. Sometimes the control group rests and sometimes it performs other tasks. We shall shortly see that there are types of transfer designs, some of which are modifications of this first type, and that a variety of designs may be employed in studies of transfer depending upon the kind of inferences one wishes to draw.

Historical Overview of Transfer. An analysis of issues and problems in transfer from 1900 until the present reveals two rather broad and quite different approaches to the study of transfer. Initially, studies of transfer were aimed at such issues as determining the gross effects of practice with one task upon another, answering questions about teaching methods, making inferences about brain physiology by way of bilateral transfer studies, and examining theoretical issues related to educational practice, such as the doctrine of formal discipline. With the exception of bilateral transfer, much of the transfer research concerned itself with problems of a practical nature, usually those dealing with educational issues. Many of these early studies of transfer, and of much of human learning, were first conducted in the classroom as distinct from the laboratory.

A great deal of the early effort in transfer was directed towards testing theoretical conceptions of transfer which had direct relevance to educational practice. One of the earliest of these efforts concerned the validity of a general conception known as the doctrine of *formal discipline*. This view contended that the "mind" was composed of several faculties, such as reasoning, memory, and judgment, and that these faculties could be trained, or strengthened,

through the study of certain kinds of subject matter. Studies such as mathematics and classical languages were regarded as especially important. For example, geometry was regarded as a good subject for improving reasoning and Latin as important because it sharpened the student's memory ability. Finally, it was argued that by strengthening certain faculties such as reasoning through the study of mathematics, one would be able to reason in a superior fashion in another but unrelated area, such as law.

Around the turn of the century this doctrine came under experimental attack. An early study by Thorndike and Woodworth (1901) critically examined the notion of formal discipline and failed to find any substantial evidence in support of it. Following their classic study, a number of investigations were conducted with little, if any, support for the doctrine resulting. As a result of their failure to find evidence for the theory of formal discipline, Thorndike and Woodworth proposed an alternate theory known as *identical elements*. This theory contended that training in one kind of activity would transfer to another as long as certain elements, or features, of the task, such as aims, methods, and approaches, were identical in the two tasks. Whereas formal discipline argued that transfer was very general and widespread, the theory of identical elements viewed transfer as more restricted in scope.

Subsequently, the identical-elements theory came under attack as a result of studies of Judd (1908) and his colleagues. Judd argued that the important condition for transfer was that the student be able to abstract general rules or principles for himself. He called this a theory of *generalization*, by which he meant that a student was able to "generalize" his experiences from one situation to another.

These early theories of transfer, perhaps better described as *points of view* rather than theories in the more formal sense, represent historical viewpoints which guided much of early research in transfer. They were all stated in rather general language, thus making them quite difficult to test in a rigorous fashion. Indeed, for this reason, Osgood (1953) has indicated that one cannot even be sure that the old doctrine of formal discipline is invalid.

Besides emphasizing educational issues, many of these early studies were essentially *nonanalytic* in character; that is, they failed to specify the precise variables which produced transfer even though positive or negative transfer may have been obtained. In a number of instances, the transfer obtained could have been due to several possible factors and the designs were such that it was difficult to unravel the effect contributed by each factor.

Later, around 1930, a shift in emphasis was seen in which laboratory rather than classroom studies became increasingly important, a trend not only true in transfer but of learning in general. Many psychologists felt that a science of behavior could be best developed through carefully controlled laboratory studies of the learning process. There was, by and large, no denial of the importance of classroom studies, but it was clearly pointed out that the complex features of the classroom environment made it difficult to discover fundamental laws of behavior.

Associated with the increase in laboratory studies were several significant changes. First, a shift occurred in the types of experiments conducted, with much greater emphasis on designs which permitted detailed analysis of the variables contributing to transfer. In other words, there was an increased emphasis on more analytic approaches in transfer designs. The beginning of this trend can be seen in the early work of McGeoch and his associates (1931), and in the work of Yum (1931) and McKinney (1933), who made precise studies of the effects of similarity on transfer. Melton's (1936) emphasis on standardization in laboratory research was also part of this trend. Psychologists became less interested

in whether or not there was transfer and much more interested in a detailed molecular analysis of the variables contributing to transfer.

A second feature which characterized this new approach was increased interest in and effort at *dimensional analysis*. Dimensional analysis involves determining the dimensions along which transfer tasks can vary. Such dimensions include similarity, complexity, and task variety, to mention a few. By analyzing the variety of task variables and their associated dimensions in a more detailed or molecular fashion it became increasingly possible to specify what precise factor or factors produced transfer.

A third trend is seen in the efforts at constructing models of transfer based on stimulus and response similarity. These efforts culminated in the models produced by Osgood (1949) and Gagné, Baker, and Foster (1950), and in more recent modifications (Dallett, 1965; Houston, 1964; Wimer, 1964). Although these models are incomplete, in the sense that they are restricted to an analysis of similarity factors in transfer, they represent attempts to summarize what is known about one class of variables and to develop a set of empirical laws. These trends in transfer research have their counterparts in other areas of learning. In general, they reflect greater sophistication in experimental design, greater concern with analytical studies, and greater interest in developing and testing more limited theoretical conceptions of transfer.

Finally, a fourth feature which characterized this new approach was a lessened interest in broad general conceptions of behavior, such as formal discipline, and greater interest in more limited conceptions of transfer. Instead of tackling all-inclusive conceptions, psychologists became interested in theories of transfer which dealt with specific processes or subprocesses influencing transfer. Examples of this kind of interest are seen in studies of stimulus predifferentiation (Arnoult, 1957), response learning in transfer (Jung, 1963; Merikle and Battig, 1963), and forward and backward associations (Ekstrand, 1966; Harcum, 1953). This approach can be characterized as a *component analysis* effort, which is the dominant methodological-conceptual approach in current transfer and retention research (Battig, 1966a; Martin, 1965; Underwood, 1964a).

The Measurement of Transfer

This section will describe several types of experimental designs and formulas used in transfer studies. It is important to note that the findings of different transfer studies depend upon the way in which transfer was measured. In addition, if we wish to compare the results of several studies which use different kinds of tasks or which measure performance at different stages, we need to know something about transfer formulas. Excellent discussions of the measurement of transfer are provided by Gagné, Foster, and Crowley (1948), Murdock (1957), and Runquist (1966).

Transfer Designs. A summary of the more frequently used transfer designs is shown in Table 17-1. Design 1 has already been described earlier. With this design, an experimental group learns Task A followed by Task B, and a control group learns only Task B. This is a frequently used design, but suffers from a major weakness because it fails to control for certain variables which may affect transfer. A number of experiments have shown that the learning of a task can be facilitated by an immediately preceding activity (Hamilton, 1950; Thune, 1950) and by previous practice on a number of similar tasks (Harlow, 1949). These effects are, respectively, warm-up and learning to learn. More will be said about these effects in a later section; for the moment they are briefly noted for purposes of understanding certain problems in transfer designs. If an

experimental group does perform superior to a control group on the transfer task one is not sure if the superior performance is due entirely to the specific features of Task A, or due to the more general effects of warm-up or learning to learn. Transfer may be due entirely to general practice effects rather than to any specific features of the initial task. In addition, transfer may be due to the summation of all three of these effects. Because Design 1 does not control for possible warm-up or learning to learn, it is not a desirable design if one wishes to know the *specific* effects of Task A. If there is no need to isolate these effects, then the design is acceptable.

Design 2 is one in which Ss are tested and matched on a portion of Task B, designated as B_1, prior to their assignment to either the experimental or control group. This method is the fore- and after-test method described by Woodworth and Schlosberg (1954). Such a procedure has the advantage of matching the two groups on their performance on B_1 so that their equivalence prior to the experiment is assured. In addition, if sufficient practice on B_1 is given, then the groups are more likely to be equal in possible warm-up effects. Unfortunately, because the experimental group still receives more practice than the control (it practices on Task A), differences in performance on Task B itself may still be a function of differences in learning to learn this type of material.

Design 3 is one in which half the Ss learn A followed by B and half learn the reverse sequence. This design is frequently used in studies of intersensory transfer where one wishes to know if transfer is greater from, say, visual to auditory, or auditory to visual systems (Holmgren, Arnoult, and Manning, 1966).

Design 4 requires that Ss in the experimental group learn Task A and then Task B; Ss in the control group learn Task A and then a similar, but not identical task, B_1. This design keeps the original task the same and introduces variations in the

Table **17-1**   Summary of Several Transfer Designs

Design	Group		Original Task	Transfer Task
1	Experimental		Learn A	Learn B
	Control		(rests)	Learn B
2	Experimental	Pretest on B_1	Learn A	Learn B
	Control	Pretest on B_1	(rests)	Learn B
3	Experimental		Learn A	Learn B
	Control		Learn B	Learn A
4	Experimental		Learn A	Learn B
	Control		Learn A	Learn B_1
5	Experimental and Control		Learn A	Learn B

transfer task. It has the important advantage of controlling the factors of warm-up and learning to learn so that differences in performance on the transfer task can be attributed to specific features of the task itself. The chief difficulty is ensuring that Tasks B and B_1 are themselves equivalent, that is, equally difficult to learn in the absence of any Task A learning. If B and B_1 are not equally difficult, then we cannot be sure that differences in performance on Tasks B and B_1 are due to transfer effects themselves, or due to differences in inherent difficulty between the tasks. In general, it is necessary to know if Tasks B and B_1 are equally difficult prior to using this design.

Design 5 requires that all Ss learn Task A and then Task B with different intervals of time elapsing between the two tasks. This design has been used extensively in studying the temporal course of transfer (Bunch and McCraven, 1938; Ellis and Burnstein, 1960). Groups learning at different time intervals serve as controls for each other.

Adjusting for Differences in Original Learning. In comparing the performance of various groups on transfer tasks, it is frequently assumed that the groups were comparable in performance on the original learning (Task A) task. If the groups were not comparable, then any differences in

transfer performance could result not only as a function of the independent variable(s), but also as a function of the *amount* of learning on the original task. This problem may be handled in one of several ways. First, a design can be employed in which all groups learn the same original task, such as in Design 4. Thus, all groups can be expected to perform at about the same level on the original task and no adjustment is required. Another procedure is to terminate practice on the original task after Ss have all reached an arbitrary criterion level. Still another procedure, which may be used when the original task is different for the various groups and differences in original learning do result, is to employ some statistical procedure such as analysis of covariance. Covariance analysis can be used to "adjust" the transfer measures for any differences in the original learning task.

Anderson (1963) has recently addressed himself to this problem in connection with comparing different experimental groups on resistance to extinction, which he regards as a special case of transfer. He reviews a variety of adjustment or "correction" procedures used in extinction studies and indicates in a general way their possible relevance to transfer; he further notes some of the limitations in adjusting for differences in original learning. This issue is also relevant to problems of measurement in retention and is discussed in the subsequent chapters on retention.

Transfer Formulas. The amount and direction (positive or negative) of transfer may be determined by employing one of several transfer formulas. It is not always necessary to use transfer formulas as one may directly compare performance on the transfer task itself for the various conditions of an experiment. If all conditions, or groups, have comparable preliminary practice, and differ only in the transfer task itself, then any differences in transfer are directly seen in Task B performance. For this, as well as other reasons, many transfer studies do not employ formulas. Nevertheless, there are good reasons for doing so, one being that transfer formulas permit the comparison of findings from different studies and from studies which use different kinds of transfer tasks. An example of this latter advantage is seen in a recent study by Vanderplas, Sanderson, and Vanderplas (1964), who compared the effects of various kinds of pretraining on several different kinds of transfer tasks. By using transfer formulas, they were able to compare the *relative* performance on the various transfer tasks which would not have been readily apparent by inspection of the raw data alone.

In order to apply a transfer formula to a given set of data, some measure of performance must have been taken. Measures which are frequently used include: (1) the number of trials required to reach a given level of mastery; (2) the amount of time required to reach a given level of mastery; (3) the level of mastery reached after a given amount of time or number of trials, such as the number of correct responses; and (4) the number of errors made in reaching a given criterion of mastery.

A simple transfer formula is described below, where E represents the mean performance of the experimental group on the transfer task (Task B) and C represents the mean performance of the control group on the transfer task. By comparing the difference between E and C groups with C itself, a percentage transfer formula can be expressed as follows:

Percentage of transfer

$$= \frac{E - C}{C} \times 100 \quad (1a)$$

This formula is appropriate if the measure of performance is such that the *larger* the value of the measure, the *better* the performance. For example, if the measure of performance is the number of correct responses, then the formula is appropriate because the number of correct responses becomes larger with better performance.

Formula (1a) must be modified by reversing the numerator to $C - E$ if the measure of performance is such that the *smaller* the value of the measure, the *better* the performance. In this case, the formula becomes:

Percentage of transfer

$$= \frac{C - E}{C} \times 100 \quad (1b)$$

This formula is appropriate with such measures as errors, trials to reach some criterion, or time. It is obvious that as errors, trials, or time are reduced in value, performance is improving.

A second type of transfer formula has been proposed by Gagné *et al.* (1948). This procedure compares the difference between the E and C groups with the maximum amount of improvement possible on the transfer task. The maximum improvement possible is indicated by the difference between the total possible score on Task B and the performance of the C group on Task B. If the measure of learning is one such as number of correct responses, as in formula (1a), and T stands for the total possible score, the formula is:

Percentage of transfer

$$= \frac{E - C}{T - C} \times 100 \quad (2a)$$

The denominator and numerator are

reversed if the measure of learning is one such as time, trials or errors, as in formula (1b).

Percentage of transfer

$$= \frac{C - E}{C - T} \times 100 \quad (2b)$$

A chief difficulty with using either formula (2a) or (2b) is that we do not always know the total possible score, T, and its determination may be difficult or impossible.

Murdock (1957) has suggested a third type of transfer formula which has a distinct advantage over the first two described. The maximum amount of positive transfer which can be obtained is 100 per cent transfer and the maximum amount of negative transfer is -100 per cent; in other words, the upper and lower limits are equal, and positive and negative transfer are symmetrical. This is accomplished by making the denominator of the formula include the performance of the E group as well as the C group. The formula is:

Percentage of transfer

$$= \frac{E - C}{E + C} \times 100 \quad (3a)$$

Like formula (1a), formula (3a) is appropriate if the measure of performance is such that the larger the value of the measure, the better the performance. If the measure of performance is such that the smaller the value of the measure, the better the performance, the formula must be modified to read:

Percentage of transfer

$$= \frac{C - E}{E + C} \times 100 \quad (3b)$$

Comparison of Formulas. A comparison of formulas (1a), (2a), and (3a) is shown in Table 17-2. Hypothetical values for E, C, and T are listed along with the percentage transfer obtained with each formula. Because different percentages of transfer are obtained with each formula, the importance of knowing what transfer formula was used in a particular study becomes obvious, especially if one wishes to compare the magnitude and direction of transfer obtained in different studies. This latter point has been strongly emphasized by both Gagné *et al.* (1948) and Murdock (1957).

Locus of Transfer. It is possible for the effects of transfer to appear during different stages of learning the transfer task. For example, transfer effects may appear only during the first few trials of the transfer task and dissipate during the later trials. Similarly, total number of trials may reflect differences among conditions in an experiment, but no differences may appear in the first few trials. For this reason, it is advantageous to take several measures of performance at various portions of the learning curve if such differences are to be reflected (Gagné *et al.*, 1948).

In addition, curve-fitting procedures for analyzing learning curves in transfer studies have been proposed by Woodworth and

Table **17-2**   Comparison of Percentage Transfer Obtained by Three Transfer Formulas

Number of Correct Responses			Percentage Transfer from Formula		
E	C	T	(1a)	(2a)	(3a)
50	0	50	$+$Infinity	$+100\%$	$+100\%$
25	15	50	$+67\%$	$+29\%$	$+25\%$
15	15	50	0%	0%	0%
15	25	50	-40%	-40%	-25%
0	50	50	-100%	$-$Infinity	-100%

Schlosberg (1954) and Rickert (1963). These procedures have in common the analysis of learning curves into slope and intercept constants and indicate that the learning curve for any transfer group can differ from that of a control group in three ways: (1) initial status, or intercept constant; (2) rate of learning; and (3) final status.

Fundamental Processes in Transfer

So far we have described transfer in a general way, indicating that it is defined in terms of the effect of previous performance, or learning, upon some subsequent performance. This effect, however, may be a result of several different factors. For instance, transfer may be due to practice effects such as learning various modes of attack, or of learning how to learn, both of which are instances of the transfer of *general* factors. In contrast, transfer may be due to *specific* factors, such as the similarity between certain features of the original and transfer tasks. In this section we shall describe some of the fundamental processes in transfer such as the transfer of general and specific factors, and distinguish among other processes such as mediation, transposition, intersensory transfer and bilateral transfer.

Transfer of General Factors. It is commonly observed that individuals improve in their ability to learn new tasks more efficiently as a result of sustained practice on a series of similar or related tasks. This progressive improvement in performance, usually reflected in an increased acquisition rate on successive tasks, is a form of transfer known as *learning to learn*. The phenomenon of learning to learn can be observed in a variety of tasks ranging from rote verbal learning to problem solving and is an instance of transfer based upon general factors.

An early study by Ward (1937) will serve to illustrate learning to learn. He required *S*s to learn successive lists of nonsense syllables at the rate of one list a day. Each list contained twelve syllables of approximately equal difficulty. On the first list *S*s required about thirty-eight trials to master the list, on the sixth list *S*s required only twenty trials to reach mastery, and by the fifteenth list *S*s required only fourteen trials to master the list. There was systematic improvement in performance on successive lists with the bulk of improvement occurring in the early lists. The usual interpretation given to this and similar findings is that *S*s are learning to transfer general methods of attack and are establishing "sets" which are appropriate for learning the material. Although the phenomenon of learning to learn is clearly established, we are still not entirely clear as to what mechanisms are precisely involved. The most promising attack on this problem has stemmed from Harlow (1949, 1959) and his students.

Although learning to learn was well established in earlier experiments (Bunch, 1944; Marx, 1944), the series of experiments reported by Harlow in 1949 served to call widespread attention to the importance of this process and the need for accounting for it in systematic formulations of the learning process. Part of the reason for Harlow's interest in learning to learn and related phenomena was his view that much of learning theory was dominated by approaches which ignored long-term studies of learning. As he put it, the majority of laboratory studies required running the animals on sufficient trials to reach some arbitrary criterion, after which they were destroyed. In contrast, Harlow argued for the advantage of studying behavior over long-term conditions of practice.

In the typical Harlow experiment, monkeys are trained on relatively simple discrimination problems. For example, a monkey is presented with two objects, a cube and a solid triangle, with a reward such as a raisin always being under one and never the other. The position of the cube and triangle is randomized so that the animal must respond to the stimulus object rather than to position cues. After the animal masters this discrimination problem, by reliably responding to the stimulus which hides the raisin, he is presented another discrimination problem. This time he might have to learn to discriminate between a large and a small triangle, again with the raisin always being under one stimulus. Successive discrimination problems are given and it is observed that the animals become progressively more efficient in learning the new problems. Indeed,

after hundreds of practice trials on successive discrimination problems, monkeys learn how to solve new discrimination problems extremely fast.

This progressive change in the shape of discrimination learning curves based upon successive problems can be seen in Fig. 17-1. The learning of the early problems takes place slowly and the curves are typical of trial-and-error learning; they also tend to be somewhat positively accelerated. On later problems learning is much faster, and after 200 problems, the animals make approximately 90 per cent correct choices on the second trial. The curve becomes

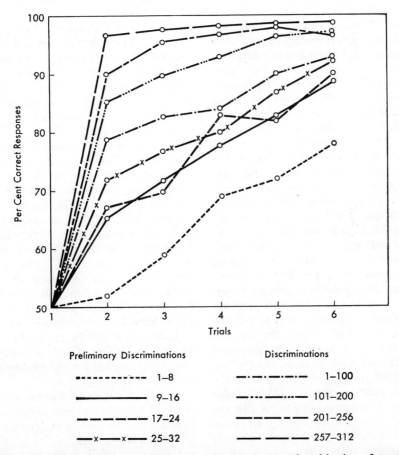

Figure 17-1. Discrimination learning curves on successive blocks of problems. (Reprinted with permission from Harlow, H. F. The formation of learning sets. *Psychol. Rev.*, 1949, **56**, 51–65.)

negatively accelerated after many trials until the animals are almost always correct on the second trial. When this occurs, Harlow contends that the animals have learned how to learn this problem, that is, they have acquired a *learning set* for this class of problems.

The initial investigations of learning to learn, or learning set formation, were largely concerned with its descriptive characteristics. More recent investigations have been oriented toward determining the conditions under which learning sets are formed, using the experimental procedures as a basis for making phylogenetic and ontogenetic comparisons, or seeking conceptual formulations designed to explain learning set phenomena. A component analysis approach is evident in research in learning set phenomena and this effort has revealed several processes or subprocesses which contribute to the net effect in interproblem transfer. These processes include attentional or perceptual mechanisms (Stollnitz, 1965), reinforcement mechanisms (Behar, 1961), and interference reduction (Harlow, 1950; Riopelle, 1953). A few examples of some of this effort will be noted.

Riopelle (1953) has presented an experimental analysis of the acquisition of learning sets for both new and reversed discrimination problems. Monkeys were given several trials of five discrimination problems per day; in addition, the stimulus objects from either the first or fourth problems were presented again with their reward value reversed. Five new problems and one reversed problem were tested each day for sixty-three days. The learning curves for the new problems paralleled those obtained in earlier studies by Harlow. In contrast, the learning curves for the reversed problem showed much slower learning; in this case, we can see that the effect of reversal is to produce an initial negative transfer, based upon stimulus generalization from one problem set to another. Ultimately, however, the initial disparity between the two groups dis-

appeared as the reversal group was given extended practice. Riopelle interpreted these findings as evidence for *transfer suppression*, that is, that performances on successive reversal problems become increasingly independent of each other with progressive training. In other words, animals can learn *not* to generalize from one problem to another.

Another interesting finding revealed by the learning set procedure throws some light on what an animal learns in a discrimination learning problem. It was long thought, for example, that animals rewarded for a position response in a discrimination learning situation would fail to learn anything about the visual aspects of discrimination. Riopelle and Chinn (1961), however, have shown that even when animals are trained to go to the right food well on the first trial, they were able to select the stimulus rewarded on this trial on the next trial 85 per cent of the time, indicating that they were learning something about the stimulus itself.

Finally, research in learning set phenomena has led Harlow to the view that only one basic process underlies discrimination learning; namely, the elimination of errors (Harlow and Hicks, 1957; Harlow, 1959). Harlow has identified at present four types of errors which he believes are fundamental in discrimination learning situations and has termed his formulation *error factor theory*. Although this is an intriguing point of view, it is questionable if this view can appropriately characterize all of learning. The simplicity of a uniprocess theory can be appealing, but it remains to be seen if such a theory can adequately account for the phenomena of learning.

A systematic analysis of learning to learn in verbal learning has been carried out by Postman and his colleagues (Postman and Schwartz, 1964; Postman, 1964; Keppel and Postman, 1966). In the first study in this series, Postman and Schwartz (1964) investigated learning to learn as a function of method of practice and class of verbal materials. Ss learned one paired-associate or one serial list consisting of either adjectives or trigrams. Half of the Ss in each of these four conditions were then shifted to a second list of paired-associate adjectives while the remaining half learned a serial list of adjectives. Interest in this problem was twofold: the Es wanted to determine if general transfer effects result when the type of material was changed and when the type of task was changed. There was evidence for general transfer in that all conditions showed improvement on second-task learning. Improvement was greater when the two tasks were similar, both in method of practice and in class of verbal materials. In general, it was concluded that transfer effects from one list to another are based in part upon specific instrumental habits which are carried over from one task to another.

In the second study in this series, Postman (1964) examined the effects of specific transfer paradigms on learning to learn. The results showed learning to learn in all paradigms; however, the degree of improvement varied as a function of transfer paradigm. This study did not, however, make it possible to determine if differences in improvement reflected the learning of skills specific to each paradigm which differ in effectiveness, or the learning of general transfer skills which are used with varying degrees of success as a function of the paradigms. The third study in this series (Keppel and Postman, 1966) attempted to assess these two possible interpretations. This was accomplished by training Ss on two lists conforming to one of four different transfer paradigms followed by one of two test lists. The basic finding was that the type of training paradigm did not affect performance differentially on the test paradigm, which led to the conclusion that the learning of skills associated with different paradigms are general rather than specific to the paradigms in which the training occurred.

Subsequent studies of learning to learn

in this series have examined a variety of problems. For instance, Postman and Stark (1967) attacked the problem of transfer from serial and paired-associate learning with an interest in defining the nature of the functional stimulus in serial learning. Subsequently, Schwenn and Postman (1967) examined the relative roles of learning and nonlearning (warm-up) activities in affecting transfer performance and concluded that for naive Ss familiarization with the learning task produces greater gain in performance than does warm-up alone. Finally, Postman (1968) examined general transfer effects in three-stage mediation paradigms and concluded that paradigm-specific modes of responding were established during the training phase.

A thorough examination of the current state of learning-set research is beyond the scope and plan of this chapter. The interested reader is directed toward the excellent summary of research on discrimination-learning sets by Miles (1965) and to the volume on nonhuman primates by Schrier, Harlow, and Stollnitz (1965).

Another type of general factor in transfer is that of *warm-up*, which is related to learning to learn. A basic difference between the two, however, is that warm-up is a much more transitory effect. The effect of warm-up on subsequent learning can be seen in a study by Hamilton (1950). He required Ss first to learn a paired-associate list of meaningful words and then gave them another list, a test list, with intervals of time ranging from eight sec. to four hours between the initial and test list. The results of learning the test list showed that it was easier to learn if practiced soon after the initial list, within about 60 min., but that the facilitating effects were smaller and fairly constant after a 60-min. interval between lists. This transitory facilitation in learning a new task was regarded by Hamilton as evidence for a warm-up effect and is usually interpreted to be the result of postural and "attentive" adjustments, acquired from practice with the original task, which transfer to the test task. Similar findings have been reported by Thune (1950) in verbal learning and by Ammons (1947) in motor-skills learning.

Transfer of Specific Factors. Transfer may depend not only upon general factors which we have just described, but also upon the presence of certain specific factors. The specific factors depend upon particular features of the tasks employed or upon the relationship between the original learning and transfer tasks. For instance, the stimuli in the original and transfer tasks can be highly similar, the consequence of which is likely to produce positive transfer. Thus, transfer may be said to depend upon the specific factor of stimulus similarity as well as upon general factors which are likely to be present. In a similar vein, transfer may also depend upon the relationship between the responses in the two tasks.

Additional specific factors which produce transfer may be seen in studies of stimulus predifferentiation in which Ss are sometimes given preliminary practice in discriminating among the task stimuli prior to learning a transfer task containing these stimuli. Similarly, Ss may be given preliminary response familiarization training, that is, training with the response components alone, prior to learning a transfer task. In both of these examples, positive transfer to a new task can be attributed to the *specific* features of the situation as well as to the likely operation of general factors. This description of specific factors in transfer serves, however, only to distinguish them from general factors. A more detailed account of specific factors will be given in the next chapter.

Mediational Processes in Transfer. The learning of a transfer task may be dependent upon the kinds and number of "associations" which exist between the original and transfer task. The study of such associations, and their effect on

transfer, provide the basis for much current work in what is called *mediation*. Typically, mediation, or mediated transfer, is studied by using the paired-associate technique (for example, Cohen and Mac-Neil, 1966). S is presented with pairs of verbal items, the first member of the pair being the stimulus item and the second member the response item. S's task is to learn to associate each response with its stimulus mate, so that when he sees the stimulus item alone he can produce the correct response. There is no necessary logical connection between the stimulus and response items, and S has to discover various cues for associating, or "hooking up," the stimulus-response pairs. An example of a stimulus-response pair is *table–road*; S would have to learn to say *road* when presented the item *table* alone.

Suppose, in the preceding example, that S is required to learn the pair *table–road* in a list of such pairs, and then is required to learn a second list of pairs, among which is *chair–road*. This second pair would be easier to learn because of the associative connection between *table* and *chair*. In other words, there would be some facilitation in learning the second pair as a result of mediation between the stimulus items.

An experiment by Bugelski and Scharlock (1952) demonstrated how language serves to mediate the learning of a paired-associate list of words. They showed that the ease of learning a third paired-associate list was dependent upon having learned two previous lists which contained items which would facilitate, or *mediate*, the learning of a third list. The task of the Ss was to learn three successive lists of paired associates. Examples of representative stimulus-response pairs in each list are shown below:

List I	List II	List III
S_1 R_1	S_2 R_2	S_1 R_2
fish-hat	*hat-book*	*fish-book*

The learning of List I served only to establish the desired associations. The response items of List I were then used as stimulus items in List II. For instance, *hat*, which was a response item in List I, became a stimulus item in List II. This procedure was assumed to strengthen the associative connection between *fish* and *book*, even though these items were never directly paired. The learning of List III served as the test for this assumption, and it was found that *S*s learned List III faster than did an appropriate control group.

In a similar vein, Russell and Storms (1955) demonstrated mediated transfer in paired-associate learning by constructing lists based upon existing associations among words. A basic difference between the two studies, however, was that Bugelski and Scharlock *experimentally produced* the associative linkages among the items by careful arrangement of word pairs, whereas Russell and Storms inferred the existence of mediation by selection of items already known to have associative linkages or connections. Words were selected from the Kent-Rosanoff list, which is made up of words that are commonly associated together. Briefly, this list was constructed by presenting *S*s with a large number of words, singly, and having them respond as fast as they could with an association. By selecting words from the Kent-Rosanoff list, Russell and Storms could infer the

likelihood of a given association to a stimulus word, and by knowing that a given response had a given associative probability, a chain of associates were constructed. For example, by examining the Kent-Rosanoff list, they knew that the most frequent associative response to the word *stem* was *flower*. In turn, the most frequent associative response to *flower* was *smell*. They reasoned that if *S*s learned to make the response *stem* to the stimulus item *cek*, that is, *cek–stem*, that it would then be easier to learn a new pair, *cek–smell*, because of the known *chain of associations* between *stem* and *smell*, than it would be to learn another pair, *cek–joy*, because *joy* had no known associative connection to *stem*.

A schematic outline of the experiment is shown in Table 17-3. *S*s in the experimental and control groups learned the same initial list of paired associates, A-B. The associative chain, B-C-D, was known to exist, based on data from the Kent-Rosanoff list. Thus, it was reasoned that the transfer list A-D would be easier to learn than A-X, because of the known chain of associations going from B to D. The results confirmed their reasoning in that the A-D list was significantly easier to learn than the A-X list.

Earlier studies of mediation, such as those just described, have served to demonstrate the existence of mediation in paired-associate learning. More recently, a

Table **17-3**   Schematic Outline of the Conditions of the Russell and Storms Experiment

	Original List	Inferred Chain	Transfer List
Experimental Group Example	Learn A-B *cek–stem*	(B-C-D) *(stem–flower–smell)*	Learn A-D *cek–smell*
Control Group Example	Learn A-B *cek–stem*	(B-C-D) *(stem–flower–smell)*	Learn A-X *cek–joy*

Adapted from Russell, W. A., and Storms, L. H. Implicit verbal chaining in paired-associate learning. *J. exp. Psychol.*, 1955, **49**, 287–293.

shift in emphasis in mediation research has taken place with greater emphasis being placed upon studies designed to demonstrate the conditions under which mediation does occur, with special emphasis on situational and task variables which affect mediation. In an important paper, Jenkins (1963) has outlined some of the details of this shift and has contended, in addition, that arguments about the nature of the "content" in mediation should be minimized with a corresponding increase in studies of the conditions of mediation.

Several trends appear evident in current research in mediation. First, there is growing doubt that mediation is a simple, associative process which can be inferred from normative data such as those obtaining with the Kent-Rosanoff list. For example, Carlin (1958) found that variations in the strength of the chain of associations did *not* produce corresponding variations in transfer. All degrees of strength of association produced significant transfer, however, when compared with controls.

Second, studies which have been designed to demonstrate the specific effects of mediation itself, as distinct from other possible sources of transfer, have not always succeeded. For example, both Crawford and Vanderplas (1959) and Barclay (1961, 1963) have failed to demonstrate any mediation effects in paired-associate learning over and above those effects which could be attributed to nonspecific sources of transfer such as learning to learn. In response to these findings, Jenkins, Foss, and Odom (1965) report evidence for mediation effects *per se* independent of warm-up and other general transfer effects. In a similar vein, Palermo (1962) found that the condition designed to produce facilitation in a paired-associate transfer task was actually inferior to a control group which could not have benefited from mediated associations. Finally, Mandler and Earhard (1964) have argued that some studies of mediation may have produced mediation effects as the result of an artifact of the particular

paradigm employed and have suggested, in turn, that some of the positive findings of mediation studies might be viewed as evidence of pseudomediation resulting from negative transfer effects in the control condition and zero transfer effects from the experimental condition. Jenkins and Foss (1965) and Schulz, Weaver, and Ginsberg (1965) have responded to this argument by testing implications of the pseudomediation argument of Mandler and Earhard, and have failed to find any but marginal evidence for pseudomediation. In turn, Earhard and Mandler (1965) have responded by contending that the data of Jenkins and Foss do, in fact, support a pseudomediation interpretation. As the matter stands at present, a resolution of this controversy seems dependent upon an analysis of unlearning mechanisms in mediation paradigms (Goulet, 1966). Although these and similar studies do not invalidate the concept of mediation, they do indicate that positive transfer effects associated with mediation can be masked by more general factors or may depend upon the careful selection of the conditions of the experiment.

A third trend is seen in the current emphasis on mediation paradigms. The simplest mediation paradigm consists of three elements which are arranged so that two of them are associated with a third. A simple three-element chain was used in the Bugelski and Scharlock study: Learn A-B, Learn B-C, Test A-C. A variation of the simple chain is Learn B-C, Learn A-B, Test A-C. All eight types of three-stage mediation paradigm are shown in Table 17-4. Four of the paradigms are chaining types (two are forward chains and two are reverse chains), two are acquired-stimulus-equivalence paradigms and two are acquired-response-equivalence paradigms.

Horton and Kjeldergaard (1961) have conducted an experiment investigating all eight paradigms using low-frequency English words as items in a paired-associate task. They found that all but paradigm III

Table **17-4** Three-Stage
Mediation Paradigm

		I	II
Simple Chains	Learn	A-B	B-C
(A→B→C)	Learn	B-C	A-B
	Test	A-C	A-C
		III	IV
Reverse Chains	Learn	B-A	C-B
(A←B←C)	Learn	C-B	B-A
	Test	A-C	A-C
		V	VI
Stimulus	Learn	A-B	C-B
Equivalence	Learn	C-B	A-B
(A→B←C)	Test	A-C	A-C
		VII	VIII
Response	Learn	B-A	B-C
Equivalence	Learn	B-C	B-A
(A←B→C)	Test	A-C	A-C

(Adapted with permission from Jenkins, J. J. Mediated associations: Paradigms and situations. In C. H. Cofer and B. S. Musgrave (Eds.), *Verbal Behavior and Learning.* New York: McGraw-Hill 1963. Pp. 210–245.)

showed significant mediation effects although there were no significant differences between the paradigms. Subsequently, Horton and Hartman (1963) reported greater mediated transfer from forward as compared to backward associations developed in the three-stage mediation paradigm.

Similarly, four-stage paradigms have recently received attention, especially those concerned with stimulus and response equivalence. Evidence for mediation effects in four-stage paradigms has been reported by Cofer and Yarczower (1957) and by McGee and Schulz (1961). An example of a four-stage paradigm is shown below:

Learn A-B
Learn C-B
Learn A-D
Test C-D

With this paradigm, it was assumed (Jenkins, 1963) that A and C become functionally equivalent stimuli during the first two stages. When a new response, D, is learned to A in stage 3, it should more likely occur to C in the test. All 16 possible paradigms were tested (eight stimulus and eight response equivalence) and *no* single paradigm produced mediation effects, in contrast with the three-stage paradigms, and in contrast with other studies (for example, McGee and Schulz, 1961).

Several hypotheses were advanced to explain these negative findings, the most obvious being that the experiment had not allowed sufficient associative strength to build up for facilitating the test list. Unfortunately, a subsequent experiment gave no support for this explanation. As the matter stands at present, Jenkins believes that other differences between the two paradigms, such as the reinforcement of specific mediation responses, individual differences in S's history, and characteristics of the tasks, may account for divergencies in findings between the two paradigms. These alternative explanations led him to conclude that future research in mediation ought to involve procedures for reinforcing the mediating responses.

Recently, James and Hakes (1965) employed a design similar to that of Jenkins (1963); however, they changed the nature of the criterion task to a matching task which proved to be a more sensitive indicator of mediation effects. In addition, they also used a self-paced paired-associate task, which can conceivably facilitate mediation during the acquisition phases. By questioning the Ss and comparing individual results, they concluded that mediation may be attempted actively, and may be used as a kind of problem-solving strategy. An implication of their argument is that one may conceive of an "active" process of mediation in a manner somewhat different from classical views of mediation, which according to James and Hakes view mediation as essentially a passive process. Although the active-passive conceptualization may not be the most useful, the value of their argument is that it certainly implies that implicit mediational responses may have instrumental properties, and that greater effort at directly producing and reinforcing these responses could represent a major advance in mediation research. An important effort in mediation is the series of investigations by Richardson and his colleagues concerning implicit verbal responses (Richardson, 1966; Richardson and Brown, 1966; Richardson, 1968). In general, these studies have been designed to test implications that follow from assumptions about implicit associative responses in mediated transfer.

As can be seen, mediation is currently an area of vigorous research activity and appears to be increasing in importance. Its usefulness is also reflected in efforts at using mediation hypotheses to account for related phenomena, such as those in problem solving (Judson and Cofer, 1956; Judson, Cofer, and Gelfand, 1956), concept formation (Goss, 1961), transfer of instrumental responses (Birge, 1941), conditioning (Shipley, 1935), sensory preconditioning (Wickens and Briggs, 1951), and concept learning (Duncan, 1965).

Transposition. A topic which has generated a considerable amount of theoretical controversy is that of transposition. This controversy concerns whether transfer in discrimination learning is based upon responding to absolute features of the stimuli or upon responding to patterns or relations among stimuli. We can illustrate this controversy by examining a simple experiment.

Chickens were trained to respond to the darker of two grays by rewarding the animals with food when they responded to the darker and by not rewarding them when they responded to the lighter (Köhler, 1925). After this discrimination was established, the animals were presented a new discrimination task, in which they had to choose between the original reinforced gray and one which was still darker. In the new task, the animals responded to the

darker of the two grays, even though they had always been rewarded for choosing the other gray. Köhler argued on the basis of these findings that the animals had learned to respond to the *relationship* between the stimuli, that is, the relationship of "darker than," rather than to the absolute properties of the stimuli. This phenomenon of responding to a new discrimination task on the basis of relationships among stimuli is called *transposition*. On theoretical grounds, it has long been argued by gestalt psychologists as evidence against strict stimulus-response conceptions of transfer in discrimination learning.

In 1937 Spence presented a theory of discrimination learning that accounts for transposition within the framework of stimulus-response theory. The advantage of his theory was that it provided a way of predicting transposition from established principles of behavior. Briefly, the theory views discrimination learning as based upon the gradual accrual of response strength. First, when a response to a particular stimulus is reinforced, a gradient of stimulus generalization about that stimulus develops. Second, when a response to another stimulus is nonreinforced, a gradient of generalized extinction about that stimulus will develop. Third, the gradients of stimulus generalization and extinction summate algebraically so that the tendency to respond to any stimulus along the dimension tested is obtained by subtracting the gradient of extinction from the gradient of generalization.

Spence demonstrated how this theory could apply to discrimination learning by first training chimpanzees to respond to a square which was 256 cm.^{2} in size and not to respond to a square which was 160 cm.^{2} in size. He then presented the animals with a new discrimination in which the stimuli were 256 and 409 cm.^{2} and found that the animals responded to the larger stimulus. In other words, the animals showed transposition.

Spence explained this relational respond-

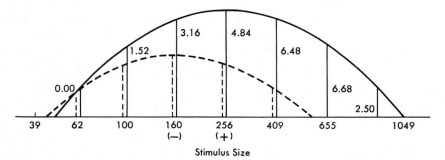

Figure 17-2. Diagrammatic representation of relations between the hypothetical generalization curves, positive and negative, after training on the stimulus combination 256 (+) and 160 (−). (Adapted from Spence, K. W. The differential response in animals to stimuli varying within a single dimension. *Psychol. Rev.*, 1937, **44**, 430–444.)

ing in terms of the algebraic summation theory described above, the details of which are shown in Fig. 17-2. Accordingly, there was some stimulus generalization from stimulus 256 to stimulus 409. Also, there was considerable generalized extinction from stimulus 160 to 265 and relatively little generalized extinction from stimulus 160 to 409. As shown in Fig. 17-2, the resulting net response strength, obtained by subtracting the gradient of extinction from the gradient of generalization, is greater for stimulus 409 than for 256. Thus the theory would predict that animals would have a greater tendency to select 409 than 256, even though they had originally been reinforced to respond to 256.

Recently, some limitations in Spence's formulation have been noted. Bugelski (1956) has pointed out that the adequacy of Spence's theory depends upon the *shape* of the generalization gradient. He notes that Spence's theory is based on the assumption that the gradients of generalization follow a concave fashion, whereas if such gradients were convex in shape, then different predictions would follow. Indeed, Bugelski suggests that the theory is useful in accounting for transposition only when the generalization gradient is concave in shape. There is no need, however, to assume that the gradient will always be concave; in fact, there is considerable evidence to indicate that the shape of the gradient can

vary depending upon a number of experimental conditions.

In a slightly different vein, Riley (1958) has contended that Spence's earlier assumption that animals do respond to the absolute properties of stimuli is itself unacceptable. Riley has proposed that the effective stimuli in a discrimination learning task must be regarded as involving a relationship between contrasting parts of a stimulus complex. As a test of this "contrast hypothesis," Riley reported that the usual breakdown in transposition with stimuli far apart (Ehrenfreund, 1952; Kendler, 1950) was not obtained as long as a contrast between the test figure and background stimulation was maintained.

More recent studies of transposition have shifted away from theoretical controversy regarding absolute versus relational responding to stimuli, and have shifted toward determining the conditions under which transposition occurs. An example of this trend can be seen in a study by Wohlwill (1962), who has shown that the tendency to make relational, as distinct from absolute, responses can depend on the way in which the stimuli are presented. Children were first presented with an array of two sets of stimuli, one group always being reinforced for choosing the smaller number of the two arrays, and the other group for making an absolute choice. During the test series, the stimuli were presented in several different ways, and both relational and absolute responses occurred. If the stimuli were presented in the form of scattered arrays of dots (perceptual series), Ss readily made a relational choice, whereas if the stimuli were presented as numerals (symbolic series), the absolute choice was made more frequently.

Intersensory Transfer. Transfer from one sense modality to another is termed *intersensory transfer*. An instance of such transfer is seen when practice in identifying visual stimuli serves to facilitate the identification of these same stimuli when they are presented tactually. A study by Gaydos (1956) illustrates intersensory transfer in the discrimination of form. Ss were given paired-associate practice in labeling nonsense forms, presented either visually or tactually, with people's names. Following preliminary practice, they then learned to name the forms which were presented in the alternate sensory mode. Gaydos found marked positive transfer in both directions, with greater transfer in going from tactual to visual training than in the opposite direction.

In a similar vein, Postman and Rosenzweig (1956) have demonstrated intersensory transfer in the recognition of verbal stimuli. Preliminary auditory or visual practice in syllable recognition was found to transfer when going to the opposite sense modality. In addition, they found that transfer was greater going from visual to auditory practice than in the opposite direction, a result which they interpreted in terms of mediation. Accordingly, they noted that during visual training Ss tended to repeat the stimulus items subvocally and that this subvocal repetition may mediate transfer to auditory recognition. On the other hand, auditory practice did not appear to produce similar subvocal reactions, which would serve to explain the lesser transfer going from auditory to visual practice.

Lifton and Goss (1962) have demonstrated aural-visual transfer in paired-associates learning. Ss practiced a list of eight paired associates—half learned them by visual presentation and half by aural presentation. After learning to a criterion of one perfect trial, Ss relearned the list with the alternate modality. Marked positive transfer was obtained in both directions, a finding that was interpreted in terms of response-mediated similarity and generalization. Accordingly, they assumed that the presentation of the same response item in the second (transfer) task would evoke response-producing stimuli, previously conditioned, which would serve to mediate learning of the second task.

A recent study by Holmgren, Arnoult, and Manning (1966) describes the results of an intersensory transfer study in paired-associates learning. Sequential patterns of tones served as stimuli for studying auditory-visual and visual-auditory transfer. The tones were presented aurally and then visually by means of oscilloscope displays of their corresponding sine waves. Despite the lack of any obvious relationship between the stimuli, intersensory positive transfer was obtained when the auditory and visual stimuli corresponded! In turn, negative transfer was obtained when the responses were reassigned in the transfer task. These results were interpreted in terms of both perceptual and mediational accounts; however, neither interpretation was unequivocally supported.

Research in intersensory transfer is still largely demonstrational in character. The phenomenon has been demonstrated but it is not yet well understood. Current attempts at explanation have tended to evoke mediation hypotheses, which appear quite reasonable. What is needed, however, are experiments directed at testing the utility of various mediation hypotheses and parametric studies directed toward determining the conditions governing intersensory transfer.

Bilateral Transfer. Many experiments have demonstrated that proficiency acquired in practicing a task with one hand will often transfer to a lesser extent to the opposite hand or leg. Such transfer is known as *bilateral transfer* and can be observed in a variety of situations. Research in this area has usually taken two directions: the first has been to use bilateral transfer as a technique for investigating, or inferring, changes in neural structure following practice with one limb; the second has been to study the conditions that govern bilateral transfer.

Examples of research of the first variety can be seen in the series of investigations carried out by Peterson and his colleagues (Peterson, 1934; Peterson and Barnett, 1961; Peterson and Devine, 1963). In one study, Peterson (1934) demonstrated that the rat's preference for one hand could be shifted to the opposite hand as a result of appropriate cortical injury or removal. Further studies were directed toward identifying the "neural equivalent of practice," an attempt to determine changes in neural structure associated with shifts in handedness observed in bilateral transfer studies.

Examples of the second variety of research can be seen in the extensive series of studies by Cook (for example, Cook, 1933; Cook, 1935), who demonstrated that bilateral transfer is greatest in the case of symmetrical members, next greatest in the limbs on the same side of the body, and least in the case of limbs diagonal to each other. Similarly, studies of bilateral transfer in pursuit rotor learning have been conducted (Kimble, 1952). A related effect known as *bilateral reminiscence* has also been demonstrated (Grice and Reynolds, 1952; Irion and Gustafson, 1952).

Recently, Walker, DeSoto, and Shelly (1957) analyzed both warm-up and reminiscence effects in bilateral transfer on a pursuit rotor task. Although bilateral reminiscence was found, as in other studies, no evidence for bilateral warm-up was obtained. Evidence was obtained, however, for unilateral warm-up, indicating that it appears specific to the set of effectors involved.

CHAPTER

18

Transfer:
Empirical Findings and
Theoretical Interpretations

In the previous chapter we examined the nature and measurement of transfer and described some of its fundamental features. In this chapter we shall outline some of the principal empirical findings in transfer with special reference to specific determinants of transfer. Finally, we shall evaluate some of the conceptual formulations which have attempted to integrate and unify various findings. This chapter is concerned with three principal issues: (1) the role of stimulus and response similarity in transfer, (2) stimulus predifferentiation, and (3) secondary variables in transfer.

A Stimulus-Response Analysis of Transfer

A longstanding effort in the history of transfer research has been the attempt to relate transfer to task similarity and, more specifically, to the dimensions of stimulus and response similarity. One of the most important of the early formulations of transfer and interference effects in reten- tion was that of the Skaggs-Robinson hypothesis (Robinson, 1927), which de- scribed the relationship between similarity and interference (and, by inference, trans- fer) as curvilinear. Interference was least with very high intertask similarity, in- creased to a maximum with moderate degrees of similarity, and decreased again at lower degrees of similarity. Subsequent research which attempted to validate this hypothesis accomplished very little, prin- cipally because of the lack of a satisfactory metric of similarity. Several investigators (Harden, 1929; Kennelly, 1941) obtained results that were in varying degrees of agree- ment with the Skaggs-Robinson hypoth- esis. However, the interpretation of these findings remains equivocal, in part because the findings cannot be related to a unitary dimension of similarity and in part because the range of tested similarity, for a single experiment, did not encompass the entire range described by the hypothesis. For the latter reason, attempts to compare empirical curves with the function described by the hypothesis remain risky.

Despite these early difficulties, researchers

in the field of transfer continued their efforts at describing relationships among transfer and various measures of similarity. This research culminated in Osgood's (1949) significant effort at summarizing the empirical studies dealing with intertask similarity, and in Gagné, Baker, and Foster's (1950) formulation which attempted to perform an analogous summary with intratask similarity. From 1950 to the present subsequent investigations of this topic have been directed principally toward further tests and refinements of these formulations, with at best only a moderate degree of success. We shall now examine these developments, especially as they relate to the problem of similarity.

Meaning of Similarity. Studies that have examined the effect of similarity on transfer have yielded the generalization that similarity between initial and transfer tasks is a major factor influencing transfer. Certainly there is general agreement that the greater the similarity between two tasks, the greater the amount of positive transfer obtained. Nevertheless, despite the fact that a number of studies conform to this generalization, it is by no means a simple or uncomplicated one, partly owing to difficulties inherent in the concept of similarity. Indeed, Noble (1957) has taken the extreme position of arguing that similarity is fundamentally nonmeasurable because it possesses the properties of nontransitivity and symmetry, which prevent it from being treated in accordance with scales having unidimensional properties.

In actual practice, similarity has been defined in several different ways: (1) Scales of similarity have been constructed based upon the judgments of Ss (Haagen, 1949; McKinney, 1933; Osgood, 1946; Rothkopf, 1957; Shepard and Chang, 1963; Yum, 1931); (2) similarity has been defined in terms of variation along some known physical dimension such as size or intensity (Grice and Saltz, 1950; Tosti and Ellis, 1964) or in terms of various statistical

distortion rules (Ellis and Feuge, 1966; LaBerge and Lawrence, 1957; Posner, 1964); (3) sometimes similarity has been defined in terms of a transfer measure itself (Gibson, 1941), which is unsatisfactory if one relates variations of this measure of similarity to transfer measured in the same fashion; (4) similarity may be defined in terms of discriminative judgments made to stimuli which vary along a single dimension, such as jnd scales (Hovland, 1937); and (5) similarity may be defined in terms of multidimensional scaling procedures (Shepard, 1958).

The scale of meaningful similarity of adjectives developed by Haagen (1949) has been frequently used in studies of verbal transfer. In order to construct this scale, Haagen presented Ss with a large number of paired adjectives, such as "complete-entire," and required them to judge each pair along a seven-point scale of similarity ranging from very great to very slight similarity. For each pair of adjectives, he obtained an average rating based on all the judgments and called this the scale value for the pair. A sample set of items from Haagen's list is shown below. A standard word is given along with three comparison words judged to be either high, moderate, or low in similarity to the standard word. For instance, "complete" and "entire" were judged to be highly similar, whereas "complete" and "perfect" were judged to be relatively low in similarity.

Standard Word	High Similarity	Moderate Similarity	Low Similarity
complete	entire	utter	perfect
beloved	cherished	prized	preferred

The fact that verbal materials may vary along several dimensions (Cofer and Foley, 1942), such as homonymity and antonymity, as well as synonymity, increases the difficulty of simple manipulation of the similarity variable. It is clear, of course, that verbal similarity is a multidimensional concept.

Another measure of similarity that has received a good deal of use is one developed by Gibson (1941), who constructed a series of perceptual designs (forms) varying in degree of similarity. An especially interesting feature of this procedure was that similarity was defined in terms of "generalization tendencies," that is, the probability of responding to a varied form as if it were an originally learned form. This procedure defines similarity in terms of one possible measure of transfer itself, probability of "generalization," and is therefore circular if one wishes to relate this measure of similarity to a measure of transfer defined in the same fashion. In other words, the Gibson measure of perceptual similarity is satisfactory only so long as an *independent* measure of transfer is employed.

Despite numerous efforts at scaling similarity, no entirely satisfactory metric has emerged. In addition, no completely adequate theoretical conception of either stimulus similarity or response similarity has yet been developed. Such a development would require a systematic conception of both the stimulus and response beyond that currently enjoyed in psychology. Despite such awesome difficulties, a body of empirical generalizations relating transfer to stimulus and response similarity has slowly emerged. We shall examine some of these generalizations and the difficulties entailed, first by examining stimulus similarity and then response similarity.

Stimulus Similarity and Transfer. The data regarding stimulus similarity and transfer tend to be quite consistent. In general, where stimuli are varied and the responses are kept identical, positive transfer increases with increasing stimulus similarity. This generalization has been supported by investigations using a wide range of learning tasks such as verbal paired associates

(Bruce, 1933), paired associates using visual forms as stimuli (Ellis and Burnstein, 1960; Hamilton, 1943; McKinney, 1933; Yum, 1931), expectancy learning (Heath, 1959), motor skills (Duncan, 1953), and mediation tasks (Ryan, 1960).

Theoretical accounts of the positive transfer effects due to stimulus similarity have traditionally employed the concept of stimulus generalization (Underwood, 1949a). Such accounts have assumed that during the learning of an S-R pair, as in a paired-associate list, there is some tendency for stimuli "similar" to the original stimulus item also to acquire some tendency toward controlling the response. In essence, there is some spread of habit strength to stimuli that share one or more dimensions of the original stimulus. This type of explanation is an instance of one of several alternative types described by Brown (1965) in which stimulus generalization is regarded as some type of covert process conceived as "explaining" or "accounting" for overt transfer.

A view currently under development by Brown (1965) equates generalization with transfer of training and attributes transfer to the presence of common stimulus components or dimensions. Such a view assumes that transfer is some function of the number of shared stimulus components. Brown (1965) notes that

. . . such a theory would hold, in the final analysis, that one stimulus can produce the same behavioral results as another only when both stimuli lead to the same neural events just prior to the final common path. At the behavioral level, two stimuli evoke the same reaction if both contain elements or components that are identical and if the reference response has been conditioned to at least one of those elements. Transfer and similarity thus reduce to stimulus-component identity (p. 22).

Such a view harkens back to earlier conceptions of transfer such as those of Thorndike (1913) and Guthrie (1930).

Response Similarity and Transfer. An early empirical generalization (Bruce, 1933; Wylie, 1919) contended that learning to make new responses to the same stimuli, in accordance with the A-B, A-C paradigm, was the basic condition for producing negative transfer. Presumably, the responses learned in the first task intrude and compete with the responses to be learned in the second task. Later studies, however, have shown that learning new responses to old stimuli may lead to *either* positive or negative transfer, depending on the presence of additional factors such as degree of response similarity (Underwood, 1951), the use of repairing procedures (Kausler and Kanoti, 1963; Porter and Duncan, 1953; Twedt and Underwood, 1959), and the use of stimulus predifferentiation paradigms (Arnoult, 1957).

A study by Underwood (1951) illustrates the conditions under which positive transfer is obtained. He required Ss to learn an initial paired-associate list of adjectives and then to learn a second list in which the stimulus items were kept identical but the responses varied through three degrees of similarity: high, moderate, and low. Response similarity was varied by selecting items from Haagen's (1949) list. The results were quite clear-cut and showed that as response similarity increased, progressively increasing amounts of positive transfer were obtained. In fact, all conditions of response similarity, even low similarity, produced some positive transfer. Additional analysis of correct responses on the first-anticipation trial of the transfer task revealed that facilitation was again an increasing function of response similarity, despite the fact that frequency of intrusions was greatest for conditions of high response similarity.

Several researchers (Duncan, 1955; Osgood, 1946; Underwood, 1951; Young, 1955) have interpreted the positive transfer effects due to response similarity in terms of a theory of response generalization. Briefly, this theory assumes that when a

response B is attached to a stimulus A, there is some tendency for responses "similar" to B to acquire some degree of associative strength to A. In effect, when a response is being attached to a stimulus, many responses similar to the reinforced response also acquire some generalized associative strength. Thus, a theory of response generalization would predict enhanced performance on the first-anticipation trial of the transfer list on the basis of generalized response tendencies developed during first-list learning.

More recently, Barnes and Underwood (1959) have proposed an alternative interpretation of positive transfer due to response similarity in terms of response mediation. They contend that direct mediation of the responses in the second list by first-list responses provides the most economical interpretation of the massive positive transfer obtained with the A-B, A-B′ paradigm. This effect presumably takes place during second-list learning in which the chain A-B-B′ is acquired. Such an explanation does not rule out the operation of response generalization, but it does appear more plausible in accounting for such findings as near perfect transfer to the second list.

Support for a response mediation interpretation was obtained by Postman (1962b) who found that first-list associations were maintained at high strength during second-list learning with an A-B, A-B′ paradigm (identical stimuli and highly similar responses), whereas first-list responses showed considerable reduction in their availability in the A-B, A-C paradigm where entirely new responses were learned. In essence, the response mediation theory is based on the established principle that words that are highly similar are likely to be strongly associated, and that such associations may mediate second-list learning. In turn, any items that have strong associative connections, regardless of their similarity, will facilitate second-list learning in the A-B, A-B′ paradigm. Underwood (1961) also believes that this same type of mediation formulation can be applied when stimulus similarity is varied between two lists, a view that is conceptually desirable, certainly from the viewpoint of economy. Two studies (Runquist and Marshall, 1963; Schulz and Lovelace, 1964) have reported data consistent with a mediation interpretation; however, Schwenn and Underwood (1965) obtained transfer results that were not entirely consistent with a mediation interpretation. Despite possible limitations, the principal importance of this alternative interpretation is that it represents a shift from generalization to mediation as a major mechanism in paired-associate transfer.

An Empirical Summary: Osgood's Transfer Surface. In 1949 Osgood presented an empirical integration of the effects of stimulus and response similarity on transfer. His review of the literature up to that time led him to make three empirical generalizations about the effects of similarity on both transfer and interference effects in retention. These generalizations are as follows: (1) In transfer paradigms where the stimuli are varied and the responses are kept the same, we find that positive transfer is obtained and increases with increasing stimulus similarity. Osgood (1949) contended that this generalization has been supported by several studies in paired-associates transfer (Hamilton, 1943; McKinney, 1933; Yum, 1933) and is consistent with the findings from studies of stimulus generalization (Hovland, 1937). (2) In transfer paradigms where the responses are varied and the stimuli remain the same, negative transfer is obtained which decreases as the similarity between the responses increases. This generalization is supported, according to Osgood (1949), by several studies (Bruce, 1933; Gibson, 1941; Wickens, 1938). (3) Finally, where both stimuli and responses are varied, negative transfer is obtained which increases as the similarity of the stimuli increases. In this

instance, Osgood (1949) indicated that studies by Gibson (1941), McGeoch and McDonald (1931) and Melton and Von Lackum (1941) offered a support.

These three generalizations are represented in a three-dimensional diagram, known as the Osgood transfer and retroaction surface, as shown in Fig. 18-1. This figure represents the effect of stimulus and response similarity on degree and direction of transfer. The vertical dimension represents degree of transfer going from maximum positive transfer through zero transfer to maximum negative transfer. The width of the figure represents the dimension of stimulus similarity ranging from functional identity of stimuli to neutrality. The length of the figure represents the dimension of response similarity, ranging from functional identity of responses through neutral or unrelated responses to responses which are opposite and finally antagonistic. The rectangular plane, which is anchored on the left at the point of zero transfer, represents zero transfer throughout the surface. The curved portion of the surface is used to indicate whether positive or negative transfer is obtained. Conceptually, we project the degree of stimulus and response similarity until the projections intersect and then determine whether the point of intersection is above or below the zero reference plane. If it is above the reference plane, transfer is positive; if it is below, transfer is negative; if it coincides with the plane, transfer is zero.

For example, we see from this figure that the conditions for maximum transfer consist of a transfer task having stimuli and responses identical to those of the original task. This is reasonable because the transfer task is merely a continuation of the original task. In addition, the figure reveals that as long as the responses are identical, any degree of stimulus similarity will yield some positive transfer. The figure also indicates that the condition for maximum negative transfer is having to make antagonistic responses to identical stimuli. Finally, it is

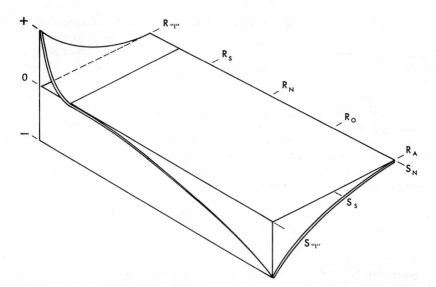

Figure 18-1.   The transfer and retroaction surface: medial plane represents effects of zero magnitude; response relations distributed along length of solid and stimulus relations along its width. (Adapted with permission from Osgood, C. E. The similarity paradox in human learning: A resolution. *Psychol. Rev.*, 1949, **56**, 132–143.)

clear that if highly similar responses are made to the same stimuli, positive transfer will occur.

Some Limitations of the Osgood Surface. In 1949 it could perhaps be said that the Osgood surface did represent reasonably the known facts about stimulus and response similarity. Nevertheless, because the surface was based on less than adequate data, subsequent investigations were directed toward filling in the gaps, especially with respect to the range of similarities that were untested at that time. Unfortunately, subsequent attempts to test the Osgood surface failed to yield consistent findings and failed to clarify, in any substantial fashion, the issues inherent in relating transfer and similarity.

For example, Bugelski and Cadwallader (1956) conducted an elaborate study in an attempt to verify Osgood's formulations. *S*s learned paired-associate lists using Gibson figures as stimuli and words as response items, and then learned transfer lists that were varied with respect to both

stimulus and response similarity. The results with respect to stimulus similarity were generally in accord with Osgood's surface; in contrast, the findings with respect to response similarity were not in accord with Osgood's predictions. When *S*s learned to make different responses, varying along a dimension of response similarity, to the same stimuli, there was no systematic decrease in transfer as the responses became less similar. Both Underwood (1961) and Dallett (1962) have noted, however, that the empirical divergence with respect to response similarity may be due to a failure to control for differences in transfer-list difficulty. The design employed by Bugelski and Cadwallader was such that all *S*s learned a common original list and different transfer lists, and no determination was made of the inherent difficulty of the transfer lists themselves. In contrast to these findings, Dallett (1962) has obtained results that were in reasonable agreement with the Osgood surface by using covariance procedures to adjust for differences in first-list learning.

At this point it can again be noted that attempts to test the Osgood surface have failed to yield consistent data. Indeed, Battig (1966a) has concluded that these and similar studies have not only failed to show much consistency with either Osgood's surface or each other, but that little has been accomplished in identifying the principal variables responsible for these inconsistencies. In general, two sources of difficulty in formulating a systematic conception that will relate transfer and similarity have been noted: (1) The lack of a satisfactory metric of similarity, along with associated conceptual difficulties, has been regarded as a principal source of difficulty. (2) Additional sources of difficulty generally relate to problems associated with confounding of variables, as was noted in the discussion of the Bugelski and Cadwallader (1956) study. All this does not mean that the Osgood surface is invalid; rather, it would seem to suggest that an adequate conceptualization of the role of intertask similarity on transfer must await the development of appropriate scales of similarity as well as other methodological developments. Some promising beginnings have been made in the direction of modifying and further developing Osgood's surface (Dallett, 1965; Houston, 1964; Thompson, 1966; Wimer, 1964). Because of divergencies among some of these modifications (Houston, 1964; Thompson, 1966), however, their ultimate usefulness remains to be seen.

The Osgood surface faces difficulty on conceptual as well as empirical grounds (Battig, 1966a; Ellis, 1965). We note in Fig. 18-1 that making a different response to the same stimuli is a condition for negative transfer, except when the responses are highly similar. In the latter situation, positive transfer is predicted. Unfortunately, the precise degree of response similarity is usually difficult to specify. In addition, it is difficult to distinguish between "opposite" and "antagonistic" responses which makes this portion of

the response-similarity dimension of limited value. Finally, there is some evidence that "opposite" verbal responses, that is, antonyms, are psychologically more similar by virtue of mediation than are "neutral" responses. On this basis, it has been suggested (Battig, 1966a) that much of the confusion about response similarity will disappear if neutrality rather than opposition or antagonism is considered as the limiting point of similarity.

Some Final Comments on Similarity. The foregoing discussion has emphasized that the problem of relating transfer and similarity will remain unsolved until a clearer conceptual formulation of similarity is developed. Several converging directions toward the solution to this problem are currently emerging, with mediation formulations being of considerable promise.

We can distinguish between two general approaches that have been taken in defining stimulus similarity. One approach has been to search for some defining property or attribute that will form a dimension of similarity and that will do so independently of Ss behavior. Here the concern is with "external" stimuli and their physical properties. This approach has typically led to either a common-element formulation (Brown, 1965) or a dimensional treatment (Ellis & Feuge, 1966). The common-element formulation assumes that a set of stimuli can be reduced to components or elements and that similarity is some function of the number of common elements. Thus, similarity reduces to a problem of the *identity* of stimulus components. The dimensional formulation, in turn, assumes that stimuli can be ordered along some physical dimension such as size or intensity. With this approach, similarity reduces to a problem of *distance* between stimuli. The principal limitation of either of these formulations is that additional factors such as sets and instructions may alter the dimensions to which S responds. In other words, common-element and dimensional formulations do not satisfactorily account for all the data.

In addition to common-element and dimensional approaches, Lawrence (1963) calls attention to a second approach which defines similarity in terms of mediation, that is, in terms of the past history of the organism. An example of this type of formulation is seen in the mechanism of acquired equivalence of cues (Goss, 1955; Miller and Dollard, 1941; Murdock, 1958), in which attaching common responses to different stimuli can mediate their equivalence through common response-produced cues. Similarly, the suggestion that the effects of both stimulus similarity (Underwood, 1961) and response similarity (Barnes and Underwood, 1959) can be accounted for in terms of mediation is another instance of this approach. The principal advantage of this approach is that it can account for similarity, defined in terms of the extent to which one stimulus can substitute for another in evoking a response, under conditions not predicted by either common-element or dimensional formulations. Nevertheless, a mediation formulation does not obviate the need for common-element and dimensional formulations. For instance, the acquired similarity of cues which is mediated by common verbal responses is always dependent upon the initial or inherent "external" similarity that exists.

In a similar vein, Miller (1959) has suggested that a formulation of response generalization, and by implication response similarity, may be interpreted in terms of the "similarity" of response-produced cues stemming from proprioceptive feedback. The essence of this view is that whenever an organism makes a response, such as making a "serve" in tennis, proprioceptive feedback to S permits him to discriminate the similarity of this to other responses, to detect if this response was executed with the proper force, and so on. In this case, S learns to make judgments about such feedback, that is, to make proprioceptive dis-

criminations; accordingly, the problem of response similarity (and response generalization) can be regarded as a special case of stimulus similarity. In this instance, response similarity, as was stimulus similarity, is defined in terms of a mediational formulation (feedback) as distinct from properties of the overt response (or stimulus).

In the present connection, it should be noted that the conceptual-methodological problems inherent in the concept of *similarity* are also shared by the concept of *distinctiveness*. Distinctiveness of stimuli may, of course, simply be regarded as a special case of low-similarity stimuli in which few common elements are shared or in which interstimulus distances are large. Nevertheless, a large body of literature about distinctiveness has emerged somewhat independently of similarity (Dollard and Miller, 1950; Miller and Dollard, 1941; Murdock, 1960) and it is convenient to use the concept in certain situations. Like similarity, we may distinguish between two kinds of distinctiveness: (1) Distinctiveness may refer to the *initial* or *primary* discriminability of a set of stimuli, such as the initial readiness or ease with which a naive organism might discriminate two tones or two wines. (2) In addition, we can conceptualize changes in distinctiveness due to *mediational* events, such as the acquired distinctiveness of cues. This type of distinctiveness might be termed secondary in the sense that it is acquired as a result of language experiences or other kinds of activity with the environment.

In summary, we can distinguish (1) primary and acquired stimulus similarity, and (2) primary and acquired response similarity. We may also distinguish between (3) primary and acquired distinctiveness of stimuli, and, by analogy, we can conceptualize (4) primary and acquired distinctiveness of responses. It would appear that a major solution to the problems of *similarity* and *distinctiveness* would be a conceptual formulation that would relate the notion of an initial or primary dimension of similarity (and distinctiveness) with that of a derived, secondary, or acquired formulation of similarity, such that an adequate account of the relationship between transfer and similarity would emerge. Promising beginnings in this direction have been suggested by Lawrence (1963), who has proposed a coding theory of the stimulus which he views as encompassing both primary and derived formulations of similarity, and Murdock (1960), who has proposed a method for quantifying the distinctiveness of unidimensional stimuli.

Stimulus Predifferentiation and Transfer

A problem which has actively engaged transfer researchers since about 1950 is that of stimulus predifferentiation. In general, studies of stimulus predifferentiation have been designed to determine what is learned about the pretraining stimuli in the A-B, A-C paradigm. In this instance, primary interest has centered on using the transfer task as an indicator of what is learned about the stimuli during A-B pretraining, as distinct from the more customary interest in second-task performance. In addition, the stimulus predifferentiation paradigm has received considerable use in attempts to test theoretical interpretations of transfer in perceptual learning (Postman, 1963; Vanderplas, 1963; Wohlwill, 1966).

Stimulus predifferentiation typically refers to the facilitation in learning a new stimulus-response task as a result of some type of preliminary training with the stimuli themselves. In addition, stimulus predifferentiation is sometimes used to identify a class of experimental *operations* as well as the *process* by which such facilitation may occur. In the typical investigation of stimulus predifferentiation Ss are given preliminary practice in attaching verbal labels, or names, to sets of stimuli and are then given a transfer task requiring them

to make qualitatively different responses to the same stimuli. Usually, the transfer task requires motor responses such as pushing switches or levers; in this fashion the two sets of responses are quite different from each other so that the positive transfer obtained *cannot* be attributed to any "similarity" between the two sets of responses. The basic features of this type of predifferentiation study are shown below:

Pretraining Task	Transfer Task
$S_0 - R_{verbal}$	$S_0 - R_{motor}$

It is reasoned that the ease of learning the transfer task, that is, of "hooking up" motor responses to the stimuli, occurs because the stimuli have become *predifferentiated* in the pretraining task. In other words, giving the various stimuli verbal labels has caused them to become less "confusing" or more "distinctive," thus making it easier to learn to attach new responses to them.

Categories of Stimulus Predifferentiation. The previous section described one type of predifferentiation in which Ss practiced attaching verbal responses to stimuli during pretraining and then learned to make different motor responses to the *same* stimuli in the transfer task. This type of predifferentiation is known as *Relevant S* pretraining—Ss are given pretraining with stimuli which are relevant (actually identical) to those used in the transfer task. There are several additional types of stimulus predifferentiation, all of which have been classified by Arnoult (1957). His classification is based upon the various kinds of activities required of S during pretraining and is outlined in Table 18-1. The transfer task is the same in all instances and consists of making different motor responses of moving a control stick up in the presence of

Table **18-1**   Various Categories of Stimulus Predifferentiation

Kind of Pretraining	Pretraining Task		Transfer Task	
	Stimuli	Verbal Responses	Stimuli	Motor Responses
Relevant S-R	Red light Green light	"Up" "Down"	Red light Green light	Up Down
Relevant S	Red light Green light	"Cow" "Horse"	Same as above	
Irrelevant S	Bright light Dim light	"Cow" "Horse"	Same as above	
Attention	Red light Green light	None None	Same as above	
No Pretraining	None		Same as above	

Adapted with permission from M. D. Arnoult, Stimulus predifferentiation: Some generalizations and hypothesis. *Psychol. Bull.*, 1957, **54**, 339–350.

a red light and down in the presence of a green light.

In the first type of pretraining, *Relevant S-R*, the stimuli in the pretraining task are the same as those in the transfer task, and the responses in the pretraining task are symbolic, or "representative," of those in the transfer task. Presumably, learning to say "up" in the presence of a red light will make it easier to learn to move a control stick in the direction of up. This type of pretraining is not, strictly speaking, a type of stimulus predifferentiation because the responses in the training and transfer task are related to each other. Thus, any transfer obtained may result from the "relatedness" of the responses as well as from stimulus familiarization.

In the second type of pretraining, *Relevant S*, the stimuli in the two tasks are the same but the responses bear no symbolic relationship to each other. This type of pretraining is typically used in tests of hypotheses about stimulus predifferentiation (Ellis and Muller, 1964; Vanderplas, Sanderson, and Vanderplas, 1964). *Irrelevant S* pretraining requires that Ss make

differential verbal responses to stimuli irrelevant to those in the transfer task. This type of training is most often used as a control for warm-up and learning-to-learn. *Attention training* requires Ss to "look at" or observe stimuli but not to label them in any way. A *No Pretraining* group is sometimes used as a control for the other conditions, but is generally unsatisfactory because it does not control for warm-up or learning-to-learn. It can, however, provide useful information if additional controls are present.

In all the categories described by Arnoult, the transfer task consists of learning to make new responses to the stimuli; in other words, a discriminative *learning* task is used as a test of the effects of various types of predifferentiation. In addition, however, *perceptual* tasks have also been used that require Ss to discriminate or to recognize stimuli rather than learn to make new responses in their presence (Arnoult, 1953; Arnoult, 1956; Ellis, Feuge, Long, and Pegram, 1964; Katz, 1963). For instance, following pretraining, S may be given a recognition test in which he has to "pick out" from an array of simillar stimuli the one or ones that he thought he experienced during pretraining.

Effects of Various Types of Pretraining on Transfer. The effects of various types of pretraining on transfer are fairly well established. Studies employing *Relevant S-R* pretraining have shown at least equal or greater positive transfer as compared with other kinds of pretraining (Arnoult, 1957). The interpretation of this finding is usually attributed to the joint effects of enhanced discriminability of the stimuli and to practice on "representative" features of the response during pretraining which presumably permit *S* to encode the response.

Relevant S pretraining has also been shown to facilitate second-task performance in a large number of experiments (Cantor, 1955; Ellis and Muller, 1964; Goss and Greenfeld, 1958; McAllister, 1953; Vanderplas, Sanderson, and Vanderplas, 1964). Facilitation on the transfer task is typically interpreted as being due to the preliminary experience with the stimuli which presumably makes them less "confusing" or more "distinctive." Exactly how the stimuli become more distinctive and precisely what mechanisms are involved is a subject of theoretical controversy, and a variety of hypotheses have been offered to account for this event (Gibson and Gibson, 1955; Goss, 1955; Hake and Ericksen, 1955; Miller and Dollard, 1941; Postman, 1955; Vanderplas, 1963). Regardless of theoretical differences in interpretation, however, the facts regarding *Relevant S* pretraining are reasonably clear.

A study by Gagné and Baker (1950) serves to illustrate the effects of *Relevant S* pretraining on transfer. One group of *S*s was given preliminary practice in learning to associate different letters of the alphabet to patches of light of varying intensity whereas another group received no preliminary practice. Both groups were then given a transfer task which required them

to learn to press a particular switch in the presence of each of the same lights. The results indicated that *S*s given preliminary practice in associating letters to lights were superior in learning the transfer task to those given no pretraining. This superiority was interpreted as indicating that pretraining served to reduce the amount of stimulus generalization among the various stimuli so that the stimuli were more distinctive to *S*. Therefore, *S* was more easily able to attach new responses to the stimuli in the transfer task.

Although this is an apparently reasonable interpretation of the effect of *Relevant S* pretraining, the design of this study makes it difficult to interpret the findings *just* in terms of reduction of intralist stimulus generalization. For example, any facilitation resulting from verbal pretraining may have been due to additional factors such as warm-up and learning to learn. Indeed, several researchers (for example, Ellis and Muller, 1964; Goss, 1953) have called attention to the importance of isolating alternative interpretations of positive transfer due to *Relevant S* pretraining before assuming that the effect is simply one of reduction in stimulus generalization or enhanced distinctiveness.

A more elaborate study by Goss and Greenfeld (1958) attempted to examine in greater detail the various conditions influencing transfer of predifferentiation. In their study several different types of pretraining were given along with several degrees of practice on the pretraining task plus a control group which received no pretraining. During pretraining *S*s engaged in one of several tasks with stimuli consisting of four lights of varying intensity. The various pretraining tasks included such activities as attaching familiar relevant labels to the stimuli, that is, learning to call them *very bright, bright, dull,* and *very dull,* labeling the stimuli with nonsense syllables, and having *S*s supply their own labels. Besides the three different verbal labeling conditions, other conditions were given which involved various combinations as follows: looking at the stimuli; looking at and discriminating among the stimuli; and looking, discriminating, and naming overtly or covertly.

Following pretraining *S*s were given a transfer task in which they had to learn to push a lever in a different direction for each of the four lights. The basic findings of the study revealed that *S*s given the various verbal labeling tasks were superior on the transfer task to those given instructions which involved various combinations of looking at, discriminating, and naming overtly or covertly. In addition, *all conditions led to superior transfer when compared with groups who only saw the stimuli*. The pronounced superiority of the various verbal labeling groups over the "seeing" group was quite striking. Goss and Greenfeld viewed their results as being consistent with an acquired distinctiveness of cues position, namely, that attaching verbal responses to the stimuli generated additional cues which served to make the stimuli more distinctive. Because they became more distinctive, the task of attaching new differential responses to them was facilitated.

Conditions of *Irrelevant S* and *Attention* pretraining have been employed in a number of studies of stimulus predifferentiation, principally as control groups. As noted earlier, *Irrelevant S* pretraining is usually employed as a control for warm-up and learning to learn. Similarly, *Attention* pretraining has been employed as a control for stimulus familiarization so that the role of the labeling activity itself can be assessed. The typical procedure is to instruct *S* to observe the pretraining stimuli (Arnoult, 1956; Ellis, Bessemer, Devine, and Trafton, 1962; Ellis and Muller, 1964), or to discriminate among them (Robinson, 1955; Vanderplas, Sanderson, and Vanderplas, 1964), and to provide an equal amount of such familiarization practice for additional *S*s who are given *Relevant S* practice. In this fashion, any superiority in performance

on the transfer task following *Relevant S* practice is attributed to events associated with *labeling* the pretraining stimuli as distinct from merely "seeing" them.

Finally, it should be noted that not all experiments have shown positive transfer effects from *Relevant S* practice (Arnoult, 1953, 1956; Robinson, 1955). In these studies, the transfer task was a *perceptual* rather than a *learning* task. This distinction has been shown to be an important one, and in part can account for some of the apparent inconsistencies in the predifferentiation literature. Although more will be said about this distinction later, it is important to note that recent investigations have clearly shown that *Relevant S* pretraining can lead to facilitation in the acquisition of instrumental responses, and under conditions in which *no* such facilitation of perceptual performance occurs (Ellis and Muller, 1964; Vanderplas, Sanderson, and Vanderplas, 1964). These findings readily attest to the significance of criterion-task variables in the transfer of stimulus predifferentiation and to the necessity of systematic interpretation of such differences.

Theoretical Interpretations of Stimulus Predifferentiation. Several theories have been proposed to account for the positive transfer effects resulting from various kinds of stimulus predifferentiation. Typically, however, these theoretical accounts have been derived from more general formulations that were initially designed to explain or encompass a large variety of behavioral phenomena. Indeed, theories of stimulus predifferentiation have usually stemmed from more general formulations of mediation theory and perceptual learning, discussions of which may be seen in several sources (Arnoult, 1957; Bevan, 1961; Ellis, 1965; Gibson, 1963; Goss, 1955; Miller and Dollard, 1941; Postman, 1963; Vanderplas, 1958, 1963; Wohlwill, 1966).

Although there is general agreement regarding the positive transfer effects stemming from predifferentiation training, especially *Relevant S* practice, there is still considerable disagreement regarding the mechanisms by which this process occurs. In general, theories of stimulus predifferentiation have differed in their emphasis upon three somewhat distinct processes in explaining facilitation in second-task performance: (1) associative or mediating processes, (2) differentiation, and (3) receptor-oriented observing responses.

Theories which have emphasized the role of associative or mediating processes have contended that stimuli become more "distinctive" as the result of the addition of response-produced cues (Goss, 1955; Lawrence, 1949, 1950; Miller and Dollard, 1941). According to the hypothesis of acquired distinctiveness of cues, attaching different verbal responses to similar stimuli tends to increase the "distinctiveness" of the stimuli. It is assumed that these verbal responses generate implicit response-produced cues which, according to one version of the hypothesis (Goss, 1955), become added to the original stimuli, thus making a more distinctive stimulus compound. In this theory "distinctiveness" is treated as an intervening variable and is typically inferred from one of three different response measures: (1) reduction in the probability of stimulus generalization following labeling practice (Birge, 1941); (2) ease of attaching different instrumental response to the pretraining stimuli following labeling practice (Gagné and Baker, 1950; Goss and Greenfeld, 1958); and (3) more direct perceptual tasks such as detection, discrimination, or recognition of the stimuli (Arnoult, 1953, 1956; Jeffrey and Bogartz, 1961; Johnson, 1964; Robinson, 1955).

In addition, the acquired "similarity" of stimuli is explained by the complementary mechanism of acquired equivalence of cues. Attaching similar or identical verbal responses to different stimuli will increase the "equivalence" of the stimuli, presumably through the addition of common response-produced cues. Both of these

conceptions imply additive processes, and hence have been regarded by Gibson and Gibson (1955) as instances of "enrichment" theories of perceptual learning. In general, such theories contend that stimuli become modified following labeling practice as a result of the addition of associations, or response-produced cues, to the stimulus impression.

In contrast to theories which emphasize the role of associations, Gibson and Gibson (1955) have proposed a somewhat different view of perceptual learning, and hence of the mechanism by which stimulus predifferentiation training facilitates second-task performance. According to their view, which they refer to as differentiation, organisms learn to distinguish various aspects of stimuli which already exist, that is, aspects which are inherent in the stimulus environment. Thus, perceptual learning consists of learning to respond to various stimuli not previously responded to rather than adding associations or response-produced cues to stimuli. Thus, perceptual learning is viewed as a *discriminative* as distinct from an *associative* process.

One difficulty in deciding between these two hypotheses lies in the fact that the role of verbal labeling practice is not entirely explicit in differentiation theory and divergent interpretations about its role have emerged. For example, Vanderplas (1963) has suggested that although the Miller-Dollard view implies a dependence on the nature of the labeling response, differentiation theory implies no such dependence. In turn, the Gibsons' position appears to imply that the verbal label may facilitate subsequent perceptual performance under conditions in which the label is in some way "relevant" to the pretraining stimuli. Finally, some experiments (for example, Robinson, 1955) have been designed so that any facilitation of second-task performance caused by verbal labeling practice would be taken as evidence of an acquired distinctiveness of cues position. In any event, attempts to make alternative predictions, and tests of these predictions derived from these formulations, fail to the extent that processes associated with verbal labeling are left unspecified or remain unclear.

Postman (1955, 1963) has criticized differentiation theory on systematic grounds by noting that it is not sufficient to contend that an organism comes to respond to new aspects of the stimulus world as a result of practice. In other words, to say that perceptual learning consists of responding to various stimuli not previously responded to is inadequate, because this is the very fact which a theory of perceptual learning must explain. In a similar vein, to assert, as does Gibson (1963), that practice serves to reduce generalization among stimuli does not distinguish differentiation theory from a distinctiveness of cues formulation because the latter also holds that perceptual learning may be accounted for in terms of reduction of stimulus generalization. Both Miller and Dollard (1941) and Goss (1955) have characterized the transfer effects of labeling practice to subsequent instrumental performance as one which involves a steepening in gradients of stimulus generalization, although for reasons presumably different from those outlined by the Gibsons.

Difficulties in comparing these two theories have arisen on methodological as well as on conceptual grounds. Neither has found unequivocal support, and where support is present, it appears to be almost invariably confounded with the nature of the transfer task (Vanderplas, 1963). For instance, studies of transfer of predifferentiation (Cantor, 1955; Gagné and Baker, 1950; Goss, 1953; Goss and Greenfeld, 1958) have usually indicated that preliminary practice in learning a different verbal label for each of a set of stimuli facilitated performance in a subsequent task when that task required making *new differential responses* to the stimuli. In contrast to such transfer studies, experiments which have employed more direct

tests of perceptual performance, such as those of recognition or discrimination (Arnoult, 1953, 1956; Campbell and Freeman, 1955; Ellis *et al.*, 1962; Robinson, 1955), following analogous labeling practice, have usually yielded negative results in that no improvement in these tasks has occurred as a result of distinctive labeling practice *per se*. Typically, the facilitation in instrumental transfer tasks following labeling practice has been interpreted as evidence in support of the hypothesis of acquired distinctiveness of cues, whereas the negative findings with perceptual tasks have been interpreted as evidence against the distinctiveness of cues hypothesis, or, as evidence consistent with the differentiation position. As noted earlier, however, such interpretations remain equivocal to the extent that processes associated with labeling practice are ambiguous or unspecified. Partly as a result of such difficulties, current emphasis in predifferentiation has tended to shift away from the testing of *alternative* theories, and has moved in the direction of formulating and testing conceptions about component processes involved.

Instances of this trend may be seen in the recent attempts to account for the role of criterion-task variables in predifferentiation. For example, Ellis and Muller (1964) have attempted to determine if the divergence in effects of labeling practice on subsequent discriminative behavior was, in fact, *task-related*. Their findings indicated that practice in giving stimuli (six-point random shapes) distinctive verbal labels led to superior performance on an instrumental transfer task (differential switch-pressing) as compared with a control group that received instructions to observe and discriminate the stimuli. In contrast, just the reverse occurred with a perceptual criterion task; *S*s given identical labeling practice were slightly inferior in a subsequent multiple shape recognition test as compared with *S*s given identical instructions to observe and discriminate. Clearly, because instructions, stimuli, labels, and amount and type of pretraining were identical for both criterion groups, the differences in effects of pretraining are related to criterion-task variables. Similarly, Vanderplas, Sanderson, and Vanderplas (1964) reported findings which were in essential agreement with those of Ellis and Muller.

The more general significance of this divergence between studies using *perceptual* tasks and those using *discriminative learning* tasks is at least twofold: first, because the transfer effects are, in fact, correlated with the nature of the criterion task, then many of the apparent inconsistencies in studies of stimulus predifferentiation can be resolved in terms of task-related variables. In addition, such a finding further reinforces the need for a taxonomy of tasks in perceptual learning, a point which has received only limited attention (Hake, 1957; Vanderplas, 1963; Wohlwill, 1958). In this connection, Kanfer (1956) has made an important distinction, the significance of which appears to have been largely overlooked until recently (Postman, 1963). Kanfer proposed that the perceptual response can be conceived as one that involves two phases: an initial identifying response to the sensory input and subsequent performance of the instrumental response. Furthermore, Kanfer noted that the experimental study of perception has usually focused on one of these phases to the neglect of the other, and that the variables governing one phase may differ from those governing the other. Certainly this view is strengthened by the results of studies of criterion-task variables (Ellis and Muller; Vanderplas *et al.*, 1964). Finally, it seems clear that considerable attention will have to be given to the development of a taxonomy of response indicators of perception if lawful relationships between conditions of stimulus predifferentiation and transfer are to emerge.

In addition, difficulties with interpretations of positive transfer in instrumental tasks may exist. For example, Ellis and Muller (1964) have suggested that if practice does increase the "distinctiveness" of the stimuli, as inferred from an instrumental transfer task, then such an increase ought to be reflected in a perceptual task as well. In other words, the fact that the "distinctiveness" of the stimuli was not similarly enhanced, as measured by a recognition test, raises some doubt about a simple distinctiveness of cues interpretation of positive transfer to an instrumental task. Ellis and Muller (1964) therefore have questioned the appropriateness of interpretations of positive transfer effects resulting from *Relevant S* training (as compared with observation controls) as being caused by the increased distinctiveness of the stimuli alone. Even though the responses in the pretraining and transfer task are qualitatively different, they propose that enhanced positive transfer in an instrumental task could occur not *only* as a result of increased distinctiveness of the stimuli, but also as a result of increased skill in production of identifying responses, a factor which may be distinguished from general practice effects. In other words, learning how to make identifying responses (labeling) during pretraining may facilitate making identifying responses (differential switch-pressing) in the transfer task as well as enhance the distinctiveness of the stimuli. Such an argument does not deny the appropriateness of a distinctiveness of cues interpretation, but contends that at least one additional factor may be present.

A third approach to the interpretation of positive transfer stemming from stimulus predifferentiation has emphasized the role of observing responses or attention. For example, Hake and Ericksen (1955) have suggested that the role of verbal labels in the pretraining task is principally one of forcing S to attend to the various cues. Such a view implies that the label helps S to select certain features of the stimuli and that it is the general labeling process rather than specific features of the labels themselves which produces positive transfer. A similar view has been proposed by Kurtz (1955), who has suggested that the role of verbal labeling practice during pretraining may be primarily one of aiding S to make appropriate observing responses during pretraining. Essentially, the role of verbal labels was conceived as one of helping to establish the appropriate observing responses during pretraining which in turn transferred to the instrumental task.

Although experimental investigations of this interpretation have left the exact role of observing responses in doubt, there is clear evidence that observing responses do mediate transfer under some conditions. For instance, Spiker (1963) and his colleagues (Cantor, 1955; Norcross, 1958; Norcross and Spiker, 1957; Reese, 1958) have shown that both observing responses and verbal labels contribute to facilitation in instrumental transfer tasks.

Along somewhat different lines, although consistent with earlier formulations concerning observing responses, Ellis *et al.*, (1964) have suggested that the findings from several studies of acquired equivalence of cues (Ellis *et al.*, 1962; Ellis and Muller, 1964; Katz, 1963) might be interpreted in terms of a *correlated practice* hypothesis. Briefly, this hypothesis contends that reduction in perceptual performance following equivalence pretraining might be explained, not in terms of acquired equivalence of cues, but rather in terms of the control that the label may exert on S's observing responses during pretraining. Under certain conditions, such as congruence or "belongingness" between stimulus and label, the label may control, or restrict, the kind of observing responses that Ss make. Accordingly, Ss will learn about fewer aspects of the stimuli, and, hence, will perform poorer on a subsequent perceptual task designed to reflect the effects of equivalence labeling practice. The essential features of the correlated practice hypothesis is that reduction in perceptual performance following equivalence pretraining may not necessarily be due to the addition

of common response-produced cues, as predicted by the hypothesis of acquired equivalence, but may instead be the result of failure to learn about certain already existing features of the stimuli.

In an attempt to test the correlated practice hypothesis, Ellis, Feuge, Long, and Pegram (1964) gave Ss forced practice in manipulating random tactual shapes, as a first approximation at controlling the amount and type of observing responses that Ss might make to the shapes. Tactual rather than visual stimuli were employed because of the greater degree of control that could be exerted over S's observation of the former. It was argued that if a correlated practice hypothesis were reasonable, then the typical reduction in perceptual performance as found, say, in a recognition test following equivalence pretraining, would not obtain because Ss would have been forced to observe the stimuli to a degree equal with that of a control group who received simple instructions to observe the stimuli. This control was approximated by requiring Ss in both equivalence and observation groups to trace 6-point random shapes with only the index finger of the preferred hand. S was required to trace the perimeter of each shape in alternating clockwise and counterclockwise directions, and other movements were not permitted. In this fashion, the equivalence and observation pretraining groups were forced to make the same observing responses and did not differ in the total amount of time spent in tracing the shapes.

In spite of the fact that both equivalence and observation pretraining groups received comparable amounts and types of practice with the stimuli, the equivalence group still made fewer correct recognitions of the stimuli in a subsequent multiple shape recognition test than did the observation group. Thus, it appears that equivalence pretraining can mediate a reduction in perceptual performance although not necessarily through the medium of correlated practice, that is, through control of observing responses during pretraining. This interpretation, of course, does not deny the possible importance of relatively central processes such as "attention" and related implicit responses which may mediate perceptual performance. Rather, it indicates only that some factor(s) other than overt observing responses *can* mediate perceptual performance. Furthermore, the problem remains as to the specification of the conditions under which overt observing responses may still mediate perceptual performance.

In summary, no single theory is adequate for accounting for the empirical phenomenon of stimulus predifferentiation. Part of this difficulty lies in incomplete or unspecified conceptualizations of the events involved. For example, experiments designed to test theories of stimulus predifferentiation must be derived from conceptions which specify the processes associated with verbal labeling practice and observing responses. In addition, the role of various task variables, including that of the transfer task itself, must be specified. Conceivably, transfer of predifferentiation can involve a variety of processes such as mediation via verbal labels, differentiation of the stimuli, overt observing responses, as well as implicit attending responses. Their exact function will not be clearly known until formulations of these processes specify their systematic status. Current trends suggest that future research will be more concerned with specification of the role of these events and with the attempt to test the effects of component processes. Instances of these trends can be seen in recent studies that are concerned with the role of stimulus and associative factors (Clark, 1965; Ellis and Feuge, 1966; Ellis, Muller, and Tosti, 1966; Homan, 1966; Johnson, 1964; Pfafflin, 1960; Ranken, 1963; Segal, 1964), response variables (Dietze, 1955; Richard, 1965), conditions of reinforcement during pre-exposure to stimuli (Bennett, 1966; Kerpelman, 1965), and task-related variables (Ellis and Muller, 1964; Jeffrey and Bogartz, 1961; Vanderplas *et al.*, 1964).

Secondary Variables Influencing Transfer

In addition to specific factors such as stimulus similarity, response similarity, and stimulus predifferentiation, transfer of training depends upon additional specific variables. These variables may be regarded as secondary in their influence because their effects are strongly determined by the similarity relationships involved. Secondary variables of known importance include: (1) degree of original-task learning, (2) time interval elapsing between tasks, (3) variety of previous tasks, and (4) task difficulty.

Degree of Original Learning. Studies that have examined the effects of degree of original learning on transfer have yielded fairly systematic results. Mandler (1962) has summarized the bulk of the research on this variable and concludes that with small amounts of initial practice there is frequently a negative transfer effect, then a return to zero transfer with more practice, and finally, increasing positive transfer with even more practice. In general, the best empirical generalization is that of a U-shaped function relating variations in degree of original learning and amount of transfer. This generalization has been supported by investigations employing a wide range of tasks such as code learning (Siipola and Israel, 1933) verbal paired associates (Bruce, 1933; Mandler and Heinemann, 1956; Underwood, 1949b), and animal learning (Bruner, Mandler, O'Dowd and Wallach, 1958; Reid, 1953; Pubols, 1956).

Some studies (for example, Underwood, 1951), however, have shown that increased practice with the original task yields only increasing amounts of positive transfer without any initial interference. These studies suggest that it is not necessarily the degree of original learning which is critical, but rather the relative strengths of the two habit systems in competition. If competition with the second task is minimal, then it is reasonable to obtain only increasing amounts of facilitation with increasing amounts of original learning. In this case, general practice effects are likely to override any slight interference tendencies, should the latter exist. Similarly, it is reasonable to expect the greatest amount of interference when the two habit systems are approximately equal in strength (Melton and Irwin, 1940; Morgan and Underwood, 1950). On this basis it would be predicted that with limited practice on the first task, maximal interference would occur during the early stages of the transfer task; in turn, with extensive practice on the first task, maximal interference would occur at some later stage of the transfer task (Underwood, 1949a).

Postman (1962a) has recently examined the generalization that positive transfer increases with the degree of first-list learning. He noted that this generalization, as far as verbal transfer is concerned, holds true as long as the responses are highly similar (Underwood, 1951), with a control condition requiring only a single list to be learned (Bruce, 1933), and in studies using the A-B, A-C paradigm, in which the specific and nonspecific transfer effects remain unseparated (Atwater, 1953; Underwood, 1949b). Consequently, Postman argued that the effect of degree of first-list learning should be determined using several basic transfer paradigms, with a nonspecific transfer group being used as a control to evaluate the other transfer paradigms.

Accordingly, Postman's (1962a) Ss learned one of four different paired-associate lists in which both stimuli and responses were selected from Haagen's (1949) list. The list conformed to four different transfer paradigms: (1) new stimuli and new responses, that is, nonspecific transfer (A-B, C-D); (2) new stimuli and old responses (A-B, C-B); (3) old stimuli and new responses (A-B, A-C); (4) old stimuli and old responses repaired (A-B, A-Br). Ss learned a list of ten paired associates to three different degrees of first-list learning: (1) to a criterion of six out of

ten correct responses; (2) perfect mastery; and (3) perfect mastery plus 50 per cent overlearning. Following the various conditions of original learning, Ss learned the same transfer lists. When compared against the nonspecific transfer control (A-B, C-D) all paradigms yielded negative transfer, using mean number of correct responses over trials 1–10 on the second list as the criterion. The amount of negative transfer was greatest for the A-B, A-Br condition, intermediate for the A-B, A-C condition, and least for the A-B, C-B condition. With increased amount of practice on the original task, the A-B, A-Br group continued to yield increasing negative transfer, but with the other groups, negative transfer increased at first and then began to decrease. Although the curves did not show a return to positive transfer, the findings were suggestive of the usual U-shaped function. In a similar study Jung (1962) obtained results that were in close agreement with those of Postman. In contrast, Spiker and Holton (1958) reported that negative transfer continued to increase as a function of the amount of first-task performance; however, this finding is not inconsistent with that of Jung or Postman because variations in degree of first-task learning did not involve overlearning.

An important feature of Postman's study is that it provides a basis for analyzing differences among paradigms using associationistic concepts. He suggested that an analysis of these differences must take into account four major sources of transfer effects: (1) learning to learn and warm-up, (2) response learning, (3) associative interference, and (4) differentiation between lists. All paradigms presumably benefit equally from the general factors of learning to learn and warm up. In turn, response learning is beneficial in the paradigms in which the responses remain the same in the two lists (A-B, C-B and A-B, A-Br). However, the facilitation caused by response learning is outweighed by the effects of associative interference (competition) such that the net effect is that of negative transfer. Postman further notes that the conditions of associative interference differ for each of the paradigms. For example, backward associations in the A-B, C-B paradigm may lead to rejection of the correct association. In turn, the assumption that interference from forward associations is greater than that from backward associations will account for the greater negative transfer produced by the A-B, A-C paradigm as compared with the A-B, C-B paradigm. Finally, the summation of interference effects from both forward and backward associations should maximize negative transfer in the A-B, A-Br paradigm.

The principal theoretical controversy regarding the effects of degree of original learning on transfer has been between those who have employed *associationistic* concepts (for example, Jung, 1965; Postman, 1962a) and those who have insisted that the data require *cognitive* as well as associationistic interpretations (for example, Mandler, 1962). Although traditional interpretations of this relationship have employed concepts derived from association theory (Melton and Irwin, 1940; Postman, 1962a; Underwood, 1949b), Mandler (1962) has recently presented a case for interpreting the data in terms of cognitive structures which emerge or develop out of associative processes. He contends that during overlearning there are developed analogic structures of the overt responses. These structures develop during the course of response integration, during which discrete parts of a response sequence come to develop as a functional unit. Once a response sequence has been integrated and acts as a unit, it develops, according to Mandler, some form of structural representation which he identifies as a "central" analogue, or, analogic structure. This analogue of the response unit can function independently of the overt responses sequence and permits symbolic activity to occur without emission of overt responses. As Mandler puts it, "structures are

developed on the basis of associationistic stimulus-response relationships but, once established, enable the organism to behave cognitively (pp. 417–418)."

The principal issue in this controversy is the extent to which the data on overlearning and transfer do, in fact, require a cognitive interpretation beyond one involving associationistic conceptions. Indeed, Mandler himself is conservative in this respect and takes the position of first examining associative and related factors before resorting to more complex interpretations involving cognitive structure. Nevertheless, he concludes that analogic structures do develop as a result of overlearning experience, and that such structures permit S to manipulate, cognitively, various responses in a problem-solving situation making only few overt errors. As a result, massive overlearning permits S to perform quite well—for example, show few errors—on the transfer task.

In response to Mandler's position, Jung (1965) has proposed that the facts of overlearning and transfer do not require a cognitive interpretation, and that traditional associative conceptions such as response competition, response availability, and differentiation can account for the data. Jung voices several objections to the need for invoking the concept of analogic structure. First, he notes that the soundness of the findings on which Mandler based his argument can be questioned. He argues that in some instances, the studies cited by Mandler lacked appropriate controls for separating the effects of specific and non-specific transfer, and as a consequence it is difficult to assess their separate roles in interpreting second-task performance. In studies employing the A-B, A-Br paradigm (for example, Mandler and Heinemann, 1956; Merikle and Battig, 1963), positive transfer has been obtained with low meaning or difficult responses whereas negative transfer can be obtained with high meaning responses (Porter and Duncan, 1953; Twedt and Underwood, 1959). In this instance, Jung argues that transfer of response learning can account for the facilitation under conditions of low meaning responses. In addition, both Jung (1962) and Postman (1962a), using appropriate nonspecific controls, failed to obtain positive transfer after extensive overlearning, suggesting that response competition between the two lists is still operative with high degree of overlearning.

Jung (1965) shows, in addition, that analysis of the "fate" of first-list associations during second-list learning (Barnes and Underwood, 1959), in the A-B, A-C paradigm, provides evidence for an associationistic interpretation of the effects of first-list overlearning on transfer. Initially, overlearning leads to greater negative transfer by increasing the availability of competing first-list associations during second-list learning; in short, a strong initial tendency for B responses to intrude in the second list occurs. In turn, with additional overlearning, list differentiation develops which eventually checks and outweighs negative transfer caused by response competition. Finally, the fact that conditions of high response meaning lead to greater negative transfer in this paradigm (Jung, 1963) may be accounted for by assuming that such responses are more available. In summary, Jung's (1965) analysis is a substantial one and provides strong support for an associationistic interpretation of the overlearning-transfer relationship in *rote* verbal learning. Moreover, efforts to test specific implications of Mandler's position by Spence (1963) and by Spence and Schulz (1965) have failed to support a cognitive interpretation. Nevertheless, their findings do not rule out the potential usefulness of cognitive interpretations in other learning situations which involve concept formation or discrimination reversal tasks.

Time Interval Between Tasks. What happens if the time interval between the original and transfer task varies over several days or weeks? Does transfer to a subsequent task decline with the passage of time, as does retention, or do the findings of transfer studies differ from those of retention? In a series of studies, Bunch and his students (Bunch, 1936; Bunch and McCraven, 1938; Bunch and Lang, 1939) demonstrated that transfer remained fairly *constant* with varying intervals of time elapsing between the two tasks. Indeed, within the time limits employed, transfer was quite stable and appeared to be remarkably independent of memory of the original task. This finding is somewhat paradoxical if one takes the view that amount of transfer from one task to another is, in a certain sense, one possible measure of retention of the original task. On the surface, it would not appear unreasonable to assume that if a task is gradually forgotten in the course of time, its transfer to a subsequent task would also show an analogous decline. As indicated, the results fail to reveal any similar decrement.

One study will illustrate the typical finding of transfer-time stability. Employing a nonspecific (A-B, C-D) transfer paradigm, Bunch and McCraven (1938) required Ss to learn an initial list of paired-associate nonsense syllables to complete mastery and then to learn a second list after intervals of zero, two, fourteen, or twenty-eight days. The results showed that Ss required approximately the same number of trials to learn the transfer list, regardless of the time interval separating the lists. In contrast, a test of retention showed a fairly systematic decline with the passage of time. Similar studies have revealed this transfer stability for several learning situations including problem solving (Bunch, 1936), maze learning (Bunch and Lang, 1939), and problem solving with school children (Gladis, 1960).

Bunch (1939) has noted one exception to this generalization about the stability of the transfer-time function. Under conditions designed to yield negative transfer, that is, one in which the cues were reversed in a T-maze learning task, transfer was found to vary systematically with the passage of time. Negative transfer effects were greatest at first, but the effect gradually shifted to that of positive transfer with longer intervals of time. Presumably, the facilitation caused by learning to learn gradually outweighed the initial interference effects associated with cue reversal, the latter effects weakening in time.

More recent studies by Ellis and his students have sought to determine the conditions under which transfer remains invariant with time. Employing an A-B, C-B paradigm, Ellis and Burnstein (1960) demonstrated that the temporal course of transfer declined with the passage of time. Subsequent studies demonstrated that this decrease did not occur, or was at best very slight, if the response items were highly meaningful (Ellis and Hunter, 1960), or if they were highly familiarized nonsense-syllable responses (Ellis and Hunter, 1961a). Finally, Ellis and Hunter (1961b) demonstrated that under conditions of non-specific transfer (A-B, C-D paradigm), transfer remained invariant with the passage of time whereas retention of the same items showed the customary loss.

These findings can be interpreted by noting that performance on the transfer task depends, in part, on the retention of the responses in the original list with the A-B, C-B paradigm. Under this circumstance, a decrease in performance over time would be expected. With highly meaningful or familiarized responses, little decrease would be expected since response availability is high. In general, the findings of Bunch and Ellis, taken together, reveal that transfer is most stable to the extent that performance on the transfer task does not depend upon retention of specific items in the task, which is the case with the non-specific paradigm. Furthermore, these findings are consistent with the extension of the two-stage theory of paired-associates learning (Underwood, Runquist, and Schulz, 1959; Underwood and Schulz, 1960) proposed by Ellis and

Burnstein (1960). Their analysis of the A-B, C-B paradigm suggested that the constancy of the transfer-time function was dependent upon the associative stage of learning. Where the response-learning stage is important, as with responses low in meaningfulness, transfer declines in the course of time.

Variety of Previous Tasks. Evidence from studies of the role of task (or stimulus) variation suggests that transfer is facilitated as a result of variation in the original task. The classic studies of both Crafts (1927) and Dashiell (1924) obtained results which indicated that, within limits, the greater the degree of variation the greater the degree of transfer. Similarly, studies by Harlow (1949) have demonstrated the importance of stimulus variation in the acquisition of learning sets. Unfortunately, Harlow's studies were such that the effects of stimulus variation were confounded with those of amount of practice; consequently, the separate effects of either variable could not be properly assessed.

A more recent study by Duncan (1958) was able to isolate the effects of sheer amount of practice from those of variety of practice, and showed that task variation is an important factor in producing positive transfer. Furthermore, Duncan's results showed that varied training on the original task produced more transfer than an equal amount of constant training. Similar findings were also reported by Morrisett and Hovland (1959), who showed that task variation produced analogous transfer effects with a problem solving task, despite the fact that variation impeded the rate of original-task learning.

The attempts to account for the superiority of varied training on transfer (for example, Duncan, 1958; Eckstrand and Wickens, 1954; Kurtz, 1955) have involved interpretations that are all quite similar. In general, the most common view is that varied training forces S to pay close attention to all stimuli on each trial, the effect of which is to teach S how to learn to look for, or attend to, stimuli. Presumably, S learns how to learn to attend, which transfers to the second task (Duncan, 1958). Similarly, Eckstrand and Wickens (1954) suggest that Ss develop a "perceptual set" whereas Kurtz (1955) suggests that S acquires "observing responses" with varied training. It is assumed that such attentional habits transfer to the second task and facilitate its acquisition, in part through minimization of both intralist and interlist interference. Finally, it should be noted that positive transfer in concept formation and problem-solving tasks caused by stimulus variation can, in part, be interpreted in terms of greater stimulus control developed during original learning.

Not all studies, however, have reported greater positive transfer as a result of varied first-task learning. For example, Adams (1954) observed that single-problem training resulted in more transfer than did a multiple-problem procedure. An analysis of his results showed that the multiple-problem group achieved a lower degree of learning within any one training problem than did the single-problem group. Indeed, this is not surprising in view of the fact that Ss received only two trials per problem. Subsequent studies by Morrisett and Hovland (1959) and by Paul and Noble (1964) revealed that the superiority of varied practice depends upon Ss receiving some optimal amount of practice on each of the problems. A high degree of learning within a single problem establishes strong stimulus-response associations whereas learning a variety of tasks presumably allows S to discriminate between relevant and irrelevant cues. In the latter case, greater stimulus control is established because of better opportunities for discrimination to occur.

Task Difficulty. Does training on an easy or a more difficult task result in greater transfer? Unfortunately, it is somewhat difficult to generalize about the role of task difficulty, in part because of conflicting results, and in part because many different kinds of tasks have been used to vary this dimension (Day, 1956). Because comparable levels of difficulty with varying tasks are sometimes difficult to assess, generalizations about the effect of gross task difficulty on transfer have been slow to emerge.

Despite this difficulty, studies of discrimination learning have yielded fairly consistent findings and indicate that training on an easy discrimination can facilitate the learning of a difficult discrimination when the stimuli are along the same dimension (for example, Lawrence, 1952; Logan, 1966; Pavlov, 1927). For example, Lawrence trained two groups of rats to discriminate between two brightness levels. One group was given training with an easy discrimination, in which the two brightnesses were quite different, and the other group received difficult discrimination training in which the two brightnesses were quite similar. Following training, all rats were tested on the difficult discrimination. The results indicated that rats trained on the easy discrimination performed better on the transfer task than did those trained originally on the difficult discrimination.

Conventionally, the interpretation of these findings assumes that training on the easier discrimination allows S to discover more readily the relevant stimulus dimension, in turn permitting him to transfer to the more difficult discrimination with greater ease. Such a view contends that discrimination learning involves two processes, the first involving the learning of appropriate observing responses to the stimuli, and the second involving development of differential response tendencies. In contrast to this two-process view, Logan (1966) has suggested that the finding of greater transfer from an easy discrimination is one that can be derived from an excitation-inhibition model (Spence, 1936) without involvement of additional perceptual principles such as learning to attend to the stimuli. By making certain arbitrary assumptions about the shape of the gradients of excitation and inhibition, he was able to show a greater discrimination index, that is, a greater difference in response tendency to the similar stimuli of the transfer task, following an easy as compared with a difficult discrimination. In addition, Logan was able to demonstrate that all easy discriminations were not equally effective in producing positive transfer. The more general importance of this work is that it represents a first step in providing a conceptual basis for dealing with the transfer-difficulty problem.

In contrast with discrimination learning, studies of pursuit-rotor and related tracking tasks have failed to show consistent findings. On the one hand, some studies (for example, Lordahl and Archer, 1958; Namikas and Archer, 1960) have shown that the more similar the original task was to the transfer task, defined in terms of tracking speed, the greater the degree of transfer. Apparently the effects of overall task similarity were so great as to override other possible effects. In general, these two studies showed that training on a pursuit-rotor task at one speed transferred best to that speed, a finding quite consistent with our knowledge about task similarity, and also consistent with micromolar approaches to learning (Logan, 1956) which imply that speed is part of what is learned in a given task. In contrast to the preceding findings, Goldstein and Newton (1962), using a complex tracking task, have indicated that training on a difficult task leads to greater transfer. In this instance, difficulty was manipulated by varying the amount of lag in the control system. Finally, other studies (Barch and Lewis, 1954; Briggs and Waters, 1958) have yielded inconclusive results.

It has been suggested (Ellis, 1965) that systematic generalizations about the role of task difficulty in transfer will not be possible until greater attention is given to the concept of difficulty. For instance, in the examples cited previously, difficulty has been described in three quite different ways:

(1) amount of difference between two stimuli, (2) response speed, and (3) feedback delay, the variation in time between Ss response to a system and subsequent system response. It is clear, then, that difficulty may involve several dimensions of a task including stimulus, response, and delay properties as well as others. It is doubtful that lawful relationships concerning difficulty and transfer will emerge until the concept is dealt with in a much more analytic fashion. Indeed, Holding (1962) has taken the position that difficulty *per se* is not an especially useful concept in predicting transfer, and that this concept must give way to a far more molecular analysis of the component aspects involved.

Component Analysis of Transfer Effects. It was briefly noted in the first chapter of this section that the current scene in transfer is characterized by a *component analysis* of the gross phenomenon of transfer into the various subprocesses which, in turn, contribute to the overall transfer. There is nothing particularly new about component analysis itself. Indeed, it is characteristic of one of several approaches which is ultimately seen in any experimental discipline as it reaches a certain stage in its development (Underwood, 1966). Component analysis seeks to isolate and study the subprocesses contributing to some gross phenomenon, such as transfer or retention, and to determine the manner in which these subprocesses interact, or are compounded, to produce some gross effect. Once the subprocesses or mechanisms are isolated, interest is then directed at determining the laws governing the relationships among the various subprocesses. In addition, interest is directed at examining the comparability of these subprocesses in various learning situations.

Component analysis represents a more sophisticated attack on the problems of transfer and retention as compared with the approach of early functionalism which concentrated on the study of gross phenomena in human learning, transfer, and retention. In addition, component analysis increases the likelihood of contact with other areas of learning at a level that can conceivably permit the detection of continuities and analogous processes. For example, the analysis of the *unlearning* mechanism in retention, as described in the last chapter of this section, marks the beginning of an effort to isolate communalities in verbal learning and conditioning phenomena. Indeed, if continuities and communalities among various learning situations are to be found, component analysis appears to be one of several efforts necessary.

Instances of component analysis were seen in several areas of transfer research described in this chapter. The most detailed example was an analysis of the transfer effects obtained with the stimulus predifferentiation paradigm. A number of conceptual mechanisms were examined which presumably contribute to the overall positive transfer effect; these mechanisms included enrichment, differentiation, observing responses, and more central attentional or perceptual mechanisms, all of which concern the subprocess of *stimulus learning* and the manner in which effects associated with this subprocess are to be interpreted. Similarly, an analysis of the effects of degree of original learning on transfer also served to portray the various subprocesses that combine to produce the gross effect: learning to learn and warm up, response learning, associative interference, and differentiation between lists. Other examples of component analysis of transfer effects can be seen in Underwood's (1964b) analysis of the A-B, C-B paradigm, Battig's

(1966a) analysis of intertask transfer, and Martin's (1965) analysis of major transfer paradigms. Martin proposes three transfer surfaces using Osgood's (1949) coordinate system to account for the effects of response availability, forward associations, and backward associations on transfer in verbal paired associates.

Analysis of the major transfer paradigms suggests that at least nine subprocesses are operating to produce a gross transfer effect. Not all of these subprocesses operate in each paradigm, but they do appear necessary in accounting for effects seen in all the major paradigms: A-B, A-C; A-B, C-B; A-B, C-D; A-B, A-Br; and A-B, A-B'. These processes include: (1) transfer of response learning, (2) transfer of stimulus learning, (3) forward associations, (4) backward associations, (5) warm-up, (6) learning to learn, (7) differentiation of stimuli from responses, (8) stimulus selection, and (9) mediation. Others may subsequently be added to the list.

Although these nine subprocesses have been identified as contributors to gross transfer effects, the manner in which they interact or go together is not yet fully conceptualized. Efforts in this direction are seen in the work of Battig (1966a) and his students, in Martin's (1965) analysis, and in the work of Ellis and his students (for example, Ellis and Muller, 1964) in the analysis of the predifferentiation paradigm. Similar analyses will be described in the remaining chapters on retention. Component analysis represents a rigorous attack on the problems of human learning, retention, and transfer; the next major step is analyzing their interaction effects.

CHAPTER 19

Retention: Nature, Measurement, and Fundamental Processes

The Nature of Retention

The study of retention involves an examination of the conditions under which learned behaviors are retained (or lost), and an analysis as well as development of conceptual formulations designed to account for these events. A comparison of retention and transfer reveals that the study of retention concerns those variables that govern the persistence of learned behaviors, whereas the study of transfer concerns those conditions of learning that influence or modify the acquisition of *new* behaviors. As such, a test for retention does not require any new learning beyond that point at which first-task learning is terminated, whereas a transfer test typically requires S to learn an additional task following first-task learning. It is true, of course, that where retention is measured by relearning procedures the test does involve additional learning; however, it is confined to an already learned event.

This distinction between retention and transfer is illustrated if the events following learning of an A-B list of paired-associates are compared. In retention, interest is in the conditions or factors that govern the subsequent strength of the A-B associations, whereas transfer deals with

the manner in which such associations influence the learning of a new list of paired associates. In addition, although it is true that retention and transfer may be distinguished by differing sets of operations, it is also true that measures of transfer can reflect the extent to which learned events are retained, thus attesting to some form of continuity between the two processes.

Although this distinction between retention and transfer roughly delimits their relative spheres of influence, it is a distinction not always adhered to in practice. As indicated, transfer measures have sometimes been used to infer the degree to which learned events have been retained. The appropriateness of such a procedure depends upon the extent to which transfer measures do, in fact, validly reflect processes involved in retention. To assume such a relationship may be reasonable under certain conditions, perhaps where a high correlation exists between measures of retention and transfer; however, these measures can yield divergent results and thus limit the usefulness of this procedure. For example, nonspecific transfer employing an A-B, C-D paradigm is known to be remarkably invariant as a function of time elapsing between the first task (A-B) and the second task (C-D), despite the fact that the retention of A-B associations decreases in the course of time (for example, Bunch and McCraven, 1938; Ellis and Hunter, 1961a.) Accordingly, a transfer measure designed to reflect the strength of A-B associations could lead to inappropriate inferences about retention in view of the temporal constancy of nonspecific transfer.

In a similar vein, a distinction between retention and learning may be drawn despite the fact that they also may be regarded as continuous processes. This continuity is seen in the fact that any trial during the course of learning some task may be regarded not only as a measure of the strength of learning at that point, but also may be regarded as a measure of what has been learned on previous trials, that is, as a measure of retention. As Underwood (1964b) has noted, however, this distinction as such fails to reveal the essential difference in the two processes because it ignores an important class of variables, namely, those variables which operate during the retention interval. Typically, the study of retention allows hours or days to elapse before a test trial is given, whereas the study of learning may allow only a few seconds or minutes between trials. As a result of this difference, it is conventionally agreed (for example, Melton, 1963) that the study of learning focuses on events that occur during the presentation of a trial or series of trials, whereas the study of retention focuses on events that occur during the interval between termination of learning and the test of retention, that is, the retention interval. Thus, the critical feature that distinguishes the study of retention from that of learning is that retention is concerned with the effective variables that operate not only during learning, but also during the retention interval. In other words, retention is concerned with the class of variables that determines the subsequent strength of a learned event, once that event has been learned to some arbitrary degree of strength. Usually, with the

exception of short-term memory, these variables are assumed to operate over a relatively long period of time.

A distinction is sometimes made between retention and forgetting (for example, Bugelski, 1956; Deese, 1958); however, it is one that is not critical from either a methodological or theoretical viewpoint. Retention is used to denote the extent to which originally learned behaviors are still available in S's repertoire, whereas forgetting refers to the *loss* of such behaviors. Thus, retention and forgetting refer to two sides of a coin, one to what is retained and the other to what is lost. Because one process is defined in terms of the other, both represent a common process, or group of subprocesses, and are governed by the same conditions. Differences in use of the terms are largely a matter of convenience or preference.

There are two principal objectives in the study of retention. One is to specify the conditions or variables that govern retention and the other is to develop conceptual formulations that will adequately account for the facts and phenomena of retention. These two objectives are interrelated and are not to be regarded as mutually exclusive. Indeed, a large number of studies have been designed to illuminate the nature of component processes in retention and to reveal the adequacy of existing theories of retention, as well as to suggest the necessity of new or modified interpretations of retention.

The concept of retention is a relational one in that, in terms of its most general usage, it is treated as an intervening variable. In this fashion the concept of retention entails the same logical considerations as do other systematic concepts of psychology such as motivation and learning. Retention is not something we directly observe; rather, retention is inferred from certain changes in S's performance, such as, for example, the ability to recall a list of paired-associate items, following specified conditions of practice with the items. More generally, retention is defined in terms of the relationship between two classes of events: specified antecedent conditions and observable behaviors. This definition may be schematized as in Fig. 19-1, in which retention is defined in terms of the relationship between specified antecedent conditions (independent variables) and observable behavior (dependent variables); as indicated, retention occupies an intermediate position characteristic of an intervening variable. Frequently, the antecedent conditions consist of various classes of practice conditions and activities interpolated between original learning and the test of retention. In turn, the observed behaviors consist of one or more measures of performance which presumably reflect the degree to which the originally learned event is retained.

As such, this definition fails to provide any distinction between subprocesses or further-refined components of retention such as immediate or long-term memory (for example, Waugh and Norman, 1965). Any effort to distinguish these and similar processes in accordance with the viewpoint just described would require additional elaboration of the events in Fig. 19-1. If real distinctions among component processes in retention do, in fact, exist, then such distinctions are to be reflected in systematic differences in observed behavior or in differences in the relationship between behavior and antecedent conditions. The essential point is that distinctions between component processes in retention are to be determined on operational grounds. The issue as to whether two distinct processes in retention exist will be discussed in a subsequent section.

Historical Overview

Here we examine issues in the history of retention, sketching only a few of the more important events from Ebbinghaus to the present. No attempt is made to present anything like an exhaustive overview; the principal objective is to illuminate some of the approaches and divergent viewpoints toward the study of retention. This section provides an overview of the following: (1) the classic work of Ebbinghaus, (2) the Gestalt reaction to Ebbinghaus's approach, (3) the study of qualitative changes in retention, including studies of perceptual memory, (4) the development of interference theory, (5) growing interest in the role of dynamic factors in retention, and (6) the current scene in retention, which is characterized by a component-analysis effort.

Ebbinghaus. Studies of the "higher mental processes" were first systematically conducted by Ebbinghaus (1885) who was concerned with the nature and course of retention. Prior to this time it was generally felt that such processes did not lend themselves readily to either experimental investigation or quantitative treatment, and hence such topics were regarded as inappropriate for scientific endeavor. Ebbinghaus was able to demonstrate, however, that not only was it possible to measure the temporal course of retention but that it was possible to study more detailed phenomena of retention such as the development of remote associations. Moreover, Ebbinghaus made significant contributions to the development of the methodology of human learning and retention. Indeed, the long-standing importance of Ebbinghaus's work is reflected in the continued influence of his methodological contributions as seen in current efforts in verbal learning and retention.

Ebbinghaus was strongly influenced by the philosophical school of British associationism, and hence was concerned with the way in which "ideas" become associated. In order to study this associative process in a way that he regarded as largely free of past experiences of the learner, he developed the nonsense syllable, a verbal unit typically

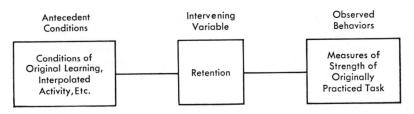

Figure 19-1. The conceptual status of retention treated as an intervening variable.

consisting of a consonant-vowel-consonant combination. Using himself as the *S*, Ebbinghaus would first learn a list of nonsense syllables, and then after varying intervals of time, he would relearn the list. In this fashion he was able to plot a curve showing ease of relearning as a function of time elapsed since original learning. The classic retention curve obtained by this method indicated that loss in retention over time showed a rather sharp negatively accelerated curve with loss greatest during the first hour and a gradual leveling out between two and six days after original learning.

Although this curve has sometimes been described as the curve of retention, it is appropriately seen as only one of several possible curves of retention. More generally, retention curves will vary with the nature of the material as well as with the method of measuring retention. Moreover, it is clear that even nonsense syllables are not free from the influence of past learning because they are known to have associative properties (for example, Glaze, 1928), thus indicating that Ebbinghaus was not, indeed, studying the development of associations purely "from scratch." Despite these considerations, it is recognized that Ebbinghaus's contributions to the study of retention stand as of prime importance.

The Gestalt Reaction. Although studying quantitative features of retention using discrete, unfamiliar material, as initiated by Ebbinghaus, is still characteristic of much of human learning research, it was not long before this approach was criticized. Gestalt

psychologists (for example, Katona, 1940) have long objected to associationistic interpretations of learning and retention and have questioned the appropriateness of using isolated verbal units, such as nonsense syllables, in studying retention. Similarly, Bartlett (1932) has argued that nonsense syllables are artificial units and not characteristic of events learned and retained in everyday life. Although it is true that such materials are not typical of those learned in everyday life, this does not invalidate their use for the experimental study of retention. Indeed one may argue that the learning of such materials bears at least some similarity to the learning of arbitrary codes and foreign language vocabulary. Furthermore, if the retention of organized materials such as poetry or prose is governed by principles quite different from those governing the retention of isolated verbal units, then this is an issue to be resolved by empirical investigation rather than by speculative debate.

The Qualitative Emphasis. A newly developing interest in *qualitative*, as distinct from quantitative, changes in retention was also part of the protest against Ebbinghaus's approach. This emphasis is reflected in the work of Bartlett (1932) who investigated changes in retention of meaningful material using the method of successive reproduction. Bartlett required his *S*s to read passages of prose material, usually brief stories, and then required reproduction of the story in successive sessions. In general, his findings indicated that familiar details tended to become elaborated and refined, with unfamiliar details dropping out or becoming simplified, along with the stereotyping of certain details. A principal feature of Bartlett's work was his emphasis on interpreting these qualitative changes in retention in terms of personal, social, and emotional characteristics of the individual learner. At this point it should be noted that this approach is not necessarily inconsistent with one that studies isolated verbal units, but rather is one that is presumably more complex in that the interpretation of such changes requires more variables to account for the facts.

An additional development that also stemmed from Gestalt conceptions of memory and perception is that of perceptual memory, that is, memory for visual forms. Gestalt theorists (for example, Koffka, 1935) have taken the position that "memory traces" of perceptual events, as inferred from changes in reproductive memory, become modified as the result of autonomous activity of the central nervous system. In brief, they postulate that certain events which are intrinsic to the central nervous system modify or change the "memory trace" so that perceived forms tend to become "better" organized and simplified. These events or forces are hypothetical in that they are never directly measured but they are presumed to be related to certain kinds of physiological processes in the cortex.

The usual procedure in tests of this theory has been to show *S*s various kinds of geometric figures and then require them to reproduce the figures on repeated occasions. Typically, the results of such studies (for example, Perkins, 1932; Wulf, 1922) show that the reproduced figures become progressively modified in such ways as to suggest increased regularity and symmetry. In turn, these changes toward a simpler or "better" figure have been interpreted by Gestalt theorists as evidence for the action of autonomous brain forces acting on the "memory trace." As we shall see subsequently, such experiments have generally been regarded as inadequate on conceptual grounds, in that simpler alternative explanations of these changes are possible, and on methodological grounds in that measures of successive reproduction yield data that are sometimes difficult to evaluate.

Despite these difficulties, interest in Gestalt conceptions of memory along with alternative accounts stimulated a long series of investigations of perceptual memory, an excellent review of which is given by Riley (1962). A major characteristic of these investigations was the gradual increase in methodological sophistication, an example of which is seen in the shift from using measures of successive reproduction to measures of recognition in which stimulus properties of the visual forms can be more precisely defined (Hebb and Foord, 1945). A second feature of studies in perceptual memory has been the increasing effort to account for changes in perceptual memory in terms of alternative interpretations which involve association theory as distinct from Gestalt formulations (Postman, 1954).

Interference. Although reactions to Ebbinghaus's approach stimulated new methods and conceptions in the study of retention, the influence of Ebbinghaus has remained remarkably strong and still reflects itself in several problem areas of retention. The stamp of the Ebbinghaus tradition is especially evident in interference conceptions of forgetting which, in brief, contend that forgetting is the result of interference from both new learning and from prior learning. In a classic paper, McGeoch (1932b) argued that forgetting was due principally to the events that intervened between learning and the test of retention, as distinct from the mere passage of time during the retention interval, a position that led to a long series of studies on interference phenomena in retention. Initially, these studies (for example, Melton and Irwin, 1940) were designed to determine the principal variables that produce interference and largely dealt with the paradigm for retroactive inhibition, a paradigm that measures the effect of some interpolated task on retention of a previously learned task. Subsequently, investigators (Barnes and Underwood, 1959; McGovern, 1964; Postman, Keppel, and Stark, 1965; Underwood, 1957; Underwood and Postman, 1960) increasingly directed their attention toward the component processes or mechanisms that produce interference such as response competition, unlearning, mediation, and stimulus and response generalization, and extraexperimental sources of interference such as letter-sequence and unit-sequence effects. An excellent summary of interference theory has been provided by Postman (1961a) and will be examined in some detail in the next chapter. For the present it is sufficient to note that the dominant position of interference theory attests to the robustness of associationistic conceptions of retention.

Dynamic Factors. Another recent trend has been the increasing interest in the role of dynamic factors, that is, motivational and emotional factors, as determinants of memory. Part of this interest stemmed from those who wished to test deductions from Freudian conceptions of memory, such as repression, which argue that unpleasant events tend to be easily forgotten because they represent a threat to the "integrity" of the individual (Rosenzweig, 1943). In addition, social psychologists have emphasized the way in which various social factors, such as political attitudes (Levine and Murphy, 1943), tend to selectively modify our retention of events. Similarly, consideration of the role of "purpose" (Russell, 1963) reflects another instance of interest in variables of this class. Although the role of such variables in influencing retention has been amply demonstrated, a principal issue that still remains is the interpretation of such complex events. Psychologists whose viewpoint is influenced by stimulus-response conceptions of be-

havior have, in many instances, attempted to interpret these memory changes in terms of "primary" principles of behavior such as, for example, those of stimulus and response generalization, whereas other psychologists have insisted that interpretations of memory will necessarily involve principles more complex than those derived from simple learning (Ausubel, 1963; Miller, 1962).

The Contemporary Scene. Today retention, like transfer, is characterized by an intensive effort to analyze the gross process of retention into its component processes or mechanisms. By the gross process of retention is meant the net outcome, as measured by some test of retention, which is the overall result of several component processes that act jointly to influence the outcome. In short, the current attack on retention can be regarded as one that is increasingly molecular with emphasis on sharp analytic separation of component processes. An important aspect of this trend is the strong conviction that the complex phenomena of retention will not be properly understood until the component processes can be analytically separated; once these processes are separated then it is felt that their independent and interactive contributions to retention can be more effectively evaluated. Thus much of the present work in retention is directed toward discovering the laws governing activity of component processes. An instance of this trend is seen in current work designed to refine interference theory which has as its goal the statement of the manner in which various processes, or subprocesses, of retention interact so as to account for forgetting (Postman, 1961b; Underwood and Postman, 1960). Another instance of this trend in component analysis is seen in the effort designed to analyze processes associated with long-term and short-term retention (Melton, 1963; Peterson, 1963; Postman, 1964; Waugh and Norman, 1965).

The Measurement of Retention

There are several measures of retention which can, under particular circumstances, reveal somewhat different aspects of the process. Indeed, the amount of retention obtained can readily vary as a function of the method of measurement as shown by the classic study of Luh (1922). Measures of retention may differ in several ways including their degree of sensitivity and their relative vulnerability to extraexperimental influences. An examination of several measures of retention will reveal some of these differences.

Recall. A straightforward method of measuring retention is that of recall. With this procedure S is required to demonstrate what he has learned by producing the correct response(s). In paired-associates learning using the anticipation procedure, S is presented with a series of stimuli one at a time and required to produce the correct response. In this case, recall is measured by the number of correct responses produced. Variations of this procedure may also be used in which S is required to recall the responses in the presence of the entire list of stimuli.

Recall may also be measured under conditions of free learning (Underwood and Keppel, 1963). In free learning S is presented with a series of items or units that he must learn as units, the order being unimportant. In addition, S knows that after presentation he will be required to recall the items in any order in which the units are available. Variations of the free-learning procedure are also employed including paced and unpaced recall (Ekstrand and Underwood, 1963). Unpaced recall allows S to produce as many responses as possible within some fixed time period, whereas paced recall gives S a limited interval to produce or anticipate a response.

Another variant of recall is that developed by Peterson and Peterson (1959) for studying short-term memory (STM). Using this procedure, they presented S with a single item for a brief study period of about 0.5 sec. and then tested for recall only once at intervals ranging from 3 to 18 sec. Even within this short interval, recall declined quite rapidly and systematically; subsequent studies (for example, Murdock, 1961) have verified this finding. A principal interest in this procedure has been to determine if STM will require fundamentally different explanatory principles than those of long-term memory (LTM), an issue that will be discussed later.

An important variant of the recall method, that of modified free recall (MFR), was first introduced by Underwood (1948) and later by Briggs (1954). MFR provides a way of assessing the relative strengths of first- and second-list associations following paired-associates learning in the A-B, A-C paradigm, or with any paradigm that contains common stimulus items. With this procedure S is presented the stimulus item (A) that is common to both lists and is required to recall either first-list (B) or second-list (C) responses. A slight modification of the procedure, designated as MMFR, in which S recalls responses from *both* lists was subsequently developed by Barnes and Underwood (1959) to investigate "what happens" to first-list associations following second-list learning. Their principal objective was to evaluate alternative accounts of transfer and retroactive inhibition in verbal learning, accounts that required the measurement of response strength of both lists for adequate assessment. Although this issue will be discussed at greater length in a later section, it is important to note that the MMFR procedure, along with additional refinements, has received extensive use in recent studies of retention and transfer (Dallett and D'Andrea, 1965; Ellington and Kausler, 1965; Postman, 1962b, 1968; and Postman, Keppel, and Stark, 1965).

The recall method may also be used in investigations of the retention of visual forms and patterns. In this instance, S is shown some form or pattern and is later asked to reproduce it as faithfully as possible. An example of this method is seen in the study by Perkins (1932) in which Ss were first shown various geometric designs and then asked to reproduce the designs on successive trials. This variation of the recall method, called *reproduction*, has received considerable use in studies of perceptual learning and memory for form, extensive discussions of which are given by Hake (1957) and by Riley (1962). The principal difficulty with this variant of the method is that changes in memory, as inferred from distortions in reproduced designs, depend upon judgments of the E which may be difficult to make and which may depend upon the "viewpoint" of the E, that is, his criteria for judgment.

The more general limitation of the recall method is that it can be relatively insensitive as compared with other measures of retention. The fact that S is unable to recall any items, say in a paired-associates list, does not necessarily imply that there is no effect from previous learning. Rather, it may simply mean that the recall method is too "demanding" (or insensitive) to reveal any effects, and that a more sensitive measure may yield evidence for some retention.

Savings. The savings method can be a more sensitive measure than recall because it may show evidence for some retention under conditions where none is obtained by recall. With this method S first learns some task to a given criterion and subsequently relearns the task. This procedure permits a comparison of the two performances in terms of a savings score, based upon such measures as time or trials to learn and then to relearn the task. A comparison of learning and relearning, using trials to learn as a criterion, yields a measure of savings as shown by the formula

Per cent saved =

$$\frac{\text{No. trials to learn} - \text{No. trials to relearn}}{\text{No. trials to learn}}$$
$$\times 100$$

For example, if it requires S thirty trials to learn a list of nonsense syllables and requires S only fifteen trials to relearn the list, a saving of 50 per cent is obtained. Even if it required S twenty-nine trials to relearn the list, some evidence for retention would be shown, thus attesting to the sensitivity of the method.

Despite the advantage of sensitivity, the savings method may be subject to extra-experimental influences during the interval prior to relearning especially if the interval is long. In addition, Bunch (1941) has noted that performance during relearning may be a function in part of S's enhanced proficiency in learning to learn and thus may yield an apparently high retention measure.

Recognition. Another method that is used in measuring retention is recognition, which requires S to select items that he has previously learned or experienced. Usually recognition requires that S select an item from an array of similar items, or items imbedded in some context; however, single-item presentation may be used in which S responds yes or no to each test item. The recognition method can, under certain circumstances, possess greater sensitivity than does the recall method because it depends upon context effects, that is, upon the material in which it is imbedded (Korn and Jahnke, 1962); nevertheless, Bahrick (1965) has argued that recognition is not *intrinsically* more sensitive than recall, but depends upon the alternatives presented in the recognition test. Furthermore, he noted that the sensitivity of a particular retention measure depends upon the momentary threshold of the measure in relation to the distribution of associative strength at the time of the test. Accordingly, recall and recognition measures might yield similar values at one time and quite different values at another. In this connection, McNulty (1965) has presented evidence which suggests that the usual superiority of recognition over recall is due, in part, to *S*'s opportunities to ultilize cues from partial learning during the recognition test. He reasoned that although *S*s learn less than the whole item, for *some* of the items, such partial learning may enable *S* to recognize a whole item correctly even though he is unable to recall the item. Accordingly, recognition will yield higher scores than recall because recognition requires learning about fewer aspects of the stimulus items than does recall. By limiting the effects of partial learning during recognition through the use of difficult distractors, that is, distractors containing elements common to both correct and incorrect alternatives on the recognition task, McNulty found that differences between recognition and recall were minimized.

Inherent in the recognition method are two principal limitations. First, the results of a recognition test depend, obviously, upon the number of alternatives present, with recognition performance decreasing as the number of alternatives increase (Murdock, 1963a). Second, recognition performance depends upon the relation of the learned material to the distractors, and to the nature of the set of distractors. For instance, if the learned material is highly distinctive a high retention score will be obtained. It is desirable to construct test alternatives (distractors) that vary in some systematic way preferably along quantitative dimensions; in this fashion, control over item homogeneity can be maintained. Accordingly, the use of recognition tasks with verbal materials may conceivably be unsatisfactory because of the difficulties associated with selecting alternatives of equal difficulty or discriminability.

Related to the second limitation of the recognition method is the fact that inter-actions among the alternatives may exist which may act to change the probability of a given selection response (Deese, 1963).

Similarly, a distractor might be more frequently recognized than a correct item under conditions in which the distractor has greater associative arousal than does the correct item. For example, following practice in paired-associates labeling of visual forms, a label might appear more "relevant" to a distractor than to the originally learned form, thus leading to more frequent selection of the distractor.

Another difficulty with the recognition method has been noted by Shepard and Teghtsoonian (1961) who found that the frequency of "false positives," that is, the selection of "new" items as "old" (familiar) ones, steadily increased as a result of ordinal-position in the test sequence. They interpreted this increase to be dependent upon the tendency of *S*'s subjective standard as to how confident he must be that an item is correct before he will call it correct to change in the course of the experiment. Thus, another source of uncontrolled error may systematically influence the recognition scores. In a successful effort to correct for this difficulty, Shepard and Chang (1963) adopted a symmetric forced-choice procedure in which *S*s were presented pairs of items, and within each pair one item was always correct and one incorrect. In this fashion, any changes in response bias or the *S*'s subjective criterion should affect both alternatives alike and presumably have little influence on *S*'s choices. Their results indicated that the percentage of correct choices was approximately constant as a function of the number of choices previously made, and that only a negligible amount of cumulative proactive interference occurred and was concentrated principally in the first few trials.

An important development in recognition memory has been the application of concepts and procedures from signal detection theory. Egan (1958) has described how a recognition memory experiment can be viewed as a yes-no task of detection in psychophysical experiments, and as a consequence, conceptual models of recognition memory have tended to be similar to models of signal detection (Bernbach, 1967; Kintsch, 1967). In yes-no studies of recognition memory the S's criterion for responding may vary in some unknown fashion. As a result the investigator may wish to separate effects caused by decision process from effects caused by memory itself. Egan has described how this separation may be accomplished by use of a receiver-operating characteristic (ROC) curve.

An interesting application of the procedure described by Shepard and Teghtsoonian has been made by Underwood (1965), who used it to study the development of implicit associative responses during the recognition test. Ss were read a list of 200 words; for each word S decided whether it had been read earlier. Certain critical stimulus words, which were presumed to arouse implicit associations, were presented early in the list, with the assumed associative words being presented later in the list. In general, the frequency of false recognitions were higher for the implicit words than for control words, thus strengthening the belief that implicit associative responses do actually occur and serve as mediators. It should also be noted that Underwood's procedure is not subject to the criticism described by Shephard and Teghtsoonian because Ss served as their own controls.

The recognition method has received considerable use in studies of perceptual memory. It has several advantages over the recall (reproduction) method in studying perceptual memory because S has only to select as distinct from reproducing (drawing) some figure or pattern; in this fashion, response biases and difficulties in judging drawings can be avoided (Carlson and Duncan, 1955; Hebb and Foord, 1945; Lovibond, 1958). Another advantage of recognition in studies of perceptual memory is that it is possible to vary systematically the alternatives along quantitative dimensions, such that the degree of difficulty and homogeneity of the alternatives can be specified (Ellis and Feuge, 1966).

We have reviewed the major ways of measuring retention along with instances of the many methodological variations that have developed. It is clear that there is no single measure of retention which is optimal under all conditions and that researchers will continue to be inventive in the development of new measures as newer attacks on problems of retention are formulated. Several of these newer developments have been outlined by Bahrick (1965) and by Bilodeau (1966), including an increasing interest in using the variance as well as the mean in estimating memory changes. We now turn our attention to a major methodological problem in retention, namely, that of measuring and controlling for differences in original learning.

Retention and the Problem of Degree of Original Learning. A fundamental problem in studies of retention, as well as transfer, extinction, generalization, and other two-stage experiments, lies in the difficulties associated with *measuring* and *equating* degree of learning on the first task. In a retention study Ss learn an initial task and, following some retention interval, are then tested for retention. Frequently, some feature of this initial task is varied so as to assess its effect on the subsequent course of retention. If, however, this feature, which is the independent variable, produces differences in terminal strength of learning, then any subsequent differences in measured performance on the retention test could result not only as a function of the independent variable that was introduced during original learning, but also as a function of differences in degree of original learning. Thus, the possibility of a serious source of confounding of variables arises in two-stage studies where the independent variable is introduced in the first stage. Principal recognition of this problem, appreciation of which does not yet seem to be widespread, has been given by Anderson (1963) and Underwood (1964b).

Let us consider a simple example. Suppose an investigator wishes to determine the effect of item meaningfulness on the retention of a serially learned list. Furthermore, assume that the high-meaning items are more rapidly learned than the low-meaning items so that performance at the end of acquisition, that is, terminal performance, differs. If we have reason to suspect that the course of retention depends on the degree of original learning, which is usually a reasonable assumption, then any differences in the amount of forgetting may reflect differences caused not only by item meaningfulness, but also by degree of original learning. As Underwood (1964b) notes, the problem becomes one of: "How does one make sure that the differences in retention (if present) can be attributed to the effects of meaningfulness *per se* rather than to the degree of learning" (p. 112)?

It has been indicated that there are two aspects to the problem of degree of original learning: the first is to *measure* reliably the strength of learning, that is, to obtain a reliable estimate of associative strength upon termination of practice on the first task; and the second is to provide a satisfactory way of *equating* degree of learning for different experimental groups after termination of original learning, should these groups differ after, say, receiving a constant number of trials on the original task. Several solutions to the problem of measuring and equating the degree of original learning have been proposed although no general solution that is entirely satisfactory for all situations has been established. The most thorough accounts of these procedures have been provided by Anderson (1963) and Underwood (1964b), only one of which will be briefly noted because a detailed description is beyond the scope of this chapter.

Underwood (1964b) notes that the number of correct responses made on the *last* anticipation trial during original learning is not an adequate measure of degree of learning at the termination of practice, since this measure does not include the growth in associative strength that occurred during that trial. As a solution to the first problem, that of measurement, Underwood recommends the use of what he calls the *single-entry projection technique*, a procedure by which the learning curve for each individual S is projected to the trial beyond the last one given. The projection to the next trial provides a very accurate estimate not only of the mean performance of the group, but also for the single S, and thus provides a more accurate score for equating degree of original learning.

In order to equate various experimental groups which, let us assume, learn different materials at different rates, Underwood proposes the *constant-trials procedure*, by which a constant number of trials is set, *differing* for each type of material, such that the mean number of correct responses anticipated is roughly the same for the different materials at the termination of original learning. The number of trials necessary to equate the different conditions can be determined by a small pilot study. Moreover, the equation need only be approximate because the projected scores will be used as the measure of terminal associative strength. Finally, Underwood notes that this procedure is applicable only when below-asymptote measures are used because no solution to the problem of measuring and equating degree of original learning is available for reliably estimating associative strength beyond asymptotic levels of performance.

Other solutions to problems stemming from differences in degree of original learning have been to use relative performance measures and to employ statistical procedures such as the analysis of covariance to adjust retention measures for differences in original-task learning (Payne, 1958). Covariance procedures, however, may not always be used because the assumptions underlying the covariance model may not have been met. Anderson (1963) makes a convincing argument for the use of parametric methods which assume some specific mathematical model for the second stage process in two-stage studies, such as resistance to extinction, and for the use of the shape function method which comprises a large class of mathematical models. Additional solutions to this problem will undoubtedly develop as awareness of the difficulties inherent in two-stage studies becomes more general.

Fundamental Processes in Retention

Up to this point we have described retention as an intervening variable which acts as a conceptual device for coordinating sets of relationships between various performance measures and various classes of independent variables. As such, retention derives its distinctive status in psychology from the *particular* class of independent variables studied and from the types of response measures examined. Its logical status, as distinguished from related concepts such as acquisition and transfer, has been noted earlier along with generally agreed-upon distinctions as outlined by Melton (1963). In this section we shall briefly describe some of the fundamental processes in retention including quantitative changes in retention, qualitative changes in retention, and short-term memory. This section is designed to provide a quite general overview of fundamental processes in retention prior to examining, in the next chapter, the major variables governing retention coupled with a summary of the current status of interference theory.

Quantitative Changes in Retention. Since the initial work of Ebbinghaus, the dominant interest of researchers in retention has been that of measuring quantitative changes in retention and determining the effective variables that govern such changes. Primary effort has been directed at reliably

measuring the amount *retained* (or forgotten), as distinct from any qualitative changes, as a function of such conditions as task, S, and method-of-measurement variables. Of particular interest has been the investigation of the variables that influence the temporal course of retention, which led to many studies of forgetting curves.

It was noted earlier that a principal contribution of Ebbinghaus was his empirical determination of retention loss as a function of time. Serving as his own S, Ebbinghaus first learned and subsequently relearned lists of nonsense syllables, thus measuring retention by the savings method. For example, Fig. 19-2 shows a plot of the results obtained by Ebbinghaus for one S who learned and relearned over 1,200 thirteen-syllable lists. The curve reveals a rapid loss at first and then a progressively slower loss in retention. Not only is this trend characteristic of classical retention curves, it is also seen to be typical of short-term memory curves (Melton, 1963; Peterson and Peterson, 1959). One significance of this common trend is to suggest that similar or even common processes may be present in the forgetting of different types of materials.

Recently Bilodeau and Levy (1964) suggested that the classical Ebbinghaus curve may not represent adequately retention loss in motor-skill tasks. They proposed a two-stage curve of forgetting in which the first stage of the retention curve is similar to that of Ebbinghaus, whereas the second stage differs radically, with retention decreasing in a positively accelerated fashion. Although the applicability of this curve to retention of verbal materials remains to be developed, the importance of this work is that it represents a challenge to traditional thinking about the measurement and nature of forgetting.

Once procedures for measuring the quantitative characteristics of retention were developed, it became a major task to determine the variables that governed

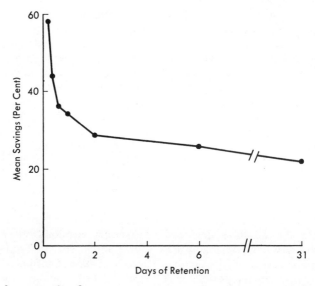

Figure 19-2.   An example of a common concave retention curve (data from Ebbing-haus, 1885: see 1913 translation). (Adapted with permission from Bilodeau, E. A. Retention. In E. A. Bilodeau (Ed.), *Acquisition of skill.* New York: Academic Press, 1966. Pp. 315–350.)

retention. The principal variables that have been investigated in quantitative studies of retention can be grouped into five categories. These are (1) the various conditions under which the original learning occurred; (2) the events that occurred *prior* to original learning; (3) the events that occurred *between* the time of original learning and the test of retention; (4) subject variables such as physiological and motivational states; and (5) the methods for measuring retention. A detailed examination of the role of these variables in retention will be made in the next chapter.

The major theoretical task in not only quantitative studies of retention, but also in qualitative studies, has been to develop an adequate conceptual system that can account for the phenomena of retention. In brief, given the facts of retention, how in turn are they to be explained? Two distinct views of the nature of retention have been developed. One view, that of *interference theory*, contends that forgetting occurs because of the interfering events of prior and/or subsequent learning (McGeoch,

1932b; Postman, 1961a). The primary task of this theory is to state the various sub-processes, or mechanisms, which produce interference and to demonstrate that these processes do, in fact, account for forgetting. The second view, that of *decay theory*, contends that "memory traces" of learned events become hypothetically internalized, and that these traces decay in accordance with certain autonomous processes. The critical difference between these two theories lies in the trace notion itself (Osgood, 1953). According to decay theory, the hypothesized traces are autonomously active and change in the course of time in accordance with principles that are independent of external changes, such as the utilization of associations. A decay theory can take the position that *some* forgetting is due to interference; however, it also contends that some forgetting is due to the autonomous decay or weakening of memory traces. In contrast, interference theory implies that there are no autonomous changes and that forgetting is due to external events, such as response competition.

Interference and decay theories emerge as alternative and competing accounts of phenomena in practically all areas of investigation in retention. These formulations are important in efforts to account for quantitative changes in retention, qualitative changes, and in efforts to distinguish short-term memory from long-term memory.

Qualitative Changes in Retention. Not only are there quantitative changes in retention but there are also changes of a qualitative kind. Thus the memory for an event may not only fade in time but it may also show *distortion*, or modification, which appears to be not merely a matter of quantitative weakening. An example of such changes was noted earlier in the description of Bartlett's (1932) studies of retention. A longstanding issue has been whether the facts of qualitative change in retention require explanatory principles that are fundamentally different from those employed in accounting for quantitative changes, or whether both kinds of changes can be accounted for in terms of some common set of principles. Furthermore, this issue is not unique to accounts of qualitative changes in retention but emerges elsewhere in the study of retention, as will be seen, for example, in the study of short-term memory which is examined in the next section.

On the one hand is a group of theorists whose bias is that of parsimony, economy, and continuity, and whose fundamental belief, or hope, is that the various phenomena of retention can be accounted for in terms of a common set of principles. Their preference is to assume that phenotypic differences in retention do not necessarily reflect noncommon underlying processes. On the other hand is another group of theorists who have taken the view that the phenomena of retention are too complex to be accounted for in terms of a common set of principles, and require instead differing sets of explanatory principles, indeed,

principles whose conceptual properties themselves differ.

Students of qualitative changes in retention (Bartlett, 1932; Katona, 1940; Koffka, 1935; Wulf, 1922) have frequently taken the position that such changes do, in fact, require additional principles beyond those usually invoked in the study of quantitative changes in retention. In general, principles derived from assumptions about the nature of perceptual organization have been invoked to account for qualitative changes coupled with the effort to view such changes as a result of central, perceptual-cognitive, determinants as distinct from more peripherally described variables. Accordingly, explanatory concepts derived from or consistent with Gestalt theory have played a prominent role in accounting for qualitative changes. Moreover, these principles are generally viewed in contrast with principles derived from associationistic conceptions of behavior as seen, for example, in interference theory.

Investigations of qualitative changes in retention have used two principal types of tasks: (1) memory for visual forms, and (2) memory for connected discourse such as prose or poetry. In both instances somewhat similar conceptual inferences have been drawn from the reported changes in memory. We noted some of the issues involved in these studies in the historical overview; however, it is instructive to examine these issues again in somewhat greater detail.

As noted earlier, Gestalt theorists have, as the result of studies of memory for visual forms, argued for a theory of retention which views changes in perceptual memory as a result of autonomous changes in the central nervous system. Briefly, they contend that changes in hypothesized "memory traces" occur as a result of activity in the central nervous system which occurs independently of task variables which may lead to interference in retention. In other words, we can logically distinguish between

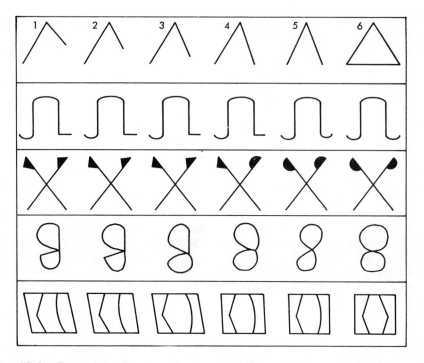

Figure 19-3. Examples of successive reproductions. The numbers represent the position of the recall period with respect to the series. (Adapted with permission from Perkins, F. T. Symmetry in visual recall. *Amer. J. Psychol.*, 1932, **44**, 473–490.)

"central" events which bring about changes in memory and more "peripheral" events which are related to interference.

This viewpoint can be illuminated by examining an experiment by Perkins (1932) which is designed to measure memory for visual forms by the method of successive reproduction. The *S*s were asked to study five visual forms that are shown to the left of the series in Fig. 19-3.

After a period of inspection each *S* was asked to reproduce (draw) the forms repeatedly. Fig. 19-3 shows five successive reproductions of each stimulus form, the first being reproduced immediately, and the others with varying retention intervals up to forty-nine days. According to the theory noted earlier, memory for visual forms should become progressively modified so as to show increased regularity and symmetry. In other words, these changes should reflect a tendency toward a "better" figure in

accordance with principles of Gestalt theory.

Inspection of these figures will reveal one of the principal difficulties in testing this theory with the method of successive reproduction. It is indeed difficult to judge the nature and direction of these changes. Moreover, even if it is agreed that the figures do show a progressive change in the direction of symmetry, it could be argued that *S* was influenced by each successive reproduction so that these changes represent only a change from one reproduction to the next as distinct from a modification of the memory trace of the original stimulus. Thus the method of successive reproduction, as used by Perkins (1932), makes it quite difficult to interpret the changes in the drawings.

Despite the difficulties encountered in Perkin's study, interest in Gestalt conceptions of memory for visual form persisted, and continued to stimulate a long series of investigations having as a major purpose the testing of the theoretical usefulness of these conceptions. Two principal conclusions have emerged in these Gestalt-oriented studies of perceptual memory: (1) the adequacy of measures of successive reproduction which are used to infer changes in "memory traces" has been seriously questioned, largely on the grounds that such measures lack "objectivity" and are difficult to interpret; and (2) the logical status of the trace concept, as employed by Gestalt theorists, has come under investigation with an increasing awareness of the difficulties associated with testing implications derived from the decay of autonomous traces. As Postman (1964) has noted, the trace concept continues to suffer from vagueness and few, if any, precise empirical implications seem to follow from the trace concept. Related to this second trend, which questions the adequacy of trace theory, is the growth of interest in alternative interpretations of perceptual memory, principally interpretations derived from association theory. An excellent account of the history of these trends has been given by Riley (1962) and only a few highlights will be mentioned.

A study by Hebb and Foord (1945) serves to illustrate some of the methodological difficulties associated with Perkins' (1932) study. Hebb and Foord used a psychophysical procedure for testing for autonomous change, in which Ss saw only two visual forms and were given only one recognition test in which they had to select forms from an array containing forms which varied systematically from the original forms. They failed to find any evidence for a progressive change in memory traces in accordance with predictions from trace theory. In subsequent studies, Carlson and Duncan (1955) and Lovibond (1958) obtained similar results and again failed to support trace-theory predictions. A principal methodological conclusion reached from these and similar studies was the desirability of using recognition as distinct from reproduction measures, and the further desirability of using single-item procedures (Carlson and Duncan, 1955).

The second major trend in studies of perceptual memory has been the increasing tendency to account for such changes in terms of principles derived from association theory. An instance of this trend is seen in a study by Postman (1954) which investigated the effects of various kinds of pretraining with visual forms on subsequent memory of the forms. A major finding of his study was the demonstration of the role of code training, that is, a set of rules by which S learns to construct pairs of visual forms, on reproductive memory. Postman demonstrated that code training becomes an increasingly important factor in determining reproductive memory with the passage of time and concluded that these performance changes can be accounted for in terms of learned responses without recourse to hypothetical changes in autonomous memory traces. As Riley (1962) notes, Postman's findings do not, of course, rule out the possibility of autonomous changes; rather, they suggest that trace theory may be unnecessary for accounting for these changes.

In recent years there has been an apparent decline of interest in Gestalt conceptions of qualitative changes in retention. Part of this decline appears to be the result of growing belief that classical Gestalt trace theory which assumes an autonomous decay of traces is difficult, if not impossible, to evaluate experimentally. In turn, alternative interpretations have been regarded as increasingly reasonable in accounting for many of these qualitative changes. Related to these developments has been the growing reliance on recognition as a method for measuring retention which permits a quantitative specification of the changes in memory. Indeed, the use of the recognition method and related psychophysical procedures allows presumed qualitative changes in retention, such as enhanced symmetry and regularity, to be treated as quantitative changes. Finally, interest among researchers in retention has been increasingly directed toward other topics such as interference theory, short-term memory, and coding processes in retention.

Short-Term Memory. An important development in the study of retention that has received substantial attention in recent years, beginning about 1958, is that of short-term memory (STM). Prior to this time many studies of STM were conducted but the majority of such studies treated STM as a *capacity* variable related to features of general intelligence. As such, STM was some capacity of the organism to be measured by classical memory span procedures. It is only as a result of more recent methodological developments in STM that the clear relevance of STM to theoretical conceptions of memory processes such as information storage and

retrieval has emerged. Of particular importance has been the issue of the "permanence" of learning and the related issue as to whether STM and long-term memory (LTM) represent fundamentally different processes, with STM being subject to rapid decay in contrast to the stability and permanence of LTM traces. Before these theoretical issues are discussed, however, we shall describe some of the experimental developments in STM.

In 1959 Peterson and Peterson described a procedure for measuring STM for single items which yielded striking results. They measured the recall of single-item trigrams, items consisting of three consonants such as CKM, after intervals of 3, 6, 9, 12, 15, and 18 sec. Each S was tested eight times at each of the recall intervals although a given trigram was used only once with each S. In order to minimize rehearsal, Ss were required to count backward by three's from a given number immediately upon hearing the trigram and continue counting until

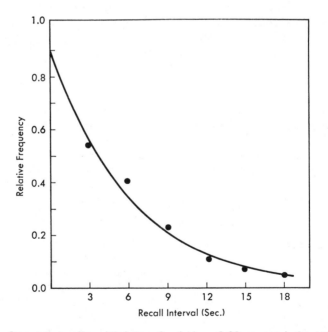

Figure 19-4.   Correct recalls with latencies below 2.83 sec. as a function of recall interval. (Adapted with permission from Peterson, L. R., and Peterson, M. J. Short-term retention of individual verbal items. *J. exp. Psychol.*, 1959, **58**, 193–198.)

the recall test. The basic findings of their study are given in Fig. 19-4 which shows a plot of the proportions of correct recalls (with latencies below 2.83 sec.) as a function of the recall interval.

Despite the extraordinary short intervals employed coupled with S's learning only a single item, the curve shows a striking decline. Indeed, after only a 3-sec. interval a considerable amount of forgetting had occurred and after 18 sec. retention was less than 10 per cent. This finding is especially noteworthy when it is considered that the verbal items were well within the memory span of the Ss.

Although Peterson and Peterson argued that the decrease in recall could not be attributed simply to the cumulative effects of prior learning, that is, proactive inhibition, which is known to be an important factor in forgetting (Underwood, 1957), subsequent investigations (Keppel and Underwood, 1962; Loess, 1964; Wickens, Born, and Allen, 1963) indicated that proactive inhibition does, indeed, develop as a function of the number of prior items learned using the Peterson and Peterson technique. The importance of this latter finding is to suggest that proactive inhibition has a similar function in both STM and LTM (Postman, 1964). Moreover, this finding would tend to support the view that STM is basically similar to LTM in contrast to the view that they represent distinct or dichotomous processes.

Subsequent investigations have verified the principal findings of Peterson and Peterson. For example, Murdock (1961) replicated the Peterson and Peterson experiment using similar trigrams and obtained a curve quite similar to that reported by the Petersons. In addition, Murdock repeated all features of their experiment except that he used words; finally, Murdock used unrelated three-word units. The basic results of Murdock's studies are shown in Fig. 19-5 along with the Petersons' results.

Fig. 19-5 indicates that single words are better retained than trigrams, although some forgetting of single words did occur. In addition, the figure indicates that the forgetting of three-word units is similar to that of trigrams. On the surface this rapid loss in retention appeared consistent with decay theory; however, this view received immediate challenge from several sources (for example, Melton, 1963; Postman, 1964).

Melton (1963) has taken the position that Murdock's findings suggest that the principal factor determining the slope of the short-term retention function was the number of "chunks" of information in the unit to be remembered. In other words, it is the chunk of information which determines the retention curve, with more rapid forgetting occurring when the unit contains more chunks. Such a view is consistent with Miller's (1956) findings regarding coding processes in memory. In addition, Melton (1963) has contended that, more generally, the rate of forgetting of a unit presented once is dependent upon the amount of *intraunit* interference and that this interference is a function of the number of chunks *encoded* within the single item as distinct from the total number of physical elements present. A considerable amount of evidence for this interpretation was assembled by Melton in studies using units with varying numbers of consonants. A major finding of these studies was that the slope of the STM curve steepened as a function of the number of consonants in the unit to be remembered. Moreover, there was only a very slight loss in retention with single-consonant units over a 32-sec. retention interval, similar to the finding of Murdock (1961) for single-word units.

Melton's (1963) findings have special significance for theories of retention, particularly so for decay and interference theories. In brief, a decay theory of retention assumes that forgetting is the result of some form of autonomous activity of the central nervous system, as distinct from sources of interference in the task, such as response competition. Melton's finding that

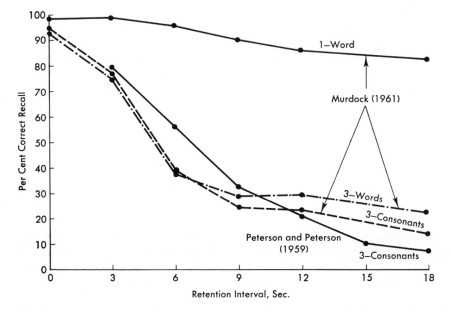

Figure 19-5.   Percentage frequency of completely correct recall of three-consonant (Peterson and Peterson, 1959; Murdock, 1961), and 1-word and 3-word units (Murdock, 1961). (Adapted with permission from Melton, A. W. Implications of short-term memory for a general theory of memory. *J. verb. Learn. verb. Behav.*, 1962, **2**, 1–21.)

the slope of the retention curve progressively steepens as a function of the number of encoded chunks would appear to be evidence against decay as a major factor in retention, although such evidence does not rule out the possibility of some autonomous decay. There are two major reasons for viewing Melton's finding on STM as evidence against decay: (1) the single consonant was well retained over a 32-sec. interval, showing almost no retention loss, despite the fact that the activities engaged by S to fill the retention interval, numerical tasks, would appear to qualify as disrupting activities; and (2) the major loss in retention was accounted for by intraunit interference as distinct from the mere passage of time. It should be cautioned that these data do not deny the possibility that some simple decay could occur because there was some forgetting of the single consonant; rather, these data strongly suggest the relative importance of interference as distinct from decay accounts of forgetting.

The second theoretical question raised by studies of STM concerns whether STM and LTM represent essentially two different processes or whether they represent a continuum. Although at present this issue remains in dispute there appears to be a moderate amount of evidence which suggests that STM and LTM are governed by similar laws and hence represent continuous processes. The distinction between STM and LTM is usually one in which STM is held to be subject to rapid decay in contrast to the stability of LTM. This distinction is arrived at, in part, from studies of STM which show a rapid loss in forgetting in the absence of rehearsal and has led to the suggestion of a dual process in memory. For example, Hebb (1949) and Broadbent (1957) have argued for a dual process in which the initial, or primary, trace declines in accordance with decay theory principles whereas a consolidated trace is prevented from decaying and is transferred into LTM storage. Once the trace is transferred into LTM storage it is then governed by the principles of associative interference (Broadbent, 1963).

Although the issue of a duplex theory of memory storage is in dispute, it is instructive to examine some of the difficulties inherent in maintaining this position. Two of these difficulties have been noted by Postman (1964) and are briefly summarized. First, Postman notes that it is uncertain if the results obtained from studies of STM and LTM are sufficiently comparable to allow a sensible judgment about the relative rates of forgetting in the two situations, and thus to infer the operation of two different processes in retention. Postman points out that the rate of forgetting is, in part, a function of the degree of original learning, and consequently it is difficult to compare the degree of learning resulting from single exposure to discrete units with the extended practice usually given with a list of items. Moreover, measures of retention in STM and LTM are usually different and hence may lead to differences in forgetting which reflect the measure itself rather than fundamental differences in processes.

Second, Postman contends that a more fundamental difficulty concerns the appropriateness of drawing inferences about the properties of a hypothetical memory trace on the basis of many studies of STM. Usually such studies employ some sort of interpolated activity during the retention interval which is designed to prevent rehearsal. The assumption has been made that such interpolated activity, although it prevents rehearsal, is not a major factor in retention loss and hence does not influence the rate of autonomous decay of the memory trace. This assumption, however, is difficult to make in view of the known similarity, in some instances, between the rehearsal task and the items learned; in addition, substantial amounts of retroactive interference have been produced in verbal learning studies even when the similarity of the two tasks is known to be low, a finding

which can be accounted for in terms of "generalized response competition" (Newton and Wickens, 1956; Postman and Riley, 1959). Thus it appears that the assumption that interpolated tasks serve principally to prevent rehearsal, and not to produce interference, must be seriously questioned, hence raising doubt about the kind of inferences one may make from these experimental designs. As Postman notes,

experimental tests of the decay hypothesis are seriously, if not fatally, handicapped by the dual requirement of measuring forgetting as a function of time and preventing rehearsal. The latter requirement makes it necessary to fill the retention interval as effectively as possible with an interpolated activity. Once that is done, the relationship between forgetting and the sheer passage of time is obscured (Postman, 1964, pp. 173–174).

This latter critique is of considerable consequence for it raises the serious question of whether decay theory, or implications from decay theory, can be properly put to test. If, indeed, it is not possible to evaluate decay theory experimentally or to determine what empirical implications follow from decay theory, then the theory is of limited value. In order to test effectively the consequences from a given theory, the empirical implications which follow from that position must be clearly specified, and adequate procedures for testing the outcomes of these implications must be available which permit unambiguous distinction from other alternatives. As long as it is possible to interpret the results of studies proposing to support decay theory in terms of interference principles the issue will remain clouded.

A detailed analysis of the principal methodological difficulties inherent in comparisons of STM and LTM experiments has been reported by Keppel (1965). These difficulties concern three considerations of experimental design which include the nature of the retention-interval activity, the measurement of immediate retention, and the type of experimental design (the use of independent versus repeated measures). For example, Keppel points out that the design for studying proactive inhibition (PI) in STM, as used by Murdock (1963b, 1964), is not exactly comparable to designs which study PI in LTM. The design for studying PI in LTM, as a function of variations in length of the retention interval, consists of experimental and control groups in which the experimental group learns an initial list prior to learning the critical list, and a control group learns only the critical list. This design is then repeated for different retention intervals. In contrast, Murdock's design, which studied the effect of PI on STM, simultaneously filled the retention interval with new items. In effect, Murdock's design introduced a factor which can clearly produce retroactive inhibition (RI), thus making his study a combination PI/RI design. In brief, careful consideration must be given to the features of the defining paradigms if one wishes to compare the phenomena of STM and LTM. Finally, any conclusions about the continuity of STM and LTM, or about the presumed similarity of processes governing these events, remains in doubt to the extent that paradigms for STM and LTM have not yet been comparable.

Along similar lines, Peterson (1966) has contended that although STM and LTM have much in common, in that interference produces forgetting in both cases, and repetition generally improves retention, an additional mechanism, that of *recency*, may operate in STM. This recency mechanism is conceptualized as a postperceptual mechanism whose role decreases with the passage of time. The consequence of this view is that a two-factor conception of memory may still be possible, although different from decay-interference distinctions.

Retention:
Empirical Findings and
Theoretical Interpretations

In the previous chapter we examined the nature and measurement of retention and described some of its fundamental characteristics. In this chapter we shall outline some of the major empirical findings in retention and examine the dominant conceptual formulation of retention; that of interference theory. This chapter is concerned with three principal issues: (1) an examination of interference phenomena in retention, (2) the role of original-learning variables influencing retention, and (3) the role of organizational factors and coding processes in retention.

Interference Phenomena in Retention

Interference theory is at present the dominant theoretical position accounting for the process of forgetting (Postman, 1961a). In general, this theory contends that events are forgotten because other learning interferes with or prevents these events from being remembered. In turn, a fundamental task of interference theory is to develop an account of the various subprocesses or mechanisms which produce

interference, and to construct the laws governing the activity of these component processes. The investigation of these subprocesses or mechanisms usually takes the form of experiments in retroactive or proactive inhibition, experiments in which two learning tasks are given S so that the influence of one task on the retention of the other can be determined.

Retroactive Inhibition. One procedure for investigating interference effects in retention is that which produces *retroactive inhibition* (RI). RI is simply the decrease in retention of an earlier-learned task caused by the effects of interpolated learning of some new task. As shown below, RI is inferred from the comparative performance of two groups, an experimental and a control group. The experimental group learns an initial task, A, and then learns a second task, B, which

	Learn	Learn	Reten- tion Test
Experi- mental	A	B	A
Control	A	... (rests) ...	A

is interpolated between the initial task and a test for retention of task A. In turn, the control group learns the initial task and is subsequently tested for retention without learning the interpolated task.

A comparison of the experimental and control groups in their performance on the retention test reveals the amount of forgetting that is due to the learning of task B. If the effect of learning the interpolated task, B, is such that the experimental group retains less than does the control group, then RI is inferred. Several component processes or mechanisms can operate to produce RI; however, it is the *net* effect or sum of all of these events that is called RI. Usually, the effect of the interpolated task is to produce interference, that is, RI; however, it is possible for the relationship of task B to A to be of such a nature that the experimental group retains more than the control, thus allowing for retroactive facilitation. In the vast majority of cases, however, interest in this paradigm has been in its interference and not its facilitative effects.

Control of the "rest" interval is an important issue in the interpretation of the results. Rarely do control Ss simply rest; rather, they engage in some task which is designed ideally to prevent simultaneously the rehearsal of task A and yet not interfere in some unspecified or *unknown* fashion with the consolidation of task A learning. For example, in studies of paired-associate learning and retention, control Ss may engage in an interpolated task such as solving mathematical problems (Postman and Stark, 1962), a task which is assumed to minimize rehearsal. In effect, Ss usually engage in some interpolated activity which is judged to be relatively unrelated to task A, and whose effect, which conceivably can produce some slight interference, can be estimated from prior experimentation.

Measurement of retention of task A (first-list) associations in studies of RI is usually accomplished by obtaining conventional anticipation measures or by employing a modified-modified free recall (MMFR) procedure as described by Barnes and Underwood (1959). Fortunately, variations in these two procedures do not produce significant differences in amounts of RI. For instance, in a study of the retention of first-list associations as a function of variations in transfer paradigms, Postman (1962b) found that measures of RI obtained from the anticipation method did not differ from those obtained by the MMFR procedure. Similarly, Houston, Garskof, Noyd, and Erskine (1965) found no significant differences in RI between a MMFR procedure and a method requiring single-list recall.

Proactive Inhibition. The second procedure which is frequently used for investigating interference effects in retention is one that produces *proactive inhibition* (PI). In general, PI is the loss in retention caused by the effects of some previously learned task. In this instance, however, the effects are due to the learning of a task prior rather than after the to-be-tested task. As shown below, the paradigm for studying PI, like that for studying RI, requires a comparison of performance between experimental and control groups. The experimental group learns an initial task (B) prior to learning task A and is then tested for retention of task A. In turn, the control group learns only task A and is subsequently tested for retention.

	Learn	Learn	Retention Test
Experimental	B	A	A
Control	. . . (rests) . . .	A	A

A comparison of the experimental and control groups in their performance on the retention test reveals the amount of forgetting that is due to the learning of task B. If the effect of learning the prior task, B, is such that the experimental group retains less of task A than does the control group, then PI is inferred. As with the RI paradigm, it is possible for B to facilitate the retention of A, thus allowing for proactive facilitation. Nevertheless, the usual procedure with this paradigm is to select tasks which are likely to produce interference so that PI effects can be studied.

It is a common procedure in some studies for the control group to rest for a period of time comparable to that required for the experimental group to learn task B, prior to learning task A. This procedure, however, can be regarded as unsatisfactory to the extent that warm-up and learning-to-learn effects in the learning of task A remain uncontrolled. The rate at which the experimental group learns task A may be faster than that of the control group, and consequently, obtained differences in the retention of A may be a result of both the interference effects of task B learning and differences in the degree of task A learning.

In order to control for this possible confounding, an additional group of control Ss is sometimes given an irrelevant task prior to learning task A. For instance, in a study of PI in paired-associate learning, Dallett (1962) required an additional control group to learn a paired-associate list containing stimuli and responses unrelated to those of task A, thus controlling for nonspecific transfer effects. In contrast, other studies (for example, Postman and Stark, 1964) have continued to employ the "traditional" control group in which Ss learn a single list and are then tested for retention, thus allowing for possible confounding of nonspecific with specific transfer effects in task A learning. In the study by Postman and Stark, however, a comparison of two transfer paradigms (A-B, A-C versus A-B, A-B') on PI was made, thus allowing for a relative comparison of PI effects. Because the investigators were interested in relative differences in PI as a function of differences in transfer

paradigms, controls for nonspecific transfer effects were unnecessary.

Variables Influencing RI and PI. A logical analysis of the RI and PI paradigms reveals those variables which are likely to be important. The principal variables that influence RI and PI are (1) the similarity between the two tasks; (2) the degree of learning of the two tasks, including their relative strengths; (3) the time interval between the various stages of learning; (4) the time interval between learning and the retention test; (5) the number of original and interpolated and/or prior-learning tasks; and (6) the extraexperimental sources of interference. No effort will be made to examine all of the variables known to influence RI and PI. A fairly recent review of the major factors influencing RI and PI has been provided by Slamecka and Ceraso (1960), and a review of the earlier RI literature has been provided by Britt (1935). Instead, representative experiments which illustrate the effects of two of the more important variables are described in the next two sections.

Similarity and Interference. Both RI and PI depend on the overall similarity between task A and B, and also on the similarity of task components, that is, of stimulus similarity and response similarity. The effect of overall task similarity on RI appears to be dependent upon the method for measuring retention. Although relatively few attempts have been made to examine this effect, studies using tests of substance or of factual retention of prose materials (for example, Ausubel, Robbins, and Blake, 1957; Hall, 1955), report minimal if any RI effects as a function of prose similarity. In contrast, Slamecka (1959, 1960) reports that RI is an increasing function of the similarity of the two tasks when measures of rote retention are employed, thus indicating that RI with connected-discourse materials is susceptible to effects similar to those obtained with other tasks such as serial lists. Similarly, Slamecka (1961) has demonstrated PI effects using prose materials which also indicate that connected discourse has the same kind of susceptibility to PI effects as do more traditional verbal-learning tasks.

The classical view that relates RI and overall task similarity, the Skaggs-Robinson hypothesis (Robinson, 1927), describes RI as a U-shaped function of the degree of similarity between the original and interpolated task. More specifically, this view contends that the recall of some task is greatest where successively practiced tasks are highly similar, is least at some point of moderate similarity, and increases again as the two tasks become still less similar. Unfortunately, experimental tests of the Skaggs-Robinson hypothesis have failed to yield entirely consistent findings (Harden, 1929; Kennelly, 1941; Robinson, 1927), and subsequent efforts at empirical integration of the data by Osgood (1949) made clear the desirability of distinguishing between stimulus and response similarity in order to assess their independent effects on RI. As a consequence, this hypothesis has been superseded by subsequent conceptual developments and methodological refinements in interference theory.

According to the transfer and retroaction surface (Osgood, 1949), it is predicted that RI is an inverse function of response similarity and that RI reaches its maximum when the response terms are opposite. In general, this relationship appears to hold when the degree of response similarity is varied *within* the same response class (Osgood, 1948; Young, 1955). Young required Ss to learn an initial (A-B) list of paired associates and then required them to learn an interpolated (A-B′) list with varying degrees of response similarity. A test for retention of A-B indicated that retention of the B responses increased as a function of interlist response similarity. Morgan and Underwood (1950) and Dallett (1962) have demonstrated that PI also varies as a func-

tion of the similarity of first and second-list responses.

In contrast, this inverse relationship between response similarity and RI does not appear to hold with variations *between* the similarity of response classes (Postman, Keppel, and Stark, 1965). Using an A-B, A-C paradigm for studying RI, with the responses drawn from different classes, they failed to support the inverse relationship predicted by Osgood. Moreover, they suggest a new principle relating RI and response similarity: "the more dissimilar the classes of responses attached to the same stimuli the more likely it becomes that the successive response systems will maintain their strengths independently of each other (Postman, Keppel, and Stark, 1965, pp. 118)."

In turn, studies of the effect of stimulus similarity on RI have shown decreasing RI as the similarity of the stimulus terms increased, when the response terms were kept identical (Bugelski and Cadwallader, 1956; Hamilton, 1943). When the response terms were varied, or unrelated, the effect of increasing stimulus similarity has been to increase RI (Bugelski and Cadwallader, 1956; Gibson, 1941; Postman, 1958). Recently, Wickelgren (1965) has demonstrated a similar relationship between RI and acoustic similarity of verbal items in short-term memory, suggesting that the similarity variable affects RI in STM in a manner analogous to LTM.

Degree of Learning and Interference. A second variable that has been extensively examined in studies of RI and PI is that of the degree of learning of either the original task or of the interfering task. With a wide range of materials, the data suggest that as the degree of original learning increases, while holding the degree of interpolated learning constant, RI tends to decrease. An early study by McGeoch (1929) provides support for this generalization. In it Ss received varying numbers of presentations of a list of nonsense syllables during learning of the original list and a constant number of presentations of the interpolated list. Similarly, more recent studies by Richardson (1956) and by Postman and Riley (1959) provide extended support for this generalization.

If the degree of interpolated learning is varied, holding the degree of original learning constant, an increase in the amount of interpolated learning tends to produce an increase in RI. This generalization is supported by the classic studies of McGeoch (1932a) and Melton and Irwin (1940) and has been confirmed by more recent studies (Briggs, 1957; Postman and Riley, 1959). In the study by Melton and Irwin (1940), Ss learned serial lists of nonsense syllables, receiving five trials on the original list and either five, ten, twenty, or forty trials on the interpolated list. With the recall score on the first relearning trial as a measure of retention, RI increased as a function of the amount of interpolated learning from five to twenty trials; however, a slight decrease in RI occurred after forty interpolated trials. Using an A-B, A-C paradigm, Thune and Underwood (1943) investigated RI in a paired-associate task in a fashion analogous to the serial learning study of Melton and Irwin, and obtained a similar relationship between RI and degree of interpolated learning.

Turning to PI, the data indicate that an increase in the degree of first-list learning, keeping second-list learning constant, produces an increase in PI (Atwater, 1953; Postman and Riley, 1959; Underwood, 1949b). In turn, PI bears a U-shaped relation to degree of second-list learning with degree of first-list learning held constant (Postman and Riley, 1959).

As noted earlier, besides similarity and degree of learning, a number of other factors influencing RI and PI have been studied. No attempt, however, has been made to examine these additional factors as their effects on RI and PI have been well described in the recent literature (Slamecka and Ceraso, 1960). The importance of

studies of RI and PI is that they have provided an analytic approach to the study of mechanisms of forgetting. Of principal interest has been the manner in which such studies reveal the nature of component processes in retention, and in their contribution to the development of an interference theory of forgetting.

Interference Theory

We noted at the beginning of this chapter that interference theory is the dominant position accounting for the phenomena of retention and that the bulk of support for the theory stems from the findings of RI and PI studies. Moreover, we noted that interference theory was not concerned just with the gross fact that individuals forget, but was more specifically concerned with analyzing the component processes or mechanisms which produce forgetting and with the development of principles governing these more molecular phenomena of retention. Probably nowhere in the study of retention is the emphasis on "component analysis" of processes more clearly evident than in the development of interference theory, with the possible exception of developments in short-term memory. An examination of the development of interference theory is now in order.

Interference theory begins with the basic assumption that forgetting is the result of other learning which prevents what initially has been learned from being remembered. It stands in contrast to decay theory and to related conceptions which contend that forgetting is the result of the autonomous decay of memory traces, or to the mere passage of time *per se*. Interference theory received strong support as a result of McGeoch's (1932b) attack on the law of disuse which led, in turn, to a series of efforts toward formalizing interference theory culminating in Postman's (1961a) important paper summarizing its status.

An early formulation of interference theory was that of the hypothesis of *response competition* as described by McGeoch (1942). According to this view, responses acquired in the original and interpolated learning tasks, and attached to similar or identical stimuli as in the A-B, A-C paradigm, remain available to S and compete with each other during S's effort to recall the original list. The degree to which the two sets of responses compete with each other depends upon similarity of the stimuli, a finding already noted in studies of RI and PI. Moreover, competition depends upon the relative strength of the two response systems, with the stronger response being given when the response systems are of unequal strength whereas responses of equal strength may block each other. Evidence for response competition is seen, for example, when S's latency for correct responses is significantly lengthened, when incorrect responses are given, or when response blocking occurs such that no response is given except when S is forced to respond as, say, in a forced-choice method.

It has been noted (Barnes and Underwood, 1959) that there are actually two components of the response competition hypothesis. The first of these is the hypothesis of *independence*, or, integrity of response systems. The second is that of *response dominance* at recall which has been noted in the previous paragraph. The independence hypothesis contends that the associative strength of the responses in the original list is maintained and is not weakened as a result of second-list learning. Although response competition between responses in the two lists may occur, there is presumably no loss of associative strength. Thus, the two responses remain intact and maintain their independence. The hypothesis of response dominance at recall accounts for the observed loss in retention by assuming that a stronger but incorrect response intrudes at recall and displaces the correct response. Thus, in the A-B, A-C paradigm a test for retention of

the B responses of the first list may yield some C responses of the interpolated list because of the presumed greater strength of the C responses.

The hypotheses of independence and response dominance are not necessarily linked (Postman, 1961a). It is possible to accept the hypothesis of response dominance at recall while simultaneously rejecting the hypothesis of independence. Indeed, recent investigations offer no support for the assumption of independence (for example, Barnes and Underwood, 1959; McGovern, 1964) whereas response dominance at recall has received considerable support.

At this point we have seen that a response competition theory that assumes displacement of one response by another in the recall task is one mechanism in interference theory. Nevertheless, response competition is not the entire picture as another mechanism, that of *unlearning*, is necessary for a more complete account of forgetting. An unlearning mechanism contends that the first-list responses in, say, an A-B, A-C paradigm are unlearned, or extinguished during second-list learning. Unlearning takes place in the following manner: to the extent that B responses intrude during A-C learning they are nonreinforced and hence should undergo experimental extinction in a manner analogous to extinction in classical or instrumental conditioning. Accordingly, a later test for retention of the B responses should show weakening to the extent that they have been nonreinforced. Furthermore, it should be noted that any evidence for unlearning stands contrary to predictions from the independence hypothesis.

Melton and Irwin (1940) first called attention to an unlearning mechanism in verbal learning in order to account for their findings regarding RI. It was their belief that this second factor coupled with the mechanism of competition between responses provided a more comprehensive account of interference in retention than

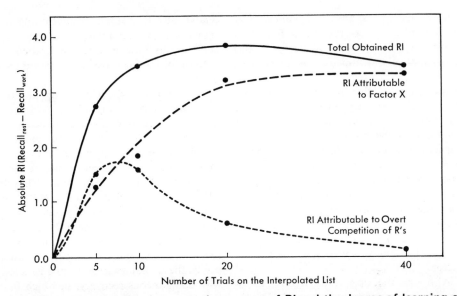

Figure 20-1.   Relationship between the amount of RI and the degree of learning of the interpolated material. The total obtained RI is the number of syllables forgotten as a consequence of the interpolated learning. The RI attributable to the overt competition of original and interpolated responses has been taken as two times the average frequency of intrusions of entire interpolated syllables during the recall trial in order to take into account the unidentified overt intrusions of parts of syllables. The curve for Factor X represents the absolute decrement in recall attributable to the factor or factors other than the overt competition of original and interpolated responses. (Adapted with permission from Melton, A. W., and Irwin, J. M. The influence of degree of interpolated learning on retroactive inhibition and the overt transfer of specific responses. *Amer. J. Psychol.*, 1940, **53**, 173–203.)

did a theory based solely on response competition. As noted earlier, their study concerned the effect of varying amounts of interpolated learning on RI in serial learning. *S*s learned an initial list of 18 nonsense syllables and then learned an interpolated list of 18 nonsense syllables for either five, ten, twenty, or forty trials, and then were tested for retention of the original list. Recall and relearning of the original list occurred after 30 min. following second-list learning. Measures of absolute RI, the difference in recall between the experimental and control group, and the number of overt interpolated-list intrusions were obtained. Melton and Irwin reasoned that the number of overt intrusions stemming from the interpolated list provided a good index of the amount of response competition between the two lists.

The major findings of their study are seen in Figure 20-1 which shows the amount of RI as a function of the number of trials on the interpolated list. The total amount of RI increased as a function of trials on the interpolated task from five to twenty trials, with a slight decrease in total RI after forty trials. In turn, the amount of RI attributable to overt response competition reached its maximum between five and ten trials of interpolated learning and then declined with further trials on the interpolated task. Of critical importance is the fact that there was no consistent relationship between the total amount of RI and that RI due to overt response competition. Since the total RI continued to increase at a point beyond which RI attributable to overt response competition increased, Melton and Irwin reasoned that some additional factor besides that of response competition must be contributing to the total RI. This additional factor was called Factor X and was tentatively identified as the unlearning of the response items in the original list. They suggested that because the original responses, when they intruded during the learning of the interpolated list, were not reinforced, they should then undergo some form of extinction and hence should be less available in S's repertoire during a subsequent recall test. Accordingly, they proposed a *two-factor theory* of RI in which response competition during recall was identified as one factor and unlearning of the original-list responses during interpolated learning was viewed as the second factor.

Although the unlearning hypothesis is not inconsistent with the response competition hypothesis, the lack of correlation between total RI and RI attributable to response competition does not, itself, require one to assume the process of unlearning. Moreover, conclusive evidence for unlearning had to await the development of procedures for measuring the strength of first-list responses independently of other possible factors contributing to RI. Accordingly, it was possible for several (Thune and Underwood, 1943; Underwood, 1945) to attribute the decline in overt intrusions at high levels of interpolated learning to increasing differentiation between the two lists as distinct from, or in addition to, unlearning. Thus a third contributor to RI, *list differentiation*, also became a possible mechanism in interference theory. A differentiation hypothesis, however, is not inconsistent with an unlearning hypothesis (Postman, 1961a). Differentiation of the two lists may develop as a result of increased practice on the interpolated task, whereas unlearning may progress simultaneously and bring about changes in the relative strengths of the competing response tendencies. Accordingly, the critical evidence for an unlearning process had to come from studies which could separate

analytically RI caused by unlearning and RI caused by differentiation. An important step in this direction occurred when the method of modified free recall (MFR) was introduced by Underwood (1948).

It was noted in the previous chapter that MFR provides a way of measuring the relative strengths of first- and second-list associations following paired-associate learning in any paradigm containing common stimulus but different response terms such as the A-B, A-C paradigm. Using the MFR procedure, Underwood (1948) found that the *relative* frequency of first-list responses increased during a 24-hr. retention interval, whereas the frequency of second-list responses declined. He interpreted these findings in terms of an analogy with spontaneous recovery, in which first-list responses undergo extinction (unlearning) during the interpolated task but recover with the passage of time. Although Underwood believed that these findings supported the usefulness of an unlearning concept, the data do not offer unequivocal support because the MFR procedure does not allow one to conclude that first-list responses are actually unavailable; rather, the procedure provides only a relative measure of response strength because S is asked to recall the dominant response, that is, the first response that "comes to mind." Accordingly, first-list responses could still be available despite the fact that they are weaker than second-list responses.

Subsequent studies by Briggs (1954) and by Briggs, Thompson, and Brogden (1954) confirmed Underwood's general findings, although any conclusions about the usefulness of the unlearning concept was still limited by the restrictions placed on the MFR procedure. Briggs (1954) required Ss to learn two successive paired-associate lists employing an A-B, A-C paradigm, and found that the mean number of B responses recalled decreased systematically as a function of increased trials on the A-C list. Accordingly, although the loss in A-B associations *could* be interpreted as evi-

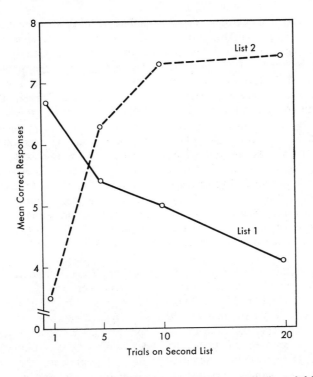

Figure 20-2. Mean number of responses correctly recalled and identified with stimulus and list in the A-B, A-C paradigm. (Adapted with permission from Barnes, J. M., and Underwood, B. J. "Fate" of first-list associations in transfer theory. *J. exp. Psychol.*, 1959, **58**, 97–105.)

dence for unlearning, this interpretation was not unequivocal since the A-B associations might still be present but were dominated by the stronger A-C associations at recall.

A critical test of the unlearning hypothesis, uncontaminated by confounding or by methodological limitations, was provided by Barnes and Underwood (1959). Their study was similar to that of Briggs (1954) except that an important methodological refinement was added, namely the use of a modified-modified free recall (MMFR) procedure. The MMFR procedure is one in which *S* is requested to recall responses from *both* lists so that actual availability of both response systems as well as relative strengths of response can be determined. Independent groups of *S*s learned two successive paired-associate lists in accord-

ance with either the A-B, A-C paradigm or the A-B, A-B′ paradigm. Following first-list learning *S*s learned a second list for either one, five, ten, or twenty trials and were then tested for recall. The *S*s were shown a list of all stimulus items and asked to write down the two responses (B and C) that had been associated with each stimulus item.

The results of the recall test following A-B, A-C learning are shown in Fig. 20-2. It can be seen that with an increase in the number of trials on the second list there is an increase in the number of second-list responses correctly recalled, whereas there is a simultaneous decrease in the number of first-list responses recalled. These data strongly support the notion of unlearning because the recall of first-list responses systematically declined as a function of the amount of interpolated learning, despite the fact that Ss were given ample opportunity to recall responses from both lists.

In contrast, the results of the recall test following A-B, A-B′ learning show no significant decline of first-list responses as a function of interpolated learning. Indeed, the B responses are almost completely available to S after twenty interpolated trials, suggesting almost no unlearning. Barnes and Underwood interpreted these data in terms of a mediation hypothesis in which the chain A-B-B′ is acquired. Most of the Ss reported using B as a mediator to learn A-B′, and B was more often recalled first until twenty interpolated trials were given. Subsequent support for a response mediation interpretation was obtained by Postman (1962b) who also found that first-list associations maintained their high strength in the A-B, A-B′ paradigm. Dallett (1964) has reported evidence, however, for some unlearning in an A-B, A-B′ paradigm, and Dallett and D'Andrea (1965) reported some reduction in RI with Ss given instructions to mediate, using an A-B, A-C paradigm.

More recent studies by Goggin (1963) and by McGovern (1964) have provided additional support for the concept of unlearning by demonstrating not only a loss in associative strength, but also a loss in forward, backward, and contextual associations. Similarly, the fact that first-list associations recover with the passage of time (for example, Birnbaum, 1965; Koppenaal, 1963), using the MMFR procedure, is a further source of support for an unlearning, or extinction, mechanism. Moreover, Ellington and Kausler (1965) have demonstrated extinction of backward associations in an A-B, C-B paradigm and loss of availability of the stimuli themselves. Finally, Garskof and Sandak (1964) have demonstrated unlearning processes using recognition memory as well as recall tasks.

Additions to Interference Theory. In addition to response competition, unlearning, and differentiation, other components of interference have been identified. One such addition may be seen in the distinction between *specific* response competition and *generalized* response competition proposed by Newton and Wickens (1956). Specific response competition refers to the displacement of a correct response by an incorrect response from the interpolated list during recall; it is in this sense that the term *response competition* has been used in previous discussion. In contrast, generalized response competition may be identified as Ss' tendency to continue responding from whatever list he last practiced, which defines a kind of "set."

Direct evidence for the usefulness of the concept of generalized response competition has been provided by Postman and Riley (1959). In their study, Ss learned serial lists of nonsense syllables in both RI and PI paradigms as a function of the degree of original and interfering learning. Fig. 20-3 presents the serial position curves for the RI and PI groups at recall. The figure shows that the curve for the RI group was considerably flatter than that of the PI group on trial 1. The flattening of the curve is most evident at the beginning of the list with the usual primacy effect being absent. On the second relearning trial the curve of the RI group begins to take on the typical bowed serial-position curve and is more comparable to the corresponding curve of the PI group. They attribute the considerable, and extremely transitory, RI for the initial part of the list (on trial 1) to generalized response competition, that is, the "set" or tendency to continue responding from the last list learned. This tendency, however, rapidly dissipates, allowing for resumption of the typical serial position curve. Although Postman (1961a) admits that the distinction between generalized and specific response competition may not always be sharp, it is still a useful concept in interference theory in that it emphasizes the fact that considerable competition may occur even when there is no evident similar-

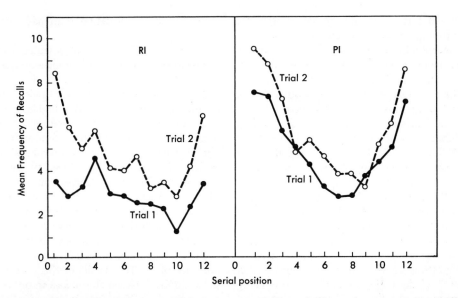

Figure 20-3. Average serial position curves of RI and PI work groups at recall. There were twenty trials of OL. (Adapted with permission from Postman, L. The present status of interference theory. In C. H. Cofer (Ed.), *Verbal learning and verbal behavior.* New York: McGraw-Hill, 1961a, 152–179.)

ity between the stimulus items in the two lists.

It is also possible to apply the notion of generalized response competition to the tendency to lose first-list associations, as revealed in an MMFR test. In other words, *S*s' tendency to adopt a "set" of giving responses from the last list learned may simultaneously inhibit the giving of first-list responses because they are viewed as inappropriate. Therefore, the possibility that generalized response competition rather than unlearning was primarily responsible for the loss of first-list associations was considered by Postman and Stark (1965). In order to test this possibility, they employed a procedure designed to minimize generalized response competition by reinstating the set to give first-list responses through use of a recitation procedure. They reasoned that the continued loss of first-list associations under conditions designed to minimize generalized response competition would, in turn, strengthen the importance of an unlearning interpretation of the loss

of first-list associations. Despite instructions designed to maximize the tendency to give first-list responses, the loss of first-list associations was not reduced. Consequently, their experiment added to the evidence that the loss of first-list associations while using a MMFR procedure may be attributed to unlearning rather than to performance set.

Postman and Stark's (1965) conclusions were restricted to paired-associate learning. As a consequence, Keppel (1966) quickly noted that it was still possible for different mechanisms of RI to operate in paired-associate and serial learning, with both unlearning and competition operating in paired-associate learning, and competition alone operating in serial learning. Using a serial version of the MMFR test, however, Keppel was able to demonstrate evidence for unlearning in serial learning and thus was able to extend the generality of the unlearning concept. In a further experiment, Keppel attempted to specify what is unlearned in serial learning in a manner analogous to McGovern's (1964) analysis of what is unlearned in paired-associate learning. Keppel noted that one may conceptualize the stimulus in serial learning as being a chain that involves the immediately preceding item, or a compound chain, a position adopted by Young (1962), or the stimulus may be conceived to be the serial position of the item itself. Testing implications of these alternative conceptions of the stimulus, Keppel concluded that a serial position hypothesis was better supported by the data.

An important development in recent years has been the growing awareness of the importance of PI as a source of interference. It was commonly believed for many years that the principal source of interference in forgetting stemmed from RI; however, in 1957 Underwood presented a convincing argument for the importance of PI, and demonstrated that PI made a much greater contribution to forgetting than had been earlier recognized.

Underwood (1957) demonstrated the significance of PI by re-examining a number of experiments in retention in which it was possible to relate list recall as a function of the number of prior lists that Ss had learned. The studies re-examined used a 24-hr. retention interval, and the retention loss obtained had typically been interpreted as evidence for RI effects produced by interference from materials learned during the 24-hr. retention interval. When recall was plotted as a function of the number of prior lists learned, however, the curve revealed a systematic decline in recall as a function of prior lists learned, attesting to the importance of PI. The results of this plot are shown in Fig. 20-4 which shows a smoothed curve fitted to the data of the various investigators.

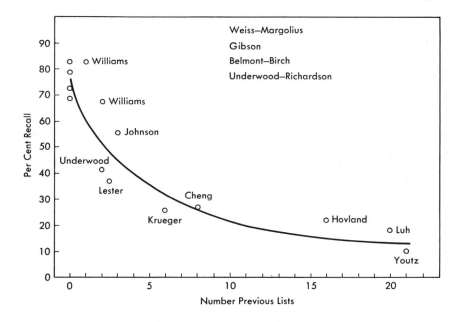

Figure 20-4. **Recall as a function of number of previous lists learned as determined from a number of studies. From left to right: Weiss and Margolius, Gibson, Belmont and Birch, Underwood and Richardson, Williams, Underwood, Lester, Johnson, Krueger, Cheng, Hovland, Luh, Youtz.** (Adapted with permission from Underwood, B. J. Interference and forgetting. *Psychol. Rev.*, 1957, **64**, 49–60.)

Underwood's analysis calls attention to the importance of extraexperimental factors in interference, that is, factors outside of the laboratory situation; moreover, he indicates that most of the extraexperimental interference is likely to stem from PI rather than RI, because the opportunities for acquiring competing habits are much greater during the long time interval prior to participation in an experiment compared with the relatively short time interval between second-list learning and the test for retention. In brief, *S* brings to the laboratory a long history of acquiring verbal habits which may clearly be a potent source of PI.

The recognition of the importance of PI and extraexperimental sources of interference led, in turn, to further efforts at expanding interference theory by Underwood and Postman (1960). Their principal effort was directed at specifying the implications of interference theory for the forgetting of different kinds of materials, which led to efforts at identifying some of the specific factors that could produce extraexperimental sources of interference. This analysis specified two sources of interference in language habits, those of *letter-sequence* interference and *unit-sequence* interference. Letter-sequence interference is likely to occur when the verbal items of a retention experiment contain sequences of letters that are different from those characteristic of *S*s' language habits. In turn, unit-sequence interference is likely to occur when the verbal unit employed, such as a CVC, elicits associations that differ from and compete with associations already existing as a result of language habits.

A number of empirical implications follow from the theoretical analysis provided by Underwood and Postman (1960). Although several of these implications have received support (Postman, 1961b), some discord has been noted in efforts to test the predicted relationship between meaningfulness and forgetting that follows from this analysis (Ekstrand and Underwood, 1965; Underwood and Keppel, 1963). The theory proposed by Underwood and Postman (1960) specifies a relationship between meaningfulness and forgetting, in which forgetting is believed to be directly related to meaningfulness with verbal units such as words, but inversely related to meaningfulness with letter sequences. Ekstrand and Underwood (1965) failed to verify this prediction in a free-learning situation and concluded that the Underwood-Postman theory is inadequate in its present form to account for these findings.

A Bit of Caution. It seems clear that the data support some form of an interference theory. Moreover, it seems reasonable to conclude that a fully developed interference theory will specify the role of the various components such as response competition (specific and general), unlearning, differentiation, and extraexperimental sources of interference in a great variety of learning situations. This is certainly the current direction of much research effort. It is tempting, perhaps, not only to conclude that interference theory is the dominant theoretical scheme, which it is, but also to conclude that it can account for all forgetting. This latter conclusion, however, would be premature, for although the data provide little support for alternative theories of forgetting, such as decay theory, it is not yet possible to rule out entirely the possibility of some decay in addition to interference. A similar point has been made by Melton (1961), who warns that we are not yet in a position to treat all long-term memory loss as the result of interference alone. Similarly, evidence from consolidation studies have suggested to some (for example, Glickman, 1961) that interference alone may not be sufficient to account for all forgetting; however, Lewis (1965) contends that adequate evidence for a consolidation notion cannot be derived from studies of electroconvulsive shock and consolidation.

Conditions of Learning
Which Influence Retention

Retention is influenced not only by interference factors, but also by variables in the original-learning situation itself. In this section the contribution of five of these variables is described: degree of learning, speed of learning, intralist similarity, meaningfulness, and distribution of practice.

Degree of Learning. The degree of learning of a given task has long been known to be a potent variable influencing retention and, more recently, the importance of this variable has been reemphasized by Underwood and Keppel (1963), who have taken the position that it is the principal original-learning variable influencing retention.

The classic study of Krueger (1929) revealed the effects of varying amounts of overlearning on retention. Ss learned a list of nouns to a criterion of one perfect recitation, or were provided additional practice bringing them to a level of either 50 or 100 per cent overlearning. Following learning, Ss were given a relearning test at various intervals of time ranging from one to twenty-eight days. The results revealed that overlearning improved retention; a diminishing returns effect was evident, however, in that the gain in retention from 50 to 100 per cent overlearning was less than the gain from the one perfect recitation criterion to 50 per cent overlearning. In a recent study Postman (1962a) replicated Krueger's study and was able to confirm his findings.

The fact that degree of original learning is a potent variable in retention has been long known, and, accordingly, researchers have typically been more interested in whether *other* original-learning variables influence retention when the degree of original learning is controlled. We noted in the last chapter that if differences in the terminal strength of learning exist as a result of some original-learning variable,

any observed difference in retention loss may be attributed to differences in degree of learning rather than to the variable studied. Moreover, it was noted that efforts at equating the degree of learning by simply varying the number of trials were inadequate (Underwood, 1964b), because differences in the rate of growth of associative strength in original learning may produce inequalities in terminal associative strength. Several procedures for equating for degree of learning (Anderson, 1963; Underwood, 1964b) were noted in the last chapter. The point to be emphasized here is that the possible confounding which may arise from a failure to control degree of learning enters into the interpretation of many retention studies. Indeed, Underwood's (1964b) analysis of the problems involved in controlling and equating degree of original learning reveals that a number of the earlier studies of retention may have confounded degree of learning with some additional original-learning variable, so that inappropriate interpretations of the data were possible. Accordingly, it is necessary to be cautious in drawing inferences from studies which have failed to control for degree of original learning or from studies in which the equating procedure can be judged to be inadequate.

Speed of Learning. Studies attempting to relate speed of learning to retention provide a good example of the confounding discussed in the previous section. An early study by Gillette (1936) suggested that fast learners retain more than slow learners under conditions in which it was *assumed* that fast and slow learners had learned an equal amount of material. Gillette used an adjusted learning procedure, in which items of a list are "dropped out" after being learned to some given criterion. Although this procedure is not satisfactory, a more serious difficulty with Gillette's study was the assumption that the terminal associative strength for all items learned was the same for both slow and fast learners.

In a re-examination of data obtained from other studies, Underwood (1954b) showed that this assumption was not, in fact, reasonable. In addition, he demonstrated that an appropriate adjusting procedure which involved successive-probability analysis of the items learned indicated that fast and slow learners show no difference in retention when associative strength at the end of learning is equivalent for the two groups.

Intralist Similarity. It is a common finding that as a list of verbal items such as words or nonsense syllables is made increasingly similar, the learning of such a list becomes more difficult. Presumably, the effect of intralist similarity on learning can be accounted for in terms of the increased generalization tendencies among the items in the list (Gibson, 1942). In contrast, increased intralist similarity does not appear to affect retention. For example, Underwood (1952) varied the similarity of lists of nonsense syllables and failed to find any effect of similarity on list recall 24 hr. after learning. In a review of the studies varying intralist similarity, Underwood (1954a) concluded that recall and intralist similarity do not appear to be related. Where they have been related, it appears that the confounding variable of degree of original learning was present.

Meaningfulness. A similar kind of issue arises when the effect of the meaningfulness of verbal materials on retention is examined. The longstanding view has been that meaningful material is retained better than nonmeaningful material (McGeoch and Irion, 1952). More recent studies, however, suggest that meaningfulness may not be a factor influencing retention when degree of learning is controlled (Ekstrand and Underwood, 1965; Underwood and Keppel, 1963).

Similarly, Underwood and Richardson (1956) failed to find significant differences in retention between items of low and high association value. In their study Ss learned lists of nonsense syllables of either low or high association value and then relearned them after 24 hr. Using both raw recall scores and successive-probability analyses of the learning data (Underwood, 1954b), they reported no difference in retention of the low- and high-meaningful items.

In contrast, Lindley (1963b) has reported that high-meaningful trigrams are better retained than low-meaningful trigrams in short-term memory. This study, however, makes the dubious assumption that the items are equal in associative strength at the end of learning because exposure time was equal. As Underwood (1964b) has noted, this assumption is probably incorrect and consequently we cannot be confident of Lindley's conclusions regarding meaningfulness and retention.

Finally, Ekstrand and Underwood (1965) have investigated the effect of item meaningfulness on retention by using a free-learning procedure. Ss learned lists of either word pairs or letter pairs of high or low meaningfulness, and after a 24-hr. retention interval were given tests of recall and relearning. Using two different methods for controlling the degree of original learning, they failed to find significant differences in retention between low- and high-meaningful word pairs or letter pairs. These findings not only reveal the importance of controlling for the degree of learning in retention studies, but provide further support for the view espoused by Underwood and Keppel (1963) that the degree of learning is the major variable affecting retention.

Distribution of Practice. A similar problem regarding the control of original learning also arises in investigations of the effect of distribution of practice on retention. Furthermore, inconsistencies in the literature have been substantial so that it is difficult to draw a firm conclusion about this variable based on many studies. Part of this difficulty is due to the failure of earlier investigations to control properly for possible differences in degree of original learning. Nevertheless, a recent study by Keppel (1964), which used appropriate procedures for controlling degree of original learning, provided substantial support for the position that distributed practice does facilitate retention for a variety of retention tasks.

Keppel required his *S*s to learn a series of four successive lists in accordance with the A-B, A-C, A-D, A-E paradigm. The first three lists were learned under identical conditions, and the variable of distributed versus massed practice was introduced in the fourth list. A distributed practice condition was compared against effects produced by two conditions of massed practice. In the first experiment, distributed practice was found to facilitate retention when measured by either recall or relearning, with an interaction between the retention interval and conditions of distribution; this interaction was seen in the rapid loss in retention under the two massed-practice conditions as compared with the slow loss in retention under distributed practice. Moreover, a follow-up of *S*s a month later revealed that the distributed practice condition still yielded superior retention.

A second experiment by Keppel indicated that distributed practice also facilitated the retention of lists conforming to the A-B$_r$ and A-C paradigms, with the effect being more pronounced for the A-B$_r$ paradigm. Finally, a third experiment indicated that distributed practice facilitated retention in short-term memory using retention intervals of 0, 30, and 90 sec.

Keppel interpreted these results by concluding that distribution of practice given during the last list of the four-list sequence allowed for greater extinction of the prior associations acquired in the first three lists, a prediction made by Underwood, Keppel, and Schulz (1962). This greater extinction, or unlearning, allowed for better retention of the last list learned because fewer responses were available to interfere with last-list retention.

Organization Factors and Coding Processes in Retention

In addition to interference factors and original-learning factors, retention is also influenced by the manner in which individuals organize and code materials. Organization variables have long been the primary interest of Gestalt psychologists (for example, Katona, 1940) and those influenced by this position. Due in large part to the considerable influence of Miller's (1956) important paper on encoding processes in memory, increasing attention has been given to the role of these variables in retention. In this section we shall examine several examples of this work, including coding processes in verbal and perceptual learning, recoding and the immediate memory span, and clustering in recall.

Coding Processes in Verbal and Perceptual Learning. The process by which an individual learns a list of paired-associate items can involve not only the establishment of associative connections between two items which make up each pair, but also the "transformation" of these items into some modified or new unit so as to facilitate their learning. For example, an item such as FAV, a syllable from Glaze's list having a 93 per cent association value, might be transformed into "favor" so that in a subsequent recall test the retrieval of FAV might occur as a result of *S* first remembering "favor," which serves as a prompt for the recall of FAV. The process by which an item is transformed, or coded, can vary in a number of ways, and the process can readily vary with *S*'s past history. For example, the item JAX is a Glaze syllable having an association value of 47 per cent, and is also the name of a beer sold in the Southern states of the United States. Accordingly, if *S* were familiar with this trade name, he might transform JAX into "beer" and then retrieve the syllable by first remembering "beer" and then recalling JAX.

A classical study that reveals the way in which coding may distort or modify the recall of visual forms was conducted by Carmichael, Hogen, and Walter (1932). Ss were shown visual forms and asked to attach a label to each form. Half of the Ss received one set of labels for each of the forms and the remaining Ss received an entirely different set of labels. Following this practice, the Ss were instructed to reproduce (draw) the forms. The Ss' drawings were frequently judged to have been influenced by the labels, and the results are today viewed as evidence of coding processes in perceptual memory.

More recently, Homan (1966) has provided further evidence for the role of coding processes in perceptual memory. He reasoned, in accordance with predictions from an hypothesis proposed by Ellis and Muller (1964), that the recognition of visual forms following various kinds of paired-associate practice ought to vary with the ease with which Ss tended to make implicit associations to the forms. This hypothesis contends that attaching distinctive verbal labels to forms will facilitate their subsequent recognition, relative to a control condition given observation practice, when the stimuli do not readily evoke implicit associations, that is, when the forms are difficult to code. In contrast, when the forms are easy to code, the attaching of labels does not facilitate subsequent recognition over and above that improvement provided by observation practice. By varying experimentally conditions designed to increase the likelihood of Ss' tendency to give implicit associative responses to visual forms, Homan found that subsequent form recognition was improved. Improvement was greatest when responses that were "representative" of the forms were made available to Ss prior to their receiving practice in observing and discriminating among the forms.

Lindley (1963a, 1963b) has provided evidence for coding processes in paired-associate verbal learning, and has demonstrated that coding can inhibit as well as facilitate retention. Underwood and Erlebacher (1965) have reported evidence for coding in free learning and paired-associate learning, and have noted that the effects of coding systems are maximal when decoding is simple. More recently, Battig (1966b) has reviewed the evidence for coding processes in paired-associate learning and concluded that coding processes play an important role in this kind of task even where extensive attempts have been made to eliminate such processes. One significant implication of the study of coding processes is that their study represents a questioning of the usefulness of the methodology and concepts growing out of traditional S-R associationistic interpretations of behavior (Battig, 1966b). The extent to which associationistic concepts can account for more complex processes in human learning and retention has emerged as a central issue, with some such as Cofer (1966) attempting to account for organizational complexity in terms of traditional S-R associationistic concepts, whereas others such as Tulving (1962, 1966) have taken the view that more complex principles, like "subjective organization," are involved. It should be clear, of course, as Kendler (1966) points out, that there is no disagreement about retention being influenced by organizational factors; the principal theoretical issue concerns the nature of the processes or mechanisms that bring about organization.

Recoding and the Immediate Memory Span. The operation of coding processes can also be seen in the immediate memory span. The immediate memory span refers to the number of items that can be immediately recalled after a single presentation. A test for digit memory span appears frequently on intelligence tests, and the normal adult can recall about seven items accurately 50 per cent of the time. The memory span, however, can be increased considerably if the items can be grouped or organized in some fashion.

The fact that individuals can code items in the immediate memory span so as to recall considerably more than seven items has been noted by Miller (1956). Miller has proposed what he calls a *chunking hypothesis*, which contends that individuals remember not only items of information, but also "chunks" of information which enable an increase in the immediate memory span. Moreover, according to Miller, individuals appear to remember a constant number of chunks or items regardless of the amount of information in each chunk. An example of coding is reported by Miller in which one of his associates studied the manner in which a long series of digits could be coded by assigning single numbers to groups of three numbers. For example, the series 010110100100110101101 could be broken up into groups such as 010-110-100-100-110-101-101 and then coded by assigning each group a number. For instance 100 could be coded as "4" and 101 as "5." In this fashion the individual could recode the entire series of twenty-one numbers into a series of seven. By recalling the rule or coding operation, the entire series could then be recalled. The manner in which such coding operations are applied to units or sequences of information are numerous and may, of course, be highly idiosyncratic. For example, a faculty colleague at New Mexico, upon receiving his new telephone number 277-4121, remarked that it was easy to remember because 41 was his chronological age and 21 was the age that he would like to be.

Evidence for coding processes is also seen in short-term memory (Murdock, 1961). Single words were found to be much more resistant to forgetting than were items consisting of three consonants. As Melton (1963) has noted, Murdock's findings suggest that the slope of the short-term memory function is strongly determined by the number of "chunks" in the item to be remembered. Similarly, Lindley and his colleagues (Lindley, 1963a and 1963b; Schaub and Lindley, 1964; Lindley and Nedler, 1965; Lindley, 1965) have examined the effects of recoding cues on short-term memory for trigrams, and have shown that recoding cues facilitate short-term memory. These studies have been designed to explore the nature and complexity of recoding cues in short-term memory, and have demonstrated (Lindley, 1965) that easy-to-decode cues have more of a facilitative effect on memory than do difficult-to-decode cues.

Clustering in Recall. Another way in which coding and organizational factors presumably influence memory is seen in studies of clustering in free recall (Cofer, 1965, 1966; Cohen, 1966; Tulving, 1966), although the interpretation of the obtained clustering in these experiments is in dispute. In free recall, or free learning, a list of words is presented to *S* and he is asked to recall the items in any order in which they occur to him. Interest in this procedure typically centers around the *order* in which the items are recalled, as compared to whatever organization existed among the items as originally presented (Cofer, 1965).

This line of investigation was initiated by Bousfield (1953) and by Jenkins and Russell (1952). These investigators were interested in the manner in which response clustering occurred in free recall. Bousfield and his students were interested in *category clustering*, the tendency of *S*s to organize items into categories representing a common class of events. For example, a list of forty items might be given to an *S*, the items composed, say of ten birds, ten cities, ten foods, and ten items of furniture. The items are presented in random order and the extent to which they are grouped together in recall is taken as evidence for category clustering. In turn, Jenkins and Russell (1952) were interested in *associative clustering*, the tendency of *S*s to recall items in clusters which are known to have associative connections. Items are presented to *S* in random order and the tendency to cluster items like *boy*, *girl*, which are known to be associated, is taken as evidence for associative clustering.

Bousfield initially interpreted category clustering by assuming the activation of superordinates by the items which were presented. For example, the items *table*, *chair*, *bed* might elicit the superordinate *furniture*. In turn, the superordinate is assumed to control the order of emission of the items in recall so that they appeared in clusters. In contrast, Jenkins and Russell did not employ this kind of explanation because the clustering they observed was based presumably on only associative factors. Indeed, Jenkins, Mink, and Russell (1958) have demonstrated that such clustering is a function of the associative strength among the items employed, and Deese (1959) has shown the number of words recalled was a function of the interitem associative strength.

Although Bousfield initially interpreted category clustering in terms of superordinates, subsequent studies (for example, Bousfield, Cohen, and Whitmarsh, 1958) led him to shift from a superordinate to an associative interpretation of clustering. In this study they found marked category clustering among lists containing items that

were high-frequency associates and relatively little clustering among categories containing low-frequency associates. Such a finding suggested that associative frequency might be a more important determinant of clustering than the use of superordinates. Moreover, this and related findings subsequently suggested to Cofer (1965) that the distinction between category and associative clustering may not be a useful one in that Ss may use either or both of these attacks in organizing material for recall.

Current research in clustering has been directed toward identifying the variables that influence recall and toward testing alternative interpretations of clustering. In a significant paper Cofer (1965) has summarized some of the important factors which influence clustering and has provided additional support for an associative interpretation of clustering. At present the major theoretical controversy which is beginning to take shape revolves around the issue regarding the extent to which associative interpretations of clustering are adequate, and to what extent additional kinds of interpretations are necessary to account for the data.

Glossary

backward association. An association formed, as in paired-associate learning, between a response and a stimulus item, so that the response item acquires some tendency to elicit the stimulus item.

clustering. The tendency to order or organize items during recall into some grouping or sequence that differs from the order present during original learning of the items, usually in terms of categorical or associational bases.

coding. The process by which an item or group of items is transformed into some modified or new unit so as to facilitate retention.

component analysis. A conceptual and methodological separation of some gross

process or phenomenon into its sub processes.

decay theory. A theory of forgetting that contends that forgetting is due to some autonomous decay of memory traces.

forward association. An association formed, as in paired-associate learning, between a stimulus and a response item, as evidenced by the tendency of that stimulus to elicit its response mate.

interference theory. A theory of forgetting that contends that events are forgotten because other learning interferes with or prevents these events from being remembered.

learning-to-learn. A progressive improvement in the case with which some new task is learned as a result of practice with a series of related or similar tasks.

mediation. The process by which implicit verbal responses, or associations, bring about transfer effects.

mixed-list design. Design in which *S*s learn both experimental and control items combined in a single list.

modified-free recall (MFR). A test of recall following the learning of two lists having common stimulus items, in which *S* is instructed to recall the *first* response that "comes to mind."

modified-modified free recall (MMFR). A test of recall, following the learning of two lists having common stimulus items, in which *S* is instructed to recall responses from *both* lists.

nonspecific transfer. Transfer of training resulting from general practice effects as distinct from specific features of the tasks.

Osgood transfer surface. A three-dimensional representation of the effects of stimulus and response similarity on transfer.

proactive inhibition (PI). Source of forgetting caused by some event learned *prior* to the learning of another event which is given a retention test.

response competition. The tendency of first-list responses, as in paired-associate learning, to intrude or displace responses during second-list learning.

retroactive inhibition (RI). Source of forgetting caused by some event learned *after* the learning of another event which is given a retention test.

short-term memory. The retention of items or events over very short time periods, usually less than 30 sec.

transfer paradigms. Schematic models that describe the interlist relationships between the original list and the transfer-task list. Frequently employed paradigms include the A-B, A-C, stimuli same, responses different; A-B, C-B, stimuli different, responses same; A-B, C-D, both stimuli and responses different; A-B, A-B$_r$, stimuli same, responses same but repaired; and, A-B, A-B′, stimuli same, responses similar. Three- and four-stage paradigms, including stimulus-equivalence and response-equivalence paradigms, are employed in the study of mediation. Other paradigms may be developed for the study of additional phenomena; for example, A-B, C-A, and A-B, B-C paradigms have been used to study response competition in backward associations.

unlearning. The loss or extinction of first-list responses during second-list learning as found, say, in the A-B, A-C paradigm.

warm-up. The transitory facilitation in learning some task as the result of prior practice with another task.

References

Adams, J. A. Multiple versus single problem training in human problem solving. *J. exp. Psychol.*, 1954, **48**, 15–18.

Ammons, R. B. Acquisition of motor skill: II. Rotary pursuit performance with continuous practice before and after a single rest. *J. exp. Psychol.*, 1947, **37**, 393–411.

Anderson, N. H. Comparison of different populations: Resistance to extinction and transfer. *Psychol. Rev.*, 1963, **70**, 162–179.

Arnoult, M. D. Transfer of predifferentiation training in simple and multiple shape discrimination. *J. exp. Psychol.*, 1953, **45**, 401–409.

Arnoult, M. D. Recognition of shapes following paired associates pretraining. In G. Finch & F. Cameron (Eds.), *Symposium on Air Force human engineering, personnel, and train-research.* Washington, D.C. (NAS-NRC Publ. No. 455). National Academy of sciences—National Research Council, **1**, 1956, Pp. 1–9.

Arnoult, M. D. Stimulus predifferentiation: Some generalization and hypothesis. *Psychol. Bull.*, 1957, **54**, 339–350.

Atwater, S. K. Proactive inhibition and associative facilitation as affected by degree of prior learning. *J. exp. Psychol.*, 1953, **46**, 400–405.

Ausubel, D. P., Robbins, L., & Blake, E., Jr. Retroactive inhibition and facilitation in the learning of school materials. *J. educ. Psychol.*, 1957, **48**, 334–343.

Ausubel, D. P. Cognitive structure and the facilitation of meaningful verbal learning. *J. Tchr. Educ.*, 1963, **14**, 217–221.

Bahrick, H. P. The ebb of retention. *Psychol. Rev.*, 1965, **72**, 60–73.

Barch, A. M., & Lewis, D. The effect of task difficulty and amount of practice on proactive transfer. *J. exp. Psychol.*, 1954, **48**, 134–142.

Barclay, A. Objective mediators in paired-associate learning. *Amer. J. Psychol.*, 1961, **74**, 373–383.

Barclay, A. Mediated transfer in verbal learning. *Psychol. Rep.*, 1963, **12**, 751–756.

Barnes, J. M., & Underwood, B. J. "Fate" of first-list associations in transfer theory. *J. exp. Psychol.*, 1959, **58**, 97–105.

Bartlett, F. C. *Remembering: A study in experimental and social psychology.* New York: Macmillan; Cambridge, England: Cambridge Univer. Press, 1932.

Battig, W. F. Facilitation and interference. In E. A. Bilodeau (Ed.), *Acquisition of skill.* New York: Academic Press, 1966a. Pp. 215–244.

Battig, W. F. Evidence for coding processes in "rote" paired-associate learning. *J. verb. Learn. verb. Behav.*, 1966b, **5**, 177–181.

Behar, I. Learned avoidance of nonreward. *Psychol. Rep.*, 1961, **9**, 43–52.

Bennett, T. L. Reinforcement and feedback in perceptual learning. Unpublished master's thesis, University of New Mexico, 1966.

Bernbach, H. A. Decision processes in memory. *Psychol. Rev.*, 1967, **74**, 462–480.

Bevan, W. Perceptual learning: an overview. *J. gen. Psychol.*, 1961, **64**, 69–99.

Bilodeau, E. A. Retention. In E. A. Bilodeau (Ed.), *Acquisition of skill.* New York: Academic Press, 1966. Pp. 315–350.

Bilodeau, E. A., & Levy, C. M. Long-term memory as a function of retention time and other conditions of training and recall. *Psychol. Rev.*, 1964, **71**, 27–41.

Birge, Jane S. The role of verbal responses in transfer. Unpublished doctoral dissertation, Yale University, 1941.

Birnbaum, I. M. Long-term retention of first-list associations in the A-B, A-C paradigm. *J. verb. Learn. verb. Behav.*, 1965, **4**, 515–520.

Bousfield, W. A. The occurrence of clustering in the recall of randomly arranged associates. *J. gen. Psychol.*, 1953, **49**, 229–240.

Bousfield, W. A., Cohen, B. H., & Whitmarsh, G. A. Associative clustering in the recall of words of different taxonomic frequencies of occurrence. *Psychol. Rep.*, 1958, **4**, 39–44.

Briggs, G. E. Acquisition, extinction and recovery functions in retroactive inhibition. *J. exp. Psychol.*, 1954, **47**, 285–293.

Briggs, G. E. Retroactive inhibition as a function of degree of original and interpolated learning. *J. exp. Psychol.*, 1957, **53**, 60–67.

Briggs, G. E., Thompson, R. F., & Brogden, W. J. Retention functions in reproductive inhibition. *J. exp. Psychol.*, 1954, **48**, 419–428.

Briggs, G. E., & Waters, L. K. Training and transfer as a function of component interaction. *J. exp. Psychol.*, 1958, **56**, 492–500.

Britt, S. H. Retroactive inhibition: a review of the literature. *Psychol. Bull.*, 1935, **32**, 381–440.

Broadbent, D. E. A mechanical model for human attention and immediate memory. *Psychol. Rev.*, 1957, **64**, 205–215.

Broadbent, D. E. Flow of information within the organism. *J. verb. Learn. verb. Behav.*, 1963, **2**, 34–39.

Brown, J. S. Generalization and discrimination. In David I. Mostofsky (Ed.), *Stimulus generalization.* Stanford, Calif.: Stanford Univer. Press, 1965. Pp. 7–23.

Bruce, R. W. Conditions of transfer of training. *J. exp. Psychol.*, 1933, **16**, 343–361.

Bruner, J. S., Mandler, J. M., O'Dowd, D., & Wallach, M. A. The role of overlearning and drive level in reversal learning. *J. comp. physiol. Psychol.*, 1958, **51**, 607–613.

Bugelski, B. R. *The psychology of learning.* New York: Holt, Rinehart, and Winston, 1956.

Bugelski, B. R., and Cadwaller, T. C. A reappraisal of the transfer and retroaction surface. *J. exp. Psychol.*, 1956, **52**, 360–366.

Bugelski, B. R., & Scharlock, D. P. An experimental demonstration of unconscious mediated association. *J. exp. Psychol.*, 1952, **44**, 334–338.

Bunch, M. E. The amount of transfer in rational learning as a function of time. *J. comp. Psychol.*, 1936, **22**, 325–337.

Bunch, M. E. Transfer of training in the mastery of an antagonistic habit after varying intervals of time. *J. comp. Psychol.*, 1939, **28**, 189–200.

Bunch, M. E. The measurement of retention by the relearning method. *Psychol. Rev.*, 1941, **48**, 450–456.

Bunch, M. E. Cumulative transfer of training under different temporal conditions. *J. comp. Psychol.*, 1944, **37**, 265–272.

Bunch, M. E., & Lang, E. S. The amount of transfer of training from partial learning after varying intervals of time. *J. comp. Psychol.*, 1939, **27**, 449–459.

Bunch, M. E., & McCraven, V. Temporal course of transfer in the learning of memory material. *J. comp. Psychol.*, 1938, **25**, 481–496.

Campbell, V., & Freeman, J. T. Some functions of experimentally-induced language in perceptual learning. *Percept. mot. Skills*, 1955, **1**, 71–79.

Cantor, G. N. Effects of three types of pretraining on discrimination learning in preschool children. *J. exp. Psychol.*, 1955, **49**, 339–342.

Cantor, J. H. Transfer of stimulus pretraining to motor paired-associate and discrimination learning tasks. In L. P. Lipsitt & C. C. Spiker (Eds.), *Advances in child development and behavior.* New York: Academic Press, 1965. Pp. 19–56.

Carlin, Jean E. Word-association strength as a variable in verbal paired-associate learning. Unpublished doctoral dissertation, University of Minnesota, 1958.

Carlson, J. B., & Duncan, C. P. A study of autonomous change in the memory trace by the method of recognition. *Amer. J. Psychol.*, 1955, **68**, 280–284.

Carmichael, L., Hogan, H. P., & Walter, A. A. An experimental study of the effect of language on the reproduction of visually perceived form. *J. exp. Psychol.*, 1932, **15**, 73–86.

Clark, H. J. Recognition memory for random shapes as a function of complexity, association value, and delay. *J. exp. Psychol.*, 1965, **69**, 590–595.

Cofer, C. N. On some factors in the organizational characteristics of free recall. *Amer. Psychologist*, 1965, **20**, 261–272.

Cofer, C. N. Some evidence for coding processes derived from clustering in free recall. *J. verb. Learn. verb. Behav.*, 1966, **5**, 188–192.

Cofer, C. N., and Foley, J. P., Jr. Mediated generalization and the interpretation of verbal behavior: I. Prolegomena. *Psychol. Rev.*, 1942, **49**, 513–540.

Cofer, C. N., & Yarczower, M. Further study of implicit verbal chaining in paired-associate learning. *Psychol. Rep.*, 1957, **3**, 453–456.

Cohen, B. H. Some-or-none characteristics of coding behavior. *J. verb. Learn. verb. Behav.*, 1966, **5**, 182–187.

Cohen, B. H., & MacNeil, D. A. A reexamination of implicit verbal chaining. *J. exp. Psychol.*, 1966, **71**, 432–437.

Cook, T. W. Studies in cross education: IV. Permanence of transfer. *J. exp. Psychol.*, 1935, **18**, 255–266.

Cook, T. W. Studies in cross education. I. Mirror tracing the star-shaped maze. *J. exp. Psychol.*, 1933, **16**, 144–210.

Crafts, L. W. Routine and varying practice as preparation for adjustment to a new situation. *Arch. Psychol.*, N.Y., 1927, **14**, No. 91.

Crawford, J. L., & Vanderplas, J. M. An experiment on the mediation of paired-associate learning. *J. Psychol.*, 1959, **47**, 87–98.

Dallett, K. M. The transfer surface reexamined. *J. verb. Learn. verb. Behav.*, 1962, **1**, 91–94.

Dallett, K. M. Proactive and retroactive inhibition in the A-B, A-B′ paradigm. *J. exp. Psychol.*, 1964, **68**, 190–200.

Dallett, K. M. A transfer surface for paradigms in which second-list S-R pairings do not correspond to first-list pairings. *J. verb. Learn. verb. Behav.*, 1965, **4**, 528–534.

Dallett, K. M., & D'Andrea, L. Mediation instructions in the A-B, A-C paradigm. *J. exp. Psychol.*, 1965, **69**, 460–466.

Dashiell, J. F. An experimental isolation of higher level habits. *J. exp. Psychol.*, 1924, **7**, 391–397.

Day, R. H. Relative task difficulty and transfer of training in skilled performance. *Psychol. Bull.*, 1956, **53**, 160–168.

Deese, J. *The psychology of learning.* New York: McGraw-Hill, 1958.

Deese, J. Influence of inter-item associative strength upon immediate free recall. *Psychol. Rep.*, 1959, **5**, 305–312.

Deese, J. Comments on Professor Murdock's paper. In C. N. Cofer & B. S. Musgrave (Eds.), *Verbal behavior and learning.* New York: McGraw-Hill, 1963. Pp. 22–25.

Dietze, D. The facilitating effect of words on discrimination and generalization. *J. exp. Psychol.*, 1955, **50**, 255–260.

Dollard, J., & Miller, N. E. *Personality and psychotherapy.* New York: McGraw-Hill, 1950.

Duncan, C. P. Transfer in motor task learning as a function of degree of first-task learning and inter-task similarity. *J. exp. Psychol.*, 1953, **46**, 445–452.

Duncan, C. P. Development of response generalization gradients. *J. exp. Psychol.*, 1955, **50**, 26–30.

Duncan, C. P. Transfer after training with single versus multiple tasks. *J. exp. Psychol.*, 1958, **55**, 63–72.

Duncan, C. P. Mediation in verbal concept learning. *J. verb. Learn. verb. Behav.*, 1965, **4**, 1–6.

Earhard, B., & Mandler, G. Pseudomediation: A reply and more data. *Psychon. Sci.*, 1965, **3**, 137–138.

Ebbinghaus, H. *Memory: A contribution to experimental psychology.* 1885. (Translated by Ruger, H. A., & Bussenius, C. E.) New York: Teachers College, 1913.

Eckstrand, G. A., & Wickens, D. D. Transfer of perceptual set. *J. exp. Psychol.*, 1954, **47**, 274–278.

Egan, J. P. Recognition memory and the operating characteristic. *Tech. Note* No. AFCRC-TN-58-51. Hearing and Communication Laboratory, Indiana University, 1958.

Ehrenfreund, D. A study of the transposition gradient. *J. exp. Psychol.*, 1952, **43**, 83–87.

Ekstrand, B. R. Backward associations. *Psychol. Bull.*, 1966, **65**, 50–64.

Ekstrand, B. R., & Underwood, B. J. Paced versus unpaced recall in free learning. *J. verb. Learn. verb. Behav.*, 1963, **2**, 288–290.

Ekstrand, B. R., & Underwood, B. J. Free learning and recall as a function of unit-sequence and letter-sequence interference. *J. verb. Learn. verb. Behav.*, 1965, **4**, 390–396.

Ellington, N. R., & Kausler, D. H. Supplementary report: "Fate" of List 1 R-S associations in transfer theory. *J. exp. Psychol.*, 1965, 207–208.

Ellis, H. C. *The transfer of learning.* New York: Macmillan, 1965.

Ellis, H. C., Bessemer, D. W., Devine, J. V., & Trafton, C. L. Recognition of random tactual shapes following predifferentiation training. *Percept. mot. Skills*, 1962, **10**, 99–102.

Ellis, H. C., & Burnstein, D. D. The effect of stimulus similarity and temporal factors in perceptual transfer of training. Tech. Rep. No. 1, 1960, Sandia Corporation, Albuquerque, New Mexico.

Ellis, H. C., & Feuge, R. L. Transfer of predifferentiation training to gradients of generalization in shape recognition. *J. exp. Psychol.*, 1966, **71**, 539–542.

Ellis, H. C., Feuge, R. L., Long, K. K., & Pegram, V. G. Evidence for acquired equivalence of cues in a perceptual task. *Percept. mot. Skills*, 1964, **19**, 159–162.

Ellis, H. C., & Hunter, J. E. Response meaningfulness and the temporal course of transfer. Tech. Rep. No. 2, 1960, Sandia Corporation, Albuquerque, New Mexico.

Ellis, H. C., & Hunter, J. E. The effect of response familiarization on the temporal course of transfer. Tech. Rep. No. 3, 1961a, Sandia Corporation, Albuquerque, New Mexico.

Ellis, H. C., & Hunter, J. E. A comparison of the temporal course of retention and non-specific transfer. Tech. Rep. No. 4, 1961b, Sandia Corporation, Albuquerque, New Mexico.

Ellis, H. C., & Muller, D. G. Transfer in perceptual learning following stimulus predifferentiation. *J. exp. Psychol.*, 1964, **68**, 388–395.

Ellis, H. C., Muller, D. G., & Tosti, D. T. Stimulus meaning and complexity as factors in the transfer of predifferentiation. *J. exp. Psychol.*, 1966, **71**, 629–633.

Gagné, R. M., & Baker, K. E. Stimulus predifferentiation as a factor in transfer of training. *J. exp. Psychol.*, 1950, **40**, 439–451.

Gagné, R. M., Baker, K. E., & Foster, H. On the relation between similarity and transfer of training in the learning of discriminative motor tasks. *Psychol. Rev.*, 1950, **57**, 67–79.

Gagné, R. M., Foster, H., & Crowley, M. E. The measurement of transfer of training. *Psychol. Bull.*, 1948, **45**, 97–130.

Garskof, B. E., & Sandak, J. M. Unlearning in recognition memory. *Psychonom. Sci.*, 1964, **1**, 197–198.

Gaydos, H. F. Intersensory transfer in the discrimination of form. *Amer. J. Psychol.*, 1956, **69**, 107–110.

Gibson, E. J. Retroactive inhibition as a function of the degree of generalization between tasks. *J. exp. Psychol.*, 1941, **28**, 93–115.

Gibson, E. J. Perceptual learning. *Ann. Rev. Psychol.*, 1963, **14**, 29–56.

Gibson, J. J., & Gibson, E. J. Perceptual learning: differentiation or enrichment? *Psychol. Rev.*, 1955, **62**, 32–41.

Gillette, A. L. Learning and retention: A comparison of three experimental procedures. *Arch. Psychol.*, 1936, No. 28.

Gladis, M. Grade differences in transfer as a function of the time interval between tasks. *J. educ. Psychol.*, 1960, **51**, 191–194.

Glaze, J. A. The association value of nonsense syllables. *J. genet. Psychol.*, 1928, **35**, 255–269.

Glickman, S. E. Perseverative neural processes and consolidation of the memory trace. *Psychol. Bull.*, 1961, **58**, 218–233.

Goggin, J. Influence of written recall measure on first-list associations. *J. exp. Psychol.*, 1963, **65**, 619–720.

Goldstein, D. A., & Newton, J. M. Transfer of training as a function of task difficulty in a complex control situation. *J. exp. Psychol.*, 1962, **63**, 370–375.

Goss, A. E. Transfer as a function of type and amount of preliminary experience with the task stimuli. *J. exp. Psychol.*, 1953, **46**, 419–428.

Goss, A. E. A stimulus-response analysis

of the interaction of cue-producing and mediating responses. *Psychol. Rev.*, 1955, **62**, 20–31.

Goss, A. E. Verbal mediating responses and concept formation. *Psychol. Rev.*, 1961, **68**, 248–298.

Goss, A. E., & Greenfeld, N. Transfer to a motor task as influenced by conditions and degree of prior discrimination training. *J. exp. Psychol.*, 1958, **55**, 258–269.

Goulet, L. R. Retroaction and the "fate" of the mediator in three stage mediation paradigms. *J. verb. Learn. verb. Behav.*, 1966, **5**, 172–176.

Grice, G. R., & Reynolds, B. Effect of varying amounts of rest on conventional and bilateral "reminiscence." *J. exp. Psychol.*, 1952, **44**, 247–252.

Grice, G. R., & Saltz, E. The generalization of an instrumental response to stimuli varying in the size dimension. *J. exp. Psychol.*, 1950, **40**, 702–708.

Guthrie, E. R. Conditioning as a principle of learning. *Psychol. Rev.*, 1930, **37**, 412–428.

Haagen, C. H. Synonymity, vividness, familiarity, and association value ratings of 400 pairs of common adjectives. *J. Psychol.*, 1949, **27**, 453–463.

Hake, H. W. *Contributions of psychology to the study of pattern vision.* Wright Air Devel. Cent. Tech. Rep. No. 57–621, 1957.

Hake, H. W., & Ericksen, C. W. Effect of number of permissible response categories on learning of a constant number of visual stimuli. *J. exp. Psychol.*, 1955, **50**, 161–167.

Hall, J. F. Retroactive inhibition in meaningful material. *J. educ. Psychol.*, 1955, **46**, 47–52.

Hamilton, C. E. The relationship between length of interval separating two tasks and performance on the second task. *J. exp. Psychol.*, 1950, **40**, 613–621.

Hamilton, R. J. Retroactive facilitation as a function of degree of generalization between tasks. *J. exp. Psychol.*, 1943, **32**, 363–376.

Harcum, E. R. Verbal transfer of overlearned forward and backward associations. *Amer. J. Psychol.*, 1953, **66**, 622–625.

Harden, L. M. A quantitative study of the

similarity factor in retroactive inhibition. *J. gen. Psychol.*, 1929, **2**, 421–430.

Harlow, H. F. The formation of learning sets. *Psychol. Rev.*, 1949, **56**, 51–65.

Harlow, H. F. Analysis of discrimination learning by monkeys. *J. exp. Psychol.*, 1950, **40**, 26–39.

Harlow, H. F. Learning set and error factor theory. In S. Koch (Ed.), *Psychology: A study of a science*. Vol. 2. New York: McGraw-Hill, 1959.

Harlow, H. F., & Hicks, L. H. Discrimination learning theory: Uniprocess vs. duoprocess. *Psychol. Rev.*, 1957, **64**, 104–109.

Heath, D. Stimulus generalization and task familiarity as determinants of expectancy generalization. *J. exp. Psychol.*, 1959, **58**, 289–294.

Hebb, D. O. *The organization of behavior*. New York: Wiley, 1949.

Hebb, D. O., & Foord, E. N. Errors of visual recognition and the nature of the trace. *J. exp. Psychol.*, 1945, **35**, 335–348.

Holding, D. H. Transfer between easy and difficult tasks. *Brit. J. Psychol.*, 1962, **53**, 397–407.

Holmgren, G. L., Arnoult, M. D., & Manning, W. H. Intermodal transfer in a paired-associates learning task. *J. exp. Psychol.*, 1966, **71**, 254–259.

Homan, L. E. Stimulus coding ability and stimulus predifferentiation. Unpublished master's thesis, University of New Mexico, 1966.

Horton, D. L., & Hartman, R. R. Verbal mediation as a function of associative directionality and exposure frequency. *J. verb. Learn. verb. Behav.*, 1963, **2**, 361–364.

Horton, D. L., & Kjeldergaard, P. M. An experimental analysis of associative factors in mediated generalization. *Psychol. Monogr.*, 1961, **75** (whole No. 515).

Houston, J. P. Verbal transfer and interlist similarities. *Psychol. Rev.*, 1964, **71**, 412–414.

Houston, J. P., Garskof, B. E., Noyd, D. E., & Erskine, J. M. First-list retention as a function of the method of recall. *J. exp. Psychol.*, 1965, **69**, 326–327.

Hovland, C. I. The generalization of conditioned responses with varying frequencies of tones. *J. gen. Psychol.*, 1937, **17**, 125–148.

Irion, A. L., & Gustafson, L. M. "Reminiscence" in bilateral transfer. *J. exp. Psychol.*, 1952, **43**, 321–323.

James, C. T., & Hakes, D. T. Mediated transfer in a four-stage, stimulus equivalence paradigm. *J. verb. Learn. verb. Behav.*, 1965, **4**, 89–93.

Jeffrey, W. E., & Bogartz, R. S. The criterion task as a factor in positive transfer following acquired distinctiveness pretraining. *Psychol. Rep.*, 1961, **8**, 15–19.

Jenkins, J. J. Mediated associations: Paradigms and situations. In C. N. Cofer & B. S. Musgrave (Eds.), *Verbal behavior and learning*. New York: McGraw-Hill, 1963. Pp. 210–245.

Jenkins, J. J., & Foss, D. J. An experimental analysis of pseudomediation. *Psychon. Sci.*, 1965, **2**, 99–100.

Jenkins, J. J., Foss, D. J., & Odom, Penelope B. Associative mediation in paired-associate learning with multiple controls. *J. verb. Learn. verb. Behav.*, 1965, **4**, 141–147.

Jenkins, J. J., Mink, W. D., & Russell, W. A. Associative clustering as a function of verbal strength. *Psychol. Rep.*, 1958, **4**, 127–136.

Jenkins, J. J., & Russell, W. A. Associative clustering during recall. *J. abnorm. soc. Psychol.*, 1952, **47**, 818–821.

Johnson, R. R. Recognition of nonsense shapes as a function of degree of congruence among components of the pretraining task. Unpublished doctoral dissertation, University of Virginia, 1964.

Judd, C. H. The relation of special training and general intelligence. *Educ. Rev.*, 1908, **36**, 42–48.

Judson, A. I., & Cofer, C. N. Reasoning as an associative process: I. "Direction" in a simple verbal problem. *Psychol. Rep.*, 1956, **2**, 469–476.

Judson, A. I., Cofer, C. N., & Gelfand, S. Reasoning as an associative process: II. "Direction" in problem solving as a function of prior reinforcement of relevant responses. *Psychol. Rep.*, 1956, **2**, 501–507.

Jung, J. Transfer of training as a function of degree of first-list learning. *J. verb. Learn. verb. Behav.*, 1962, **1**, 197–199.

Jung, J. Effects of response meaningfulness (*m*) on transfer under two different paradigms. *J. exp. Psychol.*, 1963, **65**, 377–384.

Jung, J. Comments on Mandlers' "From association to structure." *Psychol. Rev.*, 1965, **72**, 318–322.

Kanfer, F. H. Perception: identification and instrumental activity. *Psychol. Rev.*, 1956, **63**, 317–329.

Katona, G. *Organizing and memorizing.* New York: Columbia Univ. Press, 1940.

Katz, P. A. Effects of labels on children's perception and discrimination learning. *J. exp. Psychol.*, 1963, **66**, 423–428.

Kausler, D. A., and Kanoti, G. A. R–S learning and negative transfer effects with a mixed list. *J. exp. Psychol.*, 1963, **65**, 201–205

Kendler, H. H. Coding: Associationistic or organizational? *J. verb. Learn. verb. Behav.*, 1966, **5**, 198–200.

Kendler, T. S. An experimental investigation of transposition as a function of the difference between training and test stimuli. *J. exp. Psychol.*, 1950, **40**, 552–562.

Kennelly, T. W. The role of similarity in retroaction. *Arch. Psychol.*, 1941, **37**, No. 260.

Keppel, G. Facilitation in short- and long-term retention of paired associates following distributed practice in learning. *J. verb. Learn. verb. Behav.*, 1964, **3**, 91–111.

Keppel, G. Problems of method in the study of short-term memory. *Psychol. Bull.*, 1965, **63**, 1–13.

Keppel, G. Unlearning in serial learning. *J. exp. Psychol.*, 1966, **71**, 143–149.

Keppel, G., & Postman, L. Studies of learning to learn: III. Conditions of improvement in successive transfer tasks. *J. verb. Learn. verb. Behav.*, 1966, **5**, 260–267.

Keppel, G., & Underwood, B. J. Proactive inhibition in short-term retention of single items. *J. verb. Learn. verb. Behav.*, 1962, **1**, 153–161.

Kerpelman, L. C. Preexposure to visually presented forms and nondifferential reinforcement in perceptual learning. *J. exp. Psychol.*, 1965, **69**, 257–262.

Kintsch, W. Memory and decision aspects of recognition learning. *Psychol. Rev.*, 1967, **74**, 496–504.

Kimble, G. A. Transfer of work inhibition in motor learning. *J. exp. Psychol.*, 1952, **43**, 391–392.

Koffka, K. *Principles of gestalt psychology.* New York: Harcourt, Brace & World, 1935.

Köhler, W. *The mentality of apes.* New York: Harcourt, Brace & World, 1925.

Koppenaal, R. J. Time changes in the strengths of A-B, A-C lists; spontaneous recovery? *J. verb. Learn. verb. Behav.*, 1963, **2**, 310–319.

Korn, J. H., & Jahnke, J. C. Recall and recognition as measures of immediate memory. *Psychol. Rep.*, 1962, **10**, 381–382.

Krueger, W. C. F. The effect of overlearning on retention. *J. exp. Psychol.*, 1929, **12**, 71–78.

Kurtz, K. H. Discrimination of complex behavior: the relationship of training and test stimuli in transfer of discrimination. *J. exp. Psychol.*, 1955, **40**, 283–292.

LaBerge, D. L., & Lawrence, D. H. Two methods for generating matrices of forms of graded similarity. *J. Psychol.*, 1957, **43**, 77–100.

Lawrence, D. H. Acquired distinctiveness of cues: I. Transfer between discriminations on the basis of familiarity with the stimuli. *J. exp. Psychol.*, 1949, **52**, 235–243.

Lawrence, D. H. Acquired distinctiveness of cues: II. Selective association in a constant stimulus situation. *J. exp. Psychol.*, 1950, **40**, 175–188.

Lawrence, D. H. The transfer of discrimination along a continuum. *J. comp. physiol. Psychol.*, 1952, **45**, 511–516.

Lawrence, D. H. The nature of a stimulus: some relationships between learning and perception. In S. Koch (Ed.), *Psychology: A study of a science.* New York: McGraw-Hill, 1963. Pp. 179–212.

Levine, J. M., and Murphy, G. The learning and forgetting of controversial material. *J. abnorm. soc. Psychol.*, 1943, **38**, 507–517.

Lewis, D. J. Neural consolidation and electroconvulsive shock. *Psychol. Rev.*, 1965, **72**, 225–239.

Lifton, H., and Goss, A. E. Aural-visual

transfer of paired-associates learning. *J. gen. Psychol.*, 1962, **66**, 225–234.

Lindley, R. H. Association value, familiarity, and pronunciability rating in serial verbal learning. *J. exp. Psychol.*, 1963a, **65**, 347–351.

Lindley, R. H. Effects of controlled coding cues in short-term memory. *J. exp. Psychol.*, 1963b, **66**, 580–587.

Lindley, R. H. Effect of trigram-recoding cue complexity on short-term memory. *J. verb. Learn. verb. Behav.*, 1965, **4**, 274–279.

Lindley, R. H., & Nedler, S. E. Supplementary report: further effects of subject-generated recoding cues on short-term memory. *J. exp. Psychol.*, 1965, **69**, 324–325.

Loess, H. Proactive inhibition in short-term retention. *J. verb. Learn. verb. Behav.*, 1964, **3**, 362–368.

Logan, F. A. A micromolar approach to behavior theory. *Psychol. Rev.*, 1956, **63**, 63–73.

Logan, F. A. Transfer of discrimination. *J. exp. Psychol.*, 1966, **71**, 616–618.

Lordahl, D. S., & Archer, E. J. Transfer effects on a rotary pursuit task as a function of first-task difficulty. *J. exp. Psychol.*, 1958, **56**, 421–426.

Lovibond, S. H. A further test of the hypothesis of autonomous memory trace change. *J. exp. Psychol.*, 1958, **55**, 412–415.

Luh, C. W. The conditions of retention. *Psychol. Monogr.*, 1922, **31**, No. 142.

McAllister, D. E. The effects of various kinds of relevant verbal pretraining on subsequent motor performance. *J. exp. Psychol.*, 1953, **46**, 326–336.

McGee, N. E., & Schulz, R. W. Mediation in paired-associate learning. *J. exp. Psychol.*, 1961, **62**, 565–570.

McGeoch, J. A. The influence of degree of learning upon retroactive inhibition. *Amer. J. Psychol.*, 1929, **41**, 252–262.

McGeoch, J. A. The influence of degree of interpolated learning upon retroactive inhibition. *Amer. J. Psychol.*, 1932a, **44**, 695–708.

McGeoch, J. A. Forgetting and the law of disuse. *Psychol. Rev.*, 1932b, **39**, 352–370.

McGeoch, J. A. *The psychology of human learning.* New York: Longmans, Green, 1942.

McGeoch, J. A., & Irion, A. L. *The psychology of human learning.* (2nd Ed.) New York: Longmans, Green, 1952.

McGeoch, J. A., & McDonald, W. T. Meaningful relation and retroactive inhibition. *Amer. J. Psychol.*, 1931, 579–588.

McGovern, J. B. Extinction of associations in four transfer paradigms. *Psychol. Monogr.*, 1964, **78**, No. 16 (Whole No. 593).

McKinney, F. Quantitative and qualitative essential elements of transfer. *J. exp. Psychol.*, 1933, **16**, 854–864.

McNulty, J. A. An analysis of recall and recognition processes in verbal learning. *J. verb. Learn. verb. Behav.*, 1965, **4**, 430–436.

Mandler, G. From association to structure. *Psychol. Rev.*, 1962, **69**, 415–427.

Mandler, G., & Earhard, B. Pseudomediation: Is chaining an artifact? *Psychon. Sci.*, 1964, **1**, 247–247.

Mandler, G., & Heinemann, S. H. Effect of overlearning a verbal response on transfer of training. *J. exp. Psychol.*, 1956, **51**, 39–46.

Martin, E. Transfer of verbal paired associates. *Psychol. Rev.*, 1965, **72**, 327–343.

Marx, M. H. The effects of cumulative training upon retroactive inhibition and transfer. *Comp. Psychol. Monogr.*, 1944, **18**, No. 2 (Whole No. 94).

Melton, A. W. The methodology of experimental studies of human learning and retention: I. The functions of a methodology and the available criteria for evaluating different experimental methods. *Psychol. Bull.*, 1936, **33**, 305–394.

Melton, A. W. Comments on Professor Postman's paper. In C. N. Cofer (Ed.), *Verbal learning and verbal behavior.* New York: McGraw-Hill, 1961.

Melton, A. W. Implications of short-term memory for a general theory of memory. *J. verb. Learn. verb. Behav.*, 1963, **2**, 1–21.

Melton, A. W., & Irwin, J. M. The influence of degree of interpolated learning on retroactive inhibition and the overt transfer of specific responses. *Amer. J. Psychol.*, 1940, **53**, 173–203.

Melton, A. W., & von Lackum, W. J. Retroactive and proactive inhibition in retention: Evidence for a two-factor theory of retroactive inhibition. *Amer. J. Psychol.*, 1941, **54**, 157–173.

Merikle, P. M., & Battig, W. F. Transfer of training as a function of experimental paradigms and meaningfulness. *J. verb. Learn. verb. Behav.*, 1963, **2**, 485–488.

Miles, R. C. Discrimination learning sets. In A. M. Schrier, H. F. Harlow, & F. Stollnitz (Eds.), *Behavior of nonhuman primates*. New York: Academic, 1965. Pp. 51–95.

Miller, G. A. The magical number seven plus or minus two: Some limits on our capacity for processing information. *Psychol. Rev.*, 1956, **63**, 81–97.

Miller, G. A. Some psychological studies of grammar. *Amer. Psychologist*, 1962, **17**, 748–762.

Miller, N. E. Liberalization of basic S-R concepts: Extensions to conflict behavior, motivation and social learning. In S. Koch (Ed.), *Psychology: A study of a science*. Vol. 2. New York: McGraw-Hill, 1959. Pp. 196–292.

Miller, N. E., & Dollard, J. *Social learning and imitation*. New Haven: Yale Univer. Press, 1941.

Morgan, R. L., & Underwood, B. J. Proactive inhibition as a function of response similarity. *J. exp. Psychol.*, 1950, **40**, 592–603.

Morrisett, L. J., & Hovland, C. I. A comparison of three varieties of training in human problem solving. *J. exp. Psychol.*, 1959, **58**, 52–55.

Murdock, B. B., Jr. Transfer designs and formulas. *Psychol. Bull.*, 1957, **54**, 313–326.

Murdock, B. B., Jr. Effects of task difficulty, stimulus similarity, and type of response on stimulus predifferentiation. *J. exp. Psychol.*, 1958, **55**, 167–172.

Murdock, B. B., Jr. The distinctiveness of stimuli. *Psychol. Rev.*, 1960, **67**, 16–31.

Murdock, B. B., Jr. The retention of individual items. *J. exp. Psychol.*, 1961, **62**, 618–625.

Murdock, B. B., Jr. An analysis of the recognition process. In C. N. Cofer & B. S. Musgrave (Eds.), *Verbal behavior*

and learning. New York: McGraw-Hill, 1963a. Pp. 10–22.

Murdock, B. B., Jr. Short-term retention of single paired-associates. *J. exp. Psychol.*, 1963b, **65**, 433–443.

Murdock, B. B., Jr. Proactive inhibition in short-term memory. *J. exp. Psychol.*, 1964, **68**, 184–189.

Namikas, G., & Archer, E. J. Motor skill transfer as a function of intertask interval and pretransfer task difficulty. *J. exp. Psychol.*, 1960, **59**, 109–112.

Newton, J. M., & Wickens, D. D. Retroactive inhibition as a function of the temporal position of interpolated learning. *J. exp. Psychol.*, 1956, **51**, 149–154.

Noble, C. E. Psychology and the logic of similarity. *J. gen. Psychol.*, 1957, **57**, 23–43.

Norcross, K. J. The effects of discrimination performance on the similarity of previously acquired stimulus names. *J. exp. Psychol.*, 1958, **56**, 305–309.

Norcross, K. J., & Spiker, C. C. The effect of type of stimulus pretraining on discrimination performance in pre-school children. *Child Develpm.*, 1957, **28**, 70–84.

Osgood, C. E. Meaningful similarity and interference in learning. *J. exp. Psychol.*, 1946, **36**, 244–301.

Osgood, C. E. An investigation into the causes of retroactive interference. *J. exp. Psychol.*, 1948, **38**, 132–154.

Osgood, C. E. The similarity paradox in human learning: A resolution. *Psychol. Rev.*, 1949, **56**, 132–143.

Osgood, C. E. *Method and theory in experimental psychology*. New York: Oxford Univer. Press, 1953.

Palermo, D. S. Mediated association in a paired-associate task. *J. exp. Psychol.*, 1962, **64**, 234–238.

Paul, N. T., & Noble, C. E. Influence of successive habit reversals on human learning and transfer. *J. exp. Psychol.*, 1964, **68**, 37–43.

Pavlov, I. P. *Conditioned reflexes*. (Translated by G. V. Anrep.) London: Oxford Univer. Press, 1927.

Payne, R. B. An extension of Hullian theory to response decrements resulting from drugs. *J. exp. Psychol.*, 1958, **55**, 342–346.

Perkins, F. T. Symmetry in visual recall. *Amer. J. Psychol.*, 1932, **44**, 473–490.

Peterson, G. M. Mechanisms of handedness in the rat. *Comp. Psychol. Monogr.*, 1934, **9**, No. 6 (Whole No. 46).

Peterson, G. M., & Barnett, P. E. The cortical destruction necessary to produce a transfer of a forced practice function. *J. comp. physiol. Psychol.*, 1961, **54**, 382–385.

Peterson, G. M., & Devine, J. V. Transfers in handedness in the rat resulting from small cortical lesions after limited forced practice. *J. comp. physiol. Psychol.*, 1963, **4**, 752–756.

Peterson, L. R. Immediate memory: Data and theory. In C. N. Cofer & B. S. Musgrave (Eds.), *Verbal behavior and learning.* New York: McGraw-Hill, 1963. Pp. 336–353.

Peterson, L. R. Short-term verbal memory and learning. *Psychol. Rev.*, 1966, **73**, 193–207.

Peterson, L. R., & Peterson, M. J. Short term retention of individual verbal items. *J. exp. Psychol.*, 1959, **58**, 193–198.

Pfafflin, S. M. Stimulus meaning in stimulus predifferentiation. *J. exp. Psychol.*, 1960, **59**, 269–274.

Porter, L. W., & Duncan, C. P. Negative transfer in verbal learning. *J. exp. Psychol.*, 1953, **46**, 61–64.

Posner, M. I. Uncertainty as a predictor of similarity in the study of generalization. *J. exp. Psychol.*, 1964, **68**, 113–118.

Postman, L. Learned principles of organization in memory. *Psychol. Monogr.*, 1954, No. 374.

Postman, L. Association theory and perceptual learning. *Psychol. Rev.*, 1955, **62**, 348–446.

Postman, L. Mediated equivalence of stimuli and retroactive inhibition. *Amer. J. Psychol.*, 1958, **71**, 175–185.

Postman, L. The present status of interference theory. In C. N. Cofer (Ed.), *Verbal learning and verbal behavior.* New York: McGraw-Hill, 1961a.

Postman, L. Extra-experimental interference and the retention of words. *J. exp. Psychol.*, 1961b, **61**, 97–110.

Postman, L. Transfer of training as a function of experimental paradigm and degree of first-list learning. *J. verb. Learn. verb. Behav.*, 1962a, **1**, 109–118.

Postman, L. Retention of first-list associations as a function of the conditions of transfer. *J. exp. Psychol.*, 1962b, **64**, 380–387.

Postman, L. Perception and learning. In S. Koch (Ed.), *Psychology: A study of a science.* Vol. 5. New York: McGraw-Hill, 1963. Pp. 30–113.

Postman, L. Short-term memory and incidental learning. In A. W. Melton (Ed.), *Categories of human learning.* New York: Academic Press, 1964a. Pp. 145–201.

Postman, L. Studies of learning to learn: II. Changes in transfer as a function of practice. *J. verb. Learn. verb. Behav.*, 1964b, **3**, 437–447.

Postman, L. Studies of learning to learn: VI. General transfer effects in three-stage paradigms. *J. verb. Learn. verb. Behav.*, 1968, **7**, 659–664.

Postman, L., Keppel, G., & Stark, K. Unlearning as a function of the relationship between successive response classes. *J. exp. Psychol.*, 1965, **69**, 111–118.

Postman, L., & Riley, D. A. Degree of learning and interserial interference in retention. *Univer. Calif. Publ. Psychol.*, 1959, **8**, 271–396.

Postman, L., & Rosenzweig, M. R. Practice and transfer in the visual and auditory recognition of verbal stimuli. *Amer. J. Psychol.*, 1956, **69**, 209–226.

Postman, L., & Schwartz, M. Studies of learning to learn: I. Transfer as a function of method of practice and class of verbal materials. *J. verb. Learn. verb. Behav.*, 1964, **3**, 37–49.

Postman, L., & Stark, K. Retroactive inhibition as a function of set during the interpolated task. *J. verb. Learn. verb. Behav.*, 1962, **1**, 304–311.

Postman, L., & Stark, K. Proactive inhibition as a function of the conditions of transfer. *J. verb. Learn. verb. Behav.*, 1964, **3**, 249–259.

Postman, L., & Stark, K. The role of response set in tests of unlearning. *J. verb. Learn. verb. Behav.*, 1965, **4**, 315–322.

Postman, L., & Stark, K. Studies of learning to learn: IV. Transfer from serial to paired-associate learning. *J. verb. Learn. verb. Behav.*, 1967, **6**, 339–353.

Pubols, B. H. The facilitation of visual and spatial discrimination reversal by overlearning. *J. comp. physiol. Psychol.*, 1956, **49**, 243–248.

Ranken, H. B. Effects of name learning on a serial learning, position learning, and recognition learning with random shapes. *Psychol. Rep.*, 1963, **13**, 663–678.

Reese, H. W. Transfer to a discrimination task as a function of amount of stimulus predifferentiation and similarity of stimulus names. Unpublished doctoral dissertation, University of Iowa, 1958.

Reid, L. S. The development of noncontinuity behavior through continuity learning. *J. exp. Psychol.*, 1953, **46**, 107–112.

Richard, J. F. Influence of response discriminability on stimulus discriminability. *J. exp. Psychol.*, 1965, **69**, 30–35.

Richardson, J. Retention of concepts as a function of original and interpolated learning. *J. exp. Psychol.*, 1956, **51**, 358–364.

Richardson, J. The effect of B–C presentation and anticipation interval on mediated transfer. *J. verb. Learn. verb. Behav.*, 1966, **5**, 119–125.

Richardson, J. Latencies of implicit associative responses and positive transfer in paired-associate learning. *J. verb. Learn. verb. Behav.*, 1968, **7**, 638–646.

Richardson, J., & Brown, B. L. Mediated transfer in paired-associate learning as a function of presentation rate and stimulus meaningfulness. *J. exp. Psychol.*, 1966, **72**, 820–828.

Rickert, E. J. Application of Bower's association model to paired-associate transfer. Unpublished master's thesis, University of New Mexico, 1963.

Riley, D. A. The nature of the effective stimulus in animal discrimination learning: Transposition reconsidered. *Psychol. Rev.*, 1958, **65**, 1–7.

Riley, D. A. Memory for form. In L. Postman (Ed.), *Psychology in the Making.* New York: Knopf, 1962. Pp. 402–465.

Riopelle, A. J. Transfer suppression and learning sets. *J. comp. physiol. Psychol.*, 1953, **46**, 61–64.

Riopelle, A. J., & Chinn, R. McC. Position habits and discrimination learning by monkeys. *J. comp. physiol. Psychol.*, 1961, **54**, 178–180.

Robinson, E. S. The "similarity" factor in retroaction. *Amer. J. Psychol.*, 1927, **39**, 297–312.

Robinson, J. S. The effect of learning labels for stimuli on their later discrimination. *J. exp. Psychol.*, 1955, **49**, 112–115.

Rosenzweig, S. An experimental study of "repression" with special reference to need-persistive and ego-defensive reactions to frustration. *J. exp. Psychol.*, 1943, **32**, 64–74.

Rothkopf, E. Z. A measure of stimulus similarity and errors in some paired-associate learning tasks. *J. exp. Psychol.*, 1957, **53**, 94–101.

Runquist, W. N. Verbal behavior. In J. B. Sidowski (Ed.), *Experimental methods and instrumentation*, Chap. 12, Pp. 487–540, New York: McGraw-Hill, 1966.

Runquist, W. N., & Marshall, M. A. Transfer, synonymity, and anticipation interval in paired-associate verbal learning. *Amer. J. Psychol.*, 1963, **76**, 281–286.

Russell, W. A. Purpose and the problem of associative selectivity. In C. N. Cofer & B. S. Musgrave (Eds.), *Verbal behavior and learning.* New York: McGraw-Hill, 1963. Pp. 258–271.

Russell, W. A., & Storms, L. H. Implicit verbal chaining in paired-associate learning. *J. exp. Psychol.*, 1955, **49**, 287–293.

Ryan, J. J. Comparison of verbal response transfer mediated by meaningfully similar and associated stimuli. *J. exp. Psychol.*, 1960, **60**, 408–415.

Schaub, G. R., & Lindley, R. H. Effects of subject-generated recoding cues on short-term memory. *J. exp. Psychol.*, 1964, **68**, 171–175.

Schrier, A. M., Harlow, H. F., & Stollnitz, F. (Eds.), *Behavior of nonhuman primates.* Academic, 1965.

Schulz, R. W., & Lovelace, E. A. Mediation in verbal paired-associate learning: the role of temporal factors. *Psychon. Sci.*, 1964, **1**, 37–38.

Schulz, R. W., Weaver, G. E., & Ginsberg, S. Mediation with pseudomediation controlled: Chaining is not an artifact. *Psychon. Sci.*, 1965, **2**, 169–170.

Schwenn, E., & Postman, L. Studies of learning to learn: V. Gains in performance as a function of warm-up and associative practice. *J. verb. Learn. verb. Behav.*, 1967, **6**, 565–573.

Schwenn, E., & Underwood, B. J. Simulated similarity and mediation time in transfer. *J. verb. Learn. verb. Behav.*, 1965, **4**, 476–483.

Segal, E. M. Demonstration of acquired distinctiveness of cues using a paired-associate learning task. *J. exp. Psychol.*, 1964, **67**, 587–590.

Shepard, R. N. Stimulus and response generalization to distance in psychological space. *J. exp. Psychol.*, 1958, **55**, 509–523.

Shepard, R. N., & Chang, J. J. Forced-choice tests of recognition memory under steady-state conditions. *J. verb. Learn. verb. Behav.*, 1963, **2**, 93–101.

Shepard, R. N., & Teghtsoonian, M. Retention of information under conditions approaching a steady state. *J. exp. Psychol.*, 1961, **62**, 302–309.

Shipley, W. C. Indirect conditioning. *J. gen. Psychol.*, 1935, **12**, 337–357.

Siipola, E. M., & Israel, H. E. Habit interference as dependent upon stage of training. *Amer. J. Psychol.*, 1933, **45**, 205–227.

Slamecka, N. J. Studies of retention of connected discourse. *Amer. J. Psychol.*, 1959, **72**, 409–416.

Slamecka, N. J. Retroactive inhibition of connected discourse as a function of similarity of topic. *J. exp. Psychol.*, 1960, **60**, 245–249.

Slamecka, N. J. Proactive inhibition of connected discourse. *J. exp. Psychol.*, 1961, **62**, 295– 301.

Slamecka, N. J., & Ceraso, J. Retroactive and proactive inhibition of verbal learning. *Psychol. Bull.*, 1960, **57**, 449–475.

Spence, J. T. Associative interference on paired-associate lists from extra-experimental learning. *J. verb. Learn. verb. Behav.*, 1963, **2**, 329–338.

Spence, J. T., and Schulz, R. W. Negative transfer in paired-associate learning as a function of first-list trials. *J. verb. Learn. verb. Behav.*, 1965, **4**, 397–400.

Spence, K. W. The nature of discrimination learning in animals. *Psychol. Rev.*, 1936, **43**, 427–449.

Spence, K. W. The differential response in animals to stimuli varying within a single dimension. *Psychol. Rev.*, 1937, **44**, 430–444.

Spiker, C. C. Verbal factors in the discrimination learning of children. In J. C. Wright & J. Kagan (Eds.), *Basic cognitive processes in children. Monogr. Soc. Res. Child Develpm.*, 1963, **28**, No. 2 (Whole No. 86).

Spiker, C. C., & Holton, R. B. Associative interference in motor paired-associate learning. *J. exp. Psychol.*, 1958, **56**, 114–132.

Stollnitz, F. Spatial variables, observing responses, and discrimination learning sets. *Psychol. Rev.*, 1965, **72**, 247–261.

Thompson, C. P. On the incompatibility of the Houston and Osgood transfer surface. *Psychol. Rev.*, 1966, **73**, 586–588.

Thorndike, E. L. *Educational psychology. II. The psychology of learning.* New York: Teachers College, 1913.

Thorndike, E. L., & Woodworth, R. S. The influence of improvement in one mental function upon the efficiency of other functions. I; II. The estimation of magnitudes; III. Functions involving attention, observation and discrimination. *Psychol. Rev.*, 1901, **8**, 247–261, 384–395, 553–564.

Thune, L. E. The effect of different types of preliminary activities on subsequent learning of paired-associate material. *J. exp. Psychol.*, 1950, **40**, 423–438.

Thune, L. E., & Underwood, B. J. Retroactive inhibition as a function of degree of interpolated learning. *J. exp. Psychol.*, 1943, **32**, 185–200.

Tosti, D. T., & Ellis, H. C. Stimulus generalization in the absence of discrimination factors. *J. exp. Psychol.*, 1964, **68**, 595–598.

Tulving, E. Subjective organization in free recall of "unrelated" words. *Psychol. Rev.*, 1962, **69**, 344–354.

Tulving, E. Subjective organization and effects of repetition in multi-trial free-recall learning. *J. verb. Learn. verb. Behav.*, 1966, **5**, 193–197.

Twedt, H. M., & Underwood, B. J. Mixed vs. unmixed lists in transfer studies. *J. exp. Psychol.*, 1959, **58**, 111–116.

Underwood, B. J. The effect of successive interpolations on retroactive and proactive inhibition. *Psychol. Monogr.*, 1945, No. 3.

Underwood, B. J. "Spontaneous" recovery of verbal associations. *J. exp. Psychol.*, 1948, **38**, 429–439.

Underwood, B. J. *Experimental psychology.* New York: Appleton-Century-Crofts, 1949a.

Underwood, B. J. Proactive inhibition as a function of time and degree of prior learning. *J. exp. Psychol.*, 1949b, **39**, 24–34.

Underwood, B. J. Associative transfer in verbal learning as a function of response similarity and degree of first-list learning. *J. exp. Psychol.*, 1951, **42**, 44–54.

Underwood, B. J. Studies of distributed practice: VII. Learning and retention of serial nonsense lists as a function of intralist similarity. *J. exp. Psychol.*, 1952, **44**, 80–87.

Underwood, B. J. Intralist similarity in verbal learning and retention. *Psychol. Rev.*, 1954a, **61**, 160–166.

Underwood, B. J. Speed of learning and amount retained: A consideration of methodology. *Psychol. Bull.*, 1954b, **51**, 276–282.

Underwood, B. J. Interference and forgetting. *Psychol. Rev.*, 1957, **64**, 49–60.

Underwood, B. J. An evaluation of the Gibson theory of verbal learning. In C. N. Cofer (Ed.), *Verbal learning and verbal behavior.* New York: McGraw-Hill, 1961. Pp. 197–217.

Underwood, B. J. The representativeness of rote verbal learning. In A. W. Melton (Ed.), *Categories of human learning.* New York: Academic Press, 1964a. Pp. 47–78.

Underwood, B. J. Degree of learning and the measurement of forgetting. *J. verb. Learn. verb. Behav.*, 1964b, **3**, 112–129.

Underwood, B. J. False recognition produced by implicit associative responses. *J. exp. Psychol.*, 1965, **70**, 122–129.

Underwood, B. J. Motor-skills learning and verbal learning: Some observations. In E. A. Bilodeau (Ed.), *Acquisition of skill.* New York: Academic Press, 1966. Pp. 489–516.

Underwood, B. J., & Erlebacher, A. H. Studies of coding in verbal learning. *Psychol. Monogr.*, 1965, **79**, No. 13 (whole No. 606).

Underwood, B. J., & Keppel, G. Retention as a function of degree of learning and letter-sequence interference. *Psychol. Monogr.*, 1963, **77**, No. 4 (Whole No. 567).

Underwood, B. J., Keppel, G., & Schulz, R. Studies of distributed practice: XXII. Some conditions which enhance retention. *J. exp. Psychol.*, 1962, **64**, 355–363.

Underwood, B. J., & Postman, L. Extra-experimental sources of interference in forgetting. *Psychol. Rev.*, 1960, **67**, 73–95.

Underwood, B. J., & Richardson, J. The influence of meaningfulness, intralist similarity, and serial position on retention. *J. exp. Psychol.*, 1956, **52**, 119–126.

Underwood, B. J., Runquist, W. R., and Schulz, R. W. Response learning in paired-associate lists as a function of intralist similarity. *J. exp. Psychol.*, 1959, **58**, 70–78.

Underwood, B. J., & Schulz, R. W. *Meaningfulness and verbal learning.* Philadelphia: Lippincott, 1960.

Vanderplas, J. M. Transfer of training and its relation to perceptual learning and recognition. *Psychol. Rev.*, 1958, **65**, 375–385.

Vanderplas, J. M. Associative processes and task relations in perceptual learning. *Percept. mot. Skills*, 1963, **16**, 501–509.

Vanderplas, J. M., Sanderson, W. A., & Vanderplas, J. N. Some task-related determinants of transfer in perceptual learning. *Percept. mot. Skills*, 1964, **18**, 71–80.

Walker, L. C., DeSoto, C. B., & Shelly, M. W. Rest and warm-up in bilateral transfer on a pursuit rotor task. *J. exp. Psychol.*, 1957, **53**, 394–398.

Ward, L. B. Reminiscence and rote learning. *Psychol. Monogr.*, 1937, **49**, No. 220.

Waugh, N. C., & Norman, D. A. Primary memory. *Psychol. Rev.*, 1965, **72**, 89–104.

Wickelgren, W. A. Acoustic similarity and retroactive interference in short-term memory. *J. verb. Learn. verb. Behav.*, 1965, **4**, 53–61.

Wickens, D. D. The transference of conditioned excitation and conditioned inhibition from one muscle group to the antagonistic muscle group. *J. exp. Psychol.*, 1938, **22**, 101–123.

Wickens, D. D., Born, D. G., & Allen, C. K. Proactive inhibition and item similarity in short-term memory. *J. verb. Learn. verb. Behav.*, 1963, **2**, 440–445.

Wickens, D. D., & Briggs, G. E. Mediated stimulus generalization as a factor in sensory pre-conditioning. *J. exp. Psychol.*, 1951, **42**, 192–200.

Wimer, R. Osgood's transfer surface: Extension and test. *J. verb. Learn. verb. Behav.*, 1964, **3**, 274–279.

Wohlwill, J. F. The learning of absolute and relational number discriminations by children. *J. genet. Psychol.*, 1962, **101**, 217–228.

Wohlwill, J. F. Perceptual learning. *Ann. Rev. Psychol.*, 1966, **17**, 201–232.

Woodworth, R. S., & Schlosberg, H. *Experimental psychology*. New York: Holt, Rinehart, and Winston, 1954.

Wulf, F. Uber die Veranderung von Vorstellungen. *Psychol. Forsch.*, 1922, **1**, 333–373.

Wylie, H. H. An experimental study of transfer of response in the white rat. *Behav. Monogr.*, 1919, No. 16.

Young, R. K. Retroactive inhibition and proactive inhibition under varying conditions of response similarity. *J. exp. Psychol.*, 1955, **50**, 113–119.

Young, R. K. Tests of three hypotheses about the stimulus in serial learning. *J. exp. Psychol.*, 1962, **63**, 307–313.

Yum, K. W. An experimental test of the law of assimilation. *J. exp. Psychol.*, 1931, **14**, 68–82.

Suggested Readings

Adams, J. A. *Human memory*. New York: McGraw-Hill, 1967. An important source describing major theories and empirical findings of human memory in a variety of areas, including free recall, long-term memory, short-term memory, recall of motor responses, and recognition memory.

Battig, W. F. Facilitation and interference. In E. A. Bilodeau (Ed.), *Acquisition of skill*. New York: Academic Press, 1966. Pp. 215–244. A systematic treatment of the component analysis of gross transfer effects into subprocesses or mechanisms. Battig's principal thesis is that intratask interference can lead to intertask facilitation, a position that he uses to resolve several paradoxes in transfer.

Bilodeau, E. A. Retention. In E. A. Bilodeau (Ed.), *Acquisition of skill*. New York: Academic Press, 1966. Pp. 315–350. A careful re-examination of conventional beliefs about the measurement of retention. Emphasis is placed on the importance of controlling and regulating the environment in which measures of retention are obtained in a fashion analogous to that conventionally done during acquisition.

Cantor, J. H. Transfer of stimulus pretraining to motor paired-associate and discrimination learning tasks. In L. P. Lipsitt & C. C. Spiker (Eds.), *Advances in child development and behavior*. New York: Academic Press, 1965. Pp. 19–58. A recent summary of the various paradigms used in stimulus pretraining studies and the major empirical generalizations obtained. Studies using children as *S*s are emphasized.

Cofer, C. N. On some factors in the organizational characteristics of free recall. *Amer. Psychologist*, 1965, **20**, 261–272. A summary of some of the major factors influencing the order or organization of recall as compared with the order present during acquisition. Cofer contends that *S*s can employ both associational and categorical bases for clustering in recall.

Dixon, T. R., & Horton, D. L. (Eds.), *Verbal behavior and general behavior theory*. Englewood Cliffs, N.J.: Prentice-Hall, 1968. A valuable conference in which an attempt is made to relate the various specific areas of verbal learning and behavior to problems in general behavior theory.

Ellis, H. C. *The transfer of learning*. New York: Macmillan, 1965. An introductory treatment of the topic of transfer summarizing major empirical findings. Emphasis is placed on classical issues as well as on newer problem areas, including treatment of mediation, stimulus-predifferentiation, similarly effects in transfer, and the measurement of transfer.

Gagné, R. M. *The conditions of learning.* New York: Holt, Rinehart, and Winston, 1965. A description of eight hierarchical principles of learning that are used as a framework for evaluating various kinds of performance changes associated with learning. Application of these principles to educational situations is given considerable attention.

Jenkins, J. J. Mediated associations: Paradigms and situations. In C. N. Cofer & B. S. Musgrave (Eds.), *Verbal behavior and learning.* New York: McGraw-Hill, 1963. Pp. 210–245. An examination of the basic mediation paradigms with suggestions for further research. Jenkins suggests that future studies place emphasis on reinforcing mediating responses, reinforcing mediation activity on the part of *S*, and exploring the tendency of given tasks to elicit mediational activity.

Kausler, D. H. *Readings in verbal language.* New York: Wiley, 1966. An extremely valuable book in introducing the reader to the vast domain of research issues in verbal learning, transfer, and retention. Fifty-five original papers are included with introductory textual material given at each section of the book.

Martin, E. Transfer of verbal paired associates. *Psychol. Rev.*, 1965, **72**, 327–343. An extension of Osgood's coordinate system for predicting transfer to include the effects of response learning, forward associations, and backward associations. Transfer from first-task to second-task learning is viewed as some combination of these three effects.

Melton, A. W. Implications of short-term memory for a general theory of memory. *J. verb. Learn. verb. Behav.*, 1963, **2**, 1–21. A thorough account of the significance of findings in short-term memory for various conceptual issues in memory. Considerable attention is given to the distinction between short-term and long-term memory and whether these events represent continuous or dual processes.

Melton, A. W. (Ed.), *Categories of human learning.* New York: Academic Press, 1964. A symposium devoted to exploring some of the taxonomic issues in human learning. Seven categories of human learning were selected for investigation and emphasis was placed on formulating statements about each of the categories and on discovering the relatedness of the various categories.

Postman, L. The present status of interference theory. In C. N. Cofer (Ed.), *Verbal learning and verbal behavior.* New York: McGraw-Hill, 1961. An outstanding review of the development of interference theory with emphasis placed on the subprocesses involved in interference theory. Interference theory is seen to encompass several subprocesses including response competition, unlearning, differentiation, unit-sequence interference and letter-sequence interference.

Riley, D. A. Memory for form. In L. Postman (Ed.), *Psychology in the making.* New York: Knopf, 1962. Pp. 402–465. A thorough account of the research in memory for visual form. Principal emphasis is placed on methodological refinements and on a comparison of theoretical accounts of memory for visual form from Wulf to the present.

Underwood, B. J. Degree of learning and the measurement of forgetting. *J. verb. Learn. verb. Behav.*, 1964, **3**, 112–129. A major methodological analysis of base-line problems in the measurement of retention. Several methods for measuring and controlling degree of original learning are described.

VII

Motor Behavior

Jack A. Adams

University of Illinois, Urbana

Acquisition of Motor Responses

The study of motor behavior is investigation of the determinants of bodily movements, and almost always human Ss are used. Applied psychology, with a need to understand better how complex skills are learned and performed throughout many important facets of everyday life, gave early stimulation to the study of motor behavior. Many industrial jobs, like operating a lathe, require a high level of skill for success. The continuous control of automobiles, airplanes, submarines, and space vehicles involves complex motor activities, and understanding the determinants of these motor sequences is necessary for defining the personnel training programs and vehicular design that will make these man-machine systems successful.

Apart from the needs of applied psychology, there are basic scientific justifications for the study of motor behavior. Foremost is the scientific need to know determining variables for the various response classes of human and animal behavior, and motor responding is one of these classes. Just as we seek the causal variables for verbal behavior, so we seek laws for the control and prediction of motor responses. We cannot necessarily assume that the same variables apply in the same way for different classes of responding. Certain variables may be influential only for certain response classes, or other variables may be related to one response class in one way and to another response class in a different way. Because of these various possibilities, psychology is charged with mapping causal factors for the various behavioral domains, although the complexity of any behavioral situation rarely allows a domain to be isolated absolutely for study. In the laboratory we might elicit motor responses with a visual display, and thus have a task with perceptual elements that would be called a perceptual-motor task. A more complex task such as this can complicate matters a bit, but data from it are useful in understanding the compounding of response classes and for applying experimental results to practical situations where these response complexes are present. Ultimately we hope to understand how the various response classes, with their determining variables, piece together for the accurate prediction of quite complex behavior.

Another justification for the study of motor behavior is that motor responses are particularly revealing for certain phenomena. Notable is the study of work inhibition, or bodily fatigue as the layman would have it (Adams, 1964; Bilodeau and Bilodeau, 1961). Manipulating the amount of physical work is most easily done with motor movements. For example, we can ask S to lift weights repeatedly as an easy way of observing performance changes as a function of amount of physical work. Assigning motor skills a particularly useful role for the study of work inhibition does not, of course, relieve us of the scientific responsibility of understanding how work inhibition and its defining variables operate for other response classes. Nevertheless, we can make impressive progress in the early stages of a science by studying situations where a phenomenon is readily revealed. Most would agree that an early stage is where psychology now stands.

This chapter will examine salient topics for the acquisition of motor behavior, with more attention accorded to simple motor responses. No attempt will be made at a comprehensive coverage of this complex subject matter. Nor will applied ramifications of motor behavior in industrial and engineering psychology be presented.

Apparatus

As in most areas of experimental psychology, there is little standardization of apparatus. The Es use a wide variety of devices for the study of motor behavior, often arbitrary tasks of their own devising. An E decides on the variables he wishes to study, and then musters his imagination and resources to devise apparatus that allows for control and manipulation of the variables. This approach can yield apparatus with a measure of uniqueness, and a hazard is that the variables associated with this uniqueness can interact with the primary variables under investigation to yield results that conflict with other findings on the topic. An argument for some standardization of laboratory apparatus can be made if an orderly series of investigations is to be

accomplished, or meaningful replication of previous studies is to be made. On the other side of this argument, standardization can be inhibiting for new and better devices to study psychological variables, or for testing the generality of established variables in new situations. If standardization ever comes it will only be because of a strong consensus that it is the swiftest path to the achievement of laws and theory. Arguments for standardization can be countered at this time with the view that a diversity of approaches by individualistic scientists is a good tactic in these days of psychology's ebullient youth, when many of our variables are yet to be known and many of our laws are sketchy or totally unknown. Standardization might possibly be defended for psychology's gracious middle years.

In the face of apparatus heterogeneity, it is not easy to discuss equipment for the study of motor behavior. The simplest kind of motor task is the Line-Drawing Test (Thorndike, 1927) where a blindfolded S learns to draw a line of a given length. He is instructed simply "Draw a — inch line." The E reports error to S after each response, and S's skill regularly increases as a result of these operations. Not all investigators tell S the length of line to draw but rather let him discover through feedback what is required of him. The Line-Drawing Test is a good example of a motor task where S is informed of his accuracy after the movement is completed. Many tasks of the world are of this type where the correctness of behavior is not known until after the sequence is completed. Throwing darts or tossing a football pass are examples.

A second major type of motor task is illustrated by the Rotary Pursuit Test, where the task design provides S with moment-to-moment knowledge of his accuracy throughout a trial rather than after the total movement sequence has been completed. The Rotary Pursuit Test should be familiar to all students of psychology, but for the uninitiated this task has a rotary disk like a phonograph turntable that turns at 60 rpm. Set in the disk is a target about the size of a nickel, and the S has a stylus which he holds in his hand and tries to keep on the target as much as possible as it spins around. A timer runs whenever the stylus contacts the target, and the score on a practice trial is the amount of time that S has achieved the goal of staying on target. The Rotary Pursuit Test is a task where S responds to the error discrepancy between what he is required to do and what he is actually doing, and such tasks of continuous error-nulling are of a general class called *tracking tasks*. Tracking tasks are widely represented in the everyday world and they are often complex on both the display and response side. Keeping a car aligned between the road's edge and the centerline of the highway is an example of an everyday tracking task, and needs for understanding the determinants of human controlling for a wide range of vehicles from cars to spacecraft has generated a great deal of tracking research under the aegis of engineering psychology. Such research has asked how to best design tracking tasks for optimum human controlling, and how these tasks are learned. Some of the laboratory setups have used analog computers for specifying the many variables that can enter the definition of complex tracking tasks. For a discussion of tracking behavior and research, see surveys by Adams (1961a, 1967a).

A third class of motor task is discrete in nature. A discrete signal, like a light or sound, occurs and S must make a discrete response to it, like pressing a button or throwing a switch. A simple reaction time test is an example. The response is not graded and continuous, as for the Line-Drawing Test or the Rotary Pursuit Test. Rather, it is a ballistic, all-or-none response. Sometimes a series of discrete stimulus-response units are combined into a complex discrete task where S must respond to all units. Response time is the performance measure for both single and multiple

discrete tasks and, for multiple-unit tasks, error is an important measure because S must learn what response goes with what stimulus. Error also enters as a measure if S must learn the units of the complex discrete task in a defined order.

Other types of motor research devices are essentially nonlearning tasks in that they are used for the study of work inhibition (Bilodeau and Bilodeau, 1961). The acquisition of skilled movements is not involved. Rather, they are gross activities intended to create conditions of physical work. Examples are lifting weights or turning cranks. Although it might be argued that some simple learning is required for these tasks, certainly for adult Ss the learning is long completed and performance changes can be assumed to reflect primarily the effects of work on performance. Tasks where learning occurs are not avoided for the study of work inhibition, however. Work effects build rapidly on the Rotary Pursuit Test, which is a learning task, and it has been a popular device for research in this area. Despite the joint effects of work and learning variables, a great deal of importance has been learned about work inhibition from studies with the Rotary Pursuit Test.

Knowledge of Results and the Acquisition of Simple Response

This section will emphasize the acquisition of a simple motor movement sequence where S is informed of error in his movement after the response is completed. The everyday world has many examples of such situations, but the Line-Drawing Test is the prototype for this class of tasks in the laboratory. The blindfolded S responds, he is informed of the accuracy of his response relative to that which E has defined as correct, and repetition of this procedure over a series of practice trials results in regular performance improvements. The information about correctness of human response is commonly called knowledge of results (KR) by psychologists, although some find comfort in using engineering terminology and call it *information feedback*, or just *feedback*. Because KR operations are formally analogous to animal learning situations where a pellet of food or a drink of water is given as reward when a correct response is made, some refer to it as *reinforcement*. In drawing such parallels one must be cautious and not assume that the same behavioral processes are necessarily involved. What KR and animal reinforcement have in common is the identification of events which improve performance when they are administered after a response. The various types of events that work in this fashion are commonly called *empirical reinforcement events*. Informing S of his error in motor responding tends to improve his performance on the next trial. Showing S the correct verbal response by lifting the shutter of a memory drum after he has attempted to anticipate the response in paired-associate learning tends to result in better performance on the next trial. Giving an animal a pellet of food after he selects the correct arm of a T maze increases his probability of correct responding. All of these postresponse operations that increase the probability of correct responding are empirical reinforcers, and those which have no such effects are excluded from the class. It is unlikely that an animal will learn a maze if he finds a rock as reward for his successful performance.

It is implicit in the thinking of many psychologists that reinforcing events strengthen a learning or habit state of the organism that links a stimulus and a response, but we have yet to evolve a sound theory of how reinforcers function as they do either for animal or human behavior. As will be discussed shortly, there are several possibilities for explaining how KR works at the human level, and parallel controversies exist for animal learning. In the absence of a theory of reinforcement for

human learning, it is prudent to regard various KR procedures as empirical reinforcers that "work" for improving *performance*, not necessarily learning, and we can go a long way in uncovering the determinants of human behavior with this pragmatic approach. Unquestionably a greatly improved understanding will emerge when a sound theory of reinforcement is formulated, however.

KR and Response Acquisition There are two basic questions asked of how KR affects performance. First is whether performance can improve without KR. Second, what are the effects of different types of KR on performance? For the Line-Drawing Test, is qualitative feedback of "right" or "wrong" as effective for performance as a graded, quantitative error score reported in numerical units?

The first question was answered in the negative by Thorndike (1927) who found no improvement without KR, and in various contexts this finding has been upheld by others (Trowbridge and Cason, 1932; Macpherson, Dees, and Grindley, 1948; Baker and Young, 1960; Elwell and Grindley, 1938; Bilodeau, Bilodeau, and Schumsky, 1959). Thorndike's early data (1927) still stand as a good illustration. The Line-Drawing Test was used, and S drew blocks of 3-, 4-, 5-, or 6-inch lines in a session where a total of 600 lines were drawn. There were 150 lines of each of the four lengths drawn in a session. The KR was "right" or "wrong." For a 3-in. line, KR was "right" when S drew a line that was 3 in. $\pm \frac{1}{8}$ in. For other lengths the tolerance around the correct length was $\pm \frac{1}{4}$ in. On the first session the median per cent right was 34.5, and at the end of the seventh training session per cent right was 54.5. In a second study this experimental procedure was repeated for 5,400 lines but without KR. There was no significant change in per cent right from the first to the final session, and Thorndike concludes for no performance changes when KR is absent.

Seashore and Bavelas (1941) criticized Thorndike's conclusion that mere repetition of a response without KR has no effect on behavior, and they reanalyzed Thorndike's no-KR data to make their case. They agreed that S had no performance changes in regard to becoming more accurate with respect to the length of line defined by E, but they found that S improved his responses with respect to his own conception of the line's length. If S was to draw a 4-in. line, and received no KR, he would nevertheless respond to his understanding of a 4-in. line which, based on his past experience, might be, say, 5 in. His response develops less and less error around 5 in. as trials progress. Seashore and Bavelas conclude that S is getting KR from his internal, private sources and reinforcing his own conception of the line. Thus, behavior does change without external KR, although it does not improve with respect to the external task criterion which is E's frame of reference.

The second question of how types of KR affect performance was studied by Trowbridge and Cason (1932) with the Line-Drawing Test. Four groups of Ss were required to draw 3-in. lines. One group had quantitative KR where error was reported in $\frac{1}{8}$-in. units—for example, "plus two" for a response that was $\frac{1}{4}$ in. too long, or "minus one" for a response that was $\frac{1}{8}$ in. too short. A second group had qualitative KR where E reported "right" if S's response was three inches $\pm \frac{1}{8}$ in., and "wrong" otherwise. The third group had no KR, and a fourth group had irrelevant KR where E spoke a nonsense syllable after each response. The results are shown in Fig. 21-1. Type of KR is a potent performance variable, with the quantitative KR producing clear-cut superiority and rapid response acquisition. Qualitative KR is not as effective as quantitative KR, although the trend suggests that it might eventually produce the same terminal performance level. The absence of trend for the no-KR group is consistent with the

findings of Thorndike (1927) and others which were discussed, and the group with irrelevant KR also shows no trend over trials. It is noteworthy, however, that irrelevant KR has a performance level which is poorer than that for no KR. The meaningless comments by E were perhaps either distracting or led some Ss to entertain irrelevant hypotheses about the purpose of the task and to undertake modes of responding which were maladaptive as far as E's purpose for the task was concerned. Thus, Ss might have interpreted the nonsense syllable as an encoded message which carried information about what was required in the task, and they might have explored various response possibilities to see whether it would alter E's feedback in a way that could be interpreted as success. These various hypotheses had to fail and increase error because E's feedback was random.

Hardesty and Bevan (1964) report findings for reaction time that parallel those of Trowbridge and Cason. Their experimental task required the S to press a response key as rapidly as possible when a stimulus light came on. Four groups of Ss were used. A control group had no feedback, a group with quantitative KR was told their reaction time in sec. after each trial, and a group with qualitative KR was simply told "very good" or "too slow." A fourth group received both quantitative and qualitative KR. This latter group gave the best performance, with quantitative KR next, and qualitative KR ranking third. The control group performed the poorest of all.

These findings on type of KR are interesting and important for anyone attempting to apply or investigate the reinforcement operations that affect human performance, but our basic understanding of why these various types of KR work as they do is at an early level. For example, type of KR could influence habit development in the task, one's motivation to perform, or a compound of these two

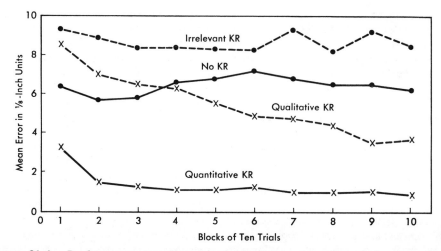

Figure 21-1. Performance in a line-drawing test as a function of the type of KR given after each response. (Drawn from tabled values in Trowbridge, Margery H., and Cason, H. An experimental study of Thorndike's theory of learning. *J. gen. Psychol.*, 1932, **7**, 245–260.)

factors. Theoretical issues for KR will be discussed more explicitly in a later part of this chapter.

Withdrawal of KR after Acquisition. What is the effect of withdrawal of KR after it has been administered for a number of trials? If one is inclined to draw parallels with studies of animal behavior, KR withdrawal is analogous to experimental extinction procedures, where reward is withheld.

We must be careful in our research design on KR withdrawal not to confound the results with forgetting. If KR withdrawal is some time after the end of acquisition trials, and there is a performance loss, we cannot be sure whether the loss is attributable to KR withdrawal or the action of forgetting processes in the time interval. Studies on KR withdrawal sometimes have had a day or so intervening between the end of acquisition trials and the test session where KR was withdrawn, so forgetting effects are inextricably bound with those of KR withdrawal in these instances. An example of this failure to control forgetting is the classic work by Thorndike (1927) and the follow-up research by Baker and Young (1960).

Acquisition and extinction trials for the Line-Drawing Test ran for several sessions, with at least a day between sessions. They found that KR withdrawal resulted in an immediate performance level that was about 50 per cent of that held on the final reinforcement session. But the long retention interval was responsible for this performance decrement rather than KR withdrawal, as Elwell and Grindley (1938) found when they compared an immediate shift to KR withdrawal with a shift after 24 hr. Starting KR withdrawal immediately gave a gradual decline in performance but its start after 24 hr. produced a large decrement. Similarly, Bilodeau, Bilodeau, and Schumsky (1959) found that immediate KR withdrawal produced a gradual decline in performance, not a precipitous drop. Bilodeau, Bilodeau, and Schumsky also found that continuing trials with KR withdrawal revealed no tendency for performance to deteriorate to the level that the naive Ss had at the start of training. Some skill residual remained. Baker and Young found the same residual advantage to persist even after 1,400 no-KR trials. Unlike the extinction of animal responses where total elimination of the skill can occur, humans retain some of their training benefits after KR is gone.

Recent thinking on the topic of *subjective reinforcement* (or self-reinforcement) is changing the conceptions that some psychologists hold about KR withdrawal (Adams, 1967b, Chapter 10). The experimental approaches to response acquisition with KR, and performance deterioration when KR is withdrawn, have closely paralleled work on acquisition and extinction in animal research, but evidence is beginning to accrue that this analogy is a trifle strained. A principal point of strain is in the conceptualization of a reinforcer as completely an external event under the control of *E*. New evidence is beginning to suggest that after training with external KR the human *S* in certain tasks will internalize the standards for response correctness and be capable of reinforcing himself after a response. It was mentioned earlier that Seashore and Bavelas (1941) criticized Thorndike's conclusion of no learning for *S*s who had no KR throughout training, and who served as the control condition for the *S*s who had KR on each trial. Learning occurred for these no-KR *S*s but with respect to *S*'s private conception of the correctness of the response. Presumably each response was compared against the internal standard and the difference between them was the KR. Without KR being present, Seashore and Bavelas revealed systematic performance changes of the kind that we ordinarily identify as learning, and they were probably the first ones to state the position that has come to be known as subjective reinforcement. Consider a British study on motor behavior by Leonard and Conrad (1963). They found that performance steadily *increased* after KR withdrawal just as if KR was being administered. Using a keyboard, *S*s were taught an arbitrary association between the keys and letters of the alphabet. After four 45-min. sessions with KR the *S*s had achieved essentially error-free response to

letters called out by an instructor. In the subsequent eight days the *S*s had 40 min. of practice a day in copying names from typed lists without KR. Speed and accuracy of response were stressed equally in the instructions. The results for the eight-day test showed no increase in errors and a steady increase in speed from thirty-five letters per min. on Day 1 to seventy letters per min. on Day 8. Apparently, after enough training with KR, the *S* was able to provide himself intrinsic KR by comparing each response with his learned internal standard and continue improvement without external KR by *E*. A discrete task like the one Leonard and Conrad used probably has a substantial verbal component in the association of the keys and letters, and it is not surprising that the area of verbal learning has demonstrated similar findings. Eimas and Zeaman (1963) and Eimas (1964) have shown that KR withdrawal for verbal paired associates is accompanied by a regular increase in speed of responding, just as in the Leonard-Conrad study. Other experiments (Richardson and Gropper, 1964; Butler and Peterson, 1965; Goss, 1965) have shown that after a series of reinforced trials in a verbal paired-associates task the *S*s will continue to increase the number of correct responses on trials without KR.

Subjective reinforcement has a long way to go before it is a secure principle in our theoretical arsenal, but certainly the data on which the idea is based urge the view that there is more to human learning than external KR. A central problem for subjective reinforcement is the conditions under which the internal reference is developed. The reference seems to develop with external KR for verbal and verbal-centered motor tasks, but what about continuous skills like the Line Drawing Test? The withdrawal of KR after an acquisition series is the condition under which performance improvement occurs if subjective reinforcement is true, and yet performance decline occurs (for example,

Bilodeau, Bilodeau, and Schumsky, 1959), although not completely to the starting level of the untrained *S*. Is it because the original training with external KR has not been carried far enough to develop an adequate internal reference? Or is subjective reinforcement particularly associated with verbal behavior, with no validity for motor responses? Motor behavior and subjective reinforcement is an unexplored region that will be revealed to us eventually.

Delay of KR. What is the effect on response acquisition of delaying KR after occurrence of the response? It should be kept in mind for this section that the concern will be with the delay between a response and its KR on a trial, as shown in Fig. 21-2, with no other *E*-instigated responses intervening. There are other KR delay possibilities which have been studied, such as one or more practice trials intervening between a response and its KR (Lavery and Suddon, 1962; Bilodeau, 1956; Lorge and Thorndike, 1935). This approach is called the trials-delay technique; in it, for example, KR for response on Trial 1 is not delivered until after Trial 5. The trials-delay method has received only passing attention from psychologists because it confounds delay *per se* with the interfering effects of responses that occur

in the delay, and disallows clean inferences about either delay or interference.

Other time variables in Fig. 21-2 are the foreperiod between onset of the ready signal and the start signal, the reaction time interval between the start signal and the onset of the response, and the interval between KR and occurrence of the response on the next trial. Because the next response is a test of how well the last reinforced response is remembered, this latter interval is the retention interval which is a key variable in studies of forgetting. This interval would also be the intertrial interval, and it is often called the post-KR delay. Some authors measure the intertrial interval as time from one response to the next (for example, Bilodeau and Bilodeau, 1958), so the student who immerses himself in the details of the literature should be alert for these different definitions. The interresponse time is a variable compounded of the KR delay and the post-KR delay, and cannot be independently manipulated without changing either the KR delay or the post-KR delay. On the other hand, KR delay and post-KR delay are independently manipulable quantities.

In general, animal studies of delay of reward have shown a decreasing efficiency of performance as a function of delay,

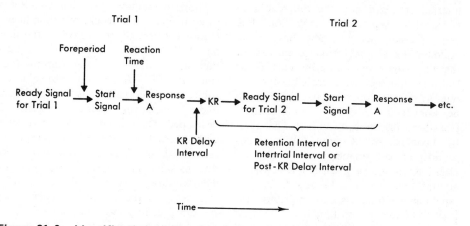

Figure 21-2. Identification of the time intervals present in simple tasks like line drawing where KR is delivered after completion of the response.

although the particular function can be complicated by other variables and does not stand in a simple relationship with delay (Kimble, 1961, pp. 150–153). Because psychologists look toward the widest generalization for their laws, it comes as a complication that human performance differs from animal findings and usually shows no effect of KR delay. Lorge and Thorndike (1935) had Ss toss balls back over their heads at an unseen target, and KR was determined by nearness of the throw to the center of the target. The KR delay periods of 0, 1, 2, 4, and 6 sec. were used, and no effects on performance were found as a function of delay. These findings are confirmed with other tasks by Bilodeau and Ryan (1960); Noble and Alcock (1958); Saltzman, Kanfer, and Greenspoon (1955); and Bilodeau and Bilodeau (1958). Moreover, these results have been validated with other response classes and do not appear to be unique for motor behavior. Bourne and Bunderson (1963) found no effect of KR delay for concept formation, and Jones and Bourne (1964, Experiments I and II) found no influence of KR delay for the learning of a verbal discrimination task.

One exception to this generalization about KR delay is continuous tracking, where delay (often called lag) seriously degrades performance (Adams, 1967a). Briefly, the gist of delay effects for tracking can be illustrated with the easy example of driving a car with delayed feedback, even though a car has a trivial delay when compared with, say, a submarine. Suppose that your car did not allow you to see the results of a steering wheel movement until 5 sec. after it occurred. If you responded at the instant the highway demanded it the car would respond five seconds too late and driving error would be disastrously large. One way to handle a system of this kind is to anticipate change in the highway and respond 5 sec. early so that correction in the car's position will coincide with change in the highway, and the difficulty of learning to anticipate is probably one of the reasons

such tasks can show poor performance. Another reason is that in a continuously moving vehicle there is very often a delay between any particular response movement and its KR, and in effect this is the trials-delay circumstance which is known to be degrading for performance (Lavery and Suddon, 1962; Bilodeau, 1956; Lorge and Thorndike, 1935).

Mechanisms of KR Delay in Simple Motor Tasks. Apparently the human has one or more effective mechanisms for bridging the KR delay interval in simple motor tasks like the Line-Drawing Test. But to say that such mechanisms exist is no more than a restatement of the finding that KR delay has the effect it does. Uncovering the nature of these mechanisms would not only give us an understanding of KR delay findings so far, but also might suggest circumstances under which KR delay would be a determining variable. Conceivably we might test a wide range of tasks and stumble upon situations (if they exist at all) where KR delay can be effective, but random hunting expeditions are usually less productive than an incisive search for basic mechanisms. When mechanisms are known and defined we can predict whether KR delay will affect performance or not in terms of whether a particular mechanism is or is not operating.

The research on KR delay has been highly empirical in asking only whether delay makes a difference for performance, but a recent study by Boulter (1964) has pushed beyond and asked about mechanisms for sustaining performance over the KR delay gap. One possibility for the mechanism could be that the motor response has internal aftereffects (motor neural traces) that are active for relatively long periods of time. The internal representation of the response is then quite active even after delay and consequently little effect of delay is found. As a second possibility the human S could capitalize on his rich language capability and use a symbolic representation of the motor response to mediate the delay. In the Line-Drawing Test, S might say to himself with some accuracy, "I moved about 5 in. that time," and then keep reminding himself "5 in." over the delay period. When E finally gives KR and says "plus 16" (assume that "plus" is overshooting and "minus" is undershooting) the S knows that 5 in. is too long and must be shortened next time. The outcome over a series of trials would be betterment of performance. Boulter reasoned that if one or both of these mechanisms were operating it should be possible to disturb them through manipulation of activities during the delay interval, and the type of activities that prove interfering should give us grounds for inferring about the mediating mechanism. The motor trace should be disturbed by other movements during the interval, and the verbal mediator should be alterable by engaging S in deliberate overt verbal activity that would deny him opportunities for covert rehearsal as an aid for remembering the verbal reference for his motor response. Boulter's task required S to move a linear slide 3 in., and it was a task similar to the Line-Drawing Test. The KR was quantitative. Four experimental groups all had KR delayed by 20 sec. in the acquisition trials. One experimental group simply rested and waited during the delay period. A second experimental group moved the metal slide back and forth during the delay period in an effort to disturb the motor trace hypothesized as the bridge for the interval. The third experimental group read from a list of random consonants during the delay in an effort to interfere with a verbal mechanism, and a fourth experimental group had both consonant reading and motor movement to cover the option that both mechanisms were operating. A control group had no delay. Forty-eight acquisition trials with KR were followed by twenty trials without KR and during which the delay interval activities were omitted. If the hypothesis concerning either the motor trace or the verbal mediator is correct, and the activities

in the delay period were properly chosen, then at least one of the experimental groups with a filled interval should have performed poorer in acquisition than the experimental group with the empty 20-sec. delay interval. None of these expectations was realized in the results. Unexpectedly, however, the three experimental groups that had motor and/or verbal activities in the delay interval performed impressively poorer than other groups on the final trials where KR was withdrawn. Boulter could not conclude for either the verbal or the motor mediator because he failed to obtain an effect in acquisition from his interfering activities. However, he did conclude that the mechanism, whatever it is, is susceptible to distortion. He reasoned that different activities in the delay interval during acquisition served to distort the stimulus context to which the response was made, and elimination of the activities when KR was withdrawn represented a different change in context for each group; hence, different performances.

In conclusion on KR delay, it is commonly heard that effective performance is dependent upon immediate KR. This generalization is or is not true, depending on whether one means acquisition trials where KR is administered or trials where KR is withdrawn. The effect of delay on response acquisition is very small or absent, or here the generalization is wrong. However, delay and the activities that fill it make a big difference for performance after KR is withdrawn, particularly if the delay interval is actively filled. If proficiency in a no-KR condition after reinforced practice is the concern, then it is wise to deliver immediate KR.

Some Theoretical Considerations. Exactly what are the changes that take place for S when KR is administered? What happens to increase the probability of motor response occurrence? Psychologists are far from agreed on the basic nature of animal reinforcement, and we are even more in the dark about why KR works to improve human performance. At least animal psychologists have shown a continuing concern about this problem but psychologists interested in human learning have been content with empirical approaches and have sidestepped the problem of why KR works as it does. It is unlikely that we will ever gain deep insight into KR delay mechanisms until we better understand what is being reinforced in motor tasks.

To illustrate the complexity of this problem let us look at the simple Line-Drawing Test and ask why KR improves performances over a series of acquisition trials. The first possibility is that KR produces an increment in a habit tendency to make the required motor response, and probably most investigators have had this view implicitly in mind. This view is one of *motor displacement habit*, or learning to displace a limb a specified amount. At the outset S makes a response of x in. displacement and this represents his habit tendencies for line drawing from past experience. These habit tendencies for inappropriate response lengths eventually extinguish with KR like "wrong" or reports of large error, and the habit tendency for the correct arm-hand displacement builds up with KR statements of "right" or of small or zero error.

But how can we be sure that S is acquiring a motor habit for arm-hand displacement? Is it possible that S is learning a *timing habit*? Rather than how much to move, S may be learning how long a time he should move. Trowbridge and Cason (1932), using the Line-Drawing Test, made interesting observations on this score. Each S was asked the following question after the experiment: "When you had drawn a line of the correct length, did you use any kind of cues in trying to draw a line of the same length again?" Of particular interest was that a number of Ss reported attempts to estimate the time required for drawing the line. Some used counting at a regular rate as a timing device; others resorted to auditory time estimation by listening to the pencil on the paper. Elwell and Grindley (1938, p. 48) report similar observations. Learning to time movements is a very critical and fundamental part of acquiring motor skills, and we know that KR is necessary for it (Slater-Hammel, 1960; Adams and Creamer, 1962a, 1962b; Adams, 1964, p. 185, 1966, 1967a).

A third possibility is that S treats the task as a problem to be solved. This is the *cognitive view*. A S might entertain various hypotheses or strategies about how to make a sequence of responses that eventually will result in zero error, and KR is used by S to confirm or disconfirm his ideas on how to attack the task and achieve the goal. Hypotheses and strategies are not easy to define and, in fact, psychologists have not yet defined them very well or devised many ways of studying them. Notwithstanding, it is becoming increasingly uncritical to bypass these complex human mechanisms that probably play a role for even simple motor activities like line drawing. As a general definition it seems fair to say that hypotheses and strategies in a motor task represent implicit verbal guidance for selecting the correct motor response from all the motor response possibilities available. The S comes to the experimental situation with a large array of problem-solving tools from his lifetime of experiences, and some of these are elicited by the task. The role of KR is to strengthen or weaken the various hypotheses and strategies that S entertains, not to strengthen or weaken the habit tendency for the motor response itself. By the cognitive view the motor response becomes a product of S's implicit, covert environment, and the KR consequences of motor responses are used for the strengthening or weakening of hypotheses or strategies, not the motor response *per se*. The distinction between a hypothesis and a strategy is somewhat arbitrary but would seem best drawn in terms of complexity. A hypothesis for line drawing might be something simple like the following: "This psychologist really wants me to move my arm until it is perpendicular to my body." A strategy would be more complex, such as, "I'll move full displacement to the right to start. If the psychologist says 'wrong' I'm probably above the target zone so next time I'll move full to the left. If he says 'wrong' again, I'm probably below the target. On the third trial I'll try something in between." A strategy like this involves a series of responses directed toward a goal, in contrast to a hypothesis which represents a single possibility for achieving a goal. How to objectify and know hypotheses and strategies is a burdensome problem for psychologists. We are only beginning to grapple with ways for knowing the hidden, under-the-skin mediational environment that determines so much of human responding. One approach is to assume hypotheses and strategies are essentially verbal and fully available through interview. By asking S how he attacked the task we can determine his hypotheses and strategies. Another way is to look at the patterning of S's motor responses and try to infer his mode of attack.

Macpherson, Dees, and Grindley (1948) apparently were the first to observe that Ss can approach a simple motor task as a problem-solving situation. They had a time and pressure experiment where the task involved how long a lever was pressed down *and* how far it was pressed. Even though Ss were given a demonstration and instructions, some used elaborate hypotheses in the task. One S thought there was a dynamo behind the apparatus and tried to figure how it functioned. Another S thought that only time of depression was relevant. Another believed that it was the rate at which the lever was released.

Annett (1959) suggested that Ss might be using a bracketing strategy in a simple lever-positioning task where Ss had to learn to displace the lever a given amount. With a bracketing strategy S would go above and below the target each time so that with successive responses he eventually homes in on the correct position. Lavery (1962) used three simple motor tasks and compared quantitative error KR (amount and direction of error) with qualitative KR where S was told only the direction of error (too high, too low). No performance differences were found for acquisition trials. With qualitative error it would seem the S had little choice but to evaluate KR reports and home in on the target by successive approximations through bracketing. The absences of differences between these conditions in Lavery's experiment could mean that Ss were using a bracketing strategy under both KR conditions, although his results do not prove it decisively. There are research directions that might produce proof, however. If the bracketing strategy is used, a series of responses should alternate between positive and negative error. The psychological literature contains no data on how responses pattern themselves around the target zone over a series of trials. Or, verbal reports, as used by Trowbridge and Cason (1932) and Macpherson, Dees, and Grindley (1948), might be used. Whatever is done, there are enough lines of preliminary evidence to suggest that a notion of KR as being simply a motor habit may be a serious simplification of the actual state of affairs. Perhaps Trowbridge and Cason (1932) were on the right track when they observed, "The motor act of drawing a line was by no means the only psychological activity taking place" (p. 253).

A fourth possibility is that *KR exerts a motivational influence* as part of its effect on performance. An increase in performance level does not necessarily mean that the strengthening of a motor habit connection, hypothesis, or strategy is the sole responsible factor. Performance level can increase with an increase in motivation too. One approach to the motivation hypothesis is the use of a nonskill task where evolvement of habits, hypotheses, or strategies is not needed for success. If KR enhances performances under these circumstances we can assume that motivation is a reasonable possibility for one of KR's influences.

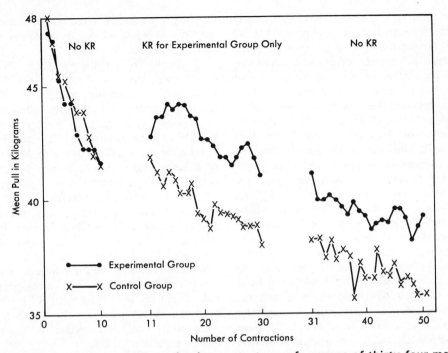

Figure 21-3. Effects of KR on the dynamometer performance of thirty-four men.
(Drawn from tabled values in Manzer, C. W. The effect of knowledge of output on muscular work. *J. exp. Psychol.*, 1935, **18**, 80–96.)

An example of a nonskill task is the well-known hand dynamometer which *S* is required to pull or squeeze at a regular rate. Score is number of pulls on a trial. Will KR affect performance in a task such as this? Arps (1917, 1920) and Crawley (1926) found positive effects for KR in simple nonskill tasks, but Manzer (1935), in a better study, made a more decisive case. The hand dynamometer was used, and each *S* pulled the dynamometer fifty times (a trial was one pull) as hard as he could. Following ten initial trials without KR for an experimental and a control group, the experimental group was told the strength of the pull on the next twenty trials while the control group continued to pull without KR. Twenty trials without KR followed for both groups. The results for thirty-four men are shown in Fig. 21-3.

It can be seen that KR markedly increased performance and that this advantage maintained itself throughout the last twenty trials where KR was absent. Because this is a nonskill task it seems reasonable to assume that KR was functioning as a motivator. The motivation may be social and competitive in that *S* might try to improve on performance which he thinks *E* will judge inadequate or which will be poorer than that of other *S*s.

Another way of testing for the motivational component of KR is to work within the context of a theory that makes assumptions about how motivation affects behavior. The theory of Clark L. Hull (1943) holds that motivation energizes all response classes, while habit is for specific stimulus-response connections with only a very limited spread to other stimuli and responses through stimulus and response generalization. If KR is in part a motivator when applied in Task A there should be improved performance (positive transfer) for completely different Tasks B, C, or D when compared to a control group that did not have prior training on Task A. However, if KR merely serves habit formation, we should not expect transfer because of marked stimulus and response dissimilarities between the tasks. This approach is similar to that of Amsel (1958, 1962) in his studies of frustration. He found that animals frustrated in one situation showed an increase in running speed when transferred to another, and he concludes for frustration being a general motivating state of affairs. No tests along this line have been made for KR and human performance but it would seem a worthwhile line of attack. One should be wary of certain hazards for this approach, however. If positive results are found, then support would be in hand for both the specific hypothesis and the theory. But if KR failed to transfer positively, then it would not be clear whether KR lacks motivational properties or whether the theory is wrong. Motivation may not energize all response classes as Hull says it does.

In conclusion on theory, these four possibilities that have been outlined for basic KR mechanisms remain to be thoroughly tested, and probably additional hypotheses will be devised. Whatever the validity of these possibilities they are important for the emphasis they give the web of influences operating in human performance situations that are seemingly very simple. But until we unscramble these matters and uncover the underlying mechanisms, we have only scratched the scientific surface. We have made use of empirical, nontheoretical research throughout this chapter in providing the fundamental facts which our mechanisms must encompass, but we remain superficial until we probe beneath and ask questions about primary mechanisms which encompass the many diverse experimental facts.

CHAPTER 22

Forgetting of Motor Responses

In the last chapter we were concerned with how motor responses are acquired, but equally important is reduction in the probability of occurrence for motor responses over periods of nonpractice. The nonpractice period is called the retention interval, and the reduction in recall is called forgetting, as everyone knows. Overall, the topic is one of memory—a term that fell into disuse for a number of years but which is used regularly now.

Memory is enjoying a lively revival in experimental psychology, and the emphasis is overdue. Learning psychologists have been concerned for a long time with the conditions under which responses are entered in the behavioral repertoire, and there is a parallel need for understanding how responses are forgotten and become unavailable to S. Even the simplest learning paradigm of several trials where the sequence is practice-rest practice-rest, and so on, contains the problem of remembering the response that was formed on earlier trials. With the usual retention interval this is a case of short-term memory over seconds or minutes (for example, Adams, 1967b) rather than long-term memory with retention intervals of hours, days, months,

and years. Thus, memory enters lawfulness for basic learning as well as fully ramifying through our practical lives.

The reader will refer to Fig. 21-2 in the last chapter and note the retention interval that is the focus here. After a response has been reinforced by KR operations we assume that an increment for the association between a stimulus and a response is formed, and this associative bond is called the *memory trace*. Habit strength is a synonym for this bond, although we discussed in the last chapter the various possibilities for what is learned in a simple motor task and the potential hazards of considering this associative mechanism as a simple motor habit. Weakening or loss of habits is all that should be admitted for the study of retention, and this restriction has not always been fully understood. Any psychological variable can conceivably change over the retention interval. Motivation can change, or recovery from the depressing effects of work inhibition can occur, and studies of this kind have often been labeled *retention*, but the plea here is for studies of forgetting to include only those investigations where performance loss over the retention interval can be attributed

495

to changes in habit. Otherwise the study of forgetting has no defined domain and is operationally meaningless.

Theories of Forgetting

It is unsatisfying for many scientists to stop at descriptive empirical data. They want to probe behind data and ask why phenomena occur. It is primary for science to collect data under controlled conditions, but the inclination to press beyond and ask about theoretical mechanisms depends on the disposition of the scientist himself. Those who are satisfied with straight empiricism without theory contend that behavioral data alone are sufficient for the scientific job of prediction, and this is true as far as it goes, but theorists contend that transcending the data with theory not only explains the data that instigated the theory but also gives the further power for predicting behavior in hitherto untested situations. It is our hope for theories of forgetting that we can predict when forgetting will occur and in what quantities.

Our theories of forgetting are not strong, and they have a long way to go for solid verification (Adams, 1967b). In the main it is fair to say they have been derived from studies of verbal behavior. An early hypothesis, and a difficult one to disprove, is the theory of the *decaying memory trace*. This view holds that memory trace is inherently unstable with respect to time, and that it weakens gradually over the retention interval. The weakened memory trace, being a prime internal agent for the response, produces a lowered performance level at recall. Forgetting, therefore, is a matter of spontaneous neural activity. The *interference theory of forgetting* has the most status currently, and it holds that events occurring during the retention interval (retroactive inhibition) or prior to original learning (proactive inhibition) are potentially interfering for criterion re-

sponses and can weaken their strength at recall (Postman, 1961). Lastly, *loss of set* is considered a process that accounts for the very temporary forgetting called warmup decrement which occurs after a period of nonpractice, and it is considered a factor operating in addition to interference with criterion responses for the task. *Set*, in this context, means favorable postural adjustments, bodily attitudes, and receptor orientations required for success in the task, and their disturbance during a retention interval results in decrement at recall. Loss of set results from interference also, but it is interference with the matrix of secondary responses supporting the criterion responses whose interference is the special concern of the interference theory of forgetting. Adams (1961b) considers that loss of set has methodological problems for motor behavior which reduce its explanatory value at this time.

Short-Term Memory for Motor Responses. Short-term memory concerns an organism's capability for retention of a response over a short period of time, usually measured in sec. or min. Span of attention or memory span, where S immediately reports back to E a series of letters or numbers presented to him, has been a long-standing interest in short-term memory for psychology. The primary emphasis for studies of memory span has often been individual differences in memory, but recent research on short-term memory has manipulated such variables as type and amount of materials, length of the retention interval, and number of practice repetitions or reinforcements, in an attempt to build data for a theory of memory. Most of the research has been done on verbal responses.

The British psychologist Brown (1958) and the American psychologists Peterson and Peterson (1959) apparently were the first to establish the experimental methods that have become widespread for the study of verbal short-term memory. A verbal unit like a nonsense syllable is presented one or

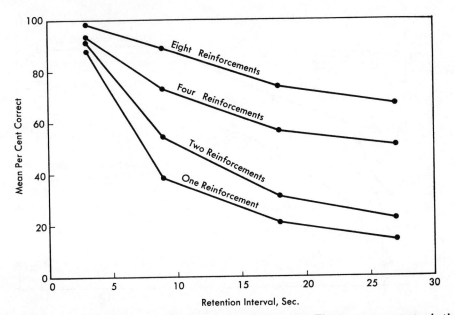

Figure 22-1. Short-term retention for a verbal response. The curve parameter is the number of practice repetitions given the response before onset of the retention interval. (Drawn from tabled values in Hellyer, S. Supplementary report: Frequency of stimulus presentation and short-term decrement in recall. *J. exp. Psychol.*, 1962, **64**, 650.)

more times. In the retention interval that follows, the S is required to repeat innocuous material like random numbers to prevent his covert rehearsal of the syllable. At the end of the retention interval the S is signaled and he attempts to recall the item. Figure 22-1 shows data by Hellyer (1962) which is representative for verbal memory studies of this kind. Depending upon the experimental condition, Hellyer's S repeated a three-consonant nonsense syllable one, two, four, or eight times and then recalled it after either 3, 9, 18, or 27 sec. Random digits were read during the brief retention interval. It can be seen that forgetting is very rapid in short-term memory, particularly when number of reinforcements is small. With a single repetition the syllable is almost completely forgotten in 27 sec. As number of reinforcements increase, however, recall level increases. One way psychologists have viewed this increase in recall as number of reinforcements increase is to hypothesize

that the memory trace gradually transitions from short-term to long-term memory with practice. Psychologists presently disagree on the need for these two compartments of verbal memory. Some argue for a continuum (Melton, 1963), but there are compelling reasons for dual compartments (Adams, 1967b). Support for a two-factor view requires evidence that the same variables and laws do not describe both short-term and long-term retention phenomena.

These data on verbal short-term memory may seem alien for a chapter on motor behavior, but they are presented as background and a basis for comparison with the work that has been done on short-term memory for motor responses. That motor short-term memory has the same rapid forgetting as verbal short-term memory has been hinted in several experiments on KR. Both Macpherson, Dees, and Grindley (1948) and Denny *et al.* (1960) found a significant worsening of performance with an increase of seconds for the retention

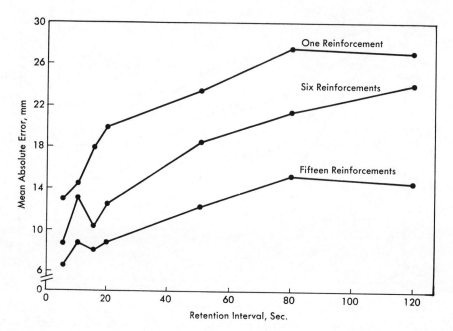

Figure 22-2. Short-term retention for a simple motor response. Curve parameter is number of repetitions of the response before onset of the retention interval. (Reprinted with permission from Adams, J. A., and Dijkstra, S. Short-term memory for motor responses. *J. exp. Psychol.*, 1966, **71**, 314–318.)

interval. More recently, Adams and Dijkstra (1966) examined the topic of motor short-term memory more systematically and asked if the same short-term forgetting functions could be found for motor responses as for verbal responses. In effect, they repeated Hellyer's experiment except that a simple linear motor response was used. If functions like those of Hellyer's were found an argument could be made for the same laws of short-term forgetting applying to both motor and verbal behavior. If different relationships emerge, a motor memory system in addition to one for verbal memory might be required and the scientific picture for memory would become complicated. Adams and Dijkstra required Ss to reach through an opaque curtain and move a metal slide along a track until it came up against a fixed stop. This defined the response length that S was to remember, just as the seeing of a nonsense syllable and saying it defines the correct

response for S in a verbal short-term memory experiment. To evaluate the effects of reinforcements or practice, one, six, or fifteen repetitions of the motor response were given. Retention intervals were either 5, 10, 15, 20, 50, 80, or 120 sec., and S waited quietly during the interval with his hand on the slide. All combinations of the various values for reinforcement and retention interval were administered. Recall was with the fixed stop removed so the slide could take on any value, and the measure of performance was absolute error, which is deviation from the correct response length irrespective of direction of error.

The results are shown in Fig. 22-2, and they parallel those of Hellyer very closely, except, of course, the curves go in the opposite direction because error and not per cent correct was the measure. Forgetting was very rapid over brief retention intervals when number of reinforcements was small, and it steadily decreased as number of reinforcements increased.

But do the findings of Adams and Dijkstra imply that verbal and motor short-term retention conform to the same laws because they have the same functional form? In the descriptive empirical sense the findings of Hellyer are much the same as those of Adams and Dijkstra, but this does not necessarily mean that the same theoretical explanation applies to both. The best explanation for verbal forgetting, both short term and long term, is interference (Adams, 1967b). If interference is the explanation for Hellyer's findings, then how does interference apply to those of Adams and Dijkstra? Proactive interference from preceding trials was not found to be a factor, and retroactive interference from events in the retention interval is hard to see because S did nothing but sit and wait for E's cue to recall the movement he had just made. One must entertain the tentative possibility that trace decay is the explanation for the Adams-Dijkstra findings and, if so, it is a different theoretical cause than the interference which explains Hellyer's data with the same functional form. If further research shows that the forgetting of motor responses is best explained by trace decay theory, then we could argue for motor memory as a compartment distinct from those that control the retention of verbal responses. Such an outcome would not be parsimonious for a theory of memory, but nature does not always abide economy of description.

Long-Term Retention of Continuous Motor Responses. Figure 22-2 shows that with practice repetitions motor retention becomes increasingly stable over time; it is puzzling in that continuous motor responses become *very* stable relative to other response classes. From our common experiences we are all familiar with the high retention for complex motor acts like riding a bicycle or ice skating. Even after comparatively long periods of no practice

we find we are able to ride a bicycle or ice skate with all the grace and coordination we had long ago. An adult can climb on a bicycle after years without practice and ride away with hardly faltering. In contrast, many other response classes are rapidly forgotten. The poem learned in the third grade has little chance of recall at all.

The high resistance of continuous motor behavior to forgetting processes has been thoroughly documented in the laboratory. A recent experiment by Fleishman and Parker (1962) nicely demonstrates that the forgetting of complex motor behavior is negligible for intervals up to twenty-four months. They used a three-dimensional tracking task that embodied some of the motor response features of flying an airplane. The motor coordinations were complex and in three dimensions (two on a stick control for the hand, one on a rudder bar for the feet), but the display was fairly simple. The S's instrument panel had two elements. One was a cathode ray tube with a dot which was programmed to move in two dimensions and S had to keep it centered with movements of his stick control. Beneath the cathode ray tube was a voltmeter whose needle deflections were centered by rudder movements. The more S kept the dot and needle centered the less his error and the better his performance. The portion of their experiment of interest here involved widely distributed original training of seventeen practice sessions spread over six weeks. Retention intervals for three different groups were nine, fourteen, and twenty-four months. The results are shown in Fig. 22-3. The acquisition curve for the training sessions is for three groups combined because they all had common treatment at this stage. High skill is indicated by the acquisition curve obtaining its asymptote and showing little inclination toward further improvement. The amounts of forgetting for the two groups that had retention intervals of 9 and 14 months were trivial, and the slightly greater forgetting for the twenty-four-

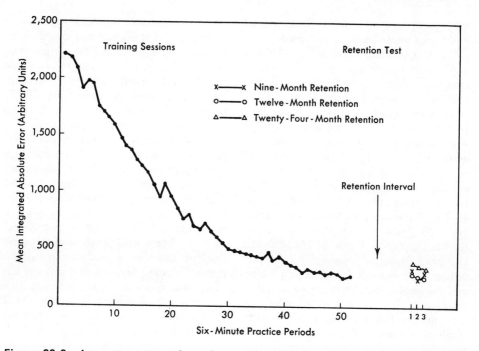

Figure 22-3. Long-term retention of a continuous motor response. (Adapted with permission from Fleishman, E. A., and Parker, J. F., Jr. Factors in the retention and relearning of perceptual-motor skills. *J. exp. Psychol.*, 1962, **64**, 215–226.)

month group is surprisingly small. Moreover, a detailed analysis of retention performance showed the forgetting loss for the twenty-four-month group, small though it was, was fleeting and temporary. After only the second minute of practice the loss for this group had almost disappeared. Fleishman and Parker conclude that the retention of continuous perceptual-motor skills is extremely high, and the small losses that do occur are recovered very rapidly in relearning. The findings are not unique. The psychological literature contains other instances of this generalization. Bell (1950) found high retention for pursuit rotor performance over a period of one year. Ammons *et al.* (1958) found very high retention of tracking performance for intervals up to two years. Mengelkoch, Adams, and Gainer (1958) used a flight simulator (a ground device for pilot training) and found very high retention of the continuous motor skills required for air-craft control over four months. There appear to be no exceptions in the psychological literature to the generalization that continuous motor responses are very well retained for long periods of time.

Why are continuous motor responses retained so much better than other response classes? There are several possibilities, none of which have received empirical verification but which seem deserving directions for research:

1. Attention must be given to *methods of measurement.* Motor error at recall may be small and corrected quickly so that the result for the performance score is a small decrement. This same kind of error response in verbal learning could be counted as a wrong response and it would not take very many of them to produce a sharp forgetting loss. Tracking behavior is continuous with respect to time and scored accordingly. Verbal behavior can also be viewed with respect to a time base line but

responses are we never treat it so. Verbal typically treated as discrete, all-or-none occurrences.

2. Assuming the *interference theory of forgetting*, unstructured everyday motor activities may have little likelihood of competing with the highly specific motor skills taught in the laboratory. Of course, one cannot simply assume the validity of an interference explanation without empirical tests, and this testing will not be easy. The interference hypothesis has attained its status in studies of verbal learning and retention, primarily because verbal behavior has received intensive investigation by psychologists and we know a great deal about verbal materials and the conditions under which interference occurs. Motor behavior, on the other hand, is a less well-developed area of psychology and we know little about the conditions that induce interference between motor responses learned in the laboratory and those performed in everyday life. One prominent approach for testing the interference theory is to have Ss learn verbal lists in the laboratory that have some likelihood of interfering with normal language habits in everyday life (Postman, 1961). Certain predictable consequences for forgetting follow from these experimental manipulations, and it is a good research strategy for assessing the theory. However, it is difficult for us at present to specify a laboratory motor task that would interfere, or not interfere, with extralaboratory motor activities. Until this methodological problem is solved, we will lack an important means for determining the relevance of interference theory for motor behavior.

3. Continuous motor responses are greatly overlearned relative to other response classes. A big problem with continuous motor tasks is that number of KR operations is indeterminate and *amount of practice* becomes a difficult quantity to control and manipulate exactly. The customary laboratory procedure is to have Ss practice on a continuous task for a fixed amount of time, but during this time there is no way of knowing the frequency of KR. How many KR events occur for S on a 1-min. trial on the Rotary Pursuit Test? Undoubtedly a great many, and with great overlearning retention is very high. A first direction for exposing the reasons for very high retention of continuous responses would be to use a motor task where number of reinforcements could be placed under explicit experimental control, and then compare its retention with that for verbal or discrete motor responses that received the same number of reinforcements.

4. Well-learned continuous motor responses may be *intrinsically* more resistant to forgetting than other well-learned response classes, and the initial gross movements tend to reinstate the kinesthetic cue set on which motor movements importantly depend, arouse the memory trace, and evoke the correct response pattern almost immediately. It is conceivable that verbal responses have a very stable memory trace also, but verbal responses do not allow immediate reinstatement of an important part of the total cue complex and retention is poor as a result.

Long-Term Retention of Discrete Motor Responses. Discrete responses are a primary category of motor behavior. A simple reaction-time test is a one-unit discrete motor task, but a common variety of discrete motor task found in and outside the laboratory has a sequence of several stimuli-response units. Performance measurement is in terms of errors and/or time to complete all units. Pertinent for our purposes here is that discrete motor responses are forgotten much more readily and completely than continuous motor responses, which is a distinction not always made by those who state the generalization that motor skills show little forgetting. Discrete responses seem to have the comparatively rapid forgetting that characterizes verbal responses. Duncan and Underwood (1952) used a six-unit discrete motor task that had six colored stimuli and six slots into which S moved a lever. The S had to learn which slot was associated with which stimulus color, and the task was to be performed as rapidly as possible. For performance measured in terms of number of correct responses on a trial they found forgetting to be a large 82 per cent over a fourteen-month retention interval. Ammons *et al.* (1958) used a fifteen-unit discrete task with low and high levels of original training (five and thirty trials), and retention intervals ranging from 1 min. to two years. The results are given in Fig. 22-4. Per cent loss

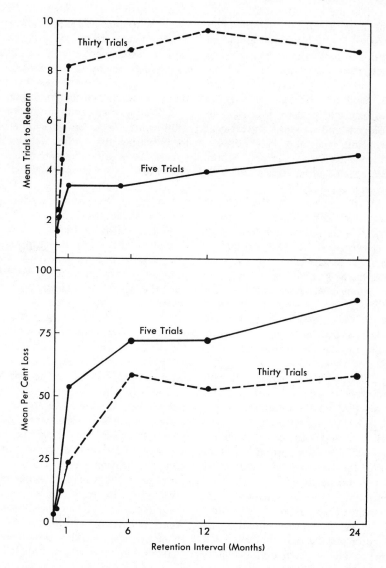

Figure 22-4. Long-term retention of discrete motor responses. Curve parameter is number of practice trials in original learning. Both per cent forgotten and trials to relearn are shown. (Adapted with permission from Ammons, R. B., *et al.* Long-term retention of perceptual-motor skills. *J. exp. Psychol.*, 1958, **55**, 318–328.)

over the retention interval was computed by a formula that expressed amount forgotten as a percentage of the amount originally learned:

Per cent loss = $100 \times$

$$\frac{(\text{First Recall Trial}) - (\text{Final Training Trial})}{(\text{First Training Trial}) - (\text{Last Training Trial})}$$

This value was computed for each S and the averages for the groups are presented in the bottom half of Fig. 22-4. A trial was once through the fifteen units, and the time to complete the trial was the score used in the formula. It can be seen that the per cent lost is very substantial and that it is larger for the small amount of original training. The top half of Fig. 22-4 shows trials to relearn the performance level of the final training trial as a function of amount of original training and retention interval. Interestingly, the groups with thirty training trials took longer to regain their lost skill even though their per cent loss was less than for groups having only five training trials. A higher level of original training pays off in a higher recall level but that which is forgotten is not easily regained when the skill is highly developed.

Aircraft pilots perform a great many discrete tasks. Starting and stopping an aircraft entail discrete response sequences. Or if an engine becomes afire, the pilot may perform several discrete responses to remedy the emergency, or attempt to remedy it. With the importance of discrete responses for flying, it is of considerable practical value to know how well discrete responses are retained and what steps must be taken to insure their high performance level in pilots. Consistent with laboratory research on the forgetting of discrete responses, research on the retention of discrete responses for aircraft has also shown rapid forgetting. Using a flight simulator, Mengelkoch, Adams and Gainer (1958) concluded that the forgetting of responses for discrete cockpit tasks over a four-month retention interval was sufficient to impair a pilot's flying efficiency and safety. They had low and high levels of original training, and they found more forgetting with the small amount of initial training but fewer trials to relearn, which confirms the findings of Ammons *et al.* (1958). Also using a flight simulator, Adams and Hufford (1962) found the forgetting of a ten-unit discrete cockpit task to be almost 100 per cent for a ten-month retention interval. Research results like these urge that training programs for the maintenance of flying proficiency give special attention to the regular retraining of discrete response sequences if the pilot is to be skillful and safe. Fortunately this problem is appreciated and the retraining of forgotten discrete responses is a standard part of flight training programs.

What explanation can we give for the rapid forgetting of discrete motor responses, particularly because continuous motor responses are retained so well? One obvious possibility that has been mentioned before is degree of learning. Like verbal responses which are also discrete, the level of original learning for discrete motor responses might be low relative to continuous motor responses. The result is that both verbal and discrete motor responses show rapid forgetting because they are not learned to a high enough level.

A second potential explanation is the interference theory of forgetting. It is defensible to consider that discrete motor responses have a verbal component and, if so, they would be subject to the same interference sources in the everyday language environment as verbal responses (Postman, 1961). Verbal guidance is a common expectation for discrete motor tasks, like S saying to himself, "Press the left-hand switch when the red light comes on." Research has shown that verbal responses can exert a considerable effect on discrete motor responses (McAllister, 1953; Solarz, 1960). Theories and empirical research on the verbal component of motor behavior, as well as other response classes, have been discussed by Arnoult (1957), Goss (1955), and Vanderplas (1958). We need techniques for measuring the degree of verbalness in motor tasks to see if verbalness and forgetting are related. Another approach would be to use techniques of verbal pretraining and specifically build a verbal component for discrete motor responses. Retention for such *S*s could then be compared with that for control *S*s who lack the experimentally trained verbal elements. Verbal pretraining techniques have been used in studies of motor learning and transfer, but they have yet to be turned toward forgetting issues.

Conclusion

The study of motor retention is not a highly developed research area, although the topic contains a number of primary issues for our scientific understanding of forgetting. The research so far has been empirical and nontheoretical. Perhaps one of the reasons for this is that motor-response classes like tracking have commanded the interest of applied psychologists who are concerned with the determinants of vehicular control. These workers have asked practical questions about how much forgetting can be expected over periods of nonpractice for skills like flying an airplane. Important as practical matters are to some, applied research usually goes only far enough to answer its pressing practical questions and leaves unanswered questions about basic variables, laws, and theory. The motor research literature has a good quantity of data for solving practical problems, and perhaps it is time to press harder for the more fundamental understanding that is lacking.

Glossary

delay of KR. In human learning situations, time delay between occurrence of a response and the reinforcing event.

discrete motor task. A motor task, like pressing a sequence of buttons, which requires a discontinuous series of discrete responses.

empirical reinforcement. Events associated with responses that result in learning but which are determined by trial-and-error empirical investigation, not theoretical rationale.

interference theory of forgetting. The theory that forgetting results from interfering events occurring prior to the learning of the criterion response (proactive inhibition), or in the retention interval (retroactive inhibition).

knowledge of results (KR). The stimulus events associated with responses in human learning experiments that result in learning. Functionally equivalent to reinforcement.

loss of set. An explanation offered to account for the portion of the forgetting decrement which is called "need to warm-up." Assumes losses in secondary behavioral components that are supportive for criterion responding, in addition to forgetting effects on the memory trace.

memory trace. The associative bond between a stimulus and a response.

self-reinforcement. The possibility that reinforcement can be internal to the *S* as well as external, as in KR.

short-term memory. A temporary memory storage system for the remembering of events over seconds or a few minutes. The scientific justification for short-term memory, as distinct from long-term memory, depends upon different behavioral laws for short-term retention paradigms.

theory of decaying memory trace. A theory of forgetting. The forgetting decrement results from spontaneous degeneration of the memory trace overtime.

tracking task. A motor control task of error-nulling. An input generates a continuously varying control problem, and the *S* responds with his control (output) to null error that is displayed to him.

References

Adams, J. A. Human tracking behavior. *Psychol., Bull.*, 1961a, **58**, 55–79.

Adams, J. A. The second facet of forgetting: A review of warm-up decrement. *Psychol. Bull.*, 1961b, **58**, 257–273.

Adams, J. A. Motor skills. *Annu. Rev. Psychol.*, 1964, **15**, 181–202.

Adams, J. A. Some mechanisms of motor responding: An examination of attention. In E. A. Bilodeau (Ed.), *Acquisition of skill*. New York: Academic Press, 1966. Pp. 169–200.

Adams, J. A. Engineering psychology. In H. Helson & W. Bevan (Eds.), *Contemporary approaches to psychology*. Princeton: Van Nostrand, 1967a.

Adams, J. A. *Human memory*. New York: McGraw-Hill, 1967b.

Adams, J. A., & Creamer, L. R. Anticipatory timing of continuous and discrete responses. *J. exp. Psychol.*, 1962a, **63**, 84–90.

Adams, J. A., & Creamer, L. R. Proprioception variables as determiners of anticipatory timing behavior. *Hum. Factors*, 1962b, **4**, 217–222.

Adams, J. A., & Dijkstra, S. Short-term memory for motor responses. *J. exp. Psychol.*, 1966, **71**, 314–318.

Adams, J. A., & Hufford, L. E. Contributions of a part-task trainer to learning and relearning of a time-shared flight maneuver. *Hum. Factors*, 1962, **4**, 159–170.

Ammons, R. B., Farr, R. G., Block, Edith, Neumann, Eva, Dey, M., Marion, R., & Ammons, Carol H. Long-term retention of perceptual-motor skills. *J. exp. Psychol.*, 1958, **55**, 318–328.

Amsel, A. The role of frustrative nonreward in noncontinuous reward situations. *Psychol. Bull.*, 1958, **55**, 102–119.

Amsel, A. Frustrative nonreward in partial reinforcement and discrimination learning: Some recent history and a theoretical extension. *Psychol. Rev.*, 1962, **69**, 306–328.

Annett, J. Some aspects of the acquisition of sensory motor skills. Unpublished doctoral dissertation, Oxford Univer., 1959.

Arnoult, M. D. Stimulus predifferentiation: some generalizations and hypotheses. *Psychol. Bull.*, 1957, **54**, 339–350.

Arps, G. F. A preliminary report on work with knowledge versus work without knowledge of results. *Psychol. Rev.*, 1917, **24**, 449–455.

Arps, G. F. Work with knowledge of results versus work without knowledge of results. *Psychol. Monogr.*, 1920, No. 125.

Baker, C. H., & Young, Phyllis. Feedback during training and retention of motor skills. *Canad. J. Psychol.*, 1960, **14**, 257–264.

Bell, H. M. Retention of pursuit rotor skill after one year. *J. exp. Psychol.*, 1950, **40**, 648–649.

Bilodeau, Ina McD. Accuracy of a simple positioning response with variation in the number of trials by which knowledge of results is delayed. *Amer. J. Psychol.*, 1956, **69**, 434–437.

Bilodeau, E. A., & Bilodeau, Ina McD. Variation of temporal intervals among critical events in five studies of knowledge of results. *J. exp. Psychol.*, 1958, **55**, 603–612.

Bilodeau, E. A., & Bilodeau, Ina McD. Motor-skills learning. *Annu. Rev. Psychol.*, 1961, **12**, 243–280.

Bilodeau, E. A., Bilodeau, Ina McD., & Schumsky, D. A. Some effects of introducing and withdrawing knowledge of results early and late in practice. *J. exp. Psychol.*, 1959, **58**, 142–144.

Bilodeau, E. A., & Ryan, F. J. A test for interaction of delay of knowledge of results and two types of interpolated activity. *J. exp. Psychol.*, 1960, **59**, 414–419.

Bourne, L. E., Jr., & Bunderson, C. V. Effects of delay of informative feedback and length of postfeedback interval on concept identification. *J. exp. Psychol.*, 1963, **65**, 1–5.

Boulter, L. R. Evaluation of mechanisms in delay of knowledge of results. *Canad. J. Psychol.*, 1964, **18**, 281–291.

Brown, J. Some tests of the decay theory of immediate memory. *Quart. J. exp. Psychol.*, 1958, **10**, 12–21.

Butler, D. C., & Peterson, D. E. Learning during "extinction" with paired associates. *J. verb. Learn. verb. Behav.*, 1965, **4**, 103–106.

Crawley, S. L. An experimental investigation of recovery from work. *Arch. Psychol.*, 1926, **13**, No. 85.

Denny, M. R., Allard, M., Hall, E., & Rokeach, M. Supplementary report: Delay of knowledge of results, knowledge of task, and intertrial interval. *J. exp. Psychol.*, 1960, **60**, 327.

Duncan, C. P., & Underwood, B. J. Retention of transfer in motor learning after 24 hours and after 14 months as a function of degree of first-task learning and inter-task similarity. USAF Wright Air Development Center, *WADC Tech. Rep. 52-224*, Oct. 1952.

Eimas, P. D. Subjective reinforcement in the paired-associate learning of retarded and normal children. *Canad. J. Psychol.*, 1964, **18**, 183–196.

Eimas, P. D., & Zeaman, D. Response speed changes in an Estes' paired-associate "miniature" experiment. *J. verb. Learn. verb. Behav.*, 1963, **1**, 384–388.

Elwell, J. L., & Grindley, G. S. The effect of knowledge of results on learning and performance. *Brit. J. Psychol.*, 1938, **29**, 39–53.

Fleishman, E. A., & Parker, J. F., Jr. Factors in the retention and relearning of perceptual-motor skill. *J. exp. Psychol.*, 1962, **64**, 215–226.

Goss, A. E. A stimulus-response analysis of the interaction of cue-producing and instrumental responses. *Psychol. Rev.*, 1955, **62**, 20–31.

Goss, A. E. Manifest strengthening of correct responses of paired-associates under postcriterion zero percent occurrence of response members. *J. gen. Psychol.*, 1965, **72**, 135–144.

Hardesty, D., & Bevan, W. Forms of orally-presented knowledge of results and serial reaction time. *Tech. Rep. No. 18*, Office of Naval Research, April 1964. Contract Nonr-3634(01).

Hellyer, S. Supplementary report: Frequency of stimulus presentation and short-term decrement in recall. *J. exp. Psychol.*, 1962, **64**, 650.

Hull, C. L. *Principles of behavior.* New York: Appleton-Century-Crofts, 1943.

Jones, R. E., & Bourne, L. E. Delay of informative feedback in verbal learning. *Canad. J. Psychol.*, 1964, **18**, 266–280.

Kimble, G. A. *Conditioning and learning.* New York: Appleton-Century-Crofts, 1961.

Lavery, J. J. Retention of simple motor skills as a function of type of knowledge of results. *Canad. J. Psychol.*, 1962, **16**, 300–311.

Lavery, J. J., & Suddon, Florence, H. Retention of simple motor skills as a function of the number of trials by which KR is delayed. *Percept. mot. Skills*, 1962, **15**, 231–237.

Leonard, J. A., & Conrad, R. Maintenance of high accuracy without augmented feedback. *Nature*, 1963, **199**, 512–513.

Lorge, L., & Thorndike, E. L. The influence of delay in the after-effect of a connection. *J. exp. Psychol.*, 1935, **18**, 186–194.

Macpherson, S. J., Dees, V., & Grindley, G. C. The effect of knowledge of results on learning and performance. II. Some characteristics of very simple skills. *Quart. J. exp. Psychol.*, 1948, **1**, 68–78.

Macpherson, S. J., Dees, V., & Grindley, G. C. The effect of knowledge of results on learning and performance: III. The influence of the time interval between trials. *Quart. J. exp. Psychol.*, 1948, **1**, 167–174.

McAllister, Dorothy E. The effects of various kinds of relevant verbal pre-training on subsequent motor performance. *J. exp. Psychol.*, 1953, **46**, 329–336.

Manzer, C. W. The effect of knowledge of output on muscular work. *J. exp. Psychol.*, 1935, **18**, 80–96.

Melton, A. W. Implications of short-term memory for a general theory of memory. *J. verb. Learn. verb. Behav.*, 1963, **2**, 1–21.

Mengelkoch, R. F., Adams, J. A., & Gainer, C. A. The forgetting of instrument flying skills as a function of the level of initial proficiency. U. S. Naval Training Device Center, *Human Engineering Tech. Rep. NAVTRADEVCEN 71-16-18*, Sept. 1958.

Noble, C. E., & Alcock, W. T. Human delayed-reward learning with different lengths of task. *J. exp. Psychol.*, 1958, **56**, 407–412.

Peterson, L. R., & Peterson, Margaret J. Short-term retention of individual verbal items. *J. exp. Psychol.*, 1959, **58**, 193–198.

Postman, L. The present status of interference theory. In C. N. Cofer (Ed.), *Verbal learning and verbal behavior*. New York: McGraw-Hill, 1961. Pp. 152–179.

Richardson, J., & Gropper, Mitsi S. Learning during recall trials. *Psychol. Rep.*, 1964, **15**, 551–560.

Saltzman, I. J., Kanfer, F. H., & Greenspoon, J. Delay of reward and human motor learning. *Psychol. Rep.*, 1955, **1**, 139–142.

Seashore, H., & Bavelas, A. The functioning of knowledge of results in Thorndike's line-drawing experiment. *Psychol. Rev.*, 1941, **48**, 155–164.

Slater-Hammel, A. T. Reliability, accuracy, and refractoriness of a transit reaction. *Res. Quart. Amer. Assoc. Health, Phys. Educ. Recreation*, 1960, **31**, 217–228.

Solarz, A. K. Latency of instrumental responses as a function of compatibility with the meaning of eliciting verbal signs. *J. exp. Psychol.*, 1960, **59**, 239–245.

Thorndike, E. L. The law of effect. *Amer. J. Psychol.*, 1927, **39**, 212–222.

Trowbridge, Margery H., & Cason, H. An experimental study of Thorndike's theory of learning. *J. gen. Psychol.*, 1932, **7**, 245–260.

Vanderplas, J. M. Transfer of training and its relation to perceptual learning and recognition. *Psychol. Rev.*, 1958, **65**, 375–385.

Suggested Readings

Adams, J. A. Human tracking behavior. *Psychol. Bull.*, 1961, **58**, 55–79. Coverage is given machine-centered points of view from engineering psychology, but primary concern is with basic processes and mechanisms of tracking behavior.

Adams, J. A. Motor skills. *Annu. Rev. Psychol.*, 1964, **15**, 181–202. This review is a follow-up of the one conducted by Bilodeau and Bilodeau in 1961, and it covers the period 1960–1963.

Adams, J. A. *Human memory*. New York: McGraw-Hill, 1967. Theory and data on the short-term and long-term retention of verbal and motor behavior.

Adams, J. A. Engineering psychology. In H. Helson & W. Bevan (Eds.), *Contemporary approaches to psychology*. Princeton: Van Nostrand, 1967. Pp. 345–383. The section on motor behavior gives special emphasis to findings that have relevance for the design and use of human tracking tasks in man-machine systems. Both single and complex multidimensional tracking tasks are discussed, as well as mathematical models of tracking behavior. Other sections of this paper examine research and issues for the visual display of information and for vigilance.

Bilodeau, E. A. (Ed). *Acquisition of skill*. New York: Academic Press, 1966. A report of a conference on motor behavior held at Tulane University in March 1965.

Bilodeau, E. A., & Bilodeau, Ina McD. Motor-skills learning. *Annu. Rev. Psychol.*, 1961, **12**, 243–280. A general review of research on motor behavior from about the end of World War II to 1960.

Index

Subjects indexed refer to a substantive discussion, a definition (*def.*), or a glossary item (*gl.*). Names of authors are included here only for individual work of substance or significance. Complete reference lists appear on pages 29-31, 111-17, 191-203, 285-96, 370-77, 464-77, and 505-507.